Praise for *Essential C# 2.0*

"*Essential C# 2.0* pulls off a very difficult task. The early chapters are comprehensible by beginning developers, while the later chapters pull no punches and provide the experienced developer with the detailed information they need to make the most of C# 2.0. Starting with the first chapter, Mark has successfully interwoven tidbits of information useful to even the most advanced developer while keeping the book approachable."

—*Chris Kinsman, chief architect, Vertafore, Microsoft Regional Director*

"How refreshing! This book deals with C# thoroughly, rather than skimming over the whole .NET framework. It is valuable to newcomers and professionals alike."

—*Jon Skeet, C# MVP*

"*Essential C# 2.0* is a one-stop shop for an experienced programmer looking to ramp up on one of the hottest languages around today. Mark delivers an intelligent and detailed tour of C#, providing newcomers to the language with a solid foundation of skill on which to build their next generation of applications."

—*Stephen Toub, technical editor, MSDN Magazine*

"This book provides complete, up-to-date coverage of all the programming constructs in C#. Masterfully organized, it allows beginning programmers to get on board and leads more experienced programmers into the world of structured programming. Because of its unwavering focus on the essential programming constructs of C#—such as generics, delegates, and much more—this book is indispensable. For programmers who want to solve their day-to-day programming issues using the latest features this modern programming language has to offer, this book is indispensable."

—*Narendra Poflee, IT integration specialist, Itron Inc.*

"*Essential C# 2.0* is an ideal book for all programmers interested in C#. If you are a beginner, you will quickly learn the basics of C# programming and become familiar with the concepts. The flow of the text is easy to follow and does a great job of not repeating concepts that have already been covered. For the experienced programmer, this book has priceless nuggets embedded with pages, making it a great read for programmers who are C#. This will be a book that I will keep next to my con

—*Michael Stokesbary, s*

Essential C# 2.0

Microsoft .NET Development Series

John Montgomery, *Series Advisor*
Don Box, *Series Advisor*
Martin Heller, *Series Editor*

The Microsoft .NET Development Series is supported and developed by the leaders and experts of Microsoft development technologies including Microsoft architects. The books in this series provide a core resource of information and understanding every developer needs in order to write effective applications and managed code. Learn from the leaders how to maximize your use of the .NET Framework and its programming languages.

Titles in the Series

For more information go to www.awprofessional.com/msdotnetseries/

Essential
C# 2.0

■ Mark Michaelis

✦✦ Addison-Wesley

Upper Saddle River, NJ • Boston • Indianapolis • San Francisco
New York • Toronto • Montreal • London • Munich • Paris • Madrid
Capetown • Sydney • Tokyo • Singapore • Mexico City

This Book Is Safari Enabled

The Safari® Enabled icon on the cover of your favorite technology book means the book is available through Safari Bookshelf. When you buy this book, you get free access to the online edition for 45 days.

Safari Bookshelf is an electronic reference library that lets you easily search thousands of technical books, find code samples, download chapters, and access technical information whenever and wherever you need it.

To gain 45-day Safari Enabled access to this book:

- Go to http://www.awprofessional.com/safarienabled
- Complete the brief registration form
- Enter the coupon code VDJ7-A2TK-ZZCA-7RLT-BW63

If you have difficulty registering on Safari Bookshelf or accessing the online edition, please e-mail customer-service@safaribooksonline.com.

Visit us on the Web: www.awprofessional.com

Library of Congress Cataloging-in-Publication Data:

Michaelis, Mark.

Essential C# 2.0 / Mark Michaelis.
  p. cm.
Includes index.
ISBN 0-321-15077-5 (pbk. : alk. paper)
1. C# (Computer program language) I. Title.

QA76.73.C154M523 2006
005.13'3—dc22

2006009699

ISBN 0-321-15077-5
Text printed in the United States on recycled paper at Courier in Stoughton, Massachusetts.
Second printing, April 2007

To my family: Elisabeth, Benjamin, Hanna, and Abigail.

Contents at a Glance

Contents

Figures

Tables

Foreword

F OR THOSE IN THE INDUSTRY who have watched the C programming language develop to embrace new concepts such as object programming (C++), ubiquity across platforms (Java), and highly structured models that form the basis of C#, it is clear that the language is well positioned to hold its own as a dominant development language.

This book has everything a developer needs to know to get up and running with the language. Many concise code samples, the use of mind maps to provide context, and the interesting way Mark contrasts C# with other languages make *Essential C# 2.0* stand out in a sea of C# books.

I have known Mark for a while now. His extensive involvement in the development of C# principles, together with his prior experience as an author of books on C++, COM+, and C#, uniquely qualify him to write the book that I believe will be a seminal reference for C#.

Further, Mark's teaching experience allows him to combine the world of technical skill with that of practical, intuitive tutorial. It begins with principles of object programming in C#, as it is a reference to verify advanced multithreading techniques in a complex system. The reader, novice or expert, will enjoy his casual style and method of eloquently communicating challenging topics.

This reference and tutorial should be on the shelf next to your workstation and carried in your backpack. Pick it up and read it! I'm confident that whether you are new or experienced with the language, you will learn something in this book that will induce an "aha!" moment!

—*Prashant Sridharan*
Microsoft Corporation
March 2006

Preface

THROUGHOUT THE HISTORY of software engineering, the methodology used to write computer programs has undergone several paradigm shifts, each building on the foundation of the former by increasing code organization and decreasing complexity. This book takes you through these same paradigm shifts.

The beginning chapters take you through **sequential programming structure** in which statements are written in the order in which they are executed. The problem with this model is that complexity increases exponentially as the requirements increase. To reduce this complexity, code blocks are moved into methods, which creates a **structured programming model**. This allows you to call the same code block from multiple locations within a program, without duplicating code. Even with this construct, however, programs quickly become unwieldy and require further abstraction. From this emerges object-oriented programming, which Chapter 5 discusses. In subsequent chapters, you continue to learn about additional methodologies, such as interface-based programming, and eventually rudimentary forms of declarative programming (in Chapter 14) via attributes.

This book has three main functions.

- It provides comprehensive coverage of the C# language, going beyond a tutorial and offering a foundation upon which you can begin effective software development projects.
- For readers already familiar with C#, this book provides insight into some of the more complex programming paradigms and provides

in-depth coverage of the features introduced in the latest version of the language, C# 2.0.

* It serves as a timeless reference, even after you gain proficiency with the language.

The key to successfully learning C# is to start coding as soon as possible. Don't wait until you are an "expert" in theory; start writing software immediately. As a believer in iterative development, I hope this book enables even a novice programmer to begin writing basic C# code by the end of Chapter 2.

A number of topics are not covered in this book. You won't find coverage of topics such as ASP.NET, ADO.NET, smart client development, distributed programming, and so on. Although these topics are relevant to the .NET framework, to do them justice requires books of their own. Fortunately, Addison-Wesley's *Microsoft .NET Development Series* provides a wealth of writing on these topics. Reading this book will prepare you to focus on and develop expertise in any of these areas. It focuses on C# and the types within the Base Class Library.

Target Audience for This Book

My challenge with this book was how to keep advanced developers awake while not abandoning beginners by using words like "assembly," "link," "chain," "thread," and "fusion," as if the topic was more appropriate for blacksmiths than for programmers. This book's primary audience is experienced developers looking to add another language to their quiver. However, I have carefully assembled this book to provide significant value to developers at all levels.

* *Beginners:* If you are new to programming, this book serves as a resource to help transition you from an entry-level programmer to a C# developer, comfortable with any C# programming task that's thrown your way. This book not only teaches you syntax, but it also trains you in good programming practices that will serve you throughout your programming career.

- *Structured programmers:* Just as it's best to learn a foreign language through immersion, learning a computer language is most effective when you begin using it before you know all the intricacies. In this vein, the book begins with a tutorial that will be comfortable for those familiar with structured programming, and by the end of Chapter 4, developers in this category should feel at home writing basic control flow programs. However, the key to excellence for C# developers is not memorizing syntax. To transition from simple programs to enter-prise development, the C# developer must think natively in terms of objects and their relationships. To this end, Chapter 5's Beginner Topics introduce classes and object-oriented development. The role of histor-ically structured programming languages such as C, COBOL, and FORTRAN is still significant but shrinking, so it behooves software engineers to become familiar with object-oriented development. C# is an ideal language for making this transition because it was designed with object-oriented development as one of its core tenets.

- *Object-based and object-oriented developers:* C++ and Java program-mers, and many experienced Visual Basic programmers, fall into this category. Many of you are already completely comfortable with semi-colons and curly braces. A brief glance at the code in Chapter 1 reveals that at its core, C# is similar to the C and C++ style languages that you already know.

- *C# professionals:* For those already versed in C#, this book provides a convenient reference for less frequently encountered syntax. Further-more, it provides answers to language details and subtleties seldom addressed. Most importantly, it presents the guidelines and patterns for programming robust and maintainable code. This book also aids in the task of teaching C# to others.

With the emergence of C# 2.0, some of the most prominent enhance-ments are:

- Partial classes (see Chapter 5)
- Global namespace qualifiers (see Chapter 9)
- Different access modifiers on property getters and setters (see Chapter 5)
- Anonymous methods (see Chapter 13)

- Generics (see Chapter 11)
- Iterator topics (see Chapter 12)

These topics are covered in detail for those not already familiar with them. Also pertinent to advanced C# development is the subject of pointers, in Chapter 17. Even experienced C# developers often do not understand this topic well.

Features of This Book

Essential C# 2.0 is a language book that adheres to the core C# Language 2.0 Specification. To help you understand the various C# constructs, it provides numerous examples demonstrating each feature. Accompanying each concept are guidelines and best practices, ensuring that code compiles, avoids likely pitfalls, and achieves maximum maintainability.

To improve readability, code is specially formatted and chapters are outlined using mind maps.

Code Samples

The code snippets in most of this text can run on any implementation of the Common Language Infrastructure (CLI), including the Mono, Rotor, and Microsoft .NET platforms. Platform- or vendor-specific libraries are seldom used, except when communicating important concepts relevant only to those platforms (appropriately handling the single-threaded user interface of Windows, for example). Any code that specifically requires C# 2.0 compliance is called out in Appendix C: C# 2.0 Topics.

Here is a sample code listing.

LISTING 1.17: Commenting Your Code

```csharp
class CommentSamples
{
  static void Main()
  {
                                      Single-Line Comment
    string firstName; // Variable for storing the first name
    string lastName;  // Variable for storing the last name

    System.Console.WriteLine("Hey you!");
```

Delimited Comment Inside Statement

```
System.Console.Write /* No new line */ (
    "Enter your first name: ");
firstName = System.Console.ReadLine();

System.Console.Write /* No new line */ (
    "Enter your last name: ");
lastName = System.Console.ReadLine();

/* Display a greeting to the console
    using composite formatting. */       Delimited Comment
System.Console.WriteLine("Your full name is {0} {1}.",
    firstName, lastName);
// ...
    }
}
```

The formatting is as follows.

- Comments are shown in italics.

    ```
    /* Display a greeting to the console
        using composite formatting. */
    ```

- Keywords are shown in bold.

    ```
    static void Main()
    ```

- Highlighted code calls out specific code snippets that may have changed from an earlier listing, or demonstrates the concept described in the text.

    ```
    System.Console.Write /* No new line */ (
    ```

    Highlighting can appear on an entire line or on just a few characters within a line.

    ```
    System.Console.WriteLine(
        "Your full name is {0} {1}.",
    ```

- Incomplete listings contain an ellipsis to denote irrelevant code that has been omitted.

    ```
    // ...
    ```

- Console output is the output from a particular listing that appears following the listing.

OUTPUT 1.4:

```
>HeyYou.exe
Hey you!
Enter your first name: Inigo
Enter your last name: Montoya
```

User input for the program appears in italics.

Although it might have been convenient to provide full code samples that you could copy into your own programs, doing so would detract you from learning a particular topic. Therefore, you need to modify the code samples before you can incorporate them into your programs. The core omission is error checking, such as exception handling. Also, code samples do not explicitly include `using System` statements. You need to assume the statement throughout all samples.

You can find sample code at http://mark.michaelis.net/EssentialCSharp and at www.awprofessional.com/title/0321150775.

Mind Maps

Each chapter's introduction includes a **mind map**, which serves as an outline that provides at-a-glance reference to each chapter's content. Here is an example (taken from Chapter 12).

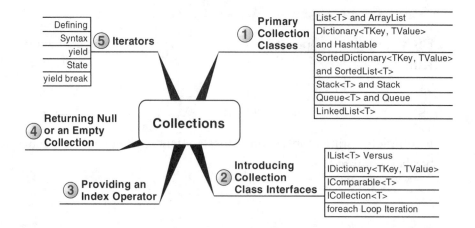

The theme of each chapter appears in the mind map's center. High-level topics spread out from the core. Mind maps allow you to absorb the flow from high-level to more detailed concepts easily, with less chance of encountering very specific knowledge that you might not be looking for.

Helpful Notes

Depending on your level of experience, special code blocks and notes will help you navigate through the text.

- *Beginner Topics* provide definitions or explanations targeted specifically toward entry-level programmers.
- *Advanced Topics* enable experienced developers to focus on the material that is most relevant to them.
- Callout notes highlight key principles in callout boxes so that readers easily recognize their significance.
- *Language Contrast* sidebars identify key differences between C# and its predecessors to aid those familiar with other languages.

How This Book Is Organized

At a high level, software engineering is about managing complexity, and it is toward this end that I have organized *Essential C# 2.0*. Chapters 1–4 introduce structured programming, which enable you to start writing simple functioning code immediately. Chapters 5–9 present the object-oriented constructs of C#. Novice readers should focus on fully understanding this section before they proceed to the more advanced topics found in the remainder of this book.

Chapters 11–13 introduce additional complexity-reducing constructs, handling common patterns needed by virtually all modern programs. This leads to dynamic programming with reflection and attributes, which is used extensively for threading and interoperability, the chapters that follow.

The book ends with a chapter on the Common Language Infrastructure, which describes C# within the context of the development platform in which it operates. This chapter appears at the end because it is not C# specific and it departs from the syntax and programming style in the rest of the book. However, this chapter is suitable for reading at any time, perhaps most appropriately immediately following Chapter 1.

Here is a description of each chapter.

- *Chapter 1—Introducing C#:* After presenting the C# `HelloWorld` program, this chapter proceeds to dissect it. This should familiarize readers with the look and feel of a C# program and provide details on how to compile and debug their own programs. It also touches on the context of a C# program's execution and its intermediate language.

- *Chapter 2—Data Types:* Functioning programs manipulate data, and this chapter introduces the primitive data types of C#. This includes coverage of two type categories, value types and reference types, along with conversion between types and support for arrays.

- *Chapter 3—Operators and Control Flow:* To take advantage of the iterative capabilities in a computer, you need to know how to include loops and conditional logic within your program. This chapter also covers the C# operators, data conversion, and preprocessor directives.

- *Chapter 4—Methods and Parameters:* This chapter investigates the details of methods and their parameters. It includes passing by value, passing by reference, and returning data via a parameter. In C#, default parameters are not supported, and this chapter explains why and how to provide the same functionality.

- *Chapter 5—Classes:* Given the basic building blocks of a class, this chapter combines these constructs together to form fully functional types. Classes form the core of object-oriented technology by defining the template for an object.

- *Chapter 6—Inheritance:* Although inheritance is a programming fundamental to many developers, C# provides some unique constructs, such as the `new` modifier. This chapter discusses the details of the inheritance syntax, including overriding.

- *Chapter 7—Interfaces:* This chapter demonstrates how interfaces are used to define the "versionable" interaction contract between classes. C# includes both explicit and implicit interface member implementation, enabling an additional encapsulation level not supported by most other languages.

- *Chapter 8—Value Types:* Although not as prevalent as defining reference types, it is sometimes necessary to define value types that behave in a fashion similar to the primitive types built into C#. This chapter describes how to define structures, while exposing the idiosyncrasies they may introduce.

- *Chapter 9—Well-Formed Types:* This chapter discusses more advanced type definition. It explains how to implement operators, such as + and cast, and describes how to encapsulate multiple classes into a single library. In addition, the chapter demonstrates defining namespaces and XML comments, and discusses how to design classes for garbage collection.

- *Chapter 10—Exception Handling:* This chapter expands on the exception-handling introduction from Chapter 4 and describes how exceptions follow a hierarchy that enables creating custom exceptions. It also includes some best practices on exception handling.

- *Chapter 11—Generics:* Generics is perhaps the core feature missing from C# 1.0. This chapter fully covers this new feature.

- *Chapter 12—Collections:* Given generics, all the collection classes in .NET 1.1 can be replaced with their generic equivalents. This chapter reviews the collection classes, along with the interfaces that define their common behavior. With minimal impact on the underlying runtime, C# 2.0 provides syntax for easier collection creation with iterators. Iterators provide a clean syntax for specifying how to loop through data within a class.

- *Chapter 13—Delegates and Events:* Delegates begin clearly distinguishing C# from its predecessors by defining patterns for handling events within code. This virtually eliminates the need for writing routines that poll. Encapsulated delegates, known as events, are a core construct of the Common Language Runtime. Anonymous methods, another C# 2.0 feature, are also presented here.

- *Chapter 14—Reflection and Attributes:* Object-oriented programming formed the basis for a paradigm shift in program structure in the late 1980s. In a similar way, attributes facilitate declarative programming and embedded metadata, ushering in a new paradigm. This chapter looks at attributes and discusses how to retrieve them via reflection. It also covers file input and output via the serialization framework within the Base Class Library.

- *Chapter 15—Multithreading:* Most modern programs require the use of threads to execute long-running tasks while ensuring active response to simultaneous events. As programs become more sophisticated, they must take additional precautions to protect data in these advanced environments. Programming multithreaded applications is complex. This chapter discusses how to work with threads and provides best practices to avoid the problems that plague multithreaded applications.

- *Chapter 16—Multithreading Patterns:* Building on the last chapter, this one demonstrates some of the built-in threading pattern support that can simplify the explicit control of multithreaded code.

- *Chapter 17—Platform Interoperability and Unsafe Code:* Given that C# is a relatively young language, far more code is written in other languages than in C#. To take advantage of this preexisting code, C# supports interoperability—the calling of unmanaged code—through P/Invoke. In addition, C# provides for the use of pointers and direct memory manipulation. Although code with pointers requires special privileges to run, it provides the power to interoperate fully with traditional C-based application programming interfaces.

- *Chapter 18—The Common Language Infrastructure:* Fundamentally, C# is the syntax that was designed as the most effective programming language on top of the underlying Common Language Infrastructure. This chapter delves into how C# programs relate to the underlying runtime and its specifications.

- *Appendix A—Downloading and Installing the C# Compiler and the CLI Platform:* This appendix provides instructions for setting up a C# compiler and the platform on which to run the code, Microsoft .NET or Mono.

- *Appendix B—Complete Source Code Listings:* In several cases, a full source code listing within a chapter would have been too long. To make these listings still available to the reader, this appendix includes the full listing from Chapters 3, 11, 12, 14, and 17.

- *Appendix C—C# 2.0 Topics:* This appendix provides a quick reference to any C# 2.0 content. It is specifically designed to help C# 1.0 programmers quickly get up to speed on the 2.0 features.

I hope you find this book to be a great resource in establishing your C# expertise and that you continue to reference it for the more obscure areas of C# and its inner workings.

Acknowledgments

NO BOOK CAN BE published by the author alone, and I am extremely grateful for the multitude of people who helped me with this one.

The order in which I thank people is not significant, except for those that come first. By far, my family has made the biggest sacrifice to allow me to complete this. Benjamin, Hanna, and (most recently) Abigail often had a Daddy distracted by this book, but Elisabeth suffered even more so. She was often left to take care of things, holding the family's world together on her own. Thanks honey!

Many technical editors reviewed each chapter in minute detail to ensure technical accuracy. I was often amazed by the subtle errors that these folks still managed to catch:

Paul Bramsman

Doug Dechow

Gerard Frantz

Anson Horton

Angelika Langer

Nicholas Paldino

Narendra Poflee

Jon Skeet

Michael Stokesbary

John Timney

Stephen Toub

In particular, Michael was a huge help in editing the technical content and serving as a sounding board as I was putting the material together, not to mention his invaluable friendship. I am also especially grateful to the C# MVPs (Nicholas and John), who know the language in certain areas second only to those on the C# team.

Thanks also to all those at Addison-Wesley, for their patience in working with me in spite of my frequent focus everywhere except on the manuscript. Thanks to:

Sheri Cain

Jessica D'Amico

Curt Johnson

Joan Murray

Stephane Nakib

Ann Wells

I especially appreciated Ann's frequent guidance and encouragement, starting back when the book was first suggested.

Prashant Sridharan, from Microsoft's Developer Division, was the one who got me started on this, and he provided me with an incredible jumpstart on the material. Thanks Prashant!

About the Author

Mark Michaelis is an enterprise architect and trainer at Itron Corporation and an IDesign architect specializing in Windows Communication Foundation (WCF) and Visual Studio Team System (VSTS). Since 1996, Mark has been recognized as a Microsoft MVP for areas such as C# and VSTS, and he serves on several Microsoft software design review teams, including C#, WCF, and VSTS. Mark holds an M.S. in computer science from the Illinois Institute of Technology, speaks at developer conferences both nationally and internationally, and has written several other books and articles.

Mark lives with his wife, Elisabeth, and three children, Benjamin, Hanna, and Abigail, in Spokane, Washington. He can be contacted via his blog, http://mark.michaelis.net, or via e-mail, mark@michaelis.net.

■1■
Introducing C#

C# IS A RELATIVELY NEW LANGUAGE that builds on features found in its predecessor C-style languages (C, C++, and Java), making it immediately familiar to many experienced programmers. Part of a larger, more complex execution platform called the Common Language Infrastructure (CLI), C# is a programming language for building software components and applications.

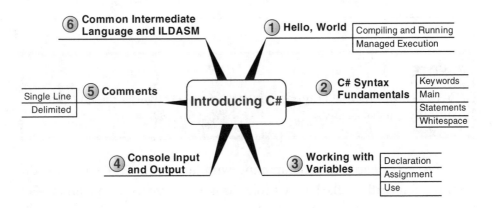

This chapter introduces C# using the traditional HelloWorld program. The chapter focuses on C# syntax fundamentals, including defining an entry point into the C# program executable. This will familiarize you with the C# syntax style and structure, and it will enable you to write the simplest of C# programs. Prior to the discussion of C# syntax fundamentals is a summary of managed execution context, which explains how a C# program executes at runtime. This chapter ends with a discussion of variable declaration, writing and retrieving data from the console, and the basics of commenting code in C#.

Hello, World

The best way to learn a new programming language is to write code. The first example is the classic HelloWorld program. In this program, you will display some text to the screen.

Listing 1.1 shows the complete HelloWorld program; in the following sections, you will compile the code.

LISTING 1.1: **HelloWorld** in C#[1]

```
class HelloWorld
{
  static void Main()
  {
    System.Console.WriteLine("Hello. My name is Inigo Montoya.");
  }
}
```

> ■ NOTE
>
> C# is a case-sensitive language: Incorrect case prevents the code from compiling successfully.

Those experienced in programming with Java, C, or C++ will immediately see similarities. Like Java, C# inherits its basic syntax from C and C++.[2] Syntactic punctuation (such as semicolons and curly braces), features (such

---

1. Refer to the movie *The Princess Bride* if you're confused about the Inigo Montoya references.
2. When creating C#, the language creators sat down with the specifications for C/C++, literally crossing out the features that they didn't like and creating a list of the ones they did like. The group also included designers with strong backgrounds in other languages.

as case sensitivity), and keywords (such as `class`, `public`, and `void`) are familiar to programmers experienced in these languages. Beginners and programmers from other languages will quickly find these constructs intuitive.

Compiling and Running the Application

The C# compiler allows any file extension for files containing C# source code, but .cs is typically used. After saving the source code to a file, developers must compile it. (Appendix A provides instructions for installing the compiler.) Because the mechanics of the command are not part of the C# standard, the compilation command varies depending on the C# compiler implementation.

If you place Listing 1.1 into a file called `HelloWorld.cs`, the compilation command in Output 1.1 will work with the Microsoft .NET compiler (assuming appropriate paths to the compiler are set up).[3]

OUTPUT 1.1:

```
>csc.exe HelloWorld.cs
Microsoft (R) Visual C# 2005 Compiler version 8.00.50727.42
for Microsoft (R) Windows (R) 2005 Framework version 2.0.50727
Copyright (C) Microsoft Corporation 2001-2005. All rights reserved.
```

Running the resulting program, `HelloWorld.exe`, displays the message shown in Output 1.2.

OUTPUT 1.2:

```
>HelloWorld.exe
Hello. My name is Inigo Montoya.
```

The program created by the C# compiler, `HelloWorld.exe`, is an **assembly**. Instead of creating an entire program that can be executed independently, developers can create a library of code that can be referenced by

---

3. Compilation using the Mono compiler, an open source compiler sponsored by Novell, is virtually identical, except that the compiler name is `mcs.exe` rather than `csc.exe`. Although I would very much like to have placed instructions for each platform here, doing so detracts from the topic of introducing C#. See Appendix A for details on Mono.

another, larger program. Libraries (or class libraries) use the filename extension .dll, which stands for Dynamic Link Library (DLL). A library is also an assembly. In other words, the output from a successful C# compile is an assembly regardless of whether it is a program or a library.

Language Contrast: Java—Filename Must Match Class Name

In Java, the filename must follow the name of the class. In C#, this convention is frequently followed but is not required. In C#, it is possible to have two classes in one file, and in C# 2.0, it's possible to have a single class span multiple files.

Managed Execution and the Common Language Infrastructure

The processor cannot directly interpret an assembly. Assemblies consist of a second language known as the Common Intermediate Language (CIL), or IL for short.

■ NOTE

A third term for CIL is *Microsoft IL (MSIL)*. This book uses the term *CIL* because it is the term adopted by the CLI standard. IL is prevalent in conversation among people writing C# code because they assume that IL refers to CIL rather than other types of intermediate languages.

The C# compiler transforms the C# source file into this intermediate language. An additional step, usually performed at execution time, is required to change the CIL code into **machine code** that the processor can understand. This involves an important element in the execution of a C# program: the **Virtual Execution System (VES)**. The VES, also casually referred to as the **runtime**, compiles CIL code as needed (this process is known as **just-in-time** compilation [**jitting**]). The code that executes under the context of an agent like the runtime is **managed code**, and the process of executing under control of the runtime is **managed execution**. It is called managed code because the runtime controls significant portions of the program's behavior by managing aspects such as memory allocation, security, and just-in-time compilation. Code that does not require the runtime in order to execute is **unmanaged code**.

■ **NOTE**

The term *runtime* can refer to either execution time or the Virtual Execution System. To help clarify, this book uses the term *execution time* to indicate when the program is executing, and it uses the term *runtime* when discussing the agent responsible for managing the execution of a C# program while it executes.

The specification for a VES is included in a broader specification known as the **Common Language Infrastructure (CLI)** specification.[4] An international standard, the CLI includes specifications for

- The VES or runtime
- The CIL
- A type system that supports language interoperability, known as the **Common Type System (CTS)**
- Guidance on how to write libraries that are accessible from CLI-compatible languages (available in the **Common Language Specification [CLS]**)
- Metadata that enables many of the services identified by the CLI (including specifications for the layout or file format of assemblies)
- A common programming framework, the Base Class Library (BCL), which developers in all languages can utilize

---

4. Miller, J., and S. Ragsdale. 2004. *The Common Language Infrastructure Annotated Standard*. Boston: Addison-Wesley.

Running within the context of a CLI implementation enables support for a number of services and features that programmers do not need to code for directly, including

- *Language interoperability:* interoperability between different source languages. This is possible because the language compilers translate each source language to the same intermediate language (CIL).
- *Type safety:* checks for conversion between types, ensuring that only conversions between compatible types will occur. This helps prevent the occurrence of buffer overruns, a leading cause of security vulnerabilities.
- *Code access security:* certification that the assembly developer's code has permission to execute on the computer.
- *Garbage collection:* memory management that automatically de-allocates space for data allocated by the runtime.
- *Platform portability:* support for potentially running the same assembly on a variety of operating systems. One obvious restriction is that no platform-dependent libraries are used; therefore, as with Java, there are inevitably some idiosyncrasies that need to be worked out.
- *BCL:* provides a large foundation of code that developers can depend on (in all CLI implementations) so that they do not have to develop the code themselves.

■ NOTE

This section gives a brief synopsis of the CLI to familiarize you with the context in which a C# program executes. It also provides a summary of some of the terms that appear throughout this book. Chapter 18 is devoted to the topic of the CLI and its relevance to C# developers. Although the chapter appears last in the book, it does not depend on any earlier chapters, so if you want to become more familiar with the CLI, you can jump to it at any time.

C# Syntax Fundamentals

Once you successfully compile and run the HelloWorld program, you are ready to start dissecting the code to learn its individual parts. First, consider the C# keywords along with the identifiers that the developer chooses.

∎ BEGINNER TOPIC

Keywords

In order for the compiler to interpret the code, certain words within C# have special status and meaning. Known as **keywords** or **reserved words**, they provide the concrete syntax that the compiler uses to interpret the expressions the programmer writes. In the HelloWorld program, class, static, and void are examples of keywords.

The compiler uses the keywords to identify the structure and organization of the code. Because the compiler interprets these words with elevated significance, you can use keywords only under the specific rules identified by the language. In other words, programming languages require that developers place keywords in only certain locations. When programmers violate these rules, the compiler will issue errors.

C# Keywords

Table 1.1 shows the C# keywords.

TABLE 1.1: C# Keywords

abstract	add*	as	base
bool	break	byte	case
catch	char	checked	class
const	continue	decimal	default
delegate	do	double	else
enum	event	explicit	extern

Continues

TABLE 1.1: C# Keywords *(Continued)*

false	finally	fixed	float
for	foreach	get[*]	goto
if	implicit	in	int
interface	internal	is	lock
long	namespace	new	null
object	operator	out	override
params	partial[*]	private	protected
public	readonly	ref	remove[*]
return	sbyte	sealed	set[*]
short	sizeof	stackalloc	static
string	struct	switch	this
throw	true	try	typeof
uint	ulong	unchecked	unsafe
ushort	using	value[*]	virtual
void	volatile	where[*]	while
yield[a]			

a Contextual keyword

C# 2.0 does not introduce any new keywords, but some C# 2.0 constructs use **contextual keywords**, which are significant only in certain locations. Outside these designated locations, contextual keywords have no special significance.[5] By this method, all C# 1.0 code is fully compatible

---

5. For example, early in the design of C# 2.0, the language designers designated yield as a keyword, and Microsoft released alpha versions of the C# 2.0 compiler, with yield as a designated keyword, to thousands of developers. However, the language designers eventually determined that by using yield return rather than yield, they could ultimately avoid adding yield as a keyword because it would have no special significance outside its proximity to return.

with the C# 2.0 standard.[6] (Table 1.1 designates contextual keywords with an asterisk.)

▪ BEGINNER TOPIC

Identifiers

In addition to the keywords defined in C#, developers may provide their own names. Programming languages refer to these names as **identifiers** since they identify constructs that the programmer codes. In Listing 1.1, `HelloWorld` and `Main` are examples of identifiers. By assigning an identifier, it is possible to refer back to the same construct using the identifier. It is important, therefore, that the names the developer assigns are meaningful rather than arbitrary. A keen ability to select succinct and indicative names is an important characteristic of a strong programmer because the resulting code is easier to understand and reuse. In some rare cases, some identifiers, like `Main`, can have a special meaning in the C# language.

Type Definition

All code in C# appears within a type definition, and the most common type definition begins with the keyword `class`. A **class definition** is the section of code that begins with `class <Identifier> { ... }`, as shown in Listing 1.2.

LISTING 1.2: Basic Class Declaration

```
class HelloWorld
{
    ...
}
```

The name used for the type (in this case, `HelloWorld`) can vary, but by convention, it should begin with a capital letter. If the name contains multiple words appended together, then each additional word should also begin with a capital letter. For this particular example, therefore, other possible names are `HelloWorld`, `HelloInigoMontoya`, and simply `Hello`.

---

6. There are some rare incompatibilities, such as C# 2.0 requiring implementation of `IDisposable` with the `using` statement, rather than simply a `Dispose()` method.

The CLI creators called this type of casing **Pascal casing** because of its popularity in the Pascal programming language. The alternative, **camel casing**, follows the same convention, except that the first letter is lowercase. Examples include `quotient`, `firstName`, and `theDreadPirateRoberts`.

Generally, programs contain multiple types, each containing multiple methods.

Main

■ BEGINNER TOPIC

What Is a Method?
Syntactically, a **method** in C# is a named block of code introduced by a method declaration (e.g., `static void Main()`) and followed by zero or more statements within curly braces. Methods perform computations and/or actions. Similar to paragraphs in written languages, methods provide a means of structuring and organizing code so that it is more readable. More importantly, methods avoid the need to duplicate code. The method declaration introduces the method and defines the method name along with the data passed to and from the method. In Listing 1.3, `Main()` followed by `{ ... }` is an example of a C# method.

The point where C# programs begin execution is the **Main method**, which begins with `static void Main()`. When you execute the program by typing `HelloWorld.exe` at the command console, the program starts up, resolves the location of `Main`, and begins executing the first statement (see Listing 1.3).

LISTING 1.3: Breaking Apart `HelloWorld`

```
class HelloWorld
{
  static void Main()         Method Declaration
  {
    System.Console.WriteLine("Hello, My name is Inigo Montoya");
  }
}
```

Method Declaration · Main · Statement · Class Definition

Although the Main method declaration can vary to some degree, `static` and the method name, `Main`, are always required.

■ ADVANCED TOPIC

Declaration of the Main Method

Although it is possible to declare the Main method without parameters or a return type, C# supports specifying either one. Listing 1.4 shows the full declaration of the Main method.

LISTING 1.4: The Main Method, with Parameters and a Return

```
static int Main(string[] args)
{
    . . .
}
```

The `args` parameter is an array of strings corresponding to the command-line parameters. However, the first element of the array is not the program name but the first command-line parameter to appear after the executable name, unlike in C and C++. To retrieve the full command used to execute the program use `System.Environment.CommandLine`.

The `int` return from `Main` is the status code and it indicates the success of the program's execution. A return of a nonzero value generally indicates an error.

Language Contrast: C++/Java—`main()` Is All Lowercase

Unlike its C-style predecessors, C# uses an uppercase M for the Main method in order to be consistent with the Pascal-based naming conventions of C#.

The designation of the `Main` method as `static` indicates that other methods may call it directly off the class definition. Without the static designation, the command console that started the program would need to perform additional work (known as **instantiation**) before calling the method. (Chapter 5 contains an entire section devoted to the topic of static members.)

Placing `void` prior to `Main()` indicates that this method does not return any data (explained further in Chapter 2).

One distinctive C/C++ style characteristic followed by C# is the use of curly braces for the body of a construct, such as the class or the method. For example, the `Main` method contains curly braces that surround its implementation; in this case, only one statement appears in the method.

Statements and Statement Delimiters

The `Main` method includes a single statement, `System.Console.Write-Line()`, which is used to write a line of text to the console. C# generally uses a semicolon to indicate the end of a **statement**, where a statement comprises one or more actions that the code will perform. Declaring a variable, controlling the program flow, and calling a method are examples of statements.

Language Contrast: Visual Basic—Line-Based Statements

Some languages are line based, meaning that without a special annotation, statements cannot span a line. Visual Basic is an example of a line-based language. It requires an underscore at the end of a line to indicate that a statement spans multiple lines.

■ ADVANCED TOPIC

Statements without Semicolons

It is only generally true that all statements in C# end with a semicolon. One example that does not include the semicolon is a `switch` statement. Because curly braces are always included in a `switch` statement, C# does not require a semicolon following the statement. In fact, code blocks themselves are considered statements (they are also composed of statements) and they don't require closure using a semicolon.

Since creation of a newline does not separate statements, you can place multiple statements on the same line and the C# compiler will interpret the line to have multiple instructions. For example, Listing 1.5 contains two statements on a single line that, in combination, display Up and Down on two separate lines.

LISTING 1.5: Multiple Statements on One Line

```
System.Console.WriteLine("Up");System.Console.WriteLine("Down");
```

C# also allows the splitting of a statement across multiple lines. Again, the C# compiler looks for a semicolon to indicate the end of a statement (see Listing 1.6).

LISTING 1.6: Splitting a Single Statement across Multiple Lines

```
System.Console.WriteLine(
    "Hello. My name is Inigo Montoya.");
```

In Listing 1.6, the original WriteLine() statement from the HelloWorld program is split across multiple lines.

Whitespace

The semicolon makes it possible for the C# compiler to ignore whitespace in code. Apart from a few exceptions, C# allows developers to insert whitespace throughout the code without altering its semantic meaning. In Listing 1.5 and Listing 1.6, it didn't matter whether a newline was inserted within a statement or between statements, and doing so had no effect on the resulting executable created by the compiler.

■ BEGINNER TOPIC

What Is Whitespace?

Whitespace is the combination of one or more consecutive formatting characters such as tab, space, and newline characters. Eliminating all whitespace between words is obviously significant, as is whitespace within a quoted string.

Frequently, programmers use whitespace to indent code for greater readability. Consider the two variations on `HelloWorld`, as shown in Listing 1.7 and Listing 1.8.

LISTING 1.7: No Indentation Formatting

```
class HelloWorld
{
static void Main()
{
System.Console.WriteLine("Hello Inigo Montoya");
}
}
```

LISTING 1.8: Removing Whitespace

```
class HelloWorld{static void Main()
{System.Console.WriteLine("Hello Inigo Montoya");}}
```

Although these two examples look significantly different from the original program, the C# compiler sees them as identical.

■ **BEGINNER TOPIC**

Formatting Code with Whitespace

Indenting the code using whitespace is important for greater readability. As you begin writing code, you need to follow established coding standards and conventions in order to enhance code readability.

The convention used in this book is to place curly braces on their own line and to indent the code contained between the curly brace pair. If another curly brace pair appears within the first pair, all the code within the second set of braces is also indented.

This is not a uniform C# standard, but a stylistic preference.

Working with Variables

Now that you've been introduced to the most basic C# program, it's time to declare a local variable. Once a variable is declared, you can assign it a value, replace that value with a new value, and use it in calculations, output, and so on. However, you cannot change the data type of the variable. In Listing 1.9, `string max` is a variable declaration.

LISTING 1.9: Declaring and Assigning a Variable

```
class MiracleMax
{
  static void Main()
  {
                Variable
       string max;
       Data Type

    max = "Have fun storming the castle!";

    System.Console.WriteLine(max);
  }
}
```

▪ BEGINNER TOPIC

Local Variables

A **variable** is a symbolic name for a storage location that the program can later assign and modify. *Local* indicates that the programmer **declared** the variable within a method.

To declare a variable is to define it, which you do by

a. Specifying the type of data to which the variable will refer
b. Assigning it an identifier (name)

Data Types

Listing 1.9 declares a variable with the data type `string`. Other common data types used in this chapter are `int` and `char`.

- `int` is the C# designation of an integer type that is 32 bits in size.
- `char` is used for a character type. It is 16 bits, large enough for (non-surrogate) Unicode characters.

The next chapter looks at these and other common data types in more detail.

■ BEGINNER TOPIC

What Is a Data Type?

The type of data that a variable declaration specifies is called a **data type**. A data type, or simply **type**, is a classification of things that share similar characteristics and behavior. For example, *animal* is a type. It classifies all things (monkeys, warthogs, and platypuses) that have animal characteristics (multicellular, capacity for locomotion, and so on). Similarly, in programming languages, a type is a definition for several items endowed with similar qualities.

Declaring a Variable

In Listing 1.9, `string max` is a variable declaration of a string type whose name is `max`. It is possible to declare multiple variables within the same statement by specifying the data type once and separating each identifier with a comma. Listing 1.10 demonstrates this.

LISTING 1.10: Declaring Two Variables within One Statement

```
string message1, message2;
```

Because a multivariable declaration statement allows developers to provide the data type only once within a declaration, all variables will be of the same type.

In C#, the name of the variable may begin with any letter or an underscore (_), followed by any number of letters, numbers, and/or underscores. By convention, however, local variable names are camel cased (the first letter in each word is capitalized, except for the first word) and do not include underscores.

Assigning a Variable

After declaring a local variable, you must assign it a value before referencing it. One way to do this is to use the = **operator**, also known as the **simple assignment operator**. Operators are symbols used to identify the function the code is to perform. Listing 1.11 demonstrates how to use the assignment operator to designate the string values to which the variables `max`[7] and `valerie` will point.

---

7. I am not using `max` to mean the math function here; I'm using it as a variable name.

Listing 1.11: Changing the Value of a Variable

```csharp
class MiracleMax
{
  static void Main()
  {
      string valerie;
      string max = "Have fun storming the castle!";

      valerie = "Think it will work?";

      System.Console.WriteLine(max);
      System.Console.WriteLine(valerie);

      max = "It would take a miracle.";
      System.Console.WriteLine(max);
  }
}
```

From this listing, observe that it is possible to assign a variable as part of the variable declaration (as it was for max), or afterward in a separate statement (as with the variable valerie). The value assigned must always be on the right side.

Running the compiled MiracleMax.exe program produces the code shown in Output 1.3.

Output 1.3:

```
>MiracleMax.exe
Have fun storming the castle!
Think it will work?
It would take a miracle.
```

C# requires that developers assign a local variable before accessing it. Additionally, an assignment returns a value. Therefore, C# allows multiple assignments within the same statement, as demonstrated in Listing 1.12.

Listing 1.12: Assignment Returning a Value That Can Be Assigned Again

```csharp
class MiracleMax
{
    // ...
    string requirements, max;
    requirements = max = "It would take a miracle.";
    // ...
}
```

Using a Variable

The result of the assignment, of course, is that you can then refer to the value using the variable identifier. Therefore, when you use the variable `max` within the `System.Console.WriteLine(max)` statement, the program displays `Have fun storming the castle!`, the value of `max`, on the console. Changing the value of `max` and executing the same `System.Console.WriteLine(max)` statement causes the new `max` value, `It would take a miracle.`, to be displayed.

■ ADVANCED TOPIC

Strings Are Immutable

All data of type `string`, whether string literals or otherwise, is immutable (or unmodifiable). For example, it is not possible to change the string `"Come As You Are"` to `"Come As You Age"`. A change like this requires that you reassign the variable to point at a new location in memory, instead of modifying the data to which the variable originally referred.

Console Input and Output

This chapter already used `System.Console.WriteLine` repeatedly for writing out text to the command console. In addition to being able to write out data, a program needs to be able to accept data that a user may enter.

Getting Input from the Console

One of the ways to retrieve text that is entered at the console is to use `System.Console.ReadLine()`. This method stops the program execution so that the user can enter characters. When the user presses the Enter key, creating a newline, the program continues. The output, also known as the **return**, from the `System.Console.ReadLine()` method is the string of text that was entered. Consider Listing 1.13 and the corresponding output shown in Output 1.4.

LISTING 1.13: Using `System.Console.ReadLine()`

```
class HeyYou
{
```

```
static void Main()
{
    string firstName;
    string lastName;

    System.Console.WriteLine("Hey you!");

    System.Console.Write("Enter your first name: ");
    firstName = System.Console.ReadLine();

    System.Console.Write("Enter your last name: ");
    lastName = System.Console.ReadLine();

    ...

}
}
```

OUTPUT 1.4:

```
>HeyYou.exe
Hey you!
Enter your first name: Inigo
Enter your last name: Montoya
```

After each prompt, this program uses the System.Console.Read-Line() method to retrieve the text the user entered and assign it to an appropriate variable. By the time the second System.Console.Read-Line() assignment completes, firstName refers to the value Inigo and lastName refers to the value Montoya.

■ ADVANCED TOPIC

System.Console.Read()

In addition to the System.Console.ReadLine() method, there is also a System.Console.Read() method. However, the data type returned by the System.Console.Read() method is an integer corresponding to the character value read, or –1 if no more characters are available. To retrieve the actual character, it is necessary to first cast the integer to a character, as shown in Listing 1.14.

LISTING 1.14: Using `System.Console.Read()`

```
int readValue;
char character;
readValue = System.Console.Read();
character = (char) readValue;
System.Console.Write(character);
```

The `System.Console.Read()` method does not return the input until the user presses the Enter key; no processing of characters will begin, even if the user types multiple characters before pressing the Enter key.

In C# 2.0, there is a new method called `System.Console.ReadKey()` which, in contrast to `System.Console.Read()`, returns the input after a single keystroke. It enables the developer to intercept the keystroke and perform actions, such as restricting the characters to numerics.

Writing Output to the Console

In Listing 1.13, you prompt the user for his first and last names using the method `System.Console.Write()` rather than `System.Console.Write-Line()`. Instead of placing a newline character after displaying the text, the `System.Console.Write()` method leaves the current position on the same line. In this way, any text the user enters will be on the same line as the prompt for input. The output from Listing 1.13 demonstrates the effect of `System.Console.Write()`.

The next step is to write the values retrieved using `System.Console.ReadLine()` back to the console. In the case of Listing 1.15, the program writes out the user's full name. However, instead of using `System.Console.WriteLine()` as before, this code will use a slight variation. Output 1.5 shows the corresponding output.

LISTING 1.15: Formatting Using `System.Console.WriteLine()`

```
class HeyYou
{
  static void Main()
  {
      string firstName;
      string lastName;
```

```
System.Console.WriteLine("Hey you!");

System.Console.Write("Enter your first name: ");
firstName = System.Console.ReadLine();

System.Console.Write("Enter your last name: ");
lastName = System.Console.ReadLine();

System.Console.WriteLine("Your full name is {0} {1}.",
    firstName, lastName);
  }
}
```

OUTPUT 1.5:

```
Hey you!
Enter your first name: Inigo
Enter your last name: Montoya
Your full name is Inigo Montoya
```

Instead of writing out Your full name is followed by another Write statement for firstName, a third Write statement for the space, and finally a WriteLine statement for lastName, Listing 1.15 writes out the entire output using **composite formatting**. With composite formatting, the code first supplies a **format string** to define the output format. In this example, the format string is "Your full name is {0} {1}.". It identifies two indexed placeholders for data insertion in the string.

Note that the index value begins at zero. Each inserted parameter (known as a **format item**) appears after the format string in the order corresponding to the index value. In this example, since firstName is the first parameter to follow immediately after the format string, it corresponds to index value 0. Similarly, lastName corresponds to index value 1.

Note that the placeholders within the format string need not appear in order. For example, Listing 1.16 switches the order of the indexed placeholders and adds a comma, which changes the way the name is displayed (see Output 1.6).

LISTING 1.16: Swapping the Indexed Placeholders and Corresponding Variables

```
System.Console.WriteLine("Your full name is {1}, {0}",
    firstName, lastName);
```

OUTPUT 1.6:

```
Hey you!
Enter your first name: Inigo
Enter your last name: Montoya
Your full name is Montoya, Inigo
```

In addition to not having the placeholders appear consecutively within the format string, it is possible to use the same placeholder multiple times within a format string. Furthermore, it is possible to omit a placeholder. It is not possible, however, to have placeholders that do not have a corresponding parameter.

Comments

In this section, you modify the program in Listing 1.15 by adding comments. In no way does this vary the execution of the program; rather, providing comments within the code makes it more understandable. Listing 1.17 shows the new code, and Output 1.7 shows the corresponding output.

LISTING 1.17: Commenting Your Code

```
class CommentSamples
{
  static void Main()
  {
                              Single-Line Comment

    string firstName; // Variable for storing the first name
    string lastName;  // Variable for storing the last name

    System.Console.WriteLine("Hey you!");

                  Delimited Comment Inside Statement
    System.Console.Write /* No new line */ (
        "Enter your first name: ");
    firstName = System.Console.ReadLine();

    System.Console.Write /* No new line */ (
        "Enter your last name: ");
    lastName = System.Console.ReadLine();

    /* Display a greeting to the console       Delimited Comment
       using composite formatting. */
    System.Console.WriteLine("Your full name is {0} {1}.",
        firstName, lastName);

    // This is the end
    // of the program listing
```

```
    }
  }
```

```
Hey you!
Enter your first name: Inigo
Enter your last name: Montoya
Your full name is Inigo Montoya
```

In spite of the inserted comments, compiling and executing the new program produces the same output as before.

Programmers use comments to describe and explain the code they are writing, especially where the syntax itself is difficult to understand, or perhaps a particular algorithm implementation is surprising. Since comments are pertinent only to the programmer reviewing the code, the compiler ignores comments and generates an assembly that is devoid of any trace that comments were part of the original source code.

Table 1.2 shows four different C# comment types. The program in Listing 1.17 includes two of these.

TABLE 1.2: C# Comment Types

Comment Type	Description	Example
Delimited comments	A forward slash followed by an asterisk, /*, identifies the beginning of a delimited comment. To end the comment use an asterisk followed by a forward slash: */. Comments of this form may span multiple lines in the code file or appear embedded within a line of code. The asterisks that appear at the beginning of the lines but within the delimiters are simply for formatting.	/*comment*/
Single-line comments	Comments may also be declared with a delimiter comprising two consecutive forward slash characters: //. The compiler treats all text from the delimiter to the end of the line as a comment. Comments of this form comprise a single line. It is possible, however, to place sequential single-line comments one after another, as is the case with the last comment in Listing 1.17.	//comment

Continues

TABLE 1.2: C# Comment Types *(Continued)*

Comment Type	Description	Example
XML delimited comments	Comments that begin with `/**` and end with `**/` are called XML delimited comments. They have the same characteristics as regular delimited comments, except that instead of ignoring XML comments entirely, the compiler can place them into a separate text file. XML delimited comments were only explicitly added in C# 2.0, but the syntax is compatible with C# 1.0.	`/**comment**/`
XML single-line comments	XML single-line comments begin with `///` and continue to the end of the line. In addition, the compiler can save single-line comments into a separate file with the XML delimited comments.	`///comment`

A more comprehensive discussion of the XML comments appears in Chapter 9, where I discuss the various XML tags that are explicitly part of the XML standard.

■ BEGINNER TOPIC

Extensible Markup Language (XML)

The Extensible Markup Language (XML) is a simple and flexible text format frequently used within web applications and for exchanging data between applications. XML is extensible because included within an XML document is information that describes the data, known as **metadata**. Here is a sample XML file.

```xml
<?xml version="1.0" encoding="utf-8" ?>
<body>
  <book title="Essential C# 2.0">
      <chapters>
          <chapter title="Introducing C#"/>
          <chapter title="Control Flow"/>
          ...
      </chapters>
  </book>
</body>
```

The file starts with a header indicating the version and character encoding of the XML file. After that appears one main "book" element. Elements begin with a word in angle brackets, such as <body>. To end an element, place the same word in angle brackets and add a forward slash to prefix the word, as in </body>. In addition to elements, XML supports attributes. title="Essential C# 2.0" is an example of an XML attribute. Note that the metadata (book title, chapter, and so on) describing the data ("Essential C# 2.0", "Control Flow") is included in the XML file. This can result in rather bloated files, but it offers the advantage that the data includes a description to aid in interpreting the data.

Common Intermediate Language and ILDASM

As mentioned earlier, the C# compiler converts C# code to CIL code and not to machine code that the processor can understand. Given an assembly (either a DLL or an executable), it is possible to view the CIL code using a CIL disassembler utility to deconstruct the assembly into its CIL representation. (The CIL disassembler is commonly referred to by its Microsoft-specific filename, ILDASM, which stands for IL Disassembler.) This program will disassemble a program or its class libraries, displaying the CIL generated by the C# compiler.

The exact command used for the CIL disassembler depends on which implementation of the CLI is used. You can execute the .NET CIL disassembler from the command line as shown in Output 1.8.

OUTPUT 1.8:

```
>ildasm /text HelloWorld.exe
```

The /text portion is used so that the output appears on the command console rather than in a new window. Similarly, the Mono disassembler implementation, which defaults to the command console, is shown in Output 1.9.

OUTPUT 1.9:

```
>monodis HelloWorld.exe
```

The stream of output that results by executing these commands is a dump of CIL code included in the `HelloWorld.exe` program. Note that CIL code is significantly easier to understand than machine code. For many developers, this may raise a concern because it is easier for programs to be decompiled and algorithms understood without explicitly redistributing the source code.

As with any program, CLI based or not, the only foolproof way of preventing disassembly is to disallow access to the compiled program altogether (for example, only hosting a program on a web site instead of distributing it out to a user's machine). However, if decreased accessibility to the source code is all that is required, there are several obfuscators. These obfuscators prevent the casual developer from accessing the code and instead create assemblies that are much more difficult and tedious to decompile into comprehensible code. Unless a program requires a high degree of algorithm security, these obfuscators are generally sufficient.

■ ADVANCED TOPIC

CIL Output for `HelloWorld.exe`

Listing 1.18 shows the CIL code created by `ILDASM`.

LISTING 1.18: Sample CIL Output

```
// Metadata version: v2.0.50727
.assembly extern mscorlib
{
  .publickeytoken = (B7 7A 5C 56 19 34 E0 89 )   // .z\V.4..
  .ver 2:0:0:0
}
.assembly HelloWorld
{
  .custom instance void
[mscorlib]System.Runtime.CompilerServices.CompilationRelaxations
Attribute::.ctor(int32) = ( 01 00 08 00 00 00 00 00 )
  .custom instance void
[mscorlib]System.Runtime.CompilerServices.RuntimeCompatibilityAt
tribute::.ctor() = ( 01 00 01 00 54 02 16 57 72 61 70 4E 6F 6E
    45 78                                   // ....T..WrapNonEx
63 65 70 74 69 6F 6E 54 68 72 6F 77 73 01 )  // ceptionThrows.
  .hash algorithm 0x00008004
  .ver 0:0:0:0
```

```
}
.module HelloWorld.exe
// MVID: {49C96993-E12B-4DD2-A127-34909F7C9A15}
.imagebase 0x00400000
.file alignment 0x00000200
.stackreserve 0x00100000
.subsystem 0x0003       // WINDOWS_CUI
.corflags 0x00000001    //  ILONLY
// Image base: 0x02EA0000

.class private auto ansi beforefieldinit HelloWorld
       extends [mscorlib]System.Object
{
  .method private hidebysig static void  Main() cil managed
  {
    .entrypoint
    // Code size       13 (0xd)
    .maxstack  8
    IL_0000:  nop
    IL_0001:  ldstr      "Hello. My name is Inigo Montoya."
    IL_0006:  call       void
[mscorlib]System.Console::WriteLine(string)
    IL_000b:  nop
    IL_000c:  ret
  } // end of method HelloWorld::Main

  .method public hidebysig specialname rtspecialname
          instance void  .ctor() cil managed
  {
    // Code size        7 (0x7)
    .maxstack  8
    IL_0000:  ldarg.0
    IL_0001:  call       instance void
[mscorlib]System.Object::.ctor()
    IL_0006:  ret
  } // end of method HelloWorld::.ctor

} // end of class HelloWorld
```

The beginning of the listing is the manifest information. It includes not only the full name of the disassembled module (HelloWorld.exe), but also all the modules and assemblies it depends on, along with their version information.

Perhaps the most interesting thing that can be gleaned from such a listing is how relatively easy it is to follow what the program is doing compared to trying to read and understand machine code (assembler). In the listing, an explicit reference to `System.Console.WriteLine()` appears. There is a lot of peripheral information to the CIL code listing, but if a developer wanted to understand the inner workings of a C# module (or any CLI-based program) without having access to the original source code, it would be relatively easy unless an obfuscator is used. In fact, several free tools are available (such as Lutz Roeder's Reflector for .NET) that can decompile from CIL to C# automatically.

SUMMARY

This chapter served as a rudimentary introduction to C#. It provided a means of familiarizing you with basic C# syntax. Because of C#'s similarity to C++ style languages, much of what I presented here should not have been new material. However, C# and managed code do have some distinct characteristics, such as compilation down to CIL. Although it is not unique, another key characteristic is that C# is entirely object oriented. Even things like reading and writing data to the console are object oriented. Object orientation is foundational to C#, and you will see this throughout this book.

The next chapter examines the fundamental data types that are part of the C# language, and discusses how you can use these data types with operands to form expressions.

■ 2 ■
Data Types

F ROM CHAPTER 1'S HelloWorld program, you got a feel for the C# language, its structure, basic syntax characteristics, and how to write the simplest of programs. This chapter continues to discuss the C# basics by investigating the fundamental C# types.

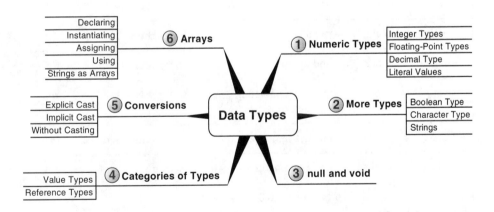

Until now, you have worked with only a few primitive data types, with little explanation. In C#, thousands of types exist, and you can combine types to create new types. A few types in C#, however, are relatively simple and are considered the building blocks of all other types. These types are **predefined types** or **primitives**. The C# language's primitive types include eight integer types, two floating-point types, a high-precision type, one Boolean type, and a character type. This chapter investigates these primitives, looks more closely at the `string` type, and introduces arrays.

Fundamental Numeric Types

The basic numeric types in C# have keywords associated with them. These types include integer types, floating-point types, and a `decimal` type to store large numbers with a high degree of accuracy.

Integer Types

There are eight C# integer types. This variety allows you to select a data type large enough to hold its intended range of values without wasting resources. Table 2.1 lists each integer type.

TABLE 2.1: Integer Types[a]

Type	Size	Range (Inclusive)	BCL Name	Signed
sbyte	8 bits	−128 and 127	System.SByte	Yes
byte	8 bits	0 and 255	System.Byte	No
short	16 bits	−32,768 and 32,767	System.Int16	Yes
ushort	16 bits	0 and 65,535	System.UInt16	No
int	32 bits	−2,147,483,648 and 2,147,483,647	System.Int32	Yes
uint	32 bits	0 and 4,294,967,295	System.UInt32	No
long	64 bits	−9,223,372,036,854,775,808 and 9,223,372,036,854,775,807	System.Int64	Yes
ulong	64 bits	0 and 18,446,744,073,709,551,615	System.UInt64	No

a. There was significant discussion among language designers and CLI designers about which types should be in the CLS. Ultimately, the decision was made to support only one type, signed or unsigned, per length. The C# designers insisted that although signed types for all lengths were acceptable in general, the byte type was an exception because unsigned bytes were more useful and common. In fact, it was argued, signed bytes could potentially cause programming problems. In the end, the C# team's perspective won out and the unsigned byte was included in the CLS instead of the signed byte.

Included in Table 2.1 (and in Tables 2.2 and 2.3) is a column for the full name of each type. All the fundamental types in C# have a short name and a full name. The full name corresponds to the type as it is named in the Base Class Library (BCL). This name is the same across all languages and it uniquely identifies the type within an assembly. Because of the fundamental nature of primitive types, C# also supplies keywords as short names or abbreviations to the full names of fundamental types. From the compiler's perspective, both names are exactly the same, producing exactly the same code. In fact, an examination of the resulting CIL code would provide no indication of which name was used.

Language Contrast: C++ — `short` Data Type

In C/C++, the `short` data type is an abbreviation for `short int`. In C#, `short` on its own is the actual data type.

Floating-Point Types (`float`, `double`)

Floating-point numbers have varying degrees of precision. If you were to read the value of a floating-point number to be 0.1, it could very easily be 0.099999999999999999 or 0.1000000000000000001 or some other number very close to 0.1. Alternatively, a large number such as Avagadro's number, 6.02E23, could be off by 9.9E9, which is something also exceptionally close to 6.02E23, considering its size. By definition, the accuracy of a floating-point number is in proportion to the size of the number it contains. Accuracy, therefore, is determined by the number of significant digits, not by a fixed value such as ±0.01.

C# supports the two floating-point number types listed in Table 2.2.

Binary numbers appear as base 10 (denary) numbers for human readability. The number of bits (binary digits) converts to 15 decimal digits, with a remainder that contributes to a sixteenth decimal digit as expressed in Table 2.2. Specifically, numbers between $1.7 * 10^{307}$ and less than $1 * 10^{308}$ have only 15 significant digits. However, numbers ranging from $1 * 10^{308}$ to $1.7 * 10^{308}$ will have 16 significant digits. A similar range of significant digits occurs with the `decimal` type as well.

TABLE 2.2: Floating-Point Types

Type	Size	Range (Inclusive)	BCL Name	Significant Digits
float	32 bits	$\pm 1.5 \times 10^{-45}$ to $\pm 3.4 \times 10^{38}$	System.Single	7
double	64 bits	$\pm 5.0 \times 10^{324}$ to $\pm 1.7 \times 10^{308}$	System.Double	15–16

Decimal Type

C# contains a numeric type with 128-bit precision (see Table 2.3). This is suitable for large and precise calculations, frequently financial calculations.

TABLE 2.3: **decimal** Type

Type	Size	Range (Inclusive)	BCL Name	Significant Digits
decimal	128 bits	1.0×10^{-28} to approximately 7.9×10^{28}	System.Decimal	28–29

Unlike floating-point numbers, the decimal type maintains exact precision for all denary numbers within its range. With the decimal type, therefore, a value of 0.1 is exactly 0.1. However, while the decimal type has greater precision than the floating-point types, it has a smaller range. Thus, conversions from floating-point types to the decimal type may result in overflow errors. Also, calculations with decimal are slightly slower.

■ ADVANCED TOPIC

Floating-Point Types and Decimals Dissected

Unless they are out of range, decimal numbers represent denary numbers exactly. In contrast, the floating-point representation of denary numbers introduces a possible rounding error. The difference between the decimal type and the C# floating-point types is that the exponent of a decimal type is a denary and the exponent of floating-point types is binary.

The exponent of a `decimal` is ±N * 10k where

- N is a positive integer represented by 96 bits.
- k is given by -28 <= k <= 0.

In contrast, a float is any number ±N * 2k where

- N is a positive integer represented by a fixed number of bits (24 for `float` and 53 for `double`).
- k is any integer ranging from -149 to +104 for `float` and -1075 to +970 for `double`.

Literal Values

A **literal value** is a representation of a constant value within source code. For example, if you want to have `System.Console.WriteLine()` print out the integer value 42 and the `double` value 1.618034 (Phi), you could use the code shown in Listing 2.1.

LISTING 2.1: Specifying Literal Values

```
System.Console.WriteLine(42);
System.Console.WriteLine(1.618034);
```

Output 2.1 shows the results of Listing 2.1.

OUTPUT 2.1:

```
42
1.618034
```

■ BEGINNER TOPIC

Use Caution When Hardcoding Values

The practice of placing a value directly into source code is called **hardcoding**, because changing the values means recompiling the code. Developers must carefully consider the choice between hardcoding values within their code and retrieving them from an external source, such as a configuration file, so that the values are modifiable without recompiling.

By default, when you specify a literal number with a decimal point, the compiler interprets it as a `double` type. Conversely, an integer value (with no decimal point) generally defaults to an `int`, assuming the value is not too large to be stored in an integer. If the value is too large, then the compiler will interpret it as a `long`. Furthermore, the C# compiler allows assignment to a numeric type other than an `int`, assuming the literal value is appropriate for the target data type. For example, `short s = 42` and `byte b = 77` are allowed. However, this is appropriate only for literal values; `b = s` is not appropriate without additional syntax, as discussed in the section Conversions between Data Types, later in this chapter.

As previously discussed in the section Fundamental Numeric Types, there are many different numeric types in C#. In Listing 2.2, a literal value is placed within C# code. Since numbers with a decimal point will default to the `double` data type, the output, shown in Output 2.2, is `1.61803398874989` (the last digit, 5, is missing), corresponding to the expected accuracy of a `double`.

LISTING 2.2: Specifying a Literal **double**

```
System.Console.WriteLine(1.618033988749895);
```

OUTPUT 2.2:

```
1.61803398874989
```

To view the intended number with its full accuracy, you must declare explicitly the literal value as a `decimal` type by appending an `m` (or `M`) (see Listing 2.3 and Output 2.3).

LISTING 2.3: Specifying a Literal **decimal**

```
System.Console.WriteLine(1.618033988749895m);
```

OUTPUT 2.3:

```
1.618033988749895
```

Now the output of Listing 2.3 is as expected: `1.618033988749895`. Note that `d` is for double. The `m` used to identify a `decimal` corresponds to its frequent use in monetary calculations.

You can also add a suffix to explicitly declare a literal as `float` or `double` by using the `f` and `d` suffixes, respectively. For integer data types, the suffixes are `u`, `l`, `lu`, and `ul`. The type of an integer literal can be determined as follows.

- Numeric literals with no suffix resolve to the first data type that can store the value in this order: `int`, `uint`, `long`, and `ulong`.
- Numeric literals with the suffix `u` resolve to the first data type that can store the value in the order `uint` and then `ulong`.
- Numeric literals with the suffix `l` resolve to the first data type that can store the value in the order `long` and then `ulong`.
- If the numeric literal has the suffix `ul` or `lu`, it is of type `ulong`.

Note that suffixes for literals are case insensitive. However, for `long`, uppercase is generally preferred because of the similarity between the lowercase letter l and the digit 1.

In some situations, you may wish to use exponential notation instead of writing out several zeroes before or after the decimal point. To use exponential notation, supply the `e` or `E` infix, follow the infix character with a positive or negative integer number, and complete the literal with the appropriate data type suffix. For example, you could print out Avagadro's number as a `float`, as shown in Listing 2.4 and Output 2.4.

LISTING 2.4: Exponential Notation

```
System.Console.WriteLine(6.023E23f);
```

OUTPUT 2.4:

```
6.023E+23
```

Hexadecimal Notation

Usually you work with numbers that are represented with a base of 10, meaning there are 10 symbols (0–9) for each digit in the number. If a number is displayed with hexadecimal notation, then it is displayed with a base of 16 numbers, meaning 16 symbols are used: 0–9, A–F (lowercase can also be used). Therefore, 0x000A corresponds to the decimal value 10 and 0x002A corresponds to the decimal value 42. The actual number is the same. Switching from hexadecimal to decimal or vice versa does not change the number itself, just the representation of the number.

Each hex digit is four bits, so a byte can represent two hex digits.

In all discussions of literal numeric values so far, I have covered only decimal type values. C# also supports the ability to specify hexadecimal values. To specify a hexadecimal value, prefix the value with 0x and then use any hexadecimal digit, as shown in Listing 2.5.

LISTING 2.5: Hexadecimal Literal Value

```
// Display the value 42 using a hexadecimal literal.
System.Console.WriteLine(0x002A);
```

Output 2.5 shows the results of Listing 2.5.

OUTPUT 2.5:

```
42
```

Note that this code still displays 42, not 0x002A.

Formatting Numbers as Hexadecimal

To display a numeric value in its hexadecimal format, it is necessary to use the x or X numeric formatting specifier. The casing determines whether the hexadecimal letters appear in lower- or uppercase. Listing 2.6 shows an example of how to do this.

LISTING 2.6: Example of a Hexadecimal Format Specifier

```
// Displays "0x2A"
System.Console.WriteLine("0x{0:X}", 42);
```

Output 2.6 shows the results.

OUTPUT 2.6:

```
0x2A
```

Note that the numeric literal (42) can be in decimal or hexadecimal form. The result will be the same.

■ **ADVANCED TOPIC**

Round-Trip Formatting

By default, `System.Console.WriteLine(1.618033988749895);` displays `1.61803398874989`, with the last digit missing. To more accurately identify the string representation of the double value it is possible to convert it using a format string and the round-trip format specifier, `R` (or `r`). `string.Format("{0:R}", 1.618033988749895)`, for example, will return the result `1.6180339887498949`.

The round-trip format specifier returns a string that, if converted back into a numeric value, will always result in the original value. Listing 2.7 demonstrates.

LISTING 2.7: Formatting Using the **R** Format Specifier

```
// ...
const double number = 1.618033988749895;
double result;
string text;

text = string.Format("{0}", number);
result = double.Parse(text);
System.Console.WriteLine("{0}: result != number",
   result != number);

text = string.Format("{0:R}", number);
result = double.Parse(text);
```

```
System.Console.WriteLine("{0}: result == number",
   result == number);
// ...
```

Output 2.7 shows the resulting output.

OUTPUT 2.7:

```
True: result != number
True: result == number
```

When assigning text the first time, there is no round-trip format specifier and, as a result, the value returned by double.Parse(text) is not the same as the original number value. In contrast, when the round-trip format specifier is used, double.Parse(text) returns the original value.

More Fundamental Types

The fundamental types discussed so far are numeric types. C# includes some additional types as well: bool, char, and string.

Boolean Type (bool)

Another C# primitive is a Boolean or conditional type, bool, which represents true or false in conditional statements and expressions. Allowable values are the keywords true and false. The BCL name for bool is System.Boolean. The literal values for a Boolean use the keywords true and false. For example, in order to compare two strings in a case-insensitive manner, you call the string.Compare() method and pass a bool literal of true (see Listing 2.8).

LISTING 2.8: A Case-Insensitive Comparison of Two Strings

```
string option;
...
int comparison = string.Compare(option, "/Help", true);
```

In this case, you make a case-insensitive comparison of the contents of the variable option with the literal text /Help and assign the result to comparison.

Although theoretically a single bit could hold the value of a Boolean, the size of `bool` is a byte.

Character Type (`char`)

A `char` type represents 16-bit characters whose set of possible values corresponds to the Unicode character set. Technically, a `char` is the same size as a 16-bit unsigned integer (`ushort`) with values between 0 and 65,535. However, `char` is a unique type in C# and code should treat it as such.

The BCL name for `char` is `System.Char`.

■ BEGINNER TOPIC

The Unicode Standard

Unicode is an international standard for representing characters found in the majority of human languages. It provides computer systems with functionality for building **localized** applications, applications that display the appropriate language and culture characteristics for different cultures.

■ ADVANCED TOPIC

16 Bits Is Too Small for All Unicode Characters

Unfortunately, not all Unicode characters are available within a 16-bit `char`. When Unicode was first started, its designers believed that 16 bits would be enough, but as more languages were supported, it was realized that this assumption was incorrect. The cumbersome result is that some Unicode characters are composed of surrogate `char` pairs totaling 32 bits.

To enter a literal character type, place the character within single quotes, as in `'A'`. Allowable characters comprise the full range of keyboard characters, including letters, numbers, and special symbols.

Some characters cannot be placed directly into the source code and instead require special handling. These characters are prefixed with a backslash (\) followed by a special character code. In combination, the backslash and special character code are an **escape sequence**. For example,

'\n' represents a newline, and '\t' represents a tab. Since a backslash indicates the beginning of an escape sequence, it can no longer identify a simple backslash; instead, you need to use '\\' to represent a single backslash character.

Listing 2.9 writes out one single quote because the character represented by \' corresponds to a single quote.

LISTING 2.9: Displaying a Single Quote Using an Escape Sequence

```
class SingleQuote
{
  static void Main()
  {
      System.Console.WriteLine('\'');
  }
}
```

In addition to showing the escape sequence, Table 2.4 includes the Unicode representation of characters.

TABLE 2.4: Escape Characters

Escape Sequence	Character Name	Unicode Encoding
\'	Single quote	0x0027
\"	Double quote	0x0022
\\	Backslash	0x005C
\0	Null	0x0000
\a	Alert (system beep)	0x0007
\b	Backspace	0x0008
\f	Form feed	0x000C
\n	Line feed (sometimes referred to as a newline)	0x000A
\r	Carriage return	0x000D
\t	Horizontal tab	0x0009

TABLE 2.4: Escape Characters *(Continued)*

Escape Sequence	Character Name	Unicode Encoding
\v	Vertical tab	0x000B
\uxxxx	Unicode character in hex	\u0029
\x[n][n][n]n	Unicode character in hex (first three placeholders are optional); variable length version of \uxxxx	\x3A
\Uxxxxxxxx	Unicode escape sequence for creating surrogate pairs	\UD840DC01 (𠀁)

You can represent any character using Unicode encoding. To do so, prefix the Unicode value with \u. You represent Unicode characters in hexadecimal notation. The letter A, for example, is the hexadecimal value 0x41; Listing 2.10 uses Unicode characters to display a smiley face (:)), and Output 2.8 shows the results.

LISTING 2.10: Using Unicode Encoding to Display a Smiley Face

```
System.Console.Write('\u003A');
System.Console.WriteLine('\u0029');
```

OUTPUT 2.8:

```
:)
```

Strings

The fundamental string type in C# is the data type string, whose BCL name is System.String. The string includes some special characteristics that may be unexpected to developers familiar with other programming languages. The characteristics include a string verbatim prefix character, @, and the fact that a string is immutable.

Literals

You can enter a literal string into code by placing the text in double quotes ("), as you saw in the HelloWorld program. Strings are composed of characters, and because of this, escape sequences can be embedded within a string.

In Listing 2.11, for example, two lines of text are displayed. However, instead of using `System.Console.WriteLine()`, the code listing shows `System.Console.Write()` with the newline character, \n. Output 2.9 shows the results.

LISTING 2.11: Using the \n Character to Insert a Newline

```
class DuelOfWits
{
  static void Main()
  {
      System.Console.Write(
          "\"Truly, you have a dizzying intellect.\"");
      System.Console.Write("\n\"Wait 'til I get going!\"\n");
  }
}
```

OUTPUT 2.9:

```
"Truly, you have a dizzying intellect."
"Wait 'til I get going!"
```

The escape sequence for double quotes differentiates the printed double quotes from the double quotes that define the beginning and end of the string.

In C#, you can use the @ symbol in front of a string to signify that a backslash should not be interpreted as the beginning of an escape sequence. The resulting **verbatim string literal** does not reinterpret just the backslash character. Whitespace is also taken verbatim when using the @ string syntax. The triangle in Listing 2.12, for example, appears in the console exactly as typed, including the backslashes, newlines, and indentation. Output 2.10 shows the results.

LISTING 2.12: Displaying a Triangle Using a Verbatim String Literal

```
class Triangle
{
  static void Main()
  {
```

```
        System.Console.Write(@ "begin
                /\
               /  \
              /    \
             /      \
            /_____\
    end");
        }
    }
```

OUTPUT 2.10:

Without the @ character, this code would not even compile. In fact, even if you changed the shape to a square, eliminating the backslashes, the code would still not compile because a newline cannot be placed directly within a string that is not prefaced with the @ symbol.

The only escape sequence the verbatim string does support is " ", which signifies double quotes and does not terminate the string.

Language Contrast: C++ — String Concatenation at Compile Time

Unlike C++, C# does not automatically concatenate literal strings. You cannot, for example, specify a string literal as follows:

```
"Major Strasser has been shot. " "Round up the usual suspects."
```

Rather, concatenation requires the use of the addition operator. (If the compiler can calculate the result at compile time, the resulting CIL code will be a single string.)

If the same literal string appears within an assembly multiple times, the compiler will define the string only once within the assembly and all variables will point to the single string literal. That way, if the same string literal containing thousands of characters was placed multiple times into the code, the resulting assembly would reflect the size of only one of them.

String Methods

The string type, like the `System.Console` type, includes several methods. There are methods, for example, for formatting, concatenating, and comparing strings.

The `Format()` method in Table 2.5 behaves exactly like the `Console.Write()` and `Console.WriteLine()` methods, except that instead of displaying the result in the console window, `string.Format()` returns the result.

All of these methods are static. This means that, to call the method, it is necessary to prefix the method name with the type that contains the method. Some of the methods in the string class, however, are instance methods. Instead of prefixing the method with the type, instance methods use the variable name (or some other reference to an instance). Table 2.6 shows a few of these methods, along with an example.

TABLE 2.5: **string** Static Methods

Statement	Example
void static **string**.Format(**string** format, ...)	**string** text, firstName, lastName; .... text = **string**.Format("Your full name is {0} {1}.",firstName, lastName); // Display // "Your full name is // <firstName> <lastName>." System.Console.WriteLine(text);
void static **string**.Concat(**string** str0, **string** str1)	**string** text, firstName, lastName; ... text = string.Concat(firstName, lastName); // Display "<firstName><lastName>", notice // that there is no space between names. System.Console.WriteLine(text);

TABLE 2.5: **string** Static Methods *(Continued)*

Statement	Example

static int
 string.Compare(
     string str0,
     string str1)
	string option;
	 ...
	 // *String comparison in which*
	 // *case matters.*
	 int result = **string**.Compare(option,
	     "/help");
	
	 // *Display:*
	 // *0 if equal*
	 // *negative if option < /help*
	 // *positive if option > /help*
	 System.Console.WriteLine(result);

	string option; ... // *Case-insensitive string comparison* **int** result = **string**.Compare(option, "/Help", **true**); // *Display:* // *0 if equal* // *< 0 if option < /help* // *> 0 if option > /help* System.Console.WriteLine(result);

TABLE 2.6: **string** Instance Methods

Statement	Example

bool StartsWith(
     string value)
 bool EndsWith(
     string value)
	string lastName
	 ...
	 bool isPhd = lastName.EndsWith("Ph.D.");
	 bool isDr = lastName.StartsWith("Dr.");

string ToLower() **string** ToUpper()	**string** severity = "warning"; // *Display the severity in uppercase* System.Console.WriteLine(severity.ToUpper());
string Trim() **string** Trim(...) **string** TrimEnd() **string** TrimStart()	// *Remove any whitespace at the start* // *or end.* username = username.Trim();

string Replace(
     string oldValue,
     string newValue)
	string filename;
	 ...
	 // *Remove ?'s altogether from the string*
	 filename = filename.Replace("?", "");;

■ ADVANCED TOPIC

C# Properties

Technically, the `Length` member referred to in the following section is not actually a method, as indicated by the fact that there are no parentheses following its call. `Length` is a property of `string`, and C# syntax allows access to a property as though it were a member variable (known in C# as a **field**). In other words, a property has the behavior of special methods called setters and getters, but the syntax for accessing that behavior is that of a field.

Examining the underlying CIL implementation of a property reveals that it compiles into two methods: `set_<PropertyName>` and `get_<PropertyName>`. Neither of these, however, is directly accessible from C# code, except through the C# property constructs.

String Length

To determine the length of a string you use a string member called `Length`. This particular member is called a **read-only property**. As such, it can't be set, nor does calling it require any parameters. Listing 2.13 demonstrates how to use the `Length` property, and Output 2.11 shows the results.

LISTING 2.13: Using **string's Length** Member

```
class PalindromeLength
{
  static void Main()
  {
      string palindrome;

      System.Console.Write("Enter a palindrome: ");
      palindrome = System.Console.ReadLine();

      System.Console.WriteLine(
          "The palindrome, \"{0}\" is {1} characters.",
          palindrome, palindrome.Length);
  }
}
```

OUTPUT 2.11:

```
Enter a palindrome: Never odd or even
The palindrome, "Never odd or even" is 17 characters.
```

The length for a string cannot be set directly; it is calculated from the number of characters in the string. Furthermore, the length of a string cannot change because a string is **immutable**.

Strings Are Immutable

The key characteristic of the `string` type is the fact that it is immutable. A string variable can be assigned an entirely new value, but for performance reasons, there is no facility for modifying the contents of a `string`. It is not possible, therefore, to convert a `string` to all uppercase letters. It is trivial to create a new string that is composed of an uppercase version of the old string, but the old string is not modified in the process. Consider Listing 2.14 as an example.

LISTING 2.14: Error; **`string`** Is Immutable

```
class Uppercase
{
  static void Main()
  {
      string text;

      System.Console.Write("Enter text: ");
      text = System.Console.ReadLine();

      // UNEXPECTED:  Does not convert text to uppercase
      text.ToUpper();

      System.Console.WriteLine(text);
  }
}
```

Output 2.12 shows the results of Listing 2.14.

OUTPUT 2.12:

```
Enter text: This is a test of the emergency broadcast system.
This is a test of the emergency broadcast system.
```

At a glance, it would appear that `text.ToUpper()` should convert the characters within `text` to uppercase. However, strings are immutable and, therefore, `text.ToUpper()` will make no such modification. Instead, `text.ToUpper()` returns a new string that needs to be saved into a variable or passed to `System.Console.WriteLine()` directly. The corrected code is shown in Listing 2.15, and its output is shown in Output 2.13.

LISTING 2.15: **Working with Strings**

```
class Uppercase
{
  static void Main()
  {
      string text, uppercase;

      System.Console.Write("Enter text: ");
      text = System.Console.ReadLine();

      // Return a new string in uppercase
      uppercase = text.ToUpper();

      System.Console.WriteLine(uppercase);
  }
}
```

OUTPUT 2.13:

```
Enter text: This is a test of the emergency broadcast system.
THIS IS A TEST OF THE EMERGENCY BROADCAST SYSTEM.
```

If the immutability of a string is ignored, mistakes similar to those shown in Listing 2.14 can occur with other string methods as well.

To actually change the value in `text`, assign the value from `ToUpper()` back into text, as in the following:

```
text = text.ToUpper();
```

System.Text.StringBuilder

If considerable string modification is needed, such as when constructing a long string in multiple steps, you should use the data type `System.Text.StringBuilder` rather than `string`. `System.Text.StringBuilder` includes methods such as `Append()`, `AppendFormat()`, `Insert()`, `Remove()`, and `Replace()`, some of which also appear on `string`. The key difference, however, is that on `System.Text.StringBuilder`, these methods will modify the data in the variable, and will not simply return a new string.

null **and** void

Two additional keywords relating to types are null and void. null is a literal value used to indicate that the data type (specifically, a reference type) is assigned nothing. void is used to indicate the absence of a type or the absence of any value altogether.

null

null can also be used as a type of string "literal." null indicates that a variable is set to nothing. Only reference types can be assigned the value null. The only reference type covered so far in this book is string; Chapter 5 covers the topic of reference types in detail. For now, suffice it to say that a reference type contains a pointer, an address, or a reference to a location in memory that is different from where the actual data resides. Code that sets a variable to null explicitly assigns the reference to point at nothing. In fact, it is even possible to check whether a reference type points to nothing. Listing 2.16 demonstrates assigning null to a string variable.

LISTING 2.16: Assigning **null** to a String

```
static void Main()
{
    string faxNumber;
    // ...

    // Clear the value of faxNumber.
    faxNumber = null;

    // ...
}
```

It is important to note that assigning the value null to a reference type is distinct from not assigning it at all. In other words, a variable that has been assigned null has still been set, and a variable with no assignment has not been set and therefore will often cause a compile error if used prior to assignment.

Assigning the value null to a string is distinctly different from assigning an empty string, "". null indicates that the variable has no value. "" indicates that there is a value: an empty string. This type of distinction can be quite useful. For example, the programming logic could interpret a `faxNumber` of `null` to mean that the fax number is unknown, while a `faxNumber` value of `""` could indicate that there is no fax number.

The `void` Nontype

Sometimes the C# syntax requires a data type to be specified but no data is passed. For example, if no return from a method is needed C# allows the use of `void` to be specified as the data type instead. The declaration of `Main` within the `HelloWorld` program is an example. Under these circumstances, the data type to specify is `void`. The use of `void` as the return type indicates that the method is not returning any data and tells the compiler not to expect a value. `void` is not a data type per se, but rather, an identification of the fact that there is no data type.

Language Contrast: C++—`void` Is a Data Type

In C++, `void` is a data type commonly used as `void**`. In C#, `void` is not considered a data type. Rather, it is used to identify that a method does not return a value.

Categories of Types

All types fall into two categories: **value types** and **reference types**. The differences between the types in each category stem from the fact that each category uses a different location in memory: Value type data is stored on the stack and reference type data is stored on the heap.

Value Types

With the exception of `string`, all the predefined types in the book so far are value types. Value types contain the value directly. In other words, the variable refers to the same location in memory where the value is stored. Because of this, when a different variable is assigned the same value, a memory copy of the original variable's value is made to the location of the new variable. A second variable of the same value type cannot refer to the same location in memory as the first variable. So changing the value of the first

variable will not affect the value in the second. Figure 2.1 demonstrates this.
`number1` refers to a particular location in memory that contains the value `42`.
After assigning `number1` to `number2`, both variables will contain the value
`42`. However, modifying either value will not affect the other.

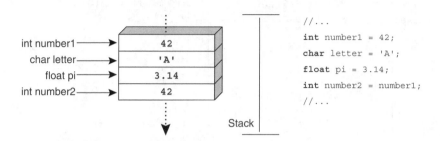

Figure 2.1: Value Types Contain the Data Directly

Similarly, passing a value type to a method such as `Console.Write-`
`Line()` will also result in a memory copy, and any changes to the parameter
value inside the method will not affect the original value within the calling
function. Since value types require a memory copy, they generally should be
defined to consume a small amount of memory (less than 16 bytes).

The amount of memory required for the value type is fixed at compile
time and will not change at runtime. This fixed size allows value types to
be stored in the area of memory known as the **stack**.

Reference Types

Reference types and the variables that refer to them point to the data storage location. Reference types store the reference (memory address) where
the data is located instead of storing the data directly. Therefore, to access
the data the runtime will read the memory location out of the variable and
then jump to the location in memory that contains the data. The memory
area of the data a reference type points to is the **heap** (see Figure 2.2).

Since accessing reference type data involves an extra hop, sometimes it
behaves slightly slower. However, a reference type does not require the same
memory copy of the data that a value type does, resulting in circumstances
when it is more efficient. When assigning one reference type variable to
another reference type variable, only a memory copy of the address occurs,

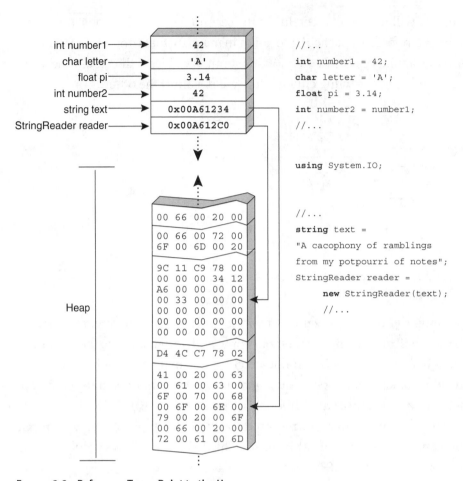

```
//...
int number1 = 42;
char letter = 'A';
float pi = 3.14;
int number2 = number1;
//...


using System.IO;


//...
string text =
"A cacophony of ramblings
from my potpourri of notes";
StringReader reader =
    new StringReader(text);
    //...
```

FIGURE 2.2: Reference Types Point to the Heap

and as such, the memory copy required by a reference type is always the size of the address itself. (A 32-bit processor will copy 32 bits and a 64-bit processor will copy 64 bits, and so on.) Obviously, not copying the data would be faster than a value type's behavior if the latter's data size is large.

Since reference types copy only the address of the data, two different variables can point to the same data. Furthermore, changing the data through one variable will change the data for the other variable as well. This happens both for assignment and for method calls. Therefore, a method can affect the data of a reference type back at the caller.

Besides `string` and any custom classes such as `Program`, all types discussed so far are value types. However, most types are reference types, and although it is possible to define custom value types, it is relatively rare to do so in comparison to the number of custom reference types.

Nullable Modifier

As I pointed out earlier, value types cannot be assigned `null` because, by definition, they can't contain references, including references to nothing. However, this presents a problem in the real world, where values are missing. When specifying a count, for example, what do you enter if the count is unknown? One possible solution is to designate a "magic" value, such as `0` or `int.Max`, but these are valid integers. Rather, it is desirable to assign `null` to the value type because this is not a valid integer.

To declare variables that can store `null` you use the nullable modifier, `?`. This C# 2.0 feature appears in Listing 2.17.

LISTING 2.17: Using the Nullable Modifier

```
static void Main()
{
    int? count = null;
    do
    {
        // ...
    }
    while(count == null);
}
```

Assigning `null` to value types is especially attractive in database programming. Frequently value type columns in database tables allow `null`s. Retrieving such columns and assigning them to corresponding fields within C# code is problematic, unless the fields can contain `null` as well. Fortunately, the nullable modifier is designed to handle such a scenario specifically.

Conversions between Data Types

Given the thousands of types predefined in the various CLI implementations and the unlimited number of types that code can define, it is important that types support conversion from one to another where it makes sense. The most common type of conversion is **casting**.

Consider the conversion between two numerical types: converting from a variable of type `long` to a variable of type `int`. A `long` type can contain values as large as 9,223,372,036,854,775,808; however, the maximum size of an `int` is 2,147,483,647. As such, that conversion could result in a loss of data—for example, if the variable of type `long` contains a value greater than the maximum size of an `int`. Any conversion that could result in a loss of data or an exception because the conversion failed requires an **explicit cast**. Conversely, a casting operation that will not lose precision and will not throw an exception regardless of the operand types is an **implicit cast**.

Explicit Cast

In C#, you cast using the **cast operator**. By specifying the type you would like the variable converted to within parentheses, you acknowledge that if an explicit cast is occurring, there may be a loss of precision and data, or an exception may result. The code in Listing 2.18 converts a `long` to an `int` and explicitly tells the system to attempt the operation.

LISTING 2.18: Explicit Cast Example

```
long longNumber = 50918309109;
int intNumber = (int) longNumber;
                ‿‿‿
               Cast Operator
```

With the cast operator, the programmer essentially says to the compiler, "Trust me, I know what I am doing. I know that the conversion could possibly not fit but I am willing to take the chance." Making such a choice will cause the compiler to allow the conversion. However, with an explicit conversion, there is still a chance that an error, in the form of an exception, might occur at runtime if the data does not convert successfully. It is, therefore, the programmer's responsibility to ensure the data will successfully convert, or else to provide the necessary code logic when it doesn't.

■ADVANCED TOPIC

Checked and Unchecked Conversions

C# provides special keywords for marking a code block to indicate what should happen if the target data type is too small to contain the assigned data.

By default, if the target data type cannot contain the assigned data, then the data will truncate during assignment. For an example, see Listing 2.19.

LISTING 2.19: Overflowing an Integer Value

```
public class Program
{
  public static void Main()
  {
      // int.MaxValue equals 2147483647
      int n = int.MaxValue;
      n = n + 1 ;
      System.Console.WriteLine(n);
  }
}
```

Output 2.14 shows the results.

OUTPUT 2.14:

```
-2147483648
```

Listing 2.19 writes the value -2147483648 to the console. However, placing the code within a **checked block**, or using the checked option when running the compiler, will cause the runtime to throw an exception of type System.OverflowException. The syntax for a checked block uses the checked keyword, as shown in Listing 2.20.

LISTING 2.20: A Checked Block Example

```
public class Program
{
  public static void Main()
  {
      checked
      {
          // int.MaxValue equals 2147483647
          int n = int.MaxValue;
          n = n + 1 ;
          System.Console.WriteLine(n);
      }
  }
}
```

Output 2.15 shows the results.

OUTPUT 2.15:

```
Unhandled Exception: System.OverflowException: Arithmetic operation
resulted in an overflow at Program.Main() in ...Program.cs:line 12
```

The result is that an exception is thrown if, within the checked block, an overflow assignment occurs at runtime.

The C# compiler provides a command-line option for changing the default checked behavior from unchecked to checked. C# also supports an unchecked block that truncates the data instead of throwing an exception for assignments within the block (see Listing 2.21).

LISTING 2.21: An Unchecked Block Example

```csharp
using System;

public class Program
{
  public static void Main()
  {
    unchecked
    {
      // int.MaxValue equals 2147483647
      int n = int.MaxValue;
      n = n + 1 ;
      System.Console.WriteLine(n);
    }
  }
}
```

Output 2.16 shows the results.

OUTPUT 2.16:

```
-2147483648
```

Even if the checked option is on during compilation, the unchecked keyword in the preceding code will prevent the runtime from throwing an exception during execution.

You cannot convert any type to any other type simply because you designate the conversion explicitly using the cast operator. The compiler will still check that the operation is valid. For example, you cannot convert a `long` to a `bool`. No such cast operator is defined, and therefore, the compiler does not allow such a cast.

Language Contrast: Converting Numbers to Booleans

It may be surprising that there is no valid cast from a numeric type to a Boolean type, since this is common in many other languages. The reason no such conversion exists in C# is to avoid any ambiguity, such as whether −1 corresponds to true or false. More importantly, as you will see in the next chapter, this also reduces the chance of using the assignment operator in place of the equality operator (avoiding `if(x=42){...}` when `if(x==42){...}` was intended, for example).

Implicit Cast

In other instances, such as going from an `int` type to a `long` type, there is no loss of precision and there will be no fundamental change in the value of the type. In these cases, code needs only to specify the assignment operator and the conversion is **implicit**. In other words, the compiler is able to determine that such a conversion will work correctly. The code in Listing 2.22 converts from an `int` to a `long` by simply using the assignment operator.

LISTING 2.22: Not Using the Cast Operator for an Implicit Cast

```
int intNumber = 31416;
long longNumber = intNumber;
```

Even when no explicit cast operator is required (because an implicit conversion is allowed), it is still possible to include the cast operator (see Listing 2.23).

LISTING 2.23: Using the Cast Operator for an Implicit Cast

```
int intNumber = 31416;
long longNumber = (long) intNumber;
```

Type Conversion without Casting

Neither an implicit nor an explicit cast is defined from a string to a numeric type, so methods such as `Parse()` are required. Each numeric data type includes a `Parse()` function that enables conversion from a string to the corresponding numeric type. Listing 2.24 demonstrates this call.

LISTING 2.24: Using **int.Parse()** to Convert a **string** to a Numeric Data Type

```
string text = "9.11E-31";
float kgElectronMass = float.Parse(text);
```

Another special type is available for converting one type to the next. The type is `System.Convert` and an example of its use appears in Listing 2.25.

LISTING 2.25: Type Conversion Using **System.Convert**

```
string middleCText = "278.4375";
double middleC = System.Convert.ToDouble(middleCText);
bool boolean = System.Convert.ToBoolean(middleC);
```

`System.Convert` supports only a predefined number of types and it is not extensible.

Furthermore, all types support a `ToString()` method that can be used to provide a string representation of a type. Listing 2.26 demonstrates how to use this method. The resulting output is shown in Output 2.17.

LISTING 2.26: Using **ToString()** to Convert to a **string**

```
bool boolean = true;
string text = boolean.ToString();
// Display "True"
System.Console.WriteLine(text);
```

OUTPUT 2.17:

```
True
```

For the majority of types, the `ToString()` method will return the name of the data type rather than a string representation of the data. The string representation is returned only if the type has an explicit implementation of `ToString()`. One last point to make is that it is possible to code custom conversion methods, and many such methods are available for classes in the runtime.

■ ADVANCED TOPIC

TryParse()

In C# 2.0, all the numeric primitive types include a static `TryParse()` method. (In C# 1.0, only `double` includes such a method.) This method is very similar to the `Parse()` method, except that instead of throwing an exception if the conversion fails, the `TryParse()` method returns `false`, as demonstrated in Listing 2.27.

LISTING 2.27: Using **TryParse()** in Place of an Invalid Cast Exception

```
double number;
string input;

System.Console.Write("Enter a number: ");
input = System.Console.ReadLine();
if (double.TryParse(input, out number))
{
    // Converted correctly, now use number
    // ...
}
else
{
    System.Console.WriteLine(
        "The text entered was not a valid number.");
}
```

Output 2.18 shows the results of Listing 2.27.

OUTPUT 2.18:

```
Enter a number: forty-two
The text entered was not a valid number.
```

The resulting value the code parses from the input `string` is returned via an `out` parameter—in this case, `number`.

The key difference between `Parse()` and `TryParse()` is the fact that `TryParse()` won't throw an exception if it fails. Frequently, the conversion from a `string` to a numeric type depends on a user entering the text.

It is expected, in such scenarios, that the user will enter invalid data that will not parse successfully. By using `TryParse()` rather than `Parse()`, you can avoid throwing exceptions in expected situations. (The expected situation in this case is that the user will enter invalid data.)

Arrays

One particular aspect of variable declaration that Chapter 1 didn't cover is array declaration. With array declaration, you can store multiple items of the same type using a single variable and still access them individually using the index when required. In C#, the array index starts at zero. Therefore, arrays in C# are **zero based**.

■ BEGINNER TOPIC

Arrays

Arrays provide a means of declaring a collection of data items that are of the same type using a single variable. Each item within the array is uniquely designated using an integer value called the **index**. The first item in a C# array is accessed using index 0. Programmers should be careful to specify an index value that is less than the array size. Since C# arrays are zero based, the index for the last element in an array is one less than the total number of items in the array.

Declaring an Array

In C#, you declare arrays using square brackets. First, you specify the type of the items within the array, followed by open and closed square brackets; then you enter the name of the variable. Listing 2.28 declares a variable called `languages` to be an array of strings.

LISTING 2.28: Declaring an Array

```
string[] languages;
```

Obviously, the first part of the array identifies the data type of the elements within the array. The square brackets that are part of the declaration identify the **rank**, or the number of dimensions, for the array; in this case it is an array of rank one. These two pieces form the data type for the variable `languages`.

Listing 2.28 defines an array with a rank of one. Commas within the square brackets define additional dimensions. Listing 2.29, for example, defines a two-dimensional array of cells for a game of chess or tic-tac-toe.

LISTING 2.29: Declaring a Two-Dimensional Array

```
//     |   |
// ---+---+---
//     |   |
// ---+---+---
//     |   |
int[,] cells;
```

In Listing 2.29, the array has a rank of two. The first dimension could correspond to cells going across and the second dimension represents cells going down. Additional dimensions are added, with additional commas, and the total rank is one more than the number of commas. Note that the number of items that occur for a particular dimension is not part of the variable declaration. This is specified when creating (instantiating) the array and allocating space for each element.

Instantiating and Assigning Arrays

Once an array is declared, you can immediately fill its values using a comma-delimited list of items enclosed within a pair of curly braces. Listing 2.30 declares an array of strings and then assigns the names of nine languages within curly braces.

LISTING 2.30: Array Declaration with Assignment

```
string[] languages = { "C#", "COBOL", "Java",
    "C++", "Visual Basic", "Pascal",
    "Fortran", "Lisp", "J#"};
```

The first item in the comma-delimited list becomes the first item in the array; the second item in the list becomes the second item in the array, and so on. The curly brackets are the notation for defining an array literal.

The assignment syntax shown in Listing 2.30 is available only if you declare and assign the value within one statement. To assign the value after declaration requires the use of the keyword new and the corresponding data type, as shown in Listing 2.31.

LISTING 2.31: Array Assignment Following Declaration

```
string[] languages;
languages = new string[]{"C#", "COBOL", "Java",
    "C++", "Visual Basic", "Pascal",
    "Fortran", "Lisp", "J#" };
```

C# also allows use of the new keyword as part of the declaration statement, so it allows the assignment and the declaration shown in Listing 2.32.

LISTING 2.32: Array Assignment with new during Declaration

```
string[] languages = new string[]{
    "C#", "COBOL", "Java",
    "C++", "Visual Basic", "Pascal",
    "Fortran", "Lisp", "J#"};
```

The use of the new keyword tells the runtime to allocate memory for the data type. It instructs the runtime to instantiate the data type—in this case, an array.

Whenever you use the new keyword as part of an array assignment, you may also specify the size of the array within the square brackets. Listing 2.33 demonstrates this syntax.

LISTING 2.33: Declaration and Assignment with the new Keyword

```
string[] languages = new string[9]{
    "C#", "COBOL", "Java",
    "C++", "Visual Basic", "Pascal",
    "Fortran", "Lisp", "J#"};
```

The array size in the initialization statement and the number of elements contained within the curly braces must match. Furthermore, it is possible to assign an array but not specify the initial values of the array, as demonstrated in Listing 2.34.

LISTING 2.34: **Assigning without Literal Values**

```
string[] languages = new string[9];
```

Assigning an array but not initializing the initial values will still initialize each element. The runtime initializes elements to their default values, as follows.

- Reference types (such as string) are initialized to `null`.
- Numeric types are initialized to zero.
- `bool` is initialized to `false`.
- `char` is initialized to `\0`.

As a result, it is not necessary to individually assign each element of an array before using it.

In C# 2.0, it is possible to use the `default()` operator to determine the default value of a data type. `default()` takes a data type as a parameter. `default(int)`, for example, returns 0 and `default(char)` returns `\0`.

Because the array size is not included as part of the variable declaration, it is possible to specify the size at runtime. For example, Listing 2.35 creates an array based on the size specified in the `Console.ReadLine()` call.

LISTING 2.35: **Defining the Array Size at Runtime**

```
string[] groceryList;
System.Console.Write("How many items on the list? ");
int size = int.Parse(System.Console.ReadLine());
groceryList = new string[size];
// ...
```

C# initializes multidimensional arrays similarly. A comma separates the size of each rank. Listing 2.36 initializes a tic-tac-toe board with no moves.

LISTING 2.36: Declaring a Two-Dimensional Array

```
int[,] cells = int[3,3];
```

Initializing a tic-tac-toe board with a specific position instead could be done as shown in Listing 2.37.

LISTING 2.37: Initializing a Two-Dimensional Array of Integers

```
int[,] cells = {
        {1, 0, 2},
        {1, 2, 0},
        {1, 2, 1}
    };
```

The initialization follows the pattern in which there is an array of three elements of type `int[]`, and each element has the same size; in this example, the size is three. Note that the dimension of each `int[]` element must be identical. The declaration shown in Listing 2.38, therefore, is not valid.

LISTING 2.38: A Multidimensional Array with Inconsistent Size, Causing an Error

```
// ERROR:  Each dimension must be consistently sized.
int[,] cells = {
        {1, 0, 2, 0},
        {1, 2, 0},
        {1, 2}
        {1}
    };
```

Representing tic-tac-toe does not require an integer in each position. One alternative is a separate virtual board for each player, with each board containing a `bool` that indicates which positions the players selected. Listing 2.39 corresponds to a three-dimensional board.

LISTING 2.39: Initializing a Three-Dimensional Array

```
bool[,,] cells;
cells = new bool[2,3,3]
  {
      // Player 1 moves           // X |   |
      { {true, false, false},     // ---+---+---
        {true, false, false},     // X |   |
        {true, false, true} },    // ---+---+---
                                  // X |   | X
```

```
    // Player 2 moves                  //    |   | O
    {   {false, false, true},          // ---+---+---
        {false, true,  false},         //    | O |
        {false, true,  true} }         // ---+---+---
                                       //    | O |
};
```

In this example, the board is initialized and the size of each rank is explicitly identified. In addition to identifying the size as part of the new expression, the literal values for the array are provided. The literal values of type bool[,,] are broken into two arrays of type bool[,], size 3x3. Each two-dimensional array is composed of three bool arrays, size 3.

As already mentioned, each dimension in a multidimensional array must be consistently sized. However, it is also possible to define a **jagged array**, which is an array of arrays. Jagged array syntax is slightly different from that of a multidimensional array, and furthermore, jagged arrays do not need to be consistently sized. Therefore, it is possible to initialize a jagged array as shown in Listing 2.40.

LISTING 2.40: Initializing a Jagged Array

```
int [][] cells = {
    new int[] {1, 0, 2, 0},
    new int[] {1, 2, 0},
    new int[] {1, 2},
    new int[] {1}
};
```

A jagged array doesn't use a comma to identify a new dimension. Rather, a jagged array defines an array of arrays. In Listing 2.40, [] is placed after the data type int[], thereby declaring an array of type int[].

Notice that a jagged array requires an array instance for each internal array. In this example, you use new to instantiate the internal element of the jagged arrays. Leaving out the instantiation would cause a compile error.

Using an Array

You access a specific item in an array using the square bracket notation, known as the **array accessor**. To retrieve the first item from an array, you specify zero as the index. In Listing 2.41, the value of the fifth item (using the index 4 because the first item is index 0) in the languages variable is stored in the variable language.

LISTING 2.41: Declaring and Accessing an Array

```
string[] languages = new string[9]{
    "C#", "COBOL", "Java",
    "C++", "Visual Basic", "Pascal",
    "Fortran", "Lisp", "J#"};
// Retrieve 3rd item in languages array (Java)
string language = languages[2];
```

The square bracket notation is also used to store data into an array. List-ing 2.42 switches the order of "C++" and "Java".

LISTING 2.42: Swapping Data between Positions in an Array

```
string[] languages = new string[9]{
    "C#", "COBOL", "Java",
    "C++", "Visual Basic", "Pascal",
    "Fortran", "Lisp", "J#"};
// Save "C++" to variable called language.
string language = languages[3];
// Assign "Java" to the C++ position.
languages[3] = languages[2];
// Assign language to location of "Java".
languages[2] = language;
```

For multidimensional arrays, an element is identified with an index for each dimension, as shown in Listing 2.43.

LISTING 2.43: Initializing a Two-Dimensional Array of Integers

```
int[,] cells = {
        {1, 0, 2},
        {0, 2, 0},
        {1, 2, 1}
    };
// Set the winning tic-tac-toe move to be player 1.
cells[1,0] = 1;
```

Jagged array element assignment is slightly different because it is con-sistent with the jagged array declaration. The first element is an array within the array of arrays. The second index specifies the item within the selected array element (see Listing 2.44).

LISTING 2.44: Declaring a Jagged Array

```
int[][] cells = {
    new int[]{1, 0, 2},
```

```
        new int[]{0, 2, 0},
        new int[]{1, 2, 1}
    };

    cells[1][0] = 1;
    // ...
```

Length

You can obtain the length of an array, as shown in Listing 2.45.

LISTING 2.45: Retrieving the Length of an Array

```
Console.WriteLine("There are {0} languages in the array.",
    languages.Length);
```

Arrays have a fixed length; they are bound such that the length cannot be changed without re-creating the array. Furthermore, overstepping the **bounds** (or length) of the array will cause the runtime to report an error. This can occur by accessing (either retrieving or assigning) the array with an index for which no element exists in the array. Such an error frequently occurs when you use the array length as an index into the array, as shown in Listing 2.46.

LISTING 2.46: Accessing Outside the Bounds of an Array, Throwing an Exception

```
string languages = new string[9];
...
// RUNTIME ERROR: index out of bounds - should
// be 8 for the last element
languages[ 4] = languages[ 9];
```

> **■. NOTE**
>
> The `Length` member returns the number of items in the array, not the highest index. The `Length` member for the `languages` variable is 9, but the highest index for the `languages` variable is 8.

It is a good practice to use `Length` in place of the hardcoded array size. To use `Length` as an index, for example, it is necessary to subtract 1 to avoid an out-of-bounds error (see Listing 2.47).

Language Contrast: C++—Buffer Overflow Bugs

Unmanaged C++ does not always check whether you overstep the bounds on an array. Not only can this be difficult to debug, but making this mistake can also result in a potential security error called a **buffer overrun**. In contrast, the Common Language Runtime protects all C# (and Managed C++) code from overstepping array bounds, eliminating the possibility of a buffer overrun issue in managed code.

LISTING 2.47: Using **Length – 1** in the Array Index

```
string languages = new string[9];
...
languages[4] = languages[languages.Length - 1];
```

To avoid overstepping the bounds on an array use Length – 1, as demonstrated in Listing 2.47, in place of a hardcoded value accessing the last item in the array.

Length returns the total number of elements in an array. Therefore, if you had a multidimensional array such as bool cells[,,] of size 2·3·3, Length would return the total number of elements, 18.

More Array Methods

Arrays include additional methods for manipulating the elements within the array. These include Sort(), BinarySearch(), Reverse(), and Clear() (see Listing 2.48).

LISTING 2.48: Additional Array Methods

```
class ProgrammingLanguages
{
  static void Main()
  {
      string[] languages = new string[]{
          "C#", "COBOL", "Java",
          "C++", "Visual Basic", "Pascal",
          "Fortran", "Lisp", "J#"};

      System.Array.Sort(languages);
```

```
        searchString = "COBOL";
        index = System.Array.BinarySearch(
            languages, searchString);
        System.Console.WriteLine(
            "The wave of the future, {0}, is at index {1}.",
            searchString, index);

        System.Console.WriteLine();
        System.Console.WriteLine("{0,-20}\t{1,-20}",
            "First Element", "Last Element");
        System.Console.WriteLine("{0,-20}\t{1,-20}",
            "-------------", "------------");
        System.Console.WriteLine("{0,-20}\t{1,-20}",
            languages[0], languages[languages.Length-1]);

        System.Array.Reverse(languages);
        System.Console.WriteLine("{0,-20}\t{1,-20}",
            languages[0], languages[languages.Length-1]);

        // Note this does not remove all items from the array.
        // Rather it sets each item to the type's default value.
        System.Array.Clear(languages, 0, languages.Length);
        System.Console.WriteLine("{0,-20}\t{1,-20}",
            languages[0], languages[languages.Length-1]);
        System.Console.WriteLine(
            "After clearing, the array size is: {0}",
            languages.Length);
    }
}
```

The results of Listing 2.48 are shown in Output 2.19.

OUTPUT 2.19:

```
The wave of the future, COBOL, is at index 1.

First Element           Last Element
-------------           ------------
C#                      Visual Basic
Visual Basic            C#

After clearing, the array size is: 9
```

Access to these methods is on the System.Array class. For the most part, using these methods is self-explanatory, except for two noteworthy items.

- Before using the `BinarySearch()` method, it is important to sort the array. If values are not sorted in increasing order, then the incorrect index may be returned. If the search element does not exist, then the value returned is negative. (Using the complement operator, `~index`, returns the first index, if any, that is larger than the searched value.)

- The `Clear()` method does not remove elements of the array and does not set the length to zero. The array size is fixed and cannot be modified. Therefore, the `Clear()` method sets each element in the array to its default value (`false`, `0`, or `null`). This explains why `Console.WriteLine()` creates a blank line when writing out the array after `Clear()` is called.

Language Contrast: Visual Basic—Redimensioning Arrays

Visual Basic includes a `Redim` statement for changing the number of items in an array. Although there is no equivalent C# specific keyword, there is a method available in .NET 2.0 that will re-create the array and then copy all the elements over to the new array. The method is called `System.Array.Resize`.

Array Instance Methods

Like strings, arrays have instance members that are accessed not from the data type, but rather, directly from the variable. `Length` is an example of an instance member because access to `Length` is through the array variable, not the class. Other significant instance members are `GetLength()`, `Rank`, and `Clone()`.

Retrieving the length of a particular dimension does not require the `Length` property. To retrieve the size of a particular rank, an array includes a `GetLength()` instance method. When calling this method, it is necessary to specify the rank whose length will be returned (see Listing 2.49).

LISTING 2.49: Retrieving a Particular Dimension's Size

```
bool[,,] cells;
cells = new bool[2,3,3];
System.Console.WriteLine(cells.GetLength(0));    // Displays 2
```

The results of Listing 2.49 appear in Output 2.20.

```
2
```

Listing 2.49 displays 2 because this is the number of elements in the first dimension.

It is also possible to retrieve the entire array's rank by accessing the array's `Rank` member. `cells.Rank`, for example, will return 3.

By default, assigning one array variable to another copies only the array reference, not the individual elements of the array. To make an entirely new copy of the array, use the array's `Clone()` method. The `Clone()` method will return a copy of the array; changing any of the members of this new array will not affect the members of the original array.

Strings as Arrays

Variables of type `string` are accessible like an array of characters. For example, to retrieve the fourth character of a string called `palindrome` you can call `palindrome[3]`. Note, however, that because strings are immutable, it is not possible to assign particular characters within a string. C#, therefore, would not allow `palindrome[3]='a'`, where `palindrome` is declared as a string. Listing 2.50 uses the array accessor to determine whether an argument on the command line is an option, where an option is identified by a dash as the first character.

LISTING 2.50: Looking for Command-Line Options

```
string[] args;
...
if(args[0][0]=='-')
{
    // This parameter is an option
}
```

This snippet uses the `if` statement, which is covered in Chapter 3. In addition, it presents an interesting example because you use the array accessor to retrieve the first element in the array of strings, `args`. Following the first array accessor is a second one, this time to retrieve the first character of the string. The code, therefore, is equivalent to that shown in Listing 2.51.

LISTING 2.51: Looking for Command-Line Options (Simplified)

```
string[] args;
...
string arg = args[0];
if(arg[0] == '-')
{
    // This parameter is an option
}
```

Not only can string characters be accessed individually using the array accessor, it is also possible to retrieve the entire string as an array of characters using the string's `ToCharArray()` method. Using this method, you could reverse the string using the `System.Array.Reverse()` method, as demonstrated in Listing 2.52, which determines if a string is a palindrome.

LISTING 2.52: Reversing a String

```
class Palindrome
{
  static void Main()
  {
      string reverse, palindrome;
      char[] temp;

      System.Console.Write("Enter a palindrome: ");
      palindrome = System.Console.ReadLine();

      // Remove spaces and convert to lowercase
      reverse = palindrome.Replace(" ", "");
      reverse = reverse.ToLower();

      // Convert to an array
      temp = reverse.ToCharArray();

      // Reverse the array
      System.Array.Reverse(temp);

      // Convert the array back to a string and
      // check if reverse string is the same.
      if(reverse == new string(temp))
      {
          System.Console.WriteLine("\"{0}\" is a palindrome.",
              palindrome);
      }
```

```
    else
    {
        System.Console.WriteLine(
            "\"{0}\" is NOT a palindrome.",
            palindrome);
    }
  }
}
```

The results of Listing 2.52 appear in Output 2.21.

OUTPUT 2.21:

```
Enter a palindrome: NeverOddOrEven
"NeverOddOrEven" is a palindrome.
```

This example uses the `new` keyword; this time, it creates a new string from the reversed array of characters.

Common Errors

This section introduced the three different types of arrays: single-dimension, multidimensional, and jagged arrays. Several rules and idiosyncrasies govern array declaration and use. Table 2.7 points out some of the most common errors and helps solidify the rules. Readers should consider reviewing the code in the Common Mistake column first (without looking at the Error Description and Corrected Code columns) as a way of verifying their understanding of arrays and their syntax.

SUMMARY

Even for experienced programmers, C# introduces several new programming constructs. For example, as part of the section on data types, this chapter covered the type `decimal` that can be used accurately for financial calculations. In addition, the chapter introduced the fact that the Boolean type, `bool`, does not convert implicitly to an integer, thereby preventing the mistaken use of the assignment operator in a conditional expression. Other unique characteristics of C# are the @ verbatim string qualifier that forces a string to ignore the escape character and the fact that the `string` data type is immutable.

TABLE 2.7: Common Array Coding Errors

Common Mistake	Error Description	Corrected Code
`int numbers[];`	The square braces for declaring an array appear after the data type, not after the variable identifier.	`int[] numbers;`

`int[] numbers;`
`numbers = {42, 84, 168};`
	When assigning an array after declaration, it is necessary to use the new keyword and then specify the data type.	`int[] numbers;`
		`numbers = new int[]{`
		`42, 84, 168 }`

`int[3] numbers =` `{ 42, 84, 168 };`	It is not possible to specify the array size as part of the variable declaration.	`int[] numbers =` `{ 42, 84, 168 };`
`int[] numbers =` `new int[];`	The array size is required at initialization time unless an array literal is provided.	`int[] numbers =` `new int[3];`

`int[] numbers =`
`new int[3]{}`
	The array size is specified as 3, but there are no elements in the array literal. The array size must match the number of elements in the array literal.	`int[] numbers =`
		`new int[3]`
		`{ 42, 84, 168 };`

`int[] numbers =`
`new int[3];`
`Console.WriteLine(`
`numbers[3]);`
	Array indexes start at zero. Therefore, the last item is one less than the array size. (Note that this is a runtime error, not a compile-time error.)	`int[] numbers =`
		`new int[3];`
		`Console.WriteLine(`
		`numbers[2]);`

TABLE 2.7: Common Array Coding Errors (Continued)

Common Mistake	Error Description	Corrected Code

`int[] numbers =`
`    new int[3];`
`numbers[numbers.Length] =`
`    42;`
	Same as previous error: 1 needs to be subtracted from the `Length` to access the last element. (Note that this is a runtime error, not a compile-time error.)	`int[] numbers =`
		`    new int[3];`
		`numbers[numbers.Length-1] =`
		`    42;`

`int[] numbers;`
`Console.WriteLine(`
`    numbers[0]);`
	`numbers` has not yet been assigned an instantiated array, and therefore, it cannot be accessed.	`int[] numbers = {42, 84};`
		`Console.WriteLine(`
		`    numbers[0]);`

`int[,] numbers =`
`    { {42},`
`      {84, 42} };`
	Multidimensional arrays must be structured consistently.	`int[,] numbers =`
		`    { {42, 168},`
		`      {84, 42} };`

`int[][] numbers =`
`    { {42, 84},`
`      {84, 42} };`
	Jagged arrays require instantiated arrays to be specified for the arrays within the array.	`int[][] numbers =`
		`    { new int[]{42, 84},`
		`      new int[]{84, 42} };`

To convert data types between each other C# includes the cast operator in both an explicit and an implicit form. In the following chapters, you will learn how to define both operator types on custom types.

This chapter closed with coverage of C# syntax for arrays, along with the various means of manipulating arrays. For many developers, the syntax can become rather daunting at first, so the section included a list of the common errors associated with coding arrays.

The next chapter looks at expressions and control flow statements. The `if` statement, which appeared a few times toward the end of this chapter, appears as well.

3
Operators and Control Flow

I N THIS CHAPTER, you will learn about operators and control flow statements. Operators provide syntax for performing different calculations
or actions appropriate for the operands within the calculation. Control
flow statements provide the means for conditional logic within a program
or looping over a section of code multiple times. After introducing the `if`
control flow statement, the chapter looks at the concept of Boolean expressions, which are embedded within many control flow statements, pointing

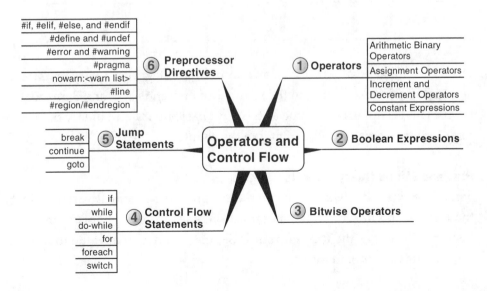

out that `ints` will not cast explicitly to `bool` and the advantages of this restriction. The chapter ends with a discussion of the primitive C# "prepro-cessor" and its accompanying directives.

Operators

Now that you have been introduced to the predefined data types (refer to Chapter 2), you can begin to learn more about how to use these data types in combination with operators in order to perform calculations. For exam-ple, you can make calculations on variables that you have declared.

■ BEGINNER TOPIC

Operators

Operators specify operations within an expression, such as a mathematical expression, to be performed on a set of values, called **operands**, to produce a new value or result. For example, in Listing 3.1 there are two operands, the numbers 4 and 2, that are combined using the subtraction operator, -. You assign the result to the variable `total`.

LISTING 3.1: A Simple Operator Example

```
total = 4 - 2;
```

Operators are generally broken down into three categories: unary, binary, and ternary, corresponding to the number of operands 1, 2, and 3, respec-tively. This section covers some of the most basic unary and binary opera-tors. Ternary operators appear later in the chapter.

Plus and Minus Unary Operators (+, –)

Sometimes you may want to change the sign of a numerical variable. In these cases, the unary minus operator (–) comes in handy. For example, Listing 3.2 changes the total current U.S. debt to a negative value to indi-cate that it is an amount owed.

LISTING 3.2: Specifying Negative Values[1]

```
// National Debt to the Penny
decimal debt = -8279328785833.43M;
```

Using the minus operator is equivalent to multiplying a number by –1.

The unary plus operator (+) has no effect on a value. It is a superfluous addition to the C# language and was included for the sake of symmetry.

Arithmetic Binary Operators (+, –, *, /, %)

Binary operators require two operands in order to process an equation: a left-hand side operand and a right-hand side operand. Binary operators also require that the code assign the resulting value to avoid losing the resulting value.

Language Contrast: C++—Operator-Only Statements

Binary operators in C# require an assignment or call; they always return a new result. Neither operand in a binary operator expression can be modified. In contrast, C++ will allow a single statement, such as 4+5, to compile even without an assignment. In C#, only assignment, call, increment, decrement, and new object expressions are allowed for operator-only statements.

The subtraction example in Listing 3.3 is an example of a binary operator—more specifically, an arithmetic binary operator. The other arithmetic binary operators are addition (+), division (/), multiplication (*), and remainder (%; sometimes called the mod operator).

LISTING 3.3: Using Binary Operators

```
class Division
{
  static void Main()
  {
      int numerator;
      int denominator;
      int quotient;
```

---

1. As of March 8, 2006.

```
       int remainder;

       System.Console.Write("Enter the numerator: ");
       numerator = int.Parse(System.Console.ReadLine());

       System.Console.Write("Enter the denominator: ");
       denominator = int.Parse(System.Console.ReadLine());

       quotient = numerator / denominator;
       remainder = numerator % denominator;

       System.Console.WriteLine(
           "{0} / {1} = {2} with remainder {3}",
           numerator, denominator, quotient, remainder);
   }
 }
```

Output 3.1 shows the results of Listing 3.3.

OUTPUT 3.1:

```
Enter the numerator: 23
Enter the denominator: 3
23 / 3 = 7 with remainder 2
```

Note the order of associativity when using binary operators. The binary operator order is from left to right. In contrast, the assignment operator order is from right to left. On its own, however, associativity does not specify whether the division will occur before or after the assignment. The order of precedence defines this. The precedence for the operators used so far is as follows:

1) *, /, and %, 2) + and -, and 3) =

Therefore, you can assume that the statement behaves as expected, with the division and remainder operators occurring before the assignment.

If you forget to assign the result of one of these binary operators, you will receive the compile error shown in Output 3.2.

OUTPUT 3.2:

```
... error CS0201: Only assignment, call, increment, decrement,
and new object expressions can be used as a statement
```

■ BEGINNER TOPIC

Associativity and Order of Precedence

As with mathematics, programming languages support the concept of **associativity**. Associativity refers to how operands are grouped and, therefore, the order in which operators are evaluated. Given a single operator that appears more than once in an expression, associative operators will produce the same result regardless of the order in which they are evaluated. Binary operators such as + and - are associative because the order in which the operators are applied is not significant; a+b+c has the same result whether a+b is performed first or b+c is performed first.

Associativity applies only when all the operators are the same. When different operators appear within a statement, the **order of precedence** for those operators dictates which operators are evaluated first. Order of precedence, for example, indicates that the multiplication operator be evaluated before the plus operator in the expression a+b*c.

Using the Plus Operator with Strings

Operators can also work with types that are not numeric. For example, it is possible to use the plus operator to concatenate two or more strings, as shown in Listing 3.4.

LISTING 3.4: Using Binary Operators with Non-Numeric Types

```
class FortyTwo
{
  static void Main()
  {
    short windSpeed = 42;
    System.Console.WriteLine(
        "The original Tacoma Bridge in Washington\nwas "
        + "brought down by a "
        + windSpeed + " mile/hour wind.");
  }
}
```

Output 3.3 shows the results of Listing 3.4.

OUTPUT 3.3:

```
The original Tacoma Bridge in Washington
was brought down by a 42 mile/hour wind.
```

Because sentence structure varies among languages in different cultures, developers should be careful not to use the plus operator with strings that require localization. Composite formatting is preferred (refer to Chapter 1).

Using Characters in Arithmetic Operations

When introducing the char type in the last chapter, I mentioned that even though it stores characters and not numbers, the char type is an integer type. It can participate in arithmetic operations with other integer types. However, interpretation of the value of the char type is not based on the character stored within it, but rather, on its underlying value. The digit 3, for example, contains a Unicode value of 0x33 (hexadecimal), which in base 10 is 51. The digit 4, on the other hand, contains a Unicode value of 0x34, or 52 in base 10. Adding 3 and 4 in Listing 3.5 results in a hexadecimal value of 0x167, or 103 in base 10, which is equivalent to the letter g.

LISTING 3.5: Using the Plus Operator with the **char** Data Type

```
int n = '3' + '4';
char c = (char)n;
System.Console.WriteLine(c);   // Writes out g.
```

Output 3.4 shows the results of Listing 3.5.

OUTPUT 3.4:

```
g
```

You can use this trait of character types to determine how far two characters are from one another. For example, the letter f is three characters away from the letter c. You can determine this value by subtracting the letter c from the letter f, as Listing 3.6 demonstrates.

LISTING 3.6: Determining the Character Difference between Two Characters

```
int distance = 'f' - 'c';
System.Console.WriteLine(distance);
```

Output 3.5 shows the results of Listing 3.6.

OUTPUT 3.5:

```
3
```

Special Floating-Point Characteristics

The floating-point types, `float` and `double`, have some special characteristics, such as the way they handle precision. This section looks at some specific examples, as well as some unique floating-point type characteristics.

A float, with seven digits of precision, can hold the value 1,234,567 and the value 0.1234567. However, if you add these two floats together, the result will be rounded to 1234567, because the decimal portion of the number is past the seven significant digits that a float can hold. This type of rounding can become significant, especially with repeated calculations or checks for equality (see the upcoming Expert Topic, Unexpected Inequality with Floating-Point Types).

Note that inaccuracies can occur with a simple assignment, such as `double number = 4.2F`. Since the double can hold a more accurate value than the `float` can store, the C# compiler will actually evaluate this expression to `double number = 4.1999998092651367;`. `4.1999998092651367` is 4.2 as a `float`, but not quite 4.2 when represented as a `double`.

▪▫ ADVANCED TOPIC

Unexpected Inequality with Floating-Point Types

The inaccuracies of floats can be very disconcerting when comparing values for equality, since they can unexpectedly be unequal. Consider Listing 3.7.

LISTING 3.7: Unexpected Inequality Due to Floating-Point Inaccuracies

```
decimal decimalNumber = 4.2M;
double doubleNumber1 = 0.1F * 42F;
double doubleNumber2 = 0.1D * 42D;
float floatNumber = 0.1F * 42F;

Trace.Assert(decimalNumber != (decimal)doubleNumber1);
// Displays: 4.2 != 4.20000006258488
System.Console.WriteLine(
    "{0} != {1}", decimalNumber, (decimal)doubleNumber1);
```

```
Trace.Assert((double)decimalNumber != doubleNumber1);
// Displays: 4.2 != 4.20000006258488
System.Console.WriteLine(
    "{0} != {1}", (double)decimalNumber, doubleNumber1);


Trace.Assert((float)decimalNumber != floatNumber);
// Displays: (float)4.2M != 4.2F
System.Console.WriteLine(
    "(float){0}M != {1}F",
    (float)decimalNumber, floatNumber);


Trace.Assert(doubleNumber1 != (double)floatNumber);
// Displays: 4.20000006258488 != 4.20000028610229
System.Console.WriteLine(
    "{0} != {1}", doubleNumber1, (double)floatNumber);


Trace.Assert(doubleNumber1 != doubleNumber2);
// Displays: 4.20000006258488 != 4.2
System.Console.WriteLine(
    "{0} != {1}", doubleNumber1, doubleNumber2);


Trace.Assert(floatNumber != doubleNumber2);
// Displays: 4.2F != 4.2D
System.Console.WriteLine(
    "{0}F != {1}D", floatNumber, doubleNumber2);


Trace.Assert((double)4.2F != 4.2D);
// Display: 4.19999980926514 != 4.2
System.Console.WriteLine(
    "{0} != {1}", (double)4.2F, 4.2D);


Trace.Assert(4.2F != 4.2D);
// Display: 4.2F != 4.2D
System.Console.WriteLine(
    "{0}F != {1}D", 4.2F, 4.2D);
```

Output 3.6 shows the results of Listing 3.7.

OUTPUT 3.6:

```
4.2 != 4.20000006258488
4.2 != 4.20000006258488
(float)4.2M != 4.2F
4.20000006258488 != 4.20000028610229
4.20000006258488 != 4.2
4.2F != 4.2D
4.19999980926514 != 4.2
4.2F != 4.2D
```

The `Assert()` methods are designed to display a dialog whenever the parameter evaluates for false. However, all of the `Assert()` statements in this code listing will evaluate to true. Therefore, in spite of the apparent equality of the values in the code listing, they are in fact not equivalent due to the inaccuracies of a `float`. Furthermore, there is not some compounding rounding error. The C# compiler performs the calculations instead of the runtime. Even if you simply assign `4.2F` rather than a calculation, the comparisons will remain unequal.

To avoid unexpected results caused by the inaccuracies of floating-point types, developers should avoid using equality conditionals with these types. Rather, equality evaluations should include a tolerance. One easy way to achieve this is to subtract one value (operand) from the other and then evaluate whether the result is less than the maximum tolerance. Even better is to use the decimal type in place of the float type.

You should be aware of some additional unique floating-point characteristics as well. For instance, you would expect that dividing an integer by zero would result in an error, and it does with precision data types such as `int` and `decimal`. `float` and `double`, however, allow for certain special values. Consider Listing 3.8, and its resulting output, Output 3.7.

LISTING 3.8: Dividing a Float by Zero, Displaying NaN

```
float n=0f;
// Displays: NaN
System.Console.WriteLine(n / 0);
```

OUTPUT 3.7:

```
NaN
```

In mathematics, certain mathematical operations are undefined. In C#, the result of dividing 0F by the value 0 results in "Not a Number," and all attempts to print the output of such a number will result in `NaN`. Similarly, taking the square root of a negative number (`System.Math.Sqrt(-1)`) will result in `NaN`.

A floating-point number could overflow its bounds as well. For example, the upper bound of a `float` type is 3.4E38. Should the number overflow that bound, the result would be stored as "positive infinity" and the output of printing the number would be `Infinity`. Similarly, the lower bound of a `float` type is –3.4E38, and assigning a value below that bound would result in "negative infinity," which would be represented by the string `-Infinity`. Listing 3.9 produces negative and positive infinity, respectively, and Output 3.8 shows the results.

LISTING 3.9: Overflowing the Bounds of a **float**

```
// Displays: -Infinity
System.Console.WriteLine(-1f / 0);
// Displays: Infinity
System.Console.WriteLine(3.402823E+38f * 2f);
```

OUTPUT 3.8:

```
-Infinity
Infinity
```

Further examination of the floating-point number reveals that it can contain a value very close to zero, without actually containing zero. If the value exceeds the threshold for the `float` or `double` type, then the value of the number can be represented as "negative zero" or "positive zero," depending on whether the number is negative or positive, and is represented in output as -0 or 0.

Parenthesis Operator

The parenthesis operator allows you to group operands and operators so that they are evaluated together. This is important because it provides a means of overriding the default order of precedence. For example, the following two expressions evaluate to something completely different:

```
(60 / 10) * 2
60 / (10 * 2)
```

The first expression is equal to 12; the second expression is equal to 3. In both cases, the parentheses affect the final value of the expression.

Sometimes the parenthesis operator does not actually change the result, because the order-of-precedence rules apply appropriately. However, it is often still a good practice to use parentheses to make the code more readable. This expression, for example:

```
fahrenheit = (celsius * 9 / 5) + 32;
```

is easier to interpret confidently at a glance than this one is:

```
fahrenheit = celsius * 9 / 5 + 32;
```

Developers should use parentheses to make code more readable, disambiguating expressions explicitly instead of relying on operator precedence.

Assignment Operators (+=, −=, *=, /=, %=)

Chapter 1 discussed the simple assignment operator, which places the value of the right-hand side of the operator into the variable on the left-hand side. Other assignment operators combine common binary operator calculations with the assignment operator. Take Listing 3.10, for example.

LISTING 3.10: Common Increment Calculation

```
int x;
x = x + 2;
```

In this assignment, you first calculate the value of x + 2 and then you assign the calculated value back to x. Since this type of operation is relatively frequent, an assignment operator exists to handle both the calculation and the assignment with one operator. The += operator increments the variable on the left-hand side of the operator with the value on the right-hand side of the operator, as shown in Listing 3.11.

LISTING 3.11: Using the += Operator

```
int x;
x += 2;
```

This code, therefore, is equivalent to Listing 3.10.

Numerous other combination assignment operators exist to provide similar functionality. You can use the assignment operator in conjunction with not only addition, but also subtraction, multiplication, division, and the remainder operators, as Listing 3.12 demonstrates.

LISTING 3.12: Other Assignment Operator Examples

```
x -= 2;
x /= 2;
x *= 2;
x %= 2;
```

Increment and Decrement Operators (++, --)

C# includes special operators for incrementing and decrementing counters. The **increment operator**, ++, increments a variable by one each time it is used. In other words, each code line shown in Listing 3.13 is equivalent.

LISTING 3.13: Increment Operator

```
spaceCount = spaceCount + 1;
spaceCount += 1;
spaceCount++;
```

Similarly, you can also decrement a variable by one using the **decrement operator**, --. Therefore, all the code lines shown in Listing 3.14 are also equivalent.

LISTING 3.14: Decrement Operator

```
lines = lines - 1;
lines -= 1;
lines--;
```

■ BEGINNER TOPIC

A Decrement Example in a Loop

The increment and decrement operators are especially prevalent in loops, such as the `while` loop. For example, Listing 3.15 uses the decrement operator in order to iterate backward through each letter in the alphabet.

LISTING 3.15: Displaying Each Character's ASCII Value in Descending Order

```
char current;
int asciiValue;
```

```
  // Set the initial value of current.
  current='z';

do
{
  // Retrieve the ASCII value of current.
  asciiValue = current;
  System.Console.Write("{0}={1}\t", current, asciiValue);

  // Proceed to the previous letter in the alphabet;
  current--;
}
while(current>='a');
```

Output 3.9 shows the results of Listing 3.15.

OUTPUT 3.9:

```
z=122   y=121   x=120   w=119   v=118   u=117   t=116   s=115   r=114
q=113   p=112   o=111   n=110   m=109   l=108   k=107   j=106   i=105
h=104   g=103   f=102   e=101   d=100   c=99    b=98    a=97
```

The increment and decrement operators are used to count how many times to perform a particular operation. Notice also that in this example, the increment operator is used on a character (`char`) data type. You can use increment and decrement operators on various data types as long as some meaning is assigned to the concept of "next" or "previous" for that data type.

Just as with the assignment operator, the increment operator also returns a value. In other words, it is possible to use the assignment operator simultaneously with the increment or decrement operator (see Listing 3.16 and Output 3.10).

LISTING 3.16: Using the Post-Decrement Operator

```
int count;
int result;
count = 0;
result = count++;
System.Console.WriteLine("result = {0} and count = {1}",
  result, count);
```

OUTPUT 3.10:

```
result = 0 and count = 1
```

You might be surprised that count is assigned to result *before* it is incremented. This is why result ends up with a value of 0 even though count ends up with a value of 1.

If you want the increment or decrement operator to take precedence over the assignment operator and to execute before assigning the value, you need to place the operator before the variable being incremented, as shown in Listing 3.17.

LISTING 3.17: Using the Pre-Increment Operator

```
int count;
int result;
count = 0;
result = ++count;
System.Console.WriteLine("result = {0} and count = {1}",
    result, count);
```

Output 3.11 shows the results of Listing 3.17.

OUTPUT 3.11:

```
result = 1 and count = 1
```

Where you place the increment or decrement operator determines the order of operations, which affects how the code functions. If the increment or decrement operator appears before the operand, then the value returned will be the new value. If x is 1, then ++x will return 2. However, if a postfix operator is used, x++, the value returned by the expression will still be 1. Regardless of whether the operator is postfix or prefix, the resulting value of x will be different. The difference between prefix and postfix behavior appears in Listing 3.18. The resulting output is shown in Output 3.12.

LISTING 3.18: Comparing the Prefix and Postfix Increment Operators

```
class IncrementExample
{
  public static void Main()
```

```
    {
        int x;

        x = 1;
        // Display 1, 2.
        Console.WriteLine("{0}, {1}", x++, x++);
        // x now contains the value 3.

        // Display 4, 5.
        Console.WriteLine("{0}, {1}", ++x, ++x);
        // x now contains the value 5.
        // ...
    }
}
```

OUTPUT 3.12:

```
1, 2
4, 5
```

As Listing 3.18 demonstrates, where the increment and decrement operators appear relative to the operand can affect the result returned from the operator. Pre-increment/decrement operators return the result after incrementing/decrementing the operand. Post-increment/decrement operators return the result before changing the operand. Developers should use caution when embedding these operators in the middle of a statement. When in doubt as to what will happen, use these operators independently, placing them within their own statements. This way, the code is also more readable and there is no mistaking the intention.

■ **ADVANCED TOPIC**

Thread-Safe Incrementing and Decrementing

In spite of the brevity of the increment and decrement operators, these operators are not atomic. A thread context switch can occur during the execution of the operator and can cause a race condition. Instead of using a lock statement to prevent the race condition, the System.Threading.Interlocked class includes the thread-safe methods Increment() and Decrement(). These methods rely on processor functions for performing fast thread-safe increments and decrements.

Constant Expressions (const)

The previous chapter discussed literal values, or values embedded directly into the code. It is possible to combine multiple literal values in a **constant expression** using operators. By definition, a constant expression is one that the C# compiler can evaluate at compile time (instead of calculating it when the program runs). For example, the number of seconds in a day can be assigned as a constant expression whose result can then be used in other expressions.

The const keyword in Listing 3.19 locks the value at compile time. Any attempt to modify the value later in the code results in a compile error.

LISTING 3.19: Declaring a Constant

```
// ...
public long Main()                    Constant Expression
{
    const int secondsPerDay = 60 * 60 * 24;
    const int secondsPerWeek = secondsPerDay * 7;
    // ...                   Constant
}
```

Note that even the value assigned to secondsPerWeek is a constant expression, because the operands in the expression are also constants, so the compiler can determine the result.

Introducing Flow Control

Toward the end of this chapter is a code listing (Listing 3.42) that shows a simple way to view a number in its binary form. Even such a simple program, however, cannot be written without using control flow statements. Such statements control the execution path of the program. This section discusses how to change the order of statement execution based on conditional checks. Later on, you will learn how to execute statement groups repeatedly through loop constructs.

A summary of the control flow statements appears in Table 3.1. Note that the General Syntax Structure column indicates common statement use, not the complete lexical structure.

An embedded-statement in Table 3.1 corresponds to any statement, including a code block (but not a declaration statement or a label).

TABLE 3.1: Control Flow Statements

Statement	General Syntax Structure	Example

`if statement`	`if (boolean-expression)`
	`    embedded-statement`
		`if (input == "quit")`
		`{`
		`    Console.WriteLine("Game end");`
		`    return;`
		`}`

	`if (boolean-expression)`
	`    embedded-statement`
	`else`
	`    embedded-statement`
		`if (input == "quit")`
		`{`
		`    Console.WriteLine("Game end");`
		`    return;`
		`}`
		`else`
		`    GetNextMove();`

`while statement`	`while (boolean-expression)`
	`    embedded-statement`
		`while (count < total)`
		`{`
		`    Console.WriteLine("count = {0}", count);`
		`    count++;`
		`}`

`do while statement`	`do`
	`    embedded-statement`
	`while (boolean-expression);`
		`do`
		`{`
		`    Console.WriteLine("Enter name:");`
		`    input = Console.ReadLine();`
		`}`
		`while (input != "exit");`

Continues

TABLE 3.1: Control Flow Statements *(Continued)*

Statement	General Syntax Structure	Example

`for` statement	`for(`*for-initializer;*
	     boolean-expression;
	     for-iterator)
	     embedded-statement
		`for (int count = 1; count <= 10; count++)`
		`{`
		`    Console.WriteLine("count = {0}", count);`
		`}`

`foreach` statement	`foreach(`*type identifier* `in`
	     expression)
	     embedded-statement
		`foreach (char letter in email)`
		`{`
		`    if(!insideDomain)`
		`    {`
		`        if (letter == '@')`
		`        {`
		`            insideDomain = true;`
		`        }`
		`        continue;`
		`    }`
		`    Console.Write(letter);`
		`}`

`continue` statement	`continue;`	

TABLE 3.1: Control Flow Statements *(Continued)*

Statement	General Syntax Structure	Example

switch statement	**switch**(governing-type-expression)
	{
	   ...
	   case const-expression:
	      statement-list
	      jump-statement
	   default:
	      statement-list
	      jump-statement
	}
		switch(*input*)
		{
		  case *"exit"*:
		  case *"quit"*:
		    Console.WriteLine("Exiting app.....");
		    break;
		  case *"restart"*:
		    Reset();
		    goto case *"start"*;
		  case *"start"*:
		    GetMove();
		    break;
		  default:
		    Console.WriteLine(input);
		    break;
		}

break statement	**break;**	
goto statement	**goto** *identifier;* **goto case** *const-expression;* **goto default;**	

Each C# control flow statement in Table 3.1 appears in the tic-tac-toe program found in Appendix B. The program displays the tic-tac-toe board, prompts each player, and updates with each move.

The remainder of this chapter looks at each statement in more detail. After covering the `if` statement, it introduces code blocks, scope, Boolean expressions, and bitwise operators before continuing with the remaining control flow statements. Readers who find the table familiar because of C#'s similarities to other languages can jump ahead to the section titled C# Preprocessor Directives, or skip forward to the conclusion.

`if` Statement

The `if` statement is one of the most common statements in C#. It evaluates a **Boolean expression** (an expression that returns a Boolean), and if the result is `true`, the following statement (or block) is executed. The general form is as follows:

```
if(boolean-expression)
   true-statement
[else
   false-statement]
```

There is also an optional `else` clause for when the Boolean expression is false. Listing 3.20 shows an example.

LISTING 3.20: `if/else` Statement Example

```csharp
class TicTacToe       // Declares the TicTacToe class.
{
  static void Main() // Declares the entry point of the program.
  {
     string input;

     // Prompt the user to select a 1 or 2 player game.
     System.Console.Write (
         "1 - Play against the computer\n" +
         "2 - Play against another player.\n" +
         "Choose:"
     );
     input = System.Console.ReadLine();

     if(input=="1")
         // The user selected to play the computer.
```

```
                System.Console.WriteLine(
                    "Play against computer selected.");
            else
                // Default to 2 players (even if user didn't enter 2).
                System.Console.WriteLine(
                    "Play against another player.");
    }
}
```

In Listing 3.20, if the user enters a 1, the program displays "Play against computer selected.". Otherwise, it displays "Play against another player.".

Nested if

Sometimes code requires multiple if statements. The code in Listing 3.21 first determines whether the user has chosen to exit by entering a number less than or equal to 0; if not, it checks whether the user knows the maximum number of turns in tic-tac-toe.

LISTING 3.21: Nested **if** Statements

```
1  class TicTacToeTrivia
2  {
3    static void Main()
4    {
5        int input;     // Declare a variable to store the input.
6
7        System.Console.Write(
8            "What is the maximum number " +
9            "of turns in tic-tac-toe?" +
10           "(Enter 0 to exit.): ");
11
12        // int.Parse() converts the ReadLine()
13        // return to an int data type.
14        input = int.Parse(System.Console.ReadLine());
15
16        if (input <= 0)
17                // Input is less than or equal to 0.
18                System.Console.WriteLine("Exiting...");
19        else
20            if (input < 9)
21                // Input is less than 9.
22                System.Console.WriteLine(
23                    "Tic-tac-toe has more than {0}" +
24                    " maximum turns.", input);
25            else
26                if(input>9)
27                    // Input is greater than 9.
28                    System.Console.WriteLine(
29                        "Tic-tac-toe has fewer than {0}" +
30                        " maximum turns.", input);
31                else
32                    // Input equals 9.
```

```
33                          System.Console.WriteLine(
34                            "Correct, " +
35                            "tic-tac-toe has a max. of 9 turns.");
36      }
37    }
```

Output 3.13 shows the results of Listing 3.21.

OUTPUT 3.13:

```
What's the maximum number of turns in tic-tac-toe? (Enter 0 to exit.): 9
Correct, tic-tac-toe has a max. of 9 turns.
```

Assume the user enters a 9 when prompted at line 14. Here is the execution path.

1. *Line 16:* Check if input is less than 0. Since it is not, jump to line 20.
2. *Line 20:* Check if input is less than 9. Since it is not, jump to line 26.
3. *Line 26:* Check if input is greater than 9. Since it is not, jump to line 33.
4. *Line 33:* Display that the answer was correct.

Listing 3.21 contains nested `if` statements. To clarify the nesting, the lines are indented. However, as you learned in Chapter 1, whitespace does not affect the execution path. Without indenting and without newlines, the execution would be the same. The code that appears in the nested `if` statement in Listing 3.22 is equivalent.

LISTING 3.22: `if/else` Formatted Sequentially

```
if (input < 0)
  System.Console.WriteLine("Exiting...");
else if (input < 9)
  System.Console.WriteLine(
      "Tic-tac-toe has more than {0}" +
      " maximum turns.", input);
else if(input>9)
  System.Console.WriteLine(
      "Tic-tac-toe has less than {0}" +
      " maximum turns.", input);
else
  System.Console.WriteLine(
      "Correct, tic-tac-toe has a maximum of 9 turns.");
```

Although the latter format is more common, in each situation, use the format that results in the clearest code.

Code Blocks ({ })

In the previous `if` statement examples, only one statement follows `if` and `else`, a single `System.Console.WriteLine()`, similar to Listing 3.23.

LISTING 3.23: **if** Statement with No Code Block

```
if(input<9)
    System.Console.WriteLine("Exiting");
```

However, sometimes you might need to execute multiple statements. Take, for example, the highlighted code block in the radius calculation in Listing 3.24.

LISTING 3.24: **if** Statement Followed by a Code Block

```
class CircleAreaCalculator
{
  static void Main()
  {
      double radius;   // Declare a variable to store the radius.
      double area;     // Declare a variable to store the area.

      System.Console.Write("Enter the radius of the circle: ");

      // double.Parse converts the ReadLine()
      // return to a double.
      radius = double.Parse(System.Console.ReadLine());

      if(radius>=0)
      {
          // Calculate the area of the circle.
          area = 3.14*radius*radius;
          System.Console.WriteLine(
              "The area of the circle is: {0}", area);
      }
      else
      {
          System.Console.WriteLine(
              "{0} is not a valid radius.", radius);
      }
  }
}
```

Output 3.14 shows the results of Listing 3.24.

OUTPUT 3.14:

```
Enter the radius of the circle: 3
The area of the circle is: 28.26
```

In this example, the `if` statement checks whether the `radius` is positive. If so, the area of the circle is calculated and displayed; otherwise, an invalid radius message is displayed.

Notice that in this example, two statements follow the first `if`. However, these two statements appear within curly braces. The curly braces combine the statements into a single unit called a **code block**.

If you omit the curly braces that create a code block in Listing 3.24, only the statement immediately following the Boolean expression executes conditionally. Subsequent statements will execute regardless of the `if` statement's Boolean expression. The invalid code is shown in Listing 3.25.

LISTING 3.25: **Relying on Indentation, Resulting in Invalid Code**

```
if(radius>=0)
  area = 3.14*radius*radius;
  System.Console.WriteLine(     // Error!! Needs code block.
      "The area of the circle is: {0}", area);
```

In C#, indentation is for code readability only. The compiler ignores it, and therefore, the previous code is semantically equivalent to Listing 3.26.

LISTING 3.26: **Semantically Equivalent to Listing 3.25**

```
if(radius>=0)
{
  area = 3.14*radius*radius;
}
System.Console.WriteLine(     // Error!! Place within code block.
  "The area of the circle is: {0}", area);
```

Programmers should take great care to avoid subtle bugs like this, perhaps even going so far as to always include a code block after a control flow statement, even if there is only one statement.

Math Constants

In Listing 3.25 and Listing 3.26, the value of pi as 3.14 was hardcoded—a crude approximation at best. There are much more accurate definitions for pi and E in the `System.Math` class. Instead of hardcoding a value, code should use `System.Math.PI` and `System.Math.E`.

Scope

Scope is the hierarchical context bound by a code block or language construct. C# prevents two declarations with the same name declared in the same scope. For example, it is not possible to define two local variables in the same code block with the same name; the code block bounds the scope. Similarly, it is not possible to define two methods called `Main()` within the same class.

Scope is hierarchical because it is not possible to define a local variable directly within a method and then to define a new variable with the same name inside an `if` block of the same method. The scope of the initial variable declaration spans the scope of all code blocks defined within the method. However, a variable declared within the `if` block will not be in the same scope as a variable defined within the `else` block. Furthermore, the same local variable name can be used within another method because the method bounds the scope of the local variable.

Scope restricts accessibility. A local variable, for example, is not accessible outside its defining method. Similarly, code that defines a variable in an `if` block makes the variable inaccessible outside the `if` block, even while still in the same method. In Listing 3.27, defining a message inside the `if` statement restricts its scope to the statement only. To avoid the error, you must declare the string outside the `if` statement.

LISTING 3.27: Variables Inaccessable Outside Their Scope

```
class Program
{
    static void Main(string[] args)
    {
        int playerCount;
        Console.Write("Enter the number of players (1 or 2):");
        if (playerCount != 1 || playerCount != 2)
```

```
    {
        string message =
            "You entered an invalid number of players.";
    }
    else
    {
        // ...
    }
    // Error:  message is not in scope.
    Console.WriteLine(message);
}
}
```

Output 3.15 shows the results of Listing 3.27.

OUTPUT 3.15:

```
Microsoft (R) Visual C# 2005 Compiler version 8.00.50727.42
for Microsoft (R) Windows (R) 2005 Framework version 2.0.50727
Copyright (C) Microsoft Corporation 2001-2005. All rights reserved.

<filename>: error CS0103: The name 'message' does not exist in the cur-
rent context
```

Boolean Expressions

The portion of the `if` statement within parentheses is the **Boolean expression**, sometimes referred to as a **conditional**. In Listing 3.28, the Boolean expression is highlighted.

LISTING 3.28: Boolean Expression

```
if(input < 9)
{
    // Input is less than 9.
    System.Console.WriteLine(
        "Tic-tac-toe has more than {0}" +
        " maximum turns.", input);
}
// ...
```

Boolean expressions appear within many control flow statements. The key characteristic is that they always evaluate to `true` or `false`. For `input<9` to be allowed as a Boolean expression, it must return a `bool`. The compiler disallows `x=42`, for example, because it assigns `x`, returning the new value, instead of checking whether `x`'s value is 42.

Language Constrast: C++ — Mistakenly Using = in Place of ==

The significant feature of Boolean expressions in C# is the elimination of a common coding error that historically appeared in C/C++. In C++, Listing 3.29 is allowed.

LISTING 3.29: C++, But Not C#, Allows Assignment As a Boolean Expression

```
if(input=9)     // COMPILE ERROR:  Allowed in C++, not in C#.
   System.Console.WriteLine(
       "Correct, tic-tac-toe has a maximum of 9 turns.");
```

Although this appears to check whether `input` equals 9, Chapter 1 showed that = represents the assignment operator, not a check for equality. The return from the assignment operator is the value assigned to the variable—in this case, 9. However, 9 is an `int`, and as such it does not qualify as a Boolean expression and is not allowed by the C# compiler.

Relational and Equality Operators

Included in the previous code examples was the use of relational operators. In those examples, relational operators were used to evaluate user input. Table 3.2 lists all the relational and equality operators.

TABLE 3.2: Relational and Equality Operators

Operator	Description	Example
<	Less than	`input<9;`
>	Greater than	`input>9;`
<=	Less than or equal to	`input<=9;`
>=	Greater than or equal to	`input>=9;`
==	Equality operator	`input==9;`
!=	Inequality operator	`input!=9;`

In addition to determining whether a value is greater than or less than another value, operators are also required to determine equivalency. You test for equivalence by using equality operators. In C#, the syntax follows the C/C++/Java pattern with ==. For example, to determine whether input equals 9 you use input==9. The equality operator uses two equal signs to distinguish it from the assignment operator, =.

The exclamation point signifies NOT in C#, so to test for inequality you use the inequality operator, !=.

The relational and equality operators are binary operators, meaning they compare two operands. More significantly, they always return a Boolean data type. Therefore, you can assign the result of a relational operator to a bool variable, as shown in Listing 3.30.

LISTING 3.30: Assigning the Result of a Relational Operator to a **bool**

```
bool result = 70 > 7;
```

In the tic-tac-toe program (see Appendix B), you use the equality operator to determine whether a user has quit. The Boolean expression of Listing 3.31 includes an OR (| |) logical operator, which the next section discusses in detail.

LISTING 3.31: Using the Equality Operator in a Boolean Expression

```
if (input == "" || input == "quit")
{
  System.Console.WriteLine("Player {0} quit!!", currentPlayer);
  break;
}
```

Logical Boolean Operators

Logical operators have Boolean operands and return a Boolean result. Logical operators allow you to combine multiple Boolean expressions to form other Boolean expressions. The logical operators are | |, &&, and ^, corresponding to OR, AND, and exclusive OR, respectively.

OR Operator (| |)

In Listing 3.31, if the user enters `quit` or presses the Enter key without typing in a value, it is assumed that she wants to exit the program. To enable two ways for the user to resign, you use the logical OR operator, `| |`.

The `| |` operator evaluates two Boolean expressions and returns a `true` value if *either* one of them is true (see Listing 3.32).

LISTING 3.32: Using the OR Operator

```
if((hourOfTheDay > 23) || (hourOfTheDay < 0))
    System.Console.WriteLine("The time you entered is invalid.");
```

Note that with the Boolean OR operator, it is not necessary to evaluate both sides of the expression. The OR operators go from left to right, so if the left portion of the expression evaluates to `true`, then the right portion is ignored. Therefore, if `hourOfTheDay` has the value `33`, `(hourOfTheDay > 23)` will return `true` and the OR operator ignores the second half of the expression. Short-circuiting an expression also occurs with the Boolean AND operator.

AND Operator (&&)

The Boolean AND operator, `&&`, evaluates to `true` only if both operands evaluate to `true`. If either operand is false, the combined expression will return `false`.

Listing 3.33 displays that it is time for work as long as the current hour is both greater than 10 and less that 24.[2] As you saw with the OR operator, the AND operator will not always evaluate the right side of the expression. If the left operand returns `false`, then the overall result will be false regardless of the right operand, so the runtime ignores the right operand.

LISTING 3.33: Using the AND Operator

```
if ((hourOfTheDay > 10) && (hourOfTheDay < 24))
    System.Console.WriteLine(
    "Hi-Ho, Hi-Ho, it's off to work we go.");
```

---

2. The typical hours that programmers work.

Exclusive OR Operator (^)

The caret symbol, ^, is the "exclusive OR" (XOR) operator. When applied to two Boolean operands, the XOR operator returns `true` only if exactly one of the operands is true, as shown in Table 3.3.

TABLE 3.3: Conditional Values for the XOR Operator

Left Operand	Right Operand	Result
True	True	False
True	False	True
False	True	True
False	False	False

Unlike the Boolean AND and Boolean OR operators, the Boolean XOR operator does not short-circuit: It always checks both operands, because the result cannot be determined unless the values of both operands are known.

Logical Negation Operator (!)

Sometimes called the NOT operator, the **logical negation operator**, !, inverts a `bool` data type to its opposite. This operator is a unary operator, meaning it requires only one operand. Listing 3.34 demonstrates how it works, and Output 3.16 shows the results.

LISTING 3.34: Using the Logical Negation Operator

```
bool result;
bool valid = false;
result = !valid;
// Displays "result = True".
System.Console.WriteLine("result = {0}", result);
```

OUTPUT 3.16:

```
result = True
```

To begin, `valid` is set to `false`. You then use the negation operator on `valid` and assign a new value to `result`.

Conditional Operator (?)

In place of an `if` statement that functionally returns a value, you can use the conditional operator instead. The conditional operator is a question mark (?), and the general format is as follows:

```
conditional? expression1: expression2;
```

The conditional operator is a ternary operator, because it has three operands: `conditional`, `expression1`, and `expression2`. If the conditional evaluates to `true`, then the conditional operator returns `expression1`. Alternatively, if the conditional evaluates to `false`, then it returns `expression2`.

Listing 3.35 is an example of how to use the conditional operator. The full listing of this program appears in Appendix B.

LISTING 3.35: Conditional Operator

```
public class TicTacToe
{
  public static string Main()
  {
      // Initially set the currentPlayer to Player 1;
      int currentPlayer = 1;

      // ...

      for (int turn = 1; turn <= 10; turn++)
      {
          // ...

          // Switch players
          currentPlayer = (currentPlayer == 2) ? 1 : 2;
      }
  }
}
```

The program swaps the current player. To do this, it checks whether the current value is 2. This is the conditional portion of the conditional statement. If the result is `true`, then the conditional operator returns the value 1. Otherwise, it returns 2. Unlike an `if` statement, the result of the conditional operator must be assigned (or passed as a parameter). It cannot appear as an entire statement on its own.

Use the conditional operator sparingly, because readability is often sacrificed and a simple `if`/`else` statement may be more appropriate.

Bitwise Operators (<<, >>, |, &, ^, ~)

An additional set of operators that is common to virtually all programming languages is the set of operators for manipulating values in their binary formats: the bit operators.

■ BEGINNER TOPIC

Bits and Bytes

All values within a computer are represented in a binary format of 1s and 0s, called **bits**. Bits are grouped together in sets of eight, called **bytes**. In a byte, each successive bit corresponds to a value of 2 raised to a power, starting from 2^0 on the right, to 2^7 on the left, as shown in Figure 3.1.

In many instances, particularly when dealing with low-level or system services, information is retrieved as binary data. In order to manipulate these devices and services, you need to perform manipulations of binary data.

As shown in Figure 3.2, each box corresponds to a value of 2 raised to the power shown. The value of the byte (8-bit number) is the sum of the powers of 2 of all of the eight bits that are set to 1.

The binary translation just described is significantly different for signed numbers. Signed numbers (`long`, `short`, `int`) are represented using a 2s complement notation. With this notation, negative numbers

0	0	0	0	0	0	0	0
2^7	2^6	2^5	2^4	2^3	2^2	2^1	2^0

FIGURE 3.1: Corresponding Placeholder Values

0	0	0	0	0	1	1	1

$$7 = 4 + 2 + 1$$

FIGURE 3.2: Calculating the Value of an Unsigned Byte

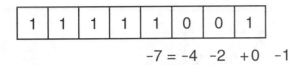

FIGURE 3.3: Calculating the Value of a Signed Byte

behave differently than positive numbers. Negative numbers are identified by a 1 in the leftmost location. If the leftmost location contains a 1, you add the locations with 0s rather than the locations with 1s. Each location corresponds to the negative power of 2 value. Furthermore, from the result, it is also necessary to subtract 1. This is demonstrated in Figure 3.3.

Therefore, 1111 1111 1111 1111 corresponds to a –1 and 1111 1111 1111 1001 holds the value –7. 1000 0000 0000 0000 corresponds to the lowest negative value that a 16-bit integer can hold.

Shift Operators (<<, >>, <<=, >>=)

Sometimes you want to shift the binary value of a number to the right or left. In executing a left shift, all bits in a number's binary representation are shifted to the left by the number of locations specified by the operand on the right of the shift operator. Zeroes are then used to backfill the locations on the right side of the binary number. A right-shift operator does almost the same thing in the opposite direction. However, if the number is negative, then the values used to backfill the left side of the binary number are ones and not zeroes. The shift operators are >> and <<, the right-shift and left-shift operators, respectively. In addition, there are combined shift and assignment operators, <<= and >>=.

Consider the following example. Suppose you had the int value –7, which would have a binary representation of 1111 1111 1111 1111 1111 1111 1111 1001. In Listing 3.36 you right-shift the binary representation of the number –7 by two locations.

LISTING 3.36: Using the Right-Shift Operator

```
int x;
x = (-7 >> 2); // 11111111111111111111111111111001 becomes
               // 11111111111111111111111111111110
```

```
// Write out "x is -2."
System.Console.WriteLine("x = {0}.", x);
```

Output 3.17 shows the results of Listing 3.36.

OUTPUT 3.17:

```
x = -2.
```

Because of the right shift, the value of the bit in the rightmost location has "dropped off" the edge and the negative bit indicator on the left shifts by two locations to be replaced with ones. The result is -2.

Bitwise Operators (&, |, ^)

In some instances, you might need to perform logical operations, such as AND, OR, and XOR, on a bit-by-bit basis for two operands. You do this via the &, |, and ^ operators, respectively.

■ BEGINNER TOPIC

Logical Operators Explained

If you have two numbers, as shown in Figure 3.4, the bitwise operations will compare the values of the locations beginning at the leftmost significant value and continuing right until the end. The value of "1" in a location is treated as "true," and the value of "0" in a location is treated as "false."

Therefore, the bitwise AND of the two values in Figure 3.4 would be the bit-by-bit comparison of bits in the first operand (12) with the bits in the second operand (7), resulting in the binary value 000000100, which is 4. Alternatively, a bitwise OR of the two values would produce 00001111, the binary equivalent of 15. The XOR result would be 00001011, or decimal 11.

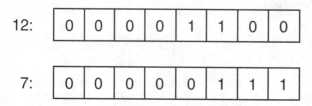

FIGURE 3.4: 12 and 7 Represented in Binary

Listing 3.37 demonstrates how to use these bitwise operators. The results of Listing 3.37 appear in Output 3.18.

LISTING 3.37: Using Bitwise Operators

```
byte and, or, xor;
and = 12 & 7;   // and = 4
or = 12 | 7;    // or = 15
xor = 12 ^ 7;   // xor = 11
System.Console.WriteLine(
    "and = {0} \nor = {1}\nxor = {2}",
    and, or, xor);
```

OUTPUT 3.18:

```
and = 4
or = 15
xor = 11
```

In Listing 3.37, the value 7 is the **mask**; it is used to expose or eliminate specific bits within the first operand using the particular operator expression.

In order to convert a number to its binary representation, you need to iterate across each bit in a number. Listing 3.38 is an example of a program that converts an integer to a string of its binary representation. The results of Listing 3.38 appear in Output 3.19.

LISTING 3.38: Getting a String Representation of a Binary Display

```
public class BinaryConverter
{
  public static void Main()
  {
      const int size = 64;
      ulong value;
      char bit;

      System.Console.Write ("Enter an integer: ");
      // Use long.Parse() so as to support negative numbers
      // Assumes unchecked assignment to ulong.
      value = (ulong)long.Parse(System.Console.ReadLine());

      // Set initial mask to 100....
      ulong mask = 1ul << size - 1;
      for (int count = 0; count < size; count++)
      {
```

```
        bit = ((mask & value) > 0) ? '1': '0';
        System.Console.WriteLine(bit);
        // Shift mask one location over to the right
        mask >>= 1;
    }
  }
}
```

OUTPUT 3.19:

```
Enter an integer: 42
000000000000000000000000000000000000000000000000000000000000101010
```

Notice that within each iteration of the for loop (discussed shortly), you use the right-shift assignment operator to create a mask corresponding to each bit in value. By using the & bit operator to mask a particular bit, you can determine whether the bit is set. If the mask returns a positive result, you set the corresponding bit to 1; otherwise, it is set to 0. In this way, you create a string representing the binary value of an unsigned long.

Listing 3.38 again used the keyword new, but this time, you instantiated a StringBuilder object, not an array. Chapter 5 covers the concept of instantiation and using the new operator in depth.

Bitwise Assignment Operators (&=, |=, ^=)

Not surprisingly, you can combine these bitwise operators with assignment operators as follows: &=, |=, and ^=. As a result, you could take a variable, OR it with a number, and assign the result back to the original variable, which Listing 3.39 demonstrates.

LISTING 3.39: Using Logical Assignment Operators

```
byte and, or, xor;
and = 12;
and &= 7;    // and = 4
or = 12;
or |= 7;    // or = 15
xor = 12;
xor ^= 7;    // xor = 11
System.Console.WriteLine(
    "and = {0} \nor = {1}\nxor = {2}",
    and, or, xor);
```

The results of Listing 3.39 appear in Output 3.20.

OUTPUT 3.20:

```
and = 4
or = 15
xor = 11
```

Bitwise Complement Operator (~)

The **bitwise complement operator** takes the complement of each bit in the operand, where the operand can be an `int`, `uint`, `long`, or `ulong`. `~1`, therefore, returns `1111 1111 1111 1111 1111 1111 1111 1110` and `~(1<<31)` returns `0111 1111 1111 1111 1111 1111 1111 1111`.

Control Flow Statements, Continued

With the additional coverage of Boolean expressions, it's time to consider more of the control flow statements supported by C#. As indicated in the introduction, many of these statements will be familiar to experienced programmers, so you can skim this section for information specific to C#. Note in particular the `foreach` loop, as this may be new to many programmers.

The `while` and `do/while` Loops

Until now, you have learned how to write programs that do something only once. However, one of the important capabilities of the computer is that it can perform the same operation multiple times. In order to do this, you need to create an instruction loop. The first instruction loop I will discuss is the `while` loop. The general form of the `while` statement is as follows:

```
while(boolean-expression )
    statement
```

The computer will repeatedly execute `statement` as long as `Boolean-expression` evaluates to `true`. If the statement evaluates to `false`, then code execution continues at the line following `statement`. The Fibonacci calculator shown in Listing 3.40 demonstrates this.

LISTING 3.40: **while** Loop Example

```csharp
class FibonacciCalculator
{
  static void Main()
  {
      decimal current;
      decimal previous;
      decimal temp;
      decimal input;

      System.Console.Write("Enter a positive integer:");

      // decimal.Parse convert the ReadLine to a decimal.
      input = decimal.Parse(System.Console.ReadLine());

      // Initialize current and previous to 1, the first
      // two numbers in the Fibonacci series.
      current = previous = 1;

      // While the current Fibonacci number in the series is
      // less than the value input by the user.
      while(current <= input)
      {
          temp = current;
          current = previous + current;
          previous = temp;
      }

      System.Console.WriteLine(
          "The Fibonacci number following this is {0}",
          current);
  }
}
```

A **Fibonacci number** is a member of the **Fibonacci series**, which includes all numbers that are the sum of the previous two numbers in the series, beginning with 1 and 1. In Listing 3.40, you prompt the user for an integer. Then you use a while loop to find the Fibonacci number that is greater than the number the user entered.

■ **BEGINNER TOPIC**

When to Use a **while** Loop

The remainder of this chapter considers other types of statements that cause a block of code to execute repeatedly. It is important to understand which loop construct to select. You use a while construct to iterate while the condition evaluates to `true`. A `for` loop is used most appropriately whenever the number of repetitions is counting from 0 to *n*. A `do/while` is similar to a `while` loop, except that it will always loop at least once.

The `do/while` loop is very similar to the `while` loop, except that it is used when the number of repetitions is from 1 to *n* and *n* is indeterminate when iterating begins. This pattern occurs most commonly when repeatedly prompting a user for input. Listing 3.41 is taken from the tic-tac-toe program.

LISTING 3.41: `do/while` Loop Example

```
// Repeatedly request player to move until they
// enter a valid position on the board.
do
{
  valid = false;

  // Request a move from the current player.
  System.Console.Write(
    "\nPlayer {0}: Enter move:", currentPlayer);
  input = System.Console.ReadLine();

  // Check the current player's input.
  // ...

} while (!valid);
```

In Listing 3.41, you always initialize `valid` to `false` at the beginning of each **iteration**, or loop repetition. Next, you prompt and retrieve the number the user input. Although not shown here, you then check whether the input was correct, and if it was, you assign `valid` equal to `true`. Since the code uses a `do/while` statement rather than a `while` statement, the user will be prompted for input at least once.

The general form of the `do/while` loop is as follows:

```
do
  statement
while(boolean-expression );
```

As with all the control flow statements, the code blocks are not part of the general form. However, a code block is generally used in place of a single statement in order to allow multiple statements.

The `for` loop

Increment and decrement operators are frequently used within a `for` loop. The `for` loop iterates a code block until a specified condition is reached in a way similar to the `while` loop. The difference is that the `for` loop has built-in syntax for initializing, incrementing, and testing the value of a counter.

Listing 3.42 shows the `for` loop used to display an integer in binary form. The results of this listing appear in Output 3.21.

LISTING 3.42: Using the `for` Loop

```
public class BinaryConverter
{
  public static void Main()
  {
      const int size = 64;
      ulong value;
      char bit;

      System.Console.Write ("Enter an integer: ");
      // Use long.Parse() so as to support negative numbers
      // Assumes unchecked assignment to ulong.
      value = (ulong)long.Parse(System.Console.ReadLine());

      // Set initial mask to 100....
      ulong mask = 1ul << size - 1;
      for (int count = 0; count < size; count++)
      {
          bit = ((mask & value) > 0) ? '1': '0';
          System.Console.WriteLine(bit);
          // Shift mask one location over to the right
          mask >>= 1;
      }
  }
}
```

OUTPUT 3.21:

```
Enter an integer: -42
1111111111111111111111111111111111111111111111111111111111010110
```

Listing 3.42 performs a bit mask 64 times, once for each bit in the number. The `for` loop declares and initializes the variable `count`, escapes once the count reaches 64, and increments the count during each iteration. Each expression within the `for` loop corresponds to a statement. (It is easy to remember that the separation character between expressions is a semicolon and not a comma, because each expression is a statement.)

You write a `for` loop generically as follows:

```
for(initial; boolean-expression; loop)
    statement
```

Here is a breakdown of the `for` loop.

- The `initial` expression performs operations that precede the first iteration. In Listing 3.42, it declares and initializes the variable `count`. The `initial` expression does not have to be a declaration of a new variable. It is possible, for example, to declare the variable beforehand and simply initialize it in the `for` loop. Variables declared here, however, are bound within the scope of the `for` statement.

- The `boolean-expression` portion of the `for` loop specifies an end condition. The loop exits when this condition is false in a manner similar to the `while` loop's termination. The `for` loop will repeat only as long as `boolean-expression` evaluates to `true`. In the preceding example, the loop exits when `count` increments to 64.

- The `loop` expression executes after each iteration. In the preceding example, `count++` executes after the right shift of the mask (`mask >>= 1`), but before the Boolean expression is evaluated. During the 64th iteration, `count` increments to 64, causing `boolean-expression` to be `false` and, therefore, terminating the loop. Because each expression can be thought of as a separate statement, each expression in the `for` loop is separated by a semicolon.

- The `statement` portion of the `for` loop is the code that executes while the conditional expression remains true.

If you wrote out each `for` loop execution step in pseudocode without using a `for` loop expression, it would look like this:

1. Declare and initialize `count` to 0.
2. Verify that `count` is less than 64.
3. Calculate `bit` and display it.
4. Shift the mask.

5. Increment `count` by one.

6. If `count<64`, then jump back to line 3.

The `for` statement doesn't require any of the elements between parentheses. `for(;;){ ... }` is perfectly valid, assuming there is still a means to escape from the loop. Similarly, the initial and loop expressions can be a complex expression involving multiple subexpressions, as shown in Listing 3.43.

LISTING 3.43: **for** Loop Using Multiple Expressions

```
for(int x=0, y=5; ((x<=5) && (y>=0)); y--, x++)
{
  System.Console.Write("{0}{1}{2}\t",
      x, (x>y? '>' : '<'), y);
}
```

The results of Listing 3.43 appear in Output 3.22.

OUTPUT 3.22:

```
0<5     1<4     2<3     3>2     4>1     5>0
```

In this case, the comma behaves exactly as it does in a declaration statement, one that declares and initializes multiple variables. However, programmers should avoid complex expressions like this one because they are difficult to read and understand.

Generically, you can write the `for` loop as a `while` loop, as shown here:

```
initial;
while(boolean-expression)
{
  statement;
  loop;
}
```

■ BEGINNER TOPIC

Choosing between **for** and **while** Loops

Although you can use the two statements interchangeably, generally you would use the `for` loop whenever there is some type of counter, and the total number of iterations is known when the loop is initialized. In contrast, you would typically use the `while` loop when iterations are not based on a count or when the number of iterations is indeterminate when iterating commences.

The `foreach` Loop

The last loop statement within the C# language is `foreach`. `foreach` is designed to iterate through a collection of items, setting an identifier to represent each item in turn. During the loop, operations may be performed on the item. One feature of the `foreach` loop is that it is not possible to accidentally miscount and iterate over the end of the collection.

The general form of the `foreach` statement is as follows:

```
foreach(type identifier in collection)
   statement;
```

Here is a breakdown of the `foreach` statement.

- `type` is used to declare the data type of the identifier for each item within the collection.
- `identifier` is a read-only variable into which the `foreach` construct will automatically assign the next item within the collection. The scope of the identifier is limited to the `foreach` loop.
- `collection` is an expression, such as an array, representing multiple items.
- `statement` is the code that executes for each iteration within the `foreach` loop.

Consider the `foreach` loop in the context of the simple example shown in Listing 3.44.

LISTING 3.44: Determining Remaining Moves Using the `foreach` Loop

```
class TicTacToe        // Declares the TicTacToe class.
{
  static void Main() // Declares the entry point of the program.
  {
      // Hardcode initial board as follows
```

```csharp
// ---+---+---
// 1 | 2 | 3
// ---+---+---
// 4 | 5 | 6
// ---+---+---
// 7 | 8 | 9
// ---+---+---
char[] cells = {
  '1', '2', '3', '4', '5', '6', '7', '8', '9'
};

System.Console.Write(
    "The available moves are as follows: ");

// Write out the initial available moves
foreach (char cell in cells)
{
  if (cell != 'O' && cell != 'X')
  {
      System.Console.Write("{0} ", cell);
  }
}
```

Output 3.23 shows the results of Listing 3.44.

OUTPUT 3.23:

```
The available moves are as follows: 1 2 3 4 5 6 7 8 9
```

When the execution engine reaches the `foreach` statement, it assigns to the variable `cell` the first item in the `cells` array—in this case, the value `'1'`. It then executes the code within the `foreach` statement block. The `if` statement determines whether the value of `cell` is `'O'` or `'X'`. If it is neither, then the value of `cell` is written out to the console. The next iteration then assigns the next array value to `cell`, and so on.

It is important to note that the compiler prevents modification of the identifier variable (`cell`) during the execution of a `foreach` loop.

Where the `switch` Statement Is More Appropriate

Sometimes you might compare the same value in several continuous `if` statements, as shown with the `input` variable in Listing 3.45.

LISTING 3.45: Checking the Player's Input with an `if` Statement

```
// ...

bool valid = false;

// Check the current player's input.
if( (input == "1") ||
  (input == "2") ||
  (input == "3") ||
  (input == "4") ||
  (input == "5") ||
  (input == "6") ||
  (input == "7") ||
  (input == "8") ||
  (input == "9") )
{
    // Save/move as the player directed.
    // ...

    valid = true;
}
else if( (input == "") || (input == "quit") )
{
    valid = true;
}
else
{
    System.Console.WriteLine(
      "\nERROR:  Enter a value from 1-9. "
      + "Push ENTER to quit");
}

// ...
```

This code validates the text entered to ensure it is a valid tic-tac-toe move. If the value of `input` were 9, for example, the program would have to perform nine different evaluations. It would be preferable to jump to the correct code after only one evaluation. To enable this, you use a `switch` statement.

The `switch` Statement

Given a variable to compare and a list of constant values to compare against, the `switch` statement is simpler to read and code than the `if` statement. The `switch` statement looks like this:

```
switch(governing-type-expression)
{
  [case constant:
      statement
      jump expression]
  [default:
      statement
      jump expression]
}
```

Here is a breakdown of the `switch` statement.

- `governing-type-expression` returns a value that is compatible with the governing types. Allowable governing data types are `sbyte`, `byte`, `short`, `ushort`, `int`, `uint`, `long`, `ulong`, `char`, `string`, and an enum-type (covered in Chapter 8).
- `constant` is any constant expression compatible with the data type of the governing type.
- `statement` is one or more statements to be executed when the governing type expression equals the constant value.
- `jump expression` is a jump statement such as a `break` or `goto` statement. If the `switch` statement appears within a loop, then `continue` is also allowed.

A `switch` statement must have at least one `case` statement or a default statement. In other words, `switch(x){}` is not valid.

Listing 3.46, with a `switch` statement, is semantically equivalent to the series of `if` statements in Listing 3.45.

LISTING 3.46: Replacing the `if` Statement with a `switch` Statement

```
static bool ValidateAndMove(
  int[] playerPositions, int currentPlayer, string input)
{
  bool valid = false;

  // Check the current player's input.
```

```csharp
switch (input)
{
  case "1" :
  case "2" :
  case "3" :
  case "4" :
  case "5" :
  case "6" :
  case "7" :
  case "8" :
  case "9" :
    // Save/move as the player directed.
    ...
    valid = true;
    break;

  case "" :
  case "quit" :
    valid = true;
    break;
  default :
    // If none of the other case statements
    // is encountered then the text is invalid.
    System.Console.WriteLine(
      "\nERROR:  Enter a value from 1-9. "
      + "Push ENTER to quit");
    break;
  }

  return valid;
}
```

In Listing 3.46, `input` is the governing type expression. Since `input` is a string, all of the constants are strings. If the value of `input` is 1, 2, ... 9, then the move is valid and you change the appropriate cell to match that of the current user's token (X or O). Once execution encounters a `break` statement, it immediately jumps to the statement following the `switch` statement.

The next portion of the switch looks for `""` or `"quit"`, and sets `valid` to `true` if `input` equals one of these values. Ultimately, the `default` label is executed if no prior `case` constant was equivalent to the governing type.

There are several things to note about the `switch` statement.

- Placing nothing within the `switch` block will generate a compiler warning, but the statement will still compile.
- `default` does not have to appear last within the `switch` statement. `case` statements appearing after `default` are evaluated.

- When you use multiple constants for one `case` statement, they should appear consecutively, as shown in Listing 3.46.
- The compiler requires a jump statement (usually a `break`).

Language Contrast: C++ — `switch` Statement Fallthrough

Unlike C++, C# does not allow a `switch` statement to fall through from one case block to the next if the `case` includes a statement. A jump statement is always required following the statement within a `case`. The C# founders believed it was better to be explicit and require the jump expression in favor of code readability. If programmers want to use a fall-through semantic, they may do so explicitly with a `goto` statement, as demonstrated in the section The `goto` Statement, later in this chapter.

Jump Statements

It is possible to alter the execution path of a loop. In fact, with jump statements, it is possible to escape out of the loop or to skip the remaining portion of an iteration and begin with the next iteration, even when the conditional expression remains true. This section considers some of the ways to jump the execution path from one location to another.

The `break` Statement

To escape out of a loop or a `switch` statement, C# uses a `break` statement. Whenever the `break` statement is encountered, the execution path immediately jumps to the first statement following the loop. Listing 3.47 examines the `foreach` loop from the tic-tac-toe program.

LISTING 3.47: Using **break** to Escape Once a Winner Is Found

```
class TicTacToe       // Declares the TicTacToe class.
{
  static void Main() // Declares the entry point of the program.
  {
      int winner=0;
      // Stores locations each player has moved.
      int[] playerPositions = {0,0};
```

```
// Hardcoded board position
// X | 2 | O
// ---+---+---
// O | O | 6
// ---+---+---
// X | X | X
playerPositions[0] = 449;
playerPositions[1] = 28;

// Determine if there is a winner
int[] winningMasks = {
    7, 56, 448, 73, 146, 292, 84, 273 };

// Iterate through each winning mask to determine
// if there is a winner.
foreach (int mask in winningMasks)
{
    if ((mask & playerPositions[0]) == mask)
    {
        winner = 1;
        break;
    }
    else if ((mask & playerPositions[1]) == mask)
    {
        winner = 2;
        break;
    }
}

System.Console.WriteLine(
    "Player {0} was the winner", winner);
    }
}
```

Output 3.24 shows the results of Listing 3.47.

OUTPUT 3.24:

```
Player 1 was the winner
```

Listing 3.47 uses a break statement when a player holds a winning position. The break statement forces its enclosing loop (or a switch statement) to cease execution, and the program moves to the next line outside of the loop. For this listing, if the bit comparison returns true (if the board holds a winning position), the break statement causes execution to jump and display the winner.

■ BEGINNER TOPIC

Bitwise Operators for Positions

The tic-tac-toe example (Appendix B) uses the bitwise operators to determine which player wins the game. First, the code saves the positions of each player into a bitmap called `playerPositions`. (It uses an array so that the positions for both players can be saved.)

To begin, both `playerPositions` are 0. As each player moves, the bit corresponding to the move is set. If, for example, the player selects cell 3, `shifter` is set to 3 – 1. The code subtracts 1 because C# is zero based and you need to adjust for 0 as the first position instead of 1. Next, the code sets `position`, the bit corresponding to cell 3, using the shift operator 000000000000001 << `shifter`, where `shifter` now has a value of 2. Lastly, it sets `playerPositions` for the current player (subtracting 1 again to shift to zero based) to 0000000000000100. Listing 3.48 uses |= so that previous moves are combined with the current move.

LISTING 3.48: Setting the Bit That Corresponds to Each Player's Move

```
int shifter;    // The number of places to shift
                // over in order to set a bit.
int position;   // The bit which is to be set.

// int.Parse() converts "input" to an integer.
// "int.Parse(input) - 1" because arrays
// are zero based.
shifter = int.Parse(input) - 1;

// Shift mask of 0000000000000000000000000000001
// over by cellLocations.
position = 1 << shifter;

// Take the current player cells and OR them to set the
// new position as well.
// Since currentPlayer is either 1 or 2,
// subtract one to use currentPlayer as an
// index in a 0-based array.
playerPositions[currentPlayer-1] |= position;
```

Later on in the program, you can iterate over each mask corresponding to winning positions on the board to determine if the current player has a winning position, as shown in Listing 3.47.

The continue Statement

In some instances, you may have a series of statements within a loop. If you determine that some conditions warrant executing only a portion of these statements for some iterations, you use the continue statement to jump to the end of the current iteration and begin the next iteration. The C# continue statement allows you to exit the current iteration (regardless of which additional statements remain) and jump to the loop conditional. At that point, if the loop conditional remains true, the loop will continue execution.

Listing 3.49 uses the continue statement so that only the letters of the domain portion of an email are displayed. Output 3.25 shows the results of Listing 3.49.

LISTING 3.49: Determining the Domain of an Email Address

```csharp
class EmailDomain
{
  static void Main()
  {
      string email;
      bool insideDomain = false;
      System.Console.WriteLine("Enter an email address: ");

      email = System.Console.ReadLine();

      System.Console.Write("The email domain is: ");

      // Iterate through each letter in the email address.
      foreach (char letter in email)
      {
          if (!insideDomain)
          {
              if (letter == '@')
              {
                  insideDomain = true;
              }
              continue;
          }

          System.Console.Write(letter);
      }
  }
}
```

OUTPUT 3.25:

```
Enter an email address:
mark@dotnetprogramming.com
The email domain is: dotnetprogramming.com
```

In Listing 3.49, if you are not yet inside the domain portion of the email address, you need to use a `continue` statement to jump to the next character in the email address.

In general, you can use an `if` statement in place of a `continue` statement, and this is usually more readable. The problem with the `continue` statement is that it provides multiple exit points within the iteration, and this compromises readability. In Listing 3.50, the sample has been rewritten, replacing the `continue` statement with the `if`/`else` construct to demonstrate a more readable version that does not use the `continue` statement.

LISTING 3.50: Replacing a **continue** with an **if** Statement

```
foreach (char letter in email)
{
  if (insideDomain)
  {
      System.Console.Write(letter);
  }
  else
  {
      if (letter == '@')
      {
          insideDomain = true;
      }
  }
}
```

The goto Statement

With the advent of object-oriented programming and the prevalence of well-structured code, the existence of a `goto` statement within C# seems like an aberration to many experienced programmers. However, C# supports `goto`, and it is the only method for supporting fallthrough within a `switch` statement. In Listing 3.51, if the `/out` option is set, code execution jumps to the `default` case using the `goto` statement; similarly for `/f`.

LISTING 3.51: Demonstrating a **switch** with **goto** Statements

```csharp
// ...
static void Main(string[] args)
{
  bool isOutputSet = false;
  bool isFiltered = false;

  foreach (string option in args)
  {
      switch (option)
      {
          case "/out":
              isOutputSet = true;
              isFiltered = false;
              goto default;
          case "/f":
              isFiltered = true;
              isRecursive = false;
              goto default;
          default:
              if (isRecursive)
              {
                  // Recurse down the hierarchy
                  // ...

              }
              else if (isFiltered)
              {
                  // Add option to list of filters.
                  // ...
              }
              break;
      }

  }

  // ...

}
```

Output 3.26 shows the results of Listing 3.51.

OUTPUT 3.26:

```
C:\SAMPLES>Generate /out fizbottle.bin /f "*.xml" "*.wsdl"
```

As demonstrated in Listing 3.51, `goto` statements are ugly. In this particular example, this is the only way to get the desired behavior of a `switch` statement. Although you can use `goto` statements outside `switch` statements, they generally cause poor program structure and you should deprecate them in favor of a more readable construct. Note also that you cannot use a `goto` statement to jump from outside a `switch` statement into a label within a `switch` statement.

C# Preprocessor Directives

Control flow statements evaluate conditional expressions at runtime. In contrast, the C# preprocessor is invoked during compilation. The preprocessor commands are directives to the C# compilers specifying the sections of code to compile and identifying how to handle specific errors and warnings. C# preprocessor commands can also provide directives to C# editors regarding the organization of code.

Language Contrast: C++—Preprocessing

Languages such as C and C++ contain a **preprocessor**, a separate utility from the compiler that sweeps over code, performing actions based on special tokens. Preprocessor directives generally tell the compiler how to compile the code in a file and do not participate in the compilation process itself. In contrast, the C# compiler handles preprocessor directives as part of the regular lexical analysis of the source code. As a result, C# does not support preprocessor macros beyond defining a constant. In fact, the term *precompiler* is generally a misnomer for C#.

Each preprocessor directive begins with a hash symbol (#), and all preprocessor directives must appear on one line. A newline rather than a semicolon indicates the end of the directive.

A list of each preprocessor directive appears in Table 3.4.

TABLE 3.4: Preprocessor Directives

Statement or Expression	General Syntax Structure	Example
#if command	**#if** preprocessor-expression code **#endif**	**#if** CSHARP2 Console.Clear(); **#endif**
#define command	**#define** conditional-symbol	**#define** CSHARP2
#undef command	**#undef** conditional-symbol	**#undef** CSHARP2
#error command	**#error** preproc-message	**#error** Buggy implementa- tion
#warning command	**#warning** preproc-message	**#warning** Needs code review
#pragma command	**#pragma** warning	**#pragma** warning disable 1030
#line command	**#line** org-line new-line **#line** default	**#line** 467 "TicTacToe.cs" ... **#line default**
#region command	**#region** pre-proc-message code **#endregion**	**#region** Methods ... **#endregion**

Excluding and Including Code (#if, #elif, #else, #endif)

Perhaps the most common use of preprocessor directives is in controlling when and how code is included. For example, to write code that could be compiled by both C# 2.0 compilers and the prior version 1.2 compilers, you use a preprocessor directive to exclude C# 2.0-specific code when compiling with a 1.2 compiler. You can see this in the tic-tac-toe example and in Listing 3.52.

LISTING 3.52: Excluding C# 2.0 Code from a C# 1.x Compiler

```
#if CSHARP2
System.Console.Clear();
#endif
```

In this case, you call the `System.Console.Clear()` method, which is available only in the 2.0 CLI version. Using the `#if` and `#endif` preprocessor directives, this line of code will be compiled only if the preprocessor symbol `CSHARP2` is defined.

Another use of the preprocessor directive would be to handle differences among platforms, such as surrounding Windows- and Linux-specific APIs with `WINDOWS` and `LINUX` `#if` directives. Developers often use these directives in place of multiline comments (`/*...*/`) because they are easier to remove by defining the appropriate symbol or via a search and replace. A final common use of the directives is for debugging. If you surround code with a `#if DEBUG`, you will remove the code from a release build on most IDEs. The IDEs define the `DEBUG` symbol by default in a debug compile and `RELEASE` by default for release builds.

To handle an else-if condition, you can use the `#elif` directive within the `#if` directive, instead of creating two entirely separate `#if` blocks, as shown in Listing 3.53.

LISTING 3.53: Using **#if**, **#elseif**, and **#endif** Directives

```
#if LINUX
...
#elif WINDOWS
...
#endif
```

Defining Preprocessor Symbols (#define, #undef)

You can define a preprocessor symbol in two ways. The first is with the `#define` directive, as shown in Listing 3.54.

LISTING 3.54: A **#define** Example

```
#define CSHARP2
```

The second method uses the `define` option when compiling for .NET, as shown in Output 3.27.

OUTPUT 3.27:

```
>csc.exe /define:CSHARP2 TicTacToe.cs
```

Output 3.28 shows the same functionality using the Mono compiler.

OUTPUT 3.28:

```
>mcs.exe -define:CSHARP2 TicTacToe.cs
```

To add multiple definitions, separate them with a semicolon. The advantage of the `define` complier option is that no source code changes are required, so you may use the same source files to produce two different binaries.

To undefine a symbol you use the `#undef` directive in the same way you use `#define`.

Emitting Errors and Warnings (#error, #warning)

Sometimes you may want to flag a potential problem with your code. You do this by inserting `#error` and `#warning` directives to emit an error or warning, respectively. Listing 3.55 uses the tic-tac-toe sample to warn that the code does not yet prevent players from entering the same move multiple times. The results of Listing 3.55 appear in Output 3.29.

LISTING 3.55: Defining a Warning with #warning

```
#warning     "Same move allowed multiple times."
```

OUTPUT 3.29:

```
Performing main compilation...
...\tictactoe.cs(471,16): warning CS1030: #warning: '"Same move allowed
multiple times."'

Build complete -- 0 errors, 1 warnings
```

By including the `#warning` directive, the compiler will report a warning, as shown in Output 3.29. This particular warning is a way of flagging the fact that there is a potential enhancement or bug within the code. It could be a simple way of reminding the developer of a pending task.

Turning Off Warning Messages (#pragma)

Warnings are helpful because they point to code that could potentially be troublesome. However, sometimes it is preferred to turn off particular warnings explicitly because they can be ignored legitimately. C# 2.0 provides the preprocessor #pragma directive for just this purpose (see Listing 3.56).

LISTING 3.56: Using the Preprocessor **#pragma** Directive to Disable the **#warning** Directive

```
#pragma warning disable  1030
```

Note that warning numbers are prefixed with the letters CS in the compiler output. However, this prefix is not used in the #pragma warning directive.

To re-enable the warning, #pragma supports the restore option following the warning, as shown in Listing 3.57.

LISTING 3.57: Using the Preprocessor **#pragma** Directive to Restore a Warning

```
#pragma warning restore  1030
```

In combination, these two directives can surround a particular block of code where the warning is explicitly determined to be irrelevant.

Perhaps one of the most common warnings to disable is CS1591, as this appears when you elect to generate XML documentation using the doc compiler option, but you neglect to document all of the public items within your program.

nowarn: <warn list> Option

In addition to the #pragma directive, C# compilers generally support the nowwarn:<warn list> option. This achieves the same result as #pragma, except that instead of adding it to the source code, you can simply insert the command as a compiler option. In addition, the nowarn option affects the entire compilation, and the #pragma option affects only the file in which it appears. Turning off the CS1591 warning, for example, would appear on the command line as shown in Output 3.30.

OUTPUT 3.30:

```
> csc /doc:generate.xml /nowarn:1591 /out:generate.exe Program.cs
```

Specifying Line Numbers (#line)

The #line directive controls on which line number the C# compiler reports an error or warning. It is used predominantly by utilities and designers that emit C# code. In Listing 3.58, the actual line numbers within the file appear on the left.

LISTING 3.58: The **#line** Preprocessor Directive

```
124        #line 113 "TicTacToe.cs"
125        #warning "Same move allowed multiple times."
126        #line default
```

Including the #line directive causes the compiler to report the warning found on line 125 as though it was on line 113, as shown in the compiler error message shown in Output 3.31.

OUTPUT 3.31:

```
Performing main compilation...
...\tictactoe.cs(113,18): warning CS1030: #warning: '"Same move allowed
multiple times."'

Build complete -- 0 errors, 1 warnings
```

Following the #line directive with default reverses the effect of all prior #line directives and instructs the compiler to report true line numbers rather than the ones designated by previous uses of the #line directive.

Hints for Visual Editors (#region, #endregion)

C# contains two preprocessor directives, #region and #endregion, that are useful only within the context of visual code editors. Code editors, such as the one in the Microsoft Visual Studio .NET IDE, can search through source code and find these directives to provide editor features when writing code. C# allows you to declare a region of code using the #region directive. You must pair the #region directive with a matching #endregion directive, both of which may optionally include a descriptive string following the directive. In addition, you may nest regions within one another.

Again, Listing 3.59 shows the tic-tac-toe program as an example.

LISTING 3.59: A **#region** and **#endregion** Preprocessor Directive

```
...
#region Display Tic-tac-toe Board

#if CSHARP2
  System.Console.Clear();
#endif

// Display the current board;
border = 0;    // set the first border (border[0] = "|")

// Display the top line of dashes.
// ("\n---+---+---\n")
System.Console.Write(borders[2]);
foreach (char cell in cells)
{
  // Write out a cell value and the border that comes after it.
  System.Console.Write(" {0} {1}", cell, borders[border]);

  // Increment to the next border;
  border++;

  // Reset border to 0 if it is 3.
  if (border == 3)
  {
      border = 0;
  }
}
#endregion Display Tic-tac-toe Board
...
```

One example of how these preprocessor directives are used is with Microsoft Visual Studio .NET. Visual Studio .NET examines the code and provides a tree control to open and collapse the code (on the left-hand side of the code editor window) that matches the region demarcated by the #region directives (see Figure 3.5).

SUMMARY

This chapter began with an introduction to the C# operators related to assignment and arithmetic. Next, you used the operators along with the const keyword to declare constant expressions. Coverage of all of the C#

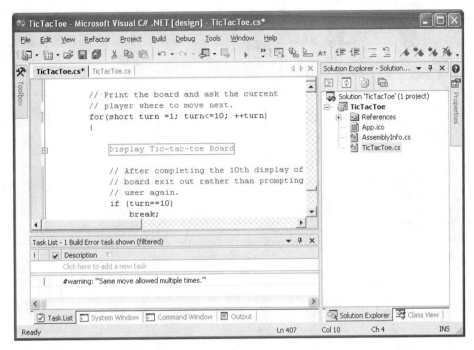

FIGURE 3.5: Collapsed Region in Microsoft Visual Studio .NET

operators was not sequential, however. Before discussing the relational and logical comparison operators, I introduced the `if` statement and the important concepts of code blocks and scope. To close out the coverage of operators I discussed the bitwise operators, especially regarding masks.

Operator precedence was discussed earlier in the chapter, but Table 3.5 summarizes the order of precedence across all operators, including several that are not yet covered.

TABLE 3.5: Operator Order of Precedence[a]

Category	Operators
Primary	`x.y  f(x)  a[x]  x++  x--  new` `typeof  checked  unchecked`
Unary	`+   -   !   ~   ++x   --x   (T)x`
Multiplicative	`*   /   %`

Continues

TABLE 3.5: Operator Order of Precedence[a] *(Continued)*

Category	Operators
Additive	+ -
Shift	<< >>
Relational and type testing	< > <= >= is as
Equality	== !=
Logical AND	&
Logical XOR	^
Logical OR	|
Conditional AND	&&
Conditional OR	||
Conditional	?:
Assignment	= *= /= %= += -= <<= >>= &= ^= |=

a Rows appear in order of precedence from highest to lowest.

Given coverage of most of the operators, the next topic was control flow statements. The last sections of the chapter detailed the preprocessor directives and the bit operators, which included code blocks, scope, Boolean expressions, and bitwise operators.

Perhaps one of the best ways to review all of the content covered in Chapters 1–3 is to look at the tic-tac-toe program found in Appendix B. By reviewing the program, you can see one way in which you can combine all that you have learned into a complete program.

■4■
Methods and Parameters

FROM WHAT YOU HAVE LEARNED about C# programming so far, you should be able to write structured programs that are similar to programs created in the 1970s. Obviously, programming has come a long way since the 1970s, and the next major programming paradigm was structured programming. Structured programming provides a construct into which statements are grouped together to form a unit. Furthermore, with structured programming, it is possible to pass data to a group of statements and then have data returned once the statements have executed.

This chapter covers how to group statements together into a method. In addition, it covers how to call a method, including how to pass data to a method and receive data from a method.

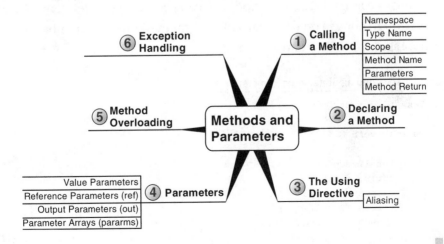

Besides the basics of calling and defining methods, this chapter also covers some slightly more advanced concepts—namely, recursion and method overloading. All method calls discussed so far and through the end of this chapter are static (a concept which Chapter 5 explores in detail).

Even as early as the `HelloWorld` program in Chapter 1, you learned how to define a method. In that example, you defined the `Main()` method. In this chapter, you will learn about method creation in more detail, including the special C# syntax for parameters that pass data to and from a method (`ref`) using a single parameter, as well as parameters that only pass data out from a method (`out`). Lastly, I will touch on some rudimentary error handling.

Calling a Method

■ BEGINNER TOPIC

What Is a Method?

Up to this point, all of the statements in the programs you have written have appeared together in one grouping called a `Main()` method. As programs become even minimally larger, a single method implementation quickly becomes difficult to maintain and complex to read through and understand.

A **method** is a means of grouping together a sequence of statements to perform a particular action. This provides greater structure and organization for the statements that comprise a program. Consider, for example, a `Main()` method that counts the lines of source code in a directory. Instead of having one large `Main()` method, you can provide a shorter version that allows you to hone in on the details of each method implementation as necessary. Listing 4.1 shows an example.

LISTING 4.1: Grouping Statements into Methods

```
class LineCount
{
  static void Main()
  {
      int lineCount;
      string files;
      DisplayHelpText();
      files = GetFiles();
      lineCount = CountLines(files);
```

```
        DisplayLineCount(lineCount);
    }
    // ...
}
```

Instead of placing all of the statements into `Main()`, the listing breaks them into groups called methods. Statements related to displaying the help text, a group of `System.Console.WriteLine()` statements, have been moved to the `DisplayHelpText()` method. All of the statements used to determine which files to count appear in the `GetFiles()` method. To actually count the files, the code calls the `CountLines()` method before displaying the results using the `DisplayLineCount()` method. With a quick glance, it is easy to review the code and gain an overview, because the method name describes the implementation.

A method is always associated with a **class**, and the class provides a means of grouping related methods together. Calling a method is conceptually the same as sending a message to a class.

Methods can receive data via **parameters**. Parameters are "variables" used for passing data from the **caller** (the method containing the method call) to the target method (`Write()`, `WriteLine()`, `GetFiles()`, `Count-Lines()`, and so on). In Listing 4.1, `files` and `lineCount` are examples of parameters passed to the `CountLines()` and `DisplayLineCount()` methods. Methods can also return data back to the caller via a **return value** (in Listing 4.1, the `GetFiles()` method call has a return value that is assigned to `files`).

To begin, you will reexamine `System.Console.Write()`, `System.Console.WriteLine()`, and `System.Console.ReadLine()` from Chapter 1. This time, look at them as examples of method calls in general, instead of looking at the specifics of printing and retrieving data from the console. Listing 4.2 shows each of the three methods in use.

LISTING 4.2: A Simple Method Call

```
class HeyYou
{
    static void Main()
    {
        string firstName;
```

```
    string lastName;

    System.Console.WriteLine("Hey you!");
```

Namespace   **Method Name**   **Parameters**

```
    System.Console.Write("Enter your first name: ");
```
      Type Name
```
    firstName = System.Console.ReadLine();

    System.Console.Write("Enter your last name: ");
    lastName = System.Console.ReadLine();

    System.Console.WriteLine("Your full name is {0} {1}.",
        firstName, lastName);
    }
}
```

The parts of the method call include the namespace, type name, method name, parameters, and return data type. A period separates each part of a fully qualified method name.

Namespace

The first item in the method call is the **namespace**. The namespace is a categorization mechanism for grouping all types related to a particular set of functionality. The namespace helps avoid type name collisions. For example, the compiler can distinguish between two types with the name "Program" as long as each type has a different namespace. The result is that the `Main` method in each class could be referred to using `Awl.Windows.Program.Main()` or `Awl.Console.Program.Main()`.

`System.Collections`, `System.Collections.Generics`, `System.IO`, and `System.Runtime.Serialization.Formatters` are valid names for a namespace. Namespaces can include periods within their names. This enables the namespaces to give the appearance of being hierarchical. This improves human readability only, since the compiler treats all namespaces at a single level. For example, `System.Collections.Generics` appears within the `System.Collections` namespace hierarchy, but to the compiler these are simply two entirely different namespaces.

In Listing 4.2, the namespace for the `Console` type is `System`. The `System` namespace contains the types that enable the programmer to perform many fundamental programming activities. Virtually all C# programs use types within the `System` namespace. Table 4.1 provides a listing of other common namespaces.

TABLE 4.1: Common Namespaces

Namespace	Description
System	Contains the definition of fundamental types, conversion between types, mathematics, program invocation, and environment management.
System.Collections	Includes types for working with collections of objects. Collections can generally follow either list or dictionary type storage mechanisms.
System.Collections.Generics	This C# 2.0 namespace works with strongly typed collections that depend on generics (type parameters).
System.Data	Contains types used for working with data that is stored within a database.
System.Drawing	Contains types for drawing to the display device and working with images.
System.IO	Contains types for working with files and directories and provides capabilities for manipulating, loading, and saving files.
System.Text	Includes types for working with strings and various text encodings, and for converting between those encodings. This namespace includes a subnamespace called `System.Text.RegularExpressions`, which provides access to regular-expression-related APIs.
System.Threading	Handles thread manipulation and multi-threaded programming.
System.Web	A collection of types that enable browser-to-server communication, generally over HTTP. The functionality within this namespace is used to support a .NET technology called ASP.NET.

Continues

TABLE 4.1: Common Namespaces *(Continued)*

Namespace	Description
System.Web.Services	Contains types that send and retrieve data over HTTP using the Simple Object Access Protocol (SOAP).
System.Windows.Forms	Includes types for creating rich user interfaces and the components within them.
System.Xml	Contains standards-based support for XML processing.

It is not always necessary to provide the namespace when calling a method. For example, if you call a method in the same namespace as the target method, then the compiler can infer the namespace to be the same as the caller's namespace. Later in this chapter, you see how the `using` directive avoids the need for a namespace qualifier as well.

Type Name

Calls to static methods (Chapter 5 covers static versus instance methods) require the type name qualifier as long as the target method is not within the same class (such as a call from `HelloWorld.Main()` to `Console.WriteLine()`). However, just as with the namespace, C# allows the elimination of the type name from a method call whenever the method is available on the containing type. (Examples of method calls like this appear in Listing 4.4.) The type name is unnecessary because the compiler infers the type from the calling method. If the compiler can make no such inference, the name must provided as part of the method call.

At their core, types are a means of grouping together methods and their associated data. For example, `Console` is the type name that contains the `Write()`, `WriteLine()`, and `ReadLine()` methods (among others). All of these methods are in the same "group" because they belong to the `Console` type.

Scope

You already learned that scope bounds declaration and accessibility. Scope also defines the inferred call context. A method call between two methods in the same namespace does not require the namespace qualifier. Similarly, two calls within the same class do not require the type name because the scope is the same.

Method Name

After specifying which type contains the method you wish to call, it is time to identify the method itself. C# always uses a period between the type name and the method name, and a pair of parentheses following the method name. Between the parentheses may appear any parameters that the method requires.

Parameters

All methods have from zero to n parameters, and each parameter in C# is of a specific data type. For example, the following method call, used in Listing 4.2, has three parameters:

```
System.Console.WriteLine(
    "Your full name is {1} {0}",lastName, firstName)
```

The first is a `string` and the second two are of type `object`. Although you pass parameter values of type `string` for the second two parameters as well, the compiler allows this because all types, including `string`, are compatible with the data type `object`.

Method Return

In contrast to `System.Console.WriteLine()`, `System.Console.Read-Line()` in Listing 4.2 does not have any parameters. However, this method happens to have a **method return**. The method return is a means of transferring results from a called method back to the caller. Because `System.Console.ReadLine()` has a return, it is possible to assign the return value to the variable `firstName`. In addition, it is possible to pass this method return as a parameter, as shown in Listing 4.3.

LISTING 4.3: Passing a Method Return As a Parameter to Another Method Call

```
class Program
{
  static void Main()
  {
      System.Console.Write("Enter your first name: ");
```

```
System.Console.WriteLine("Hello {0}!",
    System.Console.ReadLine());
    }
}
```

Instead of assigning a variable and then using it in the call to `System.Console.WriteLine()`, Listing 4.3 calls the `System.Console.ReadLine()` method within the call to `System.Console.WriteLine()`. At execution time, the `System.Console.ReadLine()` method executes first and its return is passed directly into the `System.Console.WriteLine()` method, rather than into a variable.

Not all methods return data. Both versions of `System.Console.Write()` and `System.Console.WriteLine()` are examples of such methods. As you will see shortly, these methods specify a return type of `void` just as the `HelloWorld` declaration of `Main` returned `void`.

Statement versus Method Call

Listing 4.3 provides a demonstration of the difference between a statement and a method call. Although `System.Console.WriteLine("Hello {0}!", System.Console.ReadLine());` is a single statement, it contains two method calls. A statement generally contains one or more expressions, and in this example, each expression is a method call. Therefore, method calls form parts of statements.

Although coding multiple method calls in a single statement often reduces the amount of code, it does not necessarily increase the readability and seldom offers a significant performance advantage. Developers should favor readability over brevity.

Declaring a Method

This section expands on the explanation of declaring a method (such as `Main()`) to include any parameter or a return type. Listing 4.4 contains examples of these concepts, and Output 4.1 shows the results.

LISTING 4.4: Declaring a Method

```
class IntroducingMethods
{
    static void Main()
```

```
    {
        string firstName;
        string lastName;
        string fullName;

        System.Console.WriteLine("Hey you!");

        firstName = GetUserInput("Enter your first name: ");
        lastName = GetUserInput("Enter your last name: ");

        fullName = GetFullName(firstName, lastName);

        DisplayGreeting(fullName);
    }

    static string GetUserInput(string prompt)
    {
        System.Console.Write(prompt);
        return System.Console.ReadLine();
    }

    static string GetFullName(string firstName, string lastName)
    {
        return firstName + " " + lastName;
    }

    static void DisplayGreeting(string name)
    {
        System.Console.WriteLine("Your full name is {0}.", name);
        return;
    }
}
```

OUTPUT 4.1:

```
Hey you!
Enter your first name: Inigo
Enter your last name: Montoya
Your full name is Inigo Montoya.
```

Four methods are declared in Listing 4.4. From `Main()` the code calls `GetUserInput()`, followed by a call to `GetFullName()`. Both of these methods return a value and take parameters. In addition, the listing calls `DisplayGreeting()`, which doesn't return any data. No method in C# can exist outside the confines of an enclosing class. Even the `Main` method examined in Chapter 1 must be within a class.

Language Contrast: C++/Visual Basic—Global Methods

C# provides no global method support; everything must appear within a class definition. This is why the `Main()` method was marked as `static`—the C# equivalent of a C++ global and Visual Basic module method.

■ BEGINNER TOPIC

Refactoring into Methods

The `Main()` method that is shown in Listing 4.4 results in the same behavior as does the `Main()` method that is shown in Listing 1.15, in Chapter 1. Perhaps even more noteworthy is that although both listings are trivial to follow, Listing 4.4 is easier to grasp at a glance by just viewing the `Main()` method and not worrying about the details of each called method's implementation.

Moving a set of statements into a method instead of leaving them inline within a larger method is a form of **refactoring**. Refactoring reduces code duplication, because you can call the method from multiple places instead of duplicating the code. Refactoring also increases code readability. As part of the coding process, it is a best practice to continually review your code and look for opportunities to refactor. This involves looking for blocks of code that are difficult to understand at a glance and moving them into a method with a name that clearly defines the code's behavior. This practice is often preferred over commenting a block of code, because the method name serves to describe what the implementation does.

Parameter Declaration

Consider the declaration of the `DisplayGreeting()` and `GetFullName()` methods. The text that appears between the parentheses of a method declaration is the **parameter list**. Each parameter in the parameter list includes the type of the parameter along with the parameter name. A comma separates each parameter in the list.

Behaviorally, parameters are virtually identical to local variables, and the naming convention of parameters follows accordingly. Therefore, parameter names are camel case. Also, it is not possible to declare a local variable with the same name as a parameter of the containing method, because this would create two "local variables" of the same name.

Language Contrast: Visual Basic/C++ — Default Parameters

Unlike Visual Basic and the C-style predecessors, C# does not allow specification of a default value within the method declaration so that the parameter is optional to the caller. For example, it is not possible to declare a method as follows:

```
void Method(int i=42){}
```

Optional parameter type APIs are still possible, but they are implemented via method overloading such that one version of the overloaded method does not include the parameters that are to be optional. In other words, you should define a second method with the same name (overloading it) but without the defaulted parameter. Inside this additional method, the code should assign the default value as part of the method implementation (see the section Method Overloading, later in this chapter).

Method Return Declaration

In addition to `GetUserInput()` and `GetFullName()` requiring parameters to be specified, both of these methods also include a **method return**. You can tell there is a method return because a data type appears immediately before the method name of the method declaration. For both `Get-UserInput()` and `GetFullName()`, the data type is `string`. Unlike parameters, only one method return is allowable.

Once a method includes a return data type, and assuming no error occurs, it is necessary to specify a return statement for each **code path** (or set of statements that may execute consecutively) within the method declaration. A return statement begins with the `return` keyword followed by the value the method is returning. For example, the `GetFullName()` method's return statement is `return firstName + " " + lastName`. The

C# compiler makes it imperative that the return type match the type of the data specified following the `return` keyword.

Return statements can appear in spots other than at the end of a method implementation, as long as all code paths include a return if the method has a return type. For example, an `if` or `switch` statement at the beginning of a method implementation could include a `return` statement within the conditional or `case` statement; see Listing 4.5 for an example.

LISTING 4.5: A **return** Statement before the End of a Method

```csharp
class Program
{
  static void Main()
  {
      string command;
      //...
      switch(command)
      {
          case "quit":
              return;
          // ...
      }
      // ...
  }
}
```

A `return` statement indicates a jump to the end of the method, so no break is required in a `switch` statement. Once the execution encounters a return, the method call will end.

If particular code paths include statements following the return, then the compiler will issue a warning that indicates the additional statements will never execute. In spite of the C# allowance for early returns, code is generally more readable if there is a single exit location rather than multiple returns sprinkled through various code paths of the method.

Specifying `void` as a return type indicates that there is no return from the method. As a result, the method does not support assignment to a variable or use as a parameter. Furthermore, the `return` statement becomes optional, and when it is specified, there is no value following the `return` keyword. For example, the return of `Main()` in Listing 4.4 is `void` and there is no `return` statement within the method. However, `DisplayGreeting()` includes a `return` statement that is not followed by any returned result.

Language Contrast: C++ — Header Files

Unlike C++, C# classes never separate the implementation from the declaration. In C# there is no header (.h) file or implementation (.cpp) file. Instead, declaration and implementation always appear together in the same file. In C# 2.0, it is possible to spread a class across multiple files known as partial types. However, even then the declaration of a method and the implementation of that method must remain together. For C# to declare types and methods inline makes a cleaner and more maintainable language.

The using **Directive**

It is possible to import types from one namespace into the enclosing namespace scope. As a result, it would not be necessary for the programmer to fully qualify a type. To achieve this, the C# programmer includes a using directive, generally at the top of the file. For example, in Listing 4.6, Console is not prefixed with System. Instead, it includes the using directive, using System, at the top of the listing.

LISTING 4.6: **using** Directive Example

```
// The using directive imports all types from the
// specified namespace into the enclosing scope—in
// this case, the entire file.
using System;

class HelloWorld
{
  static void Main()
  {
      // No need to qualify Console with System
      // because of the using directive above.
      Console.WriteLine("Hello, my name is Inigo Montoya");
  }
}
```

The results of Listing 4.6 appear in Output 4.2.

OUTPUT 4.2:

```
Hello, my name is Inigo Montoya
```

A using directive like using System does not enable the omission of System from a method within a more specific namespace. If code accessed a type within System.Text, for example, you would have to either include an additional using directive for System.Text, or fully qualify the type. The using directive does not import any **nested namespaces**. Nested namespaces, identified by the period in the namespace, need to be imported explicitly.

Language Contrast: Java—Wildcards in import Directive

Java allows for importing namespaces using a wildcard such as:

```
import javax.swing.*;
```

In contrast, C# does not support a wildcard using directive, and instead requires each namespace to be imported explicitly.

Language Contrast: Visual Basic .NET—Project Scope Imports Directive

Unlike C#, Visual Basic .NET supports the ability to specify the using directive equivalent, Imports, for an entire project, rather than just for a specific file. In other words, Visual Basic .NET provides a command-line means of the using directive that will span an entire compilation.

Typically, prevalent use of types within a particular namespace results in a using directive for that namespace, instead of fully qualifying all types within the namespace. Following this tendency, virtually all files include the using System directive at the top. Throughout the remainder of this book, code listings will often omit the using System directive. Other namespace directives will be included explicitly, however.

One interesting effect of the using System directive is that the string data type can be identified with varying case: String or string. The former version relies on the `using System` directive and the latter uses the `string` keyword. Both are valid C# references to the `System.String` data type, and the resulting CIL code is unaffected by which version is chosen.[1]

ADVANCED TOPIC

Nested `using` Declaratives

Not only can you have `using` declaratives at the top of a file, but you also can include them at the top of a namespace declaration. For example, if a new namespace, `Awl.Michaelis.EssentialCSharp`, were declared, it would be possible to add a `using` declarative at the top of the namespace declaration (see Listing 4.7).

LISTING 4.7: Specifying the **using** Directive inside a Namespace Declaration

```
namespace Awl.Michaelis.EssentialCSharp
{
    using System;

    class HelloWorld
    {
        static void Main()
        {
            // No need to qualify Console with System
            // because of the using directive above.
            Console.WriteLine("Hello, my name is Inigo Montoya");
        }
    }
}
```

The results of Listing 4.7 appear in Output 4.3.

OUTPUT 4.3:

```
Hello, my name is Inigo Montoya
```

The difference between placing the `using` declarative at the top of a file rather than at the top of a namespace declaration is that the declarative is

---

1. I prefer the `string` keyword, but whichever representation a programmer selects, ideally code within a project should be consistent.

active only within the namespace declaration. If the code includes a new namespace declaration above or below the `Awl.Michaelis.Essential-CSharp` declaration, then the `using System` directive within a different namespace would not be active. Code seldom is written this way, especially given the standard practice of a single type declaration per file.

Aliasing

The `using` directive also has a provision for **aliasing** a namespace or type. An alias is an alternate name that you can use within the scope to which the `using` directive applies. The two most common reasons for aliasing are to disambiguate two types that have the same name and to abbreviate a long name. In Listing 4.8, for example, the `CountDownTimer` alias is declared as a means of referring to the type `System.Timers.Timer`. Simply adding a `using System.Timers` directive will not sufficiently enable the code to avoid fully qualifying the `Timer` type. The reason is that `System.Threading` also includes a type called `Timer`, and therefore, just using `Timer` within the code will be ambiguous.

LISTING 4.8: Declaring a Type Alias

```
using System;
using System.Threading;
using CountDownTimer = System.Timers.Timer;

class HelloWorld
{
  static void Main()
  {
      CountDownTimer timer;

      // ...
  }
}
```

Listing 4.8 uses an entirely new name, `CountDownTimer`, as the alias. It is possible, however, to specify the alias as `Timer`, as shown in Listing 4.9.

LISTING 4.9: Declaring a Type Alias with the Same Name

```
using System;
using System.Threading;
```

```
// Declare alias Timer to refer to System.Timers.Timer to
// avoid code ambiguity with System.Threading.Timer
using Timer = System.Timers.Timer;

class HelloWorld
{
  static void Main()
  {
      Timer timer;

      // ...
  }
}
```

Because of the alias directive, "Timer" is not an ambiguous reference. Furthermore, to refer to the System.Threading.Timer type, you will have to either qualify the type or define a different alias.

Returns and Parameters on Main()

So far, declaration of an executable's Main() method has been the simplest declaration possible. You have not included any parameters or return types in your Main() method declarations. However, C# supports the ability to retrieve the command-line arguments when executing a program, and it is possible to return a status indicator from the Main() method.

The runtime passes the command-line arguments to Main() using a single string array parameter. All you need to do to retrieve the parameters is to access the array, as demonstrated in Listing 4.10. The purpose of this program is to download a file whose location is given by a URL. The first command-line argument identifies the URL, and the optional second argument is the filename to which to save the file. The listing begins with a switch statement that evaluates the number of parameters (args.Length) as follows.

1 If there are zero parameters, display an error indicating that it is necessary to provide the URL.

2 If there is only one argument, calculate the second argument from the first argument.

3 The presence of two arguments indicates the user has provided both the URL of the resource and the download target filename.

LISTING 4.10: Passing Command-Line Arguments to **Main**

```csharp
using System;
using System.IO;
using System.Net;

class Program
{
    static int Main(string[] args)
    {
        int result;
        string targetFileName = null;
        switch (args.Length)
        {
            case 0:
                // No URL specified, so display error.
                Console.WriteLine(
                    "ERROR:  You must specify the "
                    + "URL to be downloaded");
                break;
            case 1:
                // No target filename was specified.
                targetFileName = Path.GetFileName(args[0]);
                break;
            case 2:
                targetFileName = args[1];
                break;
        }

        if (targetFileName != null)
        {
            WebClient webClient = new WebClient();
            webClient.DownloadFile(args[0], targetFileName);
            result = 0;
        }
        else
        {
            Console.WriteLine(
                "Downloader.exe <URL> <TargetFileName>");
            result = 1;
        }
        return result;
    }
}
```

The results of Listing 4.10 appear in Output 4.4.

```
>Downloader.exe
ERROR:  You must specify the URL to be downloaded
Downloader.exe <URL> <TargetFileName>
```

If you were successful in calculating the target filename, you would use it to save the downloaded file. Otherwise, you would display the help text. The Main() method also returns an int rather than a void. This is optional for a Main() declaration, but if it is used, the program can return a status code to a caller, such as a script or a batch file. By convention, a return other than zero indicates an error.

Although all command-line arguments can be passed to Main() via an array of strings, sometimes it is convenient to access the arguments from inside a method other than Main(). The System.Environment.GetCommandLine-Args() method returns the command-line arguments array in the same form that Main(string[] args) passes the arguments into Main().

■ ADVANCED TOPIC

Disambiguate Multiple Main() Methods

If a program includes two classes with Main() methods, it is possible to specify on the command line which class to use for the Main() declaration. csc.exe includes a /m option to specify the fully qualified class name of Main().

■ BEGINNER TOPIC

Call Stack and Call Site

As code executes, methods call more methods that in turn call additional methods, and so on. In the simple case of Listing 4.4, Main() calls GetUserInput(), which in turn calls System.Console.ReadLine(), which in turn calls even more methods internally. The set of calls within calls within calls, and so on, is termed the **call stack**. As program complexity increases, the call stack generally gets larger and larger as each method calls another method. As calls complete, however, the call stack shrinks until another series of methods are invoked. The term for describing the process of removing calls from the call stack is **stack unwinding**. Stack unwinding always occurs in the reverse order of the method calls. The result of method completion is that execution will return to the **call site**, which is the location from which the method was invoked.

Parameters

So far, this chapter's examples have returned data via the method return. This section demonstrates the options of returning data via method parameters and via a variable number of parameters.

■ **BEGINNER TOPIC**

Matching Caller Variables with Parameter Names

In some of the previous listings, you matched the variable names in the caller with the parameter names in the target method. This matching is simply for readability; whether names match is entirely irrelevant to the behavior of the method call.

Value Parameters

By default, parameters are **passed by value**, which means that the variable's stack data is copied into the target parameter. For example, in Listing 4.11, each variable that `Main()` uses when calling `Combine()` will be copied into the parameters of the `Combine()` method. Output 4.5 shows the results of this listing.

LISTING 4.11: Passing Variables by Value

```
class Program
{
  static void Main()
  {
    // ...
```

```
        string fullName;
        string driveLetter = "C:";
        string folderPath  = "Data";
        string fileName     = "index.html";

        fullName = Combine(driveLetter, folderPath, fileName);

        Console.WriteLine(fullName);
        // ...
    }

    static string Combine(
        string driveLetter, string folderPath, string fileName)
    {
        string path;
        path = string.Format("{1}{0}{2}{0}{3}",
            System.IO.Path.DirectorySeparatorChar,
            driveLetter, folderPath, fileName);
        return path;
    }
}
```

OUTPUT 4.5:

```
C:\Data\index.html
```

Even if the `Combine()` method assigns `null` to `driveLetter`, `folder-Path`, and `fileName` before returning, the corresponding variables within `Main()` will maintain their original values because the variables are copied when calling a method. When the call stack unwinds at the end of a call, the copy is thrown away.

ADVANCED TOPIC

Reference Types Versus Value Types

For the purposes of this section, it is inconsequential whether the parameter passed is a value type or a reference type. The issue is whether the target method can assign the caller's original variable a new value. Since a copy is made, the caller's copy cannot be reassigned.

In more detail, a reference type variable contains an address of the memory location where the data is stored. If a reference type variable is passed by value, the address is copied from the caller to the method parameter. As a result, the target method cannot update the caller variable's address value. Alternatively, if the method parameter is a value type, the value itself is copied into the parameter, and changing the parameter will not affect the original caller's variable.

Reference Parameters (ref)

Consider Listing 4.12, which calls a function to swap two values, and Output 4.6, which shows the results.

LISTING 4.12: Passing Variables by Reference

```
class Program
{
  static void Main()
  {
      // ...
      string first = "first";
      string second = "second";
      Swap(ref first, ref second);

      System.Console.WriteLine(
          @"first = ""{0}"", second = ""{1}""",
          first, second);
      // ...
  }

  static void Swap(ref string first, ref string second)
  {
      string temp = first;
      first = second;
      second = temp;
  }
}
```

OUTPUT 4.6:

```
first = "second", second = "first"
```

The values assigned to first and second are successfully switched, even though there is no return from the Swap() method. To do this, the variables are **passed by reference**. The obvious difference between the call to Swap() and Listing 4.11's call to Combine() is the use of the keyword `ref` in front of the parameter's data type. This keyword changes the call type to be by reference, so the called method can update the original caller's variable with a new value.

When the called method specifies a parameter as `ref`, the caller is required to place `ref` in front of the variables passed. In so doing, the caller explicitly recognizes that the target method could reassign any `ref` parameters it receives. Furthermore, it is necessary to initialize variables passed as `ref` because target methods could read data from `ref` parameters without first assigning them. In Listing 4.12, for example, `temp` is assigned the value of `first`, assuming that the variable passed in `first` was initialized by the caller.

Output Parameters (`out`)

In addition to passing parameters into a method only (by value) and passing them in and back out (by reference), it is possible to pass data out only. To achieve this, code needs to decorate parameter types with the keyword `out`, as shown in the `GetPhoneButton()` method in Listing 4.13 that returns the phone button corresponding to a character.

LISTING 4.13: Passing Variables Out Only

```csharp
class ConvertToPhoneNumber
{
    static int Main(string[] args)
    {
        char button;

        if(args.Length == 0)
        {
            Console.WriteLine(
                "ConvertToPhoneNumber.exe <phrase>");
            Console.WriteLine(
                "'_' indicates no standard phone button");
            return 1;
        }
        foreach(string word in args)
        {
            foreach(char character in word)
            {
                if(GetPhoneButton(character, out button))
                {
                    Console.Write(button);
                }
```

```csharp
                else
                {
                    Console.Write('_');
                }
            }
        }
        Console.WriteLine();
        return 0;
    }


    static bool GetPhoneButton(char character, out char button)
    {
        bool success = true;
        switch( char.ToLower(character) )
        {
            case '1':
                button = '1';
                break;
            case '2': case 'a': case 'b': case 'c':
                button = '2';
                break;
            case '3': case 'd': case 'e': case 'f':
                button = '3';
                break;
            case '4': case 'g': case 'h': case 'i':
                button = '4';
                break;
            case '5': case 'j': case 'k': case 'l':
                button = '5';
                break;
            case '6': case 'm': case 'n': case 'o':
                button = '6';
                break;
            case '7': case 'p': case 'q': case 'r': case 's':
                button = '7';
                break;
            case '8': case 't': case 'u': case 'v':
                button = '8';
                break;
            case '9': case 'w': case 'x': case 'y': case 'z':
                button = '9';
                break;
            case '*':
                button = '*';
                break;
            case '0':
                button = '0';
                break;
```

```
        case '#':
            button = '#';
            break;
        case ' ':
            button = ' ';
            break;
        case '-':
            button = '-';
            break;
        default:
            // Set the button to indicate an invalid value
            button = '_';
            success = false;
            break;
        }
        return success;
    }
}
```

Output 4.7 shows the results of Listing 4.13.

OUTPUT 4.7:

```
>ConvertToPhoneNumber.exe CSharpIsGood
274277474663
```

In this example, the `GetPhoneButton()` method returns `true` if it can successfully determine the `character`'s corresponding phone button. The function also returns the corresponding button by using the button parameter which is decorated with `out`.

Whenever a parameter is marked with `out`, the compiler will check that the parameter is set for all code paths within the method. If, for example, the code does not assign `button` a value, the compiler will issue an error indicating the code didn't initialize `button`. Listing 4.13 assigns `button` to _ because even though it cannot determine the correct phone button, it is still necessary to assign a value.

Parameter Arrays (`params`)

In all the examples so far, the number of parameters is fixed by the target method declaration. However, sometimes the number of parameters may vary. Consider the `Combine()` method from Listing 4.11. In that method, you passed the drive letter, folder path, and filename. What if the number of folders in the path was more than one and the caller wanted the method to join additional folders to form the full path? Perhaps the best option would be to pass an array of strings for the folders. However, this would make the calling code a little more complex, because it would be necessary to construct an array to pass as a parameter.

For a simpler approach, C# provides a keyword that enables the number of parameters to vary in the calling code instead of being set by the target method. Before the method declaration is discussed, observe the calling code declared within `Main()`, as shown in Listing 4.14.

LISTING 4.14: Passing a Variable Parameter List

```csharp
using System.IO;

class PathEx
{
  static void Main()
  {
      string fullName;

      // ...

      // Call Combine() with four parameters
      fullName = Combine(
          Directory.GetCurrentDirectory(),
          "bin", "config", "index.html");
      Console.WriteLine(fullName);

      // ...

      // Call Combine() with only three parameters
      fullName = Combine(
          Environment.SystemDirectory,
          "Temp", "index.html");
      Console.WriteLine(fullName);

      // ...

      // Call Combine() with an array
      fullName = Combine(
          new string[] {
              "C:\", "Data",
              "HomeDir", "index.html"} );
      Console.WriteLine(fullName);
      // ...
  }
```

```
static string Combine(params string[] paths)
{
    string result = string.Empty;
    foreach (string path in paths)
    {
        result = System.IO.Path.Combine(result, path);
    }
    return result;
}
}
```

Output 4.8 shows the results of Listing 4.14.

OUTPUT 4.8:

```
C:\Data\mark\bin\config\index.html
C:\WINDOWS\system32\Temp\index.html
C:\Data\HomeDir\index.html
```

In the first call to `Combine()`, four parameters are specified. The second call contains only three parameters. In the final call, parameters are passed using an array. In other words, the `Combine()` method takes a variable number of parameters, whether separated by a comma or as a single array.

To allow this, the `Combine()` method

1. Places `params` immediately before the last parameter in the method declaration
2. Declares the last parameter as an array

With a **parameter array** declaration, it is possible to access each parameter as a member of the `params` array. In the `Combine()` method implementation, you iterate over the elements of the `paths` array and call `System.IO.Path.Combine()`. This method automatically combines the parts of the path, appropriately using the platform-specific directory-separator-character. (`PathEx.Combine()` is identical to `Path.Combine()`, except that `PathEx.Combine()` handles a variable number of parameters rather than simply two.)

There are a few notable characteristics of the parameter array.

- The parameter array is not necessarily the only parameter on a method. However, the parameter array must be the last parameter in the method declaration. Since only the last parameter may be a parameter array, a method cannot have more than one parameter array.

- The caller can specify zero parameters for the parameter array, which will result in an array of zero items.

- Parameter arrays are type safe—the type must match the type identified by the array.

- The caller can use an explicit array rather than a comma-separated list of parameters. The resulting CIL code is identical.

- If the target method implementation requires a minimum number of parameters, then those parameters should appear explicitly within the method declaration, forcing a compile error instead of relying on runtime error handling if required parameters are missing. For example, use `int Max(int first, params int[] operads)` rather than `int Max(params int[] operads)` so that at least one value is passed to `Max()`.

Using a parameter array, you can pass a variable number of parameters of the same type into a method. The section Method Overloading, later in this chapter, discusses a means of supporting a variable number of parameters that are not necessarily of the same type.

Recursion

Calling a method **recursively** or implementing the method using **recursion** refers to the fact that the method calls back on itself. This is sometimes the simplest way to implement a method. Listing 4.15 counts the lines of all the C# source files (`*.cs`) in a directory and its subdirectory.

LISTING 4.15: Returning All the Filenames, Given a Directory

```
using System.IO;

public static class LineCounter
{
  // Use the first argument as the directory
  // to search, or default to the current directory.
```

```csharp
public static void Main(string[] args)
{
    int totalLineCount = 0;
    string directory;
    if (args.Length > 0)
    {
        directory = args[0];
    }
    else
    {
        directory = Directory.GetCurrentDirectory();
    }
    totalLineCount = DirectoryCountLines(directory);
    System.Console.WriteLine(totalLineCount);
}

static int DirectoryCountLines(string directory)
{
    int lineCount = 0;
    foreach (string file in
        Directory.GetFiles(directory, "*.cs"))
    {
        lineCount += CountLines(file);
    }

    foreach (string subdirectory in
        Directory.GetDirectories(directory))
    {
        lineCount += DirectoryCountLines(subdirectory);
    }

    return lineCount;
}

private static int CountLines(string file)
{
    string line;
    int lineCount = 0;
    FileStream stream =
        new FileStream(file, FileMode.Open);
    StreamReader reader = new StreamReader(stream);
    line = reader.ReadLine();

    while(line != null)
    {
        if (line.Trim() != "")
        {
            lineCount++;
        }
        line = reader.ReadLine();
```

```
        }

    reader.Close();
    stream.Close();
    return lineCount;
  }
 }
```

Output 4.9 shows the results of Listing 4.15.

OUTPUT 4.9:

```
104
```

The program begins by passing the first command-line argument to `DirectoryCountLines()`, or by using the current directory if no argument was provided. This method first iterates through all the files in the current directory and totals the source code lines for each file. After each file in the directory, the code processes each subdirectory by passing the subdirectory back into the `DirectoryCountLines()` method, rerunning the method using the subdirectory. The same process is repeated recursively through each subdirectory until no more directories remain to process.

Readers unfamiliar with recursion may find it cumbersome at first. Regardless, it is often the simplest pattern to code, especially with hierarchical type data such as the filesystem. However, although it may be the most readable, it is generally not the fastest implementation. If performance becomes an issue, then developers should seek an alternate solution in place of a recursive implementation. The choice generally hinges on balancing readability with performance.

■ BEGINNER TOPIC

Infinite Recursion Error

A common programming error in recursive method implementations appears in the form of a stack overflow during program execution. This usually happens because of **infinite recursion**, in which the method continually calls back on itself, never reaching a point that indicates the end of the recursion. It is a good practice for programmers to review any method that uses recursion and verify that the recursion calls are finite.

Method Overloading

Listing 4.15 called `DirectoryCountLines()`, which counted the lines of `*.cs` files. However, if you want to count code in `*.h`/`*.cpp` files or in `*.vb` files, `DirectoryCountLines()` will not work. Instead, you need a method that takes the file extension, but still keeps the existing method definition so that it handles `*.cs` files by default.

All methods within a class must have a unique signature, and C# defines uniqueness by variation in the method name, parameter data types, or number of parameters. This does not include method return data types; defining two methods that have only a different return data type will cause a compile error. **Method overloading** occurs when a class has two or more methods with the same name and the parameter count and/ or data types vary between the overloaded methods.

Method overloading is a type of **operational polymorphism**. Polymorphism occurs when the same logical operation takes on many (poly) implementations (forms) because the data varies. Calling `WriteLine()` and passing a format string along with some parameters is implemented differently than calling `WriteLine()` and specifying an integer. However, logically, to the caller, the method takes care of writing the data and it is somewhat irrelevant how the internal implementation occurs. Listing 4.16 provides an example, and Output 4.10 shows the results.

LISTING 4.16: Returning All the Filenames, Given a Directory

```csharp
public static class LineCounter
{
  public static void Main(string[] args)
  {
      int totalLineCount;

      if (args.Length > 1)
      {
          totalLineCount =
              DirectoryCountLines(args[0], args[1]);
      }
      if (args.Length > 0)
```

```
    {
        totalLineCount = DirectoryCountLines(args[0]);
    }
    else
    {
        totalLineCount  = DirectoryCountLines();
    }

    System.Console.WriteLine(totalLineCount);
}

static int DirectoryCountLines()
{
    return DirectoryCountLines(
        Directory.GetCurrentDirectory());
}

static int DirectoryCountLines(string directory)
{
    return DirectoryCountLines(directory, "*.cs");
}

static int DirectoryCountLines(
    string directory, string extension)
{
    int lineCount = 0;
    foreach (string file in
        Directory.GetFiles(directory, extension))
    {
        lineCount += CountLines(file);
    }

    foreach (string subdirectory in
        Directory.GetDirectories(directory))
    {
        lineCount += DirectoryCountLines(subdirectory);
    }

    return lineCount;
}

private static int CountLines(string file)
{
    int lineCount = 0;
    string line;
    FileStream stream =
        new FileStream(file, FileMode.Open);
    StreamReader reader = new StreamReader(stream);
    line = reader.ReadLine();
    while(line != null)
    {
```

```
            if (line.Trim() == "")
            {
                lineCount++;
            }
            line = reader.ReadLine();
        }

        reader.Close();
        stream.Close();
        return lineCount;
    }
}
```

OUTPUT 4.10:

```
>LineCounter.exe .\ *.cs
28
```

The effect of method overloading is to provide optional ways to call the method. As demonstrated inside `Main()`, you can call the `Directory-CountLines()` method with or without passing the directory to search and the file extension.

Notice that the parameterless implementation of `DirectoryCount-Lines()` was changed to call the single-parameter version (`int DirectoryCountLines(string directory)`). This is a common pattern when implementing overloaded methods. The idea is that developers implement only the core logic in one method and all the other overloaded methods will call that single method. If the core implementation changes, it needs to be modified in only one location rather than within each implementation. This pattern is especially prevalent when using method overloading to enable optional parameters.

Basic Error Handling with Exceptions

An important aspect of calling methods relates to error handling; specifically, how to report an error back to the caller. This section examines how to handle error reporting via a mechanism known as **exception handling**.

With exception handling, a method is able to pass information about an error to a calling method without explicitly providing any parameters to do so. Listing 4.17 contains a slight modification to the HeyYou program from Chapter 1. Instead of requesting the last name of the user, it prompts for the user's age.

LISTING 4.17: Converting a **string** to an **int**

```
using System;

class ExceptionHandling
{
  static void Main()
  {
      string firstName;
      string ageText;
      int age;

      Console.WriteLine("Hey you!");

      Console.Write("Enter your first name: ");
      firstName = System.Console.ReadLine();

      Console.Write("Enter your age: ");
      ageText = Console.ReadLine();
      age = int.Parse(ageText);

      Console.WriteLine(
          "Hi {0}!  You are {1} months old.",
          firstName, age*12);
  }
}
```

Output 4.11 shows the results of Listing 4.17.

OUTPUT 4.11:

```
Hey you!
Enter your first name: Inigo
Enter your age: 42
Hi Inigo!  You are 504 months old.
```

The return value from System.Console.ReadLine() is stored in a variable called ageText and is then passed to a method on the int data type, called Parse(). This method is responsible for taking a string value that represents a number and converting it to an int type.

■ BEGINNER TOPIC

42 as a String Versus 42 as an Integer

C# is a strongly typed language. Therefore, not only is the data value important, but the type associated with the data is important as well. A string value of 42, therefore, is distinctly different from an integer value of 42. The string is composed of the two characters 4 and 2, whereas the `int` is the number 42.

Given the converted string, the final `System.Console.WriteLine()` statement will print the age in months by multiplying the age value by 12.

However, what happens if the user does not enter a valid integer string? For example, what happens if the user enters "forty-two"? The `Parse()` method cannot handle such a conversion. It expects the user to enter a string that contains only digits. If the `Parse()` method is sent an invalid value, it needs some way to report this fact back to the caller.

Trapping Errors

To indicate to the calling method that the parameter is invalid, `int.Parse()` will **throw an exception**. Throwing an exception will halt further execution in the current program flow and instead will jump into the first code block within the call stack that handles the exception.

Since you have not yet provided any such handling, the program reports the exception to the user as an **unhandled exception**. Assuming there is no registered debugger on the system, the error will appear on the console with a message such as that shown in Output 4.12.

OUTPUT 4.12:

```
Hey you!
Enter your first name: Inigo
Enter your age: forty-two

Unhandled Exception: System.FormatException: Input string was
      not in a correct format.
    at System.Number.ParseInt32(String s, NumberStyles style,
      NumberFormatInfo info)
    at ExceptionHandling.Main()
```

Obviously, such an error is not particularly helpful. To fix this, it is necessary to provide a mechanism that handles the error, perhaps reporting a more meaningful error message back to the user.

This is known as **catching an exception**. The syntax is demonstrated in Listing 4.18, and the output appears in Output 4.13.

LISTING 4.18: Catching an Exception

```
using System;

class ExceptionHandling
{
  static int Main()
  {
      string firstName;
      string ageText;
      int age;
      int result = 0;

      Console.Write("Enter your first name: ");
      firstName = Console.ReadLine();

      Console.Write("Enter your age: ");
      ageText = Console.ReadLine();

      try
      {
          age = int.Parse(ageText);
          Console.WriteLine(
              "Hi {0}!  You are {1} months old.",
              firstName, age*12);
      }
      catch (FormatException )
      {
          Console.WriteLine(
              "The age entered, {0}, is not valid.",
              ageText);
          result = 1;
      }
      catch(Exception exception)
      {
          Console.WriteLine(
              "Unexpected error:  {0}", exception.Message);
          result = 1;
      }
      finally
      {
          Console.WriteLine("Goodbye {0}",
```

```
                firstName);
        }

        return result;
    }
}
```

OUTPUT 4.13:

```
Enter your first name: Inigo
Enter your age: forty-two
The age entered, forty-two, is not valid.
Goodbye Inigo
```

To begin, surround the code that could potentially throw an exception (age = int.Parse()) with a **try block**. This block begins with the try keyword. It is an indication to the compiler that the developer is aware of the possibility that the code within the block could potentially throw an exception, and if it does, then one of the **catch blocks** will attempt to handle the exception.

One or more catch blocks (or the finally block) must appear immediately following a try block. The catch block header (see the Expert Topic titled Generic catch, later in this chapter) optionally allows you to specify the data type of the exception, and as long as the data type matches the exception type, the catch block will execute. If, however, there is no appropriate catch block, the exception will fall through and go unhandled as if there were no exception handling.

The resulting program flow appears in Figure 4.1.

For example, assume the user enters "forty-two" for the age. In this case, int.Parse() will throw an exception of type System.Format-Exception, and control will jump to the set of catch blocks. (System.FormatException indicates that the string was not of the correct format to be parsed appropriately.) Since the first catch block matches the type of exception that int.Parse() threw, the code inside this block will execute. If a statement within the try block throws a different exception, then the second catch block would execute because virtually all exceptions are of type System.Exception.

If there were no System.FormatException catch block, then the System.Exception catch block would execute even though int.Parse

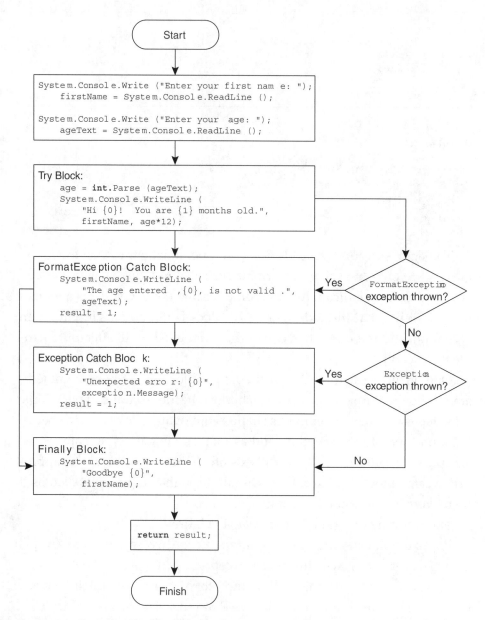

FIGURE 4.1: Exception Handling Program Flow

throws a System.FormatException. This is because a System.Format-Exception is also of type System.Exception. (System.FormatException is a more specific identification of the generic exception, System.Exception.)

Although the number of catch blocks varies, the order in which you handle exceptions is significant. Catch blocks must appear from most specific to least specific. The `System.Exception` data type is least specific and therefore it appears last. `System.FormatException` appears first because it is the most specific exception that Listing 4.18 handles.

Regardless of whether the code in the try block throws an exception, the **finally block** of code will execute. The purpose of the finally block is to provide a location to place code that will execute regardless of how the try/catch blocks exit—with or without an exception. Finally blocks are useful for cleaning up resources regardless of whether an exception is thrown. In fact, it is possible to have a try block with a finally block and no catch block. The finally block executes regardless of whether the try block throws an exception or whether a catch block is even written to handle the exception. Listing 4.19 demonstrates the try/finally block and Output 4.14 shows the results.

LISTING 4.19: Catching an Exception

```
using System;

class ExceptionHandling
{
  static int Main()
  {
      string firstName;
      string ageText;
      int age;
      int result = 0;

      Console.Write("Enter your first name: ");
      firstName = Console.ReadLine();

      Console.Write("Enter your age: ");
      ageText = Console.ReadLine();

      try
      {
          age = int.Parse(ageText);
          Console.WriteLine(
              "Hi {0}!  You are {1} months old.",
              firstName, age*12);
      }
      finally
      {
```

```
        Console.WriteLine("Goodbye {0}",
            firstName);
    }


    return result;
}
}
```

OUTPUT 4.14:

```
Enter your first name: Inigo
Enter your age: forty-two

Unhandled Exception: System.FormatException: Input string was not in a
correct format.
   at System.Number.StringToNumber(String str, NumberStyles options,
NumberBuffer& number, NumberFormatInfo info, Boolean parseDecimal)
   at System.Number.ParseInt32(String s, NumberStyles style,
NumberFormatInfo info)
   at ExceptionHandling.Main()
Goodbye Inigo
```

When this code executes, the finally block executes before displaying an unhandled exception to the user.

■ ADVANCED TOPIC

Exception Class Inheritance

All exceptions derive from System.Exception. Therefore, they can be handled by the catch(System.Exception exception) block. It is preferable, however, to include a catch block that is specific to the most derived type (System.FormatException, for example), because then it is possible to get the most information about an exception and handle it less generically. In so doing, the catch statement that uses the most derived type is able to handle the exception type specifically, accessing data related to the exception thrown, and avoiding conditional logic to determine what type of exception occurred.

This is why C# enforces that catch blocks appear from most derived to least derived. For example, a catch statement that catches System.Exception cannot appear before a statement that catches System.FormatException because System.FormatException derives from System.Exception.

A method could throw many exception types. Table 4.2 lists some of the more common ones.

TABLE 4.2: Common Exception Types

Exception Type	Description
`System.Exception`	A generic exception from which other exceptions derive
`System.ArgumentException`	A means of indicating that one of the parameters passed into the method is invalid
`System.ArgumentNullException`	Indicates that a particular parameter is `null` and that this is not valid for that parameter
`System.ApplicationException`	A custom application exception that developers can use to indicate special application errors that are not fatal
`System.FormatException`	Indicates that the string format is not valid for conversion
`System.IndexOutOfRangeException`	Indicates that an attempt was made to access an array element that does not exist
`System.InvalidCastException`	Indicates that an attempt to convert from one data type to another was not a valid conversion
`System.NotImplementedException`	Indicates that although the method signature exists, it has not been fully implemented
`System.NullReferenceException`	Thrown when code tries to access a variable that does not yet contain any data
`System.ArithmeticException`	Indicates an invalid math operation, not including divide by zero
`System.ArrayTypeMismatchException`	Occurs when attempting to store an element of the wrong type into an array
`System.StackOverflowException`	Generally indicates that there is an infinite loop in which a method is calling back into itself (known as recursion)

■ ADVANCED TOPIC

Generic `catch`

It is possible to specify a catch block that takes no parameters, as shown in Listing 4.20.

LISTING 4.20: General Catch Blocks

```
...
try
{
    age = int.Parse(ageText);
    System.Console.WriteLine(
        "Hi {0}!  You are {1} months old.",
        firstName, age*12);
}
catch (System.FormatException exception)
{
    System.Console.WriteLine(
        "The age entered ,{0}, is not valid.",
        ageText);
    result = 1;
}
catch(System.Exception exception)
{
    System.Console.WriteLine(
        "Unexpected error:  {0}", exception.Message);
    result = 1;
}
catch
{
    System.Console.WriteLine(
        "Unexpected error!");
    result = 1;
}
finally
{
    System.Console.WriteLine("Goodbye {0}",
        firstName);
}
...
```

A catch block with no data type, called a **generic catch block**, is equivalent to specifying a catch block that takes an `object` data type: for instance, `catch(object exception){...}`. And since all classes ultimately derive from `object`, a catch block with no data type must appear last.

Generic catch blocks are rarely used because there is no way to capture any information about the exception. In addition, C# doesn't support the ability to throw an exception of type `object`. (Only libraries written in languages like C++ allow exceptions of any type.)

The behavior in C# 2.0 varies slightly from the earlier C# behavior. In C# 2.0, if a language allows non-`System.Exceptions`, the object of the thrown exception will be wrapped in a `System.Runtime.CompilerServices.RuntimeWrappedException` which does derive from `System.Exception`. Therefore, all exceptions, whether deriving from `System.Exception` or not, will propagate into C# assemblies as derived from `System.Exception`.

The result is that `System.Exception` catch blocks will catch all exceptions not caught by earlier blocks, and a general catch block, following a `System.Exception` catch block, will never be invoked. Because of this, following a `System.Exception` catch block with a general catch block in C# 2.0 will result in a compiler warning indicating the general catch block will never execute.

Reporting Errors Using a `throw` Statement

Just as `int.Parse()` can throw an exception, C# allows developers to throw exceptions from their code, as demonstrated in Listing 4.21 and Output 4.15.

LISTING 4.21: Throwing an Exception

```
using System;

class ThrowingExceptions
{
  static void Main()
  {
    try
    {
        Console.WriteLine("Begin executing");
        Console.WriteLine("Throw exception...");
        throw new Exception("Arbitrary exception");
        Console.WriteLine("End executing");
    }
    catch (FormatException exception)
    {
        Console.WriteLine(
            "A FormatException was thrown");
    }
    catch(Exception exception)
    {
```

```
        Console.WriteLine(
            "Unexpected error:  {0}", exception.Message);
    }
    catch
    {
        Console.WriteLine("Unexpected error!");
    }

    Console.WriteLine(
        "Shutting down...");
    }
}
```

OUTPUT 4.15:

```
Begin executing
Throw exception...
Unexpected error:  Arbitrary exception
Shutting down...
```

As the arrows in Listing 4.21 depict, throwing an exception jumps execution from where the exception is thrown into the first catch block within the stack that is compatible with the thrown exception type. In this case, the second catch block handles the exception and writes out an error message. In Listing 4.21, there is no finally block, so execution falls through to the `System.Console.WriteLine()` statement following the try/catch block.

In order to throw an exception, it is necessary to have an instance of an exception. Listing 4.21 creates an instance using the keyword new followed by the data type of the exception. Most exception types allow a message as part of throwing the exception so that when the exception occurs, the message can be retrieved.

Sometimes a catch block will trap an exception but be unable to handle it appropriately or fully. In these circumstances, a catch block can rethrow the exception using the throw statement without specifying any exception, as shown in Listing 4.22.

LISTING 4.22: Rethrowing an Exception

```
    ...
        catch(Exception exception)
        {
            Console.WriteLine(
```

```
            "Rethrowing unexpected error:   {0}",
            exception.Message);
        throw;
    }
    ...
```

Avoid Using Exception Handling to Deal with Expected Situations

As with most languages, C# incurs a performance hit when throwing an exception, especially the first time the error-handling infrastructure needs to be loaded. For example, running Listing 4.18 and entering an invalid age demonstrates a noticeable pause while the program throws and handles the exception. Because of the performance cost associated with throwing exceptions, developers should make an effort to avoid throwing exceptions for expected conditions or normal control flow. For example, developers should expect users to enter invalid text when specifying their age.[2] Therefore, instead of relying on an exception to validate data entered by the user, developers should provide a means of checking the data before attempting the conversion. Better yet, you should prevent the user from entering invalid data in the first place.

■ ADVANCED TOPIC

Numeric Conversion with `TryParse()`

One of the problems with the `Parse()` method is that the only way to determine whether the conversion will be successful is to attempt the cast and then catch the exception if it doesn't work. Because throwing an exception is a relatively expensive operation, it is better to attempt the conversion without exception handling. In the first release of C#, the only data type that enabled this was a `double` method called `double.TryParse()`. However, the CLI added this method to all numeric primitive types in the CLI 2.0 version. It requires the use of the `out` keyword because the return from the `TryParse()` function is a `bool` rather than the converted value. Here is a code listing that demonstrates the conversion using `int.TryParse()`.

---

2. In general, developers should expect their users to perform unexpected actions, and therefore they should code defensively to handle "stupid user tricks."

```
...
if (int.TryParse(ageText, out age))
{
    System.Console.WriteLine(
        "Hi {0}!  You are {1} months old.", firstName,
        age * 12);
}
else
{
    System.Console.WriteLine(
        "The age entered ,{0}, is not valid.", ageText);
}
...
```

With the `TryParse()` method, it is no longer necessary to include a try/catch block simply for the purpose of handling the string-to-numeric conversion.

SUMMARY

This chapter discussed the details of declaring and calling methods. In many ways, this construct is identical to its declaration in C-like languages. However, the addition of the keywords `out` and `ref` are more like COM (the predecessor to CLI technology) than C-like language features. In addition to method declaration, this chapter introduced exception handling.

Methods are a fundamental construct that is a key to writing readable code. Instead of writing large methods with lots of statements, you should use methods for "paragraphs" within your code, whose lengths target roughly 10 lines or less. The process of breaking large functions into smaller pieces is one of the ways you can refactor your code to make it more readable and maintainable.

The next chapter considers the class construct and how it encapsulates methods (behavior) and fields (data) into a single unit.

■5■
Classes

YOU BRIEFLY SAW IN Chapter 1 how to declare a new class called HelloWorld. In Chapter 2, you learned about the built-in primitive types included with C#. Since you have now also learned about control flow and how to declare methods, it is time to discuss defining your own types. This is the core construct of any C# program, and the complete

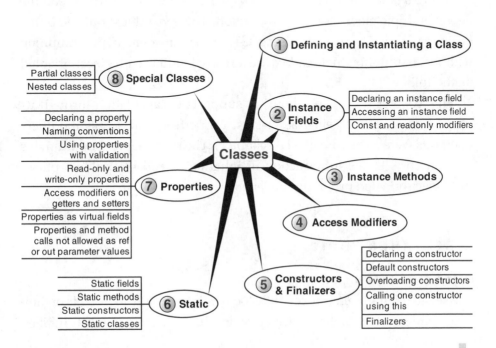

support for classes and the objects created from them is what defines C# as an object-oriented language.

This chapter introduces you to the basics of object-oriented programming using C#. A key focus is on how to define **classes**, which are the templates for objects themselves.

All of the constructs of structured programming from the previous chapters still apply within object-oriented programming. However, by wrapping those constructs within classes, you can create larger, more organized programs that are more maintainable. The transition from structured, control-flow-based programs to object-oriented programs somewhat revolutionized programming because it provided an extra level of organization. The result was that smaller programs were simplified somewhat; but more importantly, it was possible to create much larger programs because the code within those programs was better organized.

One of the key advantages of object-oriented programming is that instead of creating new programs entirely from scratch, you can assemble a collection of existing objects from prior work, extending the classes with new features, adding more classes, and then reassembling everything to provide new functionality.

Readers unfamiliar with object-oriented programming should read the Beginner Topic blocks for an introduction. The general text outside of the Beginner Topics focuses on using C# for object-oriented programming with the assumption that readers are already familiar with object-oriented methodology.

This chapter delves into how C# supports encapsulation through its support of constructs such as classes, properties, and access modifiers (methods were covered in the last chapter). The next chapter builds on this foundation with the introduction of inheritance and the polymorphism that object-oriented programming enables.

■ BEGINNER TOPIC

Object-Oriented Programming

The key to programming successfully today is in the ability to provide organization and structure to the implementation of complex requirements fulfilled in larger and larger applications. Object-oriented programming provides one of the key methodologies in accomplishing this, to the point that it is difficult for object-oriented programmers to envision transitioning back to structured programming, except for the most trivial programs.

The most fundamental construct to object-oriented programming is the class or object itself. These form a programming abstraction, model, or template of what is often a real-world concept. The class `Optical-StorageMedia`, for example, may have an `Eject()` method on it that causes a CD/DVD to eject from the player. The `OpticalStorageMedia` class is the programming abstraction of the real-world object of a CD.

Classes are the foundation for three principal characteristics of object-oriented programming: encapsulation, inheritance, and polymorphism.

Encapsulation

Encapsulation allows you to hide detail. The detail can still be accessed when necessary, but by intelligently encapsulating the detail, large programs are easier to understand, data is protected from inadvertent modification, and code is easier to maintain because the effects of a code change are bound to the scope of the encapsulation. Methods are examples of encapsulation. Although it is possible to take the code from a method and embed it directly inline with the caller's code, refactoring of code into a method provides encapsulation benefits.

Inheritance

Consider the following example: A DVD is a type of optical media. It has a specific storage capacity along with the ability to hold a digital movie. A CD is also a type of optical media but it has different characteristics. The copyright implementation on CDs is different from DVD copyright protection, and the storage capacity is different as well. Both CDs and DVDs are different from hard drives, USB drives, and floppy drives (remember those?). All fit into the category of storage media, but each has special characteristics, even for fundamental functions like the supported filesystems and whether instances of the media are read-only or read-write.

Inheritance in object-oriented programming allows you to form "is a" relationships between these similar but different items. It is a reasonable assumption that a DVD "is a" type of storage media and that a CD "is a" type of storage media, and as such, that each has storage capacity. Similarly, CDs and DVDs have "is a" relationships to the optical media type, which in turn has an "is a" relationship with the storage media type.

If you define classes corresponding to each type of storage media mentioned, you will have defined a **class hierarchy**, which is a series of "is a" relationships. The base type, from which all storage media derive, could be the class `StorageMedia`. As such, CDs, DVDs, hard drives, USB drives, and floppy drives are types of `StorageMedia`. However, CDs and DVDs don't need to derive from `StorageMedia` directly. Instead, they can derive from an intermediate type, `OpticalStorageMedia`. You can view the class hierarchy graphically using a Unified Modeling Language (UML)-like class diagram, as shown in Figure 5.1.

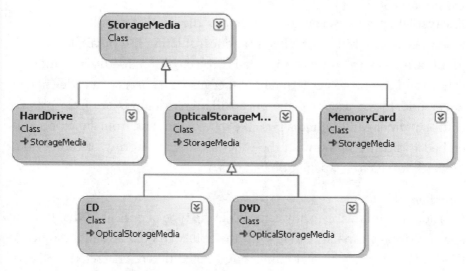

FIGURE 5.1: Class Hierarchy

The inheritance relationship involves a minimum of two classes such that one class is a more general version of the other; in Figure 5.1, `StorageMedia` is a more general version of `HardDrive`. Although the more specialized type, `HardDrive`, is a type of `StorageMedia`, the reverse is not true; a `StorageMedia` type is not necessarily a `HardDrive`. As Figure 5.1 shows, inheritance can involve more than two classes.

The more specialized type is the **derived** type or the **subtype**. The more generalized type is the **base** class or sometimes the **super** type. Other common terms for the classes in an inheritance relationship are parent and child; the former is the more generalized class.

To **derive** or **inherit** from another type is to **specialize** that type, which means to customize the base type so that it is geared for a specific purpose. Similarly, the base type is the generalized implementation of the derived types.

The key feature of inheritance is that all derived types inherit the members of the base type. Often the implementation of the base members can be modified, but regardless, the derived type contains the base type's members in addition to any other members that the derived type contains explicitly.

Derived types allow you to organize your classes into a coherent hierarchy where the "child" types have greater specificity than their "parent" types.

Polymorphism

Polymorphism comprises a word meaning "many" and a word meaning "forms." In the context of objects, polymorphism means that a single method or type can have many forms of implementation. Suppose you have a media player. It follows that the media player could play both CD music discs and DVDs containing MP3s. However, the exact implementation of the `Play()` method will vary depending on the media type. Calling `Play()` on a music CD object or `Play()` on a music DVD will play music in both cases, because each type understands the intricacies of playing. All that the media player knows about is the common base type, `OpticalStorageMedia`, and the fact that it defines the `Play()` method signature. Polymorphism is the principle that a type can take care of the exact details of a method's implementation because the method appears on multiple derived types that each share a common base type (or interface) that also contains the same method signature.

Defining and Instantiating a Class

Defining a class involves first specifying the keyword `class`, followed by an identifier, as shown in Listing 5.1.

LISTING 5.1: Defining a Class

```
class Employee
{
}
```

All code that belongs to the class will appear between the curly braces following the class declaration. Although not a requirement, generally you place each class into its own file. This makes it easier to find the code that defines a particular class, because the convention is to name the file using the class name.

Once you have defined a new class, you can use that class as though it were built into the framework. In other words, you can declare a variable of that type or define a method that takes a parameter of the new class type. Listing 5.2 demonstrates.

LISTING 5.2: Declaring Variables of the Class Type

```
class Program
{
  static void Main()
  {
      Employee employee1, employee2;
      // ...
  {

  static void IncreaseSalary(Employee employee)
  {
      // ...
  }
}
```

The curly braces under the class name declaration demarcate the scope of execution.

■ BEGINNER TOPIC

Objects and Classes Defined

In casual conversation, the terms *class* and *object* appear interchangeably. However, object and class have distinct meanings. A **class** is a template for what an object will look like at instantiation time. An **object**, therefore, is an instance of a class. Classes are like the mold for what a widget will look like. Objects correspond to widgets created by the mold. The process of creating an object from a class is **instantiation** because an object is an instance of a class.

Now that you have defined a new class type, it is time to instantiate an object of that type. Mimicking its predecessors, C# uses the new keyword to instantiate an object (see Listing 5.3).

LISTING 5.3: Instantiating a Class

```csharp
class Program
{
  static void Main()
  {
      Employee employee1 = new Employee();
      Employee employee2;
      employee2 = new Employee();

      Employee.IncreaseSalary(employee1);
  }
}
```

Not surprisingly, the assignment can occur on the same line as the declaration, or on a separate line.

Unlike the primitive types you have worked with so far, there is no literal way to specify an Employee. Instead, the new operator provides an instruction to the runtime to allocate memory for an Employee object, instantiate the object, and return a reference to the instance.

In spite of the explicit operator for allocating memory, there is no such operator for restoring the memory. Instead, the runtime automatically reclaims the memory sometime after the object is last accessible but before the application closes down. The **garbage collector** is responsible for the automatic de-allocation. It determines which objects are no longer referenced by other active objects and then de-allocates the memory for those objects. The result is that there is no compile-time-determined location where the memory will be restored to the system.

In this trivial example, no explicit data or methods are associated with an Employee and this renders the object essentially useless. The next section focuses on adding data to an object.

Language Contrast: C++—delete Operator

In contrast to C++, C# does not support the delete operator or an equivalent. Furthermore, there is no reliable way to program *deterministic destruction* (the occurrence of object destruction at a compile-time-defined location in the code).

Programmers should view the new operator as a call to instantiate an object, not as a call to allocate memory. Both objects allocated on the heap and objects allocated on the stack support the new operator, emphasizing the point that new is not about memory allocation and whether de-allocation is necessary.

■ BEGINNER TOPIC

Encapsulation Part 1: Objects Group Data with Methods

If you received a stack of index cards with employees' first names, a stack of index cards with their last names, and a stack of index cards with their salaries, the cards would be of little value unless you knew that the cards were in order in each stack. Even so, the data would be difficult to work with because determining a person's full name would require searching through two stacks. Worse, if you dropped one of the stacks, there would be no way to reassociate the first name with the last name and the salary. Instead, you would need one stack of employee cards in which all the data was grouped on one card. In this way, first names, last names, and salaries would be encapsulated together.

Outside of the object-oriented programming context, to **encapsulate** a set of items is to enclose those items within a capsule. Similarly, object-oriented programming encapsulates methods and data together into an object. This provides a grouping of all of the class **members** (the data and methods within a class) so that they no longer need to be handled individually. Instead of passing first name, last name, and salary as three separate parameters to a method, objects enable a call to pass a reference to an employee object. Once the called method receives the object reference, it can send a message (it can call a method such as AdjustSalary(), for example) on the object to perform a particular operation.

Instance Fields

One of the key purposes of object-oriented design is the grouping of data to provide structure. This section discusses how to add data to the `Employee` class. The general object-oriented term for a variable that stores data within a class is **member variable**. This term is well understood in C#, but the more accurate term is **field**, which is a named unit of storage associated with the containing type. **Instance fields** are variables declared at the class level to store data associated with an object. Hence, **association** is the relationship between the field data type and the containing field.

Declaring an Instance Field

In Listing 5.4, `Employee` has been modified to include three fields: `FirstName`, `LastName`, and `Salary`.

LISTING 5.4: Declaring Fields

```
class Employee
{
  public string FirstName;
  public string LastName;
  public string Salary;
}
```

With these fields added, it is possible to store some fundamental data with every `Employee` instance. In this case, you prefix the fields with an access modifier of `public`. `public` on a field indicates that the data within the field is accessible from classes other than `Employee` (see the section Access Modifiers, later in this chapter).

As with local variable declarations, a field declaration includes the data type to which the field refers. Furthermore, it is possible to assign fields an initial value at declaration time, as demonstrated with the `Salary` field in Listing 5.5.

LISTING 5.5: Setting Initial Values of Fields at Declaration Time

```
class Employee
{
  public string FirstName;
  public string LastName;
  public string Salary = "Not enough";
}
```

Accessing an Instance Field

You can set and retrieve the data within fields. However, the fact that the field does not include a `static` modifier indicates that it is an instance field. You can access an instance field only from an instance of the containing class (an object). You cannot access it from the class directly (without first creating an instance, in other words).

Listing 5.6 shows an updated look at the `Program` class and its utilization of the `Employee` class, and Output 5.1 shows the results.

LISTING 5.6: Accessing Fields

```
class Program
{
  static void Main()
  {
      Employee employee1 = new Employee();
      Employee employee2;
      employee2 = new Employee();

      employee1.FirstName = "Inigo";
      employee1.LastName = "Montoya";
      employee1.Salary = "Too Little";
      IncreaseSalary(employee1);
      Console.WriteLine(
          "{0} {1}: {2}",
          employee1.FirstName,
          employee1.LastName,
          employee1.Salary);
      // ...
  }

  static void IncreaseSalary(Employee employee)
  {
      employee.Salary = "Enough to survive on";
  }
}
```

OUTPUT 5.1:

```
Inigo Montoya: Enough to survive on
```

Listing 5.6 instantiates two `Employee` objects, as you saw before. Next, it sets each field, calls `IncreaseSalary()` to change the salary, and then displays each field associated with the object referenced by `employee1`.

Notice that you first have to specify which `Employee` instance you are working with. Therefore, the `employee1` variable appears as a prefix to the field name when assigning and accessing the field.

Regardless of whether fields are assigned at declaration time or within code later on, the C# compiler requires that an instance field be *definitely assigned* somewhere within the execution path prior to accessing the field. Using static code analysis, the C# compiler will report errors when instance variables are not assigned, which is sometimes rather subtle. For example, calling `if(employee1.Salary == "Too Little"){...}` before assigning a value to `employee1.Salary` will cause the compiler to report an error.

Instance Methods

One alternative to formatting the names in the `WriteLine()` method call within `Main()` is to provide a method on `Employee` that takes care of the formatting. Changing the functionality to be on `Employee` rather than on `Program` is consistent with the encapsulation of a class. Why not group the methods relating to the employee's full name with the class that contains the data that forms the name.

Listing 5.7 demonstrates the creation of such a method.

LISTING 5.7: Accessing Fields from within the Containing Class

```csharp
class Employee
{
  public string FirstName;
  public string LastName;
  public string Salary;

  public string GetName()
  {
      return FirstName + " " + LastName;
  }
}
```

There is nothing particularly special about this method compared to what you learned in Chapter 4, except that now the method accesses fields on the object instead of just local variables. In addition, the method declaration is not marked with `static`. As you will see later in this chapter, static methods cannot directly access instance fields within a class. Instead, it is necessary to obtain an instance of the class in order to call any instance member, whether a method or a field.

Given the addition of the `GetName()` method, you can update `Program.Main()` to use the new method, as shown in Listing 5.8 and Output 5.2.

LISTING 5.8: Accessing Fields from Outside the Containing Class

```csharp
class Program
{
  static void Main()
  {
      Employee employee1 = new Employee();
      Employee employee2;
      employee2 = new Employee();

      employee1.FirstName = "Inigo";
      employee1.LastName = "Montoya";
      employee1.Salary = "Too Little";
      IncreaseSalary(employee1);
      Console.WriteLine(
          "{0}: {1}",
          employee1.GetName(),
          employee1.Salary);
      // ...
  }
  // ...
}
```

OUTPUT 5.2:

```
Inigo Montoya: Enough to survive on
```

Using the `this` Keyword

You can obtain the reference to a class from within instance members that belong to the class. To indicate explicitly that the field or method accessed is an instance member of the containing class in C#, you use the keyword `this`. `this` is simply an implicit field within every class definition that returns an instance of the object itself.

For example, consider the `SetName()` method shown in Listing 5.9.

LISTING 5.9: Using `this` to Identify the Field's Owner Explicitly

```csharp
class Employee
{
  public string FirstName;
```

```
public string LastName;
public string Salary;

public string GetName()
{
    return FirstName + " " + LastName;
}

public void SetName(string newFirstName, string newLastName)
{
    this.FirstName = newFirstName;
    this.LastName = newLastName;
}
}
```

This example uses the keyword this to indicate that the fields FirstName and LastName are instance members of the class.

Language Contrast: Visual Basic—Accessing a Class Instance with Me

The C# keyword this is identical to the Visual Basic keyword Me.

You also can use the keyword this to access a class's methods explicitly. this.GetName() is allowed within the SetName() method, for example, allowing you to print out the newly assigned name (see Listing 5.10 and Output 5.3).

LISTING 5.10: Using **this** with a Method

```
class Employee
{
  // ...

  public string GetName()
  {
      return FirstName + " " + LastName;
  }

  public void SetName(string newFirstName, string newLastName)
  {
      this.FirstName = newFirstName;
      this.LastName = newLastName;
      Console.WriteLine("Name changed to '{0}'",
          this.GetName());
```

```
    }
  }

class Program
{
  static void Main()
  {
      Employee employee = new Employee();

      employee.SetName("Inigo", "Montoya");
      // ...
  }
  // ...
}
```

OUTPUT 5.3:

```
Name changed to 'Inigo Montoya'
```

In Listing 5.9 and Listing 5.10, the `this` keyword is optional, as demonstrated in the `GetName()` method where `this` is not used. However, if local variables or parameters exist with the same name as the field, then leaving off `this` would result in accessing the local variable/parameter rather than the field, so `this` would be required.

■ BEGINNER TOPIC

Relying on Coding Style to Avoid Ambiguity

In the `SetName()` method, you did not have to use the `this` keyword because `FirstName` is obviously different from `newFirstName`. Consider, however, if instead of calling the parameter "newFirstName" you called it "FirstName" (using Pascal case), as shown in Listing 5.11.

LISTING 5.11: Using **this** to Avoid Ambiguity

```
class Employee
{
  public string FirstName;
  public string LastName;
  public string Salary;

  public string GetName()
```

```
    {
        return FirstName + " " + LastName;
    }

    // Caution:  Parameter names use Pascal case
    public void SetName(string FirstName, string LastName)
    {
        this.FirstName = FirstName;
        this.LastName = LastName;
    }
}
```

In this example, it is not possible to refer to the FirstName field without explicitly indicating that the Employee object owns the variable. this acts just like the employee1 variable prefix used in the Program.Main() method (see Listing 5.8); it identifies the reference as the one on which SetName() was called.

Listing 5.11 does not follow the C# naming convention in which parameters are declared like local variables, using camel case. This can lead to subtle bugs because assigning FirstName (intending to refer to the field) to First-Name (the parameter) will still compile and even run. To avoid this problem it is a good practice to have a different naming convention for parameters and local variables than the naming convention for fields. I demonstrate one such convention later in this chapter.

Sometimes it may be necessary to use this in order to pass a reference to the currently executing object. Consider the Save() method in Listing 5.12.

LISTING 5.12: Passing **this** in a Method Call

```
class Employee
{
    public string FirstName;
    public string LastName;
    public string Salary;

    public void Save()
    {
        DataStorage.Store(this);
    }
}

class DataStorage
```

```
    {
        // Save an employee object to a file
        // named with the Employee name.
        public static void Store(Employee employee)
        {
            // ...
        }
    }
```

The `Save()` method calls a method on the `DataStorage` class, called `Store()`. The `Store()` method, however, needs to be passed the `Employee` object that needs to be persisted. This is done using the keyword `this`, which passes the instance of the `Employee` object on which `Save()` was called.

■ ADVANCED TOPIC

Storing and Loading with Files

The actual implementation of the `Store()` method inside `DataStorage` involves classes within the `System.IO` namespace, as shown in Listing 5.13. Inside `Store()`, you begin by instantiating a `FileStream` object that you associate with a file corresponding to the employee's full name. The `File-Mode.Create` parameter indicates that you want a new file to be created if there isn't already one with the `<firstname><lastname>.dat` name; if the file exists already, it will be overwritten. Next, you create a `StreamWriter` class. The `StreamWriter` class is responsible for writing text into the `FileStream`. You write the data using `WriteLine()` methods, just as though writing to the console.

LISTING 5.13: Data Persistence to a File

```
using System;
// IO namespace
using System.IO;

class DataStorage
{
    // Save an employee object to a file
    // named with the Employee name.
    // Error handling not shown.
    public static void Store(Employee employee)
```

```
   {
        // Instantiate a FileStream using FirstNameLastName.dat
        // for the filename. FileMode.Create will force
        // a new file to be created or override an
        // existing file.
        FileStream stream = new FileStream(
            employee.FirstName + employee.LastName + ".dat",
            FileMode.Create);

        // Create a StreamWriter object for writing text
        // into the FileStream
        StreamWriter writer = new StreamWriter(stream);

        // Write all the data associated with the employee.
        writer.WriteLine(employee.FirstName);
        writer.WriteLine(employee.LastName);
        writer.WriteLine(employee.Salary);

        // Close the StreamWriter and its Stream.
        writer.Close();
        stream.Close();
    }
    // ...
}
```

Once the write operations are completed, both the `FileStream` and the `StreamWriter` need to be closed so that they are not left open indefinitely while waiting for the garbage collector to run. This listing does not include any error handling, so if an exception is thrown, neither `Close()` method will be called.

The load process is similar (see Listing 5.14).

LISTING 5.14: Data Retrieval from a File

```
// IO namespace
using System;
using System.IO;

class DataStorage
{
    // ...

    public static Employee Load(string firstName, string lastName)
    {
        Employee employee = new Employee();

        // Instantiate a FileStream using FirstNameLastName.dat
        // for the filename. FileMode.Open will open
```

```
        // an existing file or else report an error.
        FileStream stream = new FileStream(
            firstName + lastName + ".dat", FileMode.Open);

        // Create a SteamReader for reading text from the file.
        StreamReader reader = new StreamReader(stream);

        // Read each line from the file and place it into
        // the associated property.
        employee.FirstName = reader.ReadLine();
        employee.LastName = reader.ReadLine();
        employee.Salary = reader.ReadLine();

        // Close the StreamReader and its Stream.
        reader.Close();
        stream.Close();

        return employee;
    }
}
```

The reverse of the save process appears in Listing 5.14, which uses a `StreamReader` rather than a `StreamWriter`. Again, `Close()` needs to be called on both `FileStream` and `StreamReader` once the data has been read.

Observe the inclusion of the `using System.IO` directive at the top of the listing. This makes each `IO` class accessible without prefixing it with the full namespace.

Access Modifiers

When declaring a field earlier in the chapter, you prefixed the field declaration with the keyword `public`. `public` is an **access modifier** that identifies the level of encapsulation associated with the member it decorates. Five access modifiers are available: `public`, `private`, `protected`, `internal`, and `protected internal`. This section considers the first two.

■ BEGINNER TOPIC

Encapsulation Part 2: Information Hiding
Besides wrapping data and methods together into a single unit, encapsulation is also about hiding the internal details of an object's data and behavior.

To some degree, methods do this; from outside a method, all that is visible to a caller is the method declaration. None of the internal implementation is visible. Object-oriented programming enables this further, however, by providing facilities for controlling the extent to which members are visible from outside the class. Members that are not visible outside the class are **private members**.

In object-oriented programming, encapsulation is the term for not only grouping data and behavior, but also hiding data within a class (the capsule) so that minimum access about the inner workings of a class is exposed outside the class.

The purpose of an access modifier is to provide encapsulation. By using `public`, you explicitly indicated that it is acceptable that the modified fields are accessible from outside the `Employee` class—in other words, that they are accessible from the `Program` class, for example.

Consider an `Employee` class that includes a `Password` field, however. It should be possible to call an `Employee` object and verify the password using a `Logon()` method. It should not be possible, however, to access the `Password` field on an `Employee` object from outside the class.

To define a `Password` field as hidden and inaccessible from outside the containing class, you use the keyword `private` for the access modifier, in place of `public` (see Listing 5.15). As a result, the `Password` field is not intended for access from inside the `Program` class, for example.

LISTING 5.15: Using the **private** Access Modifier

```
class Employee
{
    public string FirstName;
    public string LastName;
    public string Salary;
    private string Password;
    private bool IsAuthenticated;

    public bool Logon(string password)
    {
        if(Password == password)
        {
            IsAuthenticated = true;
        }
        return IsAuthenticated;
    }
}
```

```
    public bool GetIsAuthenticated()
    {
        return IsAuthenticated;
    }
    // ...
}


class Program
{
    static void Main()
    {
        Employee employee = new Employee();

        employee.FirstName = "Inigo";
        employee.LastName = "Montoya";

        // ...

        // Password is private, so it cannot be
        // accessed from outside the class.
        // Console.WriteLine(
        //     ("Password = {0}", employee.Password);
    }
    // ...
}
```

Although not shown in Listing 5.15, it is possible to decorate a method with an access modifier of `private` as well.

Note that if no access modifier is placed on a class member, the declaration will default to `private`. In other words, members are private by default and programmers need to specify explicitly that a member is to be public.

Constructors

Now that you have added fields to a class and can store data, you need to consider the validity of that data. As you saw in Listing 5.3, it is possible to instantiate an object using the `new` operator. The result, however, is the ability to create an employee with invalid data. Immediately following the assignment of `employee`, you have an `Employee` object whose name and salary are not initialized. In this particular listing, you assigned the uninitialized fields immediately following the instantiation of an employee, but if you failed to do the initialization, you would not receive a warning from the compiler. As a result, you could end up with an `Employee` object with an invalid name.

Declaring a Constructor

To correct this, you need to provide a means of specifying the required data when the object is created. You do this using a constructor, demonstrated in Listing 5.16.

LISTING 5.16: Defining a Constructor

```
class Employee
{
  // Employee constructor
  public Employee(string firstName, string lastName)
  {
    FirstName = firstName;
    LastName = lastName;
  }

  public string FirstName;
  public string LastName;
  public string Salary;

  public string GetName()
  {
      return FirstName + " " + LastName;
  }
  // ...
}
```

To define a constructor you create a method with no return type, whose method name is identical to the class name.

The constructor is the method that the code calls to create an instance of the object. In this case, the constructor takes the first name and the last name as parameters, allowing the programmer to specify these names when instantiating the Employee object. Listing 5.17 is an example of how to call a constructor.

LISTING 5.17: Calling a Constructor

```
class Program
{
  static void Main()
  {
      Employee employee;
      employee = new Employee("Inigo", "Montoya");
      employee.Salary = "Too Little";

      Console.WriteLine(
          "{0} {1}: {2}",
```

```
            employee.FirstName,
            employee.LastName,
            employee.Salary);
    }
    // ...
  }
```

Notice that the constructor returns the type of the object being instantiated (even though no return type or return statement was specified explicitly in the constructor's declaration or implementation). In addition, you have removed the initialization code for the first and last names because that occurs within the constructor. In this example, you don't initialize `Salary` within the constructor, so the code assigning the salary still appears.

Developers should take care when using both assignment at declaration time and assignment within constructors. Assignments within the constructor will occur after any assignments are made when a field is declared (such as `string Salary = "Not enough"` in Listing 5.5). Therefore, assignment within a constructor will take precedence and will override any value assigned at declaration time. This subtlety can lead to a misinterpretation of the code by a casual reader that assumes the value after instantiation is assigned at declaration time. Therefore, it is worth considering a coding style that does not mix both declaration assignment and constructor assignment within the same class.

Default Constructors

It is important to note that by adding a constructor explicitly, you can no longer instantiate an `Employee` from within `Main()` without specifying the first and last names. The code shown in Listing 5.18, therefore, will not compile.

LISTING 5.18: Default Constructor No Longer Available

```
class Program
{
  static void Main()
  {
      Employee employee;
      // ERROR:      No overload for method 'Employee'
      // takes '0' arguments.
      // employee = new Employee();
```

```
        // ...
    }
}
```

If a class has no explicitly defined constructor, then the C# compiler adds one during compilation. This constructor takes no parameters and is, therefore, the **default constructor** by definition. As soon as you add an explicit constructor to a class, the C# compiler no longer provides a default constructor. Therefore, with `Employee(string firstName, string lastName)` defined, the default constructor, `Employee()`, is not added by the compiler. You could explicitly add such a constructor, but then you would again be allowing construction of an `Employee` without specifying the employee name.

It is not necessary to rely on the default constructor defined by the compiler. It is also possible for programmers to define a default constructor explicitly, perhaps one that initializes some fields to particular values. Defining the default constructor simply involves declaring a constructor that takes no parameters.

■ **ADVANCED TOPIC**

Finalizers
Constructors define what happens during the instantiation process of a class. To define what happens when an object is destroyed C# provides the finalizer construct. Unlike destructors in C++, finalizers do not run immediately after an object goes out of scope. Rather, the finalizer executes after an object is last active and before the program shuts down. Specifically, the garbage collector identifies objects with finalizers during a garbage collection cycle, and instead of immediately de-allocating those objects, it adds them to a finalization queue. A separate thread runs through each object in the finalization queue and calls their finalizer before removing them from the queue and making them available for the garbage collector again. Chapter 9 discusses this process, along with resource cleanup, in depth.

Overloading Constructors

Constructors can be overloaded. For example, as Listing 5.19 shows, you could provide a constructor that has an employee ID with first and last names, or even just the employee ID.

LISTING 5.19: Overloading a Constructor

```csharp
class Employee
{
  public Employee(string firstName, string lastName)
  {
      FirstName = firstName;
      LastName = lastName;
  }

  public Employee(
      int id, string firstName, string lastName )
  {
      Id = id;
      FirstName = firstName;
      LastName = lastName;
  }

  public Employee(int id)
  {
      Id = id;

      // Look up employee name...
      // ...
  }

  public int Id;
  public string FirstName;
  public string LastName;
  public string Salary;

  // ...
}
```

This enables `Program.Main()` to instantiate an employee from the first and last names either by passing in the employee ID only, or by passing both the names and the IDs. You would use the constructor with both the names and the IDs when creating a new employee in the system. You would use the constructor with only the ID to load up the employee from a file or a database.

Calling Another Constructor Using `this`

Notice in Listing 5.19 that the initialization code for the `Employee` object is now duplicated in multiple places and, therefore, has to be maintained in multiple places. The amount of code is small, but there are ways to eliminate the duplication by calling one constructor from another, using **constructor initializers**. Constructor initializers determine which constructor to call before executing the implementation of the current constructor (see Listing 5.20).

LISTING 5.20: Calling One Constructor from Another

```csharp
class Employee
{
  public Employee(string firstName, string lastName)
  {
      FirstName = firstName;
      LastName = lastName;
  }

  public Employee(
      int id, string firstName, string lastName )
      : this(firstName, lastName)
  {
      Id = id;
  }

  public Employee(int id)
  {
      string firstName;
      string lastName;
      Id = id;

      // Look up employee name...
      // ...

  }
      // NOTE:  Member constructors cannot be
      // called explicitly inline
      // this(id, firstName, lastName);

  public int Id;
  public string FirstName;
  public string LastName;
  public string Salary;

  // ...
}
```

To call one constructor from another within the same class (for the same object instance) C# uses a colon followed by the `this` keyword followed by the parameter list on the callee constructor's declaration. In this case, the constructor that takes all three parameters calls the constructor that takes two. Often, the calling pattern is reversed; the constructor with the fewest parameters calls the constructor with the most parameters, passing defaults for the parameters that are not known.

■ **BEGINNER TOPIC**

Centralizing Initialization

Notice that in the `Employee(int id)` constructor implementation from Listing 5.20, you cannot call `this(firstName, LastName)` because no such parameters exist on this constructor. To enable such a pattern in which all initialization code happens through one method you must create a separate method, as shown in Listing 5.21.

LISTING 5.21: Providing an Initialization Method

```
class Employee
{
  public Employee(string firstName, string lastName)
  {
      int id;
      // Generate an employee ID...
      // ...
      Initialize(id, firstName, lastName);
  }

  public Employee(int id, string firstName, string lastName )
  {
      Initialize(id, firstName, lastName);
  }

  public Employee(int id)
  {
      string firstName;
      string lastName;
      Id = id;

      // Look up employee data
      // ...

      Initialize(id, firstName, lastName);
```

```
    }

    private void Initialize(
        int id, string firstName, string lastName)
    {
        Id = id;
        FirstName = firstName;
        LastName = lastName;
    }
    // ...
}
```

In this case, the method is called `Initialize()` and it takes both the names and the employee IDs. Note that you can continue to call one constructor from another, as you do with `Employee(string firstName, string lastName)`.

Static

The `HelloWorld` example in Chapter 1 first presented the keyword `static`; however, it did not define it fully. This section defines the `static` keyword fully.

Language Contrast: C++/Visual Basic—Global Variables and Functions

Unlike many of the languages that came before it, C# does not have global variables or global functions. All fields and methods in C# appear within the context of a class. The equivalent of a global field or function within the realm of C# is a static field or function. There is no functional difference between global variables/functions and C# static fields/methods, except that static fields/functions can include access modifiers, such as `private`, that can limit the access and provide better encapsulation.

To begin, consider an example. Assume that the employee `Id` value needs to be unique for each employee. One way to accomplish this is to store a counter to track each employee ID. If the value is stored as an instance field, however, every time you instantiate an object, a new

`NextId` field will be created such that every instance of the `Employee` object would consume memory for that field. The biggest problem is that each time an `Employee` object instantiated, the `NextId` value on all of the previously instantiated `Employee` objects would need to be updated with the next ID value. What you need is a single field that all `Employee` object instances share.

Static Fields

To define data that is available across multiple instances, you use the `static` keyword, as demonstrated in Listing 5.22.

LISTING 5.22: Declaring a Static Field

```csharp
class Employee
{
  public Employee(string firstName, string lastName)
  {
      FirstName = firstName;
      LastName = lastName;
      Id = NextId;
      NextId++;
  }

  // ...

  public static int NextId;
  public int Id;
  public string FirstName;
  public string LastName;
  public string Salary;

  // ...
}
```

In this example, the `NextId` field declaration includes the `static` modifier and therefore is called a **static field**. Unlike `Id`, a single storage location for `NextId` is shared across all instances of `Employee`. Inside the `Employee` constructor, you assign the new `Employee` object's `Id` the value of `NextId` immediately before incrementing it. When another `Employee` class is created, `NextId` will be incremented and the new `Employee` object's `Id` field will hold a different value.

Just as **instance fields** (nonstatic fields) can be initialized at declaration time, so can static fields, as demonstrated in Listing 5.23.

LISTING 5.23: Assigning a Static Field at Declaration

```csharp
class Employee
{
  // ...
  public static int NextId = 42;
  // ...
}
```

If no initialization for a static field is provided, the static field will automatically be assigned its default value (0, null, false, and so on), and it will be possible to access the static field even if it has never been explicitly assigned.

Nonstatic fields, or instance fields, have a new value for each object to which they belong. In contrast, static fields don't belong to the instance, but rather, to the class itself. As a result, you access a static field from outside a class via the class name. Consider the new `Program` class shown in Listing 5.24.

LISTING 5.24: Accessing a Static Field

```csharp
class Program
{
  static void Main()
  {
    Employee.NextId = 1000000;

    Employee employee1 = new Employee(
        "Inigo", "Montoya");
    Employee employee2 = new Employee(
        "Princess", "Buttercup");

    Console.WriteLine(
        "{0} {1} ({2})",
        employee1.FirstName,
        employee1.LastName,
        employee1.Id);
    Console.WriteLine(
        "{0} {1} ({2})",
        employee2.FirstName,
        employee2.LastName,
        employee2.Id);

    Console.WriteLine("NextId = {0}", Employee.NextId);
  }

  // ...
}
```

Output 5.4 shows the results of Listing 5.24.

OUTPUT 5.4:

```
Inigo Montoya (1000000)
Princess Buttercup (1000001)
NextId = 1000002
```

To set and retrieve the initial value of the `NextId` static field, you use the class name, `Employee`, not a variable name. The only time you can eliminate the class name is from within code that appears within the class itself. In other words, the `Employee(...)` constructor did not need to use `Employee.NextId` because the code appeared within the context of the `Employee` class itself, and therefore, the context was already understood from the scope.

Even though you refer to static fields slightly differently than instance fields, it is not possible to define a static and an instance field with the same name in the same class. The possibility of mistakenly referring to the wrong field is high, and therefore, the C# designers decided to prevent such code.

■ **BEGINNER TOPIC**

Data Can Be Associated with Both a Class and an Object

Both classes and objects can have associated data, just as can the molds and the widgets created from them.

For example, a mold could have data corresponding to the number of widgets it created, the serial number of the next widget, the current color of the plastic injected into the mold, and the number of widgets it produces per hour. Similarly, a widget has its own serial number, its own color, and perhaps the date and time when the widget was created. Although the color of the widget corresponds to the color of the plastic within the mold at the time the widget was created, it obviously does not contain data corresponding to the color of the plastic currently in the mold, or the serial number of the next widget to be produced.

In designing objects, programmers should take care to declare both fields and methods appropriately as static or instance based. In general, you should declare methods that don't access any instance data as static methods, and methods that access instance data (where the instance is not passed in as a parameter) as instance methods. Static fields store data corresponding to the class, such as defaults for new instances or the number of instances that have been created. Instance fields store data associated with the object.

Static Methods

Just like static fields, you access static methods directly off the class name (`Console.ReadLine()`, for example). Furthermore, it is not necessary to have an instance in order to access the method.

Because static methods are not referenced through a particular instance, the `this` keyword is invalid inside a static method. In fact, it is not possible to access either an instance field or an instance method directly from within a static method without a reference to the particular instance to which the field or method belongs.

Static Constructors

In addition to static fields and methods, C# also supports **static constructors**. Static constructors are provided as a means to initialize a class (not the class instance). Static constructors are not called explicitly; instead, the runtime calls static constructors automatically upon first access to the class, whether via calling a regular constructor or accessing a static method or field on the class. You use static constructors to initialize the static data within the class to a particular value, particularly when the initial value involves more complexity than a simple assignment at declaration time. Consider Listing 5.25.

LISTING 5.25: Declaring a Static Constructor

```
class Employee
{
    static Employee()
    {
        Random randomGenerator = new Random();
        NextId = randomGenerator.Next(101, 999);
    }

    // ...
```

```
    public static int NextId
    {
        get
        {
            return _NextId;
        }
        private set
        {
            _NextId = value;
        }
    }
    public static int _NextId = 42;
    // ...
}
```

Listing 5.25 assigns the initial value of NextId to be a random integer between 100 and 1,000. Because the initial value involves a method call, the NextId initialization code appears within a static constructor and not as part of the declaration.

If assignment of NextId occurs within both the static constructor and the declaration, it is not obvious what the value will be when initialization concludes. The C# compiler generates CIL in which the declaration assignment is moved to be the first statement within the static constructor. Therefore, NextId will contain the value returned by randomGenerator.Next(101, 999) instead of a value assigned during NextId's declaration. Assignments within the static constructor, therefore, will take precedence over assignments that occur as part of the field declaration, as was the case with instance fields. Note that there is no support for defining a static finalizer.

Static Classes

Some classes do not contain any instance fields. Consider, for example, a Math class that has functions corresponding to the mathematical operations Max() and Min(), as shown in Listing 5.26.

LISTING 5.26: Declaring a Static Class

```
// Static class introduced in C# 2.0
public static class SimpleMath
{
    // params allows the number of parameters to vary.
    static int Max(params int[] numbers)
    {
        // Check that there is a least one item in numbers.
```

```csharp
// ...

    int result;
    result = numbers[0];
    foreach (int number in numbers)
    {
        if(number > result)
        {
            result = number;
        }
    }
    return result;
}

// params allows the number of parameters to vary.
static int Min(params int[] numbers)
{
    // Check that there is a least one item in numbers.
    // ...

    int result;
    result = numbers[0];
    foreach (int number in numbers)
    {
        if(number < result)
        {
            result = number;
        }
    }
    return result;
}
}
```

This class does not have any instance fields (or methods), and therefore, creation of such a class would be pointless. Because of this, the class is decorated with the `static` keyword. The `static` keyword on a class provides two facilities. First, it prevents a programmer from writing code that instantiates the `SimpleMath` class. Second, it prevents the declaration of any instance fields or methods within the class. Since the class cannot be instantiated, instance members would be pointless.

C# 1.0 did not support static class declaration like this. Instead, programmers had to declare a private constructor. The private constructor prevented developers from ever instantiating an instance of the class outside of the class scope. Listing 5.27 shows the same `Math` class using a private constructor.

LISTING 5.27: Declaring a Private Constructor

```csharp
// Preventing instantiation in C# 1.0 with a private constructor.
class SimpleMath
{
    private SimpleMath() {}

    // params allows the number of parameters to vary.
    static int Max(params int[] numbers)
    {
        // ...
    }

    // params allows the number of parameters to vary.
    static int Min(params int[] numbers)
    {
        // ...
    }
}
```

The effect of using a private constructor in Listing 5.27 is very similar to the static class used in Listing 5.26, except that it is still possible to instantiate the class in Listing 5.27 from inside the class implementation. In contrast, Listing 5.26 prevents instantiation from anywhere, including from inside the class itself. Another difference between declaring a static class and using a private constructor is that instance members are allowed on a class with private constructors, but the C# 2.0 compiler will disallow any instance members on a static class.

One more distinguishing characteristic of the static class is that the C# compiler automatically marks it as `sealed`. This keyword designates the class as **inextensible**; in other words, no class can be derived from it.

`const` and `readonly` Modifiers

Two more field modifiers are related to encapsulation. The first is the `const` modifier, which you already encountered when declaring local variables. The second is `readonly`.

`const`

Just as with `const` local variables, a `const` field contains a compile-time-determined value that cannot be changed at runtime. Values such as pi make good candidates for constant field declarations. Listing 5.28 shows an example of declaring a const field.

LISTING 5.28: Declaring a Constant Field

```
class ConvertUnits
{
    public const float CentimetersPerInch = 2.54F;
    public const int CupsPerGallon = 16;
    // ...
}
```

Constant fields are static automatically, since no new field instance is required for each object instance. Declaring a constant field as static explicitly will cause a compile error.

readonly

Unlike const, the readonly modifier is available only for fields (not for local variables) and it declares that the field value is modifiable only from inside the constructor or directly during declaration. Listing 5.29 demonstrates how to declare a readonly field.

LISTING 5.29: Declaring a Field as **readonly**

```
class Employee
{
    public Employee(int id)
    {
        Id = id;
    }

    // ...
    public readonly int Id;
    public void SetId(int newId)
    {
        // ERROR:  readonly fields cannot be set
        //         outside of the constructor.
        // Id = newId
    }

    // ...
}
```

Unlike constant fields, readonly fields can vary from one instance to the next. In fact, a readonly field's value can change from its value during declaration to a new value within the constructor. Furthermore, `readonly` fields occur as either instance or static fields. Another key distinction is that you can assign the value of a `readonly` field at execution time rather than just at compile time.

Using `readonly` with an array does not freeze the contents of the array. It freezes the number of elements in the array because it is not possible to reassign the `readonly` field to a new instance. However, the elements of the array are still writeable.

Properties

The Access Modifiers section, earlier in this chapter, demonstrated how you can use the `private` keyword to encapsulate a password, preventing access from outside the class. This type of encapsulation is often too thorough, however. For example, sometimes you might need to define fields that external classes can only read but whose values you can change internally. Alternatively, perhaps you want to allow access to write some data in a class but you need to be able to validate changes made to the data. Still one more example is the need to construct the data on the fly.

Traditionally, languages enabled the features found in these examples by marking fields as private and then providing getter and setter methods for accessing and modifying the data. The code in Listing 5.30 changes both `FirstName` and `LastName` to private fields. Public getter and setter methods for each field allow their values to be accessed and changed.

LISTING 5.30: Declaring Getter and Setter Methods

```
class Employee
{

    private string FirstName;
    // FirstName getter
    public string GetFirstName()
    {
        return FirstName;
    }
    // FirstName setter
    public void SetFirstName(string newFirstName)
    {
        if(newFirstName != null && newFirstName != "")
```

```
    {
        FirstName = newFirstName;
    }
}

private string LastName;
// LastName getter
public string GetLastName()
{
    return LastName;
}
// LastName setter
public void SetLastName(string newLastName)
{
    if(newLastName != null && newLastName != "")
    {
        LastName = newLastName;
    }
}
// ...
}
```

Unfortunately, this change affects the programmability of the Employee class. No longer can you use the assignment operator to set data within the class, nor can you access data without calling a method.

Declaring a Property

Considering the frequency of this type of pattern, the C# designers decided to provide explicit syntax for it. This syntax is called a **property** (see Listing 5.31 and Output 5.5).

LISTING 5.31: Defining Properties

```
class Program
{
    static void Main()
    {
        Employee employee = new Employee("Domingo", "Montoya");

        // Call the FirstName property's setter.
        employee.FirstName = "Inigo";

        // Call the FirstName property's getter.
        Console.WriteLine(employee.FirstName);
    }
}
```

```
class Employee
{

    public Employee(string newFirstName, string newLastName)
    {
        // Use property inside the Employee
        // class as well.
        FirstName = newFirstName;
        LastName = newLastName;
    }

    // FirstName property
    public string FirstName
    {
        get
        {
            return _FirstName;
        }
        set
        {
            _FirstName = value;
        }
    }
    private string _FirstName;

    // LastName property
    public string LastName
    {
        get
        {
            return _LastName;
        }
        set
        {
            _LastName = value;
        }
    }
    private string _LastName;
    // ...
}
```

OUTPUT 5.5:

```
Inigo
```

The first thing to notice in Listing 5.31 is not the property code itself, but the code within the Program class. Although you no longer have the fields with the FirstName and LastName identifiers, you cannot see this by looking at the Program class. The API for accessing an employee's first and last names has not changed at all. It is still possible to assign the parts of the name using a simple assignment operator, for example (employee.FirstName = "Inigo").

The key feature is that properties provide an API that looks programmatically like a field. In actuality, however, no such fields exist. A property declaration looks exactly like a field declaration, but following it are curly braces in which to place the property implementation. Two optional parts make up the property implementation. The get part defines the getter portion of the property. It corresponds directly to the GetFirstName() and GetLastName() functions defined in Listing 5.30. To access the FirstName property you call employee.FirstName. Similarly, setters (the set portion of the implementation) enable the calling syntax of the field assignment:

```
employee.FirstName = "Inigo";
```

Property definition syntax uses three contextual keywords. You use the get and set keywords to identify either the retrieval or the assignment portion of the property, respectively. In addition, the setter uses the value keyword to refer to the right side of the assignment operation. When Program.Main() calls employee.FirstName = "Inigo", therefore, value is set to "Inigo" inside the setter and can be used to assign _FirstName. Listing 5.31's property implementations are the most common. When the getter is called (such as in Console.WriteLine(employee2.FirstName)), the value from the field (_FirstName) is returned.

■ ADVANCED TOPIC

Property Internals
Listing 5.32 shows that getters and setters are exposed as get_FirstName() and set_FirstName() in the CIL.

LISTING 5.32: CIL Code Resulting from Properties

```
.method public hidebysig specialname instance string
        get_FirstName()  cil managed
{
  // Code size       12 (0xc)
  .maxstack  1
  .locals init ([0] string CS$1$0000)
  IL_0000:  nop
  IL_0001:  ldarg.0
```

```
    IL_0002:  ldfld       string TicTacToe.Program::_FirstName
    IL_0007:  stloc.0
    IL_0008:  br.s        IL_000a
    IL_000a:  ldloc.0
    IL_000b:  ret
} // end of method Program:: get_FirstName

.method public hidebysig specialname instance void
        get_FirstName(string 'value')   cil managed
{
    // Code size        9 (0x9)
    .maxstack  8
    IL_0000:  nop
    IL_0001:  ldarg.0
    IL_0002:  ldarg.1
    IL_0003:  stfld       string TicTacToe.Program::_FirstName
    IL_0008:  ret
} // end of method Program:: set_FirstName
```

Just as important to their appearance as regular methods is the fact that properties are an explicit construct within the CIL, too. As Listing 5.33 shows, the getters and setters are called by CIL properties, which are an explicit construct within the CIL code. Because of this, languages and compilers are not restricted to always interpreting properties based on a naming convention. Instead, CIL properties provide a means for compilers and code editors to provide special syntax.

LISTING 5.33: Properties Are an Explicit Construct in CIL

```
    .property instance string FirstName()
    {
      .get instance string TicTacToe.Program::get_FirstName()
      .set instance void TicTacToe.Program::set_FirstName(string)
    } // end of property Program::FirstName
```

Notice that the getters and setters that are part of the property include the `specialname` metadata. This modifier is what IDEs, such as Visual Studio, use as a flag to hide the members from IntelliSense.

Naming Conventions

Because the property name is `FirstName`, the field name changed from earlier listings to `_FirstName`. Other common naming conventions for the private field that backs a property are `_firstName` and `m_FirstName` (a holdover from C++ where the m stands for member variable), as well as the camel case convention, just as with local variables.[1]

Regardless of which naming pattern you use for private fields, the coding standard for public fields and properties is Pascal case. Therefore, public properties should use the `LastName` and `FirstName` type patterns. Similarly, if no encapsulating property is created around a public field, Pascal case should be used for the field.

Static Properties

You also can declare properties as static. For example, Listing 5.34 wraps the data for the next ID into a property.

LISTING 5.34: Declaring a Static Property

```
class Employee
{
    // ...
    public static int NextId
    {
        get
        {
            return _NextId;
        }
        private set
        {
            _NextId = value;
        }
    }
    public static int _NextId = 42;
    // ...
}
```

Using Properties with Validation

Notice inside the `Employee` constructor that you use the property rather than the field for assignment as well. Although not required, the result is that any validation within the property setter will be invoked both inside and outside the class. Consider, for example, what would happen if you changed the `LastName` property so that it checked `value` for `null` or an empty string, before assigning it to _LastName (see Listing 5.35).

---

1. I prefer _FirstName because the m in front of the name is unnecessary when compared with simply _, and by using the same casing as the property, it is possible to have only one string within the Visual Studio code template expansion tools, instead of having one for both the property name and the field name.

Listing 5.35: Providing Property Validation

```csharp
class Employee
{
  // ...
  // LastName property
  public string LastName
  {
      get
      {
          return _LastName;
      }
      set
      {
          // Validate LastName assignment
          if(value == null)
          {
              // Report error
              throw new NullReferenceException();
          }
          else
          {
              // Remove any whitespace around
              // the new last name.
              value = value.Trim();
              if(value == "")
              {
                  throw new ApplicationException(
                      "LastName cannot be blank.");
              }
              else
                  _LastName = value;
          }
      }
  }
  private string _LastName;
  // ...
}
```

With this new implementation, the code throws an exception if Last-Name is assigned an invalid value, either through the constructor or via a direct assignment to LastName from inside Program.Main(). The ability to intercept an assignment and validate the parameters by providing a field-like API is one of the advantages of properties.

It is a good practice to only access a property-backing field from inside the property implementation, to always use the property rather than the field directly. In many cases, this is true even from inside the containing class because that way, when code such as validation code is added, the entire class immediately takes advantage of it. One obvious exception to this occurs when the field is marked as read-only because then the value cannot be set outside of the constructor, even in a property setter.

Although rare, it is possible to assign a value inside the setter, as Listing 5.35 does. In this case, the call to `value.Trim()` removes any whitespace surrounding the new last name value.

Read-Only and Write-Only Properties

By removing either the getter or the setter portion of a property, you can change a property's accessibility. Properties with only a setter are write-only, which is a relatively rare occurrence. Similarly, providing only a getter will cause the property to be read-only; any attempts to assign a value will cause a compile error. To make `Id` read-only, for example, you would code it as shown in Listing 5.36.

LISTING 5.36: Defining a Read-Only Property

```csharp
class Program
{
    static void Main()
    {
        Employee employee1 = new Employee(42);
        // ERROR:  Id is read-only
        // Employee.Id = 490;
    }
}


class Employee
{
    public Employee(int id)
    {
        // Use field because Id property has no setter,
        // it is read-only.
        _Id = id.ToString();
    }

    // ...
    // Id property declaration
    public string Id
    {
        get
        {
            return _Id;
        }
        // No setter provided.
    }
```

```
    private string _Id;

}
```

Listing 5.36 assigns the field from within the `Employee` constructor rather than the property (`_Id = id`). Assigning via the property causes a compile error, as it does in `Program.Main()`.

Access Modifiers on Getters and Setters

As previously mentioned, it is a good practice not to access fields from outside their properties because doing so circumvents any validation or additional logic that may be inserted. Unfortunately, C# 1.0 did not allow different levels of encapsulation between the getter and setter portions of a property. It was not possible, therefore, to create a public getter and a private setter so that external classes would have read-only access to the property while code within the class could write to the property.

In C# 2.0, support was added for placing an access modifier on either the get or the set portion of the property implementation (not on both), thereby overriding the access modifier specified on the property declaration. Listing 5.37 demonstrates how to do this.

LISTING 5.37: Placing Access Modifiers on the Setter

```
class Program
{
  static void Main()
  {
      Employee employee1 = new Employee(42);
      // ERROR:   Id is read-only outside the Employee class
      // Employee.Id = 490;
  }
}
```

```
class Employee
{
  public Employee(int id)
  {
      // Set Id property
      Id = id.ToString();
  }

  // ...
  // Id property declaration
```

```
public string Id
{
    get
    {
        return _Id;
    }
    // Providing an access modifier is in C# 2.0 only
    private set
    {
        _Id = value;
    }
}
private string _Id;

}
```

By using `private` on the setter, the property appears as read-only to classes other than `Employee`. From within `Employee`, the property appears as read/write, so you can assign the property within the constructor. When specifying an access modifier on the getter or setter, take care that the access modifier is more restrictive than the access modifier on the property as a whole. It is a compile error, for example, to declare the property as `private` and the setter as `public`.

Properties as Virtual Fields

As you have seen, properties behave like virtual fields. In some instances, you do not need a backing field at all. Instead, the property getter returns a calculated value while the setter parses the value and persists it to some other member fields, if at all. Consider, for example, the `Name` property implementation shown in Listing 5.38. Output 5.6 shows the results.

LISTING 5.38: Defining Properties

```
class Program
{
    static void Main()
    {
        Employee employee1 = new Employee(42);

        employee1.Name = "Inigo Montoya";
        Console.WriteLine(employee1.Name);

        // ...
    }
}
```

```csharp
class Employee
{
  // ...

  public Employee(string name)
  {
      Name = name;
  }

  public string FirstName
  {
      get
      {
          return _FirstName;
      }
      set
      {
          // Validate FirstName assignment
          if(value == null)
          {
              // Report error
              throw new NullReferenceException();
          }
          else
          {
              // Remove any white space around
              // the new last name.
              value = value.Trim();
              if(value == "")
              {
                  throw new ApplicationException(
                      "FirstName cannot be blank.");
              }
              else
                  _FirstName = value;
          }
      }
  }
  private string _FirstName;

  public string LastName
  {
      get
      {
          return _LastName;
      }
      set
      {
          // Validate LastName assignment
          if(value == null)
          {
              // Report error
              throw new NullReferenceException();
          }
          else
```

```
        {
            // Remove any white space around
            // the new last name.
            value = value.Trim();
            if(value == "")
            {
                throw new ApplicationException(
                    "LastName cannot be blank.");
            }
            else
                _LastName = value;
        }
    }
}
private string _LastName;

// Name property
public string Name
{
    get
    {
        return FirstName + " " + LastName;
    }
    set
    {
        // Split the assigned value into
        // first and last names.
        string[] names;
        names = value.Split(new char[]{' '});
        if(names.Length == 2)
        {
            FirstName = names[0];
            LastName = names[1];
        }
        else
        {
            // Throw an exception if the full
            // name was not assigned.
            throw new ApplicationException(
                string.Format(
                "Assigned value '{0}' is invalid", value));
        }
    }
}

// ...
}
```

OUTPUT 5.6:

```
Inigo Montoya
```

The getter for the Name property concatenates the values returned from the FirstName and LastName properties. In fact, the name value assigned is not actually stored. When the Name property is assigned, the value on the right side is parsed into its first and last name parts.

Properties and Method Calls Not Allowed as ref or out Parameter Values

C# allows properties to be used identically to fields, except when they are passed as ref or out parameter values. ref and out parameter values are internally implemented by passing the memory address to the target method. However, because properties can be virtual fields that have no backing field, or can be read/write-only, it is not possible to pass the address for the underlying storage. As a result, you cannot pass properties as ref or out parameter values. The same is true for method calls. Instead, when code needs to pass a property or method call as a ref or out parameter value, the code must first copy the value into a variable and then pass the variable. Once the method call has completed, the code must assign the variable back into the property.

Nested Classes

In addition to defining methods and fields within a class, it is also possible to define a class within a class. Such classes are **nested classes**. You use a nested class when the class makes little sense outside the context of its containing class.

Consider a class that handles the command-line options of a program. Such a class is generally unique to each program and there is no reason to make a CommandLine class accessible from outside the class that contains Main(). Listing 5.39 demonstrates such a nested class.

LISTING 5.39: Defining a Nested Class

```csharp
class Program
{
    // Define a nested class for processing the command line.
    private class CommandLine
    {
        public CommandLine(string[] arguments)
        {
            for(int argumentCounter=0;
                argumentCounter<arguments.Length;
                argumentCounter++)
```

```csharp
            {
                switch (argumentCounter)
                {
                    case 0:
                        Action = arguments[0].ToLower();
                        break;
                    case 1:
                        Id = arguments[1];
                        break;
                    case 2:
                        FirstName = arguments[2];
                        break;
                    case 3:
                        LastName = arguments[3];
                        break;
                }
            }
        }
        public string Action;
        public string Id;
        public string FirstName;
        public string LastName;
    }

    static void Main(string[] args)
    {
        CommandLine commandLine = new CommandLine(args);

        switch (commandLine.Action)
        {
            case "new":
                // Create a new employee
                // ...
                break;
            case "update":
                // Update an existing employee's data
                // ...
                break;
            case "delete":
                // Remove an existing employee's file.
                // ...
                break;
            default:
                Console.WriteLine(
                    "Employee.exe " +
              "new|update|delete <id> [firstname] [lastname]");
                break;
        }
    }
}
```

The nested class in this example is `Program.CommandLine`. As with all class members, no containing class identifier is needed from inside the containing class, so you can simply refer to it as `CommandLine`.

One unique characteristic of nested classes is the ability to specify `private` as an access modifier for the class itself. Because the purpose of this class is to parse the command line and place each argument into a separate field, `Program.CommandLine` is relevant only to the `Program` class in this application. The use of the `private` access modifier defines the intended scope of the class and prevents access from outside the class. You can do this only if the class is nested.

The `this` member within a nested class refers to an instance of the nested class, not the containing class. One way for a nested class to access an instance of the containing class is if the containing class instance is explicitly passed, such as via a constructor or method parameter.

Another interesting characteristic of nested classes is that they can access any member on the containing class, including private members. The converse to accessing private members is not true, however. It is not possible for the containing class to access a private member on the nested class.

Nested classes generally occur rarely.

Language Contrast: Java—Inner Classes

Java includes not only the concept of a nested class, but also the concept of an inner class. Inner classes correspond to objects that are associated with the containing class instance rather than just a syntactic relationship. In C#, you can achieve the same structure by including an instance field of a nested type within the class.

Partial Classes

Another language feature added in C# 2.0 is **partial classes**. Partial classes are portions of a class that the compiler can combine to form a complete class. Although you could define two or more partial classes within the same file, the general purpose of a partial class is to allow the splitting of a class definition across multiple files. Primarily this is useful for tools that are generating or modifying code. With partial classes, the tools can work on a file separate from the one the developer is manually coding.

C# 2.0 declares a partial class by appending the contextual keyword, `partial`, to the definition, as Listing 5.40 shows.

LISTING 5.40: Defining a Partial Class

```
// File: Program1.cs
partial class Program
{
}
```

```
// File: Program2.cs
partial class Program
{
}
```

In this case, each portion of `Program` is placed into a separate file, as identified by the comment. Besides their use with code generators, another common use of partial classes is to place any nested classes into their own files. This is in accordance with the coding convention that places each class definition within its own file. For example, Listing 5.41 places the `Program.CommandLine` class into a file separate from the core `Program` members.

LISTING 5.41: Defining a Nested Class in a Separate Partial Class

```
// File: Program.cs
partial class Program
{
  static void Main(string[] args)
  {
    CommandLine commandLine = new CommandLine(args);

    switch (commandLine.Action)
    {
      // ...
    }
  }
}
```

```
// File: Program+CommandLine.cs
partial class Program
{
  // Define a nested class for processing the command line.
```

```
private class CommandLine
{
    // ...
}
}
```

Partial classes do not allow extending compiled classes, classes in other assemblies. They are only a means of splitting a class implementation across multiple files within the same assembly.

SUMMARY

This chapter explained C# constructs for classes and object orientation in C#. This included a discussion of fields, and a discussion of how to access them on a class instance.

Whether to store data on a per-instance basis or across all instances of a type was a key concept discussed. Static data is associated with the class and instance data is stored on each object.

The chapter explored encapsulation in the context of access modifiers for methods and data. The C# construct of properties was introduced, and you saw how to use it to encapsulate private fields.

The next chapter focuses on how to associate classes with each other via inheritance, and the benefits derived from this object-oriented construct.

∎6∎
Inheritance

THE LAST CHAPTER DISCUSSED association relationships, how one class can reference another class or set of classes using fields or properties. This chapter looks at another relationship between classes, that of inheritance and building a class hierarchy.

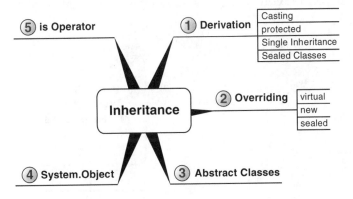

Inheritance Definitions

The previous chapter provided an overview of inheritance. Here's a review of the defined terms.

- *Derive/inherit:* Specialize a base class to include additional members or customization of the base class members.

- *Derived/sub/child type:* The specialized type that inherits the members of the more general type.
- *Base/super/parent type:* The general type whose members a derived type inherits.
- *Inheritance forms:* An "is a" relationship. The derived type is always implicitly also of the base type. Just as a hard drive is a storage device, any other type derived from the storage device type is a type of storage device.

Derivation

It is reasonably common to want to extend a given type to add functionality, such as behavior and data. The purpose of inheritance is to do exactly that. Given a `Person` class, you create an `Employee` class that additionally contains `EmployeeId` and `Department` properties. The reverse approach may also occur. Given, for example, a `Contact` class within a Personal Digital Assistant (PDA), you decide you also can add calendaring support. Toward this effort, you create an `Appointment` class. However, instead of

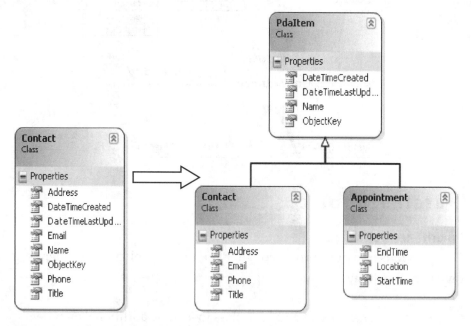

FIGURE 6.1: Refactoring into a Base Class

redefining the methods and properties that are common to both classes, you **refactor** the Contact class. Specifically, you move the common methods and properties on Contact into a base class called PdaItem from which both Contact and Appointment derive, as shown in Figure 6.1.

The common items in this case are DateTimeCreated, DateTimeLast-Updated, Name, ObjectKey, and the like. Through derivation, the methods defined on the base class, PdaItem, are accessible from all subclasses of PdaItem.

When defining a derived class, follow the class identifier with a colon and then the base class, as Listing 6.1 demonstrates.

LISTING 6.1: Deriving One Class from Another

```csharp
public class PdaItem
{
  public string Name
  {
     get { return _Name; }
     set { _Name = value; }
  }
  private string _Name;

  public string DateTimeLastUpdate
  {
     get { return _DateTimeLastUpdate; }
     set { _DateTimeLastUpdate = value; }
  }
  private string _DateTimeLastUpdate;
}
```

```csharp
// Define the Contact class as inheriting the PdaItem class
public class Contact : PdaItem
{
  public string Address
  {
     get { return _Address; }
     set { _Address = value; }
  }
  private string _Address;

  public string Phone
  {
     get { return _Phone; }
     set { _Phone = value; }
  }
  private string _Phone;
}
```

Listing 6.2 shows how to access the properties defined in Contact.

LISTING 6.2: Using Inherited Methods

```
public class Program
{
  public static void Main()
  {
      Contact contact = new Contact();
      contact.Name = "Inigo Montoya";

      // ...
  }
}
```

Even though Contact does not directly have a property called Name, all instances of Contact can still access the Name property from PdaItem and use it as though it was part of Contact. Furthermore, any additional classes that derive from Contact will also inherit the members of PdaItem, or any class from which PdaItem was derived. The inheritance chain has no practical limit and each derived class will have all the exposed members of its base class inheritance chain combined (see Listing 6.3).

LISTING 6.3: Classes Deriving from Each Other to Form an Inheritance Chain

```
public class PdaItem : object
{
  // ...
}
```

```
public class Appointment : PdaItem
{
  // ...
}
```

```
public class Contact : PdaItem
{
  // ...
}
```

```
public class Customer : Contact
{
  // ...
}
```

In other words, although Customer doesn't derive from PdaItem directly, it still inherits the members of PdaItem.

In Listing 6.3, PdaItem is shown explicitly to derive from object. Although C# allows such syntax, it is unnecessary because all objects that don't have some other derivation will derive from object, regardless of whether it is specified.

Casting between Base and Derived Types

As Listing 6.4 shows, because derivation forms an "is a" relationship, a derived type can always be directly assigned to a base type.

LISTING 6.4: Implicit Base Type Casting

```
public class Program
{
  pulic static void Main()
  {
      // Derived types can be cast implicitly to
      // base types
      Contact contact = new Contact();
      PdaItem item = contact;
      // ...

      // Base types must be cast explicitly to derived types
      contact = (Contact)item;
      // ...
  }
}
```

The derived type, Contact, is a PdaItem and can be assigned directly to a PdaItem. This is known as an **implicit cast** because no specific operator is required and the conversion will, on principal, always succeed; it will not throw an exception.

■ BEGINNER TOPIC

Casting within the Inheritance Chain

The cast to a base class does not instantiate a new instance. Instead, the same instance is simply referred to as the base type and the capabilities (the accessible members) are those of the base type. It is just like referring to a CD as a storage device. Since not all storage devices support an eject operation, a CD that is cast to a storage device cannot be ejected either, and a call to `storageDevice.Eject()` would not compile even though the instantiated object may have been a CD object that supported the `Eject()` method.

Similarly, casting down from the base class to the derived cast simply begins referring to the type more specifically, expanding the available operations. The restriction is that the actual instantiated type must be an instance of the targeted type (or something derived from it.)

The reverse, however, is not true. A `PdaItem` is not necessarily a `Contact`; it could be an `Appointment` or some other undefined, class-derived type. Therefore, casting from the base type to the derived type requires an explicit cast, which at runtime could fail. To perform an explicit cast, identify the target type within parentheses prior to the original reference, as Listing 6.4 demonstrates.

With the explicit cast, the programmer essentially communicates to the compiler to trust her, she knows what she is doing, and the C# compiler allows the conversion as long as the target type is derived from the originating type. Although the C# compiler allows an explicit conversion at compile time between potentially compatible types, the CLR will still verify the explicit cast at runtime, throwing an exception if in fact the base type is not of the targeted type.

The C# compiler allows the cast operator even when the type hierarchy allows an implicit cast. For example, the assignment from `contact` to `item` could use a cast operator as follows:

```
item = (Contact)contact;
```

or even when no cast is necessary:

```
contact = (Contact)contact;
```

Although casting between `Contact` and `PdaItem` is fully supported, casting in either direction between arrays of these types is not supported. In other words, the following, known as covariance, will not compile:

```
PdaItem[] pdaItems = (PdaItem[])new Contact[42];
```

The reverse cast, contravariance, is not supported either.

Support for Parameter Covariance and Contravariance

C#'s inheritance implementation doesn't support either **covariance** or **contravariance**. Covariance allows overriding a member by supplying a method in the derived class to be a more specialized type. For example, covariance would allow the method on a derived class, `void Draw(Widget part)`, to override the base class, perhaps an abstract member, `void Draw(Part part)`, where `Widget` derives from `Part`.

The problem with that covariance is that the base class allowed for any `Part` to be drawn, but the derived type allows for only the drawing of type `Widget`. Therefore, does the derived type handle the drawing of `Part`'s? Presumably it should, but not via the implementation of `void Draw(Widget part)`, because it handles only `Widget`. Effectively, therefore, `void Draw(Widget part)` does not override `void Draw(Part part)`, but instead, it overloads it, providing a second method with the same name. Covariance is especially questionable when overriding abstract members. An abstract member requires that the derived class implements a specific signature, and if the derived class specializes the signature, narrowing what is actually supported, then the full functionality required by the abstract method will be lacking.

Contravariance occurs when the derived type's members have broader signatures than the base type's signature. For example, the base class could have a method, `void Add(Widget widget)`, and the derived class would override the method with `void Add(Part part)`. This would allow addition of a `Part` to the class via the derived method, but since the base class always expects a `Widget`, it may call into the added item as though it was a `Widget` and fail.

Keeping with the strong type semantics of C#, neither covariance nor contravariance is supported.

■ ADVANCED TOPIC

Defining Custom Conversions

Casting between types is not limited to types within a single inheritance chain. It is possible to cast entirely unrelated types as well. The key is the provision of a conversion operator between the two types. C# allows types to include either explicit or implicit cast operators. Any time the operation could possibly fail, such as in a cast from `long` to `int`, developers should choose to define an explicit cast operator. This warns developers performing the cast to do so only when they are certain the cast will succeed, or else to be prepared to catch the exception if it doesn't. They should also use explicit casts over an implicit cast when the conversion is lossy. Converting from a `float` to an `int`, for example, truncates the decimal, which a return cast (from `int` back to `float`) would not recover.

Listing 6.5 shows implicit and explicit cast operators for `Address` to `string` and vice versa.

LISTING 6.5: Defining Cast Operators

```
class Address
{
  // ...

  public static implicit operator string(
      Address address)
  {
    // ...
  }
  public static explicit operator Address(
      string addressText)
  {
    // ...
  }
}
```

In this case, you have an implicit cast from `Address` to `string` because all `Address` objects can be converted successfully to a string. However, you have an explicit cast from `string` to `Address` because strings will not necessarily be valid addresses.

`private` Access Modifier

All `public` members of a base class are available to the derived class. However, private members are not. For example, in Listing 6.6, the `private` field, `_Name`, is not available on `Contact`.

LISTING 6.6: Private Members Are Not Inherited

```
public class PdaItem
{
  private string _Name;
```

```
      // ...
   }
```

```
public class Contact : PdaItem
{
   // ...
}
```

```
public class Program
{
   public static void Main()
   {
      Contact contact = new Contact();

      // ERROR: 'PdaItem._Name' is inaccessible
      // due to its protection level
      // contact._Name = "Inigo Montoya";
   }
}
```

As part of keeping with the principal of encapsulation, derived classes cannot access members declared as `private`. This forces the base class developer to make an explicit choice as to whether a derived class gains access to a member. In this case, the base class is defining an API in which _Name can be changed only via the `Name` property. That way, if validation is added, the derived class will gain the validation benefit automatically because it was unable to access _Name directly from the start.

protected Access Modifier

Encapsulation is finer grained than just public or private, however. It is possible to define members in base classes that only derived classes can access. Consider the `ObjectKey` property shown in Listing 6.7, for example.

LISTING 6.7: **protected** Members Are Accessible Only from Derived Classes

```
public class PdaItem
{
   protected Guid ObjectKey
   {
      get { return _ObjectKey; }
      set { _ObjectKey = value; }
   }
   private Guid _ObjectKey;

   // ...
}
```

```csharp
public class Contact : PdaItem
{
  void Save()
  {
      // Instantiate a FileStream using <ObjectKey>.dat
      // for the filename.
      FileStream stream = System.IO.File.OpenWrite(
          ObjectKey + ".dat");
      // ...
  }
}
```

```csharp
public class Program
{
  public static void Main()
  {
      Contact contact = new Contact();
      contact.Name = "Inigo Montoya";

      // ERROR:  'PdaItem.ObjectKey' is inaccessible
      // due to its protection level
      // contact.ObjectKey = Guid.NewGuid();
  }
}
```

ObjectKey is defined using the `protected` access modifier. The result is that it is accessible outside of PdaItem only from classes that derive from PdaItem. Contact derives from PdaItem and, therefore, all members of Contact have access to ObjectKey. Since Program does not derive from PdaItem, using the ObjectKey property within Program results in a compile error.

Single Inheritance

In theory, you can place an unlimited number of classes in an inheritance tree. For example, Customer derives from Contact, which derives from PdaItem, which derives from object. However, C# is a **single-inheritance**

Language Contrast: C++ — Multiple Inheritance

C#'s single inheritance is one of its significant differences from C++. It makes for a significant migration path from programming libraries such as Active Template Library (ATL), whose entire approach relies on multiple inheritance.

programming language (as is the CIL language to which C# compiles). This means that a class cannot derive from two classes directly. It is not possible, for example, to have `Contact` derive from both `PdaItem` and `Person`.

For the rare cases that require a multiple-inheritance class structure, the general solution is to use **aggregation**. Figure 6.2 shows an example of this class structure. Aggregation occurs when the association relationship defines a core part of the containing object. For multiple inheritance, this involves picking one class as the primary base class (`PdaItem`) and deriving a new class (`Contact`) from that. The second desired base class (`Person`) is added as a field in the derived class (`Contact`). Next, all the nonprivate members on the field (`Person`) are redefined on the derived

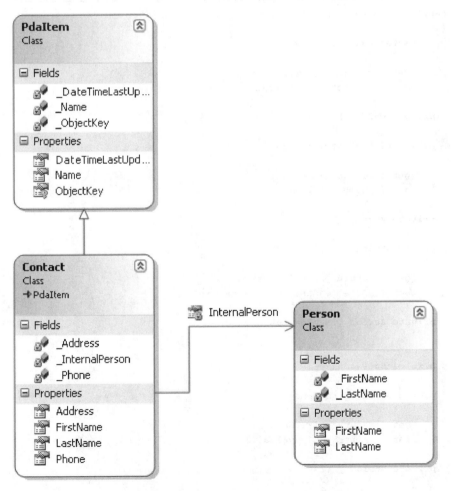

FIGURE 6.2: Working around Multiple Inheritance Using Aggregation

class (Contact) which then delegates the calls out to the field (Person). Some code duplication occurs because methods are redeclared; however, this is minimal, since the real method body is implemented only within the aggregated class (Person).

In Figure 6.2, Contact contains a private property called Internal-Person that is drawn as an association to the Person class. Contact also contains the FirstName and LastName properties but with no corresponding fields. Instead, the FirstName and LastName properties simply delegate their calls out to InternalPerson.FirstName and InternalPerson.LastName, respectively. Listing 6.8 shows the resulting code.

LISTING 6.8: Working around Single Inheritance Using Aggregation

```csharp
public class PdaItem
{
    protected Guid ObjectKey
    {
        get { return _ObjectKey; }
        set { _ObjectKey = value; }
    }
    private Guid _ObjectKey;

    public virtual string Name
    {
        get { return _Name; }
        set { _Name = value; }
    }
    private string _Name;

    public string DateTimeLastUpdate
    {
        get { return _DateTimeLastUpdate; }
        set { _DateTimeLastUpdate = value; }
    }
    private string _DateTimeLastUpdate;
}

public class Person
{
    public string FirstName
    {
        get { return _FirstName; }
        set { _FirstName = value; }
    }
    private string _FirstName;
```

```
    public string LastName
    {
        get { return _LastName; }
        set { _LastName = value; }
    }
    private string _LastName;
}

public class Contact : PdaItem
{
    private Person InternalPerson
    {
        get { return _Person; }
        set { _Person = value; }
    }
    private Person _Person;

    public string FirstName
    {
        get { return InternalPerson.FirstName; }
        set { InternalPerson.FirstName = value; }
    }

    public string LastName
    {
        get { return InternalPerson.LastName; }
        set { InternalPerson.LastName = value; }
    }

    public string Address
    {
        get { return _Address; }
        set { _Address = value; }
    }
    private string _Address;

    public string Phone
    {
        get { return _Phone; }
        set { _Phone = value; }
    }
    private string _Phone;
}
```

Another drawback is that any methods added to the field class (Person) will require manual addition to the derived class (Contact); otherwise, Contact will not expose the added functionality.

Sealed Classes

To design a class correctly that others can extend via derivation can be a tricky task that requires testing with examples to verify the derivation will work successfully. Furthermore, a slight performance overhead is associated with derived classes. To avoid some of these concerns, classes can be marked as **sealed** (see Listing 6.9).

LISTING 6.9: Preventing Derivation with Sealed Classes

```
public sealed class CommandLineParser
{
  // ...
}
```

```
// ERROR:  Sealed classes cannot be derived from
public sealed class DerivedCommandLineParser :
  CommandLineParser
{
  // ...
}
```

Sealed classes include the `sealed` modifier, and the result is that they cannot be derived. The `string` type is another example of a type that uses the `sealed` modifier to prevent derivation.

Overriding the Base Class

All `public` and `protected` members of a base class are inherited in the derived class. However, sometimes the base class does not have the optimal implementation of a particular member. Consider the `Name` property on `PdaItem`, for example. The implementation is probably acceptable when inherited by the `Appointment` class. For the `Contact` class, however, the `Name` property should return the `FirstName` and `LastName` properties combined. Similarly, when `Name` is assigned, it should be split across `FirstName` and `LastName`. In other words, the base class property declaration is appropriate for the derived class, but the implementation is not always valid. There needs to be a mechanism for **overriding** the base class implementation with a custom implementation in the derived class.

virtual Modifier

C# supports overriding on instance methods and properties but not on fields or any static members. It requires an explicit action within both the base class and the derived class. The base class must mark each member for which it allows overriding as virtual. If public or protected members do not include the virtual modifier, then subclasses will not be able to override those members.

Language Contrast: Java—Virtual Methods by Default

By default, methods in Java are virtual, and they must be explicitly sealed if nonvirtual behavior is preferred. In contrast, C# defaults to nonvirtual.

Listing 6.10 shows an example of property overriding.

LISTING 6.10: Overriding a Property

```csharp
public class PdaItem
{
    public virtual string Name
    {
        get { return _Name; }
        set { _Name = value; }
    }
    private string _Name;

    // ...
}


public class Contact : PdaItem
{
    public override string Name
    {
        get
        {
            return FirstName + " " + LastName;
        }

        set
        {
            string names = value.Split(' ');
```

```
        // Error handling not shown.
        FirstName = names[0];
        LastName = names[1];
    }
  }


  public string FirstName
  {
      get { return _FirstName; }
      set { _FirstName = value; }
  }
  private string _FirstName;

  public string LastName
  {
      get { return _LastName; }
      set { _LastName = value; }
  }
  private string _LastName;

  // ...
}
```

Not only does PdaItem include the virtual modifier on the Name property, but also, Contact's Name property is decorated with the keyword override. Eliminating virtual would result in an error and omitting override would cause a warning, as you will see shortly. C# requires the overriding methods to use the override keyword explicitly.

In other words, virtual identifies a method or property as available for replacement (overriding) in the derived type.

Language Contrast: Java and C++ — Implicit Overriding

Unlike with Java and C++, the override keyword is required on the derived class. C# does not allow implicit overriding. In order to override a method, both the base class and the derived class members must match and have corresponding virtual and override keywords. Furthermore, if specifying the override keyword, the derived implementation is assumed to hide the base class implementation.

Overloading a member causes the runtime to call the most derived implementation (see Listing 6.11).

LISTING 6.11: Runtime Calling the Most Derived Implementation of a Virtual Method

```
public class Program
{
  public static void Main()
  {
      Contact contact;
      PdaItem item;

      contact = new Contact();
      item = contact;

      // Set the name via PdaItem variable
      item.Name = "Inigo Montoya";

      // Display that FirstName & LastName
      // properties were set.
      Console.WriteLine("{0} {1}",
          contact.FirstName, contact.LastName);
  }
}
```

Output 6.1 shows the results of Listing 6.11.

OUTPUT 6.1:

```
Inigo Montoya
```

In Listing 6.11, item.Name is called, where item is declared as a PdaItem. However, the contact's FirstName and LastName are still set. The rule is that whenever the runtime encounters a virtual method, it calls the most derived and overriding implementation of the virtual member. In this case, the code instantiates a Contact and calls Contact.Name because Contact contains the most derived implementation of Name.

In creating a class, programmers should be careful when choosing to allow overriding a method, since they cannot control the derived implementation. Virtual methods should not include critical code because such methods may never be called if the derived class overrides them. Furthermore, converting a method from a virtual method to a nonvirtual method could break derived classes that override the method. This is a code-breaking change and you should avoid it, especially for assemblies intended for use by third parties.

Listing 6.12 includes a virtual `Run()` method. If the `Controller` programmer calls `Run()` with the expectation that the critical `Start()` and `Stop()` methods will be called, he will run into a problem.

LISTING 6.12: Carelessly Relying on a Virtual Method Implementation

```
public class Controller
{
  public void Start()
  {
     // Critical code
  }
  public virtual void Run()
  {
     Start();
     Stop();
  }
  public void Stop()
  {
     // Critical code
  }
}
```

In overriding `Run()`, a developer could perhaps not call the critical `Start()` and `Stop()` methods. To force the `Start()`/`Stop()` expectation, the `Controller` programmer should define the class, as shown in Listing 6.13.

LISTING 6.13: Forcing the Desirable **Run()** Semantics

```
public class Controller
{
    public void Start()
    {
       // Critical code
    }

    private void InternalRun()
    {
       Start();
       Run();
       Stop();
    }
```

```
public virtual void Run()
{
    // Default implementation
}

public void Stop()
{
    // Critical code
}
}
```

Furthermore, the `Controller` programmer should call `Run()` via `InternalRun()`, thereby forcing calls to `Start()` and `Stop()` while still allowing a custom implementation of `Run()` within a derived class.

Another drawback of virtual methods is that only at execution time is it possible to evaluate an inheritance chain to determine the most derived implementation. This results in a slight performance reduction. Rarely is this enough to avoid a virtual method when the design warrants it; however, this is a second factor indicating that virtual methods should be declared intentionally. In summary, virtual methods provide default implementations only, implementations that derived classes could override entirely. To make the best choice about virtual methods consider (and preferably implement) a specific scenario of why to define the virtual method.

Language Contrast: C++ — Dispatch Method Calls During Construction

In C++, methods called during construction will not dispatch the virtual method. Instead, during construction, the type is associated with the base type rather than the derived type, and virtual methods call the base implementation. In contrast, C# dispatches virtual method calls to the most derived type. This is consistent with the principal of calling the most derived virtual member, even if the derived constructor has not completely executed.

Finally, only instance members can be `virtual`. The CLR uses the concrete type, specified at instantiation time, to determine where to dispatch a virtual method call, so `static virtual` methods are meaningless and are not allowed.

new Modifier

When an overriding method does not use `override`, the compiler issues a warning similar to that shown in Output 6.2 or Output 6.3.

OUTPUT 6.2:

```
warning CS0114: '<derived method name>' hides inherited member
'<base method name>'. To make the current member override that implemen-
tation, add the override keyword. Otherwise add the new keyword.
```

OUTPUT 6.3:

```
warning CS0108: The keyword new is required on '<derived property name>'
because it hides inherited member '<base property name>'
```

The obvious solution is to add the `override` modifier (assuming the base member is virtual). However, as the warnings point out, the `new` modifier is also an option. Consider the scenario shown in Table 6.1.

TABLE 6.1: Why the New Modifier?

Activity	Code
| Programmer A defines class Person that includes properties FirstName and LastName. | ```csharp
public class Person
{
  public string FirstName
  {
      get { return _FirstName; }
      set { _FirstName = value; }
  }
  private string _FirstName;

  public string LastName
  {
      get { return _LastName; }
      set { _LastName = value; }
  }
  private string _LastName;
}
``` |
```

TABLE 6.1: Why the New Modifier? *(Continued)*

Activity	Code
Programmer B derives from `Person` and defines `Contact` with the additional property, `Name`. In addition, she defines the `Program` class whose `Main()` method instantiates `Contact`, assigns `Name`, and then prints out the name.	```csharp\npublic class Contact : Person\n{\n public string Name\n {\n get\n {\n return FirstName + " " + LastName;\n }\n\n set\n {\n string names = value.Split(' ');\n // Error handling not shown.\n FirstName = names[0];\n LastName = names[1];\n }\n }\n}\n```
Later, Programmer A adds the Name property but instead of implementing the getter as `FirstName + " "` `+ LastName`, she implements it as `LastName + ", "` `+ FirstName`. Furthermore, she doesn't define the property as `virtual`, and she uses the property in a `DisplayName()` method.	```csharp\npublic class Person\n{\n public string Name\n {\n get\n {\n return LastName + ", " + FirstName;\n }\n\n set\n {\n string names = value.Split(', ');\n // Error handling not shown.\n LastName = names[0];\n FirstName = names[1];\n }\n }\n public static void Display(Person person)\n {\n // Display <LastName>, <FirstName>\n Console.WriteLine(person.Name);\n }\n}\n```

Because `Person.Name` is not `virtual`, Programmer A will expect `Display()` to use the `Person` implementation, even if a `Person`-derived data type, `Contact`, is passed in. However, Programmer B would expect

`Contact.Name` to be used in all cases where the variable data type is a `Contact`. (Programmer B would have no code where `Person.Name` was used, since no `Person.Name` property existed initially.) To allow the addition of `Person.Name` without breaking either programmer's expected behavior, you cannot assume `virtual` was intended. Furthermore, since C# requires an override member to explicitly use the `override` modifier, some other semantic must be assumed, instead of allowing the addition of a member in the base class to cause the derived class to no longer compile.

The semantic is the `new` modifier, and it hides a redeclared member of the derived class from the base class. Instead of calling the most derived member, a member of the base class calls the most derived member in the inheritance chain prior to the member with the `new` modifier. If the inheritance chain contains only two classes, then a member in the base class will behave as though no method was declared on the derived class (if the derived implementation redeclared the base class member). Although the compiler will report the warning shown in either Output 6.2 or Output 6.3, if neither `override` nor `new` is specified, then `new` will be assumed, thereby maintaining the desired version safety.

Consider Listing 6.14, for example. Its output appears in Output 6.4.

LISTING 6.14: **override** versus **new** Modifier

```
public class Program
{
  public class BaseClass
  {
      public void DisplayName()
      {
          Console.WriteLine("BaseClass");
      }
  }

    public class DerivedClass : BaseClass
    {
        // Compiler WARNING... new modifier assumed.
        public virtual void DisplayName()
        {
            Console.WriteLine("DerivedClass");
        }
    }

    public class SubDerivedClass : DerivedClass
    {
```

```
        public override void DisplayName()
        {
            Console.WriteLine("SubDerivedClass");
        }
    }

    public class SuperSubDerivedClass : SubDerivedClass
    {
        public new void DisplayName()
        {
            Console.WriteLine("SuperSubDerivedClass");
        }
    }

    public static void Main()
    {
        SuperSubDerivedClass superSubDerivedClass
            = new SuperSubDerivedClass();

        SubDerivedClass subDerivedClass = superSubDerivedClass;
        DerivedClass derivedClass = superSubDerivedClass;
        BaseClass baseClass = superSubDerivedClass;

        superSubDerivedClass.DisplayName();
        subDerivedClass.DisplayName();
        derivedClass.DisplayName();
        baseClass.DisplayName();
    }
}
```

OUTPUT 6.4:

```
SuperSubDerivedClass
SubDerivedClass
SubDerivedClass
BaseClass
```

These results occur for the following reasons.

- `SuperSubDerivedClass`: `SuperSubDerivedClass.Display-Name()` displays `SuperSubDerivedClass` because there is no derived class and hence, no overload.
- `SubDerivedClass`: `SubDerivedClass.DisplayName()` is the most derived member to override a base class's virtual member. `SuperSubDerivedClass.DisplayName()` is hidden because of its new modifier.

- `SubDerivedClass`: `DerivedClass.DisplayName()` is virtual and `SubDerivedClass.DisplayName()` is the most derived member to override it. As before, `SuperSubDerivedClass.DisplayName()` is hidden because of the new modifier.

- `BaseClass`: `BaseClass.DisplayName()` does not redeclare any base class member and it is not virtual; therefore, it is called directly.

When it comes to the CIL, the new modifier has no effect on what code the compiler generates. Its only effect is to remove the compiler warning that would appear otherwise.

sealed Modifier

Just as you can prevent inheritance using the sealed modifier on a class, virtual members may be sealed, too (see Listing 6.15). This prevents a subclass from overriding a base class member that was originally declared as virtual higher in the inheritance chain. The situation arises when a subclass B overrides a base class A's member and then needs to prevent any further overriding below subclass B.

LISTING 6.15: Sealing Members

```
class A
{
  public virtual void Method()
  {
  }
}
class B : A
{
  public override sealed void Method()

  {
  }
}

class C : B
{
  // ERROR:  Cannot override sealed members
  // public override void Method()
  // {
  // }
}
```

In this example, the use of the sealed modifier on class B's Method() declaration prevents C's overriding of Method().

base Member

In choosing to redeclare a member, developers often want to invoke the member on the base class (see Listing 6.16).

LISTING 6.16: Accessing a Base Member

```csharp
public class Address
{
    public string StreetAddress;
    public string City;
    public string State;
    public string Zip;

    public override string ToString()
    {
        return string.Format("{0}" + Environment.NewLine +
            "{1}, {2}  {3}",
            StreetAddress, City, State, Zip);
    }
}

public class InternationalAddress : Address
{
    public string Country;

    public override string ToString()
    {
        return base.ToString() + Environment.NewLine +
            Country;
    }
}
```

In Listing 6.16, InternationalAddress inherits from Address and implements ToString(). To call the base class's implementation you use the base keyword. The syntax is virtually identical to this, including support for using base as part of the constructor (discussed shortly).

Parenthetically, in the Address.ToString() implementation, you are required to override as well, because ToString() is also a member of object. Any members that are decorated with override are automatically designated as virtual, so additional child classes may further specialize the implementation.

Constructors

When instantiating a derived class, the runtime first invokes the base class's constructor so that the base class initialization is not circumvented. However, if there is no accessible (nonprivate) default constructor on the base class, then it is not clear how to construct the base class and the C# compiler reports an error.

To avoid the error caused by no accessible default constructor, programmers need to designate explicitly, in the derived class constructor header, which base constructor to run (see Listing 6.17).

LISTING 6.17: Specifying Which Base Constructor to Invoke

```csharp
public class PdaItem
{
  public PdaItem(string name)
  {
     Name = name;
  }

  // ...
}
```

```csharp
public class Contact : PdaItem
{
  public Contact(string name) :
     base(name)
  {
     Name = name;
  }

  public string Name
  {
     get{  // ...}
     set{  // ...}
  }

  // ...
}
```

By identifying the base constructor in the code, you let the runtime know which base constructor to invoke before invoking the derived class constructor.

Abstract Classes

Many of the inheritance examples so far have defined a class called `PdaItem` that defines the methods and properties common to `Contact`, `Appointment`, and so on, which are type objects that derive from `PdaItem`. `PdaItem` is not intended to be instantiated itself, however. A `PdaItem` instance has no meaning by itself; it has meaning only when it is used as a base class—to share default method implementations across the set of data types that derive from it. These characteristics are indicative of the need for `PdaItem` to be an **abstract** class. Abstract classes are designed for derivation only. It is not possible to instantiate an abstract class, except in the context of instantiating a class that derives from it.

■ BEGINNER TOPIC

Abstract Classes

Abstract classes represent abstract entities. Their **abstract members** define what an object derived from an abstract entity should contain, but they don't include the implementation. Often, much of the functionality within an abstract class is unimplemented, and before a class can successfully derive from an abstract class, it needs to provide the implementation for the abstract methods in its abstract base class.

To define an abstract class, C# requires the abstract modifier to the class definition, as shown in Listing 6.18.

LISTING 6.18: Defining an Abstract Class

```csharp
// Define an abstract class
public abstract class PdaItem
{
    private string _Name;

    public PdaItem(string name)
    {
        _Name = name;
    }
}
```

```
public virtual string Name
{
    get{ return _Name; }
    set{ _Name = value; }
}
}
```

```
public class Program
{
    public void Main()
    {
        PdaItem item;
        // ERROR:  Cannot create an instance of the abstract class
        // item = new PdaItem("Inigo Montoya");
    }
}
```

Although abstract classes cannot be instantiated, this restriction is a minor characteristic of an abstract class. Their primary significance is achieved when abstract classes include **abstract members**. An abstract member is a method or property that has no implementation. Its purpose is to force all derived classes to provide the implementation.

Consider Listing 6.19.

LISTING 6.19: Defining Abstract Members

```
// Define an abstract class
public abstract class PdaItem
{
    private string _Name;
    public PdaItem(string name)
    {
        _Name = name;
    }

    public virtual string Name
    {
        get{ return _Name; }
        set{ _Name = value; };
    }

    public abstract string GetSummary();
}
```

```
public class Contact : PdaItem
{
    public override string Name
```

```
    {
        get
        {
            return FirstName + " " + LastName;
        }

        set
        {
            string names = value.Split(' ');
            // Error handling not shown.
            FirstName = names[0];
            LastName = names[1];
        }
    }

    public string FirstName
    {
        get { return _FirstName; }
        set { _FirstName = value; }
    }
    private string _FirstName;

    public string LastName
    {
        get { return _LastName; }
        set { _LastName = value; }
    }
    private string _LastName;

    public string Address
    {
        get { return _Address; }
        set { _Address = value; }
    }
    private string _Address;


    public override string GetSummary()
    {
        return string.Format(
            "FirstName: {0}\n"
            + "LastName: {1}\n"
            + "Address: {2}", FirstName, LastName, Address);
    }
    // ...
}
```

Listing 6.19 defines the GetSummary() member as abstract, and therefore, it doesn't include any implementation. Then, the code overrides it within `Contact` and provides the implementation. Because abstract members are supposed to be overridden, such members are automatically virtual and cannot be declared so explicitly. In addition, abstract members cannot be private because derived classes would not be able to see them.

Language Contrast: C++ — Pure Virtual Functions

C++ allows for the definition of abstract functions using the cryptic notation `=0`. These functions are called pure virtual functions in C++. In contrast with C#, however, C++ does not require the class itself to have any special declaration. Unlike C#'s `abstract` class modifier, C++ has no class declaration change when the class includes pure virtual functions.

If you provide no `GetSummary()` implementation in `Contact`, the compiler will report an error. By declaring an abstract member, the abstract class programmer states that in order to form an "is a" relationship with the base class type (i.e., a `PdaItem`), it is necessary to implement the abstract members, the members for which the abstract class could not provide an appropriate default implementation.

■ BEGINNER TOPIC

Polymorphism

When the implementation for the same member signature varies between two or more classes, you have a key object-oriented principal: **polymorphism**. Poly" meaning many and "morph" meaning form, polymorphism refers to the fact that there are multiple implementations of the same signature. And since the same signature cannot be used multiple times within a single class, each implementation of the member signature occurs on a different class.

The idea behind polymorphism is that the object itself knows best how to perform a particular operation. Given multiple types of documents, each document type class knows best how to perform a `Print()` method for its corresponding document type. Therefore, instead of defining a single print method that includes a `switch` statement with the special logic to print each document type, with polymorphism you call the `Print()` method corresponding to the specific type of document you wish to print. For example, calling `Print()` on a word processing document class behaves according to word processing specifics, and calling the same method on a graphics document class will result in print behavior specific to the graphic. Given the document types, however, all you have to do to print a document is to call `Print()`, regardless of the type.

Moving the custom print implementation out of a `switch` statement offers several maintenance advantages. First, the implementation appears in the context of each document type's class rather than in a location far removed; this is in keeping with encapsulation. Second, adding a new document type doesn't require a change to the `switch` statement. Instead, all that is necessary is for the new document type class to implement the `Print()` signature.

Abstract members are intended to be a way to enable polymorphism. The base class specifies the signature of the method and the derived class provides implementation (see Listing 6.20).

LISTING 6.20: Using Polymorphism to List the `PdaItems`

```
public class Program
{
  public void Main()
  {
      PdaItem[] pda = new PdaItem[3];

      Contact contact = new Contact("Sherlock Holmes");
      contact.Address = "221B Baker Street, London, England";
      pda[0] = contact;

      Appointment appointment =
          new Appointment("Soccer tournament");
      appointment.StartDateTime = new DateTime(2006, 7, 18);
      appointment.EndDateTime = new DateTime(2006, 7, 19);
      appointment.Location = "Estádio da Machava"
      pda[1] = appointment;

      contact = new Contact("Anne Frank");
      contact.Address =
```

```
                "263 Prinsengracht, Amsterdam, Netherlands";
        pda[2] = contact;

        List(pda);
    }

    public static void List(PdaItem[] items)
    {
        // Implemented using polymorphism. The derived
        // type knows the specifics of implementing
        // GetSummary().
        foreach (PdaItem item in items)
        {
            Console.WriteLine("_____");
            Console.WriteLine(item.Summary());
        }
    }
}
```

The results of Listing 6.20 appear in Output 6.5.

OUTPUT 6.5:

```
FirstName: Sherlock
LastName: Holmes
Address: 221B Baker Street, London, England

Subject: Soccer tournament
Start: 7/18/2006 12:00:00 AM
End: 7/19/2006 12:00:00 AM
Location: Estádio da Machava

FirstName: Anne
LastName: Frank
Address: 263 Prinsengracht, Amsterdam, Netherlands
```

In this way, you can call the method on the base class but the implementation is specific to the derived class.

Everything Ultimately Derives from `System.Object`

Given any object, whether a custom class or one built into the system, the methods shown in Table 6.2 will be defined.

All of these methods appear on all objects through inheritance; all objects derive (either directly or via an inheritance chain) from `object`.

TABLE 6.2: Members of **System.Object**

Method Name	Description
public virtual bool Equals(object o)	Returns true if the object supplied as a parameter is equal in *value*, not necessarily in reference, to the instance.
public virtual int GetHashCode()	Returns an integer corresponding to an evenly spread hash code. This is useful for collections such as HashTable collections.
public Type GetType()	Returns an object of type System.Type corresponding to the type of the object instance.
public static bool ReferenceEquals(**object** a, **object** b)	Returns true if the two supplied parameters refer to the same object.
public virtual string ToString()	Returns a string representation of the object instance.
public virtual void Finalize()	An alias for the destructor; informs the object to prepare for termination. C# prevents calling this method directly.
protected object MemberwiseClone()	Clones the object in question by performing a shallow copy; references are copied, but not the data within a referenced type.

Even literals include these methods, enabling somewhat peculiar-looking code like this:

```
Console.WriteLine( 42.ToString() );
```

Again, everything derives from object, even class definitions that don't have any explicit derivation. The two declarations for PdaItem in Listing 6.21, therefore, result in identical CIL.

LISTING 6.21: **System.Object** Derivation Implied When No Derivation Is Specified Explicitly

```
public class PdaItem
{
  // ...
}
```

```
public class PdaItem : object
{
  // ...
}
```

When the `object`'s default implementation isn't sufficient, programmers can override one or more of the three virtual methods. Chapter 9 describes the details for doing this.

Verifying the Underlying Type with the `is` Operator

Because C# allows casting down the inheritance chain, it is sometimes desirable to determine what the underlying type is before attempting a conversion. Also, checking the type may be necessary for type-specific actions where polymorphism was not implemented. To determine the underlying type, C# provides the `is` operator (see Listing 6.22).

LISTING 6.22: **is** Operator Determining the Underlying Type

```
public static void Save(object data)
{
    if (data is string)
    {
        data = Encrypt((string) data);
    }

    // ...
}
```

Listing 6.22 encrypts the data if the underlying type is a `string`. This is significantly different from encrypting, simply because it successfully casts to a `string` since many types support casting to a `string`, and yet their underlying type is not a `string`.

Although this capability is important, you should consider polymorphism prior to using the is operator. Polymorphism enables support for expanding a behavior to other data types without modifying the implementation that defines the behavior. For example, deriving from a common base type and then using that type as the parameter to the Save() method avoids having to check for string explicitly and enables other data types to support encryption during the save by deriving from the same base type.

Conversion Using the as Operator

The advantage of the is operator is that it enables verification that a data item is of a particular type. The as operator goes one step further. It attempts a conversion to a particular data type just like a cast does. In contrast to a cast, however, the as operator assigns null to the target if the conversion is unsuccessful. This is significant because it avoids the exception that could result from casting. Listing 6.23 demonstrates using the as operator.

LISTING 6.23: Data Conversion Using the **as** Operator

```
object Print(IDocument document)
{
  if(thing != null)
  {
      // Print document...
  }
  else
  {
  }
}

static void Main()
{
  object data;

  // ...

  Print(data as Document);
}
```

By using the `as` operator, you are able to avoid additional try-catch handling code if the conversion is invalid because the `as` operator provides a way to attempt a cast without throwing an exception if the cast fails.

One advantage of the `is` operator over the `as` operator is that the latter cannot successfully determine the underlying type. The latter potentially casts up or down an inheritance chain, as well as across to types supporting the cast operator. Therefore, unlike the `as` operator, the `is` operator can determine the underlying type.

SUMMARY

This chapter discussed how to specialize a class by deriving from it and adding additional methods and properties. This included a discussion of the `private` and `protected` access modifiers that control the level of encapsulation.

This chapter also investigated the details of overriding the base class implementation, and alternatively hiding it using the `new` modifier. To control overriding, C# provides the `virtual` modifier, which identifies to the deriving class developer which members she intends for derivation. For preventing any derivation altogether you learned about the `sealed` modifier on the class. Similarly, the `sealed` modifier on a member prevents further overriding from subclasses.

This chapter ended with a brief discussion of how all types derive from `object`. Chapter 9 discusses this derivation further, with a look at how `object` includes three virtual methods with specific rules and guidelines that govern overloading. Before you get there, however, you need to consider another programming paradigm that builds on object-oriented programming: interfaces. This is the subject of Chapter 7.

■7■
Interfaces

P OLYMORPHISM IS AVAILABLE not only via inheritance (as discussed in the previous chapter), but also via interfaces. Unlike abstract classes, interfaces cannot include any implementation. Like abstract classes, however, interfaces define a set of members that classes can rely on in order to support a particular feature.

By implementing an interface, a class defines its capabilities. The interface implementation relationship is a "can do" relationship: The class can do what the interface requires. The interface defines the contract between the classes that implement the interface and the classes that use the interface. Classes that implement interfaces define methods with the same signatures as the implemented interfaces. This chapter discusses defining, implementing, and using interfaces.

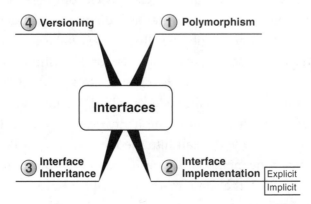

Introducing Interfaces

▪ BEGINNER TOPIC

Why Interfaces?

Implemented interfaces are like appliances with wall plugs. The wall plug is the interface that appliances support in order to receive AC power. An appliance can use that power in countless ways, but in order to plug into a wall socket, an appliance must supply a compatible wall plug. What the appliance does with the power corresponds to how an interface implementation varies from class to class. The specification that defines a wall plug is the contract that must be supported in order for an appliance to plug into the wall plug. Similarly, an interface defines a contract that a class must support in order to gain the capability that the interface provides.

Consider the following example: An innumerable number of file compression formats are available (`.zip`, `.7-zip`, `.cab`, `.lha`, `.tar`, `.tar.gz`, `.tar.bz2`, `.bh`, `.rar`, `.arj`, `.arc`, `.ace`, `.zoo`, `.gz`, `.bzip2`, `.xxe`, `.mime`, `.uue`, and `.yenc`, just to name a few). If you created classes for each compression format, you could end up with different method signatures for each compression implementation and no ability for a standard calling convention across them. Although the method signature could be defined in an abstract member of a base class, deriving from a common base type uses up a class's one and only inheritance, with an unlikely chance of sharing code across the various compression implementations, thereby making the potential of a base class implementation useless.

Instead of sharing a common base class, each compression class needs to implement a common interface. Interfaces define the contract that a class supports in order to interact with the other classes that expect the interface. Although there are many potential compression algorithms, if all of them could implement the `IFileCompression` interface and its `Compress()` and `Uncompress()` methods, then the code for calling the algorithm on any particular compression class would simply involve a cast to the `IFileCompression` interface and a call into the members, regardless of which class implemented the methods. The result is polymorphism because each compression class has the same method signature but individual implementations of that signature.

The naming convention for interfaces is to use Pascal case, with an I prefix. The IFileCompression interface shown in Listing 7.1 is an example of such a name and interface definition.

LISTING 7.1: Defining an Interface

```
interface IFileCompression
{
  void Compress(string targetFileName, string[] fileList);
  void Uncompress(
      string compressedFileName, string expandDirectoryName);
}
```

IFileCompression defines the methods a class implements to work with other compression-related classes. The power of defining the interface concerns the ability to switch between implementations without modifying the calling code, as long as each compression class implements the IFile-Compression interface.

One key characteristic of an interface is that it has no implementation and no data. Method declarations have a single semicolon in place of curly brackets after the header. Fields (data) cannot appear on an interface. When an interface requires the derived class to have certain data, it uses a property rather than a field. Since the property does not contain any implementation as part of the interface declaration, it doesn't reference a backing field.

Given that the purpose of the interface is to define the contract between multiple classes, defining private or protected members would make them inaccessible to other classes, defeating the purpose of the interface. Therefore, C# does not allow access modifiers on interface members, and instead it automatically defines them as public.

Polymorphism through Interfaces

Consider another example (see Listing 7.2): IListable defines the members a class needs to support in order for the ConsoleListControl class to display it. As such, any class that implements IListable will have the capability of using the ConsoleListControl to display itself. The IListable interface requires a read-only property, ColumnValues.

LISTING 7.2: Implementing and Using Interfaces

```csharp
interface IListable
{
  // Return the value of each column
  // in the row.
  string[] ColumnValues
  {
      get;
  }
}
```

```csharp
class Contact : PdaItem, IListable
{
  string[]ColumnValues
  {
      get
      {
        // ...
      }
  }
}
```

```csharp
class Publication : IListable
{
  string[]ColumnValues
  {
      get
      {
        // ...
      }
  }
}
```

```csharp
class Program
{
  public static void Main()
  {
      Contact[] contacts = new Contact[6];
      contacts[0] = new Contact(
          "Dick", "Traci",
          "123 Main St., Spokane, WA  99037",
          "123-123-1234");
      contacts[1] = new Contact(
          "Andrew", "Littman",
          "1417 Palmary St., Dallas, TX 55555",
          "555-123-4567");
      contacts[2] = new Contact(
          "Mary", "Hartfelt",
```

```
                "1520 Thunder Way, Elizabethton, PA 44444",
                "444-123-4567");
        contacts[3] = new Contact(
                "John", "Lindherst",
                "1 Aerial Way Dr., Monteray, NH 88888",
                "222-987-6543");
        contacts[4] = new Contact(
                "Pat", "Wilson",
                "565 Irving Dr., Parksdale, FL 22222",
                "123-456-7890");
        contacts[5] = new Contact(
                "Jane", "Doe",
                "123 Main St., Aurora, IL 66666",
                "333-345-6789");

        // Classes are cast implicitly to
        // their supported interfaces
        ConsoleListControl.List(Contact.Headers, contacts);

        Console.WriteLine();

        Publication[] publications = new Publication[3] {
            new Publication("Celebration of Discipline",
                "Richard Foster", 1978),
            new Publication("Orthodoxy",
                "G.K. Chesterton", 1908),
            new Publication(
                "The Hitchhiker's Guide to the Galaxy",
                "Douglas Adam", 1979)
            };
        ConsoleListControl.List(
            Publication.Headers, publications);
    }
}
```

```
class ConsoleListControl
{
    public static void List(string[] headers, IListable[] items)
    {
        int[] columnWidths = DisplayHeaders(headers);

        for (int count = 0; count < items.Length; count++)
        {
            string[] values = items[count].ColumnValues;
            DisplayItemRow(columnWidths, values);
        }
    }

    private static int[] DisplayHeaders(string[] headers)
    {
```

```
    // ...
    string tab = string.Empty;
    int[] columnWidths = new int[headers.Length];
    for (int count = 0; count < headers.Length; count++)
    {
        Console.Write(tab + headers[count]);
        if (tab == string.Empty)
        {
            tab = "\t";
        }
        columnWidths[count] = headers[count].Length;
    }
    Console.WriteLine();
    return columnWidths;
}

private static void DisplayItemRow(
    int[] columnWidths, string[] values)
{
    // ...
    string tab = string.Empty;
    for (int count = 0;
        count < values.Length; count++)
    {
        Console.Write(
            "{0}{1,-" + columnWidths[count] + "}",
            tab, values[count]);
        if (tab == string.Empty)
        {
            tab = "\t";
        }
    }
    Console.WriteLine();
}
}
```

The results of Listing 7.2 appear in Output 7.1

In Listing 7.2, the ConsoleListControl can display seemingly unrelated classes (Contact and Publication). A displayable class is defined simply by whether it implements the required interface. As a result, the ConsoleListControl.List() method relies on polymorphism to appropriately display whichever set of objects it is passed. Each class has its own implementation of ColumnValues, and converting a class to IListable still allows the particular class's implementation to be invoked.

OUTPUT 7.1:

```
First Name  Last Name   Phone         Address
Dick        Traci       123-123-1234  123 Main St., Spokane, WA  99037
Andrew      Littman     555-123-4567  1417 Palmary St., Dallas, TX 55555
Mary        Hartfelt    444-123-4567  1520 Thunder Way, Elizabethton, PA↵
44444
John        Lindherst   222-987-6543  1 Aerial Way Dr., Monteray, NH ↵
88888
Pat         Wilson      123-456-7890  565 Irving Dr., Parksdale, FL ↵
22222
Jane        Doe         333-345-6789  123 Main St., Aurora, IL 66666

Title                                 Author           Year
Celebration of Discipline             Richard Foster   1978
Orthodoxy                             G.K. Chesterton  1908
The Hitchhiker's Guide To The Galaxy  Douglas Adam     1979
```

Interface Implementation

Declaring a class to implement an interface is similar to deriving from a base class in that the implemented interfaces appear in a comma-separated list along with the base class (order is not significant). The only difference is that classes can implement multiple interfaces. An example appears in Listing 7.3.

LISTING 7.3: Implementing an Interface

```csharp
public class Contact : PdaItem, IListable, IComparable
{
    // ...

    #region IComparable Members
    /// <summary>
    ///
    /// </summary>
    /// <param name="obj"></param>
    /// <returns>
    /// Less than zero:    This instance is less than obj.
    /// Zero               This instance is equal to obj.
    /// Greater than zero  This instance is greater than obj.
    /// </returns>
    public int CompareTo(object obj)
    {
        int result;
        Contact contact = obj as Contact;

        if (obj == null)
        {
```

```
            // This instance is greater than obj.
            result = 1;
        }
        else if (obj == null)
        {
            throw new ArgumentException("obj is not a Contact");
        }
        else if( Contact.ReferenceEquals(this, obj) )
        {
            result = 0;
        }
        else
        {
            result = LastName.CompareTo(contact.LastName);
            if (result == 0)
            {
                result = FirstName.CompareTo(contact.FirstName);
            }
        }
        return result;
    }
    #endregion

    #region IListable Members
    string[] IListable.ColumnValues
    {
        get
        {
            // Use index to simplify swapping the order
            int index = 0;
            string[] values = new string[4];
            values[index++] = FirstName;
            values[index++] = LastName;
            values[index++] = Phone;
            values[index++] = Address;
            return values;
        }
    }
    #endregion
}
```

Once a class declares that it implements an interface, all members of the interface must be implemented. The member implementation may throw a NotImplementedException type exception in the method body, but nonetheless, the method has an implementation from the compiler's perspective.

One important characteristic of interfaces is that they can never be instantiated; you cannot use new to create an interface, and therefore, interfaces cannot even have constructors or finalizers. Interface instances are available only from types that implement them. Furthermore, interfaces cannot include static members. One key interface purpose is polymorphism, and polymorphism without an instance of the implementing type is of little value.

Each interface member behaves like an abstract method, forcing the derived class to implement the member. Therefore, it is not possible to use the abstract modifier on interface members explicitly. However, there are two variations on implementation: **explicit** and **implicit**.

Explicit Member Implementation

Explicit members are accessible only when cast to the implemented interface. For example, to call IListable.ColumnValues in Listing 7.4, you must first cast the contact to IListable because of ColumnValues's explicit implementation.

LISTING 7.4: Calling Explicit Interface Member Implementations

```
string[] values;
Contact contact1, contact2;

// ...

// ERROR:  Unable to call ColumnValues() directly
//         on a contact.
// values = contact1.ColumnValues;

// First cast to IListable.
values = ((IListable)contact2).ColumnValues;
// ...
```

The cast and the call to ColumnValues occur within the same statement in this case. Alternatively, you could assign contact2 to an IListable variable before calling ColumnValues.

Declaring an explicit interface member implementation involves prefixing the member name with the interface name (see Listing 7.5).

LISTING 7.5: Explicit Interface Implementation

```csharp
public class Contact : PdaItem, IListable, IComparable
{
    // ...

    public int CompareTo(object obj)
    {
        // ...
    }

    #region IListable Members
    string[] IListable.ColumnValues
    {
        get
        {
            // Use index to simplify swapping the order
            int index = 0;
            string[] values = new string[4];
            values[index++] = FirstName;
            values[index++] = LastName;
            values[index++] = Phone;
            values[index++] = Address;
            return values;
        }
    }
    #endregion
}
```

Listing 7.5 implements `ColumnValues` explicitly, for example, because it prefixes the property with `IListable`. Furthermore, since explicit interface implementations are directly associated with the interface, there is no need to modify them with `virtual`, `override`, or `public`, and, in fact, these modifiers are not allowed. The C# compiler assumes these modifiers; otherwise, the implementation would be meaningless.

Implicit Member Implementation

Notice that `CompareTo()` in Listing 7.5 does not include the `IComparable` prefix; it is implemented implicitly. With implicit member implementation, it is only necessary for the class member's signature to match the interface members signature. Interface member implementation does not require the `override` keyword or any indication that this member is tied to the interface. Furthermore, since the member is declared just as any other class member, code that calls implicitly implemented members can do so directly, just as it would any other class member:

```
result = contact1.CompareTo(contact2);
```

In other words, implicit member implementation does not require a cast because the member is not hidden from direct invocation on the implementing class.

Many of the modifiers disallowed on an explicit member implementation are required or are optional on an implicit implementation. For example, implicit member implementations must be `public`. Furthermore, `virtual` is optional depending on whether derived classes may override the implementation. Eliminating `virtual` will cause the member to behave as though it is `sealed`. Interestingly, `override` is not allowed because the interface declaration of the member does not include implementation, so `override` is not meaningful.

Explicit versus Implicit Interface Implementation

The key difference between implicit and explicit member interface implementation is obviously not in the method declaration, but in the accessibility from outside the class. Since explicit interface members are hidden without casting to the interface type, they provide a higher degree of encapsulation. Here are several guidelines that will help you choose between an explicit and an implicit implementation.

- Is the member a core part of the class functionality?

  Consider the `ColumnValues` property implementation on the `Contact` class. This member is not an integral part of a `Contact` type but a peripheral member probably accessed only by the `ConsoleListControl` class. As such, it doesn't make sense for the member to be immediately visible on a `Contact` object, cluttering up what could potentially already be a large list of members.

  Alternatively, consider the `IFileCompression.Compress()` member. Including an implicit `Compress()` implementation on a `ZipCompression` class is a perfectly reasonable choice, since `Compress()` is a core part of the `ZipCompression` class's behavior, so it should be directly accessible from the `ZipCompression` class.

- Is the interface member name appropriate as a class member?

  Consider an `ITrace` interface with a member called `Dump()` that writes out a class's data to a trace log. Implementing `Dump()` implicitly on a `Person` or `Truck` class would result in confusion as to what operation the method performs. Instead, it is preferable to implement the member explicitly so that only from a data type of `ITrace`, where the meaning is clearer, can the `Dump()` method be called. Consider using an explicit implementation if a member's purpose is unclear on the implementing class.

- Is there already a class member with the same name?

  Explicit interface member implementation will uniquely distinguish a member. Therefore, if there is already a method implementation on a class, a second one can be provided with the same name as long as it is an explicit interface member.

Much of the decision regarding implicit versus explicit interface member implementation comes down to intuition. However, these questions provide suggestions about what to consider when making your choice. Since changing an implementation from implicit to explicit results in a version-breaking change, it is better to err on the side of defining interfaces explicitly, allowing them to be changed to implicit later on. Furthermore, since the decision between implicit and explicit does not have to be consistent across all interface members, defining some methods as explicit and others as implicit is fully supported.

Casting between the Implementing Class and Its Interfaces

Just as with a derived class and a base type, casting from an object to its implemented interface is an implicit cast. No cast operator is required because an instance of the implementing class will always contain all the members in the interface, and therefore, the object will always cast successfully to the interface type.

Although the cast will always be successful from the implementing class to the implemented interface, many different classes could implement a particular interface, so you can never be certain that a downward cast from the interface to the implementing class will be successful. The result is that casting from an interface to its implementing class requires an explicit cast.

Interface Inheritance

Interfaces can derive from each other, resulting in an interface that inherits all the members in its base interfaces. As shown in Listing 7.6, the interfaces directly derived from IReadableSettingsProvider are the explicit base interfaces.

LISTING 7.6: Deriving One Interface from Another

```
interface IReadableSettingsProvider
{
    string GetSetting(string name, string defaultValue);
}
```

```
interface ISettingsProvider : IReadableSettingsProvider
{
    void SetSetting(string name, string value);
}
```

```
class FileSettingsProvider : ISettingsProvider
{
    #region ISettingsProvider Members
    public void SetSetting(string name, string value)
    {
        // ...
    }
    #endregion

    #region IReadableSettingsProvider Members
    public string GetSetting(string name, string defaultValue)
    {
        // ...
    }
    #endregion
}
```

In this case, ISettingsProvider derives from IReadableSettingsProvider and, therefore, inherits its members. If IReadableSettingsProvider also had an explicit base interface, ISettingsProvider would inherit those members too, and the full set of interfaces in the derivation hierarchy would simply be the accumulation of base interfaces.

It is interesting to note that if GetSetting() is implemented explicitly, it must be done using IReadableSettingsProvider. The declaration with ISettingsProvider in Listing 7.7 will not compile.

LISTING 7.7: Explicit Member Declaration without the Containing Interface (Failure)

```
// ERROR:  GetSetting() not available on ISettingsProvider
string ISettingsProvider.GetSetting(
  string name, string defaultValue)
{
  // ...
}
```

The results of Listing 7.7 appear in Output 7.2.

OUTPUT 7.2:

```
'ISettingsProvider.GetSetting' in explicit interface declaration
is not a member of interface.
```

This output appears in addition to an error indicating that IReadable-SettingsProvider.GetSetting() is not implemented. The fully qualified interface member name used for explicit interface member implementation must reference the interface name in which it was originally declared.

Even though a class implements an interface (ISettingsProvider) which is derived from a base interface (IReadableSettingsProvider), the class can still declare implementation of both interfaces overtly, as Listing 7.8 demonstrates.

LISTING 7.8: Using a Base Interface in the Class Declaration

```
class FileSettingsProvider : ISettingsProvider,
    IReadableSettingsProvider
{
    #region ISettingsProvider Members
    public void SetSetting(string name, string value)
    {
        // ...
```

```
    }
    #endregion

    #region IReadableSettingsProvider Members
    public string GetSetting(string name, string defaultValue)
    {
        // ...
    }
    #endregion
}
```

In this listing, there is no change to the interface's implementations on the class, and although the additional interface implementation declaration on the class header is superfluous, it can provide better readability.

The decision to provide multiple interfaces rather than just one combined interface depends largely on what the interface designer wants to require of the implementing class. By providing an `IReadableSettings-Provider` interface, the designer communicates that implementers are only required to implement a settings provider that retrieves settings. They do not have to be able to write to those settings. This reduces the implementation burden by not imposing the complexities of writing settings as well.

In contrast, implementing `ISettingsProvider` assumes that there is never a reason to have a class that can write settings without reading them. The inheritance relationship between `ISettingsProvider` and `IReadable-SettingsProvider`, therefore, forces the combined total of both interfaces on the `ISettingsProvider` class.

Multiple Interface Inheritance

Just as classes can implement multiple interfaces, interfaces can inherit from multiple interfaces, and the syntax is consistent with class derivation and implementation, as shown in Listing 7.9.

LISTING 7.9: Multiple Interface Inheritance

```
interface IReadableSettingsProvider
{
    string GetSetting(string name, string defaultValue);
}
```

```
interface IWriteableSettingsProvider
{
  void SetSetting(string name, string value);
}
```

```
interface ISettingsProvider : IReadableSettingsProvider,
    IWriteableSettingsProvider
{
}
```

It is unusual to have an interface with no members, but if implementing both interfaces together is predominant, it is a reasonable choice for this case. The difference between Listing 7.9 and Listing 7.6 is that it is now possible to implement `IWriteableSettingsProvider` without supplying any read capability. Listing 7.6's `FileSettingsProvider` is unaffected, but if it used explicit member implementation, specifying which interface a member belongs to changes slightly.

Implementing Multiple Inheritance via Interfaces

As Listing 7.3 demonstrated, a single class can implement any number of interfaces in addition to deriving from a single class. This feature provides a possible enhancement to work around the lack of multiple inheritance support in C# classes. The process uses aggregation as described in the previous chapter, but you can vary the structure slightly by adding an interface to the mix, as shown in Listing 7.10.

LISTING 7.10: Working around Single Inheritance Using Aggregation with Interfaces

```
public class PdaItem
{
  // ...
  protected Guid ObjectKey
  {
      get { return _ObjectKey; }
      set { _ObjectKey = value; }
  }
  private Guid _ObjectKey;

  public virtual string Name
  {
      get { return _Name; }
      set { _Name = value; }
```

```csharp
   }
   private string _Name;

   public string DateTimeLastUpdate
   {
       get { return _DateTimeLastUpdate; }
       set { _DateTimeLastUpdate = value; }
   }
   private string _DateTimeLastUpdate;
}

interface IPerson
{
    string FirstName
    {
       get;
       set;
    }

    string LastName
    {
       get;
       set;
    }
}

public class Person : IPerson
{
  // ...
  public string FirstName
  {
      get { return _FirstName; }
      set { _FirstName = value; }
  }
  private string _FirstName;

  public string LastName
  {
      get { return _LastName; }
      set { _LastName = value; }
  }
  private string _LastName;
}

public class Contact : PdaItem, IPerson
{
  private Person Person
  {
      get { return _Person; }
      set { _Person = value; }
```

```
        }
    private Person _Person;


    public string FirstName
    {
        get { return _Person.FirstName; }
        set { _Person.FirstName = value; }
    }


    public string LastName
    {
        get { return _Person.LastName; }
        set { _Person.LastName = value; }
    }


    // ...
    public string Address
    {
        get { return _Address; }
        set { _Address = value; }
    }
    private string _Address;


    public string Phone
    {
        get { return _Phone; }
        set { _Phone = value; }
    }
    private string _Phone;
}
```

IPerson ensures that the signatures between the Person members and
the same members duplicated onto Contact are consistent. The implementation is still not synonymous with multiple inheritance, however,
because new members added to Person will not be added to Contact.

■ **BEGINNER TOPIC**

Interface Diagramming
Interfaces in a UML-like figure take two possible forms. First, you can
show the interface as though it is an inheritance relationship similar to a
class inheritance, as demonstrated in Figure 7.1 between IPerson and
IContact. Alternatively, you can show the interface using a small circle,

often referred to as a lollipop, exemplified by `IPerson` and `IContact` in Figure 7.1.

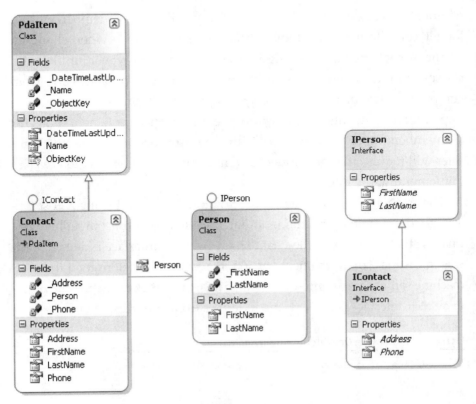

FIGURE 7.1: Working around Single Inheritances with Aggregation and Interfaces

In Figure 7.1, `Contact` derives from `PdaItem` and implements `IContact`. In addition, it aggregates the `Person` class, which implements `IPerson`. Although the Visual Studio 2005 Class Designer does not support this, interfaces are sometimes shown as using a derivation-type arrow to a class. For example, `Person` could have an arrow to `IPerson` instead of a lollipop.

Versioning

When creating a new version of a component or application that other developers have programmed against, you should not change interfaces. Because interfaces define a contract between the implementing class and the class using the interface, changing the interface is changing the contract, which will possibly break any code written against the interface.

Changing or removing a particular interface member signature is obviously a code-breaking change, as any call to that member will no longer compile without modification. The same is true when changing public or protected member signatures on a class. However, unlike with classes, adding members to an interface could also prevent code from compiling without additional changes. The problem is that any class implementing the interface must do so entirely, and implementations for all members must be provided. With new interface members, the compiler will require that developers add new interface members to the class implementing the interface.

The creation of `IDistributedSettingsProvider` in Listing 7.11 serves as a good example of extending an interface in a version-compatible way. Imagine that at first, only the `ISettingsProvider` interface is defined (as it was in Listing 7.6). In the next version, however, it is determined that per-machine settings are required. To enable this, the `IDistributedSettings-Provider` interface is created, and it derives from `ISettingsProvider`.

LISTING 7.11: Deriving One Interface from Another

```
interface IDistributedSettingsProvider : ISettingsProvider
{
  /// <summary>
  /// Get the settings for a particular machine.
  /// </summary>
  /// <param name="machineName">
  /// The machine name the setting is related to</param>
  /// <param name="name">The name of the setting</param>
  /// <param name="defaultValue">
  /// The value returned if the setting is not found.</param>
  /// <returns>The specified setting</returns>
  string GetSetting(
      string machineName, string name, string defaultValue);

  /// <summary>
  /// Set the settings for a particular machine.
  /// </summary>
  /// <param name="machineName">
  /// The machine name the setting is related to.</param>
  /// <param name="name">The name of the setting.</param>
  /// <param name="value">The value to be persisted.</param>
  /// <returns>The specified setting</returns>
```

```
   void SetSetting(
        string machineName, string name, string value);
}
```

The important factor is that programmers with classes that implement `ISettingsProvider` can choose to upgrade the implementation to include `IDistributedSettingsProvider`, or they can ignore it.

If instead of creating a new interface, the machine-related methods are added to `ISettingsProvider`, then classes implementing this interface will no longer successfully compile with the new interface definition, and instead a version-breaking change will occur.

Changing interfaces during the development phase is obviously acceptable, although perhaps laborious if implemented extensively. However, once an interface is released, it should not be changed. Instead, a second interface should be created, possibly deriving from the original interface.

(Listing 7.11 includes XML comments describing the interface members, as discussed further in Chapter 9.)

Interfaces Compared with Classes

Interfaces introduce another category of data types. (They are one of the few categories of types that don't extend `System.Object`.) Unlike classes, however, interfaces can never be instantiated. An interface instance is accessible only via a reference to an object that implements the interface. It is not possible to use the `new` operator with an interface; therefore, interfaces cannot contain any constructors or finalizers. Furthermore, static members are not allowed on interfaces.

Interfaces are closer to abstract classes, sharing such features as the lack of instantiation capability. Table 7.1 lists additional comparisons.

Given that abstract classes and interfaces have their own sets of advantages and disadvantages, you must make a cost-benefit decision based on the comparisons in Table 7.1 in order to make the right choice.

SUMMARY

Interfaces are a critical extension of object-oriented programming. Their value was accentuated during the days of Component Object Model (COM)

TABLE 7.1: Comparing Abstract Classes and Interfaces

Abstract Classes	Interfaces
Cannot be instantiated independently from their derived classes. Abstract class constructors are called only by their derived classes.	Cannot be instantiated.
Define abstract member signatures that base classes must implement.	Implementation of all members of the interface occurs in the base class. It is not possible to implement only some members within the implementing class.
Are more extensible than interfaces, without breaking any version compatibility. With abstract classes, it is possible to add additional nonabstract members that all derived classes can inherit.	Extending interfaces with additional members breaks the version compatibility.
Can include data stored in fields.	Cannot store any data. Fields can be specified only on the deriving classes. The workaround for this is to define properties, but without implementation.
Allow for (virtual) members that have implementation and, therefore, provide a default implementation of a member to the deriving class.	All members are automatically virtual and cannot include any implementation.
Deriving from an abstract class uses up a subclass's one and only base class option.	Although no default implementation can appear, classes implementing interfaces can continue to derive from one another.

programming, when interfaces defined the API between components and were critical to the versioning strategy through the life of a component.

Interfaces provide functionality similar to abstract classes but without using up the single-inheritance option, while constantly supporting derivation from multiple interfaces.

In C#, the implementation of interfaces can be either explicit or implicit, depending on whether the implementing class is to expose an interface member directly or only via a cast to the interface. Furthermore, the granularity of whether the implementation is explicit or implicit is at the member level: One member may be implicit while another on the same interface is explicit.

The next chapter looks at value types and discusses the importance of defining custom value types; at the same time, the chapter points out the subtle foibles that they can introduce.

■8■

Value Types

Y OU HAVE USED VALUE TYPES throughout this book. This chapter discusses not only using value types, but also defining custom value types. There are two categories of value types. The first category is structs. This chapter discusses how structs enable programmers to define new value types that behave very similarly to most of the predefined types discussed in Chapter 2. The key is that any newly defined value types have their own custom data and methods. The second category of value types is enums. This chapter discusses how to use enums to define sets of constant values.

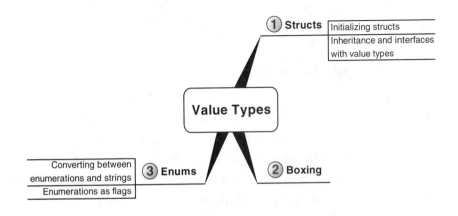

Structs

▪ BEGINNER TOPIC

Categories of Types

All types fall into two categories: reference types and value types. The differences between the types in each category stem from the fact that each category uses a different location in memory. To review, this Beginner Topic reintroduces the value type/reference type discussion to refamiliarize those who are unfamiliar with it.

Value Types

Value types directly contain their values, as shown in Figure 8.1. In other words, the variable refers to the same location in memory that the value is stored. Because of this, when a different variable is assigned the same value, a memory copy of the original variable's value is made to the location of the new variable. A second variable of the same value type cannot refer to the same location in memory as the first variable. So changing the value of the first variable will not affect the value in the second.

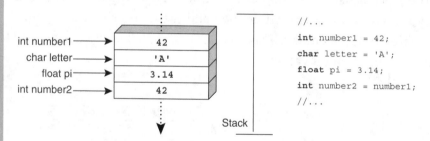

FIGURE 8.1: Value Types Contain the Data Directly

Similarly, passing a value type to a method such as `Console.WriteLine()` will also result in a memory copy, and any changes to the parameter value inside the method will not affect the original value within the calling function. Since value types require a memory copy, they generally should be defined to consume a small amount of memory (less than 16 bytes approximately).

The amount of memory that is required for the value type is fixed at compile time and will not change at runtime. This fixed size allows value types to be stored in the area of memory known as the **stack**.

Reference Types

In contrast, **reference types** and the variables that refer to them point to the data storage location (see Figure 8.2). Reference types store the reference (memory address) where the data is located, instead of the data directly. Therefore, to access the data, the runtime will read the memory location out of the variable and then jump to the location in memory that contains the data. The memory area of the data a reference type points to is the **heap**.

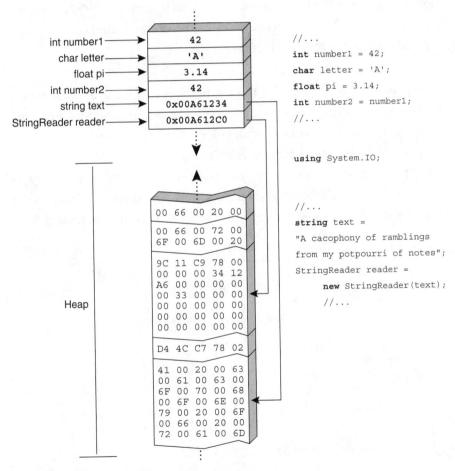

FIGURE 8.2: Reference Types Point to the Heap

Dereferencing a reference type to access its value involves an extra hop. However, a reference type does not require the same memory copy of the data that a value type does, resulting in circumstances when reference types are more efficient. When assigning one reference type variable to another reference type variable, only a memory copy of the address occurs, and as such, the memory copy required by a reference type is always the size of the address itself. (A 32-bit processor will copy 32 bits and a 64-bit processor will copy 64 bits, and so on.) Obviously, not copying the data would be faster than a value type's behavior if the data size is large.

Since reference types copy only the address of the data, two different variables can point to the same data, and changing the data through one variable will change the data for the other variable as well. This happens both for assignment and for method calls. Therefore, a method can affect the data of a reference type back at the caller.

Besides `string` and `object`, all the C# primitive types are value types. Furthermore, numerous additional value types are provided within the framework. It also is possible for developers to define their own value types that behave like user-defined primitives.

To define a custom value type, you use the same type of structure as you would to define classes and interfaces. The key difference in syntax is simply that value types use the keyword `struct`, as shown in Listing 8.1.

LISTING 8.1: Defining **struct**

```
// Use keyword struct to declare a value type.
struct Angle
{
    public Angle(int hours, int minutes, int seconds)
    {
        _Hours = hours;
        _Minutes = minutes;
        _Seconds = seconds;
    }

    public int Hours
    {
        get { return _Hours; }
    }
    private int _Hours;
```

```csharp
    public int Minutes
    {
        get { return _Minutes; }
    }
    private int _Minutes;

    public int Seconds
    {
        get { return _Seconds; }
    }
    private int _Seconds;

    public Angle Move(int hours, int minutes, int seconds)
    {
        return new Angle(
            Hours + hours,
            Minutes + minutes.
            Seconds + seconds)
    }

}

// Declaring a class - a reference type
// (declaring it as a struct would create a value type
// larger than 16 bytes.)
class Coordinate
{
  public Angle Longitude
  {
      get { return _Longitude; }
      set { _Longitude = value; }
  }
  private Angle _Longitude;

  public Angle Latitude
  {
      get { return _Latitude; }
      set { _Latitude = value; }
  }
  private Angle _Latitude;
}
```

This listing defines `Angle` as a value type that stores the hours, minutes, and seconds of an angle, either longitude or latitude. The resulting C# type is a **struct**.

> **NOTE**
>
> Although nothing in the language requires it, a good guideline is for value types to be immutable: Once you have instantiated a value type, you should not be able to modify the same instance. In scenarios where modification is desirable, you should create a new instance. Listing 8.1 supplies a `Move()` method that doesn't modify the instance of `Angle` but instead returns an entirely new instance.

Initializing structs

In addition to properties and fields, structs may contain methods and constructors. However, default (parameterless) constructors are not allowed. Sometimes (for instance, when instantiating an array) a value type's constructor will not be called because all array memory is initialized with zeroes instead. To avoid the inconsistency of default constructors being called only sometimes, C# prevents explicit definition of default constructors altogether. Because the compiler's implementation of an instance field assignment at declaration time is to place the assignment into the type's constructor, C# prevents instance field assignment at declaration time as well (see Listing 8.2).

LISTING 8.2: Initializing a **struct** Field within a Declaration, Resulting in an Error

```
struct Angle
{
  // ...
  // ERROR:  Fields cannot be initialized at declaration time
  // int _Hours = 42;
  // ...
}
```

This does not eliminate the need to initialize the field. In fact, for structs that are accessible only from within the assembly (structs decorated with internal or private modifiers), a warning is reported if the field fails to be initialized after instantiation.

Fortunately, C# supports constructors with parameters and they come with an interesting initialization requirement. They must initialize all fields within the struct. Failure to do so causes a compile error. The constructor in Listing 8.3 that initializes the property rather than the field, for example, produces a compile error.

LISTING 8.3: Accessing Properties before Initializing All Fields

```
// ERROR:   The 'this' object cannot be used before
//          all of its fields are assigned to
// public Angle(int hours, int minutes, int seconds)
// {
//     Hours = hours;      // Shorthand for this.Hours = hours;
//     Minutes = minutes   // Shorthand for this.Minutes = ...;
//     Seconds = seconds   // Shorthand for this.Seconds = ...;
// }
```

The error reports that methods and properties (Hours implies this.Hours) are accessed prior to the initialization of all fields. To resolve the issue, you need to initialize the fields directly, as demonstrated in Listing 8.1.

■ ADVANCED TOPIC

Using new with Value Types

Invoking the new operator on a reference type compiles to the CIL instruction newobj. new is available to value types as well, but in contrast, the underlying CIL instruction is initobj. This instruction initializes the memory with default values (the equivalent of assigning default(<type>) in C# 2.0).

Unlike classes, structs do not support finalizers. For local variable value types, memory is allocated on the stack, so there is no need for the garbage collector to handle the value type's cleanup and no finalizer is called before the stack is unwound. For value types that are part of a reference type, the data is stored on the heap and memory is cleaned up as part of the reference object's garbage collection.

Language Contrast: C++—struct Defines Type with Public Members

In C++, the difference between structs and classes is simply that by default, a struct's members are public. C# doesn't include this subtle distinction. The contrast is far greater in C#, where struct significantly changes the memory behavior from that of a class.

Using the `default` Operator

To provide a constructor that didn't require _Seconds would not avoid the requirement that _Seconds still required initialization. You can assign the default value of _Seconds using 0 explicitly or, in C# 2.0, using the `default` operator.

Listing 8.4 passes the default value into the `Angle` constructor that includes _Seconds. However, the default operator can be used outside of the `this` constructor call (_Seconds = default(int), for example). It is a way to specify the value for the default of a particular type.

LISTING 8.4: Using the **default** Operator to Retrieve the Default Value of a Type

```csharp
// Use keyword struct to declare a value type.
struct Angle
{
  public Angle(int hours, int minutes)
      : this( hours, minutes, default(int) )
  {
  }

  // ...
}
```

Inheritance and Interfaces with Value Types

All value types are sealed. In addition, all value types derive from System.ValueType. This means that the inheritance chain for structs is always from object to ValueType to the struct.

Value types can implement interfaces, too. Many of those built into the framework implement interfaces such as IComparable and IFormattable.

ValueType brings with it the behavior of value types, but it does not include any additional members (all of its members override object's virtual members). However, as with classes, you can override the virtual members of System.Object. The rules for overriding are virtually the same as with reference types (see Chapter 9). However, one difference is that with value types, the default implementation for GetHashCode() is to forward the call to the first non-null field within the struct. Also, Equals() makes significant use of reflection. This leads to the conclusion that if a value type is frequently used inside collections, especially dictionary-type collections that use hash codes, the value type should include overrides for both `Equals()` and `GetHashCode()`.

Boxing

Because local variable value types are stack based and their interfaces and `System.Object` are heap based, an important question to consider is what happens when a value type is converted to one of its implemented interfaces or to its root base class, `object`. The cast is known as **boxing** and it has special behavior. Casting from a value type to a reference type involves several steps.

1. First, memory is allocated on the heap that will contain the value type's data and a little overhead (a `SyncBlockIndex` and method table pointer).
2. Next, a memory copy occurs from the value type's data on the stack, into the allocated location on the heap.
3. Finally, the object or interface reference is updated to point at the location on the heap.

The reverse operation is **unboxing**. By definition, the unbox CIL instruction simply dereferences the data on the heap; it doesn't include the copy from the heap to the stack. In most cases with C#, however, a copy follows unboxing anyway.

Boxing and unboxing are important to consider because boxing has some performance and behavioral implications. Besides learning how to recognize them within C# code, a developer can count the box/unbox instructions in a particular snippet of code by looking through the CIL. Each operation has specific instructions, as shown in Table 8.1.

When boxing occurs in low volume, the performance concerns are irrelevant. However, boxing is sometimes subtle and frequent occurrences can make a difference with performance. Consider Listing 8.5 and Output 8.1.

TABLE 8.1: Boxing Code in CIL

C# Code	CIL Code

`static void Main()`
 	
`{`
 	
`    int number;`
`    object thing;`
 	
`    number = 42;`
 	
`    // Boxing`
`    thing = number;`
 	
`    // Unboxing`
`    number = (int)thing;`
 	
`    return;`
`}`
	`.method private hidebysig`
	`        static void  Main() cil managed`
	`    {`
	`    .entrypoint`
	`    // Code size       21 (0x15)`
	`    .maxstack  1`
	`    .locals init ([0] int32 number,`
	`              [1] object thing)`
	`    IL_0000:  nop`
	`    IL_0001:  ldc.i4.s    42`
	`    IL_0003:  stloc.0`
	`    IL_0004:  ldloc.0`
	`    IL_0005:  `**`box`**
	`              [mscorlib]System.Int32`
	`    IL_000a:  stloc.1`
	`    IL_000b:  ldloc.1`
	`    IL_000c:  `**`unbox.any`**
	`              [mscorlib]System.Int32`
	`    IL_0011:  stloc.0`
	`    IL_0012:  br.s        IL_0014`
	`    IL_0014:  ret`
	`} // end of method Program::Main`

LISTING 8.5: Subtle Box and Unbox Instructions

```csharp
class DisplayFibonacci
{
  static void Main()
  {

      int totalCount;
      System.Collections.ArrayList list =
          new System.Collections.ArrayList();

      Console.Write("Enter a number between 2 and 1000:");
      totalCount = int.Parse(Console.ReadLine());

      // Execution-time error:
      // list.Add(0);  // Cast to double or 'D' suffix required
                      // Whether cast or using 'D' suffix,
                      // CIL is identical.
      list.Add((double)0);
      list.Add((double)1);
      for (int count = 2; count < totalCount; count++)
      {
          list.Add(
              ((double)list[count - 1] +
```

```
                (double)list[count - 2]) );
        }

        foreach (double count in list)
        {
            Console.Write("{0}, ", count);
        }
    }
}
```

OUTPUT 8.1:

```
Enter a number between 2 and 1000:42
0, 1, 1, 2, 3, 5, 8, 13, 21, 34, 55, 89, 144, 233, 377, 610, 987, 1597,
2584, 4181, 6765, 10946, 17711, 28657, 46368, 75025, 121393, 196418,
317811, 514229, 832040, 1346269, 2178309, 3524578, 5702887, 9227465,
14930352, 24157817, 39088169, 63245986, 102334155, 165580141,
```

The code shown in Listing 8.5, when compiled, produces five box and three unbox instructions in the resulting CIL.

1. The first two box instructions occur in the initial calls to `list.Add()`. The signature for the `ArrayList` method is `int Add(object value)`. As such, any value type passed to this method is boxed.

2. Next are two unbox instructions in the call to `Add()` within the `for` loop. The return from an `ArrayList`'s index operator is always `object` because that is what `ArrayList` collects. In order to add the two values, however, you need to cast them back to `doubles`. This cast back from an object to a value type is an unbox call.

3. Now you take the result of the addition and place it into the `ArrayList` instance, which again results in a box operation. Note that the first two unbox instructions and this box instruction occur within a loop.

4. In the `foreach` loop, you iterate through each item in `ArrayList` and assign them to `count`. However, as you already saw, the items within `ArrayList` are `objects`, so assigning them to a `double` is unboxing each of them.

5. The signature for `Console.WriteLine()` that is called within the `foreach` loop is `void Console.Write(string format, object arg)`. As a result, each call to it invokes a box operation back from `double` and into `object`.

Obviously, you can easily improve this code by eliminating many of the boxing operations. Using an `object` rather than `double` in the last `foreach` loop is one improvement you can make. Another would be to change the `ArrayList` data type to one that supports a concept known as generics (see Chapter 12). The point, however, is that boxing can be rather subtle, so developers need to pay special attention and notice situations where it could potentially occur repeatedly and affect performance.

There is another unfortunate runtime-boxing-related problem. If you wanted to change the initial two `Add()` calls so that they did not use a cast (or a double literal), you would have to insert integers into the array list. Since `ints` will implicitly cast to `doubles`, this would appear to be an innocuous modification. However, the casts to `double` from within the `for` loop, and again in the assignment to `count` in the `foreach` loops, would fail. The problem is that immediately following the unbox operation is an attempt to perform a memory copy of the `int` into a `double`. You cannot do this without first casting to an `int`, because the code will throw an `InvalidCastException` at execution time. Listing 8.6 shows a similar error commented out and followed by the correct cast.

LISTING 8.6: Unboxing Must Be to the Underlying Type

```
// ...
int number;
object thing;
double bigNumber;

number = 42;
thing = number;
// ERROR: InvalidCastException
// bigNumber = (double)thing;
bigNumber = (double)(int)thing;
// ...
```

■ ADVANCED TOPIC

Value Types in the `lock` Statement

C# supports a `lock` statement for synchronizing code. The statement compiles down to `System.Threading.Monitor`'s `Enter()` and `Exit()` methods. These two methods must be called in pairs. `Enter()` records a lookup of the unique reference argument passed so that when `Exit()` is called with the same reference, the lock can be released. The trouble with using value types is the boxing. Therefore, each time `Enter()` or `Exit()` is called, a new value is created on the heap. Comparing the reference of one copy to the reference of a different copy will always return `false`, so you cannot hook up `Enter()` with the corresponding `Exit()`. Therefore, value types in the `lock()` statement are not allowed.

Listing 8.7 points out a few more runtime boxing idiosyncrasies and Output 8.2 shows the results.

LISTING 8.7: Subtle Boxing Idiosyncrasies

```
interface IAngle
{
    void MoveTo(int hours, int minutes, int seconds);
}
```

```
struct Angle : IAngle
{
    // ...


    // NOTE:  This makes Angle mutable, against the general
    //        guideline
    public void MoveTo(int hours, int minutes, int seconds)
    {
        _Hours = hours;
        _Minutes = minutes;
        _Seconds = seconds;
    }
}
```

```
class Program
{
  static void Main()
  {
    // ...

    Angle angle = new Angle(25, 58, 23);
    object objectAngle = angle;  // Box
    Console.Write( ((Angle)objectAngle).Hours);

    // Unbox and discard
    ((Angle)objectAngle).MoveTo(26, 58, 23);
    Console.Write( ((Angle)objectAngle).Hours);
```

```
        // Box, modify, and discard
        ((IAngle)angle).MoveTo(26, 58, 23);
        Console.Write(", " + ((Angle)angle).Hours);

        // Modify heap directly
        ((IAngle)objectAngle).MoveTo(26, 58, 23);
        Console.WriteLine(", " + ((Angle)objectAngle).Hours);

        // ...
    }
}
```

OUTPUT 8.2:

```
25, 25, 25, 26
```

Listing 8.7 uses the `Angle` struct and `IAngle` interface from Listing 8.1. Note also that the `IAngle.MoveTo()` interface changes `Angle` to be mutable. This brings out some of the idiosyncrasies and, in so doing, demonstrates the importance of the guideline to make structs immutable.

In the first two lines, you initialize `angle` and then box it into a variable called `objectAngle`. Next, you call `move` in order to change `Hours` to `26`. However, as the output demonstrates, no change actually occurs the first time. The problem is that in order to call `MoveTo()`, the compiler unboxes `objectAngle` and (by definition) places it on the stack. Although the stack value is successfully modified at execution time, this value is discarded and no change occurs on the heap location referenced by `objectAngle`.

In the next example, a similar problem occurs in reverse. Instead of calling `MoveTo()` directly, the value is cast to `IAngle`. The cast invokes a box instruction and the runtime copies the `angle` data to the heap. Next, the data on the heap is modified directly on the heap before the call returns. The result is that no copy back from the heap to the stack occurs. Instead, the modified heap data is ready for garbage collection while the data in `angle` remains unmodified.

In the last case, the cast to `IAngle` occurs with the data on the heap already, so no copy occurs. `MoveTo()` updates the `_Hours` value and the code behaves as desired.

■ ADVANCED TOPIC

Unboxing Avoided

As discussed earlier, the unboxing instruction does not include the copy back to the stack. In fact, some languages support the ability to access value types on the heap directly. This is generally not possible with C#. However, when accessing the boxed value via its interface, no copy is necessary.

Listing 8.7 added an interface implementation to the `Angle struct`. Listing 8.8 uses the interface to avoid unboxing.

LISTING 8.8: Avoiding Unboxing and Copying

```
int number;
object thing;
number = 42;
// Boxing
thing = number;
// No unbox instruction.
string text = ((IFormattable)thing).ToString(
    "X", null);
Console.WriteLine(text);
```

Interfaces are reference types anyway, so calling one of its members does not even require unboxing. Furthermore, calling a `struct`'s `ToString()` method (that overrides `object`'s `ToString()` method) does not require an unbox. When compiling, it is clear that a `struct`'s overriding `ToString()` method will always be called because all value types are sealed. The result is that the C# compiler can instruct a direct call to the method without unboxing.

Enums

Compare the two code snippets shown in Listing 8.9.

LISTING 8.9: Comparing an Integer with an Enum Switch

```
int connectionState;
// ...
switch (connectionState)
{
    case 0:
        // ...
        break;
```

```
    case 1:
        // ...
        break;
    case 2:
        // ...
        break;
    case 3:
        // ...
        break;
}


ConnectionState connectionState;
// ...
switch (connectionState)
{
    case ConnectionState.Connected:
        // ...
        break;
    case ConnectionState.Connecting:
        // ...
        break;
    case ConnectionState.Disconnected:
        // ...
        break;
    case ConnectionState.Disconnecting:
        // ...
        break;
}
```

Obviously, the difference in terms of readability is tremendous because in the second snippet, the cases are self-documenting to some degree. However, the performance at runtime is identical. To achieve this, the second snippet uses **enum values** in each case statement.

An enum is a type that the developer can define. The key characteristic of an enum is that it identifies a compile-time-defined set of possible values, each value referred to by name, making the code easier to read. You define an enum using a style similar to that for a class, as Listing 8.10 shows.

LISTING 8.10: Defining an Enum

```
enum ConnectionState
{
  Disconnected,
  Connecting,
  Connected,
  Disconnecting
}
```

> **NOTE**
>
> An enum is helpful even for Boolean parameters. For example, a method call such as `SetState(true)` is less readable than `SetState(DeviceState.On)`.

You refer to an enum value by prefixing it with the enum name; to refer to the `Connected` value, for example, you use `ConnectionState.Connected`. You should not use the enum names within the enum value name, to avoid the redundancy of something like `ConnectionState.ConnectionStateConnected`. By convention, the enum name itself should be singular, unless the enums are bit flags (discussed shortly).

By default, the first enum value is `0` (technically, it is `0` explicitly cast to the underlying enum type), and each subsequent entry increases by one. However, you can assign explicit values to enums, as shown in Listing 8.11.

LISTING 8.11: Defining an Enum Type

```
enum ConnectionState : short
{
  Disconnected,
  Connecting = 10,
  Connected,
  Joined = Connected,
  Disconnecting
}
```

`Disconnected` has a default value of `0`, `Connecting` has been explicitly assigned `10`, and consequently, `Connected` will be assigned `11`. `Joined` is assigned `11`, the value referred to by `Connected`. (In this case, you do not need to prefix `Connected` with the enum name, since it appears within its scope.) `Disconnecting` is `12`.

An enum always has an underlying type, which may be any of the integral types, except for `char`. In fact, the enum type's performance is equivalent to that of the underlying type. By default, the underlying value type is `int`, but you can specify a different type using inheritance type syntax. Instead of `int`, for example, Listing 8.11 uses a `short`. For consistency, the syntax emulates that of inheritance, but this doesn't actually make an inheritance relationship. The base class for all enums is

`System.Enum`. Furthermore, these classes are sealed; you can't derive from an existing enum type to add additional members.

Successful conversion doesn't work just for valid enum values. It is possible to cast 42 into a `ConnectionState`, even though there is no corresponding `ConnectionState` enum value. If the value successfully casts to the underlying type, the conversion will be successful.

The advantage to allowing casting, even without a corresponding enum value, is that enums can have new values added in later API releases, without breaking earlier versions. Additionally, the enum values provide names for the known values while still allowing unknown values to be assigned at runtime. The burden is that developers must code defensively for the possibility of unnamed values. It would be unwise, for example, to replace case `ConnectionState.Disconnecting` with `default` and expect that the only possible value for the `default` case was `ConnectionState.Disconnecting`. Instead, you should handle the `Disconnecting` case explicitly and the `Default` case should report an error or behave innocuously. As indicated before, however, conversion between the enum and the underlying type, and vice versa, involves an explicit cast, not an implicit one. For example, code cannot call `ReportState(10)` where the signature is `void ReportState(ConnectionState state)`. (The only exception is passing 0 because there is an implicit cast from 0 to any enum.) The compiler will perform a type check and require an explicit cast if the type is not identical.

Although you can add additional values to an enum in a later version of your code, you should do this with care. Inserting an enum value in the middle of an enum will bump the values of all later enums (adding `Flooded` or `Locked` before `Connected` will change the `Connected` value, for example). This will affect the versions of all code that is recompiled against the new version. However, any code compiled against the old version will continue to use the old values, making the intended values entirely different. Besides inserting an enum value at the end of the list, one way to avoid changing enum values is to assign values explicitly.

Enums are slightly different from other value types because enums derive from `System.Enum` before deriving from `System.ValueType`.

Type Compatibility between Enums

Chapter 6 discussed that C# does not support covariance (type compatibility) between arrays of derived types. For example, `Contact[]` will not cast to `PdaItem[]`. C# also does not support a direct cast between arrays of two different enums. However, there is a way to coerce the conversion by casting first to an array and then to the second enum. The requirement is that both enums share the same underlying type, and the trick is to cast first to `System.Array`, as shown at the end of Listing 8.12.

LISTING 8.12: Casting between Arrays of Enums

```
enum ConnectionState1
{
  Disconnected,
  Connecting,
  Connected,
  Disconnecting
}
```

```
enum ConnectionState2
{
  Disconnected,
  Connecting,
  Connected,
  Disconnecting
}
```

```
class Program
{
  static void Main()
  {
      ConnectionState1[] states =
          (ConnectionState2[]) (Array) new ConnectionState2[42];
  }
}
```

Converting between Enums and Strings

One of the conveniences associated with enums is the fact that the `ToString()` method, which is called by methods like `System.Console.WriteLine()`, writes out the enum value identifier:

```
System.Diagnostics.Trace.WriteLine(string.Format(
    "The Connection is currently {0}.",
    ConnectionState.Disconnecting));
```

The preceding code will write the text in Output 8.3 to the trace buffer.

OUTPUT 8.3:

```
The Connection is currently Disconnecting.
```

Conversion from a string to an enum is a little harder to find because it involves a static method on the `System.Enum` base class or, via inheritance, on the enum type. Listing 8.13 provides an example of how to do it, and Output 8.4 shows the results.

LISTING 8.13: Converting a String to an Enum

```
ThreadPriorityLevel priority = (ThreadPriorityLevel)Enum.Parse(
  typeof(ThreadPriorityLevel), "Idle");
Console.WriteLine(priority);
```

OUTPUT 8.4:

```
Idle
```

The first parameter to `Enum.Parse()` is the type, which you specify using the keyword `typeof()`. This is a compile-time way of identifying the type, like a literal for the type value (see Chapter 14).

Unfortunately, there is no `TryParse()` method, so code should include appropriate exception handling if there is a chance the string will not correspond to an enum value identifier. The key caution about casting from a string to an enum, however, is that such a cast is not localizable. Therefore, developers should use this type of cast only for messages that are not exposed to users (assuming localization is a requirement).

Enums as Flags

Many times, developers not only want enum values to be unique, but they also want to be able to combine them to represent a combinatorial value. For example, consider `System.IO.FileAttributes`. This enum, shown in Listing 8.14, indicates various attributes on a file: read-only, hidden, archive, and so on. The difference is that unlike the `ConnectionState` attribute, where each enum value was mutually exclusive, the File-Attributes enum values can and are intended for combination: A file can be both read-only and hidden. To support this, each enum value is a unique bit (or a value that represents a particular combination).

LISTING 8.14: Using Enums As Flags

```
public enum FileAttributes
{
    ReadOnly =          1<<0,    // 000000000000001
    Hidden =            1<<1,    // 000000000000010
    System =            1<<2,    // 000000000000100
    Directory =         1<<4,    // 000000000010000
    Archive =           1<<5,    // 000000000100000
    Device =            1<<6,    // 000000001000000
    Normal =            1<<7,    // 000000010000000
    Temporary =         1<<8,    // 000000100000000
    SparseFile =        1<<9,    // 000001000000000
    ReparsePoint =      1<<10,   // 000010000000000
    Compressed =        1<<11,   // 000100000000000
    Offline =           1<<12,   // 001000000000000
    NotContentIndexed = 1<<13,   // 010000000000000
    Encrypted =         1<<14,   // 100000000000000
}
```

Because enums support combined values, the guideline for the enum name of bit flags is plural.

To join enum values you use a bitwise OR operator, as shown in Listing 8.15.

LISTING 8.15: Using Bitwise OR and AND with Flag Enums

```
using System;
using System.IO;

public class Program
{
 public static void Main()
 {
    // ...

    string fileName = @"enumtest.txt";

    System.IO.FileInfo file =
        new System.IO.FileInfo(fileName);
```

```
        file.Attributes = FileAttributes.Hidden |
            FileAttributes.ReadOnly;

        Console.WriteLine("{0} | {1} = {2}",
            FileAttributes.Hidden, FileAttributes.ReadOnly,
            (int)file.Attributes);

        if ( (file.Attributes & FileAttributes.Hidden) !=
            FileAttributes.Hidden)
        {
            throw new Exception("File is not hidden.");
        }

        if (( file.Attributes & FileAttributes.ReadOnly) !=
            FileAttributes.ReadOnly)
        {
            throw new Exception("File is not read-only.");
        }

        // ...
    }
```

The results of Listing 8.15 appear in Output 8.5.

OUTPUT 8.5:

```
Hidden | ReadOnly = 3
```

Using the bitwise OR operator allows you to set the file to both read-only and hidden. In addition, you can check for specific settings using the bitwise AND operator.

Each value within the enum does not need to correspond to only one flag. It is perfectly reasonable to define additional flags that correspond to frequent combinations of values. Listing 8.16 shows an example.

LISTING 8.16: Defining Enum Values for Frequent Combinations

```
enum DistributedChannel
{
  Transacted = 1,
  Queued = 2,
  Encrypted = 4,
```

```
     Persisted = 16,
     FaultTolerant =
          Transacted | Queued | Persisted
}
```

However, you should avoid enum values corresponding to things like `Maximum` as the last enum, because `Maximum` could be interpreted as a valid enum value. To check whether a value is included within an enum use the `System.Enum.IsDefined()` method.

■ ADVANCED TOPIC

FlagsAttribute

If you decide to use flag-type values, the enum should include `Flags-Attribute`. The attribute appears in square brackets (see Chapter 14), just prior to the enum declaration, as shown in Listing 8.17.

LISTING 8.17: Using **FlagsAttribute**

```
// FileAttributes defined in System.IO.

[Flags]  // Decorating an enum with FlagsAttribute.
public enum FileAttributes
{
  ReadOnly =        1<<0,     // 000000000000001
  Hidden =          1<<1,     // 000000000000010
  // ...
}
```

```
using System;
using System.Diagnostics;
using System.IO;

class Program
{
  public static void Main()
  {
    // ...

      string fileName = @"enumtest.txt";
      FileInfo file = new FileInfo(fileName);
```

```
            file.Attributes = FileAttributes.Hidden |
                FileAttributes.ReadOnly;

            Console.WriteLine("\"{0}\" outputs as \"{1}\"",
                file.Attributes.ToString().Replace(",", " |"),
                file.Attributes);

            FileAttributes attributes =
                (FileAttributes) Enum.Parse(typeof(FileAttributes),
                file.Attributes.ToString());

            Console.WriteLine(attributes);

            // ...
    }
}
```

The results of Listing 8.17 appear in Output 8.6.

OUTPUT 8.6:

```
"ReadOnly | Hidden" outputs as "ReadOnly, Hidden"
```

The flag documents that the enum values can be combined. Furthermore, it changes the behavior of the `ToString()` and `Parse()` methods. For example, calling `ToString()` on an enum that is decorated with `Flags-Attribute` writes out the strings for each enum flag that is set. In Listing 8.17, `file.Attributes.ToString()` returns `ReadOnly, Hidden` rather than the `3` it would have returned without the `FileAttributes` flag. If two enum values are the same, the `ToString()` call would return the first value. As mentioned earlier, however, you should use this with caution because it is not localizable.

Parsing a value from a string to the enum also works. Each enum value identifier is separated by a comma.

It is important to note that `FlagsAttribute` does not automatically assign unique flag values or check that they have unique values. Doing this wouldn't make sense, since duplicates and combinations are often desirable. Instead, you must assign the values of each enum item explicitly.

SUMMARY

This chapter began with a discussion of how to define custom value types. One of the key guidelines that emerge is to create immutable value types. Boxing also was part of the value type discussion.

The idiosyncrasies introduced by boxing are subtle, and the vast majority of them lead to issues at execution time rather than at compile time. Although it is important to know about these in order to try to avoid them, in many ways, focused attention on the potential pitfalls overshadows the usefulness and performance advantages of value types. Programmers should not be overly concerned about using value types. Value types permeate virtually every chapter of this book, and yet the idiosyncrasies do not. I have staged the code surrounding each issue to demonstrate the concern, but in reality, these types of patterns rarely occur. The key to avoiding most of them is to follow the guideline of not creating mutable value types; this is why you don't encounter many of them within the primitive types.

Perhaps the only issue to occur with some frequency is repetitive boxing operations within loops. However, C# 2.0 greatly reduces the chance of this with the addition of generics, and even without that, performance is rarely affected enough to warrant avoidance until a particular algorithm with boxing is identified as a delay.

Furthermore, custom structs (value types) are relatively rare. They obviously play an important role within C# development, but when compared to the number of classes, custom structs are rare and most frequently are defined in frameworks targeted at interoperating with managed code or a particular problem space.

In addition to demonstrating structs, this chapter introduced enums. This is a standard construct available in most programming languages, and it deserves prominent consideration if you want to improve API usability and code readability.

The next chapter highlights more guidelines to creating well-formed types, both structs and otherwise. It begins by looking at overriding the virtual members of objects and defining operator-overloading methods. These two topics apply to both structs and classes, but they are somewhat more critical in completing a struct definition and making it well formed.

■9■
Well-Formed Types

T HE PREVIOUS CHAPTERS covered most of the constructs for defining classes and structs, however, several details remain concerning rounding out the type definition with fit-and-finish-type functionality. This chapter introduces how to put the final touches on a type declaration.

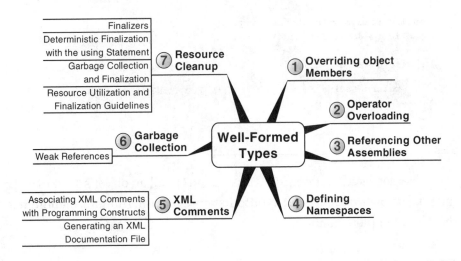

Overriding `object` Members

Chapter 6 discussed how all types derive from `object`. In addition, it reviewed each method available on `object` and discussed how some of them are virtual. This section discusses the details concerning overloading the virtual methods.

Overriding `ToString()`

By default, calling `ToString()` on any object will return the fully qualified name of the class. Calling `ToString()` on a `System.IO.FileStream` object will return the string `System.IO.FileStream`, for example. For some classes, however, `ToString()` can be more meaningful. On `string`, for example, `ToString()` returns the string value itself. Similarly, returning a `Contact`'s name would make more sense. Listing 9.1 overrides `ToString()` to return a string representation of `Coordinate`.

LISTING 9.1: Overriding **`ToString()`**

```csharp
public struct Coordinate
{
  public Coordinate(Longitude longitude, Latitude latitude)
  {
      _Longitude = longitude;
      _Latitude = latitude;
  }

  public readonly Longitude Longitude;
  public readonly Latitude Latitude;

  public override string ToString()
  {
      return string.Format("{0} {1}", Longitude, Latitude);
  }

  // ...
}
```

Write methods such as `Console.WriteLine()` call an object's `ToString()` method, so overloading it often outputs more meaningful information than the default implementation.

Overriding `GetHashCode()`

Overriding `GetHashCode()` is more complex than overriding `ToString()`. Regardless, you should override `GetHashCode()` when you are overriding `Equals()`, and there is a compiler warning to indicate this. Overriding `GetHashCode()` is also a good practice when using it as a key into a hash table collection (`System.Collections.Hashtable` and `System.Collections.Generic.Dictionary`, for example).

The purpose of the hash code is to generate a number that corresponds to the value of an object. Here are some implementation principles for a good `GetHashCode()` implementation.

- The values returned should be mostly unique. Since hash code returns only an `int`, there has to be an overlap in hash codes for objects that have potentially more values than an `int` can hold—virtually all types. (An obvious example is `long`, since there are more possible `long` values than an `int` could uniquely identify.)

- The possible hash code values should be distributed evenly over the range of an `int`. For example, creating a hash that doesn't consider the fact that distribution of a string in Latin-based languages primarily centers on the initial 128 ASCII characters would result in a very uneven distribution of string values and would not be a strong `GetHashCode()` algorithm.

- `GetHashCode()` should be optimized for performance. `GetHashCode()` is generally used in `Equals()` implementations to short-circuit a full equals comparison if the hash codes are different. As a result, it is frequently called when the type is used as a key type in dictionary collections.

- `GetHashCode()`'s returns over the life of a particular object should be constant (the same value), even if the objects data changes. In many cases, you should cache the method return to enforce this.

- Equal objects must have equal hash codes (if `a.Equals(b)`, then `a.GetHashCode() == b.GetHashCode()`).

- `GetHashCode()` should not throw any exceptions.

Consider the `GetHashCode()` implementation for the `Coordinate` type shown in Listing 9.2.

LISTING 9.2: Implementing **GetHashCode()**

```
public struct Coordinate
{
  public Coordinate(Longitude longitude, Latitude latitude)
```

```
    {
        _Longitude = longitude;
        _Latitude = latitude;
    }


    public readonly Longitude Longitude;
    public readonly Latitude Latitude;

    public override int GetHashCode()
    {
        int hashCode = Longitude.GetHashCode();
        // As long as the hash codes are not equal
        if(Longitude != Latitude)
        {
            hashCode ^= Latitude.GetHashCode();   // eXclusive OR
        }
        return hashCode;
    }

    // ...
}
```

Generally, the key is to use the XOR operator over the hash codes from the relevant types, and to make sure the XOR operands are not identical, or else the result will be all zeroes. The alternative operands, AND and OR, have similar restrictions, but the restrictions occur more frequently. Applying AND multiple times tends toward all 0 bits, and applying OR tends toward all 1 bits.

For finer-grained control, split larger-than-int types using the shift operator. For example, GetHashCode() for a long called value is implemented as follows:

```
int GetHashCode() { return ((int)value ^ (int)(value >> 32)) };
```

Also, note that if the base class is not object, then base.GetHashCode() should be included in the XOR assignment.

Finally, Coordinate does not cache the value of the hash code. Since each field in the hash code calculation is readonly, the value can't change. However, implementations should cache the hash code if calculated values could change or if a cached value could offer a significant performance advantage.

Overriding Equals()

Overriding Equals() without overriding GetHashCode() results in a warning such as that shown in Output 9.1.

OUTPUT 9.1:

```
warning CS0659: '<Class Name>' overrides Object.Equals(object o) but
does not override Object.GetHashCode()
```

Generally, programmers expect overriding `Equals()` to be trivial, but it includes a surprising number of subtleties that require careful thought and testing.

Object Identity versus Equal Object Values

Two references are identical if both refer to the same instance. `object`, and therefore, all objects, include a static method called `ReferenceEquals()` that explicitly checks for this object identity (see Figure 9.1).

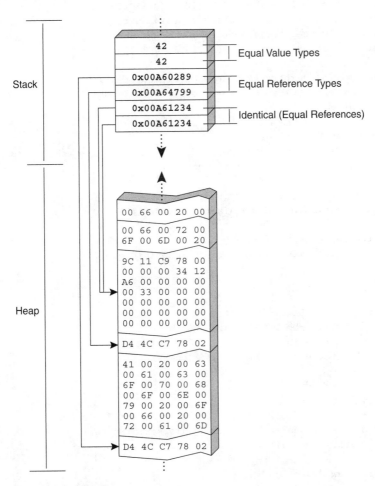

FIGURE 9.1: Identity

However, identical reference is not the only type of equality. Two object instances can also be equal if the values that identify them are equal. Consider the comparison of two `ProductSerialNumbers` shown in Listing 9.3.

LISTING 9.3: Equal

```
public sealed class ProductSerialNumber
{
  // See Appendix B
}
```

```
class Program
{
  static void Main()
  {
      ProductSerialNumber serialNumber1 =
          new ProductSerialNumber("PV", 1000, 09187234);
      ProductSerialNumber serialNumber2 = serialNumber1;
      ProductSerialNumber serialNumber3 =
          new ProductSerialNumber("PV", 1000, 09187234);

      // These serial numbers ARE the same object identity.
      if(!ProductSerialNumber.ReferenceEquals(serialNumber1,
          serialNumber2))
      {
          throw new Exception(
              "serialNumber1 does NOT " +
              "reference equal serialNumber2");
      }
      // and, therefore, they are equal
      else if(!serialNumber1.Equals(serialNumber2))
      {
          throw new Exception(
              "serialNumber1 does NOT equal serialNumber2");
      }
      else
      {
          Console.WriteLine(
              "serialNumber1 reference equals serialNumber2");
          Console.WriteLine(
              "serialNumber1 equals serialNumber2");
      }


      // These serial numbers are NOT the same object identity.
      if (ProductSerialNumber.ReferenceEquals(serialNumber1,
              serialNumber3))
      {
          throw new Exception(
```

```
            "serialNumber1 DOES reference " +
            "equal serialNumber3");
    }
    // but they are equal (assuming Equals is overloaded).
    else if(!serialNumber1.Equals(serialNumber3) ||
        serialNumber1 != serialNumber3)
    {
        throw new Exception(
            "serialNumber1 does NOT equal serialNumber3");
    }

    Console.WriteLine( "serialNumber1 equals serialNumber3" );
    Console.WriteLine( "serialNumber1 == serialNumber3" );
    }
}
```

The results of Listing 9.3 appear in Output 9.2.

OUTPUT 9.2:

```
serialNumber1 reference equals and Equals serialNumber2
serialNumber1 equals serialNumber3
serialNumber1 == serialNumber3
```

As the last assertion demonstrates with `ReferenceEquals()`, serial-Number1 and `serialNumber3` are not the same reference. However, the code constructs them with the same values and both logically associate with the same physical product. If one instance was created from data in the database and another was created from manually entered data, you would expect the instances would be equal and, therefore, that the product would not be duplicated (re-entered) in the database. Two identical references are obviously equal; however, two different objects could be equal but not reference equal. Such objects will not have identical object identities, but they may have key data that identifies them as being equal objects.

Only reference types can be reference equal, thereby supporting the concept of identity. Calling `ReferenceEquals()` on value types will always return `false` since, by definition, the value type directly contains its data, not a reference. Even when `ReferenceEquals()` passes the same variable in both (value type) parameters to `ReferenceEquals()`, the result will still be `false` because the very nature of value types is that they are copied into the parameters of the called method. Listing 9.4 demonstrates the behavior.

LISTING 9.4: Value Types Do Not Even Reference Equal Themselves

```csharp
public struct Coordinate
{
  public readonly Longitude Longitude;
  public readonly Latitude Latitude;

  // ...
}
```

```csharp
class Program
{
  public void Main()
  {
    //...

    Coordinate coordinate1 =
        new Coordinate( new Longitude(48, 52),
                        new Latitude(-2, -20));

    // Value types will never be reference equal.
    if ( Coordinate.ReferenceEquals(coordinate1,
        coordinate1) )
    {
        throw new Exception(
            "coordinate1 reference equals coordinate1");
    }

    Console.WriteLine(
        "coordinate1 does NOT reference equal itself" );
  }
}
```

In contrast to the definition of Coordinate as a reference type in Chapter 8, the definition going forward is that of a value type (struct) because the combination of Longitude and Latitude data is less than 16 bytes. (In Chapter 8, Coordinate aggregated Angle rather than Longitude and Latitude.)

Implementing Equals()

To determine whether two objects are equal (the same identifying data), you use an object's Equal() method. The implementation of this virtual method on object uses ReferenceEquals() to evaluate equality. Since this implementation is often inadequate, it is necessary to sometimes override Equals() with a more appropriate implementation.

For objects to *equal* each other, the expectation is that the identifying data within them be equal. For `ProductSerialNumbers`, for example, the `ProductSeries`, `Model`, and `Id` must be the same; however, for an `Employee` object, perhaps comparing `EmployeeIds` would be sufficient for equality. To correct `object.Equals()` implementation, it is necessary to override it. Value types, for example, override the `Equals()` implementation to instead use the fields that the type includes.

The steps for overriding `Equals()` are as follows.

1. Check for `null` if type is nullable (i.e., a reference type).
2. Check for reference equals if the data is a reference type.
3. Check for equivalent data types.
4. Possibly check for equivalent hash codes to short-circuit an extensive, field-by-field comparison.
5. Check `base.Equals()` if base class overrides `Equals()`.
6. Compare each identifying field for equality.
7. Override `GetHashCode()`.
8. Override the `==` and `!=` operators (see the next section).

Listing 9.5 shows a sample `Equals()` implementation.

LISTING 9.5: Overriding `Equals()`

```csharp
public struct Longitude
{
    // ...
}
```

```csharp
public struct Latitude
{
    // ...
}
```

```csharp
public struct Coordinate
{
    public Coordinate(Longitude longitude, Latitude latitude)
    {
        _Longitude = longitude;
        _Latitude = latitude;
    }
}
```

```csharp
    public readonly Longitude Longitude;
    public readonly Latitude Latitude;

    public override bool Equals(object obj)
    {
        // STEP 1: Check for null
        if (obj == null)
        {
            return false;
        }
        // STEP 3: equivalent data types
        if (this.GetType() != obj.GetType())
        {
            return false;
        }
        return Equals((Coordinate)obj);
    }
    public bool Equals(Coordinate obj)
    {
        // STEP 1: Check for null if nullable
        // (e.g., a reference type)
        // if (obj == null)
        // {
        //     return false;
        // }

        // STEP 2: Check for ReferenceEquals if this
        // is a reference type
        // if ( ReferenceEquals(this, obj))
        // {
        //   return true;
        // }

        // STEP 4: Possibly check for equivalent hash codes
        // if (this.GetHashCode() != obj.GetHashCode())
        // {
        //     return false;
        // }

        // STEP 5: Check base.Equals if base overrides Equals()
        // System.Diagnostics.Debug.Assert(
        //     base.GetType() != typeof(object) );
        // if ( !base.Equals(obj) )
        // {
        //     return false;
        // }

        // STEP 6: Compare identifying fields for equality.
        return ( (Longitude.Equals(obj.Longitude)) &&
            (Latitude.Equals(obj.Latitude)) );
```

```
    }

    // STEP 7: Override GetHashCode.
    public override int GetHashCode()
    {
        int hashCode = Longitude.GetHashCode();
        hashCode ^= Latitude.GetHashCode(); // Xor (eXclusive OR)
        return hashCode;
    }

}
```

In this implementation, the first two checks are relatively obvious. Checks 4–6 occur in an overload of `Equals()` that takes the `Coordinate` data type specifically. This way, a comparison of two `Coordinates` will avoid `Equals(object obj)` and its `GetType()` check altogether.

Since `GetHashCode()` is not cached and is no more efficient than step 5, the `GetHashCode()` comparison is commented out. Similarly, `base.Equals()` is not used since the base class is not overriding `Equals()`. (The assertion checks that `base` is not of type `object`, however it does not check that the base class overrides `Equals()`, which is required to appropriately call `base.Equals()`.) Regardless, since `GetHashCode()` does not necessarily return a unique value (it only identifies when operands are different), on its own it does not conclusively identify equal objects.

Like `GetHashCode()`, `Equals()` should also never throw any exceptions. It is valid to compare any object with any other object, and doing so should never result in an exception.

Guidelines for Implementing Equality

While learning the details for overriding an `object`'s virtual members, several guidelines emerge.

- `Equals()`, the `==` operator, and the `!=` operator should be implemented together.
- A type should use the same algorithm within `Equals()`, `==`, and `!=` implementations.
- When implementing `Equals()`, `==`, and `!=`, a type's `GetHashCode()` method should also be implemented.

- `GetHashCode()`, `Equals()`, `==`, and `!=` should never throw exceptions.
- When implementing `IComparable`, equality-related methods should also be implemented.

Operator Overloading

The last section looked at overriding `Equals()` and provided the guideline that the class should also implement `==` and `!=`. The term for implementing any operator is **operator overloading**, and this section describes how to do this, not only for `==` and `!=`, but also for other supported operators.

For example, `string` provides a + operator that concatenates two strings. This is perhaps not surprising, because string is a predefined type, so it could possibly have special compiler support. However, C# provides for adding + operator support to any type. Virtually all operators are supported, except for assignment operators; there is no way to change the behavior of the = operator.

Comparison Operators (==, !=, <, >, <=, >=)

Once `Equals()` is overridden, there is a possible inconsistency. Two objects could return `true` for `Equals()` but `false` for the `==` operator because `==` performs a reference equality check by default as well. To correct this it is important to overload the equals (`==`) and not equals (`!=`) operators as well.

For the most part, the implementation for these operators can delegate the logic to `Equals()`, or vice versa. However, some initial null checks are required first (see Listing 9.6).

LISTING 9.6: Implementing the == and != Operators

```
public sealed class Coordinate
{

    // ...

    public static bool operator ==(
        Coordinate leftHandSide,
        Coordinate rightHandSide)
    {
```

```
        // Check if leftHandSide is null.
        // (operator== would be recursive)
        if (ReferenceEquals(leftHandSide, null))
        {
            // Return true if rightHandSide is also null
            // but false otherwise.
            return ReferenceEquals(rightHandSide, null);
        }

        return (leftHandSide.Equals(rightHandSide));
    }

    public static bool operator !=(
        Coordinate leftHandSide,
        Coordinate rightHandSide)
    {
        return !(leftHandSide == rightHandSide);
    }

}
```

Note that to perform the null checks, you cannot use an equality check for null (`leftHandSide == null`). Doing so would recursively call back into the method, resulting in a loop until overflowing the stack. To avoid this you call `ReferenceEquals()` to check for null.

Binary Operators (+, −, *, /, %, &, |, ^, <<, >>)

You can add an `Arc` to a `Coordinate`. However, the code so far provides no support for the addition operator. Instead, you need to define such a method, as Listing 9.7 shows.

LISTING 9.7: Adding an Operator

```
struct Arc
{
    public Arc(
        Longitude longitudeDifference,
        Latitude latitudeDifference)
    {
        LongitudeDifference = longitudeDifference;
        LatitudeDifference = latitudeDifference;
    }

    public readonly Longitude LongitudeDifference;
    public readonly Latitude LatitudeDifference;
}
```

```
struct Coordinate
{
  // ...
  public static Coordinate operator +(
      Coordinate source, Arc arc)
  {
      Coordinate result = new Coordinate(
          new Longitude(
              source.Longitude + arc.LongitudeDifference),
          new Latitude(
              source.Latitude + arc.LatitudeDifference));
      return result;

  }
}
```

The +, -, *, /, %, &, |, ^, <<, and >> operators are implemented as binary
static methods where at least one parameter is of the containing type. The
method name is the operator prefixed by the word *operator* as a keyword.
As shown in Listing 9.8, given the definition of the - and + binary operators, you can add and subtract an `Arc` to and from the coordinate.

LISTING 9.8: Calling the – and + Binary Operators

```
public class Program
{
  public static void Main()
  {
      Coordinate coordinate1,coordinate2;
      coordinate1 = new Coordinate(
          new Longitude(48, 52), new Latitude(-2, -20));
      Arc arc = new Arc(new Longitude(3), new Latitude(1));
      coordinate2 = coordinate1 + arc;

      coordinate2 = coordinate2 - arc;

      coordinate2 += arc;
  }
}
```

The results of Listing 9.8 appear in Output 9.3.

OUTPUT 9.3:

```
51° 52' 0 E    -1° -20' 0 S
51° 52' 0 E    -1° -20' 0 S
54° 52' 0 E     0° -20' 0 S
```

The – and + operators on `Coordinate` return a third coordinate after subtracting `Arc`. This allows you to string multiple operators and operands together, as in `result = coordinate1 + coordinate2 + coordinate3 - coordinate4;`.

This works because the result of the first operand (`coordinate1 + coordinate2`) is another `Coordinate`, which you can then add to the next operand.

In contrast, consider if you provided a – operator that had two `Coordinates` as parameters and returned a `double` corresponding to the distance between the two coordinates. Adding a `double` to a `Coordinate` is undefined and, therefore, you could not string operators and operands. Caution is in order when defining operators that behave this way, because doing so is counterintuitive.

Combining Assignment with Binary Operators (+=, –=, *=, /=, %=, &=...)

As previously mentioned, there is no support for overloading the assignment operator. However, assignment operators in combination with binary operators (+=, –=, *=, /=, %=, &=, |=, ^=, <<=, and >>=) are effectively overloaded when overloading the binary operator. Given the definition of a binary operator without the assignment, C# automatically allows for assignment in combination with the operator. Using the definition of `Coordinate` in Listing 9.7, therefore, you can have code such as:

```
coordinate += arc;
```

which is equivalent to the following:

```
coordinate = coordinate + arc;
```

Conditional Logical Operators (&&, ||)

Like assignment operators, conditional logical operators cannot be overloaded explicitly. However, since the logical operators `&` and `|` can be overloaded, and the conditional operators comprise the logical operators, effectively it is possible to overload conditional operators. `x && y` is processed as `x & y`, where `y` must evaluate to `true`. Similarly, `x || y` is processed as `x | y` only if `x` is `false`. To enable support for evaluating a type to `true` or `false`—in an `if` statement, for example—it is necessary to override the `true`/`false` unary operators.

Unary Operators (+, -, !, ~, ++, --, `true`, `false`)

Overloading unary operators is very similar to overloading binary operators, except that they take only one parameter, also of the containing type. Listing 9.9 overloads the + and – operators for `Longitude` and `Latitude` and then uses these operators when overloading the same operators in `Arc`.

LISTING 9.9: Overloading the – and + Unary Operators

```csharp
public struct Latitude
{
    // ...
    public static Latitude operator -(Latitude latitude)
    {
        return new Latitude(-latitude.DecimalDegrees);
    }
    public static Latitude operator +(Latitude latitude)
    {
        return latitude;
    }
}

public struct Longitude
{
    // ...
    public static Longitude operator -(Longitude longitude)
    {
        return new Longitude(-longitude.DecimalDegrees);
    }
    public static Longitude operator +(Longitude longitude)
    {
        return longitude;
    }
}

public struct Arc
{
    // ...
    public static Arc operator -(Arc arc)
    {
        // Uses unary - operator defined on
        // Longitude and Latitude
        return new Arc(-arc.LongitudeDifference,
            -arc.LatitudeDifference);
    }
    public static Arc operator +(Arc arc)
    {
        return arc;
    }
}
```

Just as with numeric types, the + operator in this listing doesn't have any effect and is provided for symmetry.

Overloading `true` and `false` has the additional requirement that they both be overloaded. The signatures are the same as other operator overloads; however, the return must be a `bool`, as demonstrated in Listing 9.10.

LISTING 9.10: Overloading the **true** and **false** Operators

```
public static bool operator false(IsValid item)
{
    // ...
}
public static bool operator true(IsValid item)
{
    // ...
}
```

You can use types with overloaded `true` and `false` operators in `if`, `do`, `while`, and `for` controlling expressions.

Conversion Operators

Currently, there is no support in `Longitude`, `Latitude`, and `Coordinate` for casting to an alternate type. For example, there is no way to cast a `double` into a `Longitude` or `Latitude` instance. Similarly, there is no support for assigning a `Coordinate` using a `string`. Fortunately, C# provides for the definition of methods specifically to handle the casting of one type to another. Furthermore, the method declaration allows for specifying whether the cast is implicit or explicit.

■ ADVANCED TOPIC

Cast Operator (( ))

Implementing the explicit and implicit conversion operators is not technically overloading the cast operator (( )). However, this is effectively what takes place, so *defining a cast operator* is common terminology for implementing explicit or implicit conversion.

Defining a conversion operator is similar in style to defining any other operator, except that the "operator" is the data type of the conversion. Additionally, the `operator` keyword follows a keyword that indicates whether the conversion is implicit or explicit (see Listing 9.11).

LISTING 9.11: Providing an Implicit Conversion between **Latitude** and **double**

```
public struct Latitude
{
  // ...

  public double DecimalDegrees
  {
      get { return _DecimalDegrees; }
      set
      {
          _DecimalDegrees =
              Normalize(value);
      }
  }

  // ...

  public static implicit operator double(Latitude latitude)
  {
      return latitude.DecimalDegrees;
  }
  public static implicit operator Latitude(double degrees)
  {
      return new Latitude(degrees);
  }
}
```

With these conversion operators, you now can cast `doubles` implicitly to and from `Latitude` objects. Assuming similar conversions exist for `Longitude`, you can simplify the creation of a `Coordinate` object by specifying the decimal degrees portion of each coordinate portion (for example, `coordinate = new Coordinate(43, 172);`).

Guidelines for Conversion Operators

The difference between defining an implicit and an explicit conversion operator centers on preventing an unintentional implicit cast that results in undesirable behavior. You should be aware of two possible consequences of using the explicit conversion operator. First, conversion operators that

> **■ NOTE**
>
> Either the return or the parameter must be of the enclosing type—in support of encapsulation. C# does not allow you to specify conversions outside the scope of the converted type.

throw exceptions should always be explicit. For example, it is highly likely that a string will not conform to the appropriate format that a conversion from `string` to `Coordinate` requires. Given the chance of a failed conversion, you should define the particular conversion operator as explicit, thereby requiring that you be intentional about the conversion and that you ensure that the format is correct, or that you provide code to handle the possible exception. Frequently, the pattern for conversion is that one direction (`string` to `Coordinate`) is explicit and the reverse (`Coordinate` to `string`) is implicit.

A second consideration is the fact that some conversions will be lossy. Converting from a `float` (`4.2`) to an `int` is entirely valid, assuming an awareness of the fact that the decimal portion of the `float` will be lost. Any conversions that will lose data and not successfully convert back to the original type should be defined as explicit.

Referencing Other Assemblies

Instead of placing all code into one monolithic binary file, C# and the underlying CLI platform allow you to spread code across multiple assemblies. This enables you to reuse assemblies across multiple executables.

■ BEGINNER TOPIC

Class Libraries

The `HelloWorld.exe` program is one of the most trivial programs you can write. Real-world programs are more complex, and as complexity increases, it helps to organize the complexity by breaking programs into multiple parts. To do this, developers move portions of a program into separate compiled units called **class libraries** or, simply, **libraries**. Programs then reference and rely on class libraries to provide parts of their functionality. The power of this concept is that two programs can rely on the same class library, thereby sharing the functionality of that class library across the two programs and reducing the total amount of code needed.

In other words, it is possible to write features once, place them into a class library, and allow multiple programs to include those features by referencing the same class library. Later on, when developers fix a bug or add functionality to the class library, all the programs will have access to the increased functionality, just because they continue to reference the now improved class library.

To reuse the code within a different assembly, it is necessary to reference the assembly when running the C# compiler. Generally, the referenced assembly is a class library, and creating a class library requires a different assembly target from the default console executable targets you created thus far.

Changing the Assembly Target

The compiler allows you to create four different assembly types via the /target option.

- *Console executable:* This is the default type of assembly, and all compilation thus far has been to a console executable. (Leaving off the /target option or specifying /target:exe creates a console executable.)
- *Class library:* Classes that are shared across multiple executables are generally defined in a class library (/target:library).
- *Windows executable:* Windows executables are designed to run in the Microsoft Windows family of operating systems and outside of the command console (/target:winexe).
- *Module:* In order to facilitate multiple languages within the same assembly, code can be compiled to a module and multiple modules can be combined to form an assembly (/target:module).

Assemblies to be shared across multiple applications are generally compiled as class libraries. Consider, for example, a library dedicated to functionality around longitude and latitude coordinates. To compile the `Coordinate`, `Longitude`, and `Latitude` classes into their own library, you use the command line shown in Output 9.4.

OUTPUT 9.4:

```
>csc /target:library /out:Coordinates.dll Coordinate.cs IAngle.cs
Latitude.cs Longitude.cs Arc.cs
Microsoft (R) Visual C# 2005 Compiler version 8.00.50727.42
for Microsoft (R) Windows (R) 2005 Framework version 2.0.50727
Copyright (C) Microsoft Corporation 2001-2005. All rights reserved.
```

Assuming you use .NET and the C# compiler is in the path, this builds an assembly library called `Coordinates.dll`.

Encapsulation of Types

Just as classes serve as an encapsulation boundary for behavior and data, assemblies provide a similar boundary among groups of types. Developers can break a system into assemblies and then share those assemblies with multiple applications or integrate them with assemblies provided by third parties.

By default, a class without any access modifier is defined as `internal`. The result is that the class is inaccessible from outside the assembly. Even though another assembly references the assembly containing the class, all internal classes within the referenced assemblies will be inaccessible.

Just as `private` and `protected` provide levels of encapsulation to members within a class, C# supports the use of access modifiers at the class level for control over the encapsulation of the classes within an assembly. The access modifiers available are `public` and `internal`, and in order to expose a class outside of the assembly, the class must be marked as `public`. Therefore, before compiling the `Coordinates.dll` assembly, it is necessary to modify the type declarations as `public` (see Listing 9.12).

LISTING 9.12: Making Classes Available Outside an Assembly

```
public struct Coordinate
{
  // ...
}
```

```
public struct Latitude
{
  // ...
}
```

```
public struct Longitude
{
  // ...
}
```

```
public struct Arc
{
  // ...
}
```

Similarly, declarations such as `class` and `enum` can also be either `public` or `internal`.

■ ADVANCED TOPIC

Additional Class Access Modifiers

You can decorate nested classes with any access modifier available to other class members (`private`, for example). However, outside of the class scope, the only available access modifiers are `public` and `internal`.

The internal access modifier is not limited to type declarations. It is also available on type members. Therefore, you can designate a type as `public` but mark specific methods within the type as `internal` so that the members are available only from within the assembly. It is not possible for the members to have a greater accessibility than the type. If the class is declared as `internal`, then public members on the type will be accessible only from within the assembly.

`protected internal` is another type member access modifier. Members with an accessibility modifier of `protected internal` will be accessible from all locations within the containing assembly *and* from classes that derive from the type, even if the derived class is not in the same assembly.

■ BEGINNER TOPIC

Type Member Accessibility Modifiers

The full list of access modifiers appears in Table 9.1.

TABLE 9.1: Accessibility Modifiers

Modifier	Description
public	Declares that the member is accessible up to whatever level the type is accessible. If the class is `internal`, the member will be `internal`. Public members will be accessible from outside the assembly if the containing type is public.
internal	Accessible from within the assembly only.
private	Accessible from within the containing type, but inaccessible otherwise.
protected	Declares the member as accessible within the containing type and any subtypes derived from it, regardless of assembly.
protected internal	Accessible from anywhere within the containing assembly *and* from any types derived from the containing type, even if the derived types are within a different assembly.

Referencing an Assembly

To access code within a different assembly, the C# compiler allows the developer to reference the assembly on the command line. The option is /reference (/r is the abbreviation), followed by the list of references. The Program class listing from Listing 9.8 uses the Coordinate class, and if you place this into a separate executable, you reference Coordinates.dll using the .NET command line shown in Output 9.5.

OUTPUT 9.5:

```
csc.exe /R:Coordinates.dll Program.cs
```

The Mono command line appears in Output 9.6.

OUTPUT 9.6:

```
msc.exe /R:Coordinates.dll Program.cs
```

Defining Namespaces

As mentioned in Chapter 2, all data types are identified by the combination of their namespace and their name. For the classes you defined earlier, there was no explicit namespace declaration. Classes such as these are automatically declared as members of the default global namespace. It is highly likely that such classes will experience a name collision, which occurs when you attempt to define two classes with the same name. Once you begin referencing other assemblies from third parties, the likelihood of a name collision increases even further.

To resolve this, you should place classes into namespaces. For example, classes outside of the `System` namespace are generally placed into a namespace corresponding with the company, product name, or both. Classes from Addison-Wesley, for example, are placed into an `Awl` or `Addison-Wesley` namespace, and classes from Microsoft (not `System` classes) are located in the `Microsoft` namespace. You should use the `namespace` keyword to create a namespace and to assign a class to it, as shown in Listing 9.13.

LISTING 9.13: Defining a Namespace

```
// Define the namespace AddisonWesley
namespace AddisonWesley
{
  class Program
  {
    // ...
  }
}
// End of AddisonWesley namespace declaration
```

All content between the namespace declaration's curly brackets will then belong within the specified namespace. In Listing 9.13, `Program` is placed into the namespace `AddisonWesley`, making its full name `Addison-Wesley.Program`. Optionally, C# allows a colon after the namespace name.

Like classes, namespaces support nesting. This provides for a hierarchical organization of classes. All the `System` classes relating to network APIs are in the namespace `System.Net`, for example, and those relating to the Web are in `System.Web`.

There are two ways to nest namespaces. The first way is to nest them within each other (similar to classes), as demonstrated in Listing 9.14.

LISTING 9.14: Nesting Namespaces within Each Other

```
// Define the namespace AddisonWesley
namespace AddisonWesley
{
    // Define the namespace AddisonWesley.Michaelis
    namespace Michaelis
    {
        // Define the namespace
        // AddisonWesley.Michaelis.EssentialCSharp
        namespace EssentialCSharp
        {
            // Declare the class
            // AddisonWesley.Michaelis.EssentialCSharp.Program
            class Program
            {
                // ...
            }
        }
    }
}
// End of AddisonWesley namespace declaration
```

Such a nesting will assign the `Program` class to the `AddisonWesley.Michaelis.EssentialCSharp` namespace.

The second way is to use the full namespace in a single namespace declaration in which a period separates each identifier, as shown in Listing 9.15.

LISTING 9.15: Nesting Namespaces Using a Period to Separate Each Identifier

```
// Define the namespace AddisonWesley.Michaelis.EssentialCSharp
namespace AddisonWesley.Michaelis.EssentialCSharp
{
    class Program
    {
        // ...
    }
}
// End of AddisonWesley namespace declaration
```

Regardless of whether a namespace declaration follows Listing 9.14, Listing 9.15, or a combination of the two, the resulting CIL code will be identical. The same namespace may occur multiple times, in multiple files, and even across assemblies. For example, with the convention of one-to-one correlation between files and classes, you can define each class in its own file and surround it with the appropriate namespace declaration.

Namespace Alias Qualifier

Namespaces on their own deal with the vast majority of naming conflicts that might arise. However, sometimes (albeit rarely) conflict can arise because of an overlap in the namespace and class names. To account for this, the C# 2.0 compiler includes an option for providing an alias with the /reference option. For example, if the assemblies `CoordinatesPlus.dll` and `Coordinates.dll` have an overlapping type of `Arc`, you can reference both assemblies on the command line by assigning one or both references with a **namespace alias qualifier** that further distinguishes one class from the other. The results of such a reference appear in Output 9.7.

OUTPUT 9.7:

```
csc.exe /R:CoordPlus=CoordinatesPlus.dll /R:Coordinates.dll Program.cs
```

However, adding the alias during compilation is not sufficient on its own. In order to refer to classes in the aliased assembly, it is necessary to provide an `extern` directive that declares that the namespace alias qualifier is provided externally to the source code (see Listing 9.16).

LISTING 9.16: Using the **extern** Alias Directive

```
// extern must precede all other namespace elements
extern alias CoordPlus;

using System;
using CoordPlus::AddisonWesley.Michaelis.EssentialCSharp
// Equivalent also allowed
// using CoordPlus.AddisonWesley.Michaelis.EssentialCSharp

using global::AddisonWesley.Michaelis.EssentialCSharp
// Equivalent NOT allowed
// using global.AddisonWesley.Michaelis.EssentialCSharp
```

```
public class Program
{
  // ...
}
```

Once the `extern` alias for `CoordPlus` appears, you can reference the namespace using `CoordPlus`, followed by either two colons or a period.

To ensure that the lookup for the type occurs in the global namespace, C# 2.0 allows items to have the `global::` qualifier (but not `global.` because it could imaginably conflict with a real namespace of `global`).

XML Comments

Chapter 1 introduced comments. However, you can use XML comments for more than just notes to other programmers reviewing the source code. XML-based comments follow a practice popularized with Java. Although the C# compiler ignores all comments as far as the resulting executable goes, the developer can use command-line options to instruct the compiler[1] to extract the XML comments into a separate XML file. By taking advantage of the XML file generation, the developer can generate documentation of the API from the XML comments. In addition, C# editors can parse the XML comments in the code and display them to developers as distinct regions (for example, as a different color from the rest of the code), or parse the XML comment data elements and display them to the developer.

Figure 9.2 demonstrates how an IDE can take advantage of XML comments to assist the developer with a tip about the code he is trying to write.

These coding tips offer significant assistance in large programs, especially when multiple developers share code. For this to work, however, the developer obviously must take the time to enter the XML comments within the code and then direct the compiler to create the XML file. The next section explains how to accomplish this. (See Listing 9.17.)

---

1. The C# standard does not specify whether the C# compiler or a separate utility takes care of extracting the XML data. However, all mainstream C# compilers include the functionality via a compile switch instead of within an additional utility.

```
{
    /// <summary>
    /// Display the text specified
    /// </summary>
    /// <param name="text">The text to be displayed in the console.</param>
    static void Display(string text)
    {
        Console.WriteLine(text);
    }

    static void Main()
    {

        Display(
    }    void Naming.Display(string text)
}        text:
            The text to be displayed in the console.
```

Figure 9.2: XML Comments as Tips in Visual Studio IDE

Associating XML Comments with Programming Constructs

Consider the listing of the `DataStorage` class, as shown in Listing 9.17.

Listing 9.17: Commenting Code with XML Comments

```
/// <summary>
/// DataStorage is used to persist and retrieve
/// employee data from the files.
/// </summary>
class DataStorage
{
    /// <summary>
    /// Save an employee object to a file
    /// named with the Employee name.
    /// </summary>
    /// <remarks>
    /// This method uses
    /// <seealso cref="System.IO.FileStream"/>
    /// in addition to
    /// <seealso cref="System.IO.StreamWriter"/>
    /// </remarks>
    /// <param name="employee">
    /// The employee to persist to a file</param>
    /// <date>January 1, 2000</date>
    public static void Store(Employee employee)
    {
        // ...
    }
```

Single-Line
XML
Comment

```
/**    <summary>
 *    Loads up an employee object
 *    </summary>
 *    <remarks>
 *    This method uses
 *    <seealso cref="System.IO.FileStream"/>
 *    in addition to
 *    <seealso cref="System.IO.StreamReader"/>
 *    </remarks>
 *    <param name="firstName">
 *    The first name of the employee</param>
 *    <param name="lastName">
 *    The last name of the employee</param>
 *    <returns>
 *    The employee object corresponding to the names
 *    </returns>
 *    <date>January 1, 2000</date>**/
public static Employee Load(
    string firstName, string lastName)
{
    // ...
}
}

class Program
{
    // ...
}
```

XML
Delimited
Comment
(C# 2.0)

Listing 9.17 uses both XML delimited comments that span multiple lines, and single-line XML comments where each line requires a separate three-forward-slash delimiter (///).

Since XML comments are designed to document the API, they are intended for use only in association with C# declarations, such as the class or method shown in Listing 9.17. Any attempt to place an XML comment inline with the code, unassociated with a declaration, will result in a warning by the compiler. The compile makes the association simply because the XML comment appears immediately before the declaration.

Although C# allows any XML tag in comments, the C# standard explicitly defines a set of tags to be used. `<seealso cref="System.IO.Stream-Writer"/>` is an example of using the `seealso` tag. This tag creates a link between the text and the `System.IO.StreamWriter` class.

Generating an XML Documentation File

The compiler will check that the XML comments are well formed, and will issue a warning if they are not. To generate the XML file, you need to use the /doc option when compiling, as shown in Output 9.8.

OUTPUT 9.8:

```
>csc /doc:Comments.xml DataStorage.cs
```

The /doc option will create an XML file based on the name specified after the colon. Using the DataStorage class shown in Listing 9.17 and the compiler options listed here, the resulting CommentSamples.XML file appears as shown in Listing 9.18.

LISTING 9.18: **Comments.xml**

```xml
<?xml version="1.0"?>
<doc>
    <assembly>
        <name>DataStorage</name>
    </assembly>
    <members>
        <member name="T:DataStorage">
            <summary>
            DataStorage is used to persist and retrieve
            employee data from the files.
            </summary>
        </member>
        <member name="M:DataStorage.Store(Employee)">
            <summary>
            Save an employee object to a file
            named with the Employee name.
            </summary>
            <remarks>
            This method uses
            <seealso cref="T:System.IO.FileStream"/>
            in addition to
            <seealso cref="T:System.IO.StreamWriter"/>
            </remarks>
            <param name="employee">
            The employee to persist to a vile</param>
            <date>January 1, 2000</date>
        </member>
        <member name="M:DataStorage.Load(
                System.String,System.String)">
```

```
            <summary>
            Loads up an employee object
            </summary>
            <remarks>
            This method uses
            <seealso cref="T:System.IO.FileStream"/>
            in addition to
            <seealso cref="T:System.IO.StreamReader"/>
            </remarks>
            <param name="firstName">
            The first name of the employee</param>
            <param name="lastName">
            The last name of the employee</param>
            <returns>
            The employee object corresponding to the names
            </returns>
            <date>January 1, 2000</date>*
        </member>
    </members>
</doc>
```

The resulting file includes only the amount of metadata that is necessary to associate an element back to its corresponding C# declaration. This is important to note, because in general, it is necessary to use the XML output in combination with the generated assembly in order to produce any meaningful documentation. Fortunately, tools such as the open source project NDoc[2] can generate documentation.

Garbage Collection

Garbage collection is obviously a core function of the runtime. Its purpose is to restore memory consumed by objects that are no longer referenced. The emphasis in this statement lies with memory and references. The garbage collector is only responsible for restoring memory; it does not handle other resources such as database connections, handles (files, windows, and so on), network ports, and hardware devices such as serial ports. Also, the garbage collector determines what to clean up based on whether any references remain. Implicitly this means that the garbage collector works with reference objects and restores memory on the heap only. Additionally, it

---

2. See http://ndoc.sourceforge.net to learn more about this tool.

means that maintaining a reference to an object will prevent the garbage collector from reusing the memory consumed by the object.

■ ADVANCED TOPIC

Garbage Collection in .NET

Many details about the garbage collector pertain to the specific CLI implementation, and therefore, they could vary. This section discusses the .NET implementation, since it is the most prevalent.

In .NET, the garbage collector uses a mark-and-compact algorithm. At the beginning of a garbage collection cycle, it identifies all **root references** to objects. Root references are any references from static variables, CPU registers, and local variables or parameter instances (and f-reachable objects). Given this list, the garbage collector is able to walk the tree identified by each root reference and determine recursively all the objects to which the root references point. In this manner, the garbage collector identifies a graph of all reachable objects.

Instead of enumerating all the inaccessible objects, the garbage collector performs garbage collection by compacting all reachable objects next to each other, thereby overwriting any memory consumed by objects that are inaccessible (and, therefore, are garbage).

Locating and moving all reachable objects requires that the system maintain a consistent state while the garbage collector runs. To achieve this, all managed threads within the process halt during garbage collection. This obviously can result in brief pauses in an application, which is generally insignificant unless a particularly large garbage collection cycle is necessary. In order to reduce the likelihood of a garbage collection cycle at an inopportune time, however, the `System.GC` object includes a `Collect()` method, which can be called immediately before the critical performing code. This will not prevent the garbage collector from running, but it will reduce the likelihood that it will run, assuming no intense memory utilization occurs during the critical performance code.

One perhaps surprising aspect of .NET garbage collection behavior is that not all garbage is necessarily cleaned up during an iteration. Studies of object lifetimes reveal that recently created objects are more likely to need garbage collection than long-standing objects. Capitalizing on this behavior, the .NET garbage collector is generational, attempting to clean up short-lived objects more frequently than objects that have already survived a garbage collection iteration. Specifically, there are three generations of objects. Each time an object survives a garbage collection cycle, it is moved to the next generation, until it ends up in generation two (counting starts from zero). The garbage collector then runs more frequently for objects in generation zero than it does for objects in generation two.

Ultimately, in spite of the trepidation that .NET faced during its early beta releases when compared with unmanaged code, time has shown that .NET's garbage collection is extremely efficient. More importantly, the gains created in development productivity have far outweighed the costs in development for the few cases where managed code is dropped to optimize particular algorithms.

Weak References

All references discussed so far are **strong references** because they maintain an object's accessibility and they prevent the garbage collector from cleaning up the memory consumed by the object. The framework also supports the concept of **weak references**, however. Weak references will not prevent garbage collection on an object, but they will maintain a reference so that if the garbage collector does not clean up the object, it can be reused.

Weak references are designed for objects that are expensive to create and are too expensive to keep around. Consider, for example, a large list of objects loaded from a database and displayed to the user. The loading of this list is potentially expensive, and once the user closes the list, it should be available for garbage collection. However, if the user requests the list multiple times, a second expensive load call will always be required. However, with weak references, it is possible to use code to check whether the list has not yet been cleaned up, and if not, to rereference the same list. In this way, weak references serve as a memory cache for objects. Objects within the cache are retrieved quickly, but if the garbage collector has recovered the memory of these objects, they will need to be re-created.

Once an object (or collection of objects) is recognized for potential weak reference consideration, it needs to be assigned to `System.WeakReference` (see Listing 9.19).

LISTING 9.19: Using a Weak Reference

```
// ...

private WeakReference Data;

public FileStream GetData()
{
    FileStream data = (FileStream)Data.Target;
    if (data != null)
    {
        return data;
    }
    else
    {
        // Load data
        // ...

        // Create a weak reference
        // to data for use later.
        Data.Target = data;
    }
    return data;
}

// ...
```

Given the assignment of `WeakReference (Data)`, you can check for garbage collection by seeing if the weak reference is set to `null`. The key in doing this, however, is to first assign the weak reference to a strong reference (`FileStream data = Data`) to avoid the possibility that between checking for `null` and accessing the data, the garbage collector runs and cleans up the weak reference. The strong reference obviously prevents the garbage collector from cleaning up the object, so it must be assigned first (instead of checking `Target` for `null`).

Resource Cleanup

Garbage collection is a key responsibility of the runtime. It is important to note, however, that the garbage collection relates to memory utilization. It is not about the cleaning up of file handles, database connection strings, ports, or other limited resources.

Finalizers

Finalizers allow programmers to write code that will clean up a class's resources. However, unlike constructors that are called explicitly using the new operator, finalizers cannot be called explicitly from within the code. There is no new equivalent such as a `delete` operator. Rather, the garbage collector is responsible for calling a finalizer on an object instance. Therefore, developers cannot determine at compile time exactly when the finalizer will execute. All they know is that the finalizer will run sometime between when an object was last used and before the application shuts down. (Finalizers will execute barring process termination prior to the natural closure of the process. For instance, events such as the computer being turned off or a forced termination of the process will prevent the finalizer from running.)

The finalizer declaration is identical to the destructor syntax of C#'s predecessor—namely, C++. As shown in Listing 9.20, the finalizer declaration is prefixed with a tilde before the name of the class.

LISTING 9.20: Defining a Finalizer

```
class TemporaryFileStream
{
  public TemporaryFileStream()
  {
      Stream = new FileStream(
          File.FullName, FileMode.OpenOrCreate,
          FileAccess.ReadWrite);
  }

  // Finalizer
  ~TemporaryFileStream()
  {
      Close();
  }

  public FileStream Stream
  {
      get { return _Stream; }
        private set { _Stream = value; }
  }
  private FileStream _Stream;
```

```csharp
public FileInfo File
{
    get { return _File; }
      private set { _File = value; }
}
private FileInfo _File =
    new FileInfo(Path.GetTempFileName());

public void Close()
{
    _Stream.Close();
    File.Delete();
}
}
```

Finalizers do not allow any parameters to be passed, and as a result, finalizers cannot be overloaded. Furthermore, finalizers cannot be called explicitly. Only the garbage collector can invoke a finalizer. Therefore, access modifiers on finalizers are meaningless, and as such, they are not supported. Finalizers in base classes will be invoked automatically as part of an object finalization call.

Because the garbage collector handles all memory management, finalizers are not responsible for de-allocating memory. Rather, they are responsible for freeing up resources such as database connections and file handles, resources that require an explicit activity that the garbage collector doesn't know about.

Language Contrast: C++—Deterministic Destruction

Although finalizers are similar to destructors in C++, the fact that their execution cannot be determined at compile time makes them distinctly different. The garbage collector calls C# finalizers sometime after they were last used, but before the program shuts down; C++ destructors are automatically called when the object (not a pointer) goes out of scope.

Although running the garbage collector can be a relatively expensive process, the fact that garbage collection is intelligent enough to delay running until process utilization is somewhat reduced offers an advantage over deterministic destructors. Deterministic destructors will run at compile-time-defined locations, even when a processor is in high demand and the overall memory consuption is low.

Deterministic Finalization with the `using` Statement

The problem with finalizers on their own is that they don't support **deterministic finalization** (the ability to know when a finalizer will run). Rather, finalizers serve the important role of a backup mechanism for cleaning up resources if a developer using a class neglects to call the requisite cleanup code explicitly.

For example, consider the `TemporaryFileStream` that not only includes a finalizer but also a `Close()` method. The class uses a file resource that could potentially consume a significant amount of disk space. The developer using `TemporaryFileStream` can explicitly call `Close()` in order to restore the disk space.

Providing a method for deterministic finalization is important because it eliminates a dependency on the indeterminate timing behavior of the finalizer. Even if the developer fails to call `Close()` explicitly, the finalizer will take care of the call. The finalizer will run later than if it was called explicitly, but it will be called.

Because of the importance of deterministic finalization, the base class library includes a specific interface for the pattern and C# integrates the pattern into the language. The `IDisposable` interface defines the details of the pattern with a single method called `Dispose()`, which developers call on a resource class to "dispose" of the consumed resources. Listing 9.21 demonstrates the `IDisposable` interface and some code for calling it.

LISTING 9.21: Resource Cleanup with **`IDisposable`**

```
class TemporaryFileStream : IDisposable
{
    public TemporaryFileStream()
    {
        _Stream = new FileStream(
            File.FullName, FileMode.OpenOrCreate,
            FileAccess.ReadWrite);
    }

    ~TemporaryFileStream()
    {
        Close();
    }

    public FileStream Stream
    {
```

```csharp
        get { return _Stream; }
        private set { _Stream = value; }
    }
    private FileStream _Stream;

    public FileInfo File
    {
        get { return _File; }
        private set { _File = value; }
    }
    private FileInfo _File =
        new FileInfo(Path.GetTempFileName());

    public void Close()
    {
        _Stream.Close();
        File.Delete();
        // Turn off calling the finalizer
        System.GC.SuppressFinalize(this);
    }

    #region IDisposable Members
    public void Dispose()
    {
        Close();
    }
    #endregion
}
```

```csharp
class Program
{
  // ...
  static void Search()
  {
      TemporaryFileStream fileStream =
          new TemporaryFileStream();

      // Use temporary file stream;
      // ...

      fileStream.Dispose();

      // ...
  }
}
```

The steps for both implementing and calling the IDisposable interface are relatively simple. However, there are a couple of points you should not forget. First, there is a chance that an exception will occur between the time

`TemporaryFileStream` is instantiated and `Dispose()` is called. If this happens, `Dispose()` will not be invoked and the resource cleanup will have to rely on the finalizer. To avoid this, callers need to implement a `try/finally` block. Instead of coding such a block explicitly, C# provides a `using` statement expressly for the purpose. The resulting code appears in Listing 9.22.

LISTING 9.22: Invoking the **using** Statement

```
class Program
{
  // ...

  static void Search()
  {
      using (TemporaryFileStream fileStream1 =
          new TemporaryFileStream(),
          fileStream2 = new TemporaryFileStream())
      {
          // Use temporary file stream;
      }
  }
}
```

The resulting CIL code is identical to the code that would be created if there was an explicit `try/finally` block, where `fileStream.Dispose()` is called in the `finally` block. The `using` statement, however, provides a syntax shortcut for the `try/finally` block.

Within a `using` statement, you can instantiate more than one variable by separating each variable with a comma. The key is that all variables are of the same type and that they implement `IDisposable`. To enforce the use of the same type, the data type is specified only once rather than before each variable declaration.

■ ADVANCED TOPIC

The using Statement Prior to C# 2.0

Prior to C# 2.0, you could code a `using` statement with any type that implemented a `Dispose()` method, regardless of whether the type actually implemented the `IDisposable` interface. In C# 2.0, however, the `using` statement requires implementation of the `IDisposable` interface.

Garbage Collection and Finalization

The IDisposable pattern contains one additional important call. Back in Listing 9.21, the Close() method included a call to System.GC.Suppress-Finalize() (captured again in Listing 9.23). Its purpose was to remove the TemporaryFileStream class instance from the finalization (f-reachable) queue.

LISTING 9.23: Suppressing Finalization

```
// ...
public void Close()
{
    _Stream.Close();
    File.Delete();
    // Turn off calling the finalizer
    System.GC.SuppressFinalize(this);
}
// ...
```

The **f-reachable queue** is a list of all objects that are ready for garbage collection and that also have finalization implementations. The runtime cannot garbage collect objects with finalizers until after their finalization methods have been called. However, garbage collection itself does not call the finalization method. Rather, references to finalization objects are added to the f-reachable queue, thereby ironically delaying garbage collection. This is because the f-reachable queue is a list of "references," and as such, the objects are not garbage until after their finalization methods are called and the object references are removed from the f-reachable queue.

■ **ADVANCED TOPIC**

Resurrecting Objects

By the time an object's finalization method is called, all references to the object have disappeared and the only step before garbage collection is running the finalization code. However, it is possible to add a reference inadvertently for a finalization object back into the root reference's graph. In so doing, the rereferenced object is no longer inaccessible, and therefore, it is not ready for garbage collection. However, if the finalization method for the object has already run, it will not necessarily be run again unless it is explicitly marked for finalization (using the `GC.ReRegisterFinalize()` method).

Obviously, resurrecting objects like this is peculiar behavior and you should generally avoid it. Finalization code should be simple and should focus on cleaning up only the resources that it references.

Resource Utilization and Finalization Guidelines

When defining classes that manage resources, you should consider the following.

1. Only implement `finalize` on objects with resources that are scarce or expensive. Finalization delays garbage collection.

2. Objects with finalizers should implement `IDisposable` to support deterministic finalization.

3. Finalization methods generally invoke the same code called by `IDisposable`, perhaps simply calling the `Dispose()` method.

4. Deterministic finalization methods like `Dispose()` and `Close()` should call `System.GC.SuppressFinalize()` so that garbage collection occurs sooner and resource cleanup is not repeated.

5. Code that handles resource cleanup may be invoked multiple times and should therefore be reentrant. (For example, it should be possible to call `Close()` multiple times.)

6. Resource cleanup methods should be simple and should focus on cleaning up resources referenced by the finalization instance only. They should not reference other objects.

7. If a base class implements `Dispose()`, then the derived implementation should call the base implementation.

8. Generally, objects should be coded as unusable after `Dispose()` is called. After an object has been disposed, methods other than `Dispose()` (which could potentially be called multiple times) should throw an `ObjectDisposedException()`.

SUMMARY

This chapter provided a whirlwind tour of many topics related to building solid class libraries. All the topics pertain to internal development as well, but they are much more critical to building robust classes. Ultimately, the topic is about forming more robust and programmable APIs. In the category of robustness fit namespaces and garbage collection. Both of these items fit in the programmability category, along with the other items covered: overriding `object`'s virtual members, operator overloading, and XML comments for documentation.

Exception handling uses inheritance heavily by defining an exception hierarchy and enforcing custom exceptions to fit within this hierarchy. Furthermore, the C# compiler uses inheritance to verify catch block order. In the next chapter, you will see why inheritance is such a core part of exception handling.

■ 10 ■
Exception Handling

C HAPTER 4 DISCUSSED using the `try/catch/finally` blocks for standard exception handling. In that chapter, the catch block always caught exceptions of type `System.Exception`. This chapter defines some additional details of exception handling—specifically, details surrounding additional exception types, defining custom exceptions, and multiple catch blocks for handling each type. This chapter also details exceptions because of their reliance on inheritance.

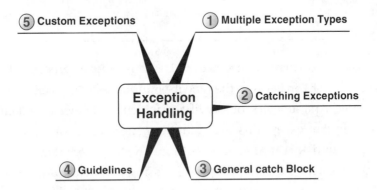

Multiple Exception Types

Listing 10.1 throws a `System.ApplicationException`, not the `System.Exception` type demonstrated in Chapter 4. C# allows code to throw any type that derives (perhaps indirectly) from `System.Exception`.

The code for throwing any exception is simply to prefix the exception instance with the keyword `throw`. The type of exception used is obviously the type that best describes the circumstances surrounding the error that caused the exception.

For example, consider the `TextNumberParser.Parse()` method in Listing 10.1.

LISTING 10.1: Throwing an Exception

```csharp
public sealed class TextNumberParser
{
  public static int Parse(string textDigit)
  {
      string[] digitTexts =
          { "zero", "one", "two", "three", "four",
              "five", "six", "seven", "eight", "nine" };

      int result = Array.IndexOf(
          digitTexts, textDigit.ToLower());

      if (result < 0)
      {
          throw new ArgumentException(
              "The argument did not represent a digit",
              "textDigit");
      }

      return result;
  }
}
```

Instead of throwing `System.Exception`, it is more appropriate to throw `ArgumentException` because the type itself indicates what went wrong and includes special parameters for identifying which parameter was at fault.

Three similar exceptions are `ArgumentException`, `ArgumentNull-Exception`, and `NullReferenceException`. `ArgumentNullException` should be thrown for the inappropriate passing of null arguments. This is a special case of an invalid parameter exception that would more generally (when it wasn't null) be thrown as an `ArgumentException` or an `ArgumentOutOfRangeException`. `NullReferenceException` is generally something that only the underlying runtime will throw with an attempt to dereference a null. Instead of causing a `NullReferenceException`, programmers should check parameters for `null` before accessing them and then throw an `ArgumentNullException`, which can provide more contextual information such as the parameter name.

Catching Exceptions

Throwing a particular exception type enables the type itself to identify the problem. It is not necessary, in other words, to catch the exception and use a `switch` statement on the exception message to determine what action to take in light of the exception. Instead, C# allows for multiple catch blocks, each targeting a specific exception type, as Listing 10.2 shows.

LISTING 10.2: Catching Different Exception Types

```csharp
public sealed class Program
{
  public static void Main()
  {
      try
      {
          // ...
          throw new ApplicationException(
              "Arbitrary exception");
          // ...
      }
      catch (NullReferenceException exception)
      {
          // Handle NullReferenceException
      }
      catch (ArgumentException exception)
      {
          // Handle ArgumentException
      }
      catch (ApplicationException exception)
      {
          // Handle ApplicationException
       }
      catch (SystemException exception)
      {
          // Handle SystemException
      }
      catch (Exception exception)
      {
          // Handle Exception
      }
  }
}
```

Listing 10.2 has five catch blocks, each handling a different type of exception. When an exception occurs, the execution will jump to the catch block with the exception type that most closely matches. The closeness of a match is determined by the inheritance chain. For example, even though the exception thrown is of type `System.Exception`, this "is a" relationship occurs through inheritance because `System.ApplicationException` derives from `System.Exception`. Since `ApplicationException` most closely matches the exception thrown, `catch(ApplicationException ...)` will catch the exception instead of the `catch(Exception ...)` block.

Catch blocks must appear in order, from most specific to most general, to avoid a compile error. For example, moving the `catch(Exception ...)` block before any of the other exceptions will result in a compile error, since all prior exceptions derive from `System.Exception` at some point in their inheritance chain.

Language Contrast: Java—Exception Specifiers

C# has no equivalent for Java's exception specifiers. With exception specifiers, the Java compiler is able to verify that all possible exceptions thrown within a function (or a function's call hierarchy) are either caught or declared as possibly rethrown. The C# team considered this option and concluded that the maintenance burden that it imposed was not worth the perceived benefit. Therefore, it is not necessary to maintain a list of all possible exceptions throughout a particular call stack, but neither is it possible to easily determine the possible exceptions. (As it turns out, this wasn't possible for Java either. Calling virtual methods or using late binding, such as reflection, made it impossible to fully resolve at compile time what exceptions a method could possibly throw.)

General Catch Block

C# requires that any object that code throws must derive from `System.Exception`. However, this requirement is not universal to all languages. C/C++, for example, allows any object type to be thrown, including managed exceptions that don't derive from `System.Exception`. In C# 1.0, the result was that method calls (into other assemblies) could potentially throw exceptions that would not be caught with a `catch(System.Exception)` block. If a different language throws a `string`, for example, the exception could go unhandled. To avoid this, C# includes a catch block that takes no parameters. The term for such a catch block is **general catch block**, and Listing 10.3 includes one.

LISTING 10.3: Catching Different Exception Types

```csharp
public sealed class Program
{
  public static void Main()
  {
      try
      {
          // ...
          throw new ApplicationException(
              "Arbitrary exception");
          // ...
      }
      catch (NullReferenceException exception)
      {
          // Handle NullReferenceException
      }
      catch (ArgumentException exception)
      {
          // Handle ArgumentException
      }
      catch (ApplicationException exception)
      {
          // Handle ApplicationException
       }
      catch (SystemException exception)
      {
          // Handle SystemException
      }
      catch (Exception exception)
      {
          // Handle Exception
      }
      catch
      {
          // Any unhandled exception
      }
  }
}
```

The general catch block will catch all exceptions, regardless of whether they derive from System.Exception, assuming an earlier catch block does not catch them. The disadvantage of such a block is simply that there is no exception instance to access and, therefore, no way to know the appropriate course of action. It wouldn't even be possible to recognize the unlikely case where such an exception is innocuous. The best course of action is to handle the exception with some cleanup code before shutting down the application. The catch block could save any volatile data, for example, before shutting down the application or rethrowing the exception.

The behavior in C# 2.0 varies slightly from the earlier C# behavior. In C# 2.0, all exceptions, whether deriving from System.Exception or not, will propagate into C# assemblies as derived from System.Exception. The result is that System.Exception catch blocks will catch all exceptions not caught by earlier blocks and a general catch block following a System.Exception catch block will never be invoked. Furthermore, general catch blocks following a System.Exception catch block will result in a compiler warning.

■ ADVANCED TOPIC

Empty Catch Block Internals

The CIL code corresponding to an empty catch block is, in fact, a catch(object) block. This means that regardless of the type thrown, the empty catch block will catch it. Interestingly, it is not possible to explicitly declare a catch(object) exception block within C# code. Therefore, there is no means of catching a non-System.Exception-derived exception and having the exception instance to scrutinize.

Ironically, unmanaged exceptions from languages like C++ generally result in System.Runtime.InteropServices.SEHException type exceptions, which derive from the System.Exception type. Therefore, not only can the unmanaged type exceptions be caught using a general catch block, but also the non-System.Exception-managed types that are thrown as well—for instance, types such as string.

Guidelines for Exception Handling

Exception handling provides much-needed structure to the error-handling mechanisms that preceded it. However, it can still make for some unwieldy results if used haphazardly. The following guidelines offer some best practices for exception handling.

- Catch only the exceptions that you can handle.

  Generally it is possible to handle some types of exceptions but not others. For example, opening a file for exclusive read-write access may throw a `System.IO.IOException` because the file is already in use. In catching this type of exception, the code can report to the user that the file is in use and allow the user the option of canceling the operation or retrying it. Only exceptions for which there is a known action should be caught. Other exception types should be left for callers higher in the stack.

- Don't hide (bury) exceptions you don't fully handle.

  New programmers are often tempted to catch all exceptions and then continue executing instead of reporting an unhandled exception to the user. However, this may result in a critical system problem going undetected. Unless code takes explicit action to handle an exception or explicitly determines certain exceptions to be innocuous, catch blocks should rethrow exceptions instead of catching them and hiding them from the caller. Predominantly, `catch(System.Exception )` and general catch blocks should occur higher in the call stack, unless the block ends by rethrowing the exception.

- Use `System.Exception` and general catch blocks rarely.

  Virtually all exceptions derive from `System.Exception`. However, the best way to handle some `System.Exceptions` is to allow them to go unhandled or to gracefully shut down the application sooner rather than later. Exceptions like `System.OutOfMemoryException` are nonrecoverable, for example, and the best course of action is to shut down the application. Such catch blocks should appear only to run cleanup or emergency code (such as saving any volatile data) before shutting down the application or rethrowing the exception with `throw;`.

- Avoid exception reporting or logging lower in the call stack.

  Often, programmers are tempted to log exceptions or report exceptions to the user at the soonest possible location in the call stack. However, these locations are seldom able to handle the exception fully and they resort to rethrowing the exception. Such catch blocks should not log the exception or report it to a user while in the bowels of the call stack. If the exception is logged and rethrown, the callers higher in the call stack may do the same, resulting in duplicate log entries of the exception. Worse, displaying the exception to the user may not be appropriate for the type of application. (Using `System.Console.WriteLine()` in a Windows application will never be seen by the user, for example, and displaying a dialog in an unattended command-line process may go unnoticed and freeze the application.) Logging- and exception-related user interfaces should be reserved for high up in the call stack.

- Use `throw;` rather than `throw <exception object>` inside a catch block.

  It is possible to rethrow an exception inside a catch block. For example, the implementation of `catch(ArgumentNullException exception)` could include a call to `throw exception`. However, rethrowing the exception like this will reset the stack trace to the location of the rethrown call, instead of reusing the original throw point location. Therefore, unless you are rethrowing with a different exception type or intentionally hiding the original call stack, use `throw;` to allow the same exception to propagate up the call stack.

- Use caution when rethrowing different exceptions.

  From inside a catch block, rethrowing a different exception will not only reset the throw point, it will also hide the original exception. To preserve the original exception set the new exception's `InnerException` property, generally assignable via the constructor. Rethrowing a different exception should be reserved for situations where

  a. Changing the exception type clarifies the problem.
     For example, in a call to `Logon(User user)`, rethrowing a different exception type is perhaps more appropriate than propagating `System.IO.IOException` when the file with the user list is inaccessible.

b. Private data is part of the original exception.

In the preceding scenario, if the file path is included in the original `System.IO.IOException`, thereby exposing private security information about the system, the exception should be wrapped. This assumes, of course, that `InnerException` is not set with the original exception.

c. The exception type is too specific for the caller to handle appropriately.

For example, instead of throwing an exception specific to a particular database system, a more generic exception is used so that database-specific code higher in the call stack can be avoided.

Defining Custom Exceptions

Once throwing an exception becomes the best course of action, it is preferable to use framework exceptions because they are well established and understood. Instead of throwing a custom invalid argument exception, for example, it is preferable to use the `System.ArgumentException` type. However, if the developers using a particular API will take special action—the exception-handling logic will vary to handle a custom exception type, for instance—it is appropriate to define a custom exception. For example, if a mapping API receives an address for which the ZIP Code is invalid, instead of throwing `System.ArgumentException`, it may be better to throw a custom `InvalidAddressException`. The key is whether the caller is likely to write a specific `InvalidAddressException` catch block with special handling rather than just a generic `System.ArgumentException` catch block.

Defining a custom exception simply involves deriving from `System.Exception` or some other exception type. Listing 10.4 provides an example.

LISTING 10.4: Creating a Custom Exception

```
class DatabaseException : System.Exception
{
  public DatabaseException(
      System.Data. SqlClient.SQLException exception)
  {
      InnerException = exception;
```

```
        // ...
    }

    public DatabaseException(
        System.Data.OracleClient.OracleException exception)
    {
        InnerException = exception;
        // ...
    }

    public DatabaseException()
    {
        // ...
    }

    public DatabaseException(string message)
    {
        // ...
    }

    public DatabaseException(
        string message, Exception innerException)
    {
        InnerException = innerException;
        // ...
    }
}
```

This custom exception might be created to wrap proprietary database exceptions. Since Oracle and SQL Server (for example) each throw different exceptions for similar errors, an application could define a custom exception that standardizes the database-specific exceptions into a common exception wrapper that the application can handle in a standard manner. That way, whether the application was using an Oracle or a SQL Server backend database, the same catch block could be used to handle the error higher up the stack.

The only requirement for a custom exception is that it derives from `System.Exception` or one of its descendents. However, there are several more good practices for custom exceptions.

- All exceptions should use the "Exception" suffix. This way, their purpose is easily established from the name.
- Generally, all exceptions should include constructors that take no parameters, a string parameter, and a parameter set of a string and an

inner exception. Furthermore, since exceptions are usually constructed within the same statement in which they are thrown, any additional exception data should also be allowed as part of the constructor. (The obvious exception to creating all these constructors is if certain data is required and a constructor circumvents the requirements.)

- The inheritance chain should be kept relatively shallow (with fewer than approximately five levels).

The inner exception serves an important purpose when rethrowing an exception that is different from the one that was caught. For example, if a `System.Data.SqlClient.SqlException` is thrown by a database call but is caught within the data access layer to be rethrown as a `DatabaseException`, then the `DatabaseException` constructor that takes the `SqlException` (or inner exception) will save the original `SqlException` in the `InnerException` property. That way, when requiring additional details about the original exception, developers can retrieve the exception from the `InnerException` property.

▪ ADVANCED TOPIC

Serializable Exceptions

Serializable objects are objects that the runtime can persist into a stream—a filestream, for example—and then reinstantiate out of the stream. In the case of exceptions, this may be necessary for certain distributed communication technologies. To support serialization, exception declarations should include the `System.SerializableAttribute` attribute or they should implement `ISerializable`. Furthermore, they must include a constructor that takes `System.Runtime.Serialization.SerializationInfo` and `System.Runtime.Serialization.StreamingContext`. Listing 10.5 shows an example of using `System.SerializableAttribute`.

LISTING 10.5: Defining a Serializable Exception

```
// Supporting serialization via an attribute
[Serializable]
class DatabaseException : System.ApplicationException
{
    // ...
```

```
    // Used for deserialization of exceptions
    public DatabaseException(
        SerializationInfo serializationInfo,
        StreamingContext context)
    {
        // ...
    }

}
```

The preceding `DatabaseException` example demonstrates both the attribute and the constructor requirement for making an exception serializable.

■ BEGINNER TOPIC

Checked and Unchecked Conversions

As first discussed in a Chapter 2 Advanced Topic, C# provides special keywords for marking a code block with instructions to the runtime of what should happen if the target data type is too small to contain the assigned data. By default, if the target data type cannot contain the assigned data, then the data will truncate during assignment. For an example, see Listing 10.6.

LISTING 10.6: Overflowing an Integer Value

```
using System;

public class Program
{
    public static void Main()
    {
        // int.MaxValue equals 2147483647
        int n = int.MaxValue;
        n = n + 1 ;
        System.Console.WriteLine(n);
    }
}
```

The results of Listing 10.6 appear in Output 10.1.

OUTPUT 10.1:

```
-2147483648
```

It writes the value -2147483648 to the console. However, placing the code within a checked block or using the checked option when running the compiler will cause the runtime to throw an exception of type System .OverflowException. The syntax for a checked block uses the checked keyword, as shown in Listing 10.7.

LISTING 10.7: A Checked Block Example

```
using System;

public class Program
{
  public static void Main()
  {
      checked
      {
          // int.MaxValue equals 2147483647
          int n = int.MaxValue;
          n = n + 1 ;
          System.Console.WriteLine(n);
      }
  }
}
```

The results of Listing 10.7 appear in Output 10.2.

OUTPUT 10.2:

```
Unhandled Exception: System.OverflowException: Arithmetic operation
resulted in an overflow. at Program.Main() in ...Program.cs:line 12
```

The result is that an exception is thrown if, within the checked block, an overflow assignment occurs at runtime.

The C# compiler provides a command-line option for changing the default checked behavior from unchecked to checked. C# also supports an unchecked block that truncates the data instead of throwing an exception for assignments within the block (see Listing 10.8).

LISTING 10.8: An Unchecked Block Example

```
using System;

public class Program
{
```

```csharp
public static void Main()
{
    unchecked
    {
        // int.MaxValue equals 2147483647
        int n = int.MaxValue;
        n = n + 1 ;
        System.Console.WriteLine(n);
    }
}
}
```

The results of Listing 10.8 appear in Output 10.3.

OUTPUT 10.3:

```
-2147483648
```

Even if the checked option is on during compilation, the unchecked keyword in the code in Listing 10.8 will prevent the runtime from throwing an exception during execution.

SUMMARY

Throwing an exception causes a significant performance hit. A single exception causes lots of runtime stack information to be loaded and processed, data that would not otherwise be loaded, and it takes a considerable amount of time. As pointed out in Chapter 4, use exceptions only to handle exceptional circumstances; APIs should provide mechanisms to check whether an exception will be thrown instead of forcing a particular API to be called in order to determine whether an exception will be thrown.

The next chapter introduces generics, a C# 2.0 feature that significantly enhances the code written in C# 1.0. In fact, it essentially deprecates any use of the System.Collections namespace, which was formerly used in nearly every project.

11

Generics

A S YOUR PROJECTS become more sophisticated, you will need a better way to reuse and customize existing software. To facilitate code reuse, especially the reuse of algorithms, C# includes a feature called **generics**. Just as methods are powerful because they can take parameters, classes that take type parameters have significantly more functionality as well, and this is what generics enable. Like their predecessor, templates, generics enable the definition of algorithms and pattern implementations once, rather than separately for each type. However, C# implements a type-safe version of templates that differs slightly in syntax and greatly in implementation from its predecessors in C++ and Java. Note that generics were added to the runtime and C# with version 2.0.

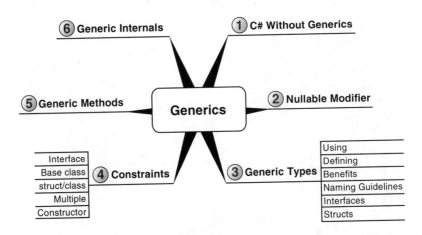

C# without Generics

I will begin the discussion of generics by examining a class that does not use generics. The class is `System.Collections.Stack`, and its purpose is to represent a collection of objects such that the last item to be added to the collection is the first item retrieved from the collection (called last in, first out, or LIFO). `Push()` and `Pop()`, the two main methods of the `Stack` class, add items to the stack and remove them from the stack, respectively. The declarations for the `Pop()` and `Push()` methods on the stack class appear in Listing 11.1.

LISTING 11.1: The **Stack** Definition Using a Data Type Object

```
public class Stack
{
   public virtual object Pop();
   public virtual void Push(object obj);
   // ...
}
```

Programs frequently use stack type collections to facilitate multiple undo operations. For example, Listing 11.2 uses the stack class for undo operations within a program which simulates the Etch A Sketch game.

LISTING 11.2: Supporting Undo in a Program Similar to the Etch A Sketch Game

```
using System;
using System.Collections;

class Program
{
  // ...

  public void Sketch()
  {
     Stack path = new Stack();
     Cell currentPosition;
     ConsoleKeyInfo key;  // New with C# 2.0

     do
     {
        // Etch in the direction indicated by the
        // arrow keys that the user enters.
        key = Move();

        switch (key.Key)
```

```
        {
            case ConsoleKey.Z:
                // Undo the previous Move.
                if (path.Count >= 1)
                {
                    currentPosition = (Cell)path.Pop();
                    Console.SetCursorPosition(
                        currentPosition.X, currentPosition.Y);
                    Undo();
                }
                break;

            case ConsoleKey.DownArrow:
            case ConsoleKey.UpArrow:
            case ConsoleKey.LeftArrow:
            case ConsoleKey.RightArrow:
                // SaveState()
                currentPosition = new Cell(
                    Console.CursorLeft, Console.CursorTop);
                path.Push(currentPosition);
                break;

            default:
                Console.Beep();  // New with C#2.0
                break;
        }

    }
    while (key.Key != ConsoleKey.X);  // Use X to quit.

    }
}

public struct Cell
{
    readonly public int X;
    readonly public int Y;
    public Cell(int x, int y)
    {
        X = x;
        Y = y;
    }
}
```

The results of Listing 11.2 appear in Output 11.1.

Using the variable path, which is declared as a System.Collec-tions.Stack, you save the previous move by passing a custom type, Cell, into the Stack.Push() method using path.Push(currentPosi-tion). If the user enters a Z (or Ctrl+Z), then you undo the previous move

OUTPUT 11.1:

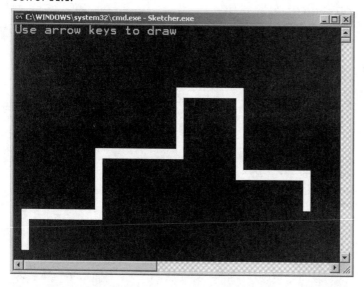

by retrieving it from the stack using a Pop() method, setting the cursor position to be the previous position, and calling Undo(). (Note that this code uses some CLR 2.0-specific console functions as well.)

Although the code is functional, there is a fundamental drawback in the System.Collections.Stack class. As shown in Listing 11.1, the Stack class collects variables of type object. Because every object in the CLR derives from object, Stack provides no validation that the elements you place into it are homogenous or are of the intended type. For example, instead of passing currentPosition, you can pass a string in which X and Y are concatenated with a decimal point between them. However, the compiler must allow the inconsistent data types because in some scenarios, it is desirable.

Furthermore, when retrieving the data from the stack using the Pop() method, you must cast the return value to a Cell. But if the value returned from the Pop() method is not a Cell type object, an exception is thrown. You can test the data type, but splattering such checks builds complexity. The fundamental problem with creating classes that can work with multiple data types without generics is that they must use a common base type, generally object data.

Using value types, such as a struct or integer, with classes that use object exacerbates the problem. If you pass a value type to the Stack.Push()

method, for example, the runtime automatically boxes it. Similarly, when you retrieve a value type, you need to explicitly unbox the data and cast the `object` reference you obtain from the `Pop()` method into a value type. While the widening operation (cast to a base class) for a reference type has a negligible performance impact, the box operation for a value type introduces nontrivial overhead.

To change the `Stack` class to enforce storage on a particular data type using the preceding C# programming constructs, you must create a specialized stack class, as in Listing 11.3.

LISTING 11.3: Defining a Specialized Stack Class

```
public class CellStack
{
  public virtual Cell Pop();
  public virtual void Push(Cell cell);
  // ...
}
```

Because `CellStack` can store only objects of type `Cell`, this solution requires a custom implementation of the stack methods, which is less than ideal.

■ BEGINNER TOPIC

Another Example: Nullable Value Types

Chapter 2 introduced the capability of declaring variables that could contain `null` by using the nullable modifier, `?`, when declaring the value type variable. C# only began supporting this in version 2.0 because the right implementation required generics. Prior to the introduction of generics, programmers faced essentially two options.

The first option was to declare a nullable data type for each value type that needs to handle null values, as shown in Listing 11.4.

LISTING 11.4: Declaring Versions of Various Value Types That Store `null`

```
struct NullableInt
{
    public int Value
    {...}
    public bool HasValue
```

```
        {...}
        ...
    }

struct NullableGuid
{
    public Guid Value
    {...}
    public bool HasValue
    {...}
    ...
}
...
```

Listing 11.4 shows implementations for only `NullableInt` and `Null-ableGuid`. If a program required additional nullable value types, you would have to create a copy with the additional value type. If the nullable implementation changed (if it supported a cast from a null to the nullable type, for example), you would have to add the modification to all of the nullable type declarations.

The second option was to declare a nullable type that contains a `Value` property of type `object`, as shown in Listing 11.5.

LISTING 11.5: Declaring a Nullable Type That Contains a **Value** Property of Type **object**

```
struct Nullable
{
    public object Value
    {...}
    public bool HasValue
    {...}
    ...
}
```

Although this option requires only one implementation of a nullable type, the runtime always boxes value types when setting the `Value` property. Furthermore, calls to retrieve data from `Nullable.Value` will not be strongly typed, so retrieving the value type will require a cast operation, which is potentially invalid at runtime.

Neither option is particularly attractive. To deal with dilemmas like this, C# 2.0 includes the concept of generics. In fact, the nullable modifier, `?`, uses generics internally.

Introducing Generic Types

Generics provide a facility for creating data structures that are specialized to handle specific types when declaring a variable. Programmers define these **parameterized types** so that each variable of a particular generic type has the same internal algorithm but the types of data and method signatures can vary based on programmer preference.

To minimize the learning curve for developers, C# designers chose syntax that matched the similar templates concept of C++. In C#, therefore, the syntax for generic classes and structures uses the same angle bracket notation to identify the data types on which the generic declaration specializes.

Using a Generic Class

Listing 11.6 shows how you can specify the actual type used by the generic class. You instruct the `path` variable to use a `Cell` type by specifying `Cell` within angle bracket notation in both the instantiation and the declaration expressions. In other words, when declaring a variable (`path` in this case) using a generic data type, C# requires the developer to identify the actual type. An example showing the new `Stack` class appears in Listing 11.6.

LISTING 11.6: Implementing Undo with a Generic **Stack** Class

```csharp
using System;
using System.Collections.Generic;

class Program
{
  // ...

  public void Sketch()
  {
      Stack<Cell> path;             // Generic variable declaration
      path = new Stack<Cell>();     // Generic object instantiation
      Cell currentPosition;
      ConsoleKeyInfo key;           // New with C# 2.0

      do
      {
          // Etch in the direction indicated by the
          // arrow keys entered by the user.
          key = Move();
```

```
        switch (key.Key)
        {
            case ConsoleKey.Z:
                // Undo the previous Move.
                if (path.Count >= 1)
                {
                    // No cast required.
                    currentPosition = path.Pop();
                    Console.SetCursorPosition(
                        currentPosition.X, currentPosition.Y);
                    Undo();
                }
                break;

            case ConsoleKey.DownArrow:
            case ConsoleKey.UpArrow:
            case ConsoleKey.LeftArrow:
            case ConsoleKey.RightArrow:
                // SaveState()
                currentPosition = new Cell(
                    Console.CursorLeft, Console.CursorTop);
                // Only type Cell allowed in call to Push().
                path.Push(currentPosition);
                break;

            default:
                Console.Beep();   // New with C#2.0
                break;
        }

    } while (key.Key != ConsoleKey.X);   // Use X to quit.
  }
}
```

The results of Listing 11.6 appear in Output 11.2.

In the `path` declaration shown in Listing 11.6, you declare and create a new instance of a `System.Collections.Generic.Stack<T>` class and specify in angle brackets that the data type used for the `path` variable is `Cell`. As a result, every object added to and retrieved from `path` is of type `Cell`. In other words, you no longer need to cast the return of `path.Pop()` or ensure that only `Cell` type objects are added to `path` in the `Push()` method. Before examining the generic advantages, the next section introduces the syntax for generic class definitions.

OUTPUT 11.2:

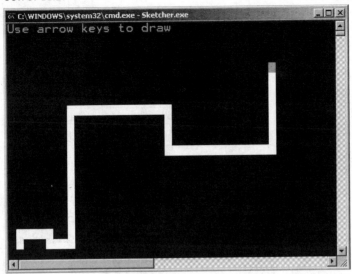

Defining a Simple Generic Class

Generics allow you to author algorithms and patterns, and reuse the code for different data types. Listing 11.7 creates a generic `Stack<T>` class similar to the `System.Collections.Generic.Stack<T>` class used in the code in Listing 11.6. You specify a **type parameter identifier** or **type parameter** (in this case, `T`) within angle brackets after the class declaration. Instances of the generic `Stack<T>` then collect the type corresponding to the variable declaration without converting the collected item to type `object`. The type parameter `T` is a placeholder until variable declaration and instantiation, when the compiler requires the code to specify the type parameter. In Listing 11.7, you can see that the type parameter will be used for the internal `Items` array, the type for the parameter to the `Push()` method, and the return type for the `Pop()` method.

LISTING 11.7: Declaring a Generic Class, **Stack<T>**

```
public class Stack<T>
{
    private T[] _Items;

    public void Push(T data)
    {
        ...
    }
```

```
public T Pop()
{
    . . .
}
}
```

Benefits of Generics

There are several advantages to using a generic class (such as the `Sys-tem.Collections.Generic.Stack<T>` class used earlier instead of the original `System.Collections.Stack` type).

1. Generics facilitate a strongly typed programming model, preventing data types other than those explicitly intended by the members within the parameterized class. In Listing 11.7, the parameterized stack class restricts you to the `Cell` data type for all instances of `Stack<Cell>`. (The statement `path.Push("garbage")` produces a compile-time error indicating that there is no overloaded method for `System.Collections.Generic.Stack<T>.Push(T)` that can work with the string `garbage`, because it cannot be converted to a `Cell`.)

2. Compile-time type checking reduces the likelihood of `InvalidCast-Exception` type errors at runtime.

3. Using value types with generic class members no longer causes a cast to `object`; they no longer require a boxing operation. (For example, `path.Pop()` and `path.Push()` do not require an item to be boxed when added or unboxed when removed.)

4. Generics in C# reduce code bloat. Generic types retain the benefits of specific class versions, without the overhead. (For example, it is no longer necessary to define a class such as `CellStack`.)

5. Performance increases because casting from an object is no longer required, thus eliminating a type check operation. Also, performance increases because boxing is no longer necessary for value types.

6. Generics reduce memory consumption because the avoidance of boxing no longer consumes memory on the heap.

7. Code becomes more readable because of fewer casting checks and because of the need for fewer type-specific implementations.

8. Editors that assist coding via some type of IntelliSense work directly with return parameters from generic classes. There is no need to cast the return data for IntelliSense to work.

At their core, generics offer the ability to code pattern implementations and then reuse those implementations wherever the patterns appear. Patterns describe problems that occur repeatedly within code, and templates provide a single implementation for these repeating patterns.

Type Parameter Naming Guidelines

Just as when you name a method parameter, you should be as descriptive as possible when naming a type parameter. Furthermore, to distinguish it as being a type parameter, the name should include a "T" prefix. For example, in defining a class such as `EntityCollection<TEntity>` you use the type parameter name "TEntity."

The only time you would not use a descriptive type parameter name is when the description would not add any value. For example, using "T" in the `Stack<T>` class is appropriate since the indication that "T" is a type parameter is sufficiently descriptive; the stack works for any type.

In the next section, you will learn about constraints. It is a good practice to use constraint descriptive type names. For example, if a type parameter must implement `IComponent`, consider a type name of "TComponent."

Generic Interfaces and Structs

C# 2.0 supports the use of generics in all parts of the C# language, including interfaces and structs. The syntax is identical to that used by classes. To define an interface with a type parameter, place the type parameter in angle brackets, as shown in the example of `IPair<T>` in Listing 11.8.

LISTING 11.8: Declaring a Generic Interface

```
interface IPair<T>
{
    T First
    {
        get;
        set;
    }
```

```
    T Second
    {
        get;
        set;
    }
}
```

This interface represents pairs of like objects, such as the coordinates of a point, a person's genetic parents, or nodes of a binary tree. The type contained in the pair is the same for both items.

To implement the interface, you use the same syntax as you would for a nongeneric class. However, implementing a generic interface without identifying the type parameter forces the class to be a generic class, as shown in Listing 11.9. In addition, this example uses a struct rather than a class, indicating that C# supports custom generic value types.

LISTING 11.9: Implementing a Generic Interface

```
public struct Pair<T>: IPair<T>
{
    public T First
    {
        get
        {
            return _First;
        }
        set
        {
            _First = value;
        }
    }
    private T _First;

    public T Second
    {
        get
        {
            return _Second;
        }
        set
        {
            _Second = value;
        }
    }
    private T _Second;
}
```

Support for generic interfaces is especially important for collection classes, where generics are most prevalent. Without generics, developers relied on a series of interfaces within the `System.Collections` namespace. Like their implementing classes, these interfaces worked only with type `object`, and as a result, the interface forced all access to and from these collection classes to require a cast. By using generic interfaces, you can avoid cast operations, because a stronger compile-time binding can be achieved with parameterized interfaces.

■ ADVANCED TOPIC

Implementing the Same Interface Multiple Times on a Single Class

One side effect of template interfaces is that you can implement the same interface many times using different type parameters. Consider the `IContainer<T>` example in Listing 11.10.

LISTING 11.10: Duplicating an Interface Implementation on a Single Class

```csharp
public interface IContainer<T>
{
    ICollection<T> Items
    {
        get;
        set;
    }
}

public class Person: IContainer<Address>,
    IContainer<Phone>, IContainer<Email>
{
    ICollection<Address> IContainer<Address>.Items
    {
        get{...}
        set{...}
    }
    ICollection<Phone> IContainer<Phone>.Items
    {
        get{...}
        set{...}
    }
    ICollection<Email> IContainer<Email>.Items
    {
        get{...}
```

```
        set{...}
    }
}
```

In this example, the `Items` property appears multiple times using an explicit interface implementation with a varying type parameter. Without generics, this is not possible, and instead, the compiler would allow only one explicit `IContainer.Items` property.

One possible improvement on `Person` would be to also implement `IContainer<object>` and to have items return the combination of all three containers (`Address`, `Phone`, and `Email`).

Defining a Constructor and a Finalizer

Perhaps surprisingly, the constructor and destructor on a generic do not require type parameters in order to match the class declaration (i.e., not `Pair<T>(){...}`). In the pair example in Listing 11.11, the constructor is declared using `public Pair(T first, T second)`.

LISTING 11.11: Declaring a Generic Type's Constructor

```
public struct Pair<T>: IPair<T>
{
    public Pair(T first, T second)
    {
        _First = first;
        _Second = second;
    }

    public T First
    {
        get{ return _First; }
        set{ _First = value; }
    }
    private T _First;

    public T Second
    {
        get{ return _Second; }
        set{ _Second = value; }
    }
    private T _Second;
}
```

Specifying a Default Value

Listing 11.1 included a constructor that takes the initial values for both
First and Second, and assigns them to _First and _Second. Since
Pair<T> is a struct, any constructor you provide must initialize all fields.
This presents a problem, however. Consider a constructor for Pair<T>
that initializes only half of the pair at instantiation time.

Defining such a constructor, as shown in Listing 11.12, causes a compile
error because the field _Second goes uninitialized at the end of the constructor. Providing initialization for _Second presents a problem since you don't
know the data type of T. If it is a reference type, then null would work, but
this would not suffice if T were a value type (unless it was nullable).

LISTING 11.12: Not Initializing All Fields, Causing a Compile Error

```
public struct Pair<T>: IPair<T>
{
  // ERROR:  Field 'Pair<T>._second' must be fully assigned
  //         before control leaves the constructor
  // public Pair(T first)
  // {
  //    _First = first;
  // }

  // ...
}
```

To deal with this scenario, C# 2.0 allows a dynamic way to code the
default value of any data type using the default operator, first discussed in
Chapter 8. In Chapter 8, I showed how the default value of int could be
specified with default(int) while the default value of a string uses
default(string) (which returns null, as it would for all reference
types). In the case of T, which _Second requires, you use default(T) (see
Listing 11.13).

LISTING 11.13: Initializing a Field with the default Operator

```
public struct Pair<T>: IPair<T>
{
  public Pair(T first)
  {
      _First = first;
      _Second = default(T);
  }
}
```

```
        // ...
    }
```

The `default` operator is allowable outside of the context of generics; any statement can use it.

Multiple Type Parameters

Generic types may employ any number of type parameters. The initial `Pair<T>` example contains only one type parameter. To enable support for storing a dichotomous pair of objects, such as a name/value pair, you need to extend `Pair<T>` to support two type parameters, as shown in Listing 11.14.

LISTING 11.14: Declaring a Generic with Multiple Type Parameters

```csharp
interface IPair<TFirst, TSecond>
{
    TFirst First
    { get; set;     }

    TSecond Second
    { get; set;     }
}

public struct Pair<TFirst, TSecond>: IPair<TFirst, TSecond>
{
    public Pair(TFirst first, TSecond second)
    {
        _First = first;
        _Second = second;
    }

    public TFirst First
    {
        get{ return _First;     }
        set{ _First = value; }
    }
    private TFirst _First;

    public TSecond Second
    {
        get{ return _Second; }
        set{ _Second = value; }
    }
    private TSecond _Second;
}
```

When you use the `Pair<TFirst, TSecond>` class, you supply multiple type parameters within the angle brackets of the declaration and instantiation statements, and then you supply matching types to the parameters of the methods when you call them, as shown in Listing 11.15.

LISTING 11.15: Using a Type with Multiple Type Parameters

```
Pair<int, string> historicalEvent =
    new Pair<int, string>(1914,
        "Shackleton leaves for South Pole on ship Endurance");
Console.WriteLine("{0}: {1}",
    historicalEvent.First, historicalEvent.Second);
```

The number of type parameters, the **arity**, uniquely distinguishes the class. Therefore, it is possible to define both `Pair<T>` and `Pair<TFirst, TSecond>` within the same namespace because of the arity variation.

Nested Generic Types

Nested types will automatically inherit the type parameters of the containing type. If the containing type includes a type parameter `T`, for example, then the type `T` will be available on the nested type as well. If the nested type includes its own type parameter named `T`, then this will hide the type parameter within the containing type and any reference to `T` in the nested type will refer to the nested `T` type parameter. Fortunately, reuse of the same type parameter name within the nested type will cause a compiler warning to prevent accidental overlap (see Listing 11.16).

LISTING 11.16: Nested Generic Types

```
class Container<T, U>
{
    // Nested classes inherit type parameters.
    // Reusing a type parameter name will cause
    // a warning.
    class Nested<U>
    {
        void Method(T param0, U param1)
        {
        }
    }
}
```

The behavior of making the container's type parameter available in the nested type is consistent with nested type behavior in the sense that private members of the containing type are also accessible from the nested type. The rule is simply that a type is available anywhere within the curly braces within which it appears.

Type Compatibility between Generic Classes with Type-Compatible Type Parameters

If you declare two variables with different type parameters using the same generic class, the variables are not type compatible; they are not **covariant**. The type parameter differentiates two variables of the same generic class but with different type parameters. For example, instances of a generic class, `Stack<Contact>` and `Stack<PdaItem>`, are not type compatible even when the type parameters are compatible. In other words, there is no built-in support for casting `Stack<Contact>` to `Stack<PdaItem>`, even though `Contact` derives from `PdaItem` (see Listing 11.17).

LISTING 11.17: **Conversion between Generics with Different Type Parameters**

```
using System.Collections.Generic;
...
// Error: Cannot convert type ...
Stack<PdaItem> exceptions = new Stack<Contact>();
```

To allow this you would have to subtly cast each instance of the type parameter, possibly an entire array or collection, which would hide a potentially significant performance cost.

Constraints

Generics support the ability to define constraints on type parameters. These constraints enforce the types to conform to various rules. Take, for example, the `BinaryTree<T>` class shown in Listing 11.18.

LISTING 11.18: **Declaring a `BinaryTree<T>` Class with No Constraints**

```
public class BinaryTree<T>
{
    public BinaryTree ( T item)
    {
        Item = item;
```

```
        }

        public T Item
        {
            get{ return _Item;      }
            set{ _Item = value; }
        }
        private T _Item;

        public Pair<BinaryTree<T>> SubItems
        {
            get{ return _SubItems; }
            set{ _SubItems = value; }
        }
        private Pair<BinaryTree<T>> _SubItems;
    }
```

(An interesting side note is that BinaryTree<T> uses Pair<T> internally, which is possible because Pair<T> is simply another type.)

Suppose you want the tree to sort the values within the Pair<T> value as it is assigned to the SubItems property. In order to achieve the sorting, the SubItems get accessor uses the CompareTo() method of the supplied key, as shown in Listing 11.19.

LISTING 11.19: Needing the Type Parameter to Support an Interface

```
    public class BinaryTree<T>
    {
        ...

        public Pair<BinaryTree<T>> SubItems
        {
            get{ return _SubItems; }
            set
            {
                IComparable first;
                // ERROR: Cannot implicitly convert type...
                first = value.First.Item;   // Explicit cast required

                if (first.CompareTo(value.Second.Item) < 0)
                {
                    // first is less than second.
                    ...
                }
                else
                {
                    // first and second are the same or
                    // second is less than first.
                    ...
                }
                _SubItems = value;
```

```
            }
        }
        private Pair<BinaryTree<T>> _SubItems;
    }
```

At compile time, the type parameter T is generic. Written as is, the compiler assumes that the only members available on T are those inherited from the base type object, since every type has object as an ancestor. (Only methods such as ToString(), therefore, are available to the key instance of the type parameter T.) As a result, the compiler displays a compilation error because the CompareTo() method is not defined on type object.

You can cast the T parameter to the IComparable interface in order to access the CompareTo() method, as shown in Listing 11.20.

LISTING 11.20: Needing the Type Parameter to Support an Interface or Exception Thrown

```
public class BinaryTree<T>
{
    ...
    public Pair<BinaryTree<T>> SubItems
    {
        get{ return _SubItems; }
        set
        {
            IComparable first;
            first = (IComparable)value.First.Item;
            if (first.CompareTo(value.Second.Item) < 0)
            {
                // first is less than second.
                ...
            }
            else
            {
                // second is less than or equal to first.
                ...
            }
            _SubItems = value;
        }
    }
    private Pair<BinaryTree<T>> _SubItems;
}
```

Unfortunately, however, if you now declare a BinaryTree class variable and supply a type parameter that does not implement the IComparable interface, you encounter an execution-time error—specifically, an `InvalidCastException`. This defeats an advantage of generics.

Language Contrast: C++—Templates

Generics in C# and the CLR differ from similar constructs in other languages. While other languages provide similar functionality, C# is significantly more type safe. Generics in C# is a language feature and a platform feature, the underlying 2.0 runtime contains deep support for generics in its engine.

C++ templates differ significantly from C# generics, because C# takes advantage of the CIL. C# generics are compiled into CIL, causing specialization to occur at execution time for each value type only when it is used, and only once for reference types.

A distinct feature not supported by C++ templates is explicit constraints. C++ templates allow you to compile a method call that may or may not belong to the type parameter. As a result, if the member does not exist in the type parameter, an error occurs, likely with a cryptic error message and referring to an unexpected location in the source code. However, the advantage of the C++ implementation is that operators (+, -, and so on) may be called on the type. C# does not support the calling of operators on the type parameter because operators are static—so they can't be identified by interfaces or base class constraints.

The problem with the error is that it occurs only when *using* the template, not when defining it. Because C# generics can declare constraints, the compiler can prevent such errors when defining the generic, thereby identifying invalid assumptions sooner. Furthermore, when declaring a variable of a generic type, the error will point to the declaration of the variable, not to the location in the generic implementation where the member is used.

It is interesting to note that Microsoft's CLI support in C++ includes both generics and C++ templates because of the distinct characteristics of each.

To avoid this exception and instead provide a compile-time error, C# enables you to supply an optional list of **constraints** for each type parameter declared in the generic class. A constraint declares the type parameter characteristics that the generic requires. You declare a constraint using the where keyword, followed by a "parameter-requirements" pair, where the parameter must be one of those defined in the generic type and the requirements are to restrict the class or interface from which the type "derives," the presence of a default constructor, or a reference/value type restriction.

Interface Constraints

In order to satisfy the sort requirement, you need to use the CompareTo() method in the BinaryTree class. To do this most effectively, you impose a constraint on the T type parameter. You need the T type parameter to implement the IComparable interface. The syntax for this appears in Listing 11.21.

LISTING 11.21: Declaring an Interface Constraint

```
public class BinaryTree<T>
    where T: System.IComparable
{
    ...
    public Pair<BinaryTree<T>> SubItems
    {
        get{ return _SubItems; }
        set
        {
            IComparable first;
            // Notice that the cast can now be eliminated.
            first = value.First.Item;

            if (first.CompareTo(value.Second.Item) < 0)
            {
                // first is less than second
                ...
            }
            else
            {
                // second is less than or equal to first.
                ...
            }
            _SubItems = value;
        }
    }
    private Pair<BinaryTree<T>> _SubItems;
}
```

Given the interface constraint addition in Listing 11.21, the compiler ensures that each time you use the `BinaryTree` class you specify a type parameter that implements the `IComparable` interface. Furthermore, you no longer need to explicitly cast the variable to an `IComparable` interface before calling the `CompareTo()` method. Casting is not even required to access members that use explicit interface implementation, which in other contexts would hide the member without a cast. To resolve what member to call, the compiler first checks class members directly, and then looks at the explicit interface members. If no constraint resolves the argument, only members of `object` are allowable.

If you tried to create a `BinaryTree<T>` variable using `System.Text`.`StringBuilder` as the type parameter, you would receive a compiler error because `StringBuilder` does not implement `IComparable`. The error is similar to the one shown in Output 11.3.

OUTPUT 11.3:

```
error CS0309: The type 'System.Text.StringBuilder>' must be convertible
to 'System.IComparable' in order to use it
as parameter 'T' in the generic type or method 'BinaryTree<T>'
```

To specify an interface for the constraint you declare an **interface constraint**. This constraint even circumvents the need to cast in order to call an explicit interface member implementation.

Base Class Constraints

Sometimes you might want to limit the constructed type to a particular class derivation. You do this using a **base class constraint**, as shown in Listing 11.22.

LISTING 11.22: Declaring a Base Class Constraint

```
public class EntityDictionary<TKey, TValue>
    : System.Collections.Generic.Dictionary<TKey, TValue>
    where TValue : EntityBase
{
    ...
}
```

In contrast to System.Collections.Generic.Dictionary<TKey, TValue> on its own, EntityDictionary<TKey, TValue> requires that all TValue types derive from the EntityBase class. By requiring the derivation, it is possible to always perform a cast operation within the generic implementation, because the constraint will ensure that all type parameters derive from the base and, therefore, that all TValue type parameters used with EntityDictionary can be implicitly converted to the base.

The syntax for the base class constraint is the same as that for the interface constraint, except that base class constraints must appear first when multiple constraints are specified. However, unlike interface constraints, multiple base class constraints are not allowed since it is not possible to derive from multiple classes. Similarly, base class constraints cannot be specified for sealed classes or specific structs. For example, C# does not allow a constraint for a type parameter to be derived from string or System.Nullable<T>.

struct/class Constraints

Another valuable generic constraint is the ability to restrict type parameters to a value type or a reference type. The compiler does not allow specifying System.ValueType as the base class in a constraint. Instead, C# provides special syntax that works for reference types as well. Instead of specifying a class from which T must derive, you simply use the keyword struct or class, as shown in Listing 11.23.

LISTING 11.23: Specifying the Type Parameter as a Value Type

```
public struct Nullable<T> :
    IFormattable, IComparable,
    IComparable<Nullable<T>>, INullable
    where T : struct
{
    // ...
}
```

Because a base class constraint requires a particular base class, using struct or class with a base class constraint would be pointless, and in fact could allow for conflicting constraints. Therefore, you cannot use struct and class constraints with a base class constraint.

There is one special characteristic for the `struct` constraint. It limits possible type parameters as being only value types while at the same time preventing type parameters that are `System.Nullable<T>` type parameters. Why? Without this last restriction, it would be possible to define the nonsense type `Nullable<Nullable<T>>`, which is nonsense because `Nullable<T>` on its own allows a value type variable that supports nulls, so a nullable-nullable type becomes meaningless. Since the nullable operator (`?`) is a C# shortcut for declaring a nullable value type, the `Nullable<T>` restriction provided by the `struct` constraint also prevents code such as the following:

```
int?? number    // Equivalent to Nullable<Nullable<int> if allowed
```

Multiple Constraints

For any given type parameter, you may specify any number of interfaces as constraints, but no more than one class, just as a class may implement any number of interfaces but inherit from only one other class. Each new constraint is declared in a comma-delimited list following the generic type and a colon. If there is more than one type parameter, each must be preceded by the `where` keyword. In Listing 11.24, the `EntityDictionary` class contains two type parameters: `TKey` and `TValue`. The `TKey` type parameter has two interface constraints, and the `TValue` type parameter has one base class constraint.

LISTING 11.24: **Specifying Multiple Constraints**

```
public class EntityDictionary<TKey, TValue>
    : Dictionary<TKey, TValue>
    where TKey : IComparable, IFormattable
    where TValue : EntityBase
{
    ...
}
```

In this case, there are multiple constraints on `TKey` itself and an additional constraint on `TValue`. When specifying multiple constraints on one type parameter, an AND relationship is assumed. `TKey` must implement `IComparable` and `IFormattable`, for example. Notice there is no comma between each `where` clause.

Constructor Constraints

In some cases, it is desirable to create an instance of a type parameter inside the generic class. In Listing 11.25, the New() method for the Entity-Dictionary<TKey, TValue> class must create an instance of the type parameter TValue.

LISTING 11.25: Requiring a Default Constructor Constraint

```
public class EntityBase<TKey>
{
    public TKey Key
    {
        get{ return _Key;  }
        set{ _Key = value; }
    }
    private TKey _Key;
}

public class EntityDictionary<TKey, TValue> :
    Dictionary<TKey, TValue>
    where TKey: IComparable, IFormattable
    where TValue : EntityBase<TKey>, new()
{
    // ...

    public TValue New(TKey key)
    {
        TValue newEntity = new TValue();
        newEntity.Key = key;
        Add(newEntity.Key, newEntity);
        return newEntity;
    }

    // ...
}
```

Because not all objects are guaranteed to have public default constructors, the compiler does not allow you to call the default constructor on the type parameter. To override this compiler restriction, you add the text new() after all other constraints are specified. This text is a **constructor constraint**, and it forces the type parameter decorated with the constructor constraint to have a default constructor. Only the default constructor constraint is available. You cannot specify a constraint for a constructor with parameters.

Constraint Inheritance

Constraints are inherited by a derived class, but they must be specified explicitly on the derived class. Consider Listing 11.26.

LISTING 11.26: Inherited Constraints Specified Explicitly

```
class EntityBase<T> where T : IComparable
{
}
```

```
// ERROR:
// The type 'T' must be convertible to 'System.IComparable'
// in order to use it as parameter 'T' in the generic type or
// method.
// class Entity<T> : EntityBase<T>
// {
// }
```

Because `EntityBase` requires that `T` implement `IComparable`, the `Entity` class needs to explicitly include the same constraint. Failure to do so will result in a compile error. This increases a programmer's awareness of the constraint in the derived class, avoiding confusion when using the derived class and discovering the constraint, but not understanding where it comes from.

■ADVANCED TOPIC

Constraint Limitations

Constraints are appropriately limited to avoid nonsense code. For example, you cannot combine a base class constraint with a `struct` or `class` constraint, nor can you use `Nullable<T>` on struct constraint type parameters. Also, you cannot specify constraints to restrict inheritance to special types such as `object`, arrays, `System.ValueType`, `System.Enum` (enum), `System.Delegate`, and `System.MulticastDelegate`.

In some cases, constraint limitations are perhaps more desirable, but they still are not supported. The following subsections provide some additional examples of constraints that are not allowed.

Operator Constraints Are Not Allowed

Another restriction on constraints is that you cannot specify a constraint that a class supports on a particular method or operator, unless that method or operator is on an interface. Because of this, the generic Add() in Listing 11.27 does not work.

LISTING 11.27: Constraint Expressions Cannot Require Operators

```
public abstract class MathEx<T>
{
    public static T Add(T first, T second)
    {
        // Error: Operator '+' cannot be applied to
        // operands of type 'T' and 'T'.
        return first + second;
    }
}
```

In this case, the method assumes that the + operator is available on all types. However, because all types support only the methods of object (which does not include the + operator), an error occurs. Unfortunately, there is no way to specify the + operator within a constraint; therefore, creating an add method like this is a lot more cumbersome. One reason for this limitation is that there is no way to constrain a type to have a static method. You cannot, for example, specify static methods on an interface.

OR Criteria Are Not Supported

If you supply multiple interfaces or class constraints for a type parameter, the compiler always assumes an AND relationship between constraints. For example, where TKey : IComparable, IFormattable requires that both IComparable and IFormattable are supported. There is no way to specify an OR relationship between constraints. Hence, an equivalent of Listing 11.28 is not supported.

LISTING 11.28: Combining Constraints Using an OR Relationship Is Not Allowed

```
public class BinaryTree<T>
    // Error:  OR is not supported.
    where T: System.IComparable || System.IFormattable<T>
{
    ...
}
```

Supporting this would prevent the compiler from resolving which method to call at compile time.

Constraints of Type Delegate and Enum Are Not Valid

Readers who are already familiar with C# 1.0 and are reading this chapter to learn 2.0 features will be familiar with the concept of delegates, which are covered in Chapter 13. One additional constraint that is not allowed is the use of any delegate type as a class constraint. For example, the compiler will output an error for the class declaration in Listing 11.29.

LISTING 11.29: Inheritance Constraints Cannot Be of Type `System.Delegate`

```
// Error:  Constraint cannot be special class 'System.Delegate'
public class Publisher<T>
    where T : System.Delegate
{

    public event T Event;
    public void Publish()
    {
        if (Event != null)
        {
            Event(this, new EventArgs());
        }
    }
}
```

All delegate types are considered special classes that cannot be specified as type parameters. Doing so would prevent compile-time validation on the call to `Event()` because the signature of the event firing is unknown with the data types `System.Delegate` and `System.MulticastDelegate`. The same restriction occurs for any enum type.

Constructor Constraints Are Allowed Only for Default Constructors

Listing 11.25 includes a constructor constraint that forces `TValue` to support a default constructor. There is no constraint to force `TValue` to support a constructor other than the default. For example, it is not possible to make `EntityBase.Key` protected and only set it in a `TValue` constructor that takes a `TKey` parameter using constraints alone. Listing 11.30 demonstrates the invalid code.

LISTING 11.30: Constructor Constraints Can Be Specified Only for Default Constructors

```
public TValue New(TKey key)
{
    // Error: 'TValue': Cannot provide arguments
    // when creating an instance of a variable type.
    TValue newEntity = null;
```

```
        // newEntity = new TValue(key);
        Add(newEntity.Key, newEntity);
        return newEntity;
    }
```

One way to circumvent this restriction is to supply a factory interface that includes a method for instantiating the type. The factory implementing the interface takes responsibility for instantiating the entity rather than the EntityDictionary itself (see Listing 11.31).

LISTING 11.31: Using a Factory Interface in Place of a Constructor Constraint

```csharp
public class EntityBase<TKey>
{
    public EntityBase(TKey key)
    {
        Key = key;
    }

    public TKey Key
    {
        get { return _key; }
        set { _key = value; }
    }
    private TKey _key;
}


public class EntityDictionary<TKey, TValue, TFactory> :
        Dictionary<TKey, TValue>
    where TKey : IComparable, IFormattable
    where TValue : EntityBase<TKey>
    where TFactory : IEntityFactory<TKey, TValue>, new()
{
    ...
    public TValue New(TKey key)
    {
        TValue newEntity = new TFactory().CreateNew(key);
        Add(newEntity.Key, newEntity);
        return newEntity;
    }
    ...
}


public interface IEntityFactory<TKey, TValue>
{
    TValue CreateNew(TKey key);
}
...
```

A declaration such as this allows you to pass the new `key` to a `TValue` constructor that takes parameters rather than the default constructor. It no longer uses the constructor constraint on `TValue` because `TFactory` is responsible for instantiating the order instead of `EntityDictionary<...>`. (One modification to the code in Listing 11.31 would be to save a copy of the factory. This would enable you to reuse the factory instead of reinstantiating it every time.)

A declaration for a variable of type `EntityDictionary<TKey, TValue, TFactory>` would result in an entity declaration similar to the `Order` entity in Listing 11.32.

LISTING 11.32: Declaring an Entity to Be Used in **EntityDictionary<...>**

```
public class Order : EntityBase<Guid>
{
  public Order(Guid key) :
      base(key)
  {
      // ...
  }
}


public class OrderFactory : IEntityFactory<Guid, Order>
{
  public Order CreateNew(Guid key)
  {
      return new Order(key);
  }
}
```

Generic Methods

You already learned that it is relatively simple to add a generic method to a class when the class is a generic. You did this in the generic class examples so far, and it also works for static methods. Furthermore, you can use generic classes within a generic class, as you did in earlier `BinaryTree` listings using the following line of code:

```
public Pair< BinaryTree<T> > SubItems;
```

Generic methods are methods that use generics even when the containing class is not a generic class or the method contains type parameters not included in the generic class type parameter list. To define generic methods, you add the type parameter syntax immediately following the method name, as shown in the `MathEx.Max<T>` and `MathEx.Min<T>` examples in Listing 11.33.

LISTING 11.33: Defining Generic Methods

```
public static class MathEx
{
  public static T Max<T>(T first, params T[] values)
      where T : IComparable
  {
      T maximum = first;
      foreach (T item in values)
      {
          if (item.CompareTo(maximum) > 0)
          {
              maximum = item;
              }
      }
      return maximum;
  }

  public static T Min<T>(T first, params T[] values)
      where T : IComparable
  {
      T minimum = first;

        foreach (T item in values)
        {
            if (item.CompareTo(minimum) < 0)
            {
                minimum = item;
            }
        }
      return minimum;
  }
}
```

You use the same syntax on a generic class when the method requires an additional type parameter not included in the class type parameter list. In this example, the method is static but C# does not require this.

Note that generic methods, like classes, can include more than one type parameter. The arity (the number of type parameters) is an additional distinguishing characteristic of a method signature.

Type Inferencing

The code used to call the `Min<T>` and `Max<T>` methods looks like that shown in Listing 11.34.

LISTING 11.34: Specifying the Type Parameter Explicitly

```
Console.WriteLine(
    MathEx.Max<int>(7, 490));
Console.WriteLine(
    MathEx.Min<string>("R.O.U.S.", "Fireswamp"));
```

The output to Listing 11.34 appears in Output 11.4.

OUTPUT 11.4:

```
490
Fireswamp
```

Not surprisingly, the type parameters, `int` and `string`, correspond to the actual types used in the generic method calls. However, specifying the type is redundant because the compiler can infer the type from the parameters passed to the method. To avoid redundancy, you can exclude the type parameters from the call. This is known as **type inferencing**, and an example appears in Listing 11.35. The output of this listing appears in Output 11.5.

LISTING 11.35: Inferring the Type Parameter

```
Console.WriteLine(
    MathEx.Max(7, 490));
Console.WriteLine(
    MathEx.Min("R.O.U.S'", "Fireswamp"));
```

OUTPUT 11.5:

```
490
Fireswamp
```

For type inferencing to be successful, the types must match the method signature. Calling the `Max<T>` method using `MathEx.Max(7.0, 490)`, for example, causes a compile error. You can resolve the error by either casting explicitly or including the type argument. Also note that you cannot perform type inferencing purely on the return type. Parameters are required for type inferencing to be allowed.

Specifying Constraints

The generic method also allows constraints to be specified. For example, you can restrict a type parameter to implement IComparable. The constraint is specified immediately following the method header, prior to the curly braces of the method block, as shown in Listing 11.36.

LISTING 11.36: Specifying Constraints on Generic Methods

```
public class ConsoleTreeControl
{
    // Generic method Show<T>
    public static void Show<T>(BinaryTree<T> tree, int indent)
        where T : IComparable
    {
        Console.WriteLine("\n{0}{1}",
            "+ --".PadLeft(5*indent, ' '),
            tree.Item.ToString());
        if (tree.SubItems.First != null)
            Show(tree.SubItems.First, indent+1);
        if (tree.SubItems.Second != null)
            Show(tree.SubItems.Second, indent+1);
    }
}
```

Notice that the Show<T> implementation itself does not use the IComparable interface. Recall, however, that the BinaryTree<T> class did require this (see Listing 11.37).

LISTING 11.37: **BinaryTree<T>** Requiring **IComparable** Type Parameters

```
public class BinaryTree<T>
    where T: System.IComparable
{
    ...
}
```

Because the BinaryTree<T> class requires this constraint on T, and because Show<T> uses BinaryTree<T>, Show<T> also needs to supply the constraint.

Casting inside a Generic Method

Sometimes you should be wary of using generics—for instance, when using it specifically to bury a cast operation. Consider the following method, which converts a stream into an object:

```
public static T Deserialize<T>(
    Stream stream, IFormatter formatter)
{
    return (T)formatter.Deserialize(stream);
}
```

The `formatter` is responsible for removing data from the stream and converting it to an object. The `Deserialize()` call on the formatter returns data of type `object`. A call to use the generic version of `Deserialize()` looks something like this:

```
string greeting =
    Deserialization.Deserialize<string>(stream, formatter);
```

The problem with this code is that to the user of the method, `Deserialize<T>()` appears to be strongly typed. However, a cast operation is still performed implicitly rather than explicitly, as in the case of the nongeneric equivalent shown here:

```
string greeting =
    (string)Deserialization.Deserialize(stream, formatter);
```

A method using an explicit cast is more explicit about what is taking place than is a generic version with a hidden cast. Developers should use care when casting in generic methods if there are no constraints to verify cast validity.

Generic Internals

Given the discussions in earlier chapters about the prevalence of objects within the CLI type system, it is no surprise that generics are also objects. In fact, the type parameter on a generic class becomes metadata that the runtime uses to build appropriate classes when needed. Generics, therefore, support inheritance, polymorphism, and encapsulation. With generics, you can define methods, properties, fields, classes, interfaces, and delegates.

To achieve this, generics require support from the underlying runtime. So, the addition of generics to the C# language is a feature of both the compiler and the platform. To avoid boxing, for example, the implementation of generics is different for value-based type parameters than for generics with reference type parameters.

■ ADVANCED TOPIC

CIL Representation of Generics

When a generic class is compiled, it is no different from a regular class. The result of the compilation is nothing but metadata and CIL. The CIL is parameterized to accept a user-supplied type somewhere in code. Suppose you had a simple `Stack` class declared as shown in Listing 11.38.

LISTING 11.38: **Stack<T>** Declaration

```
public class Stack<T> where T : IComparable
{
    T[] items;
    // rest of the class here


}
```

When you compile the class, the generated CIL is parameterized and looks something like Listing 11.39.

LISTING 11.39: CIL Code for **Stack<T>**

```
.class private auto ansi beforefieldinit
    Stack`1<([mscorlib]System.IComparable)T>
    extends [mscorlib]System.Object
{
  ...
}
```

The first notable item is the `1 that appears following `Stack` on the second line. That number is the arity. It declares the number of parameter types that the generic class will include. A declaration such as `EntityDictionary<TKey, TValue>` would have an arity of 2.

In addition, the second line of the generated CIL shows the constraints imposed upon the class. The T type parameter is decorated with an interface declaration for the IComparable constraint.

If you continue looking through the CIL, you will find that the item's array declaration of type T is altered to contain a type parameter using "exclamation point notation," new to the generics-capable version of the CIL. The exclamation point denotes the presence of the first type parameter specified for the class, as shown in Listing 11.40.

LISTING 11.40: CIL with "Exclamation Point Notation" to Support Generics

```
.class public auto ansi beforefieldinit
    'Stack'1'<([mscorlib]System.IComparable) T>
    extends [mscorlib]System.Object
{
    .field private !0[ ] items
    ...
}
```

Beyond the inclusion of the arity and type parameter in the class header and the type parameter denoted with exclamation points in code, there is little difference between the CIL generated for a generic class and the CIL generated for a nongeneric class.

Instantiating Generics Based on Value Types

When a generic type is first constructed with a value type as a type parameter, the runtime creates a specialized generic type with the supplied type parameter(s) placed appropriately in the CIL. Therefore, the runtime creates new specialized generic types for each new parameter value type.

For example, suppose some code declared a Stack constructed of integers, as shown in Listing 11.41.

LISTING 11.41: Stack<int> Definition

```
Stack<int> stack;
```

When using this type, Stack<int>, for the first time, the runtime generates a specialized version of the Stack class with int substituted for its type parameter. From then on, whenever the code uses a Stack<int>, the runtime reuses the generated specialized Stack<int> class. In Listing 11.42, you declare two instances of a Stack<int>, both using the code already generated by the runtime for a Stack<int>.

LISTING 11.42: Declaring Variables of Type **Stack<T>**

```
Stack<int> stackOne = new Stack<int>();
Stack<int> stackTwo = new Stack<int>();
```

If later in the code, you create another Stack with a different value type as its type parameter (such as a long or a user-defined struct), the runtime generates another version of the generic type. The benefit of specialized value type classes is better performance. Furthermore, the code is able to avoid conversions and boxing because each specialized generic class "natively" contains the value type.

Instantiating Generics Based on Reference Types

Generics work slightly differently for reference types. The first time a generic type is constructed with a reference type, the runtime creates a specialized generic type with object references substituted for type parameters in the CIL, not a specialized generic type based on the type parameter. Each subsequent time a constructed type is instantiated with a reference type parameter, the runtime reuses the previously generated version of the generic type, even if the reference type is different from the first reference type.

For example, suppose you have two reference types, a Customer class and an Order class, and you create an EntityDictionary of Customer types, like so:

```
EntityDictionary<Guid, Customer> customers;
```

Prior to accessing this class, the runtime generates a specialized version of the EntityDictionary class that, instead of storing Customer as the specified data type, stores object references. Suppose the next line of code creates an EntityDictionary of another reference type, called Order:

```
EntityDictionary<Guid, Order> orders =
    new EntityDictionary<Guid, Order>();
```

Unlike value types, no new specialized version of the `Entity-Dictionary` class is created for the `EntityDictionary` that uses the `Order` type. Instead, an instance of the version of `EntityDictionary` that uses `object` references is instantiated and the `orders` variable is set to reference it.

Language Contrast: Java—Generics

Sun's implementation of generics for Java occurs within the compiler entirely, not within the Java Virtual Machine. Sun did this to ensure that no updated Java Virtual Machine would need to be distributed because generics were used.

The Java implementation uses syntax similar to the templates in C++ and generics in C#, including type parameters and constraints. But because it does not treat value types differently from reference types, the unmodified Java Virtual Machine cannot support generics for value types. As such, generics in Java do not gain the execution efficiency of C#. Indeed, whenever the Java compiler needs to return data, it injects automatic downcasts from the specified constraint, if one is declared, or the base `Object` type if it is not declared. Further, the Java compiler generates a single specialized type at compile time, which it then uses to instantiate any constructed type. Finally, because the Java Virtual Machine does not support generics natively, there is no way to ascertain the type parameter for an instance of a generic type at execution time, and other uses of reflection are severely limited.

To still gain the advantage of type safety, for each object reference substituted in place of the type parameter, an area of memory for an `Order` type is specifically allocated and the pointer is set to that memory reference. Suppose you then encountered a line of code to instantiate an `EntityDictionary` of a `Customer` type as follows:

```
customers = new EntityDictionary<Guid, Customer>();
```

As with the previous use of the `EntityDictionary` class created with the `Order` type, another instance of the specialized `EntityDictionary` class (the one based on `object` references) is instantiated and the pointers contained therein are set to reference a `Customer` type specifically. This implementation of generics greatly reduces code bloat by reducing to one the number of specialized classes created by the compiler for generic classes of reference types.

Even though the runtime uses the same internal generic type definition when the type parameter on a generic reference type varies, this behavior is superseded if the type parameter is a value type. `Dictionary<int, Customer>`, `Dictionary<Guid, Order>`, and `Dictionary<long, Order>` will require new internal type definitions, for example.

SUMMARY

Generics will significantly transform C# 1.0 coding style. In virtually all cases in which programmers used `object` within C# 1.0 code, generics would be a better choice in C# 2.0 to the extent that `object` should act as a flag for a possible generics implementation. The increased type safety, cast avoidance, and reduction of code bloat offer significant improvements. Similarly, where code traditionally used the `System.Collections` namespace, `System.Collections.Generics` should be selected instead.

The next chapter looks at one of the most pervasive generic namespaces, `System.Collections.Generic`. This namespace is composed almost exclusively of generic types. It provides clear examples of how some types that originally used objects were then converted to use generics.

■ 12 ■
Collections

T HE MOST PREVALENT USE of generics in any language is in the area of collections. Collections deal with sets of like objects and with managing those objects as a group. This chapter looks at the collection classes provided with the runtime and how you use them within your applications. It also covers the various collection interfaces and how they relate to each other, and it includes a discussion of how to create custom collections using iterators. This C# 2.0 feature simplifies implementation of how the `foreach` statement iterates over the elements in a collection. Iterators not only encapsulate the internal data structure of your collection classes, but they also improve control over end-user access and the use of data within a collection.

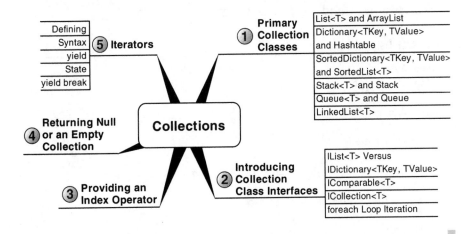

There are two types of collection-related classes: those that support generics and those that don't. This chapter primarily discusses the generic collection classes. Generally, you should use collection classes that don't support generics only when writing components that need to interoperate with earlier versions of the runtime. This is because everything that was available in the nongeneric form has a generic replacement that is strongly typed.

Primary Collection Classes

There are six key sets of collection classes, and they differ from each other in terms of how data is inserted, stored, and retrieved. Each generic class is located in the `System.Collections.Generic` namespace, and their non-generic equivalents are in the `System.Collections` namespace.

List Collections: `List<T>` and `ArrayList`

The `List<T>` class, and its nongeneric equivalent, `ArrayList`, have properties similar to an array. The key difference is that these classes automatically expand as the number of elements increases. (In contrast, an array size is constant.) Furthermore, lists can shrink via explicit calls to `TrimToSize()` or `Capacity` (see Figure 12.1 on page 422).

These classes are categorized as **list collections** whose distinguishing functionality is that each element can be individually accessed by index, just like an array. Therefore, you can set and access elements in the list collection classes using the index operator, where the index parameter value corresponds to the position of an element in the collection. Listing 12.1 shows an example, and Output 12.1 shows the results.

LISTING 12.1: Using **`List<T>`**

```csharp
using System;
using System.Collections.Generic;

class Program
{
  static void Main()
  {
      List<string> list = new List<string>();

      // Lists automatically expand as elements
      // are added.
```

```
        list.Add("Sneezy");
        list.Add("Happy");
        list.Add("Dopey");
        list.Add("Doc");
        list.Add("Sleepy");
        list.Add("Bashful");
        list.Add("Grumpy");

        list.Sort();

        Console.WriteLine(
            "In alphabetical order {0} is the "
            + "first dwarf while {1} is the last.",
            list[0], list[6]);

        list.Remove("Grumpy");
    }
}
```

OUTPUT 12.1:

```
In alphabetical order Bashful is the first dwarf while Sneezy is the last.
```

C# is zero-index based; therefore, index zero in Listing 12.1 corresponds to the first element and index 6 indicates the seventh element. Retrieving elements by index does not involve a search. It involves a quick and simple "jump" operation to a location in memory.

When you use the Add() method, elements maintain the order in which you added them. Therefore, prior to the call to Sort() in Listing 12.1, "Sneezy" is first and "Grumpy" is last. Although List<T> and ArrayList support a Sort() method, nothing states that all list collections require such a method.

There is no support for automatic sorting of elements as they are added. In other words, an explicit call to Sort() is required for the elements to be sorted (items must implement IComparable). To remove an element, you use the Remove() method.

To search either List<T> or ArrayList for a particular element, you use the Contains(), IndexOf(), LastIndexOf(), and BinarySearch() methods. The first three methods search through the array, starting at the first element (the last element for LastIndexOf()), and examine each element until

○ IList<T>
ICollection<T>
IEnumerable<T>
IList
ICollection
IEnumerable

List<T>
Generic Class

□ Properties
- Capacity
- Count
- Item
- System.Collections.Generic.ICollection<T>.IsReadOnly
- System.Collections.ICollection.IsSynchronized
- System.Collections.ICollection.SyncRoot
- System.Collections.IList.IsFixedSize
- System.Collections.IList.IsReadOnly
- System.Collections.IList.Item

□ Methods
- Add
- AddRange
- AsReadOnly
- BinarySearch (+ 2 overloads)
- Clear
- Contains
- ConvertAll<TOutput>
- CopyTo (+ 2 overloads)
- Exists
- Find
- FindAll
- FindIndex (+ 2 overloads)
- FindLast
- FindLastIndex (+ 2 overloads)
- ForEach
- GetEnumerator
- GetRange
- IndexOf (+ 2 overloads)
- Insert
- InsertRange
- LastIndexOf (+ 2 overloads)
- List (+ 2 overloads)
- Remove
- RemoveAll
- RemoveAt
- RemoveRange
- Reverse (+ 1 overload)
- Sort (+ 3 overloads)
- ToArray
- TrimExcess
- TrimToSize
- TrueForAll

○ IList
ICollection
IEnumerable
ICloneable

ArrayList
Class

□ Properties
- Capacity
- Count
- IsFixedSize
- IsReadOnly
- IsSynchronized
- Item
- SyncRoot

□ Methods
- Adapter
- Add
- AddRange
- ArrayList (+ 2 overloads)
- BinarySearch (+ 2 overloads)
- Clear
- Clone
- Contains
- CopyTo (+ 2 overloads)
- FixedSize (+ 1 overload)
- GetEnumerator (+ 1 overload)
- GetRange
- IndexOf (+ 2 overloads)
- Insert
- InsertRange
- LastIndexOf (+ 2 overloads)
- ReadOnly (+ 1 overload)
- Remove
- RemoveAt
- RemoveRange
- Repeat
- Reverse (+ 1 overload)
- SetRange
- Sort (+ 2 overloads)
- Synchronized (+ 1 overload)
- ToArray (+ 1 overload)
- TrimToSize

FIGURE 12.1: **List<>** and **ArrayList** Class Diagrams

the equivalent one is found. The execution time for these algorithms is proportional to the number of elements searched before a hit occurs. Be aware that the collection classes do not require that all the elements within the collection are unique. If two or more elements in the collection are the same, then IndexOf() returns the first index and LastIndexOf() returns the last index.

BinarySearch() uses a binary search algorithm and requires that the elements be sorted. A useful feature of the BinarySearch() method is that if the element is not found, a negative integer is returned. The bitwise complement (~) of this value is the index of the next element larger than the element being sought, or the total element count if there is no greater value. This provides a convenient means to insert new values into the list at the specific location so as to maintain sorting (see Listing 12.2).

LISTING 12.2: Using the Bit Complement of the **BinarySearch()** Result

```csharp
using System;
using System.Collections.Generic;

class Program
{
  static void Main()
  {
      List<string> list = new List<string>();
      int search;

      list.Add("public");
      list.Add("protected");
      list.Add("private");

      list.Sort();

      search = list.BinarySearch("protected internal");
      if (search < 0)
      {
        list.Insert(~search, "protected internal");
      }

      foreach (string accessModifier in list)
      {
          Console.WriteLine(accessModifier);
      }
    }
  }
```

Beware that if the list is not first sorted, an element will not necessarily be found, even if it is in the list. The results of Listing 12.2 appear in Output 12.2.

OUTPUT 12.2:

```
private
protected
protected internal
public
```

■ADVANCED TOPIC

Finding Multiple Items with `FindAll()`

Sometimes you must find multiple items within a list and your search criteria are more complex than looking for specific values. To support this, `System.Collections.Generic.List<T>` includes a `FindAll()` method. `FindAll()` takes a parameter of type `Predicate<T>`, which is a reference to a method called a delegate. Listing 12.3 demonstrates how to use the `FindAll()` method.

LISTING 12.3: Demonstrating `FindAll()` and Its Predicate Parameter

```
using System;
using System.Collections.Generic;

class Program
{
  static void Main()
  {
      List<int> list = new List<int>();
      list.Add(1);
      list.Add(2);
      list.Add(3);
      list.Add(2);

      List<int> results = list.FindAll(Even);
      Assert.AreEqual(2, results.Count);
      Assert.IsTrue(results.Contains(2));
      Assert.IsFalse(results.Contains(3));
  }

  public static bool Even(int value)
  {
      if ((value % 2) == 0)
      {
          return true;
      }
      else
      {
          return false;
      }
  }
}
```

In Listing 12.3's call to `FindAll()`, you pass a delegate instance, `Even()`. This method returns `true` when the integer argument value is even. `FindAll()` takes the delegate instance and calls into `Even()` for each item within the list (this listing uses C# 2.0's delegate type inferencing). Each time the return is `true`, it adds it to a new `List<T>` instance and then returns this instance once it has checked each item within `list`. A complete discussion of delegates occurs in Chapter 13.

Dictionary Collections: `Dictionary<TKey, TValue>` and `Hashtable`

Another category of collection classes is the dictionary classes—specifically, `Dictionary<Tkey, Tvalue>` and `Hashtable` (see Figure 12.2). Unlike the list collections, dictionary classes store name/value pairs. The name functions as a unique key that can be used to look up the corresponding element in a manner similar to that of using a primary key to access a record in a database. This adds some complexity to the access of

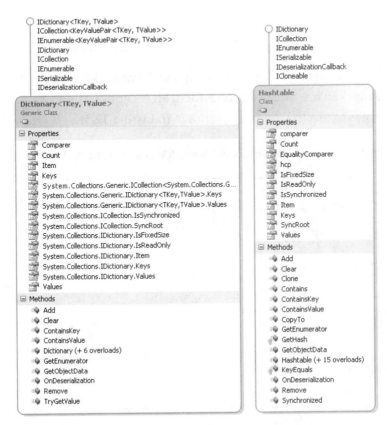

FIGURE 12.2: `Dictionary` and `Hashtable` Class Diagrams

dictionary elements, but because lookups by key are efficient operations, this is a useful collection. Note that the key may be any data type, not just a string or a numeric value.

One option for inserting elements into a dictionary is to use the Add() method, passing both the key and the value, as shown in Listing 12.4.

LISTING 12.4: Adding Items to a **Dictionary<TKey, TValue>**

```csharp
using System;
using System.Collections.Generic;

class Program
{
  static void Main()
  {
      Dictionary<Guid, string> dictionary =
          new Dictionary<Guid, string>();
      Guid key = Guid.NewGuid();

      dictionary.Add(key, "object");
  }
}
```

Listing 12.4 inserts the string "object" using a Guid as its key. If an element with the same key has already been added, an exception is thrown.

An alternative is to use the indexer, as shown in Listing 12.5.

LISTING 12.5: Inserting Items in a **Dictionary<TKey, TValue>** Using the Index Operator

```csharp
using System;
using System.Collections.Generic;

class Program
{
  static void Main()
  {
      Dictionary<Guid, string> dictionary =
          new Dictionary<Guid, string>();
      Guid key = Guid.NewGuid();

      dictionary[key] = "object";
      dictionary[key] = "byte";
  }
}
```

The first thing to observe in Listing 12.5 is that the index operator does not require an integer. Instead, the index data type is specified by the first type parameter, `TKey`, when declaring a `Dictionary<TKey, TValue>` variable (in the case of `Hashtable`, the data type is `object`). In this example, the key data type used is `Guid`, and the value data type is `string`.

The second thing to notice in Listing 12.5 is the reuse of the same index. In the first assignment, no dictionary element corresponds to `key`. Instead of throwing an out-of-bounds exception, as an array would, dictionary collection classes insert a new object. During the second assignment, an element with the specified key already exists, so instead of inserting an additional element, the existing element corresponding to `key` is updated from `"object"` to `"byte"`.

Accessing a value from a dictionary using the index operator (`[]`) with a nonexistent key throws an exception of type `System.Collections.Generic.KeyNotFoundException`. The `ContainsKey()` method, however, allows you to check whether a particular key is used before accessing its value, thereby avoiding the exception. Also, since the keys are stored in a hash algorithm type structure, the search is relatively efficient.

By contrast, checking whether there is a particular value in the dictionary collections is a time-consuming operation with linear performance characteristics. To do this you use the `ContainsValue()` method, which searches sequentially through each element in the collection.

You remove a dictionary element using the `Remove()` method, passing the key, not the element value.

There is no particular order for the dictionary classes. Elements are arranged into a hashtable type data structure using hashcodes for rapid retrieval (acquired by calling `GetHashCode()` on the key). Iterating through a dictionary class using the `foreach` loop, therefore, accesses values in no particular order. Because both the key and the element value are required to add an element to the dictionary, the data type returned from the `foreach` loop is `KeyValuePair<TKey, TValue>` for `Dictionary<TKey, TValue>`, and `DictionaryEntry` for `Hashtable`. Listing 12.6 shows a snippet of code demonstrating the `foreach` loop with the `Dictionary<TKey, TValue>` collection class. The output appears in Output 12.3

LISTING 12.6: Iterating over **Dictionary<TKey, TValue>** with **foreach**

```
using System;
using System.Collections.Generic;

class Program
{
  static void Main()
  {
      Dictionary<string,string> dictionary = new
          Dictionary<string,string>();

      int index =0;

      dictionary.Add(index++.ToString(), "object");
      dictionary.Add(index++.ToString(), "byte");
      dictionary.Add(index++.ToString(), "uint");
      dictionary.Add(index++.ToString(), "ulong");
      dictionary.Add(index++.ToString(), "float");
      dictionary.Add(index++.ToString(), "char");
      dictionary.Add(index++.ToString(), "bool");
      dictionary.Add(index++.ToString(), "ushort");
      dictionary.Add(index++.ToString(), "decimal");
      dictionary.Add(index++.ToString(), "int");
      dictionary.Add(index++.ToString(), "sbyte");
      dictionary.Add(index++.ToString(), "short");
      dictionary.Add(index++.ToString(), "long");
      dictionary.Add(index++.ToString(), "void");
      dictionary.Add(index++.ToString(), "double");
      dictionary.Add(index++.ToString(), "string");

      Console.WriteLine("Key  Value     Hashcode");
      Console.WriteLine("---  -------   --------");
      foreach (KeyValuePair<string, string> i in dictionary)
      {
          Console.WriteLine("{0,-5}{1,-9}{2}",
              i.Key, i.Value, i.Key.GetHashCode());
      }
  }
}
```

If you want to deal only with keys or only with elements within a dictionary class, they are available via the Keys and Values properties. The data type returned from these properties is of type ICollection, and it is typed in generic or nongeneric form depending on whether a Dictionary<TKey, TValue> or Hashtable collection is used. The data returned by these properties is a reference to the data within the original dictionary

OUTPUT 12.3:

```
Key  Value    Hashcode
---  -------  ----------
0    object   -842352752
1    byte     -842352753
2    uint     -842352754
3    ulong    -842352755
4    float    -842352756
5    char     -842352757
6    bool     -842352758
7    ushort   -842352759
8    decimal  -842352744
9    int      -842352745
10   sbyte    -843401329
11   short    -843466865
12   long     -843532401
13   void     -843597937
14   double   -843663473
15   string   -843729009
```

collection, so changes within the dictionary are automatically reflected in the ICollection type returned by the Keys and Values properties.

Sorted Collections: SortedDictionary<TKey, TValue> and SortedList<T>

The sorted collection classes (see Figure 12.3 on page 431) differ from unsorted implementation collections in that the elements are sorted by key for Sorted-Dictionary<TKey, TValue> and by value for SortedList<T>. (There is also a nongeneric SortedList implementation.) A foreach iteration of sorted collections returns the elements sorted in key order (see Listing 12.7).

LISTING 12.7: Using SortedDictionary<TKey, TValue>

```csharp
using System;
using System.Collections.Generic;

class Program
{
  static void Main()
  {
      SortedDictionary<string,string> sortedDictionary =
          new SortedDictionary<string,string>();

      int index =0;

      sortedDictionary.Add(index++.ToString(), "object");
      // ...
```

```
    sortedDictionary.Add(index++.ToString(), "string");

    Console.WriteLine("Key  Value     Hashcode");
    Console.WriteLine---  -------  ----------");
    foreach (
        KeyValuePair<string, string> i in sortedDictionary)
    {
        Console.WriteLine("{0,-5}{1,-9}{2}",
            i.Key, i.Value, i.Key.GetHashCode());
    }
}
}
```

The results of Listing 12.7 appear in Output 12.4.

OUTPUT 12.4:

```
Key   Value     Hashcode
---   -------   ----------
0     object    -842352752
1     byte      -842352753
10    sbyte     -843401329
11    short     -843466865
12    long      -843532401
13    void      -843597937
14    double    -843663473
15    string    -843729009
2     uint      -842352754
3     ulong     -842352755
4     float     -842352756
5     char      -842352757
6     bool      -842352758
7     ushort    -842352759
8     decimal   -842352744
9     int       -842352745
```

Note that the elements in the key are in alphabetical rather than numerical order, because the data type of the key is a string, not an integer.

When inserting or removing elements from a sorted dictionary collection, maintenance of order within the collection slightly increases execution time when compared to the straight dictionary classes described earlier. Behaviorally, there are two internal arrays, one for key retrieval and one for index retrieval. On a `System.Collections.Sorted` sorted list, indexing is supported via the `GetByIndex()` and `SetByIndex()` methods. With `System.Collections.Generic.SortedList<TKey, TValue>`, the `Keys` and `Values` properties return `IList<TKey>` and

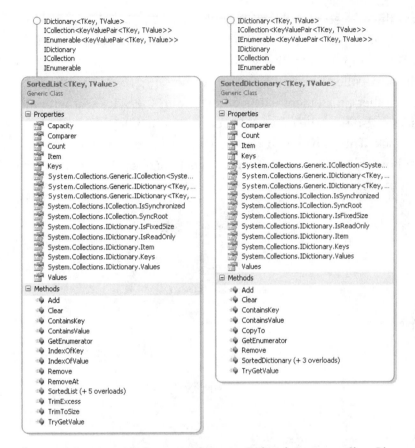

FIGURE 12.3: **SortedList<>** and **SortedDictionary<>** Class Diagrams

`IList<TValue>` instances, respectively. These methods enable the sorted list to behave both as a dictionary and as a list type collection.

Stack Collections: `Stack<T>` and `Stack`

Chapter 11 discussed the stack collection classes (see Figure 12.4). The stack collection classes are designed as last in, first out (LIFO) collections. The two key methods are `Push()` and `Pop()`.

- `Push()` places elements into the collection. The elements do not have to be unique.

- `Pop()` retrieves and removes elements in the reverse order of how they were added.

To access the elements on the stack without modifying the stack, you use the Peek() and Contains() methods. The Peek() method returns the next element that Pop() will retrieve.

As with most collection classes, you use the Contains() method to determine whether an element exists anywhere in the stack. As with all collections, it is also possible to use a foreach loop to iterate over the elements in a stack. This allows you to access values from anywhere in the stack. Note, however, that accessing a value via the foreach loop does not remove it from the stack. Only Pop() provides this functionality.

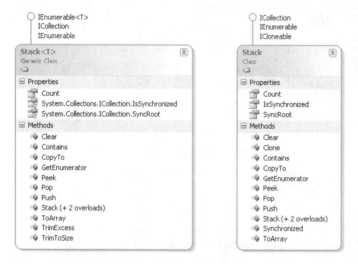

FIGURE 12.4: **Stack<T>** and **Stack** Class Diagrams

Queue Collections: Queue<T> and Queue

Queue collection classes, shown in Figure 12.5, are identical to stack collection classes, except they follow the ordering pattern of first in, first out (FIFO). In place of the Pop() and Push() methods are the Enqueue() and Dequeue() methods. The queue collection behaves like a circular array or pipe. You place objects into the queue at one end using the Enqueue() method, and you remove them from the other end using the Dequeue() method. As with stack collection classes, the objects do not have to be unique, and queue collection classes automatically increase in size as required. When data is no longer needed, you recover the capacity using the TrimToSize() method.

FIGURE 12.5: `Queue<T>` and `Queue` Class Diagrams

Linked Lists: `LinkedList<T>`

In addition, `System.Collections.Generic` supports a linked list collection that enables both forward and reverse traversal. Figure 12.6 shows the class diagram. Notice there is no corresponding nongeneric type.

Introducing Collection Class Interfaces

The previous section examined the most common collection classes and the methods that are specific to them. This section delves into the collection-related interfaces in order to understand the common capabilities of all collection classes. Understanding the interfaces implemented by a collection class gives you a quick overview of a collection's capabilities. Knowing which interfaces a collection class implements is a quick filtering mechanism for choosing the correct collection.

Figure 12.7 shows the hierarchy of interfaces that make up the collection classes.

You use these interfaces to establish capabilities such as iterating over the collection using a `foreach` loop, indexing into a collection, and determining the total number of elements in the collection. This section examines these interfaces, starting at the bottom of Figure 12.7 and moving upward.

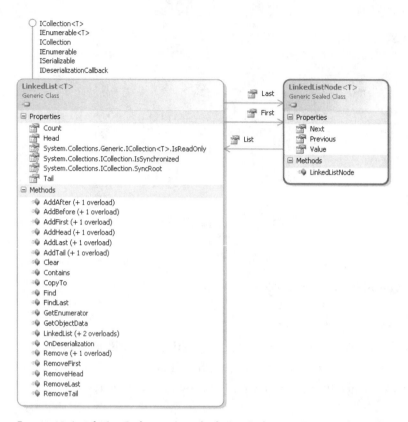

FIGURE 12.6: `LinkedList<T>` and `LinkedListNode<T>` Class Diagram

`IList<T>` versus `IDictionary<TKey, TValue>`

When selecting a collection class, the first two interfaces to look for are `IList<T>` and `IDictionary<TKey, TValue>`. These interfaces determine whether the collection type is focused on retrieval via index or retrieval via key. If the type of collection you are using should be key-centric, use a collection class that implements the `IDictionary<TKey, TValue>` interface. Alternatively, the `IList<T>` interface provides support for element retrieval via index. In other words, although both of these interfaces require that the indexer be implemented, the implementations are fundamentally different. In the case of `IList<T>`, the parameter passed to the array operator corresponds to the index of the element being retrieved, the *nth* element in the list. In the case of the `IDictionary<TKey, TValue>` interface, the parameter corresponds to the key of a previously inserted

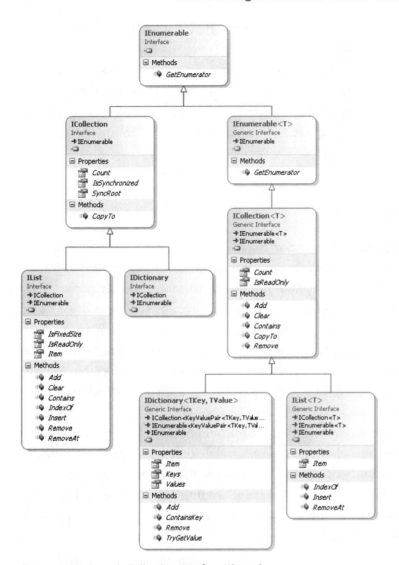

FIGURE 12.7: Generic Collection Interface Hierarchy

element. When assigning using the key, a new item will be inserted if one doesn't already exist for the specified key.

IComparable<T>

Before I discuss the next interface in Figure 12.7, I need to discuss an interface that does not appear in the diagram but is nonetheless key to both IList<T> and IDictionary<TKey, TValue>. The IComparable<T>

interface is crucial for any sorting operation by classes implementing these interfaces. For example, if the List<T>.Sort() method is called, you need a means to compare objects to determine their order. One way to do this is via the IComparable<T> interface. This interface has one method, CompareTo(). It returns an integer indicating whether the element passed is greater than, less than, or equal to the current element. For this to work the key data type needs to implement IComparable<T>.

▪ ADVANCED TOPIC

Using **IComparer<T>** for Sorting

Another way to handle custom sorting is to pass an element that implements IComparer<T> into the sort method. This interface performs a function similar to IComparable<T>, but is not generally supported directly by the element being collected. For example, consider providing an IComparable<T>.CompareTo() method for Contact. What sort order would be used: age; last name; country of residence? At issue is the fact that the sort order varies, and therefore, providing one comparison method directly on the Contact class would be an arbitrary choice.

A more appropriate solution is to provide a special sort class for each comparison implementation. Instead of the comparison method performing a comparison between the sort class instance and a single Contact instance, it would accept two Contact arguments and it would perform the comparison between these two instances. Listing 12.8 shows a sample implementation of a LastName, FirstName comparison.

LISTING 12.8: Implementing **IComparer<T>**

```
using System;
using System.Collections.Generic;

class Contact
{
  public string FirstName
  {
      get { return _FirstName; }
      set { _FirstName = value; }
  }
  private string _FirstName;
```

```csharp
    public string LastName
    {
        get { return _LastName; }
        set { _LastName = value; }
    }
    private string _LastName;
```

```csharp
using System;
using System.Collections.Generic;

    class NameComparison : IComparer<Contact>
    {
        public int Compare(Contact x, Contact y)
        {
            int result;

            if (Contact.ReferenceEquals(x, y))
            {
                result = 0;
            }
            else
            {
                if (x == null)
                {
                    result = 1;
                }
                else if (y == null)
                {
                    result = -1;
                }
                else
                {
                    result = x.LastName.CompareTo(y.LastName);
                    if (result == 0)
                    {
                        result = x.FirstName.CompareTo(
                                            y.FirstName);
                    }
                }
            }
            return result;
        }
    }
}
```

To use the new `Compare()` function you pass it to a sort method such as `List<Contact>.Sort(IComparer<Contact> comparer)`.

ICollection<T>

Both `IList<T>` and `IDictionary<TKey, TValue>` are derived from `ICollection<T>`. Furthermore, even if a collection does not implement either `IList<T>` or `IDictionary<TKey, TValue>` it will almost certainly support `ICollection<T>`. This interface is derived from `IEnumerable<T>` and includes two members: `Count` and `CopyTo()`.

- The `Count` property returns the total number of elements in the collection. Initially, it may appear that this would be sufficient to iterate through each element in the collection using a `for` loop, but in order for this to be possible the collection would also need to support retrieval by index, which the `ICollection<T>` interface does not include (although `IList<T>` does).
- The `CopyTo()` method provides the ability to convert the collection into an array. The method includes an `index` parameter so that you can specify where to insert elements in the target array. Note that to use the method you must initialize the array target with sufficient capacity, starting at the `index`, to contain all the elements in `ICollection<T>`.

Iterating Using a `foreach` Loop

Chapter 3 showed how to use a `foreach` statement to iterate over an array of elements. The syntax is simple and avoids the complication of knowing how many elements there are. The runtime does not directly support the `foreach` statement, however. Instead, the C# compiler transforms the code as described in this section.

foreach with Arrays

Consider Listing 12.9.

LISTING 12.9: **foreach** with Arrays

```
int[] array = new int[]{1, 2, 3, 4, 5, 6};

foreach (int item in array)
{
    Console.WriteLine(item);
}
```

From this code, the C# compiler creates a CIL equivalent of the `for` loop, as shown in Listing 12.10.

LISTING 12.10: Compiled Implementation of foreach with Arrays

```
int number;
int[] tempArray;
int[] array = new int[]{1, 2, 3, 4, 5, 6};

tempArray = array;
for (int counter = 0; (counter < tempArray.Length); counter++)
{
  readonly int item = tempArray[counter];

  Console.WriteLine(item);
}
```

In this example, note that `foreach` relies on support for the `Length` property and the index operator (`[]`). With the `Length` property, the C# compiler can use the `for` statement to iterate through each element in the array.

foreach with IEnumerable<T>

Although the code shown in Listing 12.10 works well on arrays where the length is fixed and the index operator is always supported, not all types of collections have a known number of elements. Furthermore, many of the collection classes, including the stack, queue, and dictionary classes, do not support retrieving elements by index. Therefore, a more general approach of iterating over collections of elements is needed. The iterator pattern provides this capability. Assuming you can determine the next element and when there are no more elements, knowing the count and supporting retrieval of elements by index is unnecessary.

The `System.Collections.Generic.IEnumerator<T>` and nongeneric `System.Collections.IEnumerator` interfaces (see Listing 12.12) are designed to enable the iterator pattern for iterating over collections of elements, rather than the length-index pattern shown in Listing 12.10. A class diagram of their relationships appears in Figure 12.8.

`IEnumerator`, which `IEnumerator<T>` derives from, includes three members. The first is `bool MoveNext()`. Using this method, you can move from one element within the collection to the next while at the same time detecting

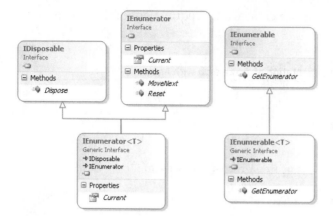

FIGURE 12.8: `IEnumerator<T>` and `IEnumerator` Interfaces

when you have enumerated through every item. The second member, a read-only property called `Current`, returns the element currently in process. `Current` is overloaded in `IEnumerator<T>`, providing a type-specific implementation of it. With these two members on the collection class, it is possible to iterate over the collection simply using a `while` loop, as demonstrated in Listing 12.11. (The last member, `Reset()`, will reset the enumeration.)

LISTING 12.11: Iterating over a Collection Using `while`

```
System.Collections.Generic.Stack<int> stack =
  new System.Collections.Generic.Stack<int>();
int number;
// ...

// This code is conceptual, not the actual code.
while (stack.MoveNext())
{
  number = stack.Current;
  Console.WriteLine(number);
}
```

In Listing 12.11, the `MoveNext()` method returns `false` when it moves past the end of the collection. This replaces the need to count elements while looping.

This example shows the gist of the C# compiler output, but it doesn't actually compile because it omits two important details about the implementation: interleaving and error handling.

State Is Shared. The problem with Listing 12.11 is that if there are two interleaving loops over the same collection, one `foreach` inside another, the collection must maintain a state indicator of the current element so that when `MoveNext()` is called, the next element can be determined. The problem is that one interleaving loop can affect the other. (The same is true of loops executed by multiple threads.)

To overcome this problem, the collection classes do not support `IEnumerator<T>` and `IEnumerator` interfaces directly. As shown in Figure 12.8, there is a second interface, called `IEnumerable<T>` (`IEnumerable` is the nongeneric version), whose only method is `GetEnumerator()`. The purpose of this method is to return an object that supports `IEnumerator<T>`. Instead of the collection class maintaining the state, a different class, usually a nested class so that it has access to the internals of the collection, will support the `IEnumerator<T>` interface and will keep the state of the iteration loop. Using this pattern, the C# equivalent of a `foreach` loop will look like the code shown in Listing 12.12.

LISTING 12.12: A Separate Enumerator Maintaining State during an Iteration

```
System.Collections.Generic.Stack<int> stack =
  new System.Collections.Generic.Stack<int>();
int number;
System.Collections.Generic.Stack<int>.IEnumerator<int>
  enumerator;

// ...

// If IEnumerable<T> is implemented explicitly,
// then a cast is required.
// ((IEnumerable)stack).GetEnumerator();
enumerator = stack.GetEnumerator();
while (enumerator.MoveNext())
{
  number = enumerator.Current;
  Console.WriteLine(number);
}
```

(Notice that if a nongeneric collection is used the enumerator will be of type `IEnumerator` rather than `IEnumerator<T>`, and an additional cast will occur when retrieving the `enumerator.Current` property.)

Error Handling. Since the classes that implement the IEnumerator<T> interface maintain the state, sometimes the state needs cleaning up after all iterations have completed. To achieve this, the IEnumerator<T> interface derives from IDisposable. Enumerators that implement IEnumerator do not necessarily implement IDisposable, but if they do, Dispose() will be called as well. This enables the calling of Dispose() after the foreach loop exits. The C# equivalent of the final CIL code, therefore, looks like Listing 12.13.

LISTING 12.13: Compiled Result of **foreach** on Collections

```
System.Collections.Generic.Stack<int> stack =
  new System.Collections.Generic.Stack<int>();
int number;
System.Collections.Generic.Stack<int>.Enumerator<int>
  enumerator;
IDisposable disposable;

enumerator = stack.GetEnumerator();
try
{
  while (enumerator.MoveNext())
  {
      number = enumerator.Current;
      Console.WriteLine(number);
  }
}
finally
{
  // Explicit cast used for IEnumerator<T>.
  disposable = (IDisposable) enumerator;
  disposable.Dispose();

  // IEnumerator will use the as operator unless IDisposable
  // support is known at compile time.
  // disposable = (enumerator as IDisposable);
  // if (disposable != null)
  // {
  //     disposable.Dispose();
  // }
}
```

Notice that because the IDisposable interface is supported by IEnumerator<T>, you can simplify the C# code with the using keyword, as shown in Listing 12.14.

LISTING 12.14: Error Handling and Resource Cleanup with **using**

```
System.Collections.Generic.Stack<int> stack =
  new System.Collections.Generic.Stack<int>();
int number;

using(
  System.Collections.Generic.Stack<int>.Enumerator<int>
      enumerator = stack.GetEnumerator())
{
  while (enumerator.MoveNext())
  {
      number = enumerator.Current;
      Console.WriteLine(number);
  }
}
```

However, recall that the `using` keyword is not directly supported by CIL either, so in reality, the former code is a more accurate C# representation of the `foreach` CIL code.

Do Not Modify Collections During foreach Iteration

Chapter 3 showed that the compiler prevents assignment of the `foreach` variable identifier (`number`). As is demonstrated in Listing 12.14, an assignment of `number` would not be a change to the collection element itself, so instead of mistakenly assuming that, the C# compiler prevents such an assignment altogether.

In addition, the element count within a collection cannot be modified during the execution of a `foreach` loop. If, for example, you called `stack.Push(42)` inside the `foreach` loop, it would be ambiguous whether the `iterator` should ignore or incorporate the change to `stack`—in other words, whether `iterator` should iterate over the newly added item or ignore it and assume the same state as when it was instantiated.

Because of this ambiguity, an exception of type `System.InvalidOper-ationException` is thrown if the collection is modified within a `foreach` loop, reporting that the collection was modified after the enumerator was instantiated.

Providing an Index Operator

The common collection interfaces provide much of the foundation for what members are needed when implementing custom collections. However, there is one more member: the **index operator**.

The index operator is a pair of square brackets that are generally used to index into a collection. Not only is this available on each collection type, but it is also a member that programmers can add to their custom classes. Listing 12.15 shows an example using `Pair<T>`.

LISTING 12.15: Defining an Index Operator

```csharp
interface IPair<T>
{
  T First
  {
      get;
  }

  T Second
  {
      get;
  }

  T this[PairItem index]
  {
      get;
  }
}


public enum PairItem
{
    First,
    Second
}


public struct Pair<T> : IPair<T>
{
  public Pair(T first, T second)
  {
      _first = first;
      _second = second;
  }
  public T First
  {
```

```csharp
        get{ return _first; }
        private set{ _first = value; }
    }
    private T _first;
    public T Second
    {
        get{ return _second; }
        private set{ _second = value; }
    }
    private T _second;

    public T this[PairItem index]
    {
        get
        {
            switch (index)
            {
                case PairItem.First:
                    return First;
                case PairItem.Second:
                    return Second;
                default :
                    throw new NotImplementedException(
                        string.Format(
                        "The enum {0} has not been implemented",
                        index.ToString()));
            }
        }
        set
        {
            switch (index)
            {
                case PairItem.First:
                    First = value;
                    break;
                case PairItem.Second:
                    Second = value;
                    break;
                default:
                    throw new NotImplementedException(
                        string.Format(
                        "The enum {0} has not been implemented",
                        index.ToString()));
            }
        }
    }
}
```

To define an index operator, you must name the member `this` and follow it with square brackets that identify the parameters. The implementation is like a property with `get` and `set` blocks. As Listing 12.15 shows, the parameter does not have to be an `int`, and in fact, the index can take multiple parameters and even be overloaded. This example uses an `enum` to reduce the likelihood that callers will supply an index for a nonexistent item.

The resulting CIL code the C# compiler creates from an index operator is a special property called `Item` that takes an argument. Properties that accept arguments cannot be created explicitly in C#, so the `Item` property is unique in this aspect. This is because any additional member with the identifier `Item`, even if it has an entirely different signature, will conflict with the compiler-created member, and will therefore not be allowed.

■ ADVANCED TOPIC

Assigning the Indexer Property Name Using `IndexerName`

As indicated earlier, the CIL property name for an indexer defaults to `Item`. Using the `IndexerNameAttribute` you can specify a different name, however. Listing 12.16, for example, changes the name to `"Entry"`.

LISTING 12.16: Changing the Indexer's Default Name

```
[System.Runtime.CompilerServices.IndexerName("Entry")]
public T this[params PairItem[] branches]
{
    // ...
}
```

This makes no difference to C# callers of the index, but it specifies the name for languages that do not support indexers directly.

Compilers consume this attribute and modify the generated CIL code. The attribute itself does not appear in the CIL output, and therefore, it is not available via reflection.

▪ ADVANCED TOPIC

Defining an Index Operator with Variable Parameters

An index operator can also take a variable parameter list. For example, Listing 12.17 defines an index operator for `BinaryTree<T>` discussed in Chapter 11 (and again in the next section).

LISTING 12.17: Defining an Index Operator with Variable Parameters

```csharp
using System;
using System.Collections.Generic;

public class BinaryTree<T>:
    IEnumerable<T>
{

  // ...

    public T this[params PairItem[] branches]
    {
        get
        {
            BinaryTree<T> currentNode = this;
            int totalLevels =
                (branches == null) ? 0 : branches.Length;
            int currentLevel = 0;

            while (currentLevel < totalLevels)
            {
                currentNode = currentNode.SubItems[
                    branches[currentLevel]];
                if (currentNode == null)
                {
                    // The binary tree at this location is null.
                    throw new IndexOutOfRangeException();
                }
                currentLevel++;
            }

            return currentNode.Value;
        }
        set
        {
            // ...
        }
    }
}
}
```

Each item within `branches` is a `PairItem` and indicates which branch to navigate down in the binary tree.

Returning `Null` or an Empty Collection

When returning an array or collection, you must indicate that there are zero items by returning either `null` or a collection instance with no items. The better choice in general is to return a collection instance with no items. In so doing, you avoid forcing the caller to check for `null` before iterating over the items in the collection. For example, given a zero-size `IEnumerable<T>` collection, the caller can immediately and safely use a `foreach` loop over the collection without concern that the internal call to `GetEnumerator()` will throw a `NullReferenceException`.

One of the few times to deviate from this guideline is when `null` is intentionally indicating something different from zero items. A `null` value for a phone number on a `string`, for example, may indicate that the phone number is not set, and an empty `string` could indicate explicitly that there is no phone number.

Iterators

Earlier, this chapter went into detail on the internals of the `foreach` loop. This section discusses how to use **iterators** to create your own implementation of the `IEnumerator<T>` and nongeneric `IEnumerator` interfaces for custom collections. Iterators provide clean syntax for specifying how to iterate on data in collection classes, especially using the `foreach` loop. The iterator allows end users of a collection to navigate its internal structure without knowledge of that structure.

▪ ADVANCED TOPIC

Origin of Iterators

In 1972, Barbara Liskov and a team of scientists at MIT began researching programming methodologies, focusing on user-defined data abstractions. To prove much of their work, they created a language called CLU that had a concept called "clusters" (CLU being the first three letters), a predecessor to the primary data abstraction programmers use today, objects. As part of their research, the team realized that although they were able to use the CLU language to abstract some data representation away from end users of their types, they consistently found themselves having to reveal the inner structure of their data in order to allow others to intelligently consume it. Through their consternation came the creation of a language construct called an iterator. (The CLU language offered many insights into what would eventually be popularized as object-oriented programming.)

If classes want to support iteration using the `foreach` loop construct, they must implement the enumerator pattern. As you saw in the earlier section, in C# the `foreach` loop construct is expanded by the compiler into the `while` loop construct based on the `IEnumerator<T>` interface that is retrieved from the `IEnumerable<T>` interface.

The problem with the enumeration pattern is that it can be cumbersome to implement manually because it maintains an internal state machine. This internal state machine may be simple for a list collection type class, but for data structures that require recursive traversal, such as binary trees, the state machine can be quite complicated. To overcome the challenges and effort associated with implementing this pattern, C# 2.0 includes a construct that makes it easier for a class to dictate how the `foreach` loop iterates over its contents.

Defining an Iterator

Iterators are a means to implement methods of a class, and they are syntactic shortcuts for the more complex enumerator pattern. When the C# compiler encounters an iterator, it expands its contents into CIL code that implements the enumerator pattern. As such, there are no runtime dependencies for implementing iterators. Because the C# compiler handles implementation through CIL code generation, there is no real runtime performance benefit to using iterators. However, there is a substantial programmer productivity gain in choosing iterators over manual implementation of the enumerator pattern. To begin, the next section examines how an iterator is defined in code.

Iterator Syntax

An iterator provides shorthand implementation of iterator interfaces, the combination of the `IEnumerable<T>` and `IEnumerator<T>` interfaces. Listing 12.18 declares an iterator for the generic `BinaryTree<T>` type by creating a `GetEnumerator()` method. In the previous chapter, you coded parts of the `BinaryTree<T>` class. In this chapter, you will add support for the iterator interfaces.

LISTING 12.18: Iterator Interfaces Pattern

```
using System;
using System.Collections.Generic;

public class BinaryTree<T>:
    IEnumerable<T>
{
    public BinaryTree ( T value)
    {
        Value = value;
    }

    #region IEnumerable<T>
    public IEnumerator<T> GetEnumerator()
    {
        ...
    }
    #endregion IEnumerable<T>

    public T Value
    {
        get{ return _value;     }
        set{ _value = value;       }
    }
    private T _value;

    public Pair<BinaryTree<T>> SubItems
    {
        get{ return _subItems; }
        set{ _subItems = value;     }
    }
    private Pair<BinaryTree<T>> _subItems;
}

public struct Pair<T>
{
    public Pair(T first, T second)
```

```
    {
        _first = first;
        _second = second;
    }
    public T First
    {
        get{ return _first; }
        private set{ _first = value; }
    }
    private T _first;
    public T Second
    {
        get{ return _second; }
        private set{ _second = value; }
    }
    private T _second;
}
```

To begin, add the declaration for the `IEnumerator<T> IEnumerable<T>.GetEnumerator()` method.

Yielding Values from an Iterator

Iterators are like functions, but instead of returning values, they *yield* them. In the case of `BinaryTree<T>`, the yield type of the iterator corresponds to the type parameter, `T`. If the nongeneric version of `IEnumerator` is used, then the return type will instead be `object`. To correctly implement the iterator pattern, you need to maintain an internal state machine in order to keep track of where you are while enumerating the collection. In the `BinaryTree<T>` case, you track which elements within the tree have already been enumerated and which are still to come.

Iterators have built-in state machines to keep track of the current and next elements. The new `yield return` statement returns values each time an iterator encounters it. Then, when the next iteration starts, the code begins executing immediately following the last `yield return` statement. In Listing 12.19, you return the C# primitive data type keywords sequentially.

LISTING 12.19: Yielding the C# Keywords Sequentially

```
using System;
using System.Collections.Generic;
```

```csharp
public class CSharpPrimitiveTypes: IEnumerable<string>
{
  public IEnumerator<string> GetEnumerator()
  {
      yield return "object";
      yield return "byte";
      yield return "uint";
      yield return "ulong";
      yield return "float";
      yield return "char";
      yield return "bool";
      yield return "ushort";
      yield return "decimal";
      yield return "int";
      yield return "sbyte";
      yield return "short";
      yield return "long";
      yield return "void";
      yield return "double";
      yield return "string";
  }


      // IEnumerator also required because IEnumerator<T>
      // derives from it.
  System.Collections.IEnumerator
      System.Collections.IEnumerable.GetEnumerator()
  {
      // Delegate to IEnumerator<string> GetEnumerator() above
      return GetEnumerator();
  }
}

public class Program
{
  static void Main()
  {
      CSharpPrimitiveTypes primitives =
          new CSharpPrimitiveTypes();

      foreach (string primitive in primitives)
      {
          Console.WriteLine(primitive);
      }
  }
}
```

The results of Listing 12.19 appear in Output 12.5.

OUTPUT 12.5:

```
object
byte
uint
ulong
float
char
bool
ushort
decimal
int
sbyte
short
long
void
double
string
```

The output from this listing is a listing of the C# primitive types.[1]

Iterators and State

When an iterator is first called in a `foreach` statement (such as `foreach primitive in primitives` in Listing 12.19), its state is initialized within the enumerator. The iterator maintains its state as long as the `foreach` statement at the call site continues to execute. When you yield a value, process it, and resume the `foreach` statement at the call site, the iterator continues where it left off the previous time around the loop and continues processing. When the `foreach` statement at the call site terminates, the iterator's state is no longer saved and it is safe to call the iterator again, knowing that it will reset to the beginning.

Figure 12.9 shows a high-level sequence diagram of what takes place. Remember that the `MoveNext()` method appears on the `IEnumerator<T>` interface.

In Listing 12.19, the `foreach` statement at the call site initiates a call to `GetEnumerator()` on the `CSharpPrimitiveTypes` instance called `primitives`. Given the iterator instance (referenced by `iterator`), `foreach` begins

---

1. In alpha versions of the C# 2.0 compiler, yield was a keyword rather than a contextual keyword. However, such a change could result in an incompatibility between C# 1.0 and C# 2.0. Instead, yield became a contextual keyword that must appear before `return`. As a result, no code-breaking change occurred because C# 1.0 did not allow any text (besides comments) prior to the `return` keyword.

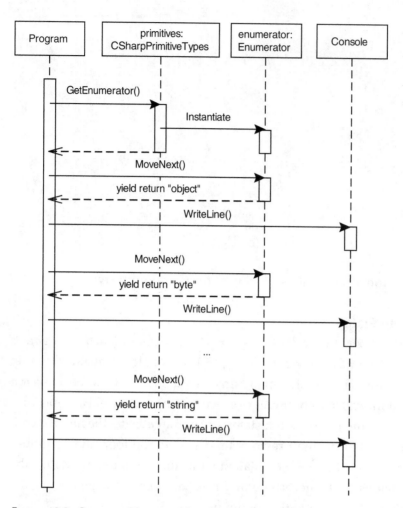

FIGURE 12.9: Sequence Diagram with `yield return`

each iteration with a call to MoveNext(). Within the iterator, you yield a value back to the foreach statement at the call site. After the yield return statement, the GetEnumerator() method seemingly pauses until the next MoveNext() request. Back at the call site, the foreach statement displays the yielded value on the screen. It then loops back around and calls MoveNext() on the iterator again. Notice that the second time, processing picks up at the second yield return statement. Once again, the foreach displays on the screen what CSharpPrimitiveTypes yielded and starts the loop again. This process continues until there are no more yield return statements within the iterator. At that point, the foreach loop at the call site terminates.

More Iterator Examples

Before you modify `BinaryTree<T>`, you must modify `Pair<T>` to support the `IEnumerable<T>` interface using an iterator. Listing 12.20 is an example that yields each element in `Pair<T>`.

LISTING 12.20: Using **yield** to Implement **BinaryTree<T>**

```csharp
public struct Pair<T>: IPair<T>,
    IEnumerable<T>
{
   public Pair(T first, T second)
   {
       _first = first;
       _second = second;
   }
   public T First
   {
       get{ return _first; }
       private set{ _first = value; }
   }
   private T _first;
   public T Second
   {
       get{ return _second; }
       private set{ _second = value; }
   }
   private T _second;

   #region IEnumerable<T>
   public IEnumerator<T> GetEnumerator()
   {
       yield return First;
       yield return Second;
   }
   #endregion IEnumerable<T>

   #region IEnumerable Members
   System.Collections.IEnumerator
       System.Collections.IEnumerable.GetEnumerator()
   {
       return GetEnumerator();
   }
   #endregion
}
```

In Listing 12.20, iterating over a `Pair<T>` data type loops twice: first through `yield return First`, and then through `yield return Second`. Each time the yield return statement within `GetEnumerator()` is encountered, the state is saved and execution appears to "jump" out of the `GetEnumerator()`

method context and into the context of the call site. When the second iteration starts, `GetEnumerator()` begins executing again with the `yield return Second` statement.

`System.Collections.Generic.IEnumerable<T>` inherits from `System.Collections.IEnumerable`. Therefore, when implementing `IEnumerable<T>`, it is also necessary to implement `IEnumerable`. In Listing 12.20 you do so explicitly, and the implementation simply involves a call to `IEnumerable<T>`'s `GetEnumerator()` implementation. This call from `IEnumerable.GetEnumerator()` to `IEnumerable<T>.GetEnumerator()` will always work because of the type compatibility (via inheritance) between `IEnumerable<T>` and `IEnumerable`. This call from x to y will work in all cases because of type compatibility between `IEnumerable` and `IEnumerator<T>`. Since the signatures for both `GetEnumerator()`s are identical (the return type does not distinguish a signature), one or both implementations must be explicit. Given the additional type safety offered by `IEnumerable<T>`'s version, you implement `IEnumerable`'s implementation explicitly.

Listing 12.21 uses the `Pair<T>.GetEnumerator()` method and displays `"Inigo"` and `"Montoya"` on two consecutive lines.

LISTING 12.21: Using **`Pair<T>.GetEnumerator()`** via **foreach**

```
Pair<string> fullname = new Pair<string>("Inigo", "Montoya");
foreach (string name in fullname)
{
    Console.WriteLine(name);
}
```

Notice that the call to `GetEnumerator()` is implicit within the `foreach` loop.

Placing a `yield return` within a Loop

It is not necessary to hardcode each `yield return` statement, as you did in both `CSharpPrimitiveTypes` and `Pair<T>`. Using the `yield return` statement, you can return values from inside a loop construct. Listing 12.22 uses a `foreach` loop. Each time the `foreach` within `GetEnumerator()` executes, it returns the next value.

LISTING 12.22: Placing `yield return` Statements within a Loop

```csharp
public class BinaryTree<T>: IEnumerable<T>
{
  // ...

  #region IEnumerable<T>
  public IEnumerator<T> GetEnumerator()
  {
      // Return the item at this node.
      yield return Value;

      // Iterate through each of the elements in the pair.
      foreach (BinaryTree<T> tree in SubItems)
      {
          if (tree != null)
          {
              // Since each element in the pair is a tree,
              // traverse the tree and yield each
              // element.
              foreach (T item in tree)
              {
                  yield return item;
              }
          }
      }
  }
  #endregion IEnumerable<T>

  #region IEnumerable Members
  System.Collections.IEnumerator
      System.Collections.IEnumerable.GetEnumerator()
  {
      return GetEnumerator();
  }
  #endregion
}
```

In Listing 12.22, the first iteration returns the root element within the binary tree. During the second iteration you traverse the pair of subelements. If the subelement pair contains a non-null value, then you traverse into that child node and yield its elements. Note that `foreach(T item in tree)` is a recursive call to a child node.

As observed with `CSharpPrimitiveTypes` and `Pair<T>`, you can now iterate over `BinaryTree<T>` using a `foreach` loop. Listing 12.23 demonstrates this, and Output 12.6 shows the results.

LISTING 12.23: Using **foreach** with **BinaryTree<string>**

```
// JFK
jfkFamilyTree = new BinaryTree<string>(
    "John Fitzgerald Kennedy");

jfkFamilyTree.SubItems = new Pair<BinaryTree<string>>(
    new BinaryTree<string>("Joseph Patrick Kennedy"),
    new BinaryTree<string>("Rose Elizabeth Fitzgerald"));

// Grandparents (Father's side)
jfkFamilyTree.SubItems.First.SubItems =
    new Pair<BinaryTree<string>>(
    new BinaryTree<string>("Patrick Joseph Kennedy"),
    new    BinaryTree<string>("Mary Augusta Hickey"));

// Grandparents (Mother's side)
jfkFamilyTree.SubItems.Second.SubItems =
    new Pair<BinaryTree<string>>(
    new BinaryTree<string>("John Francis Fitzgerald"),
    new BinaryTree<string>("Mary Josephine Hannon"));

foreach (string name in jfkFamilyTree)
{
    Console.WriteLine(name);
}
```

OUTPUT 12.6:

```
John Fitzgerald Kennedy
Joseph Patrick Kennedy
Patrick Joseph Kennedy
Mary Augusta Hickey
Rose Elizabeth Fitzgerald
John Francis Fitzgerald
Mary Josephine Hannon
```

■ BEGINNER TOPIC

struct versus class

An interesting side effect of defining `Pair<T>` as a `struct` rather than a `class` is that `SubItems.First` and `SubItems.Second` cannot be assigned directly. The following will produce a compile error indicating that `SubItems` cannot be modified, "because it is not a variable."

```
jfkFamilyTree.SubItems.First =
    new BinaryTree<string>("Joseph Patrick Kennedy");
```

The issue is that `SubItems` is a property of type `Pair<T>`, a `struct`. Therefore, when the property returns the value, a copy of _SubItems is made, and assigning `First` on a copy that is promptly lost at the end of the statement would be misleading. Fortunately, the C# compiler prevents this.

To overcome the issue don't assign it (see the approach in Listing 12.23), use `class` rather than `struct` for `Pair<T>`, don't create a `SubItems` property and instead use a field, or provide properties in `BinaryTree<T>` that give direct access to _SubItems members.

Canceling Further Iteration: `yield break`

Sometimes you might want to cancel further iteration. You can do this by including an `if` statement so that no further statements within the code are executed. However, you can also jump back to the call site, causing `MoveNext()` to return `false`. Listing 12.24 shows an example of such a method.

LISTING 12.24: Escaping Iteration via `yield break`

```
public System.Collections.Generic.IEnumerable<T>
    GetNotNullEnumerator()
{
    if((First == null) || (Second == null))
    {
        yield break;
    }
    yield return Second;
    yield return First;
}
```

This method cancels the iteration if either of the elements in the `Pair<T>` class is `null`.

A `yield break` statement is similar to placing a `return` statement at the top of a function when it is determined there is no work to do. It is a way to exit from further iterations without surrounding all remaining code with an `if` block. As such, it allows multiple exits, and therefore, you should use it with caution because casual reading of the code may miss the early exit.

■**ADVANCED TOPIC**

How Iterators Work

When the C# compiler encounters an iterator, it expands the code into the appropriate CIL for the corresponding enumerator design pattern. In the generated code, the C# compiler first creates a nested private class to implement the `IEnumerator<T>` interface, along with its `Current` property and a `MoveNext()` method. The `Current` property returns a type corresponding to the return type of the iterator. Listing 12.20 of `Pair<T>` contains an iterator that returns a `T` type. The C# compiler examines the code contained within the iterator and creates the necessary code within the `MoveNext` method and the `Current` property to mimic its behavior. For the `Pair<T>` iterator, the C# compiler generates roughly equivalent code (see Listing 12.25).

LISTING 12.25: C# Equivalent of Compiler-Generated C# Code for Iterators

```csharp
using System;
using System.Collections.Generic;

public class Pair<T> : IPair<T>, IEnumerable<T>
{
  // ...

  // The iterator is expanded into the following
  // code by the compiler
  public virtual IEnumerator<T> GetEnumerator()
  {
      __ListEnumerator result = new __ListEnumerator(0);
      result._Pair = this;
      return result;
  }
  public virtual System.Collections.IEnumerator
      System.Collections.IEnumerable.GetEnumerator()
  {
      return new GetEnumerator();
  }

  private sealed class __ListEnumerator<T> : IEnumerator<T>
  {
      public __ListEnumerator(int itemCount)
      {
          _ItemCount = itemCount;
      }
```

```
Pair<T> _Pair;
T _Current;
int _ItemCount;

public object Current
{
    get
    {
        return _Current;
    }
}

public bool MoveNext()
{
    switch (_ItemCount)
    {
        case 0:
            _Current = _Pair.First;
            _ItemCount++;
            return true;
        case 1:
            _Current = _Pair.Second;
            _ItemCount++;
            return true;
        default:
            return false;
    }
}
    }
}
```

Because the compiler takes the `yield return` statement and generates classes that correspond to what you probably would have written manually, iterators in C# exhibit the same performance characteristics as classes that implement the enumerator design pattern manually. While there is no performance improvement, the programmer productivity gained is significant.

Creating Multiple Iterators in a Single Class

Previous iterator examples implemented `IEnumerable<T>.GetEnumerator()`. This is the method that `foreach` seeks implicitly. Sometimes you might want different iteration sequences, such as iterating in reverse, filtering the results, or iterating over an object projection other than the default. You can declare additional iterators in the class by encapsulating them within properties or methods that return IEnumerable<T> or IEnumerable. If you want to iterate over the elements of Pair<T> in reverse, for example, you provide a GetReverseEnumerator() method, as shown in Listing 12.26.

LISTING 12.26: Using **yield return** in a Method That Returns **IEnumerable<T>**

```
public struct Pair<T>: IEnumerable<T>
{
    ...

    public IEnumerable<T> GetReverseEnumerator()
    {
        yield return Second;
        yield return First;
    }
    ...
}

public void Main()
{
    Pair<string> game = new Pair<string>("Redskins", "Eagles");
    foreach (string name in game.GetReverseEnumerator())
    {
        Console.WriteLine(name);
    }
}
```

Note that you return IEnumerable<T>, not IEnumerator<T>. This is different from IEnumerable<T>.GetEnumerator(), which returns IEnumerator<T>. The code in Main() demonstrates how to call GetReverseEnumerator() using a foreach loop.

yield Statement Characteristics

You can declare the yield return statement only in members that return an IEnumerator<T> or IEnumerable<T> type, or their nongeneric equivalents. More specifically, you can use yield only in GetEnumerator() methods that return IEnumerator<T>, or in methods that return IEnumerable<T> but are not called GetEnumerator().

Methods that include a yield return statement may not have a simple return. If the method uses the yield return statement, then the C# compiler generates the necessary code to maintain the state machine for the iterator. In contrast, if the method uses the `return` statement instead of `yield return`, the programmer is responsible for maintaining his own state machine and returning an instance of one of the iterator interfaces. Further, just as all code paths in a method with a return type must contain a `return` statement accompanied by a value, all code paths in an iterator must contain a `yield return` statement.

Additional restrictions on the `yield` statement that result in compiler errors are as follows.

- The `yield` statement may not appear outside a method, operator, or property accessor.
- The `yield` statement may not appear in an anonymous method (see Chapter 13).
- The `yield` statement may not appear inside the `try`, `catch`, and `finally` clauses.

SUMMARY

With the advent of generics in C# 2.0, the selection of which collection class to use will always favor generics over the nongeneric versions. In fact, C# 2.0 developers should consider the entire namespace of `System.Collections` as obsolete. In other words, don't go back and necessarily remove all code that already uses this namespace. Instead, use `System.Collections.Generics` for any new code and, over time, consider migrating existing code to use the corresponding generic collections.

Providing the `System.Collections.Generic` namespace is not the only change that C# 2.0 brings to collections. Another significant addition is the iterator. Iterators involve a new contextual keyword, `yield`, that C# uses to trigger underlying CIL code that implements the iterator pattern used by the `foreach` loop.

The next chapter looks at another C# type, delegates, and their encapsulation into events.

13

Delegates and Events

PREVIOUS CHAPTERS DISCUSSED extensively how to create classes using many of the built-in C# language facilities surrounding classes. The objects instantiated from classes encapsulate data and operations on data. As you create more and more classes, you see common patterns in the relationships between these classes. The previous chapter covered one such set of patterns.

Another pattern is to pass one or more methods to a receiver for invocation. This last pattern comprises the building blocks of larger patterns called publish-subscribe patterns. The use of methods as a data type and their support for publish-subscribe patterns is the focus of this chapter.

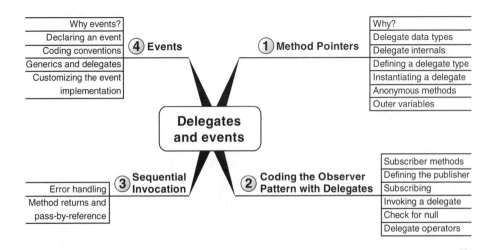

Virtually everything described within this chapter is possible to do using programming concepts that I discussed earlier in the book. However, the delegate and event constructs provide a simplified means of implementing callback and listener patterns, saving developers from reimplementing the same pattern multiple times throughout their code. By using these constructs, code becomes easier to read and write.

Method Pointers

Veteran C and C++ programmers have long used method pointers as a means to pass executable steps as parameters to another method. C# achieves the same functionality using a **delegate**, which encapsulates methods as objects, enabling an indirect method call bound at runtime. With a delegate, you can call a method chain via a single method object, create variables that refer to a method's chain, and use those data types as parameters to pass methods. Consider an example of where this is useful.

Defining the Scenario

Although not necessarily efficient, perhaps one of the simplest sort routines is a bubble sort. Listing 13.1 shows the `BubbleSort()` method.

LISTING 13.1: **BubbleSort() Method**

```
class SimpleSort
{
  public static void BubbleSort(int[] items)
  {
      int i;
      int j;
      int temp;

      for (i = items.Length - 1; i >= 0; i--)
      {
          for (j = 1; j <= i; j++)
          {
              if (items[j - 1] > items[j])
              {
                  temp = items[j - 1];
                  items[j - 1] = items[j];
                  items[j] = temp;
              }
          }
      }
```

```
        }
    }
    // ...
}
```

This method will sort an array of integers in ascending order. However, if you wanted to support the option to sort the integers in descending order, you would have essentially two options. You could duplicate the code and replace the greater-than operator with a less-than operator. Alternatively, you could pass in an additional parameter indicating how to perform the sort, as shown in Listing 13.2.

LISTING 13.2: **BubbleSort()** Method, Ascending or Descending

```
class SimpleSort
{
    ...
    public enum SortType
    {
        Ascending,
        Descending
    }

    public static void BubbleSort(int[] items, SortType sortOrder)
    {
        int i;
        int j;
        int temp;

        for (i = items.Length - 1; i >= 0; i--)
        {
            for (j = 1; j <= i; j++)
            {
                switch (sortOrder)
                {
                    case SortType.Ascending :
                        if (items[j - 1] > items[j])
                        {
                            temp = items[j - 1];
                            items[j - 1] = items[j];
                            items[j] = temp;
                        }

                        break;

                    case SortType.Descending :
                        if (items[j - 1] < items[j])
                        {
```

```
                              temp = items[j - 1];
                              items[j - 1] = items[j];
                              items[j] = temp;
                          }

                      break;
                  }
              }
          }
      }
      ...
  }
```

However, this handles only two of the possible sort orders. If you wanted
to sort them alphabetically, randomly, or via some other mechanism, it
would not take long before the number of BubbleSort() methods and
corresponding SortType values would become cumbersome.

Delegate Data Types

To reduce the amount of code duplication, you can pass in the comparison
method as a parameter to the BubbleSort() method. Moreover, in order
to pass a method as a parameter, there needs to be a data type that can represent that method—in other words, a delegate. Listing 13.3 includes a
modification to the BubbleSort() method that takes a delegate parameter. In this case, the delegate data type is GreaterThanHandler.

LISTING 13.3: **BubbleSort()** Method with Delegate Parameter

```
class DelegateSample
{
    // ...

    public static void BubbleSort(
        int[] items, GreaterThanHandler greaterThan)
    {
        int i;
        int j;
        int temp;

        for (i = items.Length - 1; i >= 0; i--)
        {
            for (j = 1; j <= i; j++)
            {
                if (greaterThan(items[j - 1], items[j]))
                {
```

```
                    temp = items[j - 1];
                    items[j - 1] = items[j];
                    items[j] = temp;
                }
            }
        }
    }
    // ...
}
```

`GreaterThanHandler` is a data type that represents a method for comparing two integers. Within the `BubbleSort()` method you then use the instance of the `GreaterThanHandler`, called `greaterThan`, inside the conditional expression. Since `greaterThan` represents a method, the syntax to invoke the method is identical to calling the method directly. In this case, `greaterThan` takes two integer parameters and returns a Boolean value that indicates whether the first integer is greater than the second one.

Perhaps more noteworthy than the particular algorithm, the `Greater-ThanHandler` delegate is strongly typed to return a `bool` and to accept only two integer parameters. Just as with any other method, the call to a delegate is strongly typed, and if the data types don't match up, then the C# compiler reports an error. Let's consider how the delegate works internally.

Delegate Internals

C# defines all delegates, including `GreaterThanHandler`, as derived indirectly from `System.Delegate`, as shown in Figure 13.1.

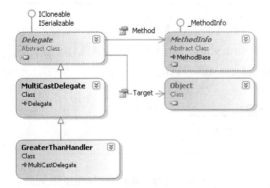

FIGURE 13.1: Delegate Types Object Model

The first property is of type `System.Reflection.MethodInfo`, which the next chapter discusses. `MethodInfo` defines the signature of a particular method, including its name, parameters, and return type. In addition to `MethodInfo`, a delegate also needs the instance of the object containing the method to invoke. This is the purpose of the second property, `Target`. In the case of a static method, `Target` corresponds to the type itself. The purpose of the `MulticastDelegate` class appears later in this chapter, in the section Multicast Delegates and the Observer Pattern.

Defining a Delegate Type

You saw how to define a method that uses a delegate, and you learned how to invoke a call to the delegate simply by treating the delegate variable as a method. However, you have yet to learn how to declare a delegate data type. For example, you have not learned how to define `GreaterThanHandler` such that it requires two integer parameters and returns a `bool`.

Although all delegate data types derive indirectly from `System.Delegate`, the C# compiler does not allow you to define a class that derives directly or indirectly (via `System.MulticastDelegate`) from `System.Delegate`. Listing 13.4, therefore, is not valid.

LISTING 13.4: **`System.Delegate`** Cannot Explicitly Be a Base Class

```
// ERROR: 'GreaterThanHandler' cannot
// inherit from special class 'System.Delegate'
public class GreaterThanHandler: System.Delegate
{
   ...
}
```

In its place, C# uses the `delegate` keyword. This keyword causes the compiler to generate a class similar to the one shown in Listing 13.4. Listing 13.5 shows the syntax for declaring a delegate data type.

LISTING 13.5: Declaring a Delegate Data Type

```
public delegate bool GreaterThanHandler (
   int first, int second);
```

In other words, the `delegate` keyword is shorthand for declaring a class derived ultimately from `System.Delegate`. In fact, if the delegate declaration appeared within another class, then the delegate type, GreaterThanHandler, would be a nested type (see Listing 13.6).

LISTING 13.6: Declaring a Nested Delegate Data Type

```
class DelegateSample
{
  public delegate bool GreaterThanHandler (
    int first, int second);
}
```

In this case, the data type would be DelegateSample.GreaterThan-Handler because it is defined as a nested class within DelegateSample.

Instantiating a Delegate

In this final step of implementing the BubbleSort() method with a delegate, you will learn how to call the method and pass a delegate instance—specifically, an instance of type GreaterThanHandler. To instantiate a delegate, you need a method that corresponds to the signature of the delegate type itself. In the case of GreaterThanHandler, that method takes two integers and returns a bool. The name of the method is not significant. Listing 13.7 shows the code for a greater-than method.

LISTING 13.7: Declaring a GreaterThanHandler-Compatible Method

```
public delegate bool GreaterThanHandler (
  int first, int second);


class DelegateSample
{


  public static void BubbleSort(
    int[] items, GreaterThanHandler greaterThan)
  {
    ...
  }


  public static bool GreaterThan(int first, int second)
  {
    return (first > second);
  }
  ...
}
```

With this method defined, you can call `BubbleSort()` and pass the delegate instance that contains this method. With C# 2.0, you simply specify the name of the delegate method (see Listing 13.8).

LISTING 13.8: Passing a Delegate Instance as a Parameter in C# 2.0

```csharp
public delegate bool GreaterThanHandler (
    int first, int second);
```

```csharp
class DelegateSample
{
  public static void BubbleSort(
      int[] items, GreaterThanHandler greaterThan)
  {
      ...
  }

  public static bool GreaterThan(int first, int second)
  {
      return (first > second);
  }

  static void Main(string[] args)
  {

      int i;
      int[] items = new int[5];

      for(i=0;i<items.Length; i++)
      {
          Console.Write("Enter an integer:");
          items[i] = int.Parse(Console.ReadLine());
      }

      BubbleSort(items, GreaterThan);

      for (i = 0; i < items.Length; i++)
      {
          Console.WriteLine(items[i]);
      }
  }

}
```

Note that the `GreaterThanHandler` delegate is a class, but you do necessarily use `new` to instantiate an instance of this class. The facility to pass the name rather than explicit instantiation is new syntax to C# 2.0. Earlier versions of the compiler require instantiation of the delegate demonstrated in Listing 13.9.

LISTING 13.9: Passing a Delegate Instance as a Parameter Prior to C# 2.0

```
public delegate bool GreaterThanHandler (
  int first, int second);
```

```
class DelegateSample
{
  public static void BubbleSort(
      int[] items, GreaterThanHandler greaterThan)
  {
      ...
  }

  public static bool GreaterThan(int first, int second)
  {
      return (first > second);
  }

  static void Main(string[] args)
  {

      int i;
      int[] items = new int[5];

      for(i=0;i<items.Length; i++)
      {
          Console.Write("Enter an integer:");
          items[i] = int.Parse(Console.ReadLine());
      }

      BubbleSort(items,
          new GreaterThanHandler(GreaterThan));

      for (i = 0; i < items.Length; i++)
      {
          Console.WriteLine(items[i]);
      }
  }

  ...
}
```

Note that C# 2.0 supports both syntaxes, but unless you are writing backward-compatible code, the 2.0 syntax is preferable.

The approach of passing the delegate to specify the sort order is significantly more flexible than the approach listed at the beginning of this chapter. With the delegate approach, you can change the sort order to be
alphabetical simply by adding an alternative delegate to convert integers
to strings as part of the comparison. Listing 13.10 shows a full listing that
demonstrates alphabetical sorting, and Output 13.1 shows the results.

LISTING 13.10: Using a Different **GreaterThanHandler**-Compatible Method

```csharp
class DelegateSample
{

    public delegate bool GreaterThanHandler(int first, int second);

    public static void BubbleSort(
        int[] items, GreaterThanHandler greaterThan)
    {
        int i;
        int j;
        int temp;

        for (i = items.Length - 1; i >= 0; i--)
        {
            for (j = 1; j <= i; j++)
            {
                if (greaterThan(items[j - 1], items[j]))
                {
                    temp = items[j - 1];
                    items[j - 1] = items[j];
                    items[j] = temp;
                }
            }
        }
    }

    public static bool GreaterThan(int first, int second)
    {
        return (first > second);
    }

    public static bool AlphabeticalGreaterThan(
        int first, int second)
    {
        int comparison;
        comparison = (first.ToString().CompareTo(
            second.ToString()));

        return (comparison > 0);
    }
```

```
static void Main(string[] args)
{

    int i;
    int[] items = new int[5];

    for(i=0;i<items.Length; i++)
    {
        Console.Write("Enter an integer:");
        items[i] = int.Parse(Console.ReadLine());
    }

        BubbleSort(items, AlphabeticalGreaterThan);

    for (i = 0; i < items.Length; i++)
    {
        Console.WriteLine(items[i]);
    }
}
}
```

OUTPUT 13.1:

```
Enter an integer:1
Enter an integer:12
Enter an integer:13
Enter an integer:5
Enter an integer:4
1
12
13
4
5
```

The alphabetic order is different from the numeric order. Note how simple it was to add this additional sort mechanism, however, compared to the process used at the beginning of the chapter.

The only changes to create the alphabetical sort order were the addition of the `AlphabeticalGreaterThan` method and then passing that method into the call to `BubbleSort()`.

Anonymous Methods

C# 2.0 also includes a feature known as **anonymous methods**. These are delegate instances with no actual method declaration. Instead, they are defined inline in the code, as shown in Listing 13.11.

LISTING 13.11: Passing an Anonymous Method

```csharp
class DelegateSample
{

    ...

    static void Main(string[] args)
    {

        int i;
        int[] items = new int[5];
        GreaterThanHandler greaterThan;

        for(i=0;i<items.Length; i++)
        {
            Console.Write("Enter an integer:");
            items[i] = int.Parse(Console.ReadLine());
        }

        greaterThan =
            delegate(int first, int second)
            {
                return (first < second);
            };

        BubbleSort(items, greaterThan);

        for (i = 0; i < items.Length; i++)
        {
            Console.WriteLine(items[i]);
        }
    }
}
```

In Listing 13.11, you change the call to BubbleSort() to use an anonymous method that sorts items in descending order. Notice that no Less-Than() method is specified. Instead, the delegate keyword is placed directly inline with the code. In this context, the delegate keyword serves as a means of specifying a type of "delegate literal," similar to how quotes specify a string literal.

You can even call the BubbleSort() method directly, without declaring the greaterThan variable (see Listing 13.12).

LISTING 13.12: Using an Anonymous Method without Declaring a Variable

```
class DelegateSample
{

  ...

  static void Main(string[] args)
  {

     int i;
     int[] items = new int[5];

     for(i=0;i<items.Length; i++)
     {
        Console.Write("Enter an integer:");
        items[i] = int.Parse(Console.ReadLine());
     }

     BubbleSort(items,
        delegate(int first, int second)
        {
           return (first < second);
        }
     );

     for (i = 0; i < items.Length; i++)
     {
        Console.WriteLine(items[i]);
     }
  }
}
```

Note that in all cases, the parameters and the return type must be compatible with the `GreaterThanHandler` data type, the delegate type of the second parameter of `BubbleSort()`.

The anonymous method does not have any intrinsic type associated with it, although implicit conversion is possible for any delegate type as long as the parameters and return type are compatible. In other words, the anonymous method is no more a `GreaterThanHandler` type than another delegate type such as `LessThanHandler`. As a result, you cannot use the `typeof()` operator (Chapter 14) on an anonymous method, and calling `GetType()` is possible only after assigning the anonymous method to a delegate variable.

■ ADVANCED TOPIC

Anonymous Method Internals

Anonymous methods are not an intrinsic construct within the CLR. Rather, they are implemented through the C# compiler. Anonymous methods provide a language construct for an inline declared delegate pattern. The C# compiler, therefore, generates the implementation code for this pattern so that the compiler automatically writes the code instead of the developer writing it manually. Given the earlier listings, therefore, the C# compiler generates CIL code that is similar to the C# code shown in Listing 13.13.

LISTING 13.13: C# Equivalent of CIL Generated by the Compiler for Anonymous Methods

```
class DelegateSample
{

  // ...

  static void Main(string[] args)
  {

      int i;
      int[] items = new int[5];

      for(i=0;i<items.Length; i++)
      {
          Console.Write("Enter an integer:");
          items[i] = int.Parse(Console.ReadLine());
      }


      BubbleSort(items, Program.__AnonymousMethod_00000000);

      for (i = 0; i < items.Length; i++)
      {
          Console.WriteLine(items[i]);
      }


  }


  private static bool __AnonymousMethod_00000000(
      int first, int second)
  {
      return first < second;
  }


}
```

In this example, an anonymous method is converted into a separately declared static method that is then instantiated as a delegate and passed as a parameter.

Outer Variables

Variables that programmers declare outside an anonymous method and access within the implementation are **outer variables**. They are available only when using anonymous methods where they are **captured** such that the C# compiler takes care of passing them, along with the delegate, and returning them at the end of the invocation. In Listing 13.14, it is relatively trivial to use an outer variable to count how many times swap is called by BubbleSort(). Output 13.2 shows the results of this listing.

LISTING 13.14: Using an Outer Variable in an Anonymous Method

```
class DelegateSample
{

    // ...

    static void Main(string[] args)
    {

        int i;
        int[] items = new int[5];
        int swapCount=0;

        for(i=0;i<items.Length; i++)
        {
            Console.Write("Enter an integer:");
            items[i] = int.Parse(Console.ReadLine());
        }

        BubbleSort(items,
            delegate(int first, int second)
            {
                bool swap = first < second;
                if(swap)
                {
                    swapCount++;
                }
                return swap;
            }
        );

        for (i = 0; i < items.Length; i++)
        {
```

```
            Console.WriteLine(items[i]);
        }

            Console.WriteLine("Items were swapped {0} times.",
                    swapCount);
    }
}
```

OUTPUT 13.2:

```
Enter an integer:5
Enter an integer:1
Enter an integer:4
Enter an integer:2
Enter an integer:3
5
4
3
2
1
Items were swapped 4 times.
```

swapCount appears outside the anonymous method and is incremented inside it. After calling the BubbleSort() method, swapCount is printed out to the console.

As this code demonstrates, the C# compiler takes care of generating CIL code that passes swapCount by reference between the anonymous method and the call site, even though there is no parameter to pass swapCount within the anonymous delegate, nor within the BubbleSort() method.

■ ADVANCED TOPIC

Outer Variable Internals

The CIL code generated by the C# compiler for outer variables is more complex than the code for a simple anonymous method because the outer variable must pass to and from the call site in a thread-safe manner. Listing 13.15 shows the C# equivalent of the CIL code used to implement outer variables.

LISTING 13.15: C# Equivalent of CIL Code Generated by Compiler for Outer Variables

```
class DelegateSample
{
```

```
// ...

   private sealed class __LocalsDisplayClass_00000001
{
   public int swapCount;
   public bool __AnonymousMethod_00000000(
       int first, int second)
   {
       bool swap = first < second;

       if (swap)
       {
           swapCount++;
       }

       return swap;
   }
}
```

...

```
static void Main(string[] args)
{

   int i;
   int swapCount=0;
   int[] items = new int[5];

   for(i=0;i<items.Length; i++)
   {
       Console.Write("Enter an integer:");
       items[i] = int.Parse(Console.ReadLine());
   }

   __LocalsDisplayClass_00000001 handler =
       new __LocalsDisplayClass_00000001();

   handler.swapCount = swapCount;

   BubbleSort(items, handler.__AnonymousMethod_00000000);

   swapCount = handler.swapCount;

   for (i = 0; i < items.Length; i++)
   {
       Console.WriteLine(items[i]);
   }

   Console.WriteLine("Items were swapped {0} times.",
                     swapCount);
   }
}
```

Multicast Delegates and the Observer Pattern

In this chapter, you've seen how to store a single method inside an instance of a delegate type and invoke that method via the delegate. Delegates are more than storage mechanisms for a single method, however. A single delegate variable can reference a series of delegates in which each successive one points to a succeeding delegate in the form of a chain, sometimes known as a **multicast delegate**. All delegates are multicast delegates, but so far, they have supported only a single callback (a multiplicity of one).

The C# implementation of multicast delegates is a common pattern that would otherwise require significant manual code. Known as the **observer** or **publish-subscribe pattern**, it represents scenarios where notifications of single events, such as a change in object state, are broadcast to multiple subscribers.

Coding the Observer Pattern with Delegates

Consider a temperature control example, where a heater and a cooler are hooked up to the same thermostat. In order for a unit to turn on and off appropriately, you notify the unit of changes in temperature. One thermostat publishes temperature changes to multiple subscribers—the heating and cooling units. The next section investigates the code.[1]

Defining Subscriber Methods

Begin by defining the `Heater` and `Cooler` objects (see Listing 13.16).

LISTING 13.16: **Heater** and **Cooler** Event Subscriber Implementations

```
class Cooler
{
  public Cooler(float temperature)
  {
      Temperature = temperature;
  }

  public float Temperature
  {
      get{return _Temperature;}
```

---

1. In this example, I use the term *thermostat* because people more commonly think of it in the context of heating and cooling systems. Technically, however, *thermometer* would be more appropriate.

```csharp
        set{_Temperature = value;}
    }
    private float _Temperature;

    public void OnTemperatureChanged(float newTemperature)
    {
        if (newTemperature > Temperature)
        {
            System.Console.WriteLine("Cooler: On");
        }
        else
        {
            System.Console.WriteLine("Cooler: Off");
        }
    }
}

class Heater
{
    public Heater(float temperature)
    {
        Temperature = temperature;
    }

    public float Temperature
    {
        get
        {
            return _Temperature;
        }
        set
        {
            _Temperature = value;
        }
    }
    private float _Temperature;

    public void OnTemperatureChanged(float newTemperature)
    {
        if (newTemperature < Temperature)
        {
            System.Console.WriteLine("Heater: On");
        }
        else
        {
            System.Console.WriteLine("Heater: Off");
        }
    }
}
```

The two classes are essentially identical, with the exception of the temperature comparison. (In fact, you could eliminate one of the classes if you used a delegate as a method pointer for comparison within the OnTemperature-Changed method.) Each class stores the temperature for when to turn on the unit. In addition, both classes provide an OnTemperatureChanged() method. Calling the OnTemperatureChanged() method is the means to indicate to the Heater and Cooler classes that the temperature has changed. The method implementation uses newTemperature to compare against the stored trigger temperature to determine whether to turn on the device.

The OnTemperatureChanged() methods are the subscriber methods. It is important that they have the parameters and a return type that matches the delegate from the Thermostat class, which is discussed next.

Defining the Publisher

The Thermostat class is responsible for reporting temperature changes to the heater and cooler object instances. The Thermostat class listing appears in Listing 13.17.

LISTING 13.17: Defining the Event Publisher, **Thermostat**

```
public class Thermostat
{
    // Define the delegate data type
    public delegate void TemperatureChangeHandler(
        float newTemperature);

    // Define the event publisher
    public TemperatureChangeHandler OnTemperatureChange
    {
        get{ return _OnTemperatureChange;}
        set{ _OnTemperatureChange = value;}
    }
    private TemperatureChangeHandler _OnTemperatureChange;

    public float CurrentTemperature
    {
        get{return _CurrentTemperature;}
        set
        {
            if (value != CurrentTemperature)
            {
                _CurrentTemperature = value;
            }
```

```
        }
    }
    private float _CurrentTemperature;
}
```

The first member of the `Thermostat` class is the `TemperatureChange-Handler` delegate. Although not a requirement, `Thermostat.Temperature-ChangeHandler` is a nested delegate because its definition is specific to the `Thermostat` class. The delegate defines the signature of the subscriber methods. Notice, therefore, that in both the `Heater` and `Cooler` classes, the `OnTemperatureChanged()` methods match the signature of `Tempera-tureChangeHandler`.

In addition to defining the delegate type, `Thermostat` also includes a property called `OnTemperatureChange` that is of the `OnTemperature-ChangeHandler` delegate type. `OnTemperatureChange` stores a list of sub-scribers. Notice that only one delegate field is required to store all the subscribers. In other words, both the `Cooler` and the `Heater` classes will receive notifications of a change in the temperature from this single publisher.

The last member of `Thermostat` is the `CurrentTemperature` property. This sets and retrieves the value of the current temperature reported by the `Thermostat` class.

Hooking Up the Publisher and Subscribers

Finally, put all these pieces together in a `Main()` method. Listing 13.18 shows a sample of what `Main()` could look like.

LISTING 13.18: Hooking Up the Publisher and Subscribers

```
class Program
{
  public static void Main()
  {
      Thermostat thermostat = new Thermostat();
      Heater heater = new Heater(60);
      Cooler cooler = new Cooler(80);
      string temperature;

      // Using C# 2.0 syntax.
      thermostat.OnTemperatureChange +=
          heater.OnTemperatureChanged;
      thermostat.OnTemperatureChange +=
          cooler.OnTemperatureChanged;
```

```
        Console.Write("Enter temperature: ");
        temperature = Console.ReadLine();
        thermostat.CurrentTemperature = int.Parse(temperature);
    }
}
```

The code in this listing has registered two subscribers (`heater.OnTemperatureChanged` and `cooler.OnTemperatureChanged`) to the `OnTemperatureChange` delegate by directly assigning them using the `+=` operator. As noted in the comment, you need to use the new operator with the `TemperatureChangeHandler` constructor if you are not using C# 2.0.

By taking the temperature value the user has entered, you can set the `CurrentTemperature` of `thermostat`. However, you have not yet written any code to publish the change temperature event to subscribers.

Invoking a Delegate

Every time the `CurrentTemperature` property on the `Thermostat` class changes, you want to **invoke the delegate** to notify the subscribers (`heater` and `cooler`) of the change in temperature. To do this, modify the `CurrentTemperature` property to save the new value and publish a notification to each subscriber. The code modification appears in Listing 13.19.

LISTING 13.19: Invoking a Delegate without Checking for **null**

```
public class Thermostat
{
    ...
    public float CurrentTemperature
    {
        get{return _CurrentTemperature;}
        set
        {
            if (value != CurrentTemperature)
            {
                _CurrentTemperature = value;

                // INCOMPLETE:  Check for null needed
                // Call subscribers
                OnTemperatureChange(value);
            }
        }
    }
    private float _CurrentTemperature;
}
```

Now the assignment of `CurrentTemperature` includes some special logic to notify subscribers of changes in `CurrentTemperature`. The call to notify all subscribers is simply the single C# statement, `OnTemperature-Change(value)`. This single statement publishes the temperature change to the `cooler` and `heater` objects. Here, you see in practice that the ability to notify multiple subscribers using a single call is why delegates are more specifically known as multicast delegates.

Check for Null

One important part of publishing an event code is missing from Listing 13.19. If no subscriber registered to receive the notification, then `OnTemperature-Change` would be `null` and executing the `OnTemperatureChange(value)` statement would throw a `NullReferenceException`. To avoid this, it is necessary to check for `null` before firing the event. Listing 13.20 demonstrates how to do this.

LISTING 13.20: Invoking a Delegate

```
public class Thermostat
{
  . . .
  public float CurrentTemperature
  {
      get{return _CurrentTemperature;}
      set
      {
          if (value != CurrentTemperature)
          {
              _CurrentTemperature = value;
              // If there are any subscribers
              // then notify them of changes in
              // temperature
              TemperatureChangeHandler localOnChange =
                  OnTemperatureChange;
              if(localOnChange != null)
              {
                  // Call subscribers
                  localOnChange(value);
              }
          }
      }
  }
  private float _CurrentTemperature;
}
```

Instead of checking for `null` directly, first assign `OnTemperatureChange` to a second delegate variable, `handlerCopy`. This simple modification ensures that if all `OnTemperatureChange` subscribers are removed (by a different thread) between checking for `null` and sending the notification, you won't fire a `NullReferenceException`.

One more time: Remember to check the value of a delegate for `null` before invoking it.

■ ADVANCED TOPIC

-= Operator for a Delegate Returns a New Instance

Given that a delegate is a reference type, it is perhaps somewhat surprising that assigning a local variable and then using that local variable is sufficient for making the null check thread safe. Since `localOnChange` points at the same location that `OnTemperatureChange` points, one would think that any changes in `OnTemperatureChange` would be reflected in `localOnChange` as well.

This is not the case because effectively, any calls to `OnTemperatureChange -= <listener>` will not add a new delegate to `OnTemperatureChange`, but rather, will assign it an entirely new multicast delegate without having any effect on the original multicast delegate to which `localOnChange` also points.

Delegate Operators

To combine the two subscribers in the `Thermostat` example, you used the `+=` operator. This takes the first delegate and adds the second delegate to the chain so that one delegate points to the next. Now, after the first delegate's method is invoked, it calls the second delegate. To remove delegates from a delegate chain, use the `-=` operator, as shown in Listing 13.21.

LISTING 13.21: Using the += and -= Delegate Operators

```
// ...
Thermostat thermostat = new Thermostat();
Heater heater = new Heater(60);
Cooler cooler = new Cooler(80);
```

```
Thermostat.TemperatureChangeHandler delegate1;
Thermostat.TemperatureChangeHandler delegate2;
Thermostat.TemperatureChangeHandler delegate3;

// use Constructor syntax prior to C# 2.0.
delegate1 = heater.OnTemperatureChanged;
delegate2 = cooler.OnTemperatureChanged;

Console.WriteLine("Invoke both delegates:");
delegate3 = delegate1;
delegate3 += delegate2;
delegate3(90);

Console.WriteLine("Invoke only delegate2");
delegate3 -= delegate1;
delegate3(30);
// ...
```

The results of Listing 13.21 appear in Output 13.3.

OUTPUT 13.3:

```
Invoke both delegates:
Heater: Off
Cooler: On
Invoke only delegate2
Cooler: Off
```

Furthermore, you can also use the + and – operators to combine delegates, as Listing 13.22 shows.

LISTING 13.22: Using the + and – Delegate Operators

```
// ...
Thermostat thermostat = new Thermostat();
Heater heater = new Heater(60);
Cooler cooler = new Cooler(80);

Thermostat.TemperatureChangeHandler delegate1;
Thermostat.TemperatureChangeHandler delegate2;
Thermostat.TemperatureChangeHandler delegate3;

// Note: Use new Thermostat.TemperatureChangeHandler(
//       cooler.OnTemperatureChanged) for versions
//       of C# prior to version 2.0.
delegate1 = heater.OnTemperatureChanged;
delegate2 = cooler.OnTemperatureChanged;
```

```
Console.WriteLine("Combine delegates using + operator:");
delegate3 = delegate1 + delegate2;
delegate3(60);

Console.WriteLine("Uncombine delegates using - operator:");
delegate3 = delegate3 - delegate2;
delegate3(60);
// ...
```

Use of the assignment operator clears out all previous subscribers and allows you to replace them with new subscribers. This is an unfortunate characteristic of a delegate. It is simply too easy to mistakenly code an assignment when, in fact, the += operator is intended. The solution, called events, appears in the Events section, later in this chapter.

It should be noted that both the + and – operators and their assignment equivalents, += and -=, are implemented internally using the static methods `System.Delegate.Combine()` and `System.Delegate.Remove()`. Both methods take two parameters of type `delegate`. The first method, `Combine()`, joins the two parameters so that the first parameter points to the second within the list of delegates. The second, `Remove()`, searches through the chain of delegates specified in the first parameter and then removes the delegate specified by the second parameter.

One interesting thing to note about the `Combine()` method is that either or both of the parameters can be `null`. If one of them is `null`, then `Combine()` returns the non-`null` parameter. If both are `null`, then `Combine()` returns `null`. This explains why you can call `thermostat.OnTemperatureChange += heater.OnTemperatureChanged;` and not throw an exception, even if the value of `thermostat.OnTemperatureChange` is not yet assigned.

Sequential Invocation

The process of notifying both `heater` and `cooler` appears in Figure 13.2.

Although you coded only a single call to `OnTemperatureChange()`, the call is broadcast to both subscribers so that from that one call, both `cooler` and `heater` are notified of the change in temperature. If you added more subscribers, they too would be notified by `OnTemperatureChange()`.

Although a single call, `OnTemperatureChange()`, caused the notification of each subscriber, they are still called sequentially, not simultaneously, because a single delegate can point to another delegate that can, in turn, point to additional delegates.

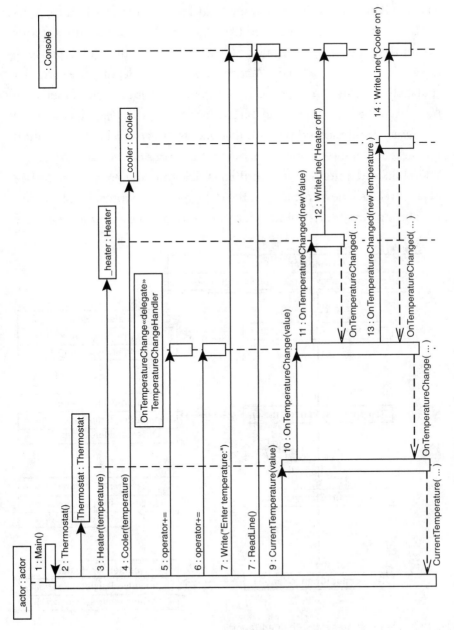

FIGURE 13.2: Delegate Invocation Sequence Diagram

■ ADVANCED TOPIC

Multicast Delegate Internals

To understand how events work, you need to revisit the first examination of the `System.Delegate` type internals. Recall that the `delegate` keyword is an alias for a type derived from `System.MulticastDelegate`. In turn, `System.MulticastDelegate` is derived from `System.Delegate`, which, for its part, comprises an object reference and a method pointer (of type `System.Reflection.MethodInfo`). When you create a delegate, the compiler automatically employs the `System.MulticastDelegate` type rather than the `System.Delegate` type. The `MulticastDelegate` class includes an object reference and method pointer, just like its `Delegate` base class, but it also contains a reference to another `System.MulticastDelegate` object.

When you add a method to a multicast delegate, the `MulticastDelegate` class creates a new instance of the delegate type, stores the object reference and the method pointer for the added method into the new

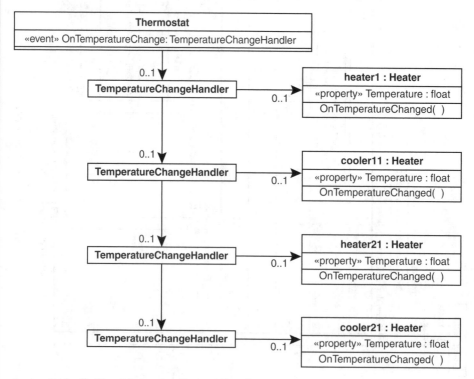

FIGURE 13.3: Multicast Delegates Chained Together

instance, and adds the new delegate instance as the next item in a list of delegate instances. In effect, the `MulticastDelegate` class maintains a linked list of `Delegate` objects. Conceptually, you can represent the thermostat example as shown in Figure 13.3.

When invoking the multicast, each delegate instance in the linked list is called sequentially. Generally, delegates are called in the order they were added, but this behavior is not specified within the CLI specification, and furthermore, it can be overridden. Therefore, programmers should not depend on an invocation order.

Error Handling

Error handling makes awareness of the sequential notification critical. If one subscriber throws an exception, later subscribers in the chain do not receive the notification. Consider, for example, if you changed the Heater's `OnTemperatureChanged()` method so that it threw an exception, as shown in Listing 13.23.

LISTING 13.23: **`OnTemperatureChanged()`** Throwing an Exception

```
class Heater
{
    ...
    public void OnTemperatureChanged(float newTemperature)
    {
        throw new NotImplementedException();
    }
    ...
}
```

Figure 13.4 shows an updated sequence diagram. Even though `cooler` subscribed to receive messages, the `heater` exception terminates the chain and prevents the `cooler` object from receiving notification.

To avoid this problem so that all subscribers receive notification, regardless of the behavior of earlier subscribers, you must manually enumerate through the list of subscribers and call them individually. Listing 13.24 shows the updates required in the `CurrentTemperature` property. The results appear in Output 13.4.

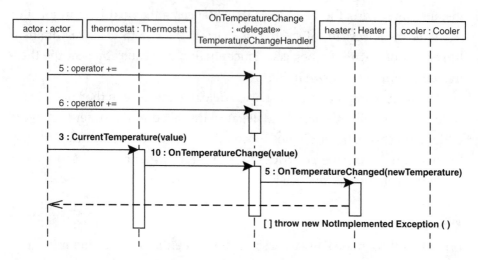

FIGURE 13.4: Delegate Invocation with Exception Sequence Diagram

LISTING 13.24: Handling Exceptions from Subscribers

```
public class Thermostat
{
    // Define the delegate data type
    public delegate void TemperatureChangeHandler(
        float newTemperature);

    // Define the event publisher
    public event TemperatureChangeHandler OnTemperatureChange;

    public float CurrentTemperature
    {
        get{return _CurrentTemperature;}
        set
        {
            if (value != CurrentTemperature)
            {
                _CurrentTemperature = value;
                if(OnTemperatureChange != null)
                {
                    foreach(
                        TemperatureChangeHandler handler in
                        OnTemperatureChange.GetInvocationList() )
                    {
                        try
                        {
                            handler(value);
                        }
                        catch(Exception exception)
                        {
```

```
                              Console.WriteLine(exception.Message);
                          }
                      }
                  }
              }
          }
      }
      private float _CurrentTemperature;
  }
```

OUTPUT 13.4:

```
Enter temperature: 45
The method or operation is not implemented.
Cooler: Off
```

This listing demonstrates that you can retrieve a list of subscribers from a delegate's `GetInvocationList()` method. Enumerating over each item in this list returns the individual subscribers. If you then place each invocation of a subscriber within a try/catch block, you can handle any error conditions before continuing with the enumeration loop. In this sample, even though `heater.OnTemperatureChanged()` throws an exception, `cooler` still receives notification of the temperature change.

Method Returns and Pass-By-Reference

There is another scenario where it is useful to iterate over the delegate invocation list instead of simply activating a notification directly. This scenario relates to delegates that either don't return `void` or have `ref` or `out` parameters. In the thermostat example so far, the `OnTemperature-Handler` delegate had a return type of `void`. Furthermore, it did not include any parameters that were `ref` or `out` type parameters, parameters that return data to the caller. This is important because an invocation of a delegate potentially triggers notification to multiple subscribers. If the subscribers return a value, it is ambiguous which subscriber's return value would be used.

If you changed `OnTemperatureHandler` to return an enumeration value, indicating whether the device was on because of the temperature change, the new delegate would look like Listing 13.25.

LISTING 13.25: Declaring a Delegate with a Method Return

```
public enum Status
{
    On,
    Off
}


// Define the delegate data type
public delegate Status TemperatureChangeHandler(
    float newTemperature);
```

All subscriber methods would have to use the same method signature as the delegate, and therefore, each would be required to return a status value. Assuming you invoke the delegate in a similar manner as before, what will the value of status be in Listing 13.26, for example?

LISTING 13.26: Invoking a Delegate Instance with a Return

```
Status status = OnTemperatureChange(value);
```

Since `OnTemperatureChange` potentially corresponds to a chain of delegates, `status` reflects only the value of the last delegate. All other values are lost entirely.

To overcome this issue, it is necessary to follow the same pattern that you used for error handling. In other words, you must iterate through each delegate invocation list, using the `GetInvocationList()` method, to retrieve each individual return value. Similarly, delegate types that use `ref` and `out` parameters need special consideration.

Events

There are two key problems with the delegates as you have used them so far. To overcome these issues, C# uses the keyword `event`. In this section, you will see why you would use events, and how they work.

Why Events?

This chapter has covered all that you need to know about how delegates work. However, weaknesses in the delegate structure may inadvertently allow the programmer to introduce a bug. The issues relate to encapsulation, that neither the subscription nor the publication of events can be sufficiently controlled.

Encapsulating the Subscription

As demonstrated earlier, it is possible to assign one delegate to another using the assignment operator. Unfortunately, this capability introduces a common source for bugs. Consider Listing 13.27.

LISTING 13.27: Using the Assignment Operator = Rather Than +=

```
class Program
{
  public static void Main()
  {
      Thermostat thermostat = new Thermostat();
      Heater heater = new Heater(60);
      Cooler cooler = new Cooler(80);
      string temperature;

      // Note: Use new Thermostat.TemperatureChangeHandler(
      //       cooler.OnTemperatureChanged) if not C# 2.0.
      thermostat.OnTemperatureChange =
          heater.OnTemperatureChanged;

      // Bug:  assignment operator overrides
      // previous assignment.
      thermostat.OnTemperatureChange =
          cooler.OnTemperatureChanged;

      Console.Write("Enter temperature: ");
      temperature = Console.ReadLine();
      thermostat.CurrentTemperature = int.Parse(temperature);
  }
}
```

Listing 13.27 is almost identical to Listing 13.21 except that instead of using the += operator, you use a simple assignment operator. As a result, when code assigns cooler.OnTemperatureChanged to OnTemperature-Change, heater.OnTemperatureChanged is cleared out because an entirely new chain is assigned to replace the previous one. The potential for mistakenly using an assignment operator, when in fact the += assignment was intended, is so high that it would be preferable if the assignment operator were not even supported for objects, outside of the containing class. It is the purpose of the event keyword to provide additional encapsulation such that you cannot inadvertently cancel other subscribers.

Encapsulating the Publication

The second important difference between delegates and events is that events ensure that only the containing class can trigger an event notification. Consider Listing 13.28.

LISTING 13.28: Firing the Event from Outside the Events Container

```
class Program
{
  public static void Main()
  {
      Thermostat thermostat = new Thermostat();
      Heater heater = new Heater(60);
      Cooler cooler = new Cooler(80);
      string temperature;

      // Note: Use new Thermostat.TemperatureChangeHandler(
      //       cooler.OnTemperatureChanged) if not C# 2.0.
      thermostat.OnTemperatureChange +=
          heater.OnTemperatureChanged;

      thermostat.OnTemperatureChange +=
          cooler.OnTemperatureChanged;

      thermostat.OnTemperatureChange(42);
  }
}
```

In Listing 13.28, Program is able to invoke the OnTemperatureChange delegate even though the CurrentTemperature on thermostat did not change. Program, therefore, triggers a notification to all thermostat subscribers that the temperature changed, but in reality, there was no change in the thermostat temperature. As before, the problem with the delegate is that there is insufficient encapsulation. Thermostat should prevent any other class from being able to invoke the OnTemperatureChange delegate.

Declaring an Event

C# provides the event keyword to deal with both of these problems. event modifies a field declaration, as shown in Listing 13.29.

LISTING 13.29: Using the **event** Keyword with the Event-Coding Pattern

```csharp
public class Thermostat
{
    public class TemperatureArgs: System.EventArgs
    {
        public TemperatureArgs( float newTemperature )
        {
            NewTemperature = newTemperature;
        }

        public float NewTemperature
        {
            get{return _newTemperature;}
            set{_newTemperature = value;}
        }
        private float _newTemperature;
    }

    // Define the delegate data type
    public delegate void TemperatureChangeHandler(
        object sender, TemperatureArgs newTemperature);

    // Define the event publisher
    public event TemperatureChangeHandler OnTemperatureChange;

    public float CurrentTemperature
    {
        ...
    }
    private float _CurrentTemperature;
}
```

The new `Thermostat` class has four changes from the original class. First, the `OnTemperatureChange` property has been removed, and instead, `OnTemperatureChange` has been declared as a public field. This seems contrary to solving the earlier encapsulation problem. It would make more sense to increase the encapsulation, not decrease it by making a field public. However, the second change was to add the `event` keyword immediately before the field declaration. This simple change provides all the encapsulation needed. By adding the `event` keyword, you prevent use of the assignment operator on a public delegate field (for example, `thermostat.OnTemperatureChange = cooler.OnTemperatureChanged`). In addition, only the containing class is able to invoke the delegate that triggers the publication to all subscribers (for example, disallowing `thermostat.OnTemperatureChange(42)` from outside the class). In other words, the `event` keyword provides the needed encapsulation that prevents any external class from publishing an event or unsubscribing previous subscribers they did not add.

This resolves the two issues with plain delegates and is one of the key reasons for the `event` keyword in C#.

Coding Conventions

All you need to do to gain the desired functionality is to take the original delegate variable declaration, change it to a field, and add the `event` keyword. With these two changes, you provide the necessary encapsulation and all other functionality remains the same. However, an additional change occurs in the delegate declaration in the code in Listing 13.29. To follow standard C# coding conventions, you changed `OnTemperatureChangeHandler` so that the single `temperature` parameter was replaced with two new parameters, `sender` and `temperatureArgs`. This change is not something that the C# compiler will enforce, but passing two parameters of these types is the norm for declaring a delegate intended for an event.

The first parameter, `sender`, should contain an instance of the class that invoked the delegate. This is especially helpful if the same subscriber method registers with multiple events—for example, if the `heater.OnTemperatureChanged` event subscribes to two different `Thermostat` instances. In such a scenario, either `Thermostat` instance can trigger a call to `heater.OnTemperatureChanged`. In order to determine which instance of `Thermostat` triggered the event, you use the `sender` parameter from inside `Heater.OnTemperatureChanged()`.

The second parameter, `temperatureArgs`, is of type `Thermostat.TemperatureArgs`. Using a nested class is appropriate because it conforms to the same scope as the `OnTemperatureChangeHandler` delegate itself. The important part about `TemperatureArgs`, at least as far as the coding convention goes, is that it derives from `System.EventArgs`. The only significant property on `System.EventArgs` is `Empty` and it is used to indicate that there is no event data. When you derive `TemperatureArgs` from `System.EventArgs`, however, you add an additional property, `NewTemperature`, as a means to pass the temperature from the thermostat to the subscribers.

To summarize the coding convention for events: The first argument, `sender`, is of type `object` and it contains a reference to the object that invoked the delegate. The second argument is of type `System.EventArgs` or something that derives from `System.EventArgs` but contains additional data about the event. You invoke the delegate exactly as before, except for the additional parameters. Listing 13.30 shows an example.

LISTING 13.30: Firing the Event Notification

```
public class Thermostat
{
    . . .
    public float CurrentTemperature
    {
        get{return _CurrentTemperature;}
        set
        {
            if (value != CurrentTemperature)
            {
                _CurrentTemperature = value;
                // If there are any subscribers
                // then notify them of changes in
                // temperature
                if(OnTemperatureChange != null)
                {
                    // Call subscribers
                    OnTemperatureChange(
                        this, new TemperatureArgs(value) );
                }
            }
        }
    }
    private float _CurrentTemperature;
}
```

You usually specify the sender using the container class (`this`) because that is the only class that can invoke the delegate for events.

In this example, the subscriber could cast the sender parameter to `Thermostat` and access the current temperature that way, as well as via the `TemperatureArgs` instance. However, the current temperature on the `Thermostat` instance may change via a different thread. In the case of events that occur due to state changes, passing the previous value along with the new value is a frequent pattern used to control what state transitions are allowable.

Generics and Delegates

The previous section mentioned that the typical pattern for defining delegate data is to specify the first parameter, `sender`, of type `object` and the second parameter, `eventArgs`, to be a type deriving from `System.Event-Args`. One of the more cumbersome aspects of delegates in C# 1.0 is that you have to declare a new delegate type whenever the parameters on the handler change. Every creation of a new derivation from `System.Event-Args` (a relatively common occurrence) required the declaration of a new delegate data type that uses the new `EventArgs` derived type. For example, in order to use `TemperatureArgs` within the event notification code in Listing 13.30, it is necessary to declare the delegate type `Temperature-ChangeHandler` that has `TemperatureArgs` as a parameter.

With generics, you can use the same delegate data type in many locations with a host of different parameter types, and remain strongly typed. Consider the delegate declaration example shown in Listing 13.31.

LISTING 13.31: Declaring a Generic Delegate Type

```
public delegate void EventHandler<T>(object sender, T e)
   where T : EventArgs;
```

Using `EventHandler<T>`, each class that requires a particular `sender-EventArgs` pattern need not declare its own delegate definition. Instead, they can all share the same one, changing the thermostat example as shown in Listing 13.32.

LISTING 13.32: Using Generics with Delegates

```
public class Thermostat
{
  public class TemperatureArgs: System.EventArgs
  {
      public TemperatureArgs( float newTemperature )
      {
          NewTemperature = newTemperature;
      }

      public float NewTemperature
      {
          get{return _newTemperature;}
          set{_newTemperature = value;}
      }
      private float _newTemperature;
  }

// TemperatureChangeHandler no longer needed
// public delegate void TemperatureChangeHandler(
```

```
    // object sender, TemperatureArgs newTemperature);

    // Define the event publisher without using
    //       TemperatureChangeHandler
    public event EventHandler<TemperatureArgs>
        OnTemperatureChange;

    public float CurrentTemperature
    {
        ...
    }
    private float _CurrentTemperature;
}
```

Listing 13.32 assumes, of course, that `EventHandler<T>` is defined somewhere. In fact, `System.EventHandler<T>`, as just declared, is included in the 2.0 framework class library. Therefore, in the majority of circumstances when using events in C# 2.0, it is not necessary to declare a custom delegate data type.

Note that `System.EventHandler<T>` restricts T to derive from `EventArgs` using a constraint, exactly what was necessary to correspond with the general convention for the event declaration of C# 1.0.

■ ADVANCED TOPIC

Event Internals

Events restrict external classes from doing anything other than adding subscribing methods to the publisher via the += operator and then unsubscribing using the -= operator. In addition, they restrict classes, other than the containing class, from invoking the event. To do this the C# compiler takes the public delegate variable with its event keyword modifier and declares the delegate as private. In addition, it adds a couple of methods and two special event blocks. Essentially, the event keyword is a C# shortcut for generating the appropriate encapsulation logic. Consider the example in the event declaration shown in Listing 13.33.

LISTING 13.33: Declaring the **OnTemperatureChange** Event

```
    public class Thermostat
    {
        // Define the delegate data type
        public delegate void TemperatureChangeHandler(
```

```
    object sender, TemperatureArgs newTemperature);

public event TemperatureChangeHandler OnTemperatureChange

    ...
}
```

When the C# compiler encounters the event keyword, it generates CIL code equivalent to the C# code shown in Listing 13.34.

LISTING 13.34: C# Equivalent of the Event CIL Code Generated by the Compiler

```
public class Thermostat
{
    // Define the delegate data type
    public delegate void TemperatureChangeHandler(
        object sender, TemperatureArgs newTemperature);

    // Declaring the delegate field to save the
    // list of subscribers.
    private TemperatureChangeHandler OnTemperatureChange;

    public void add_OnTemperatureChange(
        TemperatureChangeHandler handler)
    {
        System.Delegate.Combine(OnTemperatureChange, handler);
    }

    public void remove_OnTemperatureChange(
        TemperatureChangeHandler handler)
    {
        System.Delegate.Remove(OnTemperatureChange, handler);
    }

    public event TemperatureChangeHandler OnTemperatureChange
    {
        add
        {
            add_OnTemperatureChange(value)
        }
        remove
        {
            remove_OnTemperatureChange(value)
        }
    }
}
```

In other words, the code shown in Listing 13.33 is the C# shorthand that the compiler uses to trigger the code expansion shown in Listing 13.34.

The C# compiler first takes the original event definition and defines a private delegate variable in its place. By doing this, the delegate becomes unavailable to any external class, even to classes derived from it.

Next, the C# compiler defines two methods, add_OnTemperature-Change() and remove_OnTemperatureChange(), where the OnTemperatureChange suffix is taken from the original name of the event. These methods are responsible for implementing the += and -= assignment operators, respectively. As Listing 13.34 shows, these methods are implemented using the static System.Delegate.Combine() and System.Delegate.Remove() methods, discussed earlier in the chapter. The first parameter passed to each of these methods is the private TemperatureChangeHandler delegate instance, OnTemperatureChange.

Perhaps the most curious part of the code generated from the event keyword is the last part. The syntax is very similar to that of a property's getter and setter methods except that the methods are add and remove. The add block takes care of handling the += operator on the event by passing the call to add_OnTemperatureChange(). In a similar manner, the remove block operator handles the -= operator by passing the call onto remove_OnTemperatureChange.

It is important to notice the similarities between this code and the code generated for a property. Readers will recall that the C# implementation of a property is to create get_<propertyname> and set_<propertyname> and then to pass calls to the get and set blocks on to these methods. Clearly, the event syntax is very similar.

Another important characteristic to note about the generated CIL code is that the CIL equivalent of the event keyword remains in the CIL. In other words, an event is something that the CIL code recognizes explicitly; it is not just a C# construct. By keeping an equivalent event keyword in the CIL code, all languages and editors are able to provide special functionality because they can recognize the event as a special class member.

Customizing the Event Implementation

The code for += and -= that the compiler generates can be customized. Consider, for example, changing the scope of the OnTemperatureChange delegate so that it is protected rather than private. This, of course, would allow classes derived from Thermostat to access the delegate directly instead of being limited to the same restrictions as external classes. To enable this, C# allows the same property as the syntax shown in Listing 13.32. In other words, C# allows you to define custom `add` and `remove` blocks to provide implementation for each aspect of the event encapsulation. Listing 13.35 provides an example.

LISTING 13.35: Custom **add** and **remove** Handlers

```csharp
public class Thermostat
{
    public class TemperatureArgs: System.EventArgs
    {
        ...
    }

    // Define the delegate data type
    public delegate void TemperatureChangeHandler(
        object sender, TemperatureArgs newTemperature);

    // Define the event publisher
    public event TemperatureChangeHandler OnTemperatureChange
    {
        add
        {
            System.Delegate.Combine(value, _OnTemperatureChange);
        }
        remove
        {
            System.Delegate.Remove(_OnTemperatureChange, value);
        }
    }
    protected TemperatureChangeHandler _OnTemperatureChange;

    public float CurrentTemperature
    {
        ...
    }
    private float _CurrentTemperature;
}
```

In this case, the delegate that stores each subscriber, _OnTemperature-Change, was changed to `protected`. In addition, implementation of the add block switches around the delegate storage so that the last delegate added to the chain is the first delegate to receive a notification.

SUMMARY

This chapter began with a discussion of delegates and their use as method pointers and callbacks. Next, it discussed the full potential of a delegate within the observer pattern. Now that you have described events, it is worth mentioning that in general, method pointers are the only cases where it is advisable to work with a delegate variable outside of the context of an event. In other words, given the additional encapsulation features of an event and the ability to customize the implementation when necessary, the best practice is always to use events for the observer pattern.

This chapter also introduced two syntaxes for creating delegate instances. C# 2.0 allows the assigning of delegates directly, by just using the method's name. Prior to this, it was necessary to explicitly instantiate delegates using the new operator. Throughout the remainder of the book, I will show only the C# 2.0 syntax. (This will cause some of the remaining code not to compile on version 1.0 compilers without modification to use explicit delegate instantiation.)

It may take a little practice to be able to code delegates and events from scratch without sample code. However, they are a critical foundation to the asynchronous, multithreaded coding of the next chapter.

■ 14 ■
Reflection and Attributes

ATTRIBUTES ARE A MEANS of inserting additional metadata into an assembly and associating the metadata with a programming construct such as a class, method, or property. This chapter investigates the details surrounding attributes that are built into the framework, as well as how to define custom attributes. In order to take advantage of custom attributes, it is necessary to identify them. This is handled through reflection. This chapter begins with a look at reflection, including how it can be used to dynamically bind at runtime and call a member using its name at compile time. This is frequently performed within tools such as a code generator. In addition, reflection is used at execution time when the callee is unknown.

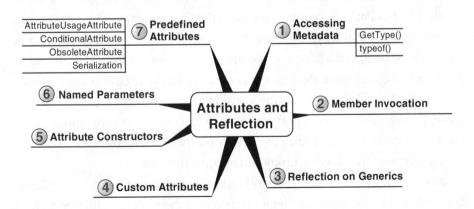

Reflection

Using reflection, it is possible to do the following.

- Access the metadata for types within an assembly. This includes constructs such as the full type name, member names, and any attributes decorating a construct.
- Dynamically invoke a type's member at runtime using the metadata, rather than a compile-time-defined binding.

Reflection is the process of examining the metadata within an assembly. Traditionally, when code compiles down to a machine language, all the metadata (such as type and method names) about the code is discarded. In contrast, when C# compiles into the CIL, it maintains most of the metadata about the code. Furthermore, using reflection, it is possible to enumerate through all the types within an assembly and search for those that match certain characteristics. You access a type's metadata through instances of `System.Type`, and this object includes methods for enumerating the type instance's members. Furthermore, it is possible to invoke those members on particular objects that are of the examined type.

The facility for reflection enables a host of new paradigms that are unavailable otherwise. For example, reflection enables you to enumerate over all the types within an assembly, along with their members, and in the process create stubs for documentation of the assembly API. You can then combine the metadata retrieved from reflection with the XML document created from XML comments (using the `/doc` switch) to create the API documentation. Similarly, programmers use reflection metadata to generate code for persisting (serializing) business objects into a database. It could also be used in a list control that displays a collection of objects. Given the collection, a list control could use reflection to iterate over all the properties of an object in the collection, defining a column within the list for each property. Furthermore, by invoking each property on each object, the list control could populate each row and column with the data contained in the object, even though the data type of the object is unknown at compile time.

`XmlSerializer`, `ValueType`, and `DataBinder` are a few of the classes in the framework that use reflection for portions of their implementation as well.

Accessing Metadata Using `System.Type`

The key to reading a type's metadata is to obtain an instance of `System .Type` that represents the target type instance. `System.Type` provides all the methods for retrieving the information about a type. You can use it to answer questions such as the following.

- What is the type's name (`Type.Name`)?
- Is the type public (`Type.IsPublic`)?
- What is the type's base type (`Type.BaseType`)?
- Does the type support any interfaces (`Type.GetInterfaces()`)?
- Which assembly is the type defined in (`Type.Assembly`)?
- What are a type's properties, methods, fields, and so on (`Type.Get-Properties()`, `Type.GetMethods()`, `Type.GetFields()`, etc.)?
- What attributes decorate a type (`Type.GetCustomAttributes()`)?

There are more such members, but in summary, they all provide information about a particular type. The key, obviously, is to obtain a reference to a type's `Type` object. The two primary ways to do this are through `object.GetType()` and `typeof()`.

GetType()

`object` includes a `GetType()` member, and therefore, all types include this function. You call `GetType()` to retrieve an instance of `System.Type` corresponding to the original object. Listing 14.1 demonstrates this, using a `Type` instance from `DateTime`. Output 14.1 shows the results.

LISTING 14.1: Using `Type.GetProperties()` to Obtain an Object's Public Properties

```
DateTime dateTime = new DateTime();
//
Type type = dateTime.GetType();
foreach (
    System.Reflection.PropertyInfo property in
        type.GetProperties())
{
    Console.WriteLine(property.Name);
}
```

OUTPUT 14.1:

```
Date
Day
DayOfWeek
DayOfYear
Hour
Kind
Millisecond
Minute
Month
Now
UtcNow
Second
Ticks
TimeOfDay
Today
Year
```

After calling `GetType()`, you iterate over each `System.Reflection.PropertyInfo` instance returned from `Type.GetProperties()` and display the property names. The key to calling `GetType()` is that you must have an object instance. However, sometimes no such instance is available. Static classes, for example, cannot be instantiated, so there is no way to call `GetType()`.

typeof()

Another way to retrieve a `Type` object is with the `typeof` expression. `typeof` binds at compile time to a particular `Type` instance, and it takes a type directly as a parameter. Listing 14.2 demonstrates the use of `typeof` with `Enum.Parse()`.

LISTING 14.2: Using **typeof()** to Create a **System.Type** Instance

```
using System.Diagnostics;
// ...
    ThreadPriorityLevel priority;
    priority = (ThreadPriorityLevel)Enum.Parse(
        typeof(ThreadPriorityLevel), "Idle");
// ...
```

`Enum.Parse()` takes a `Type` object identifying an enum and then converts a string to the specific enum value. In this case, it converts `"Idle"` to `System.Diagnostics.ThreadPriorityLevel.Idle`.

Member Invocation

The possibilities with reflection don't stop with retrieving the metadata. The next step is to take the metadata and dynamically invoke the members they reference. Consider the possibility of defining a class to represent an application's command line. The difficulty with a CommandLineInfo class such as this has to do with populating the class with the actual command-line data that started the application. However, using reflection, you can map the command-line options to property names and then dynamically set the properties at runtime. Listing 14.3 demonstrates this example.

LISTING 14.3: Dynamically Invoking a Member

```
using System;
using System.Diagnostics;

public partial class Program
{
  public static void Main(string[] args)
  {
      string errorMessage;
      CommandLineInfo commandLine = new CommandLineInfo();
      if (!CommandLineHandler.TryParse(
          args, commandLine, out errorMessage))
      {
          Console.WriteLine(errorMessage);
          DisplayHelp();
      }

      if (commandLine.Help)
      {
          DisplayHelp();
      }
      else
      {
          if (commandLine.Priority !=
              ProcessPriorityClass.Normal)
          {
              // Change thread priority
          }

      }
      // ...

  }

  private static void DisplayHelp()
```

```
        {
            // Display the command-line help.
        }
    }
```

```
using System;
using System.Diagnostics;

public partial class Program
{
    private class CommandLineInfo
    {
        public bool Help
        {
            get { return _Help; }
            set { _Help = value; }
        }
        private bool _Help;

        public string Out
        {
            get { return _Out; }
            set { _Out = value; }
        }
        private string _Out;

        public ProcessPriorityClass Priority
        {
            get { return _Priority; }
            set { _Priority = value; }
        }
        private ProcessPriorityClass _Priority =
            ProcessPriorityClass.Normal;
    }
}
```

```
using System;
using System.Diagnostics;
using System.Reflection;

public class CommandLineHandler
{
    public static void Parse(string[] args, object commandLine)
    {
        string errorMessage;
        if (!TryParse(args, commandLine, out errorMessage))
        {
            throw new ApplicationException(errorMessage);
        }
```

```
        }

public static bool TryParse(string[] args, object commandLine,
    out string errorMessage)
{
    bool success = false;
    errorMessage = null;
    foreach (string arg in args)
    {
        string option;
        if (arg[0] == '/' || arg[0] == '-')
        {
            string[] optionParts = arg.Split(
                new char[] { ':' }, 2);

            // Remove the slash/dash
            option = optionParts[0].Remove(0, 1);
            PropertyInfo property =
                commandLine.GetType().GetProperty(option,
                    BindingFlags.IgnoreCase |
                    BindingFlags.Instance |
                    BindingFlags.Public);
            if (property != null)
            {
                if (property.PropertyType == typeof(bool))
                {
                    // Last parameters for handling indexers
                    property.SetValue(
                        commandLine, true, null);
                    success = true;
                }
                else if (
                    property.PropertyType == typeof(string))
                {
                    property.SetValue(
                        commandLine, optionParts[1], null);
                    success = true;
                }
                else if (property.PropertyType.IsEnum)
                {
                    try
                    {
                        property.SetValue(commandLine,
                            Enum.Parse(
                                typeof(ProcessPriorityClass),
                                optionParts[1], true),
                            null);
                        success = true;
                    }
                    catch (ArgumentException )
                    {
                        success = false;
                        errorMessage =
                            string.Format(
                                "The option '{0}' is " +
```

```
                              "invalid for '{1}'",
                          optionParts[1], option);
                 }
             }
             else
             {
                 success = false;
                 errorMessage = string.Format(
                     "Data type '{0}' on {1} is not"
                     + " supported.",
                     property.PropertyType.ToString(),
                     commandLine.GetType().ToString());
             }
         }
         else
         {
             success = false;
             errorMessage = string.Format(
                 "Option '{0}' is not supported.",
                 option);
         }
     }
 }
 return success;
 }
}
```

Although Listing 14.3 is long, the code is relatively simple. `Main()` begins by instantiating a `CommandLineInfo` class. This type is defined specifically to contain the command-line data for this program. Each property corresponds to a command-line option for the program where the command line is as shown in Output 14.2.

OUTPUT 14.2:

```
Compress.exe /Out:<file name> /Help
   /Priority:RealTime|High|AboveNormal||Normal|BelowNormal|Idle
```

The `CommandLineInfo` object is passed to the `CommandLineHandler`'s `Try-Parse()` method. This method begins by enumerating through each option and separating out the option name (`Help` or `Out`, for example). Once the name is determined, the code reflects on the `CommandLineInfo` object, looking for an instance property with the same name. If the property is found, it assigns the property using a call to `SetValue()` and specifying the data corresponding to the property type. (For arguments, this call accepts the object on which to set the value, the new value, and an additional `index` parameter that is `null` unless the property is an indexer.) This listing handles three property types: Boolean, string, and enum. In the case of enums, you parse the option value and assign the property the text's enum equivalent. Assuming the `TryParse()` call was successful, the method exits and the `CommandLineInfo` object is initialized with the data from the command line.

Interestingly, in spite of the fact that `CommandLineInfo` is a private class nested within `Program`, `CommandLineHandler` has no trouble reflecting over it and even invoking its members. In other words, reflection is able to circumvent accessibility rules as long as appropriate code access security (CAS) permissions are established. If, for example, `Out` was private, it would still be possible for the `TryParse()` method to assign it a value. Because of this, it would be possible to move `CommandLineHandler` into a separate assembly and share it across multiple programs, each with their own `CommandLineInfo` class.

In this particular example, you invoke a member on `CommandLineInfo` using `PropertyInfo.SetValue()`. Not surprisingly, `PropertyInfo` also includes a `GetValue()` method for retrieving data from the property. For a method, however, there is a `MethodInfo` class with an `Invoke()` member. Both `MethodInfo` and `PropertyInfo` derive from `MemberInfo` (although indirectly), as shown in Figure 14.1.

The CAS permissions are set up to allow private member invocation in this case because the program runs from the local computer, and by default, locally installed programs are part of the trusted zone and have appropriate permissions granted. Programs run from a remote location will need to be explicitly granted such a right.

Reflection on Generic Types

Just as you can use reflection on nongeneric types, the 2.0 framework has provisions for reflecting on generic types. Runtime reflection on generics determines whether a class or method contains a generic type, and any type parameters or arguments it may contain.

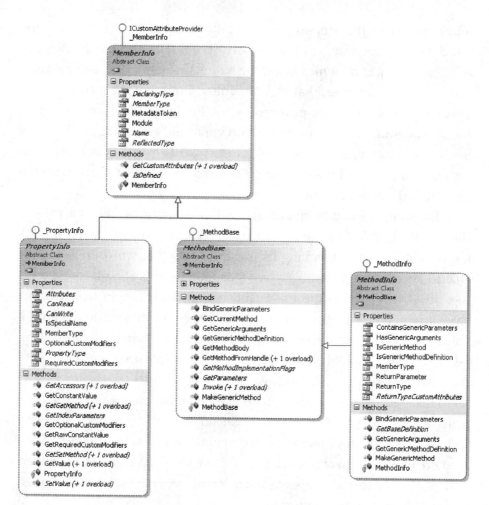

FIGURE 14.1: **MemberInfo** Derived Classes

Determining the Type of Type Parameters

In the same way that you can use a `typeof` operator with nongeneric types to retrieve an instance of `System.Type`, you can use the `typeof` operator on type parameters in a generic type or generic method. Listing 14.4 applies the `typeof` operator to the type parameter in the `Add` method of a `Stack` class.

LISTING 14.4: Declaring the **Stack<T>** Class

```
public class Stack<T>
{
    ...
```

```
    public void Add(T i)
    {
        . . .
        Type t = typeof(T);
        . . .
    }
    . . .
}
```

Once you have an instance of the `Type` object for the type parameter, you may then use reflection on the type parameter itself to determine its behavior and tailor the `Add` method to the specific type more effectively.

Determining Whether a Class or Method Supports Generics

In the `System.Type` class for CLI 2.0, a handful of new methods determine whether a given type supports generic parameters and arguments. A generic argument is a type parameter supplied when a generic class is instantiated. You can determine whether a class or method contains generic parameters that have not yet been set by querying the `Type.ContainsGenericParameters Boolean` property, as demonstrated in Listing 14.5.

LISTING 14.5: Reflection with Generics

```
using System;

public class Program
{
  static void Main()
  {
      Type type;
      type = typeof(System.Nullable<>);
      Console.WriteLine(type.ContainsGenericParameters);
      Console.WriteLine(type.IsGenericType);

      type = typeof(System.Nullable<DateTime>);
      Console.WriteLine(!type.ContainsGenericParameters);
      Console.WriteLine(type.IsGenericType);
  }
}
```

Output 14.3 shows the results of Listing 14.5.

`Type.IsGenericType` is a Boolean property that evaluates whether a type is generic.

OUTPUT 14.3:

```
True
True
True
True
```

Obtaining Type Parameters for a Generic Class or Method

You can obtain a list of generic arguments, or type parameters, from a generic class by calling the GetGenericArguments() method. The result is an array of System.Type instances that corresponds to the order in which they are declared as type parameters to the generic class. Listing 14.6 reflects into a generic type and obtains each type parameter. Output 14.4 shows the results.

LISTING 14.6: Using Reflection with Generic Types

```csharp
using System;
using System.Collections.Generic;

Stack<int> s = new Stack<int>();

Type t = s.GetType();

foreach(Type types in t.GetGenericArguments())
{
    System.Console.WriteLine(
        "Type parameter: " + types.FullName);
}
```

OUTPUT 14.4:

```
Type parameter: System.Int32
```

Attributes

Before delving into details on how to program attributes, you should consider a use case that demonstrates its utility. In the CommandLineHandler example in Listing 14.3, you dynamically set a class's properties based on the command-line option matching the property name. This approach is insufficient, however, when the command-line option is an invalid property name. /?, for example, cannot be supported. Furthermore, this mechanism doesn't provide any way of identifying which options are required versus which are optional.

Instead of relying on an exact match between the option name and the property name, attributes provide a way of identifying additional metadata about the decorated construct—in this case, the option that the attribute decorates. With attributes, you can decorate a property as `Required` and provide a `/?` option alias. In other words, attributes are a means of associating additional data with a property (and other constructs).

Attributes appear within square brackets preceding the construct they decorate. For example, you can modify the `CommandLineInfo` class to include attributes as shown in Listing 14.7.

LISTING 14.7: Decorating a Property with an Attribute

```csharp
class CommandLineInfo
{
    [CommandLineSwitchAlias ("?")]
    public bool Help
    {
        get { return _Help; }
        set { _Help = value; }
    }
    private bool _Help;


    [CommandLineSwitchRequired]
    public string Out
    {
        get { return _Out; }
        set { _Out = value; }
    }
    private string _Out;


    public System.Diagnostics.ProcessPriorityClass Priority
    {
        get { return _Priority; }
        set { _Priority = value; }
    }
    private System.Diagnostics.ProcessPriorityClass _Priority =
        System.Diagnostics.ProcessPriorityClass.Normal;
}
```

In Listing 14.7, the `Help` and `Out` properties are decorated with attributes. The purpose of these attributes is to allow an alias of `/?` for `/Help`, and to indicate that `/Out` is a required parameter. The idea is that from within the `CommandLineHandler.TryParse()` method, you enable support for option aliases and, assuming the parsing was successful, you can check that all the required switches were specified.

There are two ways to combine attributes on the same construct. You can either separate the attributes with commas within the same square brackets, or place each attribute within its own square brackets, as shown in Listing 14.8.

LISTING 14.8: Decorating a Property with Multiple Attributes

```
[CommandLineSwitchRequired]
[CommandLineSwitchAlias("FileName")]
public string Out
{
    get { return _Out; }
    set { _Out = value; }
}
```

```
[CommandLineSwitchRequired,
CommandLineSwitchAlias("FileName")]
public string Out
{
    get { return _Out; }
    set { _Out = value; }
}
```

In addition to decorating properties, developers can use attributes to decorate classes, interfaces, structs, enums, delegates, events, methods, constructors, fields, parameters, return values, assemblies, type parameters, and modules. For the majority of these, applying an attribute involves the same square bracket syntax shown in Listing 14.8. However, this syntax doesn't work for return values, assemblies, and modules.

Assembly attributes are used to add additional metadata about the assembly. Visual Studio's Project Wizard, for example, generates an `AssemblyInfo.cs` file that includes a host of attributes about the assembly. Listing 14.9 is an example of such a file.

LISTING 14.9: Assembly Attributes within `AssemblyInfo.cs`

```
using System.Reflection;
using System.Runtime.CompilerServices;
using System.Runtime.InteropServices;
```

```
// General information about an assembly is controlled
// through the following set of attributes. Change these
// attribute values to modify the information
// associated with an assembly.
[assembly: AssemblyTitle("CompressionLibrary")]
[assembly: AssemblyDescription("")]
[assembly: AssemblyConfiguration("")]
[assembly: AssemblyCompany("Michaelis.net")]
[assembly: AssemblyProduct("CompressionLibrary")]
[assembly: AssemblyCopyright("Copyright © Michaelis.net 2006")]
[assembly: AssemblyTrademark("")]
[assembly: AssemblyCulture("")]

// Setting ComVisible to false makes the types in this
// assembly not visible to COM components. If you need to
// access a type in this assembly from COM, set the ComVisible
// attribute to true on that type.
[assembly: ComVisible(false)]

// The following GUID is for the ID of the typelib if this
// project is exposed to COM
[assembly: Guid("417a9609-24ae-4323-b1d6-cef0f87a42c3")]

// Version information for an assembly consists
// of the following four values:
//
//      Major Version
//      Minor Version
//      Build Number
//      Revision
//
// You can specify all the values or you can
// default the Revision and Build Numbers
// by using the '*' as shown below:
[assembly: AssemblyVersion("1.0.0.0")]
[assembly: AssemblyFileVersion("1.0.0.0")]
```

The `assembly` attributes define things like company, product, and assembly version number. Similar to `assembly`, identifying an attribute usage as `module` requires prefixing it with `module:`. The restriction on `assembly` and `module` attributes is that they appear after the `using` directive but before any namespace or class declarations.

Return attributes, such as the one shown in Listing 14.10, appear before a method declaration but use the same type of syntax structure.

LISTING 14.10: Specifying a Return Attribute

```
[return: Description(
    "Returns true if the object is in a valid state.")]
public bool IsValid()
{
  // ...
  return true;
}
```

In addition to `assembly:` and `return:`, C# allows for explicit target identifications of `module`, `class:`, and `method:`, corresponding to attributes that decorate the module, class, and method. `class:` and `method:`, however, are optional, as demonstrated earlier.

One of the conveniences of using attributes is that the language takes into consideration the attribute naming convention, which is to place `Attribute` at the end of the name. However, in all the attribute *uses* in the preceding listings, no such suffix appears, despite the fact that each attribute used follows the naming convention. This is because although the full name (`DescriptionAttribute`, `AssemblyVersionAttribute`, and so on) is allowed when applying an attribute, C# makes the suffix optional and generally, no such suffix appears when *applying* an attribute; it appears only when defining one or using the attribute inline (such as `typeof(DescriptionAttribute)`).

Custom Attributes

Defining a custom attribute is relatively trivial. Attributes are objects; therefore, to define an attribute, you need to define a class. The characteristic that turns a general class into an attribute is that it derives from `System.Attribute`. Therefore, you can create a `CommandLineSwitch-RequiredAttribute` class, as shown in Listing 14.11.

LISTING 14.11: Defining a Custom Attribute

```
public class CommandLineSwitchRequiredAttribute : Attribute
{
}
```

With that simple definition, you now can use the attribute as demonstrated in Listing 14.7. So far, no code responds to the attribute; therefore, the Out property that includes the attribute will have no effect on command-line parsing.

Looking for Attributes

In addition to providing properties for reflecting on a type's members, Type includes methods to retrieve the Attributes decorating that type. Similarly, all the reflection types (PropertyInfo and MethodInfo, for example) include members for retrieving a list of attributes that decorate a type. Listing 14.12 defines a method to return a list of required switches that are missing from the command line.

LISTING 14.12: Retrieving a Custom Attribute

```
using System;
using System.Collections.Specialized;
using System.Reflection;

public class CommandLineSwitchRequiredAttribute : Attribute
{
  public static string[] GetMissingRequiredOptions(
      object commandLine)
  {
      StringCollection missingOptions = new StringCollection();
      PropertyInfo[] properties =
          commandLine.GetType().GetProperties();

      foreach (PropertyInfo property in properties)
      {
          Attribute[] attributes =
              (Attribute[])property.GetCustomAttributes(
                  typeof(CommandLineSwitchRequiredAttribute),
                  false);
          if ((attributes.Length > 0) &&
              (property.GetValue(commandLine, null) == null))
          {
              if (property.GetValue(commandLine, null) == null)
              {
                  missingOptions.Add(property.Name);
              }
          }
      }
      string[] results = new string[missingOptions.Count];
      missingOptions.CopyTo(results, 0);
      return results;
  }
}
```

The code that checks for an attribute is relatively simple. Given a `Prop-ertyInfo` object (obtained via reflection), you call `GetCustom-Attributes()` and specify the attribute sought, followed by whether to check any overloaded methods. (Alternatively, you can call the `GetCustom-Attributes()` method without the attribute type to return all of the attributes.)

Although it is possible to place code for finding the `Command-LineSwitchRequiredAttribute` attribute within the `CommandLineHandler`'s code directly, it makes for better object encapsulation to place the code within the `CommandLineSwitchRequiredAttribute` class itself. This is frequently the pattern for custom attributes. What better location to place code for finding an attribute than in a static method on the attribute class?

Initializing an Attribute through a Constructor

The call to `GetCustomAttributes()` returns an array of objects that will successfully cast to an `Attribute` array. However, since the attribute in this example didn't have any instance members, the only metadata information that it provided in the returned attribute was whether it appeared. Attributes can also encapsulate data, however. Listing 14.13 defines a `CommandLineAliasAttribute` attribute. This is another custom attribute, and it provides alias command-line options. For example, you can provide command-line support for `/Help` or `/?` as an abbreviation. Similarly, `/S` could provide an alias to `/Subfolders` that indicates that the command should traverse all the subdirectories.

To support this, you need to provide a constructor on the attribute. Specifically, for the alias you need a constructor that takes a string argument. (Similarly, if you want to allow multiple aliases, you need to define an attribute that has a `params string` array for a parameter.)

LISTING 14.13: Providing an Attribute Constructor

```
public class CommandLineSwitchAliasAttribute : Attribute
{
    public CommandLineSwitchAliasAttribute(string alias)
    {
        Alias = alias;
    }
```

```
    public string Alias
    {
        get { return _Alias; }
        set { _Alias = value; }
    }
    private string _Alias;
}
```

```
class CommandLineInfo
{
    [CommandLineSwitchAliasAttribute("?")]
    public bool Help
    {
        get { return _Help; }
        set { _Help = value; }
    }
    private bool _Help;

    // ...
}
```

The only restriction on the constructor is that when applying an attribute to a construct, only literal values and types (like `typeof(int)`) are allowed as arguments. This is to enable their serialization into the resulting CIL. It is not possible, therefore, to call a static method when applying an attribute; in addition, providing a constructor that takes arguments of type `System.DateTime` would be of little value, since there is no `System.DateTime` literal.

Given the constructor call, the objects returned from `Property-Info.GetCustomAttributes()` will be initialized with the specified constructor arguments, as demonstrated in Listing 14.14.

LISTING 14.14: Retrieving a Specific Attribute and Checking Its Initialization

```
PropertyInfo property =
    typeof(CommandLineInfo).GetProperty("Help");
CommandLineSwitchAliasAttribute attribute =
    (CommandLineSwitchAliasAttribute)
        property.GetCustomAttributes(
        typeof(CommandLineSwitchAliasAttribute), false)[0];
if(attribute.Alias == "?")
{
    Console.WriteLine("Help(?)");
};
```

Furthermore, as Listing 14.15 and Listing 14.16 demonstrate, you can use similar code in a `GetSwitches()` method on `CommandLineAlias-Attribute` that returns a dictionary collection of all the switches, including those from the property names, and associate each name with the corresponding attribute on the command-line object.

LISTING 14.15: Retrieving Custom Attribute Instances

```csharp
using System;
using System.Reflection;
using System.Collections.Generic;

public class CommandLineSwitchAliasAttribute : Attribute
{
  public CommandLineSwitchAliasAttribute(string alias)
  {
    Alias = alias;
  }

  public string Alias
  {
    get { return _Alias; }
    set { _Alias = value; }
  }
  private string _Alias;

  public static Dictionary<string, PropertyInfo> GetSwitches(
    object commandLine)
  {
    PropertyInfo[] properties = null;
    Dictionary<string, PropertyInfo> options =
      new Dictionary<string, PropertyInfo>();

    properties = commandLine.GetType().GetProperties(
      BindingFlags.Public | BindingFlags.NonPublic |
      BindingFlags.Instance);
    foreach (PropertyInfo property in properties)
    {
      options.Add(property.Name.ToLower(), property);
      foreach (CommandLineSwitchAliasAttribute attribute in
        property.GetCustomAttributes(
          typeof(CommandLineSwitchAliasAttribute), false))
      {
        options.Add(attribute.Alias.ToLower(), property);
      }
    }
    return options;
  }
}
```

LISTING 14.16: Updating `CommandLineHandler.TryParse()` to Handle Aliases

```csharp
using System;
using System.Reflection;
using System.Collections.Generic;

public class CommandLineHandler
{
  // ...

  public static bool TryParse(
      string[] args, object commandLine,
      out string errorMessage)
  {
      bool success = false;
      errorMessage = null;

      Dictionary<string, PropertyInfo> options =
          CommandLineSwitchAliasAttribute.GetSwitches(
              commandLine);

      foreach (string arg in args)
      {
          PropertyInfo property;
          string option;
          if (arg[0] == '/' || arg[0] == '-')
          {
              string[] optionParts = arg.Split(
                  new char[] { ':' }, 2);
              option = optionParts[0].Remove(0, 1).ToLower();

              if (options.TryGetValue(option, out property))
              {
                  success = SetOption(
                      commandLine, property,
                      optionParts, ref errorMessage);
              }
              else
              {
                  success = false;
                  errorMessage = string.Format(
                      "Option '{0}' is not supported.",
                      option);
              }
          }
      }

      return success;
  }

    private static bool SetOption(
        object commandLine, PropertyInfo property,
```

```
        string[] optionParts, ref string errorMessage)
    {
        bool success;

        if (property.PropertyType == typeof(bool))
        {
            // Last parameters for handling indexers
            property.SetValue(
                commandLine, true, null);
            success = true;
        }
        else
        {

            if ((optionParts.Length < 2)
                || optionParts[1] == ""
                || optionParts[1] == ":")
            {
                // No setting was provided for the switch.
                success = false;
                errorMessage = string.Format(
                    "You must specify the value for the {0} option.",
                    property.Name);
            }
            else if (
                property.PropertyType == typeof(string))
            {
                property.SetValue(
                    commandLine, optionParts[1], null);
                success = true;
            }
            else if (property.PropertyType.IsEnum)
            {
                success = TryParseEnumSwitch(
                    commandLine, optionParts,
                    property, ref errorMessage);
            }
            else
            {
                success = false;
                errorMessage = string.Format(
                    "Data type '{0}' on {1} is not supported.",
                    property.PropertyType.ToString(),
                    commandLine.GetType().ToString());
            }
        }
        return success;
    }
}
```

■ BEGINNER TOPIC

Using `Hashtable` Rather Than `Dictionary<TKey, TValue>`

Listing 14.15 uses the generic collection `Dictionary<string, Property-Info>`. Unfortunately, this is not available prior to 2.0, and instead, you have to use `System.Collections.Hashtable`. This is virtually a search-and-replace substitution, except in the call to `TryGetValue()`, which is not available on `Hashtable`. In that case, you can retrieve the value using the index operator and then check for `null`, as follows:

```
if((property = (PropertyInfo)options[option])!=null)
{ // ... }
```

`System.AttributeUsageAttribute`

Most attributes are intended to decorate only particular constructs. For example, it makes no sense to allow `CommandLineOptionAttribute` to decorate a class or an assembly. Those contexts would be meaningless. To avoid inappropriate use of an attribute, custom attributes can be decorated with `System.AttributeUsageAttribute`. Listing 14.17 (for `Command-LineOptionAttribute`) demonstrates how to do this.

LISTING 14.17: **Restricting the Constructs an Attribute Can Decorate**

```
[AttributeUsage(AttributeTargets.Property)]
public class CommandLineSwitchAliasAttribute : Attribute
{
  // ...
}
```

If the attribute is used inappropriately, as it is in Listing 14.18, it will cause a compile-time error, a characteristic unique to predefined attributes (see page 535), as Output 14.5 demonstrates.

LISTING 14.18: **`AttributeUsageAttribute` Restricting Where to Apply an Attribute**

```
// ERROR: The attribute usage is restricted to properties
[CommandLineSwitchAlias("?")]
class CommandLineInfo
{
}
```

OUTPUT 14.5:

```
...Program+CommandLineInfo.cs(24,17): error CS0592: Attribute
'CommandLineSwitchAlias' is not valid on this declaration type. It is
valid on 'property, indexer' declarations only.
```

AttributeUsageAttribute's constructor takes an AttributesTargets flag. This enum provides a list of all the possible targets that the runtime allows an attribute to decorate. For example, if you also allowed CommandLineSwitchAliasAttribute on a field, you would update the AttributeUsageAttribute application as shown in Listing 14.19.

LISTING 14.19: Limiting an Attribute's Usage with **AttributeUsageAttribute**

```
// Restrict the attribute to properties and methods
[AttributeUsage(
   AttributeTargets.Field | AttributeTargets.Property)]
public class CommandLineSwitchAliasAttribute : Attribute
{
   // ...
}
```

Named Parameters

In addition to restricting what an attribute can decorate, AttributeUsageAttribute provides a mechanism for allowing duplicates of the same attribute on a single construct. The syntax appears in Listing 14.20.

LISTING 14.20: Using a Named Parameter

```
[AttributeUsage(AttributeTargets.Property, AllowMultiple=true)]
public class CommandLineSwitchAliasAttribute : Attribute
{
   // ...
}
```

The syntax is different from the constructor initialization syntax discussed earlier. The AllowMultiple parameter is a **named parameter**, which is a designation that is unique to attributes. Named parameters provide a mechanism for setting specific public properties and fields within the attribute constructor call, even though the constructor includes no corresponding parameters. The named attributes are optional designations, but they provide a means of setting additional instance data on the attribute without providing a constructor parameter for the purpose. In this case, `AttributeUsageAttribute` includes a public member called `AllowMultiple`. Therefore, you can set this member using a named parameter assignment when you use the attribute. Assigning named parameters must occur as the last portion of a constructor, following any explicitly declared constructor parameters.

Named parameters allow for assigning attribute data without providing constructors for every conceivable combination of which attribute properties are specified and which are not. Since many of an attribute's properties may be optional, this is a useful construct in many cases.

▪ BEGINNER TOPIC

FlagsAttribute

Chapter 8 introduced enums and included an Expert Topic in regard to `FlagsAttribute`. This is a framework-defined attribute that targets enums which represent flag type values. Here is similar text as a Beginner Topic, starting with the sample code shown in Listing 14.21.

LISTING 14.21: Using **FlagsAttribute**

```
// FileAttributes defined in System.IO.

[Flags]   // Decorating an enum with FlagsAttribute.
public enum FileAttributes
{
  ReadOnly =          2^0,      // 000000000000001
  Hidden =            2^1,      // 000000000000010
  // ...
}
```

```
using System;
using System.Diagnostics;
using System.IO;

class Program
{
  public static void Main()
  {
    // ...
```

```
        string fileName = @"enumtest.txt";
        FileInfo file = new FileInfo(fileName);

        file.Attributes = FileAttributes.Hidden |
            FileAttributes.ReadOnly;

        Console.WriteLine("\"{0}\" outputs as \"{1}\"",
            file.Attributes.ToString().Replace(",", "  |"),
            file.Attributes);

        FileAttributes attributes =
            (FileAttributes) Enum.Parse(typeof(FileAttributes),
            file.Attributes.ToString());

        Console.WriteLine(attributes);

        // ...
    }
}
```

Output 14.6 shows the results of Listing 14.21.

OUTPUT 14.6:

```
"ReadOnly | Hidden" outputs as "ReadOnly, Hidden"
```

The flag documents that the enumeration values can be combined. Furthermore, it changes the behavior of the ToString() and Parse() methods. For example, calling ToString() on an enumeration that is decorated with FlagsAttribute writes out the strings for each enumeration flag that is set. In Listing 14.21, file.Attributes.ToString() returns "Read-Only, Hidden" rather than the 3 it would have returned without the FileAttributes flag. If two enumeration values are the same, the ToString() call would return the first one. As mentioned earlier, however, you should use this with caution because it is not localizable.

Parsing a value from a string to the enumeration also works. Each enumeration value identifier is separated by a comma.

It is important to note that FlagsAttribute does not automatically assign the unique flag values or check that they have unique values. The values of each enumeration item still must be assigned explicitly.

Predefined Attributes

The `AttributeUsageAttribute` attribute has a special characteristic that you didn't see in the custom attributes you have created thus far in this book. This attribute affects the behavior of the compiler, causing the compiler to sometimes report an error. Unlike the reflection code you wrote earlier for retrieving `CommandLineRequiredAttribute` and `CommandLineSwitchAliasAttribute`, `AttributeUsageAttribute` has no runtime code; instead, it has built-in compiler support.

`AttributeUsageAttribute` is a predefined attribute. Not only do such attributes provide additional metadata about the constructs they decorate, but also the runtime and compiler behave differently in order to facilitate these attributes' functionality. Attributes like `AttributeUsageAttribute`, `FlagsAttribute`, `ObsoleteAttribute`, and `ConditionalAttribute` are examples of predefined attributes. They include special behavior that only the CLI provider or compiler can offer because there are no extension points for additional noncustom attributes. In contrast, custom attributes are entirely passive. Listing 14.21 includes a couple of predefined attributes; Chapter 15 includes a few more.

System.ConditionalAttribute

Within a single assembly, the `System.Diagnostics.ConditionalAttribute` attribute behaves a little like the `#if`/`#endif` preprocessor identifier. However, instead of eliminating the CIL code from the assembly, `System.Diagnostics.ConditionalAttribute` will optionally cause the call to behave like a **no-op**, an instruction that does nothing. Listing 14.22 demonstrates the concept, and Output 14.7 shows the results.

LISTING 14.22: Using Reflection with Generic Types

```csharp
#define CONDITION_A

using System;
using System.Diagnostics;

public class Program
{
```

```
public static void Main()
{
    Console.WriteLine("Begin...");
    MethodA();
    MethodB();
    Console.WriteLine("End...");
}


[Conditional("CONDITION_A")]
static void MethodA()
{
    Console.WriteLine("MethodA() executing...");
}


[Conditional("CONDITION_B")]
static void MethodB()
{
    Console.WriteLine("MethodB() executing...");
}
}
```

OUTPUT 14.7:

```
Begin...
MethodA() executing...
End...
```

This example defined CONDITION_A, so MethodA() executed normally. CONDITION_B, however, was not defined through either #define or by using the csc.exe /Define option. As a result, all calls to Program.MethodB() from within this assembly will do nothing and don't even appear in the code.

Functionally, ConditionalAttribute is similar to placing a #if/ #endif around the method invocation. The syntax is cleaner, however, because developers create the effect by adding the ConditionalAttribute attribute to the target method without making any changes to the caller itself.

Note that the C# compiler notices the attribute on a called method during compilation, and assuming the preprocessor identifier exists, it eliminates any calls to the method. Note also that ConditionalAttibute does not affect the compiled CIL code on the target method itself (besides the addition of the attribute metadata). Instead, it affects the call site during compilation by removing the calls. This further distinguishes Conditional-Attribute from #if/#endif when calling across assemblies. Because the decorated method is still compiled and included in the target assembly, the determination of whether to call a method is based not on the preprocessor identifier in the callee's assembly, but rather, on the caller's assembly. In other words, if you create a second assembly that defines CONDITION_B, any calls to Program.MethodB() from the second assembly will execute. This is a useful characteristic in many tracing and testing scenarios. In fact, calls to System.Diagnostics.Trace and System.Diagnostics.Debug use this trait with ConditionalAttributes on TRACE and DEBUG preprocessor identifiers.

Because methods don't execute whenever the preprocessor identifier is not defined, ConditionalAttribute may not be used on methods that include an out parameter or specify a return other than void. Doing so causes a compile-time error. This makes sense because possibly none of the code within the decorated method will execute, so it is unknown what to return to the caller. Similarly, properties cannot be decorated with ConditionalAttribute. The AttributeUsage (see the section titled System.AttributeUsageAttribute, earlier in this chapter) for ConditionalAttribute is AttributeTargets.Class (starting in .NET 2.0) and AttributeTargets.Method. This allows the attribute to be used on either a method or a class. However, the class usage is special because Conditional-Attribute is allowed only on System.Attribute-derived classes.

When ConditionalAttribute decorates a custom attribute, a feature started in .NET 2.0, the latter can be retrieved via reflection only if the conditional string is defined in the calling assembly. Without such a conditional string, reflection that looks for the custom attribute will fail to find it.

System.ObsoleteAttribute

As mentioned earlier, predefined attributes affect the compiler's and/or the runtime's behavior. ObsoleteAttribute provides another example of attributes affecting the compiler's behavior. The purpose of Obsolete-Attribute is to help with the versioning of code, providing a means of indicating to callers that a particular member is no longer current. Listing 14.23 is an example of `ObsoleteAttribute` usage. As Output 14.8 shows, any callers that compile code that invokes a member marked with `Obsolete-Attribute` will cause a compile-time warning, optionally an error.

LISTING 14.23: Using **ObsoleteAttribute**

```
class Program
{
  public static void Main()
  {
      ObsoleteMethod();
  }

  [Obsolete]
  public static void ObsoleteMethod()
  {
  }
}
```

OUTPUT 14.8:

```
c:\SampleCode\ObsoleteAttributeTest.cs(24,17): warning CS0612:
Program.ObsoleteMethod()' is obsolete
```

In this case, `ObsoleteAttribute` simply displays a warning. However, there are two additional constructors on the attribute. One of them, `ObsoleteAttribute(string message)`, appends the additional message argument to the compiler's obsolete message. The second, however, is a `bool error` parameter that forces the warning to be recorded as an error instead.

`ObsoleteAttribute` allows third parties to notify developers of deprecated APIs. The warning (not an error) allows the original API to work until the developer is able to update the calling code.

Serialization-Related Attributes

Using predefined attributes, the framework supports the capacity to serialize objects onto a stream so that they can be deserialized back into objects at a later time. This provides a means of easily saving a document type object to disk before shutting down an application. Later on, the document may be deserialized so that the user can continue to work on it.

In spite of the fact that an object can be relatively complex and include links to many other types of objects that also need to be serialized the serialization framework is easy to use. In order for an object to be serializable, the only requirement is that it includes a `System.Serializable-Attribute`. Given the attribute, a formatter class reflects over the serializable object and copies it into a stream (see Listing 14.24).

LISTING 14.24: Saving a Document Using `System.SerializableAttribute`

```
using System;
using System.IO;
using System.Runtime.Serialization.Formatters.Binary;

class Program
{
  public static void Main()
  {
      Stream stream;
      Document documentBefore = new Document();
      documentBefore.Title =
          "A cacophony of ramblings from my potpourri of notes";
      Document documentAfter;

      using (stream = File.Open(
          documentBefore.Title + ".bin", FileMode.Create))
      {
          BinaryFormatter formatter =
              new BinaryFormatter();
          formatter.Serialize(stream, documentBefore);
      }

      using (stream = File.Open(
          documentBefore.Title + ".bin", FileMode.Open))
      {
          BinaryFormatter formatter =
              new BinaryFormatter();
          documentAfter = (Document)formatter.Deserialize(
              stream);
      }

      Console.WriteLine(documentAfter.Title);
  }
}
```

```
// Serializable classes use SerializableAttribute.
[Serializable]
class Document
{
```

```
    public string Title = null;
    public string Data = null;

    [NonSerialized]
    public long _WindowHandle = 0;

    class Image
    {
    }
    [NonSerialized]
    private Image Picture = new Image();
}
```

Output 14.9 shows the results of Listing 14.24.

OUTPUT 14.9:

```
A cacophony of ramblings from my potpourri of notes
```

Listing 14.24 serializes and deserializes a Document object. Serialization involves instantiating a formatter (this example uses System.Runtime .Serialization.Formatters.Binary.BinaryFormatter) and calling Serialization() with the appropriate stream object. Deserializing the object simply involves a call to the formatter's Deserialize() method, specifying the stream that contains the serialized object as an argument. However, since the return from Deserialize() is of type object, you also need to cast it specifically to the type that was serialized.

Notice that serialization occurs for the entire object graph (all the items associated with the serialized object [Document] via a field). Therefore, all fields in the object graph also must be serializable.

System.NonSerializable. Fields that are not serializable should be decorated with the System.NonSerializable attribute. This tells the serialization framework to ignore them. The same attribute should appear on fields that should not be persisted for use case reasons. Passwords and Windows handles are good examples of fields that should not be serialized: Windows handles because they change each time a window is re-created and passwords because data serialized into a stream is not encrypted and can easily be accessed. Consider the Notepad view of the serialized document in Figure 14.2.

FIGURE 14.2: **BinaryFormatter** Does Not Encrypt Data

Listing 14.24 set the `Title` field and the resulting `*.BIN` file includes the text in plain view.

Providing Custom Serialization. One way to add encryption is to provide custom serialization. Ignoring the complexities of encrypting and decrypting, this requires implementing the `ISerializable` interface in addition to using `SerializableAttribute`. The interface only requires the `GetObjectData()` method to be implemented. However, this is sufficient only for serialization. In order to also support deserialization, it is necessary to provide a constructor that takes parameters of type `System.Runtime.Serialization.SerializationInfo` and `System.Runtime.Serialization.StreamingContext` (see Listing 14.25).

LISTING 14.25: Implementing **System.Runtime.Serialization.ISerializable**

```csharp
using System;
using System.Runtime.Serialization;

[Serializable]
class EncryptableDocument :
    ISerializable
{
  public EncryptableDocument(){ }

  enum Field
  {
      Title,
      Data
  }
  public string Title;
  public string Data;

  public static string Encrypt(string data)
  {
```

```
        string encryptedData = data;
        // Key-based encryption ...
        return encryptedData;
    }


    public static string Decrypt(string encryptedData)
    {
        string data = encryptedData;
      // Key-based decryption...
        return data;
    }


#region ISerializable Members
    public void GetObjectData(
        SerializationInfo info, StreamingContext context)
    {
        info.AddValue(
            Field.Title.ToString(), Title);
        info.AddValue(
            Field.Data.ToString(), Encrypt(Data));
    }


    public EncryptableDocument(
        SerializationInfo info, StreamingContext context)
    {
        Title = info.GetString(
            Field.Title.ToString());
        Data = Decrypt(info.GetString(
            Field.Data.ToString()));
    }
#endregion
}
```

Essentially, the `System.Runtime.Serialization.Serialization-Info` object is a collection of name/value pairs. When serializing, the `GetObject()` implementation calls `AddValue()`. To reverse the process, you call one of the `Get*()` members. In this case, you encrypt and decrypt prior to serialization and deserialization, respectively.

Versioning the Serialization. One more serialization point deserves mentioning: versioning. Objects such as documents may be serialized using one version of an assembly and deserialized using a newer version, sometimes the reverse. Without paying attention, however, version incompatibilities can easily be introduced, sometimes unexpectedly. Consider the scenario shown in Table 14.1.

TABLE 14.1: Deserialization of a New Version Throws an Exception

Step	Description	Code

0	Define a class decorated with `System.SerializableAttribute`.	```[Serializable]```
		```class Document```
		```{```

1	Add a field or two (public or private) of any serializable type.	``` public string Title;```
		``` public string Data;```
		```}```

2	Serialize the object to a file called `*.v1.bin`.	```Stream stream;```
		```Document documentBefore = new Document();```
		```documentBefore.Title =```
		``` "A cacophony of ramblings from my potpourri of notes";```
		```Document documentAfter;```
		
		```using (stream = File.Open(```
		``` documentBefore.Title + ".bin",```
		``` FileMode.Create))```
		```{```
		``` BinaryFormatter formatter =```
		``` new BinaryFormatter();```
		``` formatter.Serialize(```
		``` stream, documentBefore);```
		```}```

Continues

TABLE 14.1: Deserialization of a New Version Throws an Exception *(Continued)*

Step	Description	Code
3	Add an additional field to the serializable class.	```[Serializable]
class Document
{
public string Title;
public string Author;
public string Data;
}```
4	Deserialize the *v1.bin file into the new object (Document) version.	```using (stream = File.Open(
documentBefore.Title + ".bin",
FileMode.Open))
{
BinaryFormatter formatter =
new BinaryFormatter();
documentAfter =
(Document)formatter.Deserialize(
stream);
}```

544

Surprisingly, even though all you did was to add a new field, deserializing the original file throws a `System.Runtime.Serialization.SerializationException`. This is because the formatter looks for data corresponding to the new field within the stream. Failure to locate such data throws an exception.

To avoid this, the 2.0 framework includes a `System.Runtime.Serialization.OptionalFieldAttribute`. When you require backward compatibility, you must decorate serialized fields—even private ones—with `OptionalFieldAttribute` (unless, of course, a latter version begins to require it).

Unfortunately, `System.Runtime.Serialization.OptionalFieldAttribute` is not supported in the earlier framework version. Instead, it is necessary to implement `ISerializable`, just as you did for encryption, saving and retrieving only the fields that are available. Assuming the addition of the `Author` field, for example, the implementation shown in Listing 14.26 is required for backward-compatibility support prior to the 2.0 framework:

LISTING 14.26: Backward Compatibility Prior to the 2.0 Framework

```
[Serializable]
public class VersionableDocument : ISerializable
{
    enum Field
    {
        Title,
        Author,
        Data,
    }

    public VersionableDocument()
    {
    }

    public string Title;
    public string Author;
    public string Data;

    #region ISerializable Members
    public void GetObjectData(
        SerializationInfo info, StreamingContext context)
    {
        info.AddValue(Field.Title.ToString(), Title);
        info.AddValue(Field.Author.ToString(), Author);
        info.AddValue(Field.Data.ToString(), Data);
```

```
        }
    public VersionableDocument(
        SerializationInfo info, StreamingContext context)
    {
        foreach(SerializationEntry entry in info)
        {
            switch ((Field)Enum.Parse(typeof(Field), entry.Name))
            {
                case Field.Title:
                    Title = info.GetString(
                        Field.Title.ToString());
                    break;
                case Field.Author:
                    Author = info.GetString(
                        Field.Author.ToString());
                    break;
                case Field.Data:
                    Data = info.GetString(
                        Field.Data.ToString());
                    break;
            }
        }
    }
    #endregion
}
```

Serializing in `GetObjectData()` simply involves serializing all fields (assume here that version 1 does not need to open documents from version 2). On deserialization, however, you can't simply call `GetString("Author")` because if no such entry exists, it will throw an exception. Instead, iterate through all the entries that are in `info` and retrieve them individually.

■ ADVANCED TOPIC

System.SerializableAttribute and the CIL

In many ways, the serialize attributes behave just like custom attributes. At runtime, the formatter class searches for these attributes, and if the attributes exist, the classes are formatted appropriately. One of the characteristics that make `System.SerializableAttribute` not just a custom attribute, however, is the fact that the CIL has a special header notation for serializable classes. Listing 14.27 shows the class header for the `Person` class in the CIL.

LISTING 14.27: The CIL for **SerializableAttribute**

```
class auto ansi serializable nested private
  beforefieldinit Person
  extends [mscorlib]System.Object
{
} // end of class Person
```

In contrast, attributes (including most predefined attributes) generally appear within a class definition (see Listing 14.28).

LISTING 14.28: The CIL for Attributes in General

```
.class private auto ansi beforefieldinit Person
      extends [mscorlib]System.Object
{
  .custom instance void CustomAttribute::.ctor() =
      ( 01 00 00 00 )
} // end of class Person
```

In Listing 14.28, CustomAttribute is the full name of the decorating attribute.

SerializableAttribute translates to a set bit within the metadata tables. This makes SerializableAttribute a **pseudoattribute**, an attribute that sets bits or fields in the metadata tables.

SUMMARY

This chapter discussed how to use reflection to read the metadata that is compiled into the CIL. Using reflection, you saw how to provide a late binding in which the code to call is defined at execution time rather than at compile time. Although reflection is entirely feasible for deploying a dynamic system, it is considerably slower than statically linked (compile-time), defined code. This tends to make it more prevalent and useful in development tools.

Reflection also enables the retrieval of additional metadata decorating various constructs in the form of attributes. Typically custom attributes are sought using reflection. It is possible to define your own custom attributes that insert additional metadata of your own choosing into the CIL. At run-time, it is then possible to retrieve this metadata and use it within the programming logic.

Many view attributes as a precursor to a concept known as aspect-oriented programming, in which you add functionality through constructs such as attributes instead of manually implementing the functionality wherever it is needed. It will take some time before you see true aspects within C# (if ever); however, attributes provide a clear steppingstone in that direction, without forcing a significant risk to the stability of the language.

The next chapter looks at multithreading, where attributes are used for synchronization.

■ 15 ■
Multithreading

T HIS CHAPTER DISCUSSES how to write multithreaded code. To do
this, you delve into the System.Threading namespace that contains
the API for manipulating threads. In addition, the chapter introduces a C#
keyword that makes multithreaded programming synchronization easier.

Except for Listing 15.1, this chapter uses the C# 2.0 syntax to create delegates. In other words, it does not explicitly instantiate the delegate before
registering for an event. Instead, it passes the method name directly.

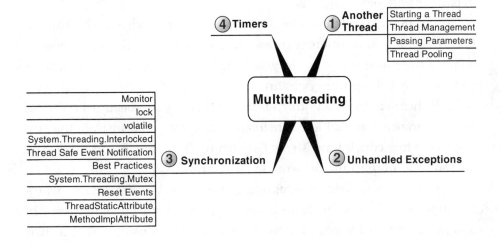

■ BEGINNER TOPIC

Thread Basics

A **thread** is a sequence of instructions that is executing. A program that enables more than one sequence to execute concurrently is **multithreaded**. For example, in order to import a large file while simultaneously allowing a user to click Cancel, a developer creates an additional thread to perform the import. By performing the import on a different thread, the program can cancel instead of freezing the user interface until the import completes.

An operating system simulates multiple threads via a mechanism known as **time slicing**. Even with multiple processors, there is generally a demand for more threads than there are processors, and as a result, time slicing occurs. Time slicing is a mechanism whereby the operating system switches execution from one thread (sequence of instructions) to the next so quickly that it appears the threads are executing simultaneously.

The effect is similar to that of a fiber optic telephone line in which the fiber optic line represents the processor and each conversation represents a thread. A (single-mode) fiber optic telephone line can send only one signal at a time, but many people can hold simultaneous conversations over the line. The fiber optic channel is fast enough to switch between conversations so quickly that each conversation appears to be uninterrupted. Similarly, each thread of a multithreaded process appears to run continuously in parallel with other threads.

Since a thread is often waiting for various events, such as an I/O operation, switching to a different thread results in more efficient execution, because the processor is not idly waiting for the operation to complete. However, switching from one thread to the next does create some overhead. If there are too many threads, the switching overhead overwhelms the appearance that multiple threads are executing, and instead, the system slows to a crawl; time is spent switching from one thread to another instead of accomplishing the work of each thread.

Even readers new to programming will have heard the term *multithreading* before, most likely in a conversation about its complexity. In designing both the C# language and the framework, considerable time was spent on simplifying the programming API that surrounds multithreaded programming. However, considerable complexity remains, not so much in writing a program that has multiple threads, but in doing so in a manner that maintains atomicity, avoids deadlocks, and does not introduce execution uncertainty such as race conditions.

Atomicity

Consider code that transfers money from a bank account. First, the code verifies whether there are sufficient funds; if there are, the transfer occurs. If after checking the funds, execution switches to a thread that removes the funds, an invalid transfer may occur when execution returns to the initial thread. Controlling account access so that only one thread can access the account at a time fixes the problem and makes the transfer **atomic**. An atomic operation is one that either completes all of its steps fully, or restores the state of the system back to its original state. A bank transfer should be an atomic operation because it involves two steps. In the process of performing those steps, it is possible to lose operation atomicity if another thread modifies the account before the transfer is complete.

Identifying and implementing atomicity is one of the primary complexities of multithreaded programming.

The complexity increases because the majority of C# statements are not necessarily atomic. _Count++, for example, is a simple statement in C#, but it translates to multiple instructions for the processor.

1. The processor reads the data in _Count.
2. The processor calculates the new value.
3. _Count is assigned a new value (even this may not be atomic).

After the data is accessed, but before the new value is assigned, a different thread may modify the original value (perhaps also checking the value prior to modifying it), creating a **race condition** because the value in Count has, for at least one thread's perspective, changed unexpectedly.

Deadlock

To avoid such race conditions, languages support the ability to restrict blocks of code to a specified number of threads, generally one. However, if the order of lock acquisition between threads varies, a **deadlock** could occur such that threads freeze, each waiting for the other to release their lock.

For example:

	Thread A	Thread B
Time	Acquires a lock on a	Acquires a lock on b
	Requests a lock on b	Requests a lock on a
	Deadlocks, waiting for b	Deadlocks, waiting for a

At this point, each thread is waiting on the other thread before proceeding, so each thread is blocked, leading to an overall deadlock in the execution of that code.

Uncertainty

The problem with code that is not atomic or causes deadlocks is that it depends on the order in which processor instructions across multiple threads occur. This dependency introduces uncertainty concerning program execution. The order in which one instruction will execute relative to an instruction in a different thread is unknown. Many times, the code will appear to behave uniformly, but occasionally it won't, and this is the crux of multithreaded programming. Because such race conditions are difficult to replicate in the laboratory, much of the quality assurance of multithreaded code depends on long-running stress tests and manual code analysis/reviews.

Running and Controlling a Separate Thread

Chapter 14 discussed delegates and events. Programming multiple threads with C# depends heavily on the syntax of delegates. In order to start a new thread, it is necessary to call a delegate that contains the code for the separate thread. Listing 15.1 provides a simple example, and Output 15.1 on page 554 shows the results.

LISTING 15.1: Starting a Method in a Separate Thread

```
using System;
using System.Threading;
```

```
public class RunningASeparateThread
{
  public const int Repetitions = 1000;

  public static void Main()
  {
      ThreadStart threadStart = new ThreadStart(DoWork);
      Thread thread = new Thread(threadStart);
      thread.Start();
      for (int count = 0; count < Repetitions; count++)
      {
          Console.Write('-');
      }
      thread.Join();
  }

  public static void DoWork()
  {
      for (int count = 0; count < Repetitions; count++)
      {
          Console.Write('.');
      }
  }
}
```

The code that is to run in a new thread appears in the DoWork() method. This method prints . to the console repeatedly during each iteration within a loop. Besides the fact that it contains code for starting another thread, the Main() method is virtually identical in structure to DoWork(), except that it displays -. The resulting output from the program is a series of dashes until the thread context switches, at which time the program displays periods until the next thread switch, and so on. (On Windows, it is possible to increase the chances of a thread context switch by using Start /low /b <program.exe> to execute the program. This will assign the entire process a lower priority, causing its threads to be interrupted more frequently, and thus causing more frequent thread switches.)

Starting a Thread

In order for DoWork() to run under the context of a different thread, you must first instantiate a System.Threading.ThreadStart delegate around the DoWork() method. Next, you pass the ThreadStart delegate instance to

OUTPUT 15.1:

the `System.Threading.Thread` constructor before commencing execution of the thread with a call to `thread.Start()`.

In Listing 15.1, you instantiate the thread in two separate steps, explicitly instantiating a `System.Threading.ThreadStart` instance and assigning it to a variable before instantiating the `System.Threading.Thread` object. As Listing 15.2 demonstrates, you could combine both statements, or you could use C# 2.0's delegate inference to avoid any explicit syntax to instantiate `ThreadStart` and instead pass `DoWork` directly into `System.Threading.Thread`'s constructor.

LISTING 15.2: Creating a Thread Using C# 2.0 Syntax

```
using System;
using System.Threading;

public class RunningASeparateThread
{
```

```
    // ...

public static void Main()
{
    // Requires C# 2.0
    Thread thread = new Thread(DoWork);
    thread.Start();
    // ...
}

public static void DoWork()
{
    // ...
}
}
```

You can elect not to declare a `ThreadStart` variable in C# 1.0, but you cannot avoid explicit instantiation of the `ThreadStart` instance.

Starting a thread simply involves a call to `Thread.Start()`. As soon as the `DoWork()` method begins execution, the call to `Thread.Start()` returns and executes the `for` loop in the `Main()` method. The threads are now independent and neither waits for the other. The output from Listing 15.1 and Listing 15.2 will intermingle the output of each thread, instead of creating a series of . followed by -.

■ BEGINNER TOPIC

Static and Instance `ThreadStart` Methods

This example uses a static `ThreadStart`-compatible method. As you learned in Chapter 14, it is also possible to use instance methods as delegates, explicitly identifying the object that contains the method (for example, `this.Find`, which is equivalent to `new ThreadStart(Find)`). You can also specify methods on other objects by prefixing the method name with the instance identifier (for example, `song.Play`).

Thread Management

Threads include a number of methods and properties for managing their execution.

Join()

Once threads are started, you can cause a "wait for completion" with a call to thread.Join(). The calling thread will wait until the thread instance terminates. The Join() method is overloaded to take either an int or a TimeSpan to support a maximum time to wait for thread completion before continuing execution.

IsBackGround

Another thread configuration option is the thread.IsBackGround property. By default, a thread is a foreground thread, meaning the process will not terminate until the thread completes. In contrast, setting the IsBackGround property to true will allow process execution to terminate prior to a thread's completion.

Priority

When using the Join() method, you can increase or decrease the thread's priority by setting the Priority to a new ThreadPriority enum value (Lowest, BelowNormal, Normal, AboveNormal, Highest).

ThreadState

A thread's state is accessible through the ThreadState property, a more precise reflection of the Boolean IsAlive property. The ThreadState enum flag values are Aborted, AbortRequested, Background, Running, Stopped, StopRequested, Suspended, SuspendRequested, Unstarted, and WaitSleepJoin. The flag names indicate activities that may occur on a thread. Two noteworthy methods are Thread.Sleep() and Abort().

Thread.Sleep()

Thread.Sleep() is a static method that pauses the current thread for a period. A single parameter (in milliseconds, or a TimeSpan) specifies how long the active thread waits before continuing execution. This enables switching to a different thread for a specific period.

This method is not for accurate timing. Returns can occur hundreds of milliseconds *before* or *after* the specified time.

Abort()

A thread's `Abort()` method causes a `ThreadAbortException` to be thrown within the target thread. The problem is that `Thread.Abort()` introduces uncertainty into the thread's behavior. In .NET 1.x, if the abort interrupts execution of a `finally` block, the remaining code within that block will never run. Furthermore, `Abort()` may fail because the aborted thread could have a `catch` block that handles the `ThreadAbortException` and calls `Thread.ResetAbort()`, or the thread could currently be running unmanaged code which will not throw the `ThreadAbortException` until the code returns. Except in rare circumstances, developers should consider the `Abort()` method to be a last resort.

In .NET 2.0, if the abort interrupts execution of a `finally` block, then its effect will be delayed until the conclusion of the `finally` block (and any additional `finally` blocks within the call stack).

Passing Parameters to Threads

The code in Listing 15.2 was relatively simple. A significant missing item was to pass data from the main thread to the second thread. In C# 1.0, this was cumbersome because the `Thread` constructor could handle only the `System.Threading.ThreadStart` delegate type, and it did not take parameters. However, C# 2.0 includes an additional thread constructor, one that takes the `System.Threading.ParameterizedThreadStart` delegate type. This delegate takes a parameter of type `object`, making it possible to pass multiple data elements to the thread by wrapping them in a custom class or a collection. Listing 15.3 demonstrates a simple character-passing example, and Output 15.2 shows the results.

LISTING 15.3: Using **`ParameterizedThreadStart`** to Pass Data

```
using System;
using System.Threading;
```

```
class PassingParametersUsingParameterizedThreadStart
{
    public const int Repetitions = 1000;
    public static void Main()
    {
        // DoWork() now matches the signature of
        // ParameterizedThreadStart rather than ThreadStart.
        Thread thread = new Thread(DoWork);
        thread.Start('.');

        for (int count = 0; count < Repetitions; count++)
        {
            Console.Write('-');
        }

        thread.Join();
    }

    public static void DoWork(object state)
    {
        for (int count = 0; count < Repetitions; count++)
        {
            Console.Write(state);
        }
    }
}
```

In cases where the new thread requires multiple pieces of data, you must declare a type to hold this data for the new thread. You pass this data as an instance of the new type (see Listing 15.4).

LISTING 15.4: Using **ParameterizedThreadStart** to Pass Multiple Data Elements

```
using System;
using System.Threading;

struct DoWorkData
{
    public DoWorkData(int repetitions, char character)
    {
        _Repetitions = repetitions;
        _Character = character;
    }
    public int Repetitions
    {
        get { return _Repetitions; }
    }
```

OUTPUT 15.2:

```
...................................-----------------------------------------
---------------------------------------------------------------------------
---------------------------------------------------------------------------
---------------------------------------------------------------------------
---------------------------------------------------------------------------
---------------------------------------------------------------...........
...........................................................................
...........................................................................
...........................................................................
...........................................................................
...........................................................................
...........................................................................
..........................-------------------------------------------------
---------------------------------------------------------------------------
---------------------------------------------------------------------------
---------------------------------------------------------------------------
---------------------------------------------------------------------------
---------------------------------------------------------.........
...........................................................................
...........................................................................
...........................................................................
...........................................................................
...........................................................................
......-.--------------------------------------------------------------------
---------------------------------------------------------------------------
---------------------------------------------------------------------.....
...........................................................................
...........................................................................
...........................................................................
...........................................................................
.............................
```

```csharp
    private int _Repetitions;

    public char Character
    {
        get { return _Character; }
    }
    private char _Character;

}
class PassingMultipleParametersUsingParameterizedThreadStart
{
  public static void Main()
  {
      const int repetitions = 1000;

      // DoWork() now matches the signature of
      // ParameterizedThreadStart rather than ThreadStart.
      Thread thread = new Thread(DoWork);
      thread.Start( new DoWorkData(repetitions, '.') );
```

```
        for (int count = 0; count < repetitions; count++)
        {
            Console.Write('-');
        }

        thread.Join();
    }
    public static void DoWork(object state)
    {
        DoWorkData data = (DoWorkData)state;
        for (int count = 0; count < data.Repetitions; count++)
        {
            Console.Write(data.Character);
        }
    }
}
```

The results of Listing 15.4 appear in Output 15.3. An alternative to declaring a type is to pass an array or collection.

OUTPUT 15.3:

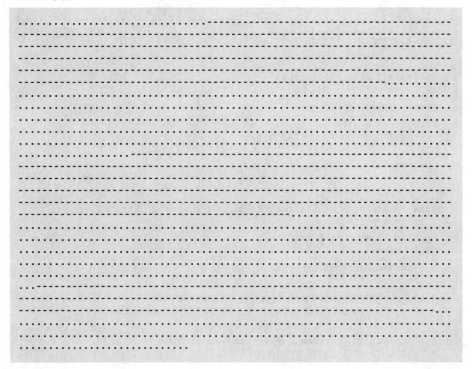

C# 1.0 does not support the `ParameterizedThreadStart` delegate. An alternative method to pass data in C# 1.0 is to store it in a location accessible from both threads. The problem is associating a thread with its own data. It is sometimes necessary to define a class that contains the thread delegate, instantiate this new class, set the shared data, and call the thread to start the delegate associated with the new class method. For many scenarios, this is overkill. The `ThreadPool` class, described next, is a simpler mechanism.

Thread Pooling

Regardless of the number of processors, excess threads affect performance. `System.Threading.ThreadPool` manages threads, including the reuse of expired threads, based on resources.

Accessing threads in `ThreadPool` is similar to explicit use of the `Thread` class. However, as Listing 15.5 shows, `ThreadPool` has the advantage of passing parameters even in the 1.0 implementation, where `ParameterizedThreadStart` is unavailable.

LISTING 15.5: Using **ThreadPool** Instead of Instantiating Threads Explicitly

```csharp
using System;
using System.Threading;

public class ThreadPools
{
  public const int Repetitions = 1000;
  public static void Main()
  {
      ThreadPool.QueueUserWorkItem(DoWork, '.');

      for (int count = 0; count < Repetitions; count++)
      {
          Console.Write('-');
      }

      // Pause until the thread completes
      Thread.Sleep(1000);
  }
  public static void DoWork(object state)
  {
```

```
    for (int count = 0; count < Repetitions; count++)
    {
        Console.Write(state);
    }
  }
}
```

The results of Listing 15.5 appear in Output 15.4. Output 15.4 shows the same intermingling of . and – as Output 15.3 does. The thread pool class does not return a handle to the thread itself, which prevents the calling thread from controlling it with the thread management functions described earlier in the chapter, or easily monitoring its state to determine when it completes. Assuming these deficiencies are not critical, developers should consider using the thread pool over explicit thread creation. This provides more-efficient execution on single- and multiprocessor computers as well as a simple means for passing arbitrary data, even within the 1.0 framework.

OUTPUT 15.4:

Unfortunately, however, thread pool use is not without its pitfalls. Activities like I/O operations and other framework methods that internally use the thread pool can consume threads as well. Consuming all threads within the pool can delay execution and, in extreme cases, cause a deadlock.

Unhandled Exceptions

To catch all exceptions from a thread, you surround the initial thread start method with a try/catch/finally block, just as you would for all code within `Main()`. However, what happens if a third-party component creates an alternate thread and throws an unhandled exception from that thread? A try/catch block in `Main()` will not catch an exception in an alternate thread. Even if it did, the code could never appropriately recover from all possible exceptions and continue executing. The general unhandled-exceptions guideline is for the program to shut down and restart in a clean state, instead of behaving erratically or hanging because of an invalid state.

Instead of crashing suddenly or ignoring the exception entirely if it occurs on an alternate thread, it is often desirable to save any working data and/or log the exception for error reporting and future debugging. This requires a mechanism to register for notifications of unhandled exceptions.

Registering for unhandled exceptions on the main application domain occurs via an application domain's `UnhandledException` event. Listing 15.6 demonstrates that process, and Output 15.5 shows the results.

LISTING 15.6: Registering for Unhandled Exceptions

```csharp
using System;
using System.Threading;

public class MultiThreadedExceptionHandling
{
  static void Main()
  {
      try
      {
          // Register a callback to receive notifications
          // of any unhandled exception.
```

```
        AppDomain.CurrentDomain.UnhandledException +=
            OnUnhandledException;

    Thread thread =
        new Thread(ThrowException);
    thread.Start();
    // ...

    // Wait for the unhandled exception to fire
    Thread.Sleep(10000);

    Console.WriteLine("Still running...");
}
finally
{
    Console.WriteLine("Exiting...");
}
}
```

```
static void OnUnhandledException(
    object sender, UnhandledExceptionEventArgs eventArgs)
{
    Console.WriteLine("ERROR:{0}", eventArgs.ExceptionObject);
}

public static void ThrowException()
{
    throw new ApplicationException("Arbitrary exception");
}
}
```

OUTPUT 15.5:

```
Still running...
Exiting...
```

The UnhandledException callback will fire for all unhandled exceptions on threads within the application domain, including the main thread. This is a notification mechanism, not a mechanism to catch and process exceptions so that the application can continue. After the event, the application should be programmed to exit.

Synchronization

Running a new thread is a relatively simple programming task. What makes multithreaded programming difficult, however, is recognizing the data that multiple threads could access simultaneously. The program needs to synchronize such data, the **state**, in order to prevent simultaneous access. Consider Listing 15.7.

LISTING 15.7: Unsynchronized State

```csharp
using System;
using System.Threading;

class RaceCondition
{
    const int _Total = int.MaxValue;
    static long _Count = 0;

    public static void Main()
    {
        Thread thread = new Thread(Decrement);
        thread.Start();

        // Increment
        for (int i = 0; i < _Total; i++)
        {
            _Count++;
        }

        thread.Join();
        Console.WriteLine("Count = {0}", _Count);
    }

    static void Decrement()
    {
        for (int i = 0; i < _Total; i++)
        {
            _Count--;
        }
    }
}
```

The results of Listing 15.7 appear in Output 15.6.

OUTPUT 15.6:

```
Count = 113449949
```

The output is not 0, as it would have been if `Decrement()` was called directly rather than on a separate thread. Instead, a race condition is introduced because the `_Count++` and `_Count--` statements are able to interrupt each other. Although in C# these statements appear to be one operation, each takes three steps, as discussed earlier in this chapter.

The problem with this is that a thread context switch could take place during any of these steps. Consider the sample execution in Table 15.1.

TABLE 15.1: **Sample Pseudocode Execution**

Main Thread	Decrement Thread	Count
...	...	...
Copy the value 0 out of `_Count`.		0
Increment the copied value (0), resulting in 1.		0
Copy the resulting value (1) into `_Count`.		1
Copy the value 1 out of `_Count`.		1
	Copy the value 1 out of `_Count`.	1
Increment the copied value (1), resulting in 2.		1
Copy the resulting value (2) into `_Count`.		2
	Decrement the copied value (1), resulting in 0.	2
	Copy the resulting value (0) into `_Count`.	0
...	...	...

Table 15.1 shows a thread context switch by the transition of instructions appearing from one column to the other. The value of _Count after a particular line has completed appears in the last column. In this sample execution, _Count++ executes twice and _Count-- occurs once. However, the resulting _Count value is 0, not 1. Copying a result back to _Count essentially wipes out any _Count value changes that occurred since the read of _Count on the same thread.

The problem in Listing 15.7 is a **race condition**, which occurs when multiple threads have simultaneous access to the same data elements. As this sample execution demonstrates, simultaneous access to data by multiple threads undermines data integrity, even on a single-processor computer. To remedy this, the code needs synchronization around the data (state). Code or data that is appropriately synchronized for simultaneous access by multiple threads is known as **thread safe**.

There is one important point to note about atomicity of reading and writing to variables. The runtime guarantees that a type whose size is no bigger than a native integer will not be read or written only partially. Assuming a 32-bit operating system, therefore, reads and writes to an int (System.Int32) will be atomic. However, reads and writes to a long (System.Int64), for example, will not be guaranteed to be atomic. Therefore, write operations to change a long variable may be interrupted after copying only 32 bits, resulting in the reading of an incorrect value.

■ **BEGINNER TOPIC**

Multiple Threads and Local Variables
Note that it is not necessary to synchronize local variables. Local variables are loaded onto the stack and each thread has its own logical stack. Therefore, each local variable has its own instance for each method call. Local variables are not shared across method calls; therefore, they are also not shared between multiple threads.

However, this does not mean local variables are entirely without concurrency issues. A local variable of a reference type could be passed to an alternate thread, making the data within the variable accessible across multiple threads.

Synchronization Using Monitor

To synchronize two threads so that they cannot execute particular sections of code simultaneously, you need a **monitor** to block the second thread from entering a protected code section until the first thread has exited that particular section. The monitor functionality is part of a class called System .Threading.Monitor, and the beginning and end of protected code sections are marked with calls to the static methods Monitor.Enter() and Monitor.Exit(), respectively.

Listing 15.8 demonstrates synchronization using the Monitor class explicitly. As this listing shows, it is important that all code between calls to Monitor.Enter() and Monitor.Exit() be surrounded with a try/ finally block. Without this, an exception could occur within the protected section and Monitor.Exit() may never be called, thereby blocking other threads indefinitely.

LISTING 15.8: Synchronizing with a Monitor Explicitly

```
using System;
using System.Threading;

class SynchronizationWithMonitorsExplicitly
{
    readonly static object _Sync = new object();
    const int _Total = int.MaxValue;
    static long _Count = 0;

    public static void Main()
    {
        Thread thread = new Thread(Decrement);
        thread.Start();

        // Increment
        for (int i = 0; i < _Total; i++)
```

```
    {
        Monitor.Enter(_Sync);
        try
        {
            _Count++;
        }
        finally
        {
            Monitor.Exit(_Sync);
        }
    }

    thread.Join();
    Console.WriteLine("Count = {0}", _Count);
}

static void Decrement()
{
    for (int i = 0; i < _Total; i++)
    {
        Monitor.Enter(_Sync);
        try
        {
            _Count--;
        }
        finally
        {
            Monitor.Exit(_Sync);
        }
    }
}
}
```

The results of Listing 15.8 appear in Output 15.7.

OUTPUT 15.7:

```
Count = 0
```

Note that `Monitor.Enter()` and `Monitor.Exit()` are associated with each other by sharing the same object reference passed as the parameter (in this case, `_Sync`).

Using the `lock` Keyword

Because of the frequent need for synchronization using `Monitor` in multithreaded code, and the fact that the try/finally block could easily be forgotten, C# provides a special keyword to handle this locking synchronization pattern. Listing 15.9 demonstrates the use of the new `lock` keyword, and Output 15.8 shows the results.

LISTING 15.9: Synchronizing Using the `lock` Keyword

```csharp
using System;
using System.Threading;

class SynchronizationUsingLock
{
    readonly static object _Sync = new object();
    const int _Total = int.MaxValue;
    static long _Count = 0;

    public static void Main()
    {
        Thread thread = new Thread(Decrement);
        thread.Start();

        // Increment
        for (int i = 0; i < _Total; i++)
        {
            lock (_Sync)
            {
                _Count++;
            }
        }

        thread.Join();
        Console.WriteLine("Count = {0}", _Count);
    }

    static void Decrement()
    {
        for (int i = 0; i < _Total; i++)
        {
            lock (_Sync)
            {
                _Count--;
            }
        }
    }
}
```

OUTPUT 15.8:

```
Count = 0
```

By locking the section of code accessing _Count (using either lock or Monitor), you are making the Main() and Decrement() methods thread safe, meaning they can be safely called from multiple threads simultaneously.

Synchronization does not come without a cost. First, synchronization has an impact on performance. Listing 15.9, for example, takes an order-of-magnitude longer to execute than Listing 15.7 does, which demonstrates lock's relatively slow execution compared to the execution of incrementing and decrementing the count.

Even when lock is insignificant in comparison with the work it synchronizes, programmers should avoid indiscriminately adding synchronization, thus avoiding the complexities of deadlocks and unnecessary constraints on multiprocessor computers. The general best practice for object design is to synchronize static state and to leave out synchronization from any instance data. Programmers that allow multiple threads to access a particular object must provide their own synchronization for the object. Any class that explicitly deals with threads itself is likely to want to make instances thread safe to some extent.

Choosing a lock Object

Regardless of whether using the lock keyword or the Monitor class explicitly, it is crucial that programmers carefully select the lock object.

In the previous examples, the synchronization variable, _Sync, is declared as both private and read only. It is declared as read only to ensure that the value is not changed between calls to Monitor.Enter() and Monitor.Exit(). This is important because there would otherwise be no correlation between the entering and exiting of the synchronized block of code.

Similarly, the code declares _Sync as private so that no other synchronization block outside the class can synchronize on the same object instance, thereby inappropriately causing the code to block.

If the data is public, then the synchronization object could be public so that other classes can synchronize using the same synchronization object instance. The problem is that this makes deadlock avoidance more difficult. Fortunately, the need for this pattern occurs rarely. For public data, it is preferable to leave synchronization entirely outside the class, allowing the calling code to take locks with its own synchronization object.

One more important factor is that the synchronization object cannot be a value type. If the `lock` keyword is used on a value type, then the compiler will report an error. (In the case of the `System.Threading.Monitor` class, however, no such error will occur at compile time. Instead, the code will throw an exception with the call to `Monitor.Exit()`, indicating there was no corresponding `Monitor.Enter()` call.) The issue is that when using a value type, the runtime makes a copy of the value, places it in the heap (boxing occurs), and passes the boxed value to `Monitor.Enter()`. Similarly, `Monitor.Exit()` receives a boxed copy of the original variable. The result is that `Monitor.Enter()` and `Monitor.Exit()` receive different synchronization object instances so that no correlation between the two calls occurs.

Why to Avoid Locking on `this` and `typeof(type)`

One common pattern is to lock on the `this` keyword for instance data in a class, and on the type instance obtained from `typeof(type)` (for example, `typeof(MyType)`) for static data. Such a pattern provides a synchronization target for all states associated with a particular object instance when `this` is used, and all static data for a type when `typeof(type)` is used. The problem is that the synchronization target that `this` (or `typeof(type)`) points to could participate in the synchronization target for an entirely different synchronization block created in an entirely unrelated block of code. In other words, although only the code within the instance itself can block using the `this` keyword, the caller that created the instance can still pass that instance into a synchronization lock.

The result is that two different synchronization blocks that synchronize two entirely different sets of data could potentially block each other. Although perhaps unlikely, sharing the same synchronization target could have an unintended performance impact and, in extreme cases, even cause a deadlock. Instead of locking on `this` or even `typeof(type)`, it is better to define a private, read-only field on which no one will block, except for the class that has access to it.

Declaring Fields as `volatile`

On occasion, the compiler may optimize code in such a way that the instructions don't occur in the exact order they are coded, or some instructions are optimized out. Such optimizations are generally innocuous when code executes on one thread. However, with multiple threads, such optimizations may have unintended consequences because the optimizations may change the order of execution of a field's read or write operations relative to an alternate thread's access to the same field.

One way to stabilize this is to declare fields using the `volatile` keyword. This keyword forces all reads and writes to the `volatile` field to occur at the exact location the code identifies instead of at some other location that the optimization produces. The `volatile` modifier identifies that the field is susceptible to modification by the hardware, operating system, or another thread. As such, the data is "volatile," and the keyword instructs the compilers and runtime to handle it more exactly.

Using the `System.Threading.Interlocked` Class

Within a particular process, you have all the necessary tools for handling synchronization. However, synchronization with `System.Threading.Monitor` is a relatively expensive operation and there is an alternative solution, generally supported by the processor directly, that targets specific synchronization patterns.

Listing 15.10 sets `_Data` to a new value as long as the preceding value was `null`. As indicated by the method name, this pattern is the Compare/Exchange pattern. Instead of manually placing a lock around behaviorally equivalent compare and exchange code, the `Interlocked.CompareExchange()` method provides a built-in method for a synchronous operation that does the same check for a value (`null`) and swaps the first two parameters if the value is equal. Table 15.2 shows other synchronization methods supported by `Interlocked`.

LISTING 15.10: Synchronizing Using **System.Threading.Interlocked**

```csharp
class SynchronizationUsingInterlocked
{
    private static object _Data;

    // Initialize data if not yet assigned.
    static void Initialize(object newValue)
    {
        // If _Data is null then set it to newValue.
        Interlocked.CompareExchange(
            ref _Data, newValue, null);
    }

    // ...
}
```

TABLE 15.2: **Interlock's** Synchronization-Related Methods

Method Signature	Description
`public static T CompareExchange<T>( T location, T value, T comparand );`	Checks `location` for the value in `comparand`. If the values are equal, it sets `location` to `value` and returns the original data stored in `location`.
`public static T Exchange<T>( T location, T value );`	Assigns `location` with `value` and returns the previous value.
`public static int Decrement( ref int location );`	Decrements `location` by one. It is equivalent to the – operator, except `Decrement` is thread safe.
`public static int Increment( ref int location );`	Increments `location` by one. It is equivalent to the ++ operator, except `Increment()` is thread safe.
`public static int Add( ref int location, int value );`	Adds `value` to `location` and assigns `location` the result.
`public static long Read( ref long location );`	Returns a 64-bit value in a single atomic operation.

Most of these methods are overloaded with additional data type signatures, such as support for `long`. Table 15.2 provides the general signatures and descriptions. For example, the threading namespace does not include generic method signatures until C# 2.0, although earlier versions do include nongeneric equivalents.

Note that `Increment()` and `Decrement()` can be used in place of the synchronized `++` and `--` operators from Listing 15.9, and doing so will yield better performance. Also note that if a different thread accessed `location` using a noninterlocked method, then the two accesses would not be synchronized correctly.

Event Notification with Multiple Threads

One area where developers often overlook synchronization is when firing events. The unsafe thread code for publishing an event is similar to Listing 15.11.

LISTING 15.11: Firing an Event Notification

```
// Not thread safe
if(OnTemperatureChanged != null)
{
    // Call subscribers
    OnTemperatureChanged(
        this, new TemperatureEventArgs(value) );
}
```

This code is valid when it appears in an instance method that multiple threads do not access. However, when multiple threads may access it, the code is not atomic. It is possible that between the time when `OnTempera-tureChange` is checked for `null` and the event is actually fired, `OnTemperatureChange` could be set to `null`, thereby throwing a `Null-ReferenceException`. In other words, if multiple threads could possibly access a delegate simultaneously, it is necessary to synchronize the assignment and firing of the delegate.

Fortunately, the operators for adding and removing listeners are thread safe and static (operator overloading is done with static methods). To correct Listing 15.11 and make it thread safe, assign a copy, check the copy for `null`, and fire the copy (see Listing 15.12).

LISTING 15.12: Thread-Safe Event Notification

```
// ...
TemperatureChangedHandler localOnChange =
    OnTemperatureChanged;
if(localOnChanged != null)
{
    // Call subscribers
    localOnChanged(
      this, new TemperatureEventArgs(value) );
}
// ...
```

Given that a delegate is a reference type, it is perhaps surprising that assigning a local variable and then firing with the local variable is sufficient for making the null check thread safe. Since localOnChange points to the same location that OnTemperatureChange points to, one would think that any changes in OnTemperatureChange would be reflected in localOnChange as well.

However, this is not the case because any calls to OnTemperatureChange += <listener> will not add a new delegate to OnTemperatureChange, but rather, will assign it an entirely new multicast delegate without having any effect on the original multicast delegate to which localOnChange also points. This makes the code thread safe because only one thread will access the localOnChange instance, and OnTemperatureChange will be an entirely new instance if listeners are added or removed.

Synchronization Design Best Practices

Along with the complexities of multithreaded programming come several best practices for handling the complexities.

Avoiding Deadlock

With the introduction of synchronization comes the potential for deadlock. Deadlock occurs when two or more threads wait for each other to release a synchronization lock. For example, Thread 1 requests a lock on _Sync1, and then later requests a lock on _Sync2 before releasing the lock on _Sync1. At the same time, Thread 2 requests a lock on _Sync2, followed by a lock on _Sync1, before releasing the lock on _Sync2. This sets the stage for the deadlock. The deadlock actually occurs if both Thread 1 and Thread 2 successfully acquire their initial locks (_Sync1 and _Sync2, respectively) before obtaining their second locks.

Two conditions cause the deadlock: Two or more threads need to lock on the same two or more synchronization targets, and the locks are requested in different orders. To avoid deadlocks like this, developers should be careful when acquiring multiple locks to code each thread to obtain the locks in the same order.

For each synchronization mechanism discussed here, a single thread cannot cause a deadlock with itself. If a thread acquires a lock and then recursively calls back on the same method and re-requests the lock, the thread will not block because it already is the owner of the lock. (Although not discussed in this chapter, System.Threading.Semaphore is one example of a synchronization mechanism that could potentially deadlock with itself.)

When to Provide Synchronization

As already discussed, all static data should be thread safe. Therefore, synchronization needs to surround static data. Generally, this means that programmers should declare private static variables and then provide public methods for modifying the data. Such methods should internally handle the synchronization.

In contrast, instance state is not expected to include synchronization. Synchronization significantly decreases performance and increases the chance of a lock contention or deadlock. With the exception of classes that are explicitly designed for multithreaded access, programmers sharing objects across multiple threads are expected to handle their own synchronization of the data being shared.

Avoiding Unnecessary Locking

Although not at the cost of data integrity, programmers should avoid synchronization where possible. For example, if static method A() calls static method B() and both methods include taking locks, the redundant locks will decrease performance and perhaps decrease scalability. Carefully code APIs to minimize the number of locks required.

More Synchronization Types

In addition to `System.Threading.Monitor` and `System.Threading`
`.Interlocked`, several more synchronization techniques are available.

System.Threading.Mutex

`System.Threading.Mutex` is virtually identical in concept to the `System`
`.Threading.Monitor` class, except that the `lock` keyword does not use it,
and it synchronizes across multiple processes. Using the `Mutex` class, you can
synchronize access to a file or some other cross-process resource. Since `Mutex`
is a cross-process resource, .NET 2.0 added support to allow for setting the
access control via a `System.Security.AccessControl.MutexSecurity`
object. One use for the `Mutex` class is to limit an application so that it cannot
run multiple times simultaneously, as Listing 15.13 demonstrates.

LISTING 15.13: Creating a Single Instance Application

```csharp
using System;
using System.Threading;
using System.Reflection;

class Program
{
    public static void Main()
    {
        // Indicates whether this is the first
        // application instance
        bool firstApplicationInstance;

        // Obtain the mutex name from the full assembly name.
        string mutexName =
            Assembly.GetEntryAssembly().FullName;

        using( Mutex mutex = new Mutex(false, mutexName,
            out firstApplicationInstance) )
        {

            if(!firstApplicationInstance)
            {
                Console.WriteLine(
                    "This application is already running.");
            }
            else
            {
                Console.WriteLine("ENTER to shutdown");
                Console.ReadLine();
```

```
            }
         }
      }
   }
```

The results from running the first instance of the application appear in Output 15.9.

OUTPUT 15.9:

```
ENTER to shutdown
```

The results of the second instance of the application while the first instance is still running appear in Output 15.10.

OUTPUT 15.10:

```
This application is already running.
```

In this case, the application can run only once on the machine, even if it is launched by different users. To restrict the instances to once per user, prefix `Assembly.GetEntryAssembly().FullName` with `System.Windows .Forms.Application.UserAppDataPath.Replace("\\", "+")` instead. This requires a reference to the `System.Windows.Forms` assembly.

Reset Events: *ManualResetEvent* and *AutoResetEvent*

One way to control uncertainty about when particular instructions in a thread will execute relative to instructions in another thread is with reset events, of which there are two. In spite of the term *events*, reset events have nothing to do with C# delegates and events. Instead, reset events are a way to force code to wait for the execution of another thread until the other thread signals. These are especially useful for testing multi-threaded code because it is possible to wait for a particular state before verifying the results.

The reset event types are `System.Threading.AutoResetEvent` and `System.Threading.ManualResetEvent`. The key methods on the reset events are `Set()` and `WaitHandle()`. Calling the `WaitHandle()` method will cause a thread to block until a different thread calls Set(), or until the wait period times out. Listing 15.14 demonstrates how this works, and Output 15.11 shows the results.

LISTING 15.14: Waiting for **AutoResetEvent**

```
using System;
using System.Threading;

public class AutoResetEventSample
{
    static AutoResetEvent ResetEvent = new AutoResetEvent(false);

    public static void DoWork()
    {
        Console.WriteLine("DoWork() started....");
        Thread.Sleep(1000);
        Console.WriteLine("DoWork() ending....");
        // Signal to ResetEvent.WaitOne().
        ResetEvent.Set();
    }

    public static void Main()
    {
        Console.WriteLine("Application started....");
        Thread thread = new Thread(DoWork);
        Console.WriteLine("Starting thread....");
        thread.Start();
        // Block until ResetEvent.Set() is called.
        ResetEvent.WaitOne();
        Console.WriteLine("Application shutting down....");
    }
}
```

OUTPUT 15.11:

```
Application started....
Starting thread....
DoWork() started....
DoWork() ending....
Application shutting down....
```

Listing 15.14 begins by starting a new thread. Following thread.Start(), it calls ResetEvent.WaitOne(). This causes the thread executing Main() to suspend and wait for the AutoResetEvent called ResetEvent to be set. The thread running DoWork() continues, however. Inside DoWork() is a call to `ResetEvent.Set()`, and once this method has been called, the call to `ResetEvent.WaitOne()` back in `Main()` is signaled, meaning it is allowed to continue. As a result, `DoWork()` started and `DoWork()` ending appear before `Application shutting down....` in spite of the fact that `DoWork()` includes a call to `Thread.Sleep()` and `DoWork()` is running on a different thread.

Calling a reset event's `WaitOne()` method blocks the calling thread until another thread signals and allows the blocked thread to continue. Instead of blocking indefinitely, `WaitOne()` includes a parameter, either in milliseconds or as a `TimeSpan` object, for the maximum amount of time to block. When specifying a timeout period, the return from `WaitOne()` will be `false` if the timeout occurs before the reset event is signaled.

The only difference between `System.Threading.AutoResetEvent` and `System.Threading.ManualResetEvent` is the fact that `AutoReset-Event` will automatically switch to an unsignaled state after calling `Set()`. As a result, a second call to `WaitOne()` will automatically be blocked until another call to `Set()` occurs. Given this behavior, it is possible for two different threads to call `WaitOne()` simultaneously, and only one will be allowed to continue with each call to `Set()`. In contrast, `Manual-ResetEvent` will require a call to `Reset()` before it will block any additional threads.

The remainder of this chapter, and Chapter 16, use a call to an `AutoRe-setEvent`'s `Set()` method within the worker thread's implementation. In addition, `AutoResetEvent`'s `WaitOne()` method blocks on `Main()`'s thread until `Set()` has been called. In this way, it demonstrates that the worker thread executes before `Main()` exits.

Although not exactly the same, `System.Threading.Monitor` includes `Wait()` and `Pulse()` methods that provide similar functionality to reset events in some circumstances.

ThreadStaticAttribute

In some cases, using synchronization locks can lead to unacceptable performance and scalability restrictions. In other instances, providing synchronization around a particular data element may be too complex, especially when it is added after the original coding.

One alternate solution to synchronization is **thread local storage**. Thread local storage creates a new instance of a static field for every thread. This provides each thread with its own instance; as a result, there is no need for synchronization, as there is no point in synchronizing data that occurs within only a single thread's context.

Decorating a field with a `ThreadStaticAttribute`, as in Listing 15.15, designates it as one instance per thread.

LISTING 15.15: Using the **ThreadStaticAttribute**

```
class ThreadStaticData
{
    const int _Total = short.MaxValue;

    [ThreadStatic]
    static long _Count = 0;

    public static void Main()
    {
        Thread thread = new Thread(Decrement);
        thread.Start();

        // Increment
        for (int i = 0; i < _Total; i++)
        {
            _Count++;
        }

        thread.Join();
        Console.WriteLine("Count = {0}", _Count);
    }

    static void Decrement()
    {
        for (int i = 0; i < _Total; i++)
        {
            _Count--;
        }
    }
}
```

The results of Listing 15.15 appear in Output 15.12.

OUTPUT 15.12:

```
Count = 32767
```

As Output 15.12 demonstrates, the value of _Count for the thread executing Main() is never decremented by the thread executing Decrement(). Since _Count is decorated by the ThreadStaticAttribute, the thread running Main() and the thread running Decrement() are operating on entirely different instances of _Count.

There is one important caveat to the ThreadStaticAttribute. If the value of _Count is assigned during declaration—private int _Count = 42, for example—then only the thread static instance associated with the thread running the constructor will be initialized. In Listing 15.15, only the thread executing Main() will have a thread local storage variable of _Count that is initialized. The value of _Count that Decrement() decrements will never be initialized. Similarly, if a constructor initializes a thread local storage field, only the constructor calling thread will have an initialized thread local storage instance. For this reason, it is a good practice to initialize a thread local storage field within the method that is initially called by each thread.

The decision to use thread local storage requires some degree of cost-benefit analysis. For example, consider using thread local storage for a database connection. Depending on the database management system, database connections are relatively expensive, so creating a connection for every thread could be costly. Similarly, locking a connection so that all database calls are synchronized places a significantly lower ceiling on scalability. Each pattern has its costs and benefits, and the correct choice depends largely on the individual implementation.

Another reason to use ThreadStatic is to make commonly needed context information available to other methods without explicitly passing the data via parameters. If multiple methods in the call stack require user security information, for example, you can pass the data using thread local storage fields instead of as parameters. This keeps APIs cleaner while still making the information available to methods in a thread-safe manner.

Synchronizing a Method Using MethodImplAttribute

The last synchronization method to point out is the MethodImpl-Attribute. Used in conjunction with the MethodImplOptions.Synchronized method, this attribute marks a method as synchronized so that only one thread can execute the method at a time. In the current implementation, this causes the JIT to treat the method as though it was surrounded by `lock(this)`. Such an implementation means that, in fact, the method and all other methods on the same class, decorated with the same attribute and enum, are synchronized, not just each method relative to itself. In other words, given two or more methods on the same class decorated with the attribute, only one of them will be able to execute at a time and the one executing will block all calls by other threads to itself or to any other method in the class with the same decoration.

Timers

One area where threading issues relating to the user interface may arise unexpectedly is when using one of the timer classes. The trouble is that when timer notification callbacks fire, the thread on which they fire may not be the user interface thread, and therefore, it cannot safely access user interface controls and forms (see Chapter 16).

Several timer classes are available, including `System.Windows.Forms` `.Timer`, `System.Timers.Timer`, and `System.Threading.Timer`. In creating `System.Windows.Forms.Timer`, the development team designed it specifically for use within a rich client user interface. Programmers can drag it onto a form as a nonvisual control and control the behavior from within the Properties window. Most importantly, it will always safely fire an event from a thread that can interact with the user interface.

The other two timers are very similar. `System.Threading.Timer` is essentially a lighter-weight implementation of `System.Timers.Timer`. Specifically, `System.Threading.Timer` does not derive from `System.Component-Model.Component`, and therefore, it cannot be used as a component within a component container, something that implements `System.Component-Model.IContainer`. Another difference is that `System.Threading.Timer` enables the passing of state, an object parameter, from the call to start the timer and then into the call that fires the timer notification. The remaining differences are simply in the API usability with `System.Timers.Timer` supporting a synchronization object and having calls that are slightly more intuitive. Both `System.Timers.Timer` and `System.Threading.Timer` are designed for use in server-type processes, and neither should interact directly with the user interface. Furthermore, both timers use the system thread pool. Table 15.3 provides an overall comparison of the various timers.

TABLE 15.3: Overview of the Various Timer Characteristics

Feature Description	System.Timers.Timer	System.Threading.Timer	System.Windows.Forms.Timer
Support for adding and removing listeners after the timer is instantiated	Yes	No	Yes
Supports callbacks on the user interface thread	Yes	No	Yes
Calls back from threads obtained from the thread pool	Yes	Yes	No
Supports drag-and-drop in the Windows Forms Designer	Yes	No	Yes
Suitable for running in a multithreaded server environment	Yes	Yes	No

Continues

TABLE 15.3: Overview of the Various Timer Characteristics *(Continued)*

Feature Description	`System.Timers.Timer`	`System.Threading.Timer`	`System.Windows.Forms.Timer`
Includes support for passing arbitrary state from the timer initialization to the callback	No	Yes	No
Implements `IDisposable`	Yes	Yes	Yes
Supports on-off callbacks as well as periodic repeating callbacks	Yes	Yes	Yes
Accessible across application domain boundaries	Yes	Yes	Yes
Supports `IComponent`; hostable in an `IContainer`	Yes	No	Yes

Using `System.Windows.Forms.Timer` is a relatively obvious choice for user interface programming. The only caution is that a long-running operation on the user interface thread may delay the arrival of a timer's expiration. Choosing between the other two options is less obvious, and generally, the difference between the two is insignificant. If hosting within an `IContainer` is necessary, then `System.Timers.Timer` is the right choice. However, if no specific `System.Timers.Timer` feature is required, then choose `System.Threading.Timer` by default, simply because it is a slightly lighter-weight implementation.

Listing 15.16 and Listing 15.17 provide sample code for using `System.Timers.Timer` and `System.Threading.Timer`, respectively. Their code is very similar, including the fact that both support instantiation within a `using` statement because both support `IDispose`. The output for both listings is identical, as shown in Output 15.13.

LISTING 15.16: Using **System.Timers.Timer**

```
using System;
using System.Timers;
using System.Threading;
// Because Timer exists in both the System.Timers and
// System.Threading namespaces, you disambiguate "Timer"
// using an alias directive.
using Timer = System.Timers.Timer;

 class UsingSystemTimersTimer
 {
     private static int _Count=0;
     private static readonly AutoResetEvent _ResetEvent =
         new AutoResetEvent(false);
     private static int _AlarmThreadId;

     public static void Main()
     {
         using( Timer timer = new Timer() )
         {
             // Initialize Timer
             timer.AutoReset = true;
             timer.Interval = 1000;
             timer.Elapsed += new ElapsedEventHandler(Alarm);

             timer.Start();

             // Wait for Alarm to fire for the 10th time.
             _ResetEvent.WaitOne();
         }
```

```
        // Verify that the thread executing the alarm
        // Is different from the thread executing Main
        if(_AlarmThreadId ==
            Thread.CurrentThread.ManagedThreadId)
        {
            throw new ApplicationException(
                "Thread Ids are the same.");
        }

        if(_Count < 9)
        {
            throw new ApplicationException(" _Count < 9");
        };

        Console.WriteLine(
            "(Alarm Thread Id) {0} != {1} (Main Thread Id)",
            _AlarmThreadId,
            Thread.CurrentThread.ManagedThreadId);
        Console.WriteLine("Final Count = {0}", _Count);
    }

    static void Alarm(object sender, ElapsedEventArgs eventArgs)
    {
        _Count++;

        Console.WriteLine("{0}:- {1}",
            eventArgs.SignalTime.ToString("T"),
            _Count);

        if (_Count >= 9)
        {
            _AlarmThreadId =
                Thread.CurrentThread.ManagedThreadId;
            _ResetEvent.Set();
        }
    }
}
```

In Listing 15.16, you have using directives for both System.Threading and System.Timers. This makes the Timer type ambiguous. Therefore, use an alias to explicitly associate Timer with System.Timers.Timer.

One noteworthy characteristic of System.Threading.Timer is that it takes the callback delegate and interval within the constructor.

LISTING 15.17: Using System.Threading.Timer

```
using System;
using System.Threading;

class UsingSystemThreadingTimer
{
```

```csharp
private static int _Count=0;
private static readonly AutoResetEvent _ResetEvent =
    new AutoResetEvent(false);
private static int _AlarmThreadId;

public static void Main()
{
    // Timer(callback, state, dueTime, period)
    using( Timer timer = new Timer(Alarm, null, 0, 1000) )
    {
    // Wait for Alarm to fire for the 10th time.
    _ResetEvent.WaitOne();
    }

    // Verify that the thread executing the alarm
    // Is different from the thread executing Main
    if(_AlarmThreadId ==
        Thread.CurrentThread.ManagedThreadId)
    {
        throw new ApplicationException(
            "Thread Ids are the same.");
    }
    if(_Count < 9)
    {
        throw new ApplicationException(" _Count < 9");
    };

    Console.WriteLine(
        "(Alarm Thread Id) {0} != {1} (Main Thread Id)",
        _AlarmThreadId,
        Thread.CurrentThread.ManagedThreadId);
    Console.WriteLine("Final Count = {0}", _Count);
}

static void Alarm(object state)
{
    _Count++;

    Console.WriteLine("{0}:- {1}",
        DateTime.Now.ToString("T"),
        _Count);

    if (_Count >= 9)
    {
        _AlarmThreadId =
            Thread.CurrentThread.ManagedThreadId;
        _ResetEvent.Set();
    }
}
}
```

OUTPUT 15.13:

```
12:19:36 AM:- 1
12:19:37 AM:- 2
12:19:38 AM:- 3
12:19:39 AM:- 4
12:19:40 AM:- 5
12:19:41 AM:- 6
12:19:42 AM:- 7
12:19:43 AM:- 8
12:19:44 AM:- 9
(Alarm Thread Id) 4 != 1 (Main Thread Id)
Final Count = 9
```

You can change the interval or time due after instantiation on `System`
`.Threading.Timer` via the `Change()` method. However, you cannot
change the callback listeners after instantiation. Instead, you must create a
new instance.

SUMMARY

This chapter delved into the details surrounding the creation and manipulation of threads. In addition to introducing the framework-related classes
and the `lock` keyword, this chapter gave an overview of what makes multithreaded programming difficult. In summary, the difficulty concerns not
the APIs themselves, but rather, the uncertainty that multithreaded programming can introduce unless appropriate synchronization is in place.

The next chapter takes multithreaded programming in the framework a
little further by explaining how to place common multithreading scenarios
within a pattern so that you do not need to reinvent the design for solving
the scenarios.

◼ 16 ◼
Multithreading Patterns

C HAPTER 15 FOCUSED on managing threads and synchronizing the data that the threads share. As developers write more multithreaded code, a common set of scenarios and programming patterns for handling those scenarios emerges. The key scenarios relate to notifications of when a thread completes and notifications about the progress on the threads' status. In addition, there is some built-in C# functionality for calling methods asynchronously, regardless of whether their signatures match `ThreadStart`. Most importantly, going with built-in patterns like this significantly reduces the effort in programming to solve these types of scenarios from scratch.

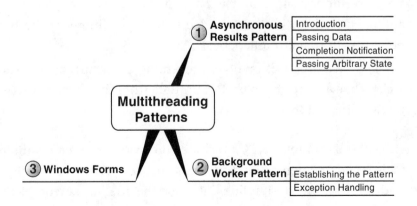

The two patterns specifically designed for these scenarios are the asynchronous results pattern and the background worker pattern, and this chapter investigates both. This chapter breaks down how to code these patterns into a step-by-step process, and it points out some important characteristics of Windows Forms programming.

Asynchronous Results Pattern

Multithreaded programming includes the following complexities.

1. *Monitoring the thread state for completion.* This includes determining when a thread has completed, preferably not by polling the thread's state or by blocking and waiting with a call to `Join()`.
2. *Passing data to and from the thread.* Calling arbitrary methods asynchronously is cumbersome because they do not necessarily support `ThreadState-` or `ParameterizedThreadStart`-compatible signatures.
3. *Thread pooling.* This avoids the significant cost of starting and tearing down threads. In addition, thread pooling avoids the creation of too many threads, such that the system spends more time switching threads than running them.
4. *Providing atomicity across operations and synchronizing data access.* Adding synchronization around groups of operations ensures that operations execute as a single unit and are appropriately interrupted by another thread. Locking is provided so that two different threads do not access the data simultaneously.
5. *Avoiding deadlocks.* This involves preventing the occurrence of deadlocks while attempting to protect the data from simultaneous access by two different threads.

To deal with this complexity, C# includes the **asynchronous results pattern**. This section demonstrates how to use the asynchronous results pattern and shows how it simplifies at least the first three complexities associated with multithreading.

Introducing the Asynchronous Results Pattern

With the asynchronous results pattern, you do not code using the `Thread` class explicitly. Instead, you use delegate instances. Consider the code in Listing 16.1.

LISTING 16.1: Asynchronous Results Pattern Example

```csharp
using System;
using System.Threading;

public class AsyncResultPatternIntroduction
{

  delegate void WorkerThreadHandler();

  public static AutoResetEvent ResetEvent =
    new AutoResetEvent(false);

  public static void Main()
  {
      Console.WriteLine("Application started....");

      WorkerThreadHandler workerMethod = null
      IAsyncResult asyncResult = null;

      try
      {
          workerMethod =
              new WorkerThreadHandler(DoWork);
          Console.WriteLine("Starting thread....");
          IAsyncResult asyncResult =
              workerMethod.BeginInvoke(null, null);

          // Display periods as progress bar.
          while(!asyncResult.AsyncWaitHandle.WaitOne(
              1000, false))
          {
              Console.Write('.');
          }
          Console.WriteLine();
          Console.WriteLine("Thread ending....");
      }
      finally
      {
          if (workerMethod != null && asyncResult != null)
          {
              workerMethod.EndInvoke(asyncResult);
          }
      }
      Console.WriteLine("Application shutting down....");
```

```
    }

    public static void DoWork()
    {
        // TODO:  Replace all the pseudocode below
        // with a real implementation of a long-
        // running operation
        Console.WriteLine("\nDoWork() started....");
        Thread.Sleep(1000);
        Console.WriteLine("\nDoWork() ending....");
    }
}
```

The results of Listing 16.1 appear in Output 16.1.

OUTPUT 16.1:

```
Application started....
Starting thread....
 .
DoWork() started....
...................
DoWork() ending....
Thread ending....
Application shutting down....
```

Main() begins by instantiating a delegate of type WorkerThreadHandler. As part of the instantiation, the DoWork() method is specified as the method to execute on a different thread. This line is similar to the instantiation of ThreadStart in Chapter 15, except you use your own delegate type, WorkerThreadHandler, rather than one built into the framework. As you shall see shortly, this allows you to pass custom parameters to the thread.

Next, the code calls BeginInvoke(). This method will start the DoWork() method on a thread from the thread pool and then return immediately. This allows you to run other code asynchronously with the DoWork() method. In this example, you print periods while waiting for the DoWork() method to complete.

You monitor the DoWork() method state through a call to IAsync-Result.AsyncWaitHandle.WaitOne() on asyncResult. Like AutoReset-Event.WaitOne(), IAsyncResult.AsyncWaitHandle.WaitOne() will return false if the timeout (1000 milliseconds) expires before the thread ends. As a result, the code prints periods to the screen each second during which the `DoWork()` method is executing. In this example, the mock work in `DoWork()` is to pause for one second.

Finally, the code calls `EndInvoke()`. It is important to pass to `EndInvoke()` the `IAsyncResult` reference returned when calling `BeginInvoke()`. `IAsyncResult` contains the data about the executing worker thread. If the thread identified by the `IAsyncResult` parameter is still executing, then `EndInvoke()` will block and wait for the `DoWork()` method to complete. `EndInvoke()` does not abort a thread, but blocks the thread until it is done. In this example, there is no blocking because you poll the thread's state in the `while` loop and call `EndInvoke()` only after the thread has completed.

Passing Data to and from an Alternate Thread

The introductory example in Listing 16.1 didn't pass any data to or receive any data back from the alternate thread. This is rather limiting. Passing data using fields is an option, but in addition to being cumbersome, such a solution requires the programmer of the called method to explicitly code for an asynchronous call, rather than just an arbitrary method that the caller wants to invoke asynchronously. In other words, the called method must explicitly access its required data from the member fields instead of having the data passed in via a parameter. Fortunately, the asynchronous results pattern handles this explicitly.

To begin, you need to change the delegate data type to match the signature of the method you are calling asynchronously. Consider, for example, a method called `GetFiles()` that returns an array of filenames that match a particular search pattern. Listing 16.2 shows such a method.

LISTING 16.2: Target Method Sample for an Asynchronous Invocation

```csharp
public static string[] GetFiles(
    string searchPattern, bool recurseSubdirectories)
{
    string[] results = null;

    // Search for files matching the pattern.
    StringCollection files = new StringCollection();
    string directory;
    directory = Path.GetDirectoryName(searchPattern);
    if ((directory == null) || (directory.Trim().Length == 0))
    {
```

```csharp
            directory = Directory.GetCurrentDirectory();
        }

        files.AddRange(GetFiles(searchPattern));

        if (recurseSubdirectories)
        {
            foreach (string subDirectory in
                Directory.GetDirectories(directory))
            {
                files.AddRange(GetFiles(
                    Path.Combine(
                        subDirectory,
                        Path.GetFileName(searchPattern)),
                    true));
            }
        }

        results = new string[files.Count];
        files.CopyTo(results, 0);

        return results;
    }

    public static string[] GetFiles(string searchPattern)
    {
        string[] fileNames;
        string directory;

        // Set directory , default to the current if the
        // is none specified in the searchPattern.
        directory = Path.GetDirectoryName(searchPattern);
        if ((directory == null) || (directory.Trim().Length == 0))
        {
            directory = Directory.GetCurrentDirectory();
        }

        fileNames = Directory.GetFiles(
            Path.GetFullPath(directory),
            Path.GetFileName(searchPattern));

        return fileNames;
    }
```

As input parameters, this method takes the search pattern and a `bool` indicating whether to search subdirectories. It returns an array of strings. Since the method could potentially take some time to execute, you decide (perhaps after implementing the method) to call it asynchronously.

In order to call GetFiles() asynchronously using the asynchronous results pattern, you need a delegate to match the method signature. Listing 16.3 declares such a delegate instead of relying on an existing delegate type.

LISTING 16.3: Asynchronous Results with Completed Notification

```
delegate string[] GetFilesHandler(
    string searchPattern, bool recurseSubdirectories);
```

Given the delegate, you can declare a delegate instance and call Begin-Invoke(). Notice that the signature for BeginInvoke() is different from the signature in the asynchronous results pattern in Listing 16.1. Now there are four parameters. The last two correspond to the callback and state parameters. These parameters were in the BeginInvoke() call of Listing 16.1 and will be investigated shortly. There are two new parameters at the beginning, however, and this is not because BeginInvoke() is overloaded. The new parameters are searchPattern and recurseSubdirectories, which correspond to the GetFilesHandler delegate. This enables a call to GetFiles() using the asynchronous results pattern while passing in the data that GetFiles() needs (see Listing 16.4).

LISTING 16.4: Passing Data Back and Forth Using the Asynchronous Results Pattern

```
using System;
using System.IO;
using System.Threading;
using System.IO;

public class FindFiles
{
    private static void DisplayHelp()
    {
        Console.WriteLine(
            "FindFiles.exe <search pattern> [/S]\n" +
            "\n" +
            "search pattern     " +
            "The directory and pattern to search\n" +
            "                   e.g. C:\\Windows\\*.dll\n" +
            "/s                 Search subdirectories");
    }


    delegate string[] GetFilesHandler(
        string searchPattern, bool recurseSubdirectories);
```

```csharp
public static void Main(string[] args)
{
    string[] files;
    string searchPattern;
    bool recurseSubdirectories = false;
    IAsyncResult result = null;

    // Assign searchPattern & recurseSubdirectories
    switch (args.Length)
    {
        case 2:
            if (args[1].Trim().ToUpper() == "/S")
            {
                recurseSubdirectories = true;
            }
            goto case 1;
        case 1:
            searchPattern = args[0];
            // Validate search pattern
            // ...
            break;
        default:
            DisplayHelp();
            return;
    }

    GetFilesHandler asyncGetFilesHandler= GetFiles;

    Console.WriteLine("Searching: {0}",  searchPattern );
    if (recurseSubdirectories)
    {
        Console.WriteLine("\trecursive...");
    }
    result = asyncGetFilesHandler.BeginInvoke(
        searchPattern, recurseSubdirectories,
        null, null);

    // Display periods every second to indicate
    // the program is running and not frozen.
    while(!result.AsyncWaitHandle.WaitOne(1000, false))
    {
        Console.Write('.');
    }
    Console.WriteLine("");

    // Retrieve the results
    files = (string[])asyncGetFilesHandler.EndInvoke(result);

    // Display the results
    foreach (string file in files)
```

```
    {
        // Display only the filename, not the directory
        Console.WriteLine(Path.GetFileName(file));
    }
}

public static string[] GetFiles(
    string searchPattern, bool recurseSubdirectories)
{
    string[] results = null;

    // ...

    return results;
}
}
```

The results of Listing 16.4 appear in Output 16.2.

```
Searching: C:\Samples\*.cs
    recursive...

AsyncResultPatternIntroduction.cs
FindFilesWithoutNotificationOrState.cs
FindFilesWithNotification.cs
FindFiles.cs
AutoResetEventSample.cs
RunningASeparateThread.cs
```

As demonstrated in Listing 16.4, you also need to retrieve the data returned from `GetFiles()`. The return from `GetFiles()` is retrieved in the call to `EndInvoke()`. Just as the `BeginInvoke()` method signature was generated by the compiler to match all input parameters on the delegate, the `EndInvoke()` signature matches all the output parameters. The return from `getFilesMethod.EndInvoke()`, therefore, is a `string[]`, matching the return of `GetFiles()`. In addition to the return, any parameters marked as `ref` or `out` would be part of the `EndInvoke()` signature as well.

Consider a delegate type that includes `out` and `ref` parameters, as shown in Figure 16.1.

An `in` parameter, such as `data`, only appears in the `BeginInvoke()` call because only the caller needs to pass such parameters. Similarly, an `out` parameter, `changeDescription`, only appears in the `EndInvoke()`

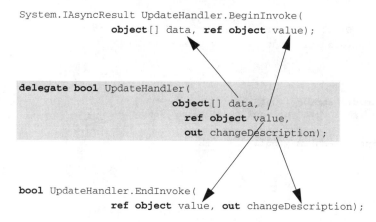

```
System.IAsyncResult UpdateHandler.BeginInvoke(
                object[] data, ref object value);
```

```
delegate bool UpdateHandler(
                     object[] data,
                     ref object value,
                     out changeDescription);
```

```
bool UpdateHandler.EndInvoke(
                ref object value, out changeDescription);
```

FIGURE 16.1: Delegate Parameter Distribution to **BeginInvoke()** and **EndInvoke()**

signature. Notice, however, that the `ref` parameter (`value`) appears in both `BeginInvoke()` and `EndInvoke()`, since a `ref` parameter is passed into both the function and a parameter via which data will be returned.

In summary, all delegates created by the C# compiler include the `BeginInvoke()` and `EndInvoke()` methods, and these are generated based on the delegate parameters.

Receiving Notification of Thread Completion

Listing 16.1 and Listing 16.4 poll to determine whether the `DoWork()` or `GetFiles()` method is running. Since polling is generally not very efficient or convenient, a notification mechanism that fires an event once the thread has completed is preferable. This is what the `AsyncCallback` delegate type is for, and an instance of this delegate is passed as the second-to-last parameter of `BeginInvoke()`. Given an `AsyncCallback` instance, the async pattern will invoke the callback delegate once the method has completed. Listing 16.5 provides an example, and Output 16.3 shows the results.

LISTING 16.5: Asynchronous Results with Completed Notification

```
using System;
using System.IO;
using System.Runtime.Remoting.Messaging;
using System.Threading;
using System.IO;

public class FindFilesWithNotifications
```

```
{
    // DisplayHelp() method
    // ...

    delegate string[] GetFilesHandler(
        string searchPattern, bool recurseSubdirectories);

    public static void Main(string[] args)
    {
        string searchPattern;
        bool recurseSubdirectories = false;
        IAsyncResult result = null;

        // Assign searchPattern & recurseSubdirectories
        // ...

        GetFilesHandler asyncGetFilesHandler = GetFiles;

        Console.WriteLine("Searching: {0}", args[0]);
        if (recurseSubdirectories)
        {
            Console.WriteLine("\trecursive...");
        }
        Console.WriteLine("Push ENTER to cancel/exit...");

        result = asyncGetFilesHandler.BeginInvoke(
            args[0], recurseSubdirectories,
            SearchCompleted, null);

        Console.ReadLine();

    }


    public static string[] GetFiles(
        string searchPattern, bool recurseSubdirectories)
    {
        string[] files = null;

        // Search for files matching the pattern.
        // See Listing 16.2.
        // ...

        return files;
    }

    public static void SearchCompleted(IAsyncResult result)
    {
        AsyncResult asyncResult = (AsyncResult)result;
        GetFilesHandler handler =
            (GetFilesHandler)asyncResult.AsyncDelegate;
        string[] files = handler.EndInvoke(result);
```

```
        foreach (string file in files)
        {
            Console.WriteLine(Path.GetFileName(file));
        }
    }
}
```

OUTPUT 16.3:

```
Searching: C:\Samples\*.cs
        recursive...
Push ENTER to cancel/exit...
AsyncResultPatternIntroduction.cs
FindFilesWithoutNotificationOrState.cs
FindFilesWithNotification.cs
FindFiles.cs
AutoResetEventSample.cs
RunningASeparateThread.cs
```

Callback notification when the worker thread completes provides a key benefit of using the asynchronous results pattern over manual thread manipulation. For example, it allows developers to display a widget to indicate that a task has completed.

As already demonstrated, `EndInvoke()` can be called from within `Main()` using the delegate instance and the `IAsyncResult` reference returned from `BeginInvoke()`. However, `EndInvoke()` will block until the asynchronous call completes. As a result, it is preferable to call `EndInvoke()` from within the callback. To accomplish this, the callback function casts its `IAsyncResult` parameter, but the cast is unintuitive. The data type is `AsyncResult`, but the namespace is the unintuitive `System.Runtime.Remoting.Messaging`. `SearchCompleted()` demonstrates the code for calling `EndInvoke()` from within the thread completion callback. Listing 16.6 shows the fully qualified call.

LISTING 16.6: Calling **EndInvoke()** from within Asynchronous Callback

```
    ...
    public static void SearchCompleted(IAsyncResult result)
    {
        System.Runtime.Remoting.Messaging.AsyncResult asyncResult
            =(System.Runtime.Remoting.Messaging.AsyncResult)result;
        GetFilesHandler handler =
            (GetFilesHandler)asyncResult.AsyncDelegate;
        string[] files = handler.EndInvoke(result);
        ...
    }
```

Passing Arbitrary State

The last parameter in the `BeginInvoke()` call is of type `object`, and it provides a mechanism for passing arbitrary data to the callback method (`SearchCompleted()`). Consider a situation in which multiple threads were started one after the other, and in each case the callback was to the same `AsyncCallback` delegate instance. The problem is that from within the async callback delegate you don't correlate which completed call to `GetFiles()` corresponds to which call that initiated the `GetFiles()` method. For example, you cannot print out which search results correspond to which `searchPattern`.

Fortunately, this is the purpose of the last parameter in `Begin-Invoke()`. Listing 16.7 starts the `GetFiles()` method for each search pattern passed in the command line. In each call, you pass the search pattern (`arg`) twice to `asyncGetFilesHandler.BeginInvoke()`: once as a parameter to the `GetFiles()` method that is to run asynchronously, and once as the last parameter to be accessed from inside `SearchCompleted()`.

LISTING 16.7: Asynchronous Results with Completed Notification

```csharp
using System;
using System.IO;
using System.Runtime.Remoting.Messaging;
using System.IO;

public class FindFiles
{
  delegate string[] GetFilesHandler(
      string searchPattern, bool recurseSubdirectories);

  public static void Main(string[] args)
  {
      bool recurseSubdirectories = true;
      IAsyncResult[] result = new IAsyncResult[args.Length];
      int count = 0;

      foreach(string arg in args)
      {
          if (arg.Trim().ToUpper() == "/S")
          {
              recurseSubdirectories = true;
              break;
          }
      }
```

```csharp
        GetFilesHandler asyncGetFilesHandler = GetFiles;

        Console.WriteLine("Searching: {0}",
            string.Join(", ", args));
        if (recurseSubdirectories)
        {
            Console.WriteLine("\trecursive...");
        }
        Console.WriteLine("Push ENTER to cancel/exit...");

        foreach (string arg in args)
        {
            if (arg.Trim().ToUpper() != "/S")
            {
                result[count] = asyncGetFilesHandler.BeginInvoke(
                    arg, recurseSubdirectories,
                    SearchCompleted, arg );
            }
            count++;
        }
        Console.ReadLine();
    }

    public static string[] GetFiles(
      string searchPattern, bool recurseSubdirectories)
    {
        string[] files;

        // Search for files matching the pattern.
        // See Listing 16.2.
        // ...

        return files;
    }

    public static void SearchCompleted(IAsyncResult result)
    {
        string searchPattern = (string)result.AsyncState;
        Console.WriteLine("{0}:", searchPattern);
        AsyncResult asyncResult = (AsyncResult)result;
        GetFilesHandler handler =
            (GetFilesHandler)asyncResult.AsyncDelegate;
        string[] files = handler.EndInvoke(result);
        foreach (string file in files)
        {
            Console.WriteLine("\t"+ Path.GetFileName(file));
        }
    }
}
```

The results of Listing 16.7 appear in Output 16.4.

OUTPUT 16.4:

```
Searching: C:\Samples\*.cs, C:\Samples\*.exe
    recursive...
Push ENTER to cancel/exit...
C:\Samples\*.cs
 AsyncResultPatternIntroduction.cs
 FindFilesWithoutNotificationOrState.cs
 FindFilesWithNotification.cs
 FindFiles.cs
 AutoResetEventSample.cs
C:\Samples\*.exe
 FindFiles.exe
```

Since the listing passes `arg` (the search pattern) in the call to `BeginInvoke()`, it can retrieve the search pattern from the `IAsyncResult` parameter of `SearchCompleted()`. To do this, it accesses the `IAsyncResult.Async-State` property. Because it is of type `object`, the `string` data type passed during `BeginInvoke()` needs to be downcast to `string`. In this way, it can display the search pattern above the list of files that meet the search pattern.

Asynchronous Results Conclusions

One of the key features that the asynchronous results pattern offers is that the caller determines whether to call a method asynchronously. The called object may choose to provide asynchronous methods explicitly, perhaps even using the asynchronous results pattern internally. However, this is not a requirement for the caller to make an asynchronous call.

Called methods may choose to provide asynchronous APIs explicitly when the called class can implement the asynchronous functionality more efficiently than the caller can, or when it is determined that asynchronous method calls are likely, such as with methods that are relatively slow. If it is determined that a method should explicitly provide an asynchronous calling pattern, it is a good practice for the API to follow the asynchronous results design pattern. An explicit implementation, therefore, should include methods that correspond to `BeginInvoke()`, along with events that callers can subscribe to in order to be notified when a thread completes.

For example, in .NET 2.0, the `System.Net.WebClient` class includes asynchronous method calls for downloading files. To begin the download, it includes the `DownloadFileAsync()` method. Additionally, the caller can register for notification when the download is complete using the `DownloadFileCompleted` event.

The .NET 2.0 implementation of `System.Net.WebClient` also includes a `DownloadProgressChanged` event for publishing when a download operation successfully transfers some of its data, as well as a `CancelAsync()` method to discontinue the download. These are not explicitly part of the asynchronous results pattern, and therefore, they are not available unless provided by the called class explicitly. These methods are another reason why programmers may explicitly implement asynchronous APIs, instead of just relying on the caller to use the asynchronous results pattern. To help with such methods, .NET 2.0 includes the `System.ComponentModel.BackgroundWorker` class.

Although not supplied by `System.Net.WebClient`, a method corresponding to `EndInvoke()` is also a nice addition for explicitly implemented asynchronous calls.

The asynchronous results pattern relies on the built-in thread pool that provides support for reusing threads rather than always creating new ones. The pool has a number of threads, dependent on the number of processors, and the thread pool will wait for a free thread before servicing the request. If a request for a new thread is needed but the creation of a new thread would undermine the value of multithreading (because the cost of an additional thread would outweigh its benefit), the thread pool won't allocate a thread until another thread is released back to the thread pool.

Background Worker Pattern

Frequently with multithreaded operations, you not only want to be notified when the thread completes, but you also want the method to provide an update on the status of the operation. Often, users want to be able to cancel long-running tasks. The .NET Framework 2.0 includes a `BackgroundWorker` class for programming this type of pattern.

Listing 16.8 is an example of this pattern. It calculates pi to the number of digits specified.

LISTING 16.8: Using the Background Worker Pattern

```csharp
using System;
using System.Threading;
using System.ComponentModel;
using System.Text;

public class PiCalculator
{
    public static BackgroundWorker calculationWorker =
        new BackgroundWorker();
    public static AutoResetEvent resetEvent =
        new AutoResetEvent(false);

    public static void Main()
    {
        int digitCount;

        Console.Write(
            "Enter the number of digits to calculate:");
        if (int.TryParse(Console.ReadLine(), out digitCount))
        {
            Console.WriteLine("ENTER to cancel");
            // C# 2.0 Syntax for registering delegates
            calculationWorker.DoWork += CalculatePi;
            // Register the ProgressChanged callback
            calculationWorker.ProgressChanged +=
                UpdateDisplayWithMoreDigits;
            calculationWorker.WorkerReportsProgress = true;
            // Register a callback for when the
            // calculation completes
            calculationWorker.RunWorkerCompleted +=
                new RunWorkerCompletedEventHandler(Complete);
            calculationWorker.WorkerSupportsCancellation = true;

            // Begin calculating pi for up to digitCount digits
            calculationWorker.RunWorkerAsync(digitCount);

            Console.ReadLine();
            // If cancel is called after the calculation
            // has completed it doesn't matter.
            calculationWorker.CancelAsync();
            // Wait for Complete() to run.
            resetEvent.WaitOne();
        }
        else
        {
            Console.WriteLine(
                "The value entered is an invalid integer.");
        }
    }


    private static void CalculatePi(
```

```csharp
    object sender, DoWorkEventArgs eventArgs)
{
    int digits = (int)eventArgs.Argument;

    StringBuilder pi = new StringBuilder("3.", digits + 2);
    calculationWorker.ReportProgress(0, pi.ToString());

    // Calculate rest of pi, if required
    if (digits > 0)
    {
        for (int i = 0; i < digits; i += 9)
        {

            // Calculate next i decimal places
            int nextDigit = PiDigitCalculator.StartingAt(
                i + 1);
            int digitCount = Math.Min(digits - i, 9);
            string ds = string.Format("{0:D9}", nextDigit);
            pi.Append(ds.Substring(0, digitCount));

            // Show current progress
            calculationWorker.ReportProgress(
                0, ds.Substring(0, digitCount));

            // Check for cancellation
            if (calculationWorker.CancellationPending)
            {
                // Need to set Cancel if you need to
                // distinguish how a worker thread completed
                // i.e., by checking
                // RunWorkerCompletedEventArgs.Cancelled
                eventArgs.Cancel = true;
                break;
            }
        }
    }

    eventArgs.Result = pi.ToString();
}

private static void UpdateDisplayWithMoreDigits(
    object sender, ProgressChangedEventArgs eventArgs)
{
    string digits = (string)eventArgs.UserState;

    Console.Write(digits);
}


static void Complete(
    object sender, RunWorkerCompletedEventArgs eventArgs)
```

```
    {
        // ...
    }
}
```

```
public class PiDigitCalculator
{
    // ...
}
```

Establishing the Pattern

The process of hooking up the background worker pattern is as follows.

1. Register the long-running method with the `Background-Worker.DoWork` event. In this example, the long-running task is the call to `CalculatePi()`.

2. To receive progress or status notifications, hook up a listener to `Back-groundWorker.ProgressChanged` and set `Background-Worker.WorkerReportsProgress` to true. In Listing 16.8, the `UpdateDisplayWithMoreDigits()` method takes care of updating the display as more digits become available.

3. Register a method (`Complete()`) with the `BackgroundWorker.Run-WorkerCompleted` event.

4. Assign the `WorkerSupportsCancellation` property to support cancellation. Once this property is assigned the value `true`, a call to `BackgroundWorker.CancelAsync` will set the `DoWorkEvent-Args.CancellationPending` flag.

5. Within the `DoWork`-provided method (`CalculatePi()`), check the `DoWorkEventArgs.CancellationPending` property and exit the method when it is `true`.

6. Once everything is set up, you can start the work by calling `Back-groundWorker.RunWorkerAsync()` and providing a state parameter that is passed to the specified `DoWork()` method.

When it is broken down into steps, the background worker pattern is relatively easy to follow and provides the advantage over the asynchronous results pattern of a mechanism for cancellation and progress notification. The drawback is that you cannot use it arbitrarily on any method. Instead, the `DoWork()` method has to conform to a `System.ComponentModel` `.DoWorkEventHandler` delegate, which takes arguments of type `object` and `DoWorkEventArgs`. If this isn't the case, then a wrapper function is required. The cancellation- and progress-related methods also require specific signatures, but these are in control of the programmer setting up the background worker pattern.

Exception Handling

If an unhandled exception occurs while the background worker thread is executing, then the `RunWorkerCompletedEventArgs` parameter of the `RunWorkerCompleted` delegate (`Completed`'s `eventArgs`) will have an `Error` property set with the exception. As a result, checking the `Error` property within the `RunWorkerCompleted` callback in Listing 16.9 provides a means of handling the exception.

LISTING 16.9: Handling Unhandled Exceptions from the Worker Thread

```
// ...
static void Complete(
    object sender, RunWorkerCompletedEventArgs eventArgs)
{
    Console.WriteLine();
    if (eventArgs.Cancelled)
    {
        Console.WriteLine("Cancelled");
    }
    else if (eventArgs.Error != null)
    {
        // IMPORTANT: check error to retrieve any exceptions.
        Console.WriteLine(
            "ERROR: {0}", eventArgs.Error.Message);
    }
    else
    {
        Console.WriteLine("Finished");
    }
    resetEvent.Set();
}
// ...
```

It is important that the code check `eventArgs.Error` inside the `RunWorkerCompleted` callback. Otherwise, the exception will go undetected; it won't even be reported to `AppDomain`.

Windows Forms

One more important threading concept relates to user interface development using the System.Windows.Forms namespace. The Microsoft Windows suite of operating systems uses a single-threaded, message-processing-based user interface. This means that only one thread at a time should access the user interface, and any alternate thread interaction should be marshaled via the Windows message pump. The process involves calling a component's InvokeRequired property to determine if marshaling is necessary. Internally, Invoke() will check InvokeRequired anyway, but it can be more efficient to do so beforehand explicitly. Listing 16.10 demonstrates this pattern.

LISTING 16.10: Accessing the User Interface via **Invoke()**

```
using System;
using System.Drawing;
using System.Threading;
using System.Windows.Forms;

class Program : Form
{
    private System.Windows.Forms.ProgressBar _ProgressBar;

    [STAThread]
    static void Main()
    {
        Application.Run(new Program());
    }

    public Program()
    {
        InitializeComponent();
        ThreadStart threadStart = Increment;
        threadStart.BeginInvoke(null, null);
    }

    void UpdateProgressBar()
    {
        if (_ProgressBar.InvokeRequired)
        {
            MethodInvoker updateProgressBar = UpdateProgressBar;
            _ProgressBar.Invoke(updateProgressBar);
        }
        else
        {
            _ProgressBar.Increment(1);
```

```
        }
    }

    private void Increment()
    {
        for (int i = 0; i < 100; i++)
        {
            UpdateProgressBar();
            Thread.Sleep(100);
        }

        if (InvokeRequired)
        {
            // Close cannot be called directly from
            // a non-UI thread.
            Invoke(new MethodInvoker(Close));
        }
        else
        {
            Close();
        }
    }

    private void InitializeComponent()
    {
        _ProgressBar = new ProgressBar();
        SuspendLayout();

        _ProgressBar.Location = new Point(13, 17);
        _ProgressBar.Size = new Size(267, 19);

        ClientSize = new Size(292, 53);
        Controls.Add(this._ProgressBar);
        Text = "Multithreading in Windows Forms";
        ResumeLayout(false);
    }
}
```

This program displays a window that contains a progress bar that automatically starts incrementing. Once the progress bar reaches 100 percent, the dialog box closes.

Notice from Listing 16.10 that you have to check `InvokeRequired` twice, and then the marshal calls across to the user interface thread if it returns `true`. In both cases, the marshaling involves instantiating a `MethodInvoker` delegate that is then passed to `Invoke()`. Since marshaling across to another thread could be relatively slow, an asynchronous invocation of the call is also available via `BeginInvoke()` and `EndInvoke()`.

`Invoke()`, `BeginInvoke()`, `EndInvoke()`, and `InvokeRequired` comprise the members of the `System.ComponentModel.ISynchronizeInvoke` interface which is implemented by `System.Windows.Forms.Control`, from which Windows Forms controls derive.

■ ADVANCED TOPIC

Controlling the COM Threading Model with the `STAThreadAttribute`

With COM, four different apartment-threading models determine the threading rules relating to calls between COM objects. Fortunately, these rules—and the complexity that accompanied them—have disappeared from .NET as long as the program invokes no COM components. The general approach to handling COM Interop is to place all .NET components within the main, single-threaded apartment by decorating a process's `Main` method with the `System.STAThreadAttribute`. In so doing, it is not necessary to cross apartment boundaries to invoke the majority of COM components. Furthermore, apartment initialization does not occur, unless a COM Interop call is made.

COM Interop is not necessarily an explicit action by the developer. Microsoft implemented many of the components within the .NET Framework by creating a runtime callable wrapper (RCW) rather than rewriting all the COM functionality within managed code. As a result, COM calls are often made unknowingly. To ensure that these calls are always made from a single-threaded apartment, it is generally a good practice to decorate the main method of all Windows Forms executables with the `System.STAThreadAttribute`.

SUMMARY

This chapter used a step-by-step approach to setting up both the asynchronous results pattern and the background worker pattern. The asynchronous results pattern provides support for calling any method asynchronously, even a method written by a third party. It includes a notification mechanism about method execution completion via a callback on a delegate passed when setting up the pattern. One drawback to the asynchronous results pattern is that there is no inherent mechanism for posting the status of the asynchronous method. However, the .NET Framework 2.0 provides this functionality in a second multithreading pattern called the background worker pattern. The key about this pattern is that it includes support for notification of status (without polling), completion, and errors. To support this, however, the pattern requires special code hooks within the asynchronously invoked method. This prevents developers from using it on methods for which they have no source code, or if they are unwilling to code special hooks. Calling long-running methods provided by third parties, for example, prevents the support for embedding the callback hooks within the methods.

The next chapter investigates another fairly complex .NET technology: that of marshaling calls out of .NET and into managed code using P/Invoke. In addition, it introduces a concept known as unsafe code, which is used to access memory pointers directly, as in C++.

17

Platform Interoperability and Unsafe Code

C# HAS GREAT CAPABILITIES, but sometimes it still isn't sufficient and you need to escape out of all the safety it provides and step back into the world of memory addresses and pointers. C# supports this in three ways. The first way is to go through Platform Invoke (P/Invoke) and calls into APIs exposed by unmanaged DLLs. The second is through **unsafe code**, which enables access to memory pointers and addresses. Frequently, code uses these features in combination. The third way, which is not covered in this text, is through COM interoperability.

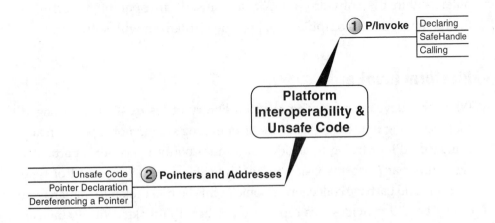

This chapter culminates with a small program that determines whether the computer is a virtual computer. The code requires that you do the following:

1. Call into an operating system DLL and request allocation of a portion of memory for executing instructions
2. Write some assembler instructions into the allocated area
3. Inject an address location into the assembler instructions
4. Execute the assembler code

Aside from the P/Invoke and unsafe constructs covered here, the final listing demonstrates the full power of C# and the fact that the capabilities of unmanaged code are still accessible from C# and managed code.

■ **BEGINNER TOPIC**

What Is a Virtual Computer?

A **virtual computer** (or virtual machine), also called a **guest computer**, is virtualized or emulated through software running on the host operating system and interacting with the host computer's hardware. For example, virtual computer software (such as VMWare Workstation and Microsoft Virtual PC) can be installed on a computer running a recent version of Windows. Once the software is installed, users can configure a guest computer within the software, boot it, and install an operating system as though it was a real computer, not just one virtualized with software.

Platform Invoke

Whether a developer is trying to call a library of his existing unmanaged code, accessing unmanaged code in the operating system not exposed in any managed API, or trying to achieve maximum performance for a particular algorithm that performs faster by avoiding the runtime overhead of type checking and garbage collection, at some point she must call into unmanaged code. The CLI provides this capability through P/Invoke. With P/Invoke, you can make API calls into exported functions of unmanaged DLLs.

All of the APIs invoked in this section are Windows APIs. Although the same APIs are not available on other platforms, developers can still use P/Invoke for APIs native to their platform, or for calls into their own DLLs. The guidelines and syntax are the same.

Declaring External Functions

Once the target function is identified, the next step of P/Invoke is to declare the function with managed code. Just like all regular methods that belong to a class, you need to declare the targeted API within the context of a class, but by using the `extern` modifier. Listing 17.1 demonstrates how to do this.

LISTING 17.1: Declaring an External Method

```
using System;
using System.Runtime.InteropServices;
class VirtualMemoryManager
{
  [DllImport("kernel32.dll", EntryPoint="GetCurrentProcess")]
  internal static extern IntPtr GetCurrentProcessHandle();
}
```

In this case, the class is `VirtualMemoryManager`, because it will contain functions associated with managing memory. (This particular function is available directly off the `System.Diagnostics.Processor` class, so there is no need to declare it in real code.)

`extern` methods are always static and don't include any implementation. Instead, the `DllImport` attribute, which accompanies the method declaration, points to the implementation. At a minimum, the attribute needs the name of the DLL that defines the function. The runtime determines the function name from the method name. However, it is possible to override this default using the `EntryPoint` named parameter to provide the function name. (The .NET platform will automatically attempt calls to the Unicode [...W] or ASCII [...A] API version.)

It this case, the external function, `GetCurrentProcess()`, retrieves a pseudohandle for the current process which you will use in the call for virtual memory allocation. Here's the unmanaged declaration:

```
HANDLE GetCurrentProcess();
```

Parameter Data Types

Assuming the developer has identified the targeted DLL and exported function, the most difficult step is identifying or creating the managed data types that correspond to the unmanaged types in the external function.[1] Listing 17.2 shows a more difficult API.

LISTING 17.2: The **VirtualAllocEx()** API

```
LPVOID VirtualAllocEx(
    HANDLE hProcess,          // The handle to a process. The
                              // function allocates memory within
                              // the virtual address space of this
                              // process.
    LPVOID lpAddress,         // The pointer that specifies a
                              // desired starting address for the
                              // region of pages that you want to
                              // allocate. If lpAddress is NULL,
                              // the function determines where to
                              // allocate the region.
    SIZE_T dwSize,            // The size of the region of memory to
                              // allocate, in bytes. If lpAddress
                              // is NULL, the function rounds dwSize
                              // up to the next page boundary.
    DWORD flAllocationType,   // The type of memory allocation.
    DWORD flProtect);         // The type of memory allocation.
```

VirtualAllocEx() allocates virtual memory that the operating system specifically designates for execution or data. To call it, you also need corresponding definitions in managed code for each data type; although common in Win32 programming, HANDLE, LPVOID, SIZE_T, and DWORD are undefined in the CLI managed code. The declaration in C# for Virtual-AllocEx(), therefore, is shown in Listing 17.3.

LISTING 17.3: Declaring the **VirtualAllocEx()** API in C#

```
using System;
using System.Runtime.InteropServices;
class VirtualMemoryManager
{
    [DllImport("kernel32.dll")]
    internal static extern IntPtr GetCurrentProcess();
```

---

1. One particularly helpful resource for declaring Win32 APIs is www.pinvoke.net. This provides a great starting point for many APIs, helping to avoid some of the subtle problems that can arise when coding an external API call from scratch.

```
[DllImport("kernel32.dll", SetLastError = true)]
private static extern IntPtr VirtualAllocEx(
    IntPtr hProcess,
    IntPtr lpAddress,
    IntPtr dwSize,
    AllocationType flAllocationType,
    uint flProtect);
}
```

One distinct characteristic of managed code is the fact that primitive data types such as `int` do not change size based on the processor. Whether 16, 32, or 64 bits, `int` is always 32 bits. In unmanaged code, however, memory pointers will vary depending on the processor. Therefore, instead of mapping types such as `HANDLE` and `LPVOID` simply to `int`s, you need to map to `System.IntPtr`, whose size will vary depending on the processor memory layout. This example also uses an `AllocationType` enum, which I discuss in the section Simplifying API Calls with Wrappers, later in this chapter.

Using `ref` Rather Than Pointers

Frequently, unmanaged code uses pointers for pass-by-reference parameters. In these cases, P/Invoke doesn't require that you map the data type to a pointer in managed code. Instead, you map the corresponding parameters to `ref` (or `out`), depending on whether the parameter is in-out or just out. In Listing 17.4, `lpflOldProtect`, whose data type is `PDWORD`, is an example that returns the "pointer to a variable that receives the previous access protection of the first page in the specified region of pages."

LISTING 17.4: Using `ref` and `out` Rather Than Pointers

```
class VirtualMemoryManager
{
    // ...
    [DllImport("kernel32.dll", SetLastError = true)]
    static extern bool VirtualProtectEx(
        IntPtr hProcess, IntPtr lpAddress,
        IntPtr dwSize, uint flNewProtect,
        ref uint lpflOldProtect);
}
```

In spite of the fact that `lpflOldProtect` is documented as `[out]`, the description goes on to mention that the parameter must point to a valid variable and not NULL. The inconsistency is confusing, but common. The guideline is to use ref rather than out for P/Invoke type parameters since the callee can always ignore the data passed with ref, but the converse will not necessarily succeed.

The other parameters are virtually the same as VirtualAllocEx(), except that the lpAddress is the address returned from Virtual-AllocEx(). In addition, flNewProtect specifies the exact type of memory protection: page execute, page read-only, and so on.

Using StructLayoutAttribute for Sequential Layout

Some APIs involve types that have no corresponding managed type. To call these requires redeclaration of the type in managed code. You declare the unmanaged COLOREF struct, for example, in managed code (see Listing 17.5).

LISTING 17.5: Declaring Types from Unmanaged Structs

```
[StructLayout(LayoutKind.Sequential)]
struct ColorRef
{
  public byte Red;
  public byte Green;
  public byte Blue;
  // Turn off warning about not accessing Unused.
  #pragma warning disable 414
  private byte Unused;
  #pragma warning restore 414

  public ColorRef(byte red, byte green, byte blue)
  {
      Blue = blue;
      Green = green;
      Red = red;
      Unused = 0;
  }
}
```

Various Microsoft Windows color APIs use COLORREF to represent RGB colors (levels of red, green, and blue).

The key in this declaration is StructLayoutAttribute. By default, managed code can optimize the memory layouts of types, so layouts may not be sequential from one field to the next. To force sequential layouts so that a type maps directly and can be copied bit for bit (blitted) from managed to unmanaged code and vice versa, you add the StructLayout-Attribute with the LayoutKind.Sequential enum value. (This is also useful when writing data to and from filestreams where a sequential layout may be expected.)

Since the unmanaged (C++) definition for struct does not map to the C# definition, there is not a direct mapping of unmanaged struct to managed struct. Instead, developers should follow the usual C# guidelines about whether the type should behave like a value or a reference type, and whether the size is small (approximately less than 16 bytes).

Error Handling

One inconvenient characteristic of Win32 API programming is the fact that it frequently reports errors in inconsistent ways. For example, some APIs return a value (0, 1, false, and so on) to indicate an error, and others set an out parameter in some way. Furthermore, the details of what went wrong require additional calls to the GetLastError() API and then an additional call to FormatMessage() to retrieve an error message corresponding to the error. In summary, Win32 error reporting in unmanaged code seldom occurs via exceptions.

Fortunately, the P/Invoke designers provided a mechanism for handling this. To enable this, given the SetLastError named parameter of the DllImport attribute is true, it is possible to instantiate a System .ComponentModel.Win32Exception() that is automatically initialized with the Win32 error data immediately following the P/Invoke call (see Listing 17.6).

LISTING 17.6: Win32 Error Handling

```
class VirtualMemoryManager
{
  [DllImport("kernel32.dll", ", SetLastError = true)]
  private static extern IntPtr VirtualAllocEx(
      IntPtr hProcess,
      IntPtr lpAddress,
      IntPtr dwSize,
      AllocationType flAllocationType,
      uint flProtect);

  // ...
```

```csharp
[DllImport("kernel32.dll", SetLastError = true)]
static extern bool VirtualProtectEx(
    IntPtr hProcess, IntPtr lpAddress,
    IntPtr dwSize, uint flNewProtect,
    ref uint lpflOldProtect);

[Flags]
private enum AllocationType : uint
{
    // ...
}

[Flags]
private enum ProtectionOptions
{
    // ...
}

[Flags]
private enum MemoryFreeType
{
    // ...
}

public static IntPtr AllocExecutionBlock(
    int size, IntPtr hProcess)
{
    IntPtr codeBytesPtr;
    codeBytesPtr = VirtualAllocEx(
        hProcess, IntPtr.Zero,
        (IntPtr)size,
        AllocationType.Reserve | AllocationType.Commit,
        (uint)ProtectionOptions.PageExecuteReadWrite);

    if (codeBytesPtr == IntPtr.Zero)
    {
        throw new System.ComponentModel.Win32Exception();
    }

    uint lpflOldProtect = 0;
    if (!VirtualProtectEx(
        hProcess, codeBytesPtr,
        (IntPtr)size,
        (uint)ProtectionOptions.PageExecuteReadWrite,
        ref lpflOldProtect))
    {
        throw new System.ComponentModel.Win32Exception();
    }
    return codeBytesPtr;
}
```

```
    public static IntPtr AllocExecutionBlock(int size)
    {
        return AllocExecutionBlock(
            size, GetCurrentProcessHandle());
    }
}
```

This enables developers to provide the custom error checking that each API uses while still reporting the error in a standard manner.

Listing 17.1 and Listing 17.3 declared the P/Invoke methods as internal or private. Except for the simplest of APIs, wrapping methods in public wrappers that reduce the complexity of the P/Invoke API calls is a good guideline that increases API usability and moves toward object-oriented type structure. The `AllocExecutionBlock()` declaration in Listing 17.6 provides a good example of this.

Using `SafeHandle`

Frequently, P/Invoke involves a resource, such as a window handle, that code needs to clean up after using it. Instead of requiring developers to remember this and manually code it each time, it is helpful to provide a class that implements `IDisposable` and a finalizer. In Listing 17.7, for example, the address returned after `VirtualAllocEx()` and `Virtual-ProtectEx()` requires a follow-up call to `VirtualFreeEx()`. To provide built-in support for this, you define a `VirtualMemoryPtr` class that derives from `System.Runtime.InteropServices.SafeHandle` (this is new in .NET 2.0).

LISTING 17.7: Managed Resources Using `SafeHandle`

```
public class VirtualMemoryPtr :
    System.Runtime.InteropServices.SafeHandle
{
    public VirtualMemoryPtr(int memorySize) :
        base(IntPtr.Zero, true)
    {
        ProcessHandle =
            VirtualMemoryManager.GetCurrentProcessHandle();
        MemorySize = (IntPtr)memorySize;
        AllocatedPointer =
            VirtualMemoryManager.AllocExecutionBlock(
            memorySize, ProcessHandle);
```

```
            Disposed = false;
        }

    public readonly IntPtr AllocatedPointer;
    readonly IntPtr ProcessHandle;
    readonly IntPtr MemorySize;
    bool Disposed;

    public static implicit operator IntPtr(
        VirtualMemoryPtr virtualMemoryPointer)
    {
        return virtualMemoryPointer.AllocatedPointer;
    }


    // SafeHandle abstract member
    public override bool IsInvalid
    {
        get
        {
            return Disposed;
        }
    }


    // SafeHandle abstract member
    protected override bool ReleaseHandle()
    {
        if (!Disposed)
        {
            Disposed = true;
            GC.SuppressFinalize(this);
            VirtualMemoryManager.VirtualFreeEx(ProcessHandle,
                AllocatedPointer, MemorySize);
        }
        return true;
    }
}
```

System.Runtime.InteropServices.SafeHandle includes the abstract
members IsInvalid and ReleaseHandle(). In the latter, you place
your cleanup code; the former indicates whether the cleanup code has
executed yet.

With VirtualMemoryPtr, you can allocate memory simply by instantiating the type and specifying the needed memory allocation.

■ ADVANCED TOPIC

Using `IDisposable` Explicitly in Place of `SafeHandle`

In C# 1.0, `System.Runtime.InteropServices.SafeHandle` is not available. Instead, a custom implementation of `IDisposable`, as shown in Listing 17.8, is necessary.

LISTING 17.8: Managed Resources without **SafeHandle** but Using **IDisposable**

```csharp
public struct VirtualMemoryPtr : IDisposable
{
    public VirtualMemoryPtr(int memorySize)
    {
        ProcessHandle =
            VirtualMemoryManager.GetCurrentProcessHandle();
        MemorySize = (IntPtr)memorySize;
        AllocatedPointer =
            VirtualMemoryManager.AllocExecutionBlock(
            memorySize, ProcessHandle);
        Disposed = false;
    }

    public readonly IntPtr AllocatedPointer;
    readonly IntPtr ProcessHandle;
    readonly IntPtr MemorySize;
    bool Disposed;

    public static implicit operator IntPtr(
        VirtualMemoryPtr virtualMemoryPointer)
    {
        return virtualMemoryPointer.AllocatedPointer;
    }

    #region IDisposable Members
    public void Dispose()
    {
        if (!Disposed)
        {
            Disposed = true;
            GC.SuppressFinalize(this);
            VirtualMemoryManager.VirtualFreeEx(ProcessHandle,
                AllocatedPointer, MemorySize);
        }
    }
    #endregion
}
```

In order for `VirtualMemoryPtr` to behave with value type semantics, you need to implement it as a `struct`. However, the consequence of this is there can be no finalizer, since value types are not managed by the garbage collector. This means the developer using the type must remember to clean up the code. There is no fallback mechanism if he doesn't.

The second restriction is not to pass or copy the instance outside the method. This is a common guideline of `IDisposable` implementing types. Their scope should be left within a `using` statement and they should not be passed as parameters to other methods that could potentially save them beyond the life of the `using` scope.

Calling External Functions

Once you declare the P/Invoke functions, you invoke them just as you would any other class member. The key, however, is that the imported DLL must be in the path, including the executable directory, so that it can be successfully loaded. Listing 17.6 and Listing 17.7 provide demonstrations of this. However, they rely on some constants.

Since `flAllocationType` and `flProtect` are flags, it is a good practice to provide constants or enums for each. Instead of expecting the caller to define these, encapsulation suggests you provide them as part of the API declaration, as shown in Listing 17.9.

LISTING 17.9: Encapsulating the APIs Together

```
class VirtualMemoryManager
{
  // ...

  /// <summary>
  /// The type of memory allocation. This parameter must
  /// contain one of the following values.
  /// </summary>
  [Flags]
  private enum AllocationType : uint
  {
      /// <summary>
      /// Allocates physical storage in memory or in the
      /// paging file on disk for the specified reserved
      /// memory pages. The function initializes the memory
      /// to zero.
      /// </summary>
```

```
    Commit = 0x1000,
    /// <summary>
    /// Reserves a range of the process's virtual address
    /// space without allocating any actual physical
    /// storage in memory or in the paging file on disk.
    /// </summary>
    Reserve = 0x2000,
    /// <summary>
    /// Indicates that data in the memory range specified by
    /// lpAddress and dwSize is no longer of interest. The
    /// pages should not be read from or written to the
    /// paging file. However, the memory block will be used
    /// again later, so it should not be decommitted. This
    /// value cannot be used with any other value.
    /// </summary>
    Reset = 0x80000,
    /// <summary>
    /// Allocates physical memory with read-write access.
    /// This value is solely for use with Address Windowing
    /// Extensions (AWE) memory.
    /// </summary>
    Physical = 0x400000,
    /// <summary>
    /// Allocates memory at the highest possible address.
    /// </summary>
    TopDown = 0x100000,
}


/// <summary>
/// The memory protection for the region of pages to be
/// allocated.
/// </summary>
[Flags]
private enum ProtectionOptions : uint
{
    /// <summary>
    /// Enables execute access to the committed region of
    /// pages. An attempt to read or write to the committed
    /// region results in an access violation.
    /// </summary>
    Execute = 0x10,
    /// <summary>
    /// Enables execute and read access to the committed
    /// region of pages. An attempt to write to the
    /// committed region results in an access violation.
    /// </summary>
    PageExecuteRead = 0x20,
    /// <summary>
    /// Enables execute, read, and write access to the
    /// committed region of pages.
```

```
        /// </summary>
        PageExecuteReadWrite = 0x40,
        // ...
    }


    /// <summary>
    /// The type of free operation
    /// </summary>
    [Flags]
    private enum MemoryFreeType : uint
    {
        /// <summary>
        /// Decommits the specified region of committed pages.
        /// After the operation, the pages are in the reserved
        /// state.
        /// </summary>
        Decommit = 0x4000,
        /// <summary>
        /// Releases the specified region of pages. After this
        /// operation, the pages are in the free state.
        /// </summary>
        Release = 0x8000
    }

    // ...
}
```

The advantage of enums is that they group together each value. Furthermore, they limit the scope to nothing else besides these values.

Simplifying API Calls with Wrappers

Whether it is error handling, structs, or constant values, one goal of good
API developers is to provide a simplified managed API that wraps the
underlying Win32 API. For example, Listing 17.10 overloads Virtual-
FreeEx() with public versions that simplify the call.

LISTING 17.10: Wrapping the Underlying API

```
class VirtualMemoryManager
{
    // ...

    [DllImport("kernel32.dll", SetLastError = true)]
    static extern bool VirtualFreeEx(
        IntPtr hProcess, IntPtr lpAddress,
        IntPtr dwSize, IntPtr dwFreeType);
```

```
    public static bool VirtualFreeEx(
        IntPtr hProcess, IntPtr lpAddress,
        IntPtr dwSize)
    {
        bool result = VirtualFreeEx(
            hProcess, lpAddress, dwSize,
            (IntPtr)MemoryFreeType.Decommit);
        if (!result)
        {
            throw new System.ComponentModel.Win32Exception();
        }
        return result;
    }
    public static bool VirtualFreeEx(
        IntPtr lpAddress, IntPtr dwSize)
    {
        return VirtualFreeEx(
            GetCurrentProcessHandle(), lpAddress, dwSize);
    }

    [DllImport("kernel32", SetLastError = true)]
    static extern IntPtr VirtualAllocEx(
        IntPtr hProcess,
        IntPtr lpAddress,
        IntPtr dwSize,
        AllocationType flAllocationType,
        uint flProtect);

    // ...
}
```

Function Pointers Map to Delegates

One last P/Invoke key is that function pointers in unmanaged code map to delegates in managed code. To set up a Microsoft Windows timer, for example, you would provide a function pointer that the timer could call back on, once it had expired. Specifically, you would pass a delegate instance that matched the signature of the callback.

Guidelines

Given the idiosyncrasies of P/Invoke, there are several guidelines to aid in the process of writing such code.

- Check that no managed classes already expose the APIs.
- Define API external methods as private or, in simple cases, internal.

- Provide public wrapper methods around the external methods that handle the data type conversions and error handling.
- Overload the wrapper methods and provide a reduced number of required parameters by inserting defaults for the extern method call.
- Use `enum` or `const` to provide constant values for the API as part of the API's declaration.
- For all P/Invoke methods that support `GetLastError()`, be sure to assign the `SetLastError` named attribute to `true`. This allows the reporting of errors via `System.ComponentModel.Win32Exception`.
- Wrap resources, such as handles, into classes that derive from `System.Runtime.InteropServices.SafeHandle` or that support `IDisposable`.
- Function pointers in unmanaged code map to delegate instances in managed code. Generally, this requires the declaration of a specific delegate type that matches the signature of the unmanaged function pointer.
- Map input/output and output parameters to `ref` parameters instead of relying on pointers.

The last bullet implies C#'s support for pointers, described in the next section.

Pointers and Addresses

On occasion, developers will want to be able to access and work with memory, and with pointers to memory locations, directly. This is necessary for certain operating system interaction as well as with certain types of time-critical algorithms. To support this, C# requires use of the unsafe code construct.

Unsafe Code

One of C#'s great features is the fact that it is strongly typed and supports type checking throughout the runtime execution. What makes this feature especially great is that it is possible to circumvent this support and manipulate memory and addresses directly. You would do this when working with things like memory-mapped devices, or if you wanted to implement time-critical algorithms. The key is to designate a portion of the code as unsafe.

Unsafe code is an explicit code block and compilation option, as shown in Listing 17.11. The unsafe modifier has no effect on the generated CIL code itself. It is only a directive to the compiler to permit pointer and address manipulation within the unsafe block. Furthermore, *unsafe* does not imply *unmanaged*.

LISTING 17.11: Designating a Method for Unsafe Code

```
class Program
{
  unsafe static int Main(string[] args)
  {
      // ...
  }
}
```

You can use unsafe as a modifier to the type or to specific members within the type.

In addition, C# allows unsafe as a statement that flags a code block to allow unsafe code (see Listing 17.12).

LISTING 17.12: Designating a Code Block for Unsafe Code

```
class Program
{
  static int Main(string[] args)
  {
      unsafe
      {
          // ...
      }
  }
}
```

Code within the unsafe block can include unsafe constructs such as pointers.

■ NOTE

It is important to note that it is necessary to explicitly indicate to the compiler that unsafe code is supported.

From the command line, this requires the /unsafe switch. For example, to compile the previous code, you need to use the command shown in Output 17.1.

OUTPUT 17.1:

```
csc.exe /unsafe Program.cs
```

You need to use the /unsafe switch because unsafe code opens up the possibility of buffer overflows and similar possibilities that expose the potential for security holes. The /unsafe switch includes the ability to directly manipulate memory and execute instructions that are unmanaged. Requiring /unsafe, therefore, makes the choice of potential exposure explicit.

Pointer Declaration

Now that you have marked a code block as unsafe, it is time to look at how to write unsafe code. First, unsafe code allows the declaration of a pointer. Consider the following example.

```
byte* pData;
```

Assuming pData is not null, its value points to a location that contains one or more sequential bytes; the value of pData represents the memory address of the bytes. The type specified before the * is the **referent** type, or the type located where the value of the pointer refers. In this example, pData is the pointer and byte is the referent type, as shown in Figure 17.1.

Because pointers (which are just byte values) are not subject to garbage collection, C# does not allow referent types other than **unmanaged types**,

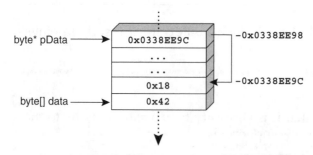

FIGURE 17.1: Pointers Contain the Address of the Data

which are types that are not reference types, are not generics, and do not contain reference types. Therefore, the following is not valid:

```
string* pMessage
```

Neither is this:

```
ServiceStatus* pStatus
```

where `ServiceStatus` is defined as shown in Listing 17.13; the problem again is that `ServiceStatus` includes a `string` field.

LISTING 17.13: Invalid Referent Type Example

```
struct ServiceStatus
{
    int State;
    string Description;   // Description is a reference type
}
```

Language Contrast: C/C++—Pointer Declaration

In C/C++, multiple pointers within the same declaration are declared as follows:

```
int *p1, *p2;
```

Notice the * on `p2`; this makes `p2` an `int*` rather than an `int`. In contrast, C# always places the * with the data type:

```
int* p1, p2;
```

The result is two variables of type `int*`. The syntax matches that of declaring multiple arrays in a single statement:

```
int[] array1, array2;
```

Pointers are an entirely new category of type. Unlike structs, enums, and classes, pointers don't ultimately derive from `System.Object`.

In addition to custom structs that contain only unmanaged types, valid referent types include enums, predefined value types (`sbyte`, `byte`, `short`, `ushort`, `int`, `uint`, `long`, `ulong`, `char`, `float`, `double`, `decimal`, and `bool`), and pointer types (such as `byte**`). Lastly, valid syntax includes `void*` pointers, which represent pointers to an unknown type.

Assigning a Pointer

Once code defines a pointer, it needs to assign a value before accessing it. Just like other reference types, pointers can hold the value `null`; this is their default value. The value stored by the pointer is the address of a location. Therefore, in order to assign it, you must first retrieve the address of the data.

You could explicitly cast an integer or a long into a pointer, but this rarely occurs without a means of determining the address of a particular data value at execution time. Instead, you need to use the address operator (`&`) to retrieve the address of the value type:

```
byte* pData = &bytes[0];  // Compile error
```

The problem is that in a managed environment, data can move, thereby invalidating the address. The error message is "You can only take the address of [an] unfixed expression inside of a fixed statement initializer." In this case, the byte referenced appears within an array and an array is a reference type (a moveable type). Reference types appear on the heap and are subject to garbage collection or relocation. A similar problem occurs when referring to a value type field on a moveable type:

```
int* a = &"message".Length;
```

Either way, to complete the assignment, the data needs to be a value type, fixed, or explicitly allocated on the call stack.

Fixing Data

To retrieve the address of a moveable data item, it is necessary to fix, or pin, the data, as demonstrated in Listing 17.14.

LISTING 17.14: Fixed Statement

```
byte[] bytes = new byte[24];
fixed (byte* pData = &bytes[0])  // pData = bytes also allowed
```

```
{
    // ...
}
```

Within the code block of a fixed statement, the assigned data will not move. In this example, `bytes` will remain at the same address, at least until the end of the fixed statement.

The fixed statement requires the declaration of the pointer variable within its scope. This avoids accessing the variable outside of the fixed statement, when the data is no longer fixed. However, it is the programmer's responsibility to ensure that he doesn't assign the pointer to another variable that survives beyond the scope of the fixed statement—possibly in an API call, for example. Similarly, using `ref` or `out` parameters will be problematic for data that will not survive beyond the method call.

Since a string is an invalid referent type, it would appear invalid to define pointers to strings. However, as in C++, internally a string is a pointer to the first character of an array of characters, and it is possible to declare pointers to characters using `char*`. Therefore, C# allows declaring a pointer of type `char*` and assigning it to a string within a fixed statement. The fixed statement prevents the movement of the string during the life of the pointer. Similarly, it allows any moveable type that supports an implicit conversion to a pointer of another type, given a fixed statement.

You can replace the verbose assignment of `&bytes[0]` with the abbreviated `bytes`, as shown in Listing 17.15.

LISTING 17.15: Fixed Statement without Address or Array Indexer

```
byte[] bytes = new byte[24];
fixed (byte* pData = bytes)
{
    // ...
}
```

Depending on the frequency and time to execute, fixed statements have the potential to cause fragmentation in the heap because the garbage collector cannot compact fixed objects. To reduce this problem, the best practice is to pin blocks early in the execution and to pin fewer large blocks rather than many small blocks. .NET 2.0 reduces the .NET Framework problem as well, due to some additional fragmentation-aware code.

Allocating on the Stack

You should use the fixed statement on an array to prevent the garbage collector from moving the data. However, an alternative is to allocate the array on the call stack. Stack allocated data is not subject to garbage collection or to the finalizer patterns that accompany it. Like referent types, the requirement is that the `stackalloc` data is an array of unmanaged types. For example, instead of allocating an array of bytes on the heap, you can place it onto the call stack, as shown in Listing 17.16.

LISTING 17.16: Allocating Data on the Call Stack

```
byte* bytes = stackalloc byte[42];
```

Because the data type is an array of unmanaged types, it is possible for the runtime to allocate a fixed buffer size for the array and then to restore that buffer once the pointer goes out of scope. Specifically, it allocates `sizeof(T) * E`, where `E` is the array size and `T` is the referent type. Given the requirement of using `stackalloc` only on an array of unmanaged types, the runtime restores the buffer back to the system simply by unwinding the stack, eliminating the complexities of iterating over the f-reachable queue and compacting reachable data. Therefore, there is no way to explicitly free `stackalloc` data.

Dereferencing a Pointer

Accessing the value of a type referred to by a pointer requires that you dereference the pointer, placing the indirection operator prior to the pointer type. `byte data = *pData;`, for example, dereferences the location of the `byte` referred to by `pData` and returns the single `byte` at that location.

Using this principle in unsafe code allows the unorthodox behavior of modifying the "immutable" string, as shown in Listing 17.17. In no way is this recommended, but it does expose the potential of low-level memory manipulation.

LISTING 17.17: Modifying an Immutable String

```
string text = "S5280ft";
Console.Write("{0} = ", text);
unsafe // Requires /unsafe switch.
{
```

```
fixed (char* pText = text)
{
    char* p = pText;
    *++p = 'm';
    *++p = 'i';
    *++p = 'l';
    *++p = 'e';
    *++p = ' ';
    *++p = ' ';
}
}
Console.WriteLine(text);
```

The results of Listing 17.17 appear in Output 17.2.

OUTPUT 17.2:

```
S5280ft = Smile
```

In this case, you take the original address and increment it by the size of the referent type (`sizeof(char)`), using the preincrement operator. Next, you dereference the address using the indirection operator and then assign the location with a different character. Similarly, using the + and − operators on a pointer changes the address by the `* sizeof(T)` operand, where `T` is the referent type.

Similarly, the comparison operators (`==`, `!=`, `<`, `>`, `<=`, and `=>`) work to compare pointers translating effectively to the comparison of address location values.

One restriction on the dereferencing operator is the inability to dereference a `void*`. The `void*` data type represents a pointer to an unknown type. Since the data type is unknown, it can't be dereferenced to another type. Instead, to access the data referenced by a `void*`, you must cast it to first assign it to any other pointer type and then to dereference the later type, for example.

You can achieve the same behavior as Listing 17.17 by using the index operator rather than the indirection operator (see Listing 17.18).

LISTING 17.18: Modifying an Immutable with the Index Operator in Unsafe Code

```
string text;
text = "S5280ft";
Console.Write("{0} = ", text);
```

```
Unsafe   // Requires /unsafe switch.
{
    fixed (char* pText = text)
    {
        pText[1] = 'm';
        pText[2] = 'i';
        pText[3] = 'l';
        pText[4] = 'e';
        pText[5] = ' ';
        pText[6] = ' ';
    }
}
Console.WriteLine(text);
```

The results of Listing 17.18 appear in Output 17.3.

OUTPUT 17.3:

```
S5280ft = Smile
```

Modifications such as those in Listing 17.17 and Listing 17.18 lead to unexpected behavior. For example, if you reassigned `text` to `"S5280ft"` following the `Console.WriteLine()` statement and then redisplayed `text`, the output would still be `Smile` because the address of two equal string literals is optimized to one string literal referenced by both variables. In spite of the apparent assignment

```
text = "S5280ft";
```

after the unsafe code in Listing 17.17, the internals of the string assignment are an address assignment of the modified `"S5280ft"` location, so `text` is never set to the intended value.

Accessing the Member of a Referent Type

Dereferencing a pointer makes it possible for code to access the members of the referent type. However, this is possible without the indirection operator (&). As Listing 17.19 shows, it is possible to directly access a referent type's members using the -> operator (shorthand for (*p)).

LISTING 17.19: Directly Accessing a Referent Type's Members

```
unsafe
{
```

```
Angle angle = new Angle(30, 18, 0);
Angle* pAngle = &angle;
System.Console.WriteLine("{0}° {1}' {2}",
    pAngle->Hours, pAngle->Minutes, pAngle->Seconds);
}
```

The results of Listing 17.19 appear in Output 17.4.

OUTPUT 17.4:

```
30° 18' 0
```

SUMMARY

This chapter's introduction outlined the low-level access to the underlying operating system that C# exposes. To summarize this, consider the Main() function listing for determining whether execution is with a virtual computer (see Listing 17.20).

LISTING 17.20: Designating a Block for Unsafe Code

```
using System.Runtime.InteropServices;

class Program
{
  unsafe static int Main(string[] args)
  {
      // Assign redpill
      byte[] redpill = {
          0x0f, 0x01, 0x0d,           // asm SIDT instruction
          0x00, 0x00, 0x00, 0x00,     // placeholder for an address
          0xc3};                      // asm return instruction

          unsafe
          {
          fixed (byte* matrix = new byte[6],
              redpillPtr = redpill)
          {
              // Move the address of matrix immediately
              // following the SIDT instruction of memory.
              *(uint*)&redpillPtr[3] = (uint)&matrix[0];

              using (VirtualMemoryPtr codeBytesPtr =
                  new VirtualMemoryPtr(redpill.Length))
              {
                  Marshal.Copy(
                      redpill, 0,
```

```
                           codeBytesPtr, redpill.Length);

                    MethodInvoker method =

   (MethodInvoker)Marshal.GetDelegateForFunctionPointer(
                        codeBytesPtr, typeof(MethodInvoker));

                    method();
                }
                if (matrix[5] > 0xd0)
                {
                    Console.WriteLine("Inside Matrix!\n");
                    return 1;
                }
                else
                {
                    Console.WriteLine("Not in Matrix.\n");
                    return 0;
                }
            } // fixed
        } // unsafe
    }
}
```

The results of Listing 17.20 appear in Output 17.5.

OUTPUT 17.5:

```
Inside Matrix!
```

In this case, you use a delegate to trigger execution of the assembler code. The delegate is declared as follows:

```
delegate void MethodInvoker();
```

This book has demonstrated the power, flexibility, consistency, and fantastic structure of C#. This chapter demonstrated the ability, in spite of such high-level programming capabilities, to perform very low-level operations as well.

Before ending the book, the next chapter briefly describes the underlying execution platform and shifts the focus from the C# language to the broader platform in which C# programs execute.

◾18◾
The Common Language Infrastructure

O NE OF THE FIRST ITEMS that C# programmers encounter beyond the syntax is the context under which a C# program executes. This chapter discusses the underpinnings of how C# handles memory allocation and de-allocation, type checking, interoperability with other languages, cross-platform execution, and support for programming metadata. In other words, this chapter investigates the Common Language Infrastructure (CLI) on which C# relies both at compile time and during execution. It covers the execution engine that governs a C# program at

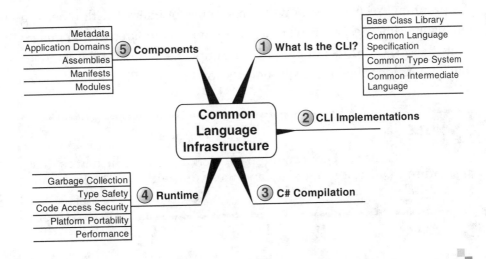

runtime and how C# fits into a broader set of languages that are governed by the same execution engine. Because of C#'s close ties with this infrastructure, most of the features that come with the infrastructure are made available to C#.

Defining the Common Language Infrastructure (CLI)

Instead of generating instructions that a processor can interpret directly, the C# compiler generates instructions in an intermediate language, the **Common Intermediate Language** (**CIL**). A second compilation step occurs, generally at execution time, converting the CIL to **machine code** that the processor can understand. Conversion to machine code is still not sufficient for code execution, however. It is also necessary for a C# program to execute under the context of an agent. The agent responsible for managing the execution of a C# program is the **Virtual Execution System** (**VES**), generally more casually referred to as the **runtime**. (Note that the runtime in this context does not refer to a time, such as execution time; rather, the runtime—the Virtual Execution System—is an agent responsible for managing the execution of a C# program.) The runtime is responsible for loading and running programs and providing additional services (security, garbage collection, and so on) to the program as it executes.

The specification for the CIL and the runtime is contained within an international standard known as the **Common Language Infrastructure** (**CLI**). This is a key specification for understanding the context in which a C# program executes and how it can seamlessly interact with other programs and libraries, even when they are written in alternate languages. Note that the CLI does not prescribe the implementation for the standard, but rather, identifies the requirements for how a CLI platform should

---

▪ NOTE

Note the similarity between these two acronyms and the names they stand for. Take care to understand these upfront to avoid confusion later on.

behave once it conforms to the standard. This provides CLI implementers with the flexibility to innovate where necessary, while still providing enough structure that programs created by one platform can execute on a different CLI implementation, and even on a different operating system.

Contained within the CLI standard are specifications for the following:

- The Virtual Execution System (VES, or runtime)
- The Common Intermediate Language (CIL)
- The Common Type System (CTS)
- The Common Language Specification (CLS)
- Metadata
- The Framework

This chapter broadens your view of C# to include the CLI, which is critical to how C# programs operate and interact with programs and with the operating system.

CLI Implementations

There are currently four predominant implementations of the CLI, each with an accompanying implementation of a C# compiler. Table 18.1 describes these implementations.

TABLE 18.1: Primary C# Compilers

Compiler	Description
Microsoft Visual C# .NET Compiler	Microsoft's .NET C# compiler is dominant in the industry, but it is limited to running on the Windows family of operating systems. You can download it free as part of the Microsoft .NET Framework SDK from http://msdn.microsoft.com/netframework/downloads/updates/default.aspx.
Mono Project	The Mono Project is an open source implementation sponsored by Ximian and designed to provide a Windows-, Linux-, and UNIX-compatible version of the CLI specification and C# compiler. Source code and binaries are available at www.go-mono.com.

Continues

TABLE 18.1: Primary C# Compilers *(Continued)*

Compiler	Description
DotGNU	This is focused on creating platform-portable applications that will run under both the .NET and the DotGNU.Portable.NET implementations of the CLI. This implementation is available from www.dotgnu.org. Supported operating systems include GNU/Linux *BSD, Cygwin/Mingw32, Mac OS X, Solaris, AIX, and PARISC. DotGNU and Mono have used portions of each other's libraries at various times.
Rotor	The Rotor program, also known as the Shared Source CLI, is an implementation of the CLI that Microsoft developed to run on Windows, Mac OS X, and FreeBSD. Both the implementation and the source code are available free at http://msdn.microsoft.com/net/sscli. Note that although the source code is available for download, Microsoft has not licensed Rotor for developing commercial applications and instead has targeted it as a learning tool.

Although none of these platforms and compilers would have any problems with the source code shown in Chapter 1, note that each CLI and C# compiler implementation is at a different stage of compliance with the specifications. For example, some implementations will not compile all the C# 2.0 syntax. All implementations, however, are intended to comply with the ECMA-334 specification for C# 1.0[1] and the ECMA-335 specification for the CLI 1.2.[2] Furthermore, many implementations include prototype features prior to the establishment of those features in standards.

C# Compilation to Machine Code

The `HelloWorld` program listing from Chapter 1 is obviously C# code, and you compiled it for execution using the C# compiler. However, the processor still cannot directly interpret compiled C# code. An additional compilation step is required to convert the result of C# compilation into machine code.

1. This is available for free via mail, or via download at www.ecma-international.org/publications/standards/Ecma-334.htm.
2. This is available for free via mail, or via download at www.ecma-international.org/publications/standards/Ecma-335.htm.

Furthermore, the execution requires the involvement of an agent that adds additional services to the C# program, services that it was not necessary to code for explicitly.

All computer languages define syntax and semantics for programming. Since languages such as C and C++ compile to machine code, the platform for these languages is the underlying operating system and machine instruction set, be it Microsoft Windows, Linux, UNIX, or others. Languages such as C# are different; the underlying platform is the runtime (or VES).

CIL is what the C# compiler produces after compiling. It is termed a "common intermediate language" (CIL) because an additional step is required to transform the CIL into something that processors can understand. (Figure 18.1 shows the process.) In other words, C# compilation requires two steps:

1. Conversion from C# to CIL by the C# compiler
2. Conversion from CIL to instructions that the processor can execute

The runtime is able to understand CIL statements and compile them to machine code. Generally, a **component** within the runtime performs this compilation from CIL to machine code. This component is the **just-in-time (JIT) compiler**, and **jitting** can occur when the program is installed or executed. Most CLI implementations favor execution-time compilation of the CIL, but the CLI does not specify when the compilation needs to occur. In fact, the CLI even allows the CIL to be interpreted rather than compiled, similar to the way many scripting languages work. In addition, .NET includes a tool called NGEN that enables compilation to machine code prior to actually running the program. This preexecution-time compilation needs to take place on the computer that the program will be executing because it will evaluate the machine characteristics (processor, memory, and so on) in order to generate more efficient code. The advantage of using NGEN at installation (or at any time prior to execution) is that you can reduce the need for the jitter to run at startup, thereby decreasing startup time.

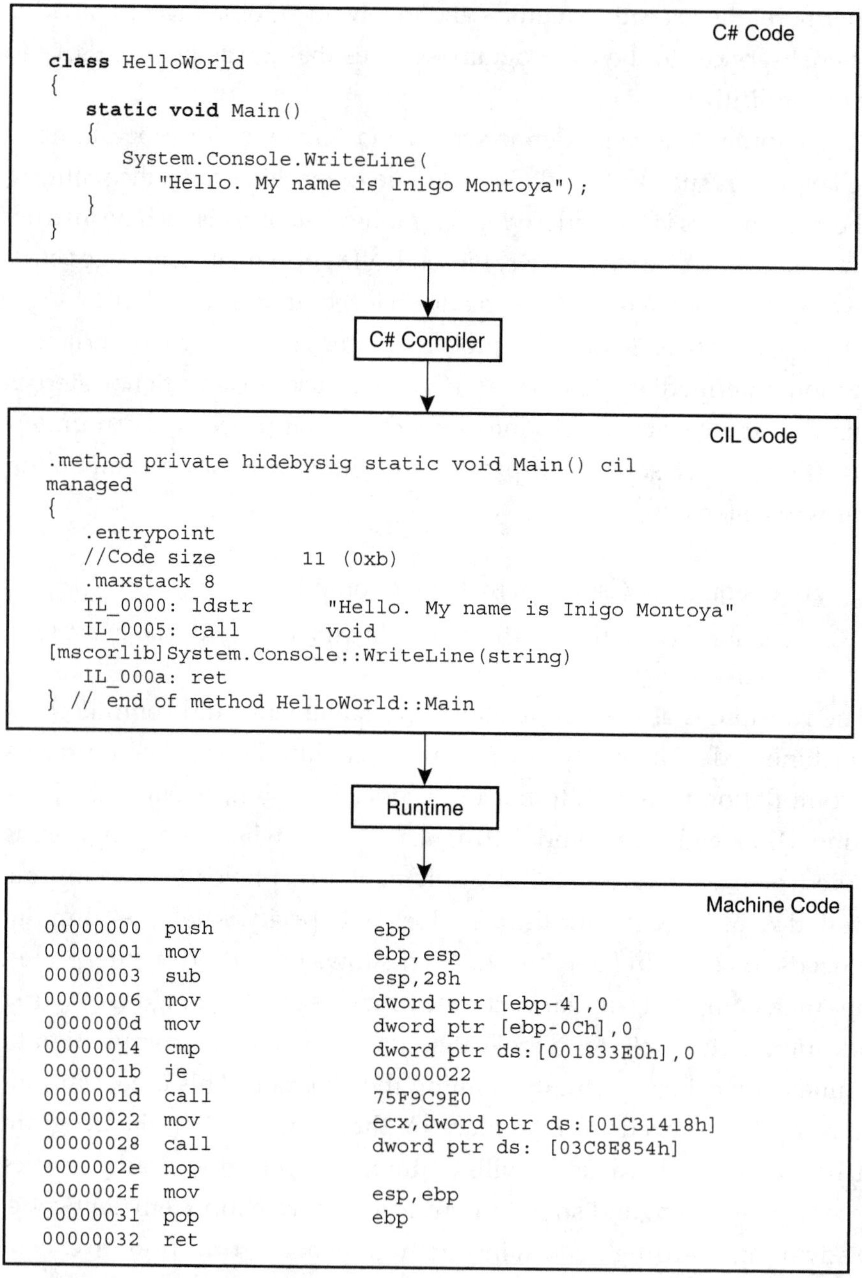

```
                                                                  C# Code
   class HelloWorld
   {
       static void Main()
       {
           System.Console.WriteLine(
               "Hello. My name is Inigo Montoya");
       }
   }
```

C# Compiler

```
                                                                  CIL Code
   .method private hidebysig static void Main() cil
   managed
   {
       .entrypoint
       //Code size        11 (0xb)
       .maxstack 8
       IL_0000: ldstr      "Hello. My name is Inigo Montoya"
       IL_0005: call       void
   [mscorlib]System.Console::WriteLine(string)
       IL_000a: ret
   } // end of method HelloWorld::Main
```

Runtime

```
                                                              Machine Code
   00000000   push            ebp
   00000001   mov             ebp,esp
   00000003   sub             esp,28h
   00000006   mov             dword ptr [ebp-4],0
   0000000d   mov             dword ptr [ebp-0Ch],0
   00000014   cmp             dword ptr ds:[001833E0h],0
   0000001b   je              00000022
   0000001d   call            75F9C9E0
   00000022   mov             ecx,dword ptr ds:[01C31418h]
   00000028   call            dword ptr ds: [03C8E854h]
   0000002e   nop
   0000002f   mov             esp,ebp
   00000031   pop             ebp
   00000032   ret
```

FIGURE 18.1: Compiling C# to Machine Code

Runtime

Even after the runtime converts the CIL code to machine code and starts to execute, it continues to maintain control of its execution. The code that executes under the context of an agent such as the runtime is **managed code**, and the process of executing under control of the runtime is **managed execution**. The control over execution transfers to the data, making it **managed data** because memory for the data is automatically allocated and de-allocated by the runtime.

Somewhat inconsistently, the term *Common Language Runtime* (CLR) is not technically a generic term that is part of the CLI. Rather, CLR is the Microsoft-specific implementation of the runtime for the .NET platform. Regardless, CLR is casually used as a generic term for *runtime*, and the technically accurate term, *Virtual Execution System*, is seldom used outside the context of the CLI specification.

Because an agent controls program execution, it is possible to inject additional services into a program, even though programmers did not explicitly code for them. Managed code, therefore, provides information to allow these services to be attached. Among other items, managed code enables the location of metadata about a type member, exception handling, access to security information, and the capability to walk the stack. The remainder of this section includes a description of some additional services made available via the runtime and managed execution. The CLI does not explicitly require all of them, but the established CLI platforms have an implementation of each.

Garbage Collection

Garbage collection is the process of automatically allocating and de-allocating memory based on the program's needs. This is a significant programming problem for languages that don't have an automated system for doing this. Without the garbage collector, programmers must remember to always restore any memory allocations they make. Forgetting to do so, or doing so repeatedly for the same memory allocation, introduces memory leaks or corruption into the program, something exacerbated by long-running programs such as web servers. Because of the runtime's built-in support for garbage collection, programmers targeting runtime execution can focus on adding program features rather than "plumbing" related to memory management.

Language Contrast: C++ — Deterministic Destruction

The exact mechanics for how the garbage collector works are not part of the CLI specification; therefore, each implementation can take a slightly different approach. (In fact, garbage collection is one item not explicitly required by the CLI.) One key concept that may take C++ programmers a little getting used to is that garbage-collected objects are not necessarily collected *deterministically* (at well-defined, compile-time-known locations). In fact, objects can be garbage collected anytime between when they are last accessed and when the program shuts down. This includes collection prior to falling out of scope, or waiting until well after an object instance is accessible by the code.

It should be noted that the garbage collector only takes responsibility for handling memory management. It does not provide an automated system for managing resources unrelated to memory. Therefore, if an explicit action to free a resource (other than memory) is required, programmers using that resource should utilize special CLI-compatible programming patterns that will aid in the cleanup of those resources (see Chapter 9).

Garbage Collection on .NET

The .NET platform implementation of garbage collection uses a generational, compacting, mark-and-sweep-based algorithm. It is generational because objects that have lived for only a short period will be cleaned up sooner than objects that have already survived garbage collection sweeps because they were still in use. This conforms to the general pattern of memory allocation that objects that have been around longer will continue to outlive objects that have only recently been instantiated.

Additionally, the .NET garbage collector uses a mark-and-sweep algorithm. During each garbage collection execution, it marks objects that are to be de-allocated and compacts together the objects that remain so that there is no "dirty" space between them. The use of compression to fill in the space left by de-allocated objects often results in faster instantiation of new objects (than with unmanaged code), because it is not necessary to search through memory to locate space for a new allocation. This also decreases the chance of paging because more objects are located in the same page, which improves performance as well.

The garbage collector takes into consideration the resources on the machine and the demand on those resources at execution time. For example, if memory on the computer is still largely untapped, the garbage collector is less likely to run and take time to clean up those resources, an optimization rarely taken by platforms and languages that are not based on garbage collection.

Type Safety

One of the key advantages the runtime offers is checking conversions between types, or **type checking**. Via type checking, the runtime prevents programmers from unintentionally introducing invalid casts that can lead to buffer overrun vulnerabilities. Such vulnerabilities are one of the most common means of breaking into a computer system, and having the runtime automatically prevent these is a significant gain.[3] Type checking provided by the runtime ensures that

- Both variables and the data the variables refer to are typed and that the type of the variable is compatible with the data that it refers to.

- It is possible to locally analyze a type (without analyzing all of the code in which the type is used) to determine what permissions will be required to execute that type's members.

- Each type has a compile-time-defined set of methods and the data they contain. The runtime enforces rules about what classes can access those methods and data. Methods marked as "private," for example, are accessible only by the containing type.

---

3. Assuming you are not the unscrupulous type that is looking for such vulnerabilities.

■ ADVANCED TOPIC

Circumventing Encapsulation and Access Modifiers

Given appropriate permissions, it is possible to circumvent encapsulation and access modifiers via a mechanism known as **reflection**. Reflection provides late binding by enabling support for browsing through a type's members, looking up the names of particular constructs within an object's metadata, and invoking the type's members.

Code Access Security

The runtime can make security checks as the program executes, allowing and disallowing the specific types of operations depending on permissions. Permission to execute a specific function is not restricted to authentication of the user running the program. The runtime also controls execution based on who created the program and whether they are a trusted provider. Permissions can be tuned such that partially trusted providers can read and write files from controlled locations on the disk, but they are prevented from accessing other locations (such as email addresses from an email program) for which the provider has not been granted permission. Identification of a provider is handled by certificates that are embedded into the program when the provider compiles the code.

Platform Portability

One theoretical feature of the runtime is the opportunity it provides for C# code and the resulting programs to be **platform portable**, capable of running on multiple operating systems and executing on different CLI implementations. Portability in this context is not limited to the source code such that recompiling is necessary. A single CLI module compiled for one platform should run on any CLI-compatible platform without needing to be recompiled. This portability occurs because the work of porting the code lies in the hands of the runtime implementation rather than the application developer.

The restriction is, of course, that no platform-specific APIs are used. Because of this restriction, many developers forgo CLI platform-neutral code in favor of accessing the underlying platform functionality, rather than writing it all from scratch.

The platform portability offered by .NET, DotGNU, Rotor, and Mono varies depending on the goals of the platform developers. For obvious reasons, .NET was targeted to run only on the Microsoft series of operating systems. Rotor, also produced by Microsoft, was primarily designed as a means for teaching and fostering research into future CLI development. Its inclusion of support for FreeBSD proves the portability characteristics of the CLI. Some of the libraries included in .NET (such as WinForms, ASP.NET, ADO.NET, and more) are not available in Rotor.

DotGNU and Mono were initially targeted at Linux but have since been ported to many different operating systems. Furthermore, the goal of these CLIs was to provide a means for taking .NET applications and porting them to operating systems in addition to those controlled by Microsoft. In so doing, there is a large overlap between the APIs found in .NET and those available in Mono and DotGNU.

Performance

Many programmers accustomed to writing unmanaged code will correctly point out that managed environments impose overhead on applications, no matter how simple. The trade-off is one of increased development productivity and reduced bugs in managed code versus runtime performance. The same dichotomy emerged as programming went from assembler to higher-level languages like C, and from structured programming to object-oriented development. In the vast majority of scenarios, development productivity wins out, especially as the speed and reduced price of hardware surpass the demands of applications. Time spent on architectural design is much more likely to yield big performance gains than the complexities of a low-level development platform. In the climate of security holes caused by buffer overruns, managed execution is even more compelling.

Undoubtedly, certain development scenarios (device drivers, for example) may not yet fit with managed execution. However, as managed execution increases in capability and sophistication, many of these performance considerations will likely vanish. Unmanaged execution will then be reserved for development where precise control or circumvention of the runtime is deemed necessary.[4]

Furthermore, the runtime introduces several factors that can contribute to improved performance over native compilation. For example, because translation to machine code takes place on the destination machine, the resulting compiled code matches the processor and memory layout of that machine, resulting in performance gains generally not leveraged by nonjitted languages. Also, the runtime is able to respond to execution conditions that direct compilation to machine code rarely takes into account. If, for example, there is more memory on the box than is required, unmanaged languages will still deallocate their memory at deterministic, compile-time-defined execution points in the code. Alternatively, jit-compiled languages will need to de-allocate memory only when it is running low or when the program is shutting down. Even though jitting can add a compile step to the execution process, code efficiencies that a jitter can insert lead to performance rivaling that of programs compiled directly to machine code. Ultimately, CLI programs are not necessarily faster than non-CLI programs, but their performance is competitive.

Application Domains

By introducing a layer between the program and the operating system, it is possible to implement virtual processes or applications known as **application domains (app domains)**. An application domain behaves like an operating system process in that it offers a level of isolation between other application domains. For example, an app domain has its own virtual memory allocation, and communication between application domains requires distributed communication paradigms, just as it would between two operating system processes. Similarly, static data is not shared between application domains, so static constructors run for each application domain, and assuming a single thread per application domain, there is no need to synchronize the static data because each application has its own instance of the data. Furthermore, each application domain has its own

---

4. Indeed, Microsoft has indicated that managed development will be the predominant means of writing applications for its Windows platform in the future, even those applications that integrate with the operating system.

threads, and just like with an operating system process, threads cannot cross application domain boundaries.

The point of an application domain is that operating systems are considered relatively expensive. With application domains, you can avoid this additional expense by running multiple application domains within a single process. For example, you can use a single process to host a series of web sites. However, you can isolate the web sites from each other by placing them in their own application domain. In summary, application domains represent a virtual process on a layer between an operating system process and the threads.

Assemblies, Manifests, and Modules

Included in the CLI is the specification of the CIL output from a source language compiler, usually an assembly. In addition to the CIL instructions themselves, an assembly includes a **manifest** which is made up of the following:

- The types that an assembly defines and imports
- Version information about the assembly itself
- Additional files the assembly depends on
- Security permissions for the assembly

The manifest is essentially a header to the assembly, providing all the information about what an assembly is composed of, along with the information that uniquely identifies it.

Assemblies can be class libraries or the executables themselves, and one assembly can reference other assemblies (which, in turn, can reference more assemblies), thereby establishing an application composed of many components rather than one large, monolithic program. This is an important feature that modern programming platforms take for granted, because it significantly improves maintainability and allows a single component to be shared across multiple programs.

In addition to the manifest, an assembly contains the CIL code within one or more modules. Generally, the assembly and the manifest are combined into a single file, as was the case with `HelloWorld.exe` in Chapter 1.

However, it is possible to place modules into their own separate files and then use an assembly linker (al.exe) to create an assembly file that includes a manifest that references each module.[5] This not only provides another means of breaking a program into components, but it also enables the development of one assembly using multiple source languages.

Casually, the terms *module* and *assembly* are somewhat interchangeable. However, the term *assembly* is predominant for those talking about CLI-compatible programs or libraries. Figure 18.2 depicts the various component terms.

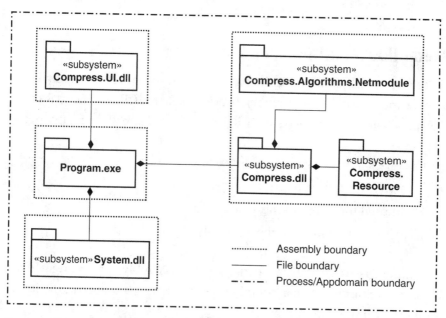

FIGURE 18.2: Assemblies with the Modules and Files They Reference

Note that both assemblies and modules can also reference files such as resource files that have been localized to a particular language. Although it is rare, two different assemblies can reference the same module or file.

In spite of the fact that an assembly can include multiple modules and files, there is only one version number for the entire group of files and it

---

5. This is partly because one of the primary CLI IDEs, Visual Studio .NET, lacks functionality for working with assemblies composed of multiple modules. Current implementations of Visual Studio .NET do not have integrated tools for building multimodule assemblies, and when they use such assemblies, the IntelliSense does not fully function.

is placed in the assembly manifest. Therefore, the smallest versionable component within an application is the assembly, even if that assembly is composed of multiple files. If you change any of the referenced files— even to release a patch—without updating the assembly manifest, you will violate the integrity of the manifest and the entire assembly itself. As a result, assemblies form the logical construct of a component or unit of deployment.

> **■ NOTE**
>
> Assemblies form the smallest unit that can be versioned and installed, not the individual modules that comprise them.

Even though an assembly (the logical construct) could consist of multiple modules, most assemblies contain only one. Furthermore, Microsoft now provides an `ILMerge.exe` utility for combining multiple modules and their manifests into a single file assembly.

Because the manifest includes a reference to all the files an assembly depends on, it is possible to use the manifest to determine an assembly's dependencies. Furthermore, at execution time, the runtime needs to examine only the manifest to determine what files it requires. Only tool vendors distributing libraries shared by multiple applications (Microsoft, for example) need to register those files at deployment time. This makes deployment significantly easier. Often, deployment of a CLI-based application is referred to as **xcopy deployment**, after the Windows `xcopy` command that simply copies files to a selected destination.

Language Contrast: COM DLL Registration

Unlike Microsoft's COM files of the past, CLI assemblies rarely require any type of registration. Instead, it is possible to deploy applications by copying all the files that comprise a program into a particular directory, and then executing the program.

Common Intermediate Language (CIL)

Considering the Common Language Infrastructure (CLI) name, another important feature of the CIL and the CLI is to support the interaction of multiple languages within the same application (instead of portability of source code across multiple operating systems). As a result, the CIL is the intermediate language not only for C#, but also for many other languages, including Visual Basic .NET, the Java-like language of J#, some incantations of Smalltalk, C++, and a host of others (more than 20 at the time of this writing, including versions of COBOL and FORTRAN). Languages that compile to the CIL are **source languages** and each has a custom compiler that converts the source language to the CIL. Once compiled to the CIL, the source language is insignificant. This powerful feature enables the development of libraries by different development groups across multiple organizations, without concern for the language choice of a particular group. Thus, the CIL enables programming language interoperability as well as platform portability.

> **■ NOTE**
>
> A powerful feature of the CLI is support for multiple languages. This enables the creation of programs using multiple languages and the accessibility of libraries written in one language from code written in a different language.

Common Type System (CTS)

Regardless of the programming language, the resulting program operates internally on data types; therefore, the CLI includes the **Common Type System** (**CTS**). The CTS defines how types are structured and laid out in memory, as well as the concepts and behaviors that surround types. It includes type manipulation directives alongside the information about the data stored within the type. The CTS standard applies to how types appear and behave at the external boundary of a language because the purpose of the CTS is to achieve interoperability between languages.

It is the responsibility of the runtime at execution time to enforce the contracts established by the CTS.

Within the CTS, types are broken down into two categories.

- **Values** are bit patterns used to represent basic types, like integers and characters, as well as more complex data in the form of structures. Each value type corresponds to a separate type designation not stored within the bits itself. The separate type designation refers to the type definition that provides the meaning of each bit within the value and the operations that the value supports.

- **Objects** contain within them the object's type designation. (This helps in enabling type checking.) Objects have identity that makes each instance unique. Furthermore, objects have slots that can store other types (either values or object references). Unlike values, changing the contents of a slot does not change the identity of the object.

These two categories of types translate directly to C# syntax that provides a means of declaring each type.

Common Language Specification (CLS)

Since the language integration advantages provided by the CTS generally outweigh the costs of implementing it, the majority of source languages support the CTS. However, there is also a subset of CTS language conformance called the **Common Language Specification** (CLS). Its focus is toward library implementations. It targets library developers, providing them with standards for writing libraries that are accessible from the majority of source languages, regardless of whether the source languages using the library are CTS compliant. It is called the Common Language Specification because it is intended to also encourage CLI languages to provide a means of creating interoperable libraries, or libraries that are accessible from other languages.

For example, although it is perfectly reasonable for a language to provide support for an unsigned integer, such a type is not included as part of the CLS. Therefore, developers implementing a class library should not externally expose unsigned integers because doing so would cause the library to be less accessible from CLS-compliant source languages that do not support unsigned integers. Ideally, therefore, any development of libraries that is to be accessible from multiple languages should conform to the CLS specification. Note that the CLS is not concerned with types that are not exposed externally to the assembly.

Base Class Library (BCL)

In addition to providing a platform in which CIL code can execute, the CLI also defines a core set of class libraries that programs may employ, called the **Base Class Library** (BCL). These libraries provide foundational types and APIs, allowing the program to interact with the runtime and underlying operating system in a consistent manner. The BCL includes support for collections, simple file access, some security, fundamental data types (`string`, and so on), streams, and the like.

Similarly, there is a Microsoft-specific library called the **Framework Class Library** (FCL) that adds to this and includes support for rich client user interfaces, web user interfaces, database access, distributed communication, and more.

Metadata

In addition to execution instructions, CIL code includes **metadata** about the types and files included in a program. The metadata includes the following:

- Descriptions of each type within a program or class library
- The manifest information containing data about the program itself, along with the libraries it depends on
- Custom attributes embedded in the code, providing additional information about the constructs the attributes decorate

The metadata is not a cursory, nonessential add-on to the CIL. Instead, it forms a core part of the CLI implementation. It provides the representation and the behavior information about a type and includes location information about which assembly contains a particular type definition. It serves a key role in saving data from the compiler and making it accessible at execution time to debuggers and the runtime. This data is not only available in the CIL code, but also is accessible during machine code execution so that the runtime can continue to make any necessary type checks.

Metadata provides a mechanism for the runtime to handle a mixture of native and managed code execution. Also, it increases code and execution robustness because it smoothes the migration from one library version to the next, replacing compile-time-defined binding with a load-time implementation.

All header information about a library and its dependencies is in a portion of the metadata known as the manifest. As a result, the manifest portion of the metadata enables developers to determine a module's dependencies, including information about particular versions of the dependencies and signatures of who created the module. At execution time, the runtime uses the manifest to determine what dependent libraries to load, whether the libraries or main program have been tampered with, and whether assemblies are missing.

The metadata also contains **custom attributes** that may decorate the code. Attributes provide additional metadata about CIL instructions that are accessible via the program at execution time.

Metadata is available at execution time by a mechanism known as **reflection**. With reflection, it is possible to look up a type or its member at execution time and then invoke that member or determine whether a construct is decorated with a particular attribute. This provides **late binding**, determining what code to execute at execution time rather than at compile time. Reflection can even be used for generating documentation by iterating through metadata and copying it into a help document of some kind (see Chapter 14).

SUMMARY

This chapter described many new terms and acronyms that are important to understanding the context under which C# programs run. The preponderance of three-letter acronyms can be confusing. Table 18.2 provides a summary list of the terms and acronyms that are part of the CLI.

TABLE 18.2: Common C#-Related Acronyms

Acronym	Definition	Description
.NET	None	Microsoft's implementation of the entire CLI stack. Includes the CLR, CIL, and various languages, all of which are CLS compliant.
BCL	Base Class Library	The portion of the CLI specification that defines the collection, threading, console, and other base classes necessary to build virtually all programs.
C#	None	A programming language. Note that separate from the CLI standard there is a C# Language Specification, also ratified by the ECMA and ISO standards bodies.
CIL (IL)	Common Intermediate Language	The language of the CLI specification that defines the instructions for the code executable on implementations of the CLI. This is sometimes also referred to as IL or Microsoft IL (MSIL) to distinguish it from other intermediate languages. (To indicate that it is a standard broader than Microsoft, CIL is preferred over MSIL and even IL.)
CLI	Common Language Infrastructure	The specification that defines the intermediate language, base classes, and behavioral characteristics which enable implementers to create Virtual Execution Systems and compilers in which source languages are interoperable on top of a common execution environment.
CLR	Common Language Runtime	Microsoft's implementation of the runtime, as defined in the CLI specification.
CLS	Common Language Specification	The portion of the CLI specification that defines the core subset of features which source languages *must* support in order to be executable on runtimes implemented according to the CLI specification.
CTS	Common Type System	A standard generally implanted by CLI-compliant languages that defines the representation and behavior of types that the language exposes visibly outside of a module. It includes concepts for how types can be combined to form new types.

TABLE 18.2: Common C#-Related Acronyms *(Continued)*

Acronym	Definition	Description
FCL	.NET Framework Class Library	The class library that comprises Microsoft's .NET Framework. It includes Microsoft's implementation of the BCL as well as a large library of classes for such things as web development, distributed communication, database access, rich client user interface development, and a host of others.
VES (runtime)	Virtual Execution System	An agent that manages the execution of a program that is compiled for the CLI.

◾A◾
Downloading and Installing the C# Compiler and the CLI Platform

T O COMPILE AND RUN C# programs, it is necessary to install a version of the compiler and the CLI platform.

Microsoft's .NET

The predominant CLI platform is Microsoft .NET and this is the platform of choice for development on Microsoft Windows.

- The minimum installation that includes the compiler and the .NET Framework with C# 2.0 syntax support is the redistributable package for the .NET Framework 2.0 or higher. This is available at http://msdn.microsoft.com/netframework/downloads/updates/default.aspx.
- For a rich IDE that includes IntelliSense and support for project files, install a version of the Visual Studio 2005 IDE or later. This includes Visual C# Express, which is available free at http://lab.msdn.microsoft.com/express/vcsharp/default.aspx.

For command-line compilation, regardless of a Visual Studio install or only the runtime, you must set the PATH environment variable to include the C# compiler, CSC.EXE.

Setting Up the Compiler Path with Microsoft .NET

If Visual Studio .NET is installed on your computer, open the command prompt from the Start menu by selecting All Programs->Microsoft Visual Studio .NET->Visual Studio Tools->Visual Studio Command Prompt. This command prompt places CSC.EXE in the path to be available for execution from any directory.

Without Visual Studio .NET installed, no special compiler command prompt item appears in the Start menu. Instead, you need to reference the full compiler pathname explicitly or add it to the path. The compiler is located at %Windir%\Microsoft.NET\Framework\<version>, where <version> is the version of the .NET Framework (v1.0.3705, v1.1.4322, v2.0.50727, and so on) and %Windir% is the environment variable that points to the location of the Windows directory. To add this location to the path use Set PATH=%PATH%;%Windir%\Microsoft.NET\Framework\<version>, again substituting the value of <version> appropriately. Output A.1 provides an example.

OUTPUT A.1:

```
Set PATH=%PATH%;%Windir%\Microsoft.NET\Framework\v2.0.50727
```

Once the path includes the framework, it is possible to use the .NET C# compiler, CSC.EXE, without providing the full path to its location.

Mono

For CLI development on platforms other than Microsoft Windows, consider Mono, which is a platform you can download at www.mono-project.com. As with the .NET platform, Mono requires the full path to the C# compiler if it is not already in the search path. The default installation path on Linux is /usr/lib/mono/<version> and the compiler is gmcs.exe or mcs.exe, depending on the version. (If Mono is installed on Microsoft Windows, the default path is `%ProgramFiles%\Mono-<version>\lib\mono\<version>\`.)

One option for a Linux version that includes an installation of Mono is Monoppix. This builds on the CD-bootable Linux distribution known as Knoppix and is available for download at www.monoppix.com.

Instead of CSC.EXE, the Mono platform's compiler is MCS.EXE or GMCS.EXE, depending on the compiler version. Therefore, the command for compiling `HelloWorld.cs` is as shown in Output A.2.

OUTPUT A.2:

```
C:\SAMPLES>msc.exe HelloWorld.cs
```

Unfortunately, the Linux environment cannot run the resulting binaries directly; instead, it requires explicit execution of the runtime using `mono.exe`, as shown in Output A.3.

OUTPUT A.3:

```
C:\SAMPLES>mono.exe HelloWorld.exe
Hello. My name is Inigo Montoya.
```

B

Complete Source Code Listings

M ANY OF THE CHAPTERS in this book have source code spread over multiple listings. When listings are large, this makes the code difficult to follow. This appendix includes the code listings as one program, making the individual listings easier to understand as a whole.

Chapters 3 and 4

LISTING B.1: Tic-Tac-Toe

```csharp
#define CSHARP2

using System;

#pragma warning disable 1030 // Disable user-defined warnings

// The TicTacToe class enables two players to
// play tic-tac-toe.
class TicTacToeGame        // Declares the TicTacToeGame class
{
  static void Main()  // Declares the entry point to the program
  {
      // Stores locations each player has moved.
      int[] playerPositions = { 0, 0 };

      // Initially set the currentPlayer to Player 1;
      int currentPlayer = 1;
```

```csharp
        // Winning player
        int winner = 0;

        string input = null;


        // Display the board and
        // prompt the current player
        // for their next move.
        for (int turn = 1; turn <= 10; ++turn)
        {
            DisplayBoard(playerPositions);

            #region Check for End Game
            if (EndGame(winner, turn, input))
            {
                break;
            }
            #endregion Check for End Game

            input = NextMove(playerPositions, currentPlayer);

            winner = DetermineWinner(playerPositions);

            // Switch players
            currentPlayer = (currentPlayer == 2) ? 1 : 2;
        }
    }

    private static string NextMove(int[] playerPositions,
                int currentPlayer)
    {
        string input;

        // Repeatedly prompt the player for a move
        // until a valid move is entered.
        bool validMove;
        do
        {
            // Request a move from the current player.
            System.Console.Write("\nPlayer {0} - Enter move:",
                    currentPlayer);
            input = System.Console.ReadLine();
            validMove = ValidateAndMove(playerPositions,
                        currentPlayer, input);
        } while (!validMove);

        return input;
    }
```

```csharp
static bool EndGame(int winner, int turn, string input)
{
    bool endGame = false;
    if (winner > 0)
    {
        System.Console.WriteLine("\nPlayer {0} has won!!!!",
                    winner);
        endGame = true;
    }
    else if (turn == 10)
    {
        // After completing the 10th display of the
        // board, exit out rather than prompting the
        // user again.
        System.Console.WriteLine("\nThe game was a tie!");
        endGame = true;
    }
    else if (input == "" || input == "quit")
    {
        // Check if user quit by hitting Enter without
        // any characters or by typing "quit".
        System.Console.WriteLine("The last player quit");
        endGame = true;
    }
    return endGame;
}

static int DetermineWinner(int[] playerPositions)
{
    int winner = 0;

    // Determine if there is a winner
    int[] winningMasks = {
        7, 56, 448, 73, 146, 292, 84, 273};

    foreach (int mask in winningMasks)
    {
        if ((mask & playerPositions[0]) == mask)
        {
            winner = 1;
            break;
        }
        else if ((mask & playerPositions[1]) == mask)
        {
            winner = 2;
            break;
        }
    }
    return winner;
}
```

```csharp
static bool ValidateAndMove(
  int[] playerPositions, int currentPlayer, string input)
{
    bool valid = false;

    // Check the current player's input.
    switch (input)
    {
        case "1":
        case "2":
        case "3":
        case "4":
        case "5":
        case "6":
        case "7":
        case "8":
        case "9":
#warning "Same move allowed multiple times."
            int shifter;   // The number of places to shift
            // over in order to set a bit.
            int position;  // The bit which is to be set.

            // int.Parse() converts "input" to an integer.
            // "int.Parse(input) - 1" because arrays
            // are zero based.
            shifter = int.Parse(input) - 1;

            // Shift mask of 00000000000000000000000000000001
            // over by cellLocations.
            position = 1 << shifter;

            // Take the current player cells and OR them to set
            // the new position as well.
            // Since currentPlayer is either 1 or 2 you
            // subtract one to use currentPlayer as an
            // index in a 0-based array.
            playerPositions[currentPlayer - 1] |= position;

            valid = true;
            break;

        case "":
        case "quit":
            valid = true;
            break;

        default:
            // If none of the other case statements
            // is encountered, then the text is invalid.
```

```
                    System.Console.WriteLine(
                        "\nERROR:  Enter a value from 1-9. "
                        + "Push ENTER to quit");
                    break;
            }

            return valid;
        }

        static void DisplayBoard(int[] playerPositions)
        {
            // This represents the borders between each cell
            // for one row.
            string[] borders = {
    "|", "|", "\n---+---+---\n", "|", "|",
    "\n---+---+---\n", "|", "|", ""
            };

            // Display the current board;
            int border = 0;  // set the first border (border[0] = "|")

#if CSHARP2
            System.Console.Clear();
#endif

            for (int position = 1;
                position <= 256;
                position <<= 1, border++)
            {
                char token = CalculateToken(
                    playerPositions, position);

                // Write out a cell value and the border that
                // comes after it.
                System.Console.Write(" {0} {1}",
                    token, borders[border]);
            }
        }

        static char CalculateToken(
            int[] playerPositions, int position)
        {
            // Initialize the players to 'X' and 'O'
            char[] players = {'X', 'O'};

            char token;
            // If player has the position set,
            // then set the token to that player.
            if ((position & playerPositions[0]) == position)
            {
```

```csharp
            // Player 1 has that position marked
            token = players[0];
        }
        else if ((position & playerPositions[1]) == position)
        {
            // Player 2 has that position marked
            token = players[1];
        }
        else
        {
            // The position is empty.
            token = ' ';
        }
        return token;
    }


#line 113 "TicTacToe.cs"
    // Generated code goes here
#line default
}
```

Chapter 9

LISTING B.2: ProductSerialNumber

```csharp
public sealed class ProductSerialNumber
{
    public ProductSerialNumber(
        string productSeries, int model, long id)
    {
        ProductSeries = productSeries;
        Model = model;
        Id = id;
    }

    public readonly string ProductSeries;
    public readonly int Model;
    public readonly long Id;

    public override int GetHashCode()
    {
        int hashCode = ProductSeries.GetHashCode();
        hashCode ^= Model;  // Xor (eXclusive OR)
        hashCode ^= Id.GetHashCode();  // Xor (eXclusive OR)
        return hashCode;
    }
```

```csharp
public override bool Equals(object obj)
{
    if (obj == null)
    {
        return false;
    }
    if (ReferenceEquals(this, obj))
    {
        return true;
    }
    if (this.GetType() != obj.GetType())
    {
        return false;
    }
    return Equals((ProductSerialNumber)obj);
}


public bool Equals(ProductSerialNumber obj)
{
    // STEP 3: Possibly check for equivalent hash codes
    // if (this.GetHashCode() != obj.GetHashCode())
    // {
    //     return false;
    // }

    // STEP 4: Check base.Equals if base overrides Equals()
    // System.Diagnostics.Debug.Assert(
    //     base.GetType() != typeof(object));
    // if ( base.Equals(obj) )
    // {
    //     return false;
    // }

    // STEP 1: Check for null
    return ((obj != null)
        // STEP 5: Compare identifying fields for equality.
        && (ProductSeries == obj.ProductSeries) &&
        (Model == obj.Model) &&
        (Id == obj.Id));
}


public static bool operator ==(
    ProductSerialNumber leftHandSide,
    ProductSerialNumber rightHandSide)
{

    // Check if leftHandSide is null.
    // (operator== would be recursive)
```

```csharp
        if (ReferenceEquals(leftHandSide, null))
        {
            // Return true if rightHandSide is also null
            // but false otherwise.
            return ReferenceEquals(rightHandSide, null);
        }

        return (leftHandSide.Equals(rightHandSide));
    }

    public static bool operator !=(
        ProductSerialNumber leftHandSide,
        ProductSerialNumber rightHandSide)
    {
        return !(leftHandSide == rightHandSide);
    }
}
```

Chapter 12

LISTING B.3: Binary Tree and Pair

```csharp
public enum PairItem
{
    First,
    Second
}
```

```csharp
interface IPair<T>
{
    T First
    {
        get;
        set;
    }

    T Second
    {
        get;
        set;
    }

    T this[PairItem index]
    {
        get;
        set;
    }
}
```

```csharp
using System.Collections;
using System.Collections.Generic;

public struct Pair<T> : IPair<T>, IEnumerable<T>
{
    public Pair(T first)
    {
        _First = first;
        _Second = default(T);
    }
    public Pair(T first, T second)
    {
        _First = first;
        _Second = second;
    }
    public T First
    {
        get
        {
            return _First;
        }
        set
        {
            _First = value;
        }
    }
    private T _First;


    public T Second
    {
        get
        {
            return _Second;
        }
        set
        {
            _Second = value;
        }
    }
    private T _Second;

    [System.Runtime.CompilerServices.IndexerName("Entry")]
    public T this[PairItem index]
    {
        get
        {
            switch (index)
            {
                case PairItem.First:
```

```csharp
                    return First;
                case PairItem.Second:
                    return Second;
                default:
                    throw new NotImplementedException(
                        string.Format(
                        "The enum {0} has not been implemented",
                        index.ToString()));
            }
        }
        set
        {
            switch (index)
            {
                case PairItem.First:
                    First = value;
                    break;
                case PairItem.Second:
                    Second = value;
                    break;
                default:
                    throw new NotImplementedException(
                        string.Format(
                        "The enum {0} has not been implemented",
                        index.ToString()));
            }
        }
    }


    #region IEnumerable<T> Members
    public IEnumerator<T> GetEnumerator()
    {
        yield return First;
        yield return Second;
    }
    #endregion


    #region IEnumerable Members
    IEnumerator IEnumerable.GetEnumerator()
    {
        return GetEnumerator();
    }
    #endregion


    public IEnumerable<T> GetReverseEnumerator()
    {
        yield return Second;
        yield return First;
    }
```

```csharp
    // Listing 12.24
    public IEnumerable<T> GetNotNullEnumerator()
    {
        if ((First == null) || (Second == null))
        {
            yield break;
        }
        yield return Second;
        yield return First;
    }
}
```

```csharp
using System.Collections;
using System.Collections.Generic;

public interface IBinaryTree<T>
{
    T Item
    {
        get;
        set;
    }
    Pair<IBinaryTree<T>> SubItems
    {
        get;
        set;
    }
}
public class BinaryTree<T> : IEnumerable<T>
{
    public BinaryTree(T value)
    {
        Value = value;
    }

    public T Value
    {
        get { return _Value; }
        set { _Value = value; }
    }
    private T _Value;

    public Pair<BinaryTree<T>> SubItems
    {
        get { return _SubItems; }
        set
        {
            IComparable first;
            first = (IComparable)value.First.Value;
```

```csharp
            if (first.CompareTo(value.Second.Value) < 0)
            {
                // first is less than second.
            }
            else
            {
                // first and second are the same or
                // second is less than first.
            }
            _SubItems = value;
        }
    }
    private Pair<BinaryTree<T>> _SubItems;

    public T this[params PairItem[] branches]
    {
        get
        {
            BinaryTree<T> currentNode = this;
            int totalLevels =
                (branches == null) ? 0 : branches.Length;
            int currentLevel = 0;

            while (currentLevel < totalLevels)
            {
                currentNode =
                    currentNode.SubItems[branches[currentLevel]];
                if (currentNode == null)
                {
                    // The binary tree at this location is null.
                    throw new IndexOutOfRangeException();
                }
                currentLevel++;
            }


            return currentNode.Value;
        }
    }
    #region IEnumerable<T>
    // Listing 12.22
    public IEnumerator<T> GetEnumerator()
    {
        // Return the item at this node.
        yield return Value;

        // Iterate through each of the elements in the pair.
        foreach (BinaryTree<T> tree in SubItems)
        {
            if (tree != null)
            {
```

```
                // Since each element in the pair is a tree,
                // traverse the tree and yield each
                // element.
                foreach (T item in tree)
                {
                    yield return item;
                }
            }
        }
    }
}
#endregion IEnumerable<T>


#region IEnumerable Members
IEnumerator IEnumerable.GetEnumerator()
{
    return GetEnumerator();
}
#endregion
}
```

Chapter 14

LISTING B.4: Command-Line Attributes

```
using System;
using System.Diagnostics;

public partial class Program
{
  public static void Main(string[] args)
  {
      string errorMessage;
      CommandLineInfo commandLine = new CommandLineInfo();
      if (!CommandLineHandler.TryParse(
          args, commandLine, out errorMessage))
      {
          Console.WriteLine(errorMessage);
          DisplayHelp();
      }

      if (commandLine.Help)
      {
          DisplayHelp();
      }
      else
      {
          if (commandLine.Priority !=
```

```csharp
                        ProcessPriorityClass.Normal)
            {
                // Change thread priority
            }

        }
        // ...

    }

    private static void DisplayHelp()
    {
            // Display the command-line help.
            Console.WriteLine(
                "Thankyou for contacting the help text");  }
}
```

```csharp
using System;
using System.Diagnostics;

public partial class Program
{
    private class CommandLineInfo
    {
        [CommandLineSwitchAlias("?")]
        public bool Help
        {
            get { return _Help; }
            set { _Help = value; }
        }
        private bool _Help;

        [CommandLineSwitchRequired]
        [CommandLineSwitchAlias("FileName")]
        public string Out
        {
            get { return _Out; }
            set { _Out = value; }
        }
        private string _Out;

        public ProcessPriorityClass Priority
        {
            get { return _Priority; }
            set { _Priority = value; }
        }
        private ProcessPriorityClass _Priority =
            ProcessPriorityClass.Normal;

    }
}
```

```csharp
using System;
using System.Diagnostics;
using System.Reflection;

public class CommandLineHandler
{
    public static void Parse(string[] args, object commandLine)
    {
        string errorMessage;
        if (!TryParse(args, commandLine, out errorMessage))
        {
            throw new ApplicationException(errorMessage);
        }
    }

    public static bool TryParse(string[] args, object commandLine,
        out string errorMessage)
    {
        bool success = false;
        errorMessage = null;
        foreach (string arg in args)
        {
            string option;
            if (arg[0] == '/' || arg[0] == '-')
            {
                string[] optionParts = arg.Split(
                    new char[] { ':' }, 2);

                // Remove the slash|dash
                option = optionParts[0].Remove(0, 1);
                PropertyInfo property =
                    commandLine.GetType().GetProperty(option,
                        BindingFlags.IgnoreCase |
                        BindingFlags.Instance |
                        BindingFlags.Public);
                if (property != null)
                {
                    if (property.PropertyType == typeof(bool))
                    {
                        // Last parameters for handling indexers
                        property.SetValue(
                            commandLine, true, null);
                        success = true;
                    }
                    else if (
                        property.PropertyType == typeof(string))
                    {
                        property.SetValue(
                            commandLine, optionParts[1], null);
                        success = true;
```

```
                        }
                        else if (property.PropertyType.IsEnum)
                        {
                            try
                            {
                                property.SetValue(commandLine,
                                    Enum.Parse(
                                        typeof(ProcessPriorityClass),
                                        optionParts[1], true),
                                    null);
                                success = true;
                            }
                            catch (ArgumentException )
                            {
                                success = false;
                                errorMessage =
                                    string.Format(
                                        "The option '{0}' is " +
                                        "invalid for '{1}'",
                                        optionParts[1], option);
                            }
                        }
                        else
                        {
                            success = false;
                            errorMessage = string.Format(
                                "Data type '{0}' on {1} is not"
                                + " supported.",
                                property.PropertyType.ToString(),
                                commandLine.GetType().ToString());
                        }
                    }
                    else
                    {
                        success = false;
                        errorMessage = string.Format(
                            "Option '{0}' is not supported.",
                            option);
                    }
                }
            }
        return success;
    }
}


using System;
using System.Collections.Specialized;
using System.Reflection;
```

```csharp
[AttributeUsage(AttributeTargets.Property, AllowMultiple = false)]
public class CommandLineSwitchRequiredAttribute : Attribute
{
  public static string[] GetMissingRequiredOptions(
      object commandLine)
  {
      StringCollection missingOptions = new StringCollection();
      PropertyInfo[] properties =
          commandLine.GetType().GetProperties();

      foreach (PropertyInfo property in properties)
      {
          Attribute[] attributes =
              (Attribute[])property.GetCustomAttributes(
                  typeof(CommandLineSwitchRequiredAttribute),
                  false);
          if ((attributes.Length > 0) &&
              (property.GetValue(commandLine, null) == null))
          {
              if (property.GetValue(commandLine, null) == null)
              {
                  missingOptions.Add(property.Name);
              }
          }
      }
      string[] results = new string[missingOptions.Count];
      missingOptions.CopyTo(results, 0);
      return results;
  }
}
```

```csharp
using System;
using System.Reflection;
using System.Collections.Generic;

[AttributeUsage(AttributeTargets.Property)]
public class CommandLineSwitchAliasAttribute : Attribute
{
  public CommandLineSwitchAliasAttribute(string alias)
  {
      Alias = alias;
  }

  public string Alias
  {
      get { return _Alias; }
      set { _Alias = value; }
  }
  private string _Alias;
```

```csharp
    public static Dictionary<string, PropertyInfo> GetSwitches(
        object commandLine)
    {
        PropertyInfo[] properties = null;
        Dictionary<string, PropertyInfo> options =
            new Dictionary<string, PropertyInfo>();

        properties = commandLine.GetType().GetProperties(
            BindingFlags.Public | BindingFlags.NonPublic |
            BindingFlags.Instance);
        foreach (PropertyInfo property in properties)
        {
            options.Add(property.Name.ToLower(), property);
            foreach (CommandLineSwitchAliasAttribute attribute in
                property.GetCustomAttributes(
                typeof(CommandLineSwitchAliasAttribute), false))
            {
                options.Add(attribute.Alias.ToLower(), property);
            }
        }
        return options;
    }
}
```

```csharp
using System;
using System.Reflection;
using System.Collections.Generic;

public class CommandLineHandler
{
  // ...

  public static bool TryParse(
      string[] args, object commandLine,
      out string errorMessage)
  {
      bool success = false;
      errorMessage = null;

      Dictionary<string, PropertyInfo> options =
          CommandLineSwitchAliasAttribute.GetSwitches(
              commandLine);

      foreach (string arg in args)
      {
          PropertyInfo property;
          string option;
          if (arg[0] == '/' || arg[0] == '-')
          {
              string[] optionParts = arg.Split(
```

```
                        new char[] { ':' }, 2);
                option = optionParts[0].Remove(0, 1).ToLower();

                if (options.TryGetValue(option, out property))
                {
                    success = SetOption(
                        commandLine, property,
                        optionParts, ref errorMessage);
                }
                else
                {
                    success = false;
                    errorMessage = string.Format(
                        "Option '{0}' is not supported.",
                        option);
                }
            }
        }

        return success;
    }

    private static bool SetOption(
        object commandLine, PropertyInfo property,
        string[] optionParts, ref string errorMessage)
    {
        bool success;

        if (property.PropertyType == typeof(bool))
        {
            // Last parameters for handling indexers
            property.SetValue(
                commandLine, true, null);
            success = true;
        }
        else
        {

            if ((optionParts.Length < 2)
                || optionParts[1] == ""
                || optionParts[1] == ":")
            {
                // No setting was provided for the switch.
                success = false;
                errorMessage = string.Format(
                    "You must specify the value for the {0} option.",
                    property.Name);
            }
            else if (
                property.PropertyType == typeof(string))
```

```
            {
                property.SetValue(
                    commandLine, optionParts[1], null);
                success = true;
            }
            else if (property.PropertyType.IsEnum)
            {
                success = TryParseEnumSwitch(
                    commandLine, optionParts,
                    property, ref errorMessage);
            }
            else
            {
                success = false;
                errorMessage = string.Format(
                    "Data type '{0}' on {1} is not supported.",
                    property.PropertyType.ToString(),
                    commandLine.GetType().ToString());
            }
        }
        return success;
    }
}
```

Chapter 17

LISTING B.5: Virtual Computer Detection Using P/Invoke

```csharp
using System.Runtime.InteropServices;

class Program
{
    delegate void MethodInvoker();

    unsafe static int Main(string[] args)
    {
        // Assign redpill
        byte[] redpill = {
            0x0f, 0x01, 0x0d,         // asm SIDT instruction
            0x00, 0x00, 0x00, 0x00,   // placeholder for an address
            0xc3};                    // asm return instruction

        unsafe
        {
            fixed (byte* matrix = new byte[6],
                redpillPtr = redpill)
            {
                // Move the address of matrix immediately
                // following the SIDT instruction of memory.
```

```
                *(uint*)&redpillPtr[3] = (uint)&matrix[0];

                using (VirtualMemoryPtr codeBytesPtr =
                    new VirtualMemoryPtr(redpill.Length))
                {
                    Marshal.Copy(
                        redpill, 0,
                        codeBytesPtr, redpill.Length);

                    MethodInvoker method =
(MethodInvoker)Marshal.GetDelegateForFunctionPointer(
                        codeBytesPtr, typeof(MethodInvoker));

                    method();
                }
                if (matrix[5] > 0xd0)
                {
                    Console.WriteLine("Inside Matrix!\n");
                    return 1;
                }
                else
                {
                    Console.WriteLine("Not in Matrix.\n");
                    return 0;
                }
            } // fixed
        } // unsafe
    }
}
```

```
public class VirtualMemoryPtr :
    System.Runtime.InteropServices.SafeHandle
{
    public VirtualMemoryPtr(int memorySize) :
        base(IntPtr.Zero, true)
    {
        ProcessHandle =
            VirtualMemoryManager.GetCurrentProcessHandle();
        MemorySize = (IntPtr)memorySize;
        AllocatedPointer =
            VirtualMemoryManager.AllocExecutionBlock(
            memorySize, ProcessHandle);
        Disposed = false;
    }

    public readonly IntPtr AllocatedPointer;
    readonly IntPtr ProcessHandle;
    readonly IntPtr MemorySize;
    bool Disposed;
```

```csharp
    public static implicit operator IntPtr(
        VirtualMemoryPtr virtualMemoryPointer)
    {
        return virtualMemoryPointer.AllocatedPointer;
    }


    // SafeHandle abstract member
    public override bool IsInvalid
    {
        get
        {
            return Disposed;
        }
    }


    // SafeHandle abstract member
    protected override bool ReleaseHandle()
    {
        if (!Disposed)
        {
            Disposed = true;
            GC.SuppressFinalize(this);
            VirtualMemoryManager.VirtualFreeEx(ProcessHandle,
                AllocatedPointer, MemorySize);
        }
        return true;
    }
}
```

```csharp
class VirtualMemoryManager
{

    /// <summary>
    /// The type of memory allocation. This parameter must
    /// contain one of the following values.
    /// </summary>
    [Flags]
    private enum AllocationType : uint
    {
        /// <summary>
        /// Allocates physical storage in memory or in the
        /// paging file on disk for the specified reserved
        /// memory pages. The function initializes the memory
        /// to zero.
        /// </summary>
        Commit = 0x1000,
        /// <summary>
        /// Reserves a range of the process's virtual address
        /// space without allocating any actual physical
```

```csharp
    /// storage in memory or in the paging file on disk.
    /// </summary>
    Reserve = 0x2000,
    /// <summary>
    /// Indicates that data in the memory range specified by
    /// lpAddress and dwSize is no longer of interest. The
    /// pages should not be read from or written to the
    /// paging file. However, the memory block will be used
    /// again later, so it should not be decommitted. This
    /// value cannot be used with any other value.
    /// </summary>
    Reset = 0x80000,
    /// <summary>
    /// Allocates physical memory with read-write access.
    /// This value is solely for use with Address Windowing
    /// Extensions (AWE) memory.
    /// </summary>
    Physical = 0x400000,
    /// <summary>
    /// Allocates memory at the highest possible address.
    /// </summary>
    TopDown = 0x100000,
}


/// <summary>
/// The memory protection for the region of pages to be
/// allocated.
/// </summary>
[Flags]
private enum ProtectionOptions : uint
{
    /// <summary>
    /// Enables execute access to the committed region of
    /// pages. An attempt to read or write to the committed
    /// region results in an access violation.
    /// </summary>
    Execute = 0x10,
    /// <summary>
    /// Enables execute and read access to the committed
    /// region of pages. An attempt to write to the
    /// committed region results in an access violation.
    /// </summary>
    PageExecuteRead = 0x20,
    /// <summary>
    /// Enables execute, read, and write access to the
    /// committed region of pages.
    /// </summary>
    PageExecuteReadWrite = 0x40,
    // ...
}
```

```csharp
/// <summary>
/// The type of free operation
/// </summary>
[Flags]
private enum MemoryFreeType : uint
{
    /// <summary>
    /// Decommits the specified region of committed pages.
    /// After the operation, the pages are in the reserved
    /// state.
    /// </summary>
    Decommit = 0x4000,
    /// <summary>
    /// Releases the specified region of pages. After this
    /// operation, the pages are in the free state.
    /// </summary>
    Release = 0x8000
}


[DllImport("kernel32.dll", EntryPoint="GetCurrentProcess")]
internal static extern IntPtr GetCurrentProcessHandle();

[DllImport("kernel32.dll")]
internal static extern IntPtr GetCurrentProcess();

[DllImport("kernel32.dll", SetLastError = true)]
private static extern IntPtr VirtualAllocEx(
    IntPtr hProcess,
    IntPtr lpAddress,
    IntPtr dwSize,
    AllocationType flAllocationType,
    uint flProtect);

// ...
[DllImport("kernel32.dll", SetLastError = true)]
static extern bool VirtualProtectEx(
    IntPtr hProcess, IntPtr lpAddress,
    IntPtr dwSize, uint flNewProtect,
    ref uint lpflOldProtect);

public static IntPtr AllocExecutionBlock(
    int size, IntPtr hProcess)
{
    IntPtr codeBytesPtr;
    codeBytesPtr = VirtualAllocEx(
        hProcess, IntPtr.Zero,
        (IntPtr)size,
        AllocationType.Reserve | AllocationType.Commit,
        (uint)ProtectionOptions.PageExecuteReadWrite);
```

```csharp
    if (codeBytesPtr == IntPtr.Zero)
    {
        throw new System.ComponentModel.Win32Exception();
    }

    uint lpflOldProtect = 0;
    if (!VirtualProtectEx(
        hProcess, codeBytesPtr,
        (IntPtr)size,
        (uint)ProtectionOptions.PageExecuteReadWrite,
        ref lpflOldProtect))
    {
        throw new System.ComponentModel.Win32Exception();
    }
    return codeBytesPtr;
}

public static IntPtr AllocExecutionBlock(int size)
{
    return AllocExecutionBlock(
        size, GetCurrentProcessHandle());
}

[DllImport("kernel32.dll", SetLastError = true)]
static extern bool VirtualFreeEx(
    IntPtr hProcess, IntPtr lpAddress,
    IntPtr dwSize, IntPtr dwFreeType);
public static bool VirtualFreeEx(
    IntPtr hProcess, IntPtr lpAddress,
    IntPtr dwSize)
{
    bool result = VirtualFreeEx(
        hProcess, lpAddress, dwSize,
        (IntPtr)MemoryFreeType.Decommit);
    if (!result)
    {
        throw new System.ComponentModel.Win32Exception();
    }
    return result;
}
public static bool VirtualFreeEx(
    IntPtr lpAddress, IntPtr dwSize)
{
    return VirtualFreeEx(
        GetCurrentProcessHandle(), lpAddress, dwSize);
}

}
```

C
C# 2.0 Topics

READERS ALREADY FAMILIAR with C# 1.0 will want to scan through the book for material specific to C# 2.0 in order to upgrade their skills. This appendix contains a list of all the C# 2.0 material that appears in the book.

TABLE C.1: Topics by Page Number

Page Number	Topic Title
4, 234–236	Support for a single class spanning multiple files (partial classes)
8	No new keywords, contextual keywords only
20	`System.Console.Readkey()`
24, 350–351	XML delimited comments
53	Nullable modifier (?)
59, 183–184	`TryParse()` supported on all numeric types
63, 304	`default()` operator
134	`#pragma` enables support for turning off warning messages
181	General exception blocks (`catch{}`) produce a warning
181, 370	All exceptions derive from `System.Exception`

Continues

TABLE C.1: Topics by Page Number *(Continued)*

Page Number	Topic Title
216–217	Static classes
228–229	Access modifiers on property getters and setters
348–349	Namespace alias qualifier
361	`using` statement operands must support `IDisposable`
379–418	Generics (Chapter 11)
385–396	Generic types
396–409	Generic constraints
409–413	Generic methods
419–433	Generic collections
433–443	Generic interfaces
448–463	Iterators and `yield return` statements
471–475	Delegate instantiation shorthand
475–481	Anonymous methods
501–503	Generics and delegates
517–520	Reflection on generic types
545	`System.Runtime.Serialization.OptionalFieldsAttribute`
557–560	`System.Threading.ParameterizedThreadStart`
574	Generic `System.Threading.Interlocked` methods
578	Support for access control on `System.Threading.Mutex`
606	`System.Net.WebClient` asynchronous methods
606–610	`System.Threading.BackgroundWorker`
632	`System.Runtime.InteropServices.SafeHandle`

Table C.2: Topics by Title

Topic Title	Page Number
`#pragma` enables support for turning of warning messages	134
Access modifiers on property getters and setters	228–229
All exceptions derive from `System.Exception`	181, 370
Anonymous methods	475–481
`default()` operator	63, 304
Delegate instantiation shorthand	471–475
General exception blocks (`catch{}`) produce a warning	181
Generic collections	419–433
Generic constraints	396–409
Generic interfaces	433–443
Generic methods	409–413
Generic `System.Threading.Interlocked` methods	574
Generic types	385–396
Generics (Chapter 11)	379–418
Generics and delegates	501–503
Iterators and `yield return` statements	448–463
Namespace alias qualifier	348–349
No new keywords, contextual keywords only	8
Nullable modifier (?)	53
Reflection on generic types	517–520
Static classes	216–217

Continues

TABLE C.2: Topics by Title *(Continued)*

Topic Title	Page Number
Support for a single class spanning multiple files (partial classes)	4, 234–236
Support for access control on `System.Threading.Mutex`	578
`System.Console.Readkey()`	20
`System.Net.WebClient` asynchronous methods	606
`System.Runtime.InteropServices.SafeHandle`	632
`System.Runtime.Serialization.OptionalFieldsAttribute`	545
`System.Threading.BackgroundWorker`	606–610
`System.Threading.ParameterizedThreadStart`	557–560
`TryParse()` supported on all numeric types	59, 183–184
`using` statement operands must support `IDisposable`	361
XML delimited comments	24, 350–351

Index

SYMBOLS

! (logical negation) operator, 106
!= (not equals) operator, 103, 334–335
" (double quotes), 41
(hash) symbol, 130
% (remainder) operator, 79–80
&& (AND) operator, 105
  flag enums, 317–319
  overloading, 337
() (cast) operator, 339–340
* (multiplication) operator, 79–80
++ (increment) operator, 88–91
+ (plus) operator, 78–79, 81–82
-- (decrement) operator, 88–91
- (delete) operator, 192
- (minus) operator, 78–79
- (subtraction) operator, 79–80
/ (division) operator, 79–80
/// (three-forward-slash delimiter), 351
; (semicolons), statements without, 12–13
< (less than) operator, 103
<= (less than or equal to) operator, 103
== (equals) operator, 103, 334–335
= operator, 16
> (greater than) operator, 103
>= (greater than or equal to) operator, 103
? (conditional) operator, 107
@ character, 43
[ ] (index) operator, 426, 444–448
\n (newline) character, 42
\( ) (parenthesis) operator (delete slash),
  86–87

^ (exclusive OR) operator, 106
{ } (curly braces), 61
  code blocks, 99–101
| | (OR) operator, 104, 105
  flag enums, 317–319
  overloading, 337
~ (bitwise complement) operator, 113, 423

A

Abort() method, 557
abstract classes, 263–268
  interfaces, comparing, 294
abstract members, defining, 264–265
access
  base members, 261
  code, 6
  code, security, 650
  fields, 196
  instance fields, 194–195
  interfaces, 611–612
  metadata, 511–512
  modifiers. *See* access modifiers
  property-backing fields, 226
  referent type members, 638–639
  scope, 101–102
  static fields, 213
access modifiers, 202–204, 345
  classes, 344
  encapsulation, circumventing, 650
  private, 244–245
  properties, 228–229
  protected, 245–246

Microsoft .NET Development Series

.NET Framework Standard Library Annotated Reference
Volume 1: Base Class Library and Extended Numerics Library
Brad Abrams

0321154894

.NET Framework Standard Library Annotated Reference
Volume 2: Networking Library, Reflection Library and XML Library
Brad Abrams
Tamara Abrams

0321194454

.NET Web Services
Architecture and Implementation
Keith Ballinger

0321113594

A Developer's Guide to SQL Server 2005
Bob Beauchemin
Dan Sullivan

0321382188

The .NET Developer's Guide to Windows Security
Keith Brown

0321228359

Visual Studio Tools for Office
Using C# with Excel, Word, Outlook, and InfoPath
Eric Carter
Eric Lippert

0321334884

Visual Studio Tools for Office
Using Visual Basic 2005 with Excel, Word, Outlook, and InfoPath
Eric Carter
Eric Lippert

0321411757

GDI+ Programming with C#
Mahesh Chand

0321160770

The C# Programming Language
Second Edition
Anders Hejlsberg
Scott Wiltamuth
Peter Golde

0321334434

ADO.NET and System.Xml v. 2.0
The Beta Version
Alex Homer
Dave Sussman
Mark Fussell

0321247124

ASP.NET 2.0 Illustrated
Alex Homer
Dave Sussman

0321418344

ASP.NET v. 2.0–
The Beta Version
Alex Homer
Dave Sussman
Rob Howard

0321257278

Data Binding with Windows Forms 2.0
Programming Smart Client Data Applications with .NET
Brian Noyes

032126892X

Essential ASP.NET
with Examples in C#
Fritz Onion

0201760401

Essential ASP.NET
with Examples in Visual Basic .NET
Fritz Onion

0201760398

Windows Forms Programming in Visual Basic .NET
Chris Sells
Justin Gehtland

0321125193

The Visual Basic .NET Programming Language
Paul Vick

0321169514

For more information go to www.awprofessional.com/msdotnetseries/

A First Look at SQL Server 2005 for Developers

Bob Beauchemin
Niels Berglund
Dan Sullivan

0321180593

Essential .NET
Volume 1
The Common Language Runtime

Don Box
with Chris Sells

0201734117

Framework Design Guidelines
Conventions, Idioms, and Patterns for Reusable .NET Libraries

Krzysztof Cwalina
Brad Abrams

0321246756

Effective Use of Microsoft Enterprise Library
Building Blocks for Creating Enterprise Applications and Services

Len Fenster

0321334213

Software Engineering with Microsoft Visual Studio Team System

Sam Guckenheimer
with Juan J. Perez

0321278720

The .NET Developer's Guide to Directory Services Programming

Joe Kaplan
Ryan Dunn

0321350170

Essential C#

Mark Michaelis

0321150775

The Common Language Infrastructure Annotated Standard

Jim Miller
Susann Ragsdale

0321154932

Enterprise Services with the .NET Framework
Developing Distributed Business Solutions with .NET Enterprise Services

Christian Nagel

032124673X

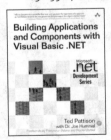

Building Applications and Components with Visual Basic .NET

Ted Pattison
with Dr. Joe Hummel

0201734958

eXtreme .NET
Introducing eXtreme Programming Techniques to .NET Developers

Dr. Neil Roodyn

0321303636

Windows Forms 2.0 Programming

Chris Sells
Michael Weinhardt

0321267966

Windows Forms Programming in C#

Chris Sells

0321116208

Programming in the .NET Environment

Damien Watkins
Mark Hammond
Brad Abrams

0201770180

Pragmatic ADO.NET
Data Access for the Internet World

Shawn Wildermuth

0201745682

.NET Compact Framework Programming with C#

Paul Yao
David Durant

0321174038

.NET Compact Framework Programming with Visual Basic .NET

Paul Yao
David Durant

0321174046